Communicating Effectively

Eighth Edition

Communicating Effectively

Saundra Hybels

Richard L. Weaver II

McGraw Hill

Boston   Burr Ridge, IL   Dubuque, IA   Madison, WI   New York   San Francisco   St. Louis
Bangkok   Bogotá   Caracas   Kuala Lumpur   Lisbon   London   Madrid   Mexico City
Milan   Montreal   New Delhi   Santiago   Seoul   Singapore   Sydney   Taipei   Toronto

The McGraw·Hill Companies

McGraw Hill **Higher Education**

COMMUNICATING EFFECTIVELY
Published by McGraw-Hill, a business unit of The McGraw-Hill Companies, Inc., 1221 Avenue of the Americas, New York, NY, 10020. Copyright © 2007, 2004, 2001, 1998, 1995, 1992, 1989, 1986 by The McGraw-Hill Companies, Inc. All rights reserved. No part of this publication may be reproduced or distributed in any form or by any means, or stored in a database or retrieval system, without the prior written consent of The McGraw-Hill Companies, Inc., including, but not limited to, in any network or other electronic storage or transmission, or broadcast for distance learning.
Some ancillaries, including electronic and print components, may not be available to customers outside the United States.

This book is printed on acid-free paper.

1 2 3 4 5 6 7 8 9 0 DOW/DOW 0 9 8 7 6

ISBN 0-07-319339-9 (student edition)
ISBN 0-07-319347-X (author annotated edition)

Editor in Chief: *Emily Barrosse*
Publisher: *Phillip A. Butcher*
Executive Editor: *Suzanne Earth*
Senior Developmental Editor: *Jennie Katsaros*
Freelance Permissions Coordinator: *Judy Brody*
Senior Marketing Manager: *Leslie Oberhuber*
Managing Editor: *Jean Dal Porto*
Project Manager: *Jean R. Starr*
Art Director: *Jeanne Schreiber*
Lead Designer: *Gino Cieslik*
Art Editor: *Emma C. Ghiselli*
Photo Research Coordinator: *Nora Agbayani*
Cover Credit: *(left to right)* © *Stockbyte;* © *Getty;* © *Getty;* © *Getty*
Senior Media Project Manager: *Nancy Garcia*
Senior Production Supervisor: *Carol A. Bielski*
Composition: *Electronic Publishing Services Inc., NYC*
Printing: *45 # Pub Matte Plus, R.R. Donnelley/Willard, Ohio*

Credits: The credits section for this book begins on page C-1 and is considered an extension of the copyright page.

Library of Congress Cataloging-in-Publication Data

Hybels, Saundra.
    Communicating Effectively / Saundra Hybels, Richard L. Weaver II.—8th ed.
      p. cm.
    Includes biographical references and index.
    ISBN-13: 978-0-07-319339-7 (pbk. : alk. paper)
    ISBN-10: 0-07-319339-9 (pbk. : alk. paper)
    ISBN-13: 978-0-07-319347-2 (AIE : pbk. : alk. paper)
    ISBN-10: 0-07-319347-X (AIE : pbk. : alk. paper)
    1. Oral Communication. I. Weaver, Richard L., 1941– II. Title
P95.H9 2007
302.2'242—dc22
                                                2005054036

The Internet addresses listed in the text were accurate at the time of publication. The inclusion of a Web site does not indicate an endorsement by the authors of McGraw-Hill, and McGraw-Hill does not guarantee the accuracy of the information presented at these sites. **www.mhhe.com**

www.mhhe.com

Brief Contents

Basic Principles of Communication — Part One

- Chapter 1   **The Communication Process**   2
- Chapter 2   **Self, Perception, and Communication**   28
- Chapter 3   **Intercultural Communication**   54
- Chapter 4   **Listening**   78
- Chapter 5   **Verbal Communication**   104
- Chapter 6   **Nonverbal Communication**   130

Interpersonal Communication — Part Two

- Chapter 7   **Interpersonal Relationships**   154
- Chapter 8   **Evaluating and Improving Relationships**   182
- Chapter 9   **Communication at Work: Professional Communication**   208

Communicating in Groups — Part Three

- Chapter 10   **Small-Group Participation**   230
- Chapter 11   **Group Leadership and Conflict Management**   256

Computer-Mediated Communication — Part Four

- Appendix A   **Computer-Mediated Communication (CMC)**   276

Communicating in Public — Part Five

- Appendix B   **A Quick Guide to Public Speaking**   286
- Chapter 12   **Getting Started and Finding Speech Material**   288
- Chapter 13   **Organizing and Outlining the Speech**   312
- Chapter 14   **Delivering the Speech**   342
- Chapter 15   **The Informative Speech**   370
- Chapter 16   **The Persuasive Speech**   396

References   R-1
Glossary   G-1
Credits   C-1
Index   I-1

Contents

Preface xiii

Part One
Basic Principles of Communication

1 The Communication Process 2

Everyone Needs Communication Skills 4

Strategic Flexibility (SF) 6
  Creativity 7

Communication Is a Process 8
  A Definition of Communication 8
  The Elements of Communication 8

Communication Is a Transaction 13
  The Three Principles of Transactional Communication 13

Types of Communication 15
  Intrapersonal Communication 15
  Interpersonal Communication 15
  Small-Group Communication 17
  Computer-Mediated Communication 18
  Public Communication 18
  Intercultural Communication 18

Ethical Communication 20

Communicating Effectively 21
  Where to Begin 22

The Internet and the Communication Process 23

Chapter Review 26
  Summary 26
  Key Terms and Concepts 27
  Questions to Review 27

2 Self, Perception, and Communication 28

The Role of Self and Perception in Communicating Effectively and Strategic Flexibility 30

Self-Concept 31
  Reflected Appraisals 32
  Social Comparisons 33
  Self-Perception 35
  Gender, Sex, and Self-Concept 36
  Psychological Safety and Risk 37

Can You Improve Your Self-Concept? 38
  Where Should Change Begin? 38
  What Do You Want to Change about Yourself? 40
  Are Your Circumstances Keeping You from Changing? 40
  Are You Willing to Take Some Chances? 40
  What Would Be a Realistic Goal? 40
  Can You Discipline Yourself? 41
  Are There People Who Will Support You? 41
  Can You Be More You-Centered? 41

The Map Is Not the Territory 41

The Internet, Self, and Communication 44

Perception 45
  The Perceptual Process 45
  Deletions, Distortions, and Generalizations 46
  Perceptual Filters 47
  Adjusting to Perceptual Influences 48

Chapter Review 52
  Summary 52
  Key Terms and Concepts 53
  Questions to Review 53

3 Intercultural Communication 54

The Role of Intercultural Communication in Communicating Effectively and Strategic Flexibility 56
  In Communicating Effectively 56
  In Strategic Flexibility 57

What Is Culture? 57

You Are a Cultural Being 58

The Importance of Studying Intercultural Communication 60

Intercultural Communication and the Communication Model 62

Studying Cultural Differences 63
Power Distance 63
Individualism versus Collectivism 64
Femininity versus Masculinity 64
Uncertainty Avoidance 65
Long-Term Orientation 65
High Context versus Low Context 65

Barriers to Intercultural Communication 66
Ethnocentrism 66
Stereotyping 66
Prejudice 67
Discrimination 67

Dealing with Barriers to Intercultural Communication 68
Communication between Nondominant- and Dominant-Group Members 68
The Consequences of Nondominant- and Dominant-Group Communication 71

Improving Intercultural Communication 72

The Internet and Intercultural Communication 74

Chapter Review 76
Summary 76
Key Terms and Concepts 76
Questions to Review 77

4 Listening 78

The Role of Listening in Communicating Effectively and Strategic Flexibility 80

Remembering Information 83

Note-Taking Skills 84

Listening Styles 85
Culture and Listening 86
Gender and Listening 87

The Difficulty of Listening 88

Learning to Listen 90

Three Kinds of Listening 92
Active Listening 93
Critical Listening 94
Empathic Listening 95

Talking So Others Will Listen 98

The Internet and Listening 100

Chapter Review 102
Summary 102
Key Terms and Concepts 102
Questions to Review 103

5 Verbal Communication 104

The Role of Verbal Communication in Communicating Effectively and Strategic Flexibility 107
Communicating Effectively 107
Strategic Flexibility 108

How Words Work 109

People Determine Meanings 112

The Language Environment 113
People, Purposes, and Rules 113
Appropriate Language 114
Specialization 114

Style, Roles, and Group Memberships 116
Gender and Language 116
Culture and Language 119
Speaking and Writing 120

Working on Your Communication 122
What Do You Want to Say? 122
How Do You Want to Say It? 122
To Whom Are You Talking? 124
What Metamessages Are You Sending? 125
Ethics 125

The Internet and Verbal Communication 126

Chapter Review 128
Summary 128
Key Terms and Concepts 129
Questions to Review 129

6 Nonverbal Communication 130

The Role of Nonverbal Communication in Communicating Effectively and Achieving Strategic Flexibility 132
Communicating Effectively 132
Strategic Flexibility 133

Differences between Verbal and Nonverbal Communication 134

Characteristics of Nonverbal Communication 134
Nonverbal Communication Is Culturally Determined 134

Nonverbal Messages May Conflict with Verbal Messages 135
Nonverbal Messages Are Largely Unconscious 135
Nonverbal Communication Shows Your Feelings and Attitudes 135
Nonverbal Communication Varies by Gender 136

Types of Nonverbal Communication 136
Paralanguage 136
Body Movement 138
Eye Messages 139
Attractiveness 139
Clothing 140
Body Adornment 141
Space and Distance 142
Touch 144
Smell 145
Time 146

Functions of Nonverbal Communication 147

Improving Your Nonverbal Communication 148
How Do People React to You? 148
Can Videotapes Help Your Nonverbal Communication? 148
Is Your Nonverbal Communication Appropriate to the Role You Are Playing? 149
How Do You Use Your Space? 149
How Do You Use Time? 149

The Internet and Nonverbal Communication 149

Chapter Review 152
Summary 152
Key Terms and Concepts 152
Questions to Review 153

Part Two
Interpersonal Communication

7 Interpersonal Relationships 154

Emotional Intelligence 156
Being Self-Aware 156
Managing Emotions 157
Motivating Yourself 157
Recognizing Emotions in Others 158
Handling Relationships 158

The Importance of Emotional Intelligence to Strategic Flexibility 158

Attraction to Others 159
Physical Attraction 160
Perceived Gain 160
Similarities 160
Differences 161
Proximity 161
Cyberattraction 161

Motives for Interpersonal Communication 162
Pleasure 162
Affection 162
Inclusion 162
Escape 163
Relaxation 163
Control 163
Health 163
Cybermotivation 163

Talking to Each Other 164
Roles, Relationships, and Communication 164
Beginning Conversations: The Art of Small Talk 164
Bids and the Bidding Process 166
Owned Messages 167

Self-Disclosure: Important Talk 168
The Importance of Self-Disclosure 168
The Process of Self-Disclosure 170
Self-Disclosure and Intimacy: Rewards and Fears 171
When Should Self-Disclosure Occur? 172

Essential Elements of Good Relationships 173
Verbal Skills 173
Emotional Expressiveness 173
Conversational Focus 174
Nonverbal Analysis 175
Conversational Encouragement 175
Care and Appreciation 175
Commitment 176
Adaptation 176

The Internet and Interpersonal Relationships 177

Chapter Review 180
Summary 180
Key Terms and Concepts 180
Questions to Review 181

8 Evaluating and Improving Relationships 182

The Stages of a Relationship 185
   Coming Together 186
   Coming Apart 189

Evaluating Relationships: Ask the Right Questions 192
   Ask Yourself Questions 192
   Ask Questions about Your Partner 192
   Ask Questions about Rewards and Costs 193
   Ask Questions about Roles 194

Improving Relationships: Use Communication Strategies 195
   Aggressive Talk and Aggression 196
   Regrettable Talk 197
   Criticism and Complaints 197
   Avoidance 199
   Defensive Communication 199
   Avoiding Defense Communication: A Practical Example 201

Resolving Conflict 202
   The Bottom Line 203

The Internet and Evaluating and Improving Relationships 203

Chapter Review 206
   Summary 206
   Key Terms and Concepts 206
   Questions to Review 207

9 Communicating at Work: Professional Communication 208

Principles of Professional Conduct 210

Interviews 211
   The Information Interview 212
   Information Interviews as Precursors to Job Interviews 217
   The Employment Interview 219

Cultural Differences in the Workplace 222

Gender Differences in the Workplace 223

Communicating within a Professional Atmosphere 224

Dealing with Conflict at Work 224

The Internet and Professional Communication 226

Chapter Review 228
   Summary 228
   Key Terms and Concepts 229
   Questions to Review 229

Part Three
Communicating in Groups

10 Small-Group Participation 230

Why Learn about Small Groups? 233

Characteristics of Small Groups 234
   Cultural Values 234
   Group Norms 235
   Group Rules 236

Types of Groups 236

Small-Group Effectiveness 237
   Workable Size 237
   An Appropriate Meeting Place 238
   Suitable Seating Arrangements 238
   Cohesiveness and Commitment 239
   Groupthink 239
   Teams versus Groups 241

Discussion in Groups 241
   Choosing a Topic 242
   Identifying the Problem 243
   Analyzing the Problem 243
   Finding and Evaluating Solutions 245
   Reevaluating Solutions 246

Participating in Group Discussion 247
   Task Roles 248
   Maintenance Roles 249
   Dysfunctional Roles 250

The Internet and Small-Group Participation 251

Chapter Review 254
   Summary 254
   Key Terms and Concepts 254
   Questions to Review 255

11 Group Leadership and Conflict Management 256

What Is a Leader? 258

How Leaders Influence Followers 258
 Reward Power 259
 Coercive Power 259
 Legitimate Power 259
 Expert Power 259
 Referent Power 259

How People Become Leaders 259
 Personality Traits 260
 Situational Factors 260
 Strategic Flexibility 260

Approaches to Leadership 261
 Traditional Leadership Styles 261
 Functional Leadership 262
 Shared Leadership 262
 Situational Leadership 263

Leading the Group 264
 Listening 264
 Maintaining Neutrality and Objectivity 265
 Establishing Procedures 265
 Finding Solutions 265
 Helping the Group to Progress 267
 Seeking Diversity 267
 Raising Questions 267
 Focusing on Answers 268
 Delegating Responsibility 268
 Encouraging Social Interaction 268
 Sharing a Vision 268

Conflict in Groups 269
 The Value of Substantive Conflict 269
 Managing Group Conflict 270

The Internet, Group Leadership, and Conflict Management 272

Chapter Review 274
 Summary 274
 Key Terms and Concepts 274
 Questions to Review 275

Part Four
Computer-Mediated Communication

Appendix A Computer-Mediated Communication (CMC) 276

CMC and Literacy 277

CMC and the Communication Model 277

Why Choose CMC over FtFC? 279
 Personal Needs 279
 Interpersonal Needs 280
 Experimentation 281

CMC and Developing Online Credibility 281
 The Importance of Language 281
 Essential Criteria 281

Virtual Communities 282
 Credibility in Virtual Communities 282
 Values of Virtual Communities 282
 Blogs as Virtual Communities 282

How Do Ethics Relate to CMC? 283
 Before You Write or Post 283
 Before You Read 283

Chapter Review 285
 Summary 285
 Key Terms and Concepts 285
 Questions to Review 285

Part Five
Communicating in Public 286

Appendix B A Quick Guide to Public Speaking 286

Preparation 286

Delivery 287

12 Getting Started and Finding Speech Material 288

Why Study Public Speaking? 290

Knowledge of Public Speaking 290

Public Speaking and the Elements of Communication 290

Preparation for Public Speaking 291
- *Finding a Topic* 291
- *Narrowing the Topic* 292
- *Selecting a Purpose* 293
- *Analyzing the Audience* 295
- *Analyzing the Occasion* 300
- *Researching Your Topic: Where to Look* 301
- *Supporting Material: What to Look For* 304

The Internet and Getting Started 308

Chapter Review 310
- *Summary* 310
- *Key Terms and Concepts* 310
- *Questions to Review* 311

13 Organizing and Outlining the Speech 312

Principles of Organization 316
- *Relate Points to Your Specific Purpose and Central Idea* 316
- *Distinguish between Main and Minor Points* 316
- *Phrase All Points in Full Sentences* 316
- *Give All Points a Parallel Structure* 317

Patterns of Organization 318
- *Time Order* 318
- *Spatial Order* 319
- *Cause-and-Effect Order* 320
- *Problem–Solution Order* 320
- *Motivated Sequence* 322
- *Topical Order* 322

The Speech Introduction 323
- *State Your Purpose, Central Idea, and Main Points* 323
- *Get Attention* 323
- *Additional Tips for Introductions* 326

The Speech Conclusion 327
- *Summarize Your Main Ideas* 327
- *Include a Quotation* 327
- *Inspire Your Audience to Action* 328
- *Additional Tips for Conclusions* 328

Speech Transitions 328
- *Tips for Transitions* 328

Preparing an Outline 329
- *The Outline Format* 329
- *Full-Sentence and Keyword Outlines* 330

The Reference List 330

The Internet and Organizing and Outlining the Speech 331

Sample Outline 334

Chapter Review 340
- *Key Terms and Concepts* 340
- *Questions to Review* 341

14 Delivering the Speech 342

Characteristics of Good Delivery 344
- *Conversational Quality* 345
- *Attentiveness* 346
- *Immediacy* 346
- *Directness* 347

Types of Delivery 347
- *Impromptu Speaking* 347
- *Speaking from a Manuscript* 348
- *Speaking from Memory* 348
- *Extemporaneous Speaking* 349

How You Look 349
- *Appearance* 349
- *Body Language* 350
- *Eye Contact* 350
- *Facial Expression* 350
- *Gestures* 351
- *Posture* 351

How You Sound 351
- *Volume* 351
- *Using a Microphone* 351
- *Pace* 352

Pitch and Inflection 352
Enunciation 352

Using Visual Support 353
Types of Visual Support 353
Rules for Using Visual Support 360

Public Speaking Anxiety 361
A Good Place to Begin 361
Other Strategies for Reducing Anxiety 362

Rehearsing Your Speech 363
Preparing Your Speech 363
Trying Out Your Speech 364
Rehearsing Actual Delivery 364

The Internet and Delivering the Speech 365

Chapter Review 368
Summary 368
Key Terms and Concepts 368
Questions to Review 368

15 The Informative Speech 370

Goals of an Informative Speaker 373
Increasing Understanding 373
Getting Attention 374
Helping Retention 375

Types of Informative Speeches 375
Objects 375
Processes 375
Events 375
Concepts 376
Overarching Principles 376

Strategies for Informative Speeches 376
Defining 376
Describing 378
Explaining 379

Arousing Interest in Your Topic 381
Arouse Curiosity 381
Present Anecdotes 381
Build Anticipation 382
Build Suspense 382
Other Techniques for Getting Attention 382

Getting Listeners Involved 383
Get the Audience to Participate 384
Ask Rhetorical Questions 384
Solicit Questions from the Audience 384

Presentations 385
Thorough Preparation 385
Natural Delivery 386
Effective Visuals 387

The Internet and the Informative Speech 387

Sample Speech 389

Chapter Review 394
Summary 394
Key Terms and Concepts 394
Questions to Review 395

16 The Persuasive Speech 396

Persuasion and the Communication Model 398

What Is Persuasion, and What Is Its Purpose? 399

Values, Beliefs, and Attitudes 399
Values 400
Beliefs 400
Attitudes 401

Why Persuasion Is Difficult 401

Strategies of Persuasion 403
Determine Your Purpose 403
Analyze Your Audience 404
Appeal to Your Audience Using Logic 404
Appeal to Your Audience Using Emotion 409
Use Research to Prove Your Points 411
Choose Your Language Carefully 412
Appeal to Your Audience Using Your Credibility 412
Expertise 412
Dynamism 413
Trustworthiness 413
Ethics 413

Structure Your Material Effectively 414
Questions of Fact, Value, and Policy 414
One-Sided versus Two-Sided Arguments 416
Order of Presentation 416

The Internet and the Persuasive Speech 418

Sample Speech 419

Chapter Review 426
Summary 426
Key Terms and Concepts 426
Questions to Review 427

Glossary G-1
References R-1
Credits C-1
Index I-1

Preface

Communicating Effectively, Eighth Edition, is written for students taking speech communication classes for the first time. The book covers the theory and practice of interpersonal, group, and public communication. The overall approach of the book is pragmatic, so that students can see and appreciate the practical application of the ideas, concepts, and theories in their own lives and in the lives of people who are close to them.

APPROACH

There are four specific approaches that appear throughout the eighth edition. The first is simply an answer to the question, "Why study this?" This approach begins in Chapter 1 in the opening section entitled "Everyone Needs Communication Skills," but it continues in the following chapters with sections such as "The Role of Self and Perception in Communication," and "The Role of Intercultural Communication in Communicating Effectively and Strategic Flexibility." Similar sections occur in the chapters on verbal and nonverbal communication. The hope is that by the time readers have finished Chapter 6, "Nonverbal Communication," they will not just understand the importance of communicating effectively but recognize, too, how communicating effectively depends on strategic flexibility.

The second approach is introduced in Chapter 1, integrated into each of the following chapters, and then added as marginal comments wherever appropriate throughout every chapter. It is called strategic flexibility (SF), which is a value-added system students can use to add to, improve upon, and increase their communication skills. SF means expanding your communication repertoire (your collection or stock of communication behaviors that can readily be brought into use) to enable you to use the best skill or behavior available for a particular situation. It is a "value-added" concept because students can use it to build on the skills they already possess. The six-step program for applying SF to real-life situations includes the steps—1) anticipate, 2) assess, 3) evaluate, 4) select, 5) apply, and 6) re-assess and re-evaluate. The importance of SF is that most people believe they already communicate well enough, perhaps, even very well; thus, they don't need a course in or book on speech communication. SF is a concept that honors those beliefs and yet suggests that communication repertoires can be expanded, and the more expansion that occurs, the more likely people can "use the best skill or behavior available for particular situations." Simply put, they have more tools in their toolbox.

The third approach has to do with the influence of the Internet. Each chapter ends with a section on "The Internet" as it relates to the content of that chapter. Although several of these sections make specific reference to particular websites, most reveal Internet influences. With the near-universal acceptance and use of the Internet, these sections offer valuable insights regarding the impact, advantages, and limitations of Internet use in all the contexts discussed throughout this textbook.

The fourth approach is a continuation of the applied, problem-solution approach explained in previous editions. This approach can be seen in the chapter on intercultural communication where we ask, "How do you study culture?" In response, the six dimensions or frameworks for studying cultural differences are explained as solutions, and each solution is followed by a corresponding, student-oriented example, so that students see the theory in use. There are numerous examples throughout the book, but another obvious one occurs in the chapter on interpersonal relationships where the perplexing problem is, "What is the glue that holds relationships together?" According to John Gottman and his team of relationship researchers, the answer is "bids and responses to bids."

Each of these approaches has the same purpose: to make the book readable, interesting, and challenging. Most important, however, is that they make the book immediate and relevant: they bring communication into the day-to-day lives of students.

ORGANIZATION AND COVERAGE

Part One is devoted to the principles of communication. Chapters 1 through 6 present a model of communication, relate communication both to the self and culture, and show how communication works, both verbally and nonverbally, in our encounters with others. Chapter 3, Intercultural Communication, explains different frameworks for studying cultural differences, barriers to intercultural communication, and ways to improve it.

The second part of the book focuses on interpersonal and small-group communication as well as professional communication or communicating at work. Chapters 7 and 8 cover interpersonal relationships, their dynamics, and how they can be evaluated and improved. Chapter 9 discusses principles of professional conduct, information interviews, information interviews as precursors to job interviews, employment interviews, cultural and gender differences in the workplace, communicating within a professional atmosphere, dealing with conflict at work, dealing with supervisors and managers, dealing with customers, as well as the section on "The Internet and Professional Communication." Chapter 10 examines Small-Group Participation, and Chapter 11 discusses Group Leadership and Conflict Management.

New to the eighth edition is an in-text appendix on Computer-Mediated Communication (CMC). This new chapter discusses the importance of CMC, what it is, how it relates to the communication model, why people choose CMC over face-to-face communication, CMC and developing online credibility, virtual communities (and blogs) and their significance, and how ethics relates to CMC.

The third part of the book examines public communication. Chapter 12 covers getting started and finding speech material; Chapter 13 treats organization and outlining; Chapter 14 discusses delivery; and Chapters 15 and 16 deal with informative and persuasive speaking respectively.

One of the goals for the text is to present the world beyond our local communities. Although this is true throughout the book, it is especially true in Chapter 3, Intercultural Communication, the in-text Appendix, Computer-Mediated Communication, and in the sections on the Internet at the end of each chapter.

NEW TO THIS EDITION

The eighth edition includes a significant number of changes, more than in any other edition in the history of this book. There are two motives for the extensive changes: 1. to streamline the edition to more effectively meet the needs of both instructors and students and 2. to make the book even more practical, current, and relevant.

- Strategic Flexibility

    Chapter 1 introduces the concept of strategic flexibility (SF). As noted earlier, strategic flexibility means expanding your communication repertoire (your collection or stock of communication behaviors that can readily be brought into use) to enable you to use the best skill or behavior available for a particular situation. It is a "value-added" concept because students can use it to build on the skills they already possess. The method includes six steps—1) anticipate, 2) assess, 3) evaluate, 4) select, 5) apply, and 6) re-assess and re-evaluate. These steps are re-introduced and reinforced in each chapter throughout the book, and each time SF is relevant to the content of a chapter, there is a marginal SF icon and comment at that point.

- Impact of the Internet

    At the end of every chapter there is a section on the Internet. The information in those sections, for the most part, discusses the impact, implications, advantages, and limitations of Internet use, rather than offering a variety of URLs (Internet addresses) and Web-based links. The purpose of these sections is well described in a sentence contained in the section "The Internet and Intercultural Communication": "All those with access to the Internet now have the opportunity to expand their horizons by learning how to communicate, relate, collaborate, and understand their changing world."

- Listening

    The chapter on listening is re-written and now depends on the Integrative Listening Model (ILM) framework. The chapter includes strategies for remembering information, as well as new sections on "Note-taking Skills," "Culture and Listening," and "The Difficulty of Listening."

- Interpersonal Relationships

    Chapter 7 is streamlined with a new focus on friendships and serious interpersonal relationships. There are new sections, too, on cyber attraction, cyber communication, and cyber motivation, and this chapter now includes the section "Essential Elements of Good Relationships," and the section on the Internet mentions the overall benefits of Internet usage to developing interpersonal relationships as well as the benefits for online dating.

- Evaluating and Improving Relationships

    Chapter 8 is focused and streamlined as well with a new section on "Evaluating Relationships: Ask the Right Questions," which includes questions partners need to ask themselves, about their partners, about rewards and costs, and about roles. There are sections, too, on how to deal with aggressive talk, regrettable talk, criticism and complaints, avoidance, and defensive communication. A new section on "The Bottom Line" reports results of "The Institute for American Values." The section "The Internet and Evaluating and Improving Relationships" is one of the most extensive. It discusses Internet deception and the red flags to look for, precautions to take in making a transition from virtual to real world, precautions for meeting in person (after connecting online), precautions for meeting outside your area, and precautions, too, for freeing yourself from trouble.

- Communicating at Work or Professional Communication

    Chapter 9 takes a new direction, focusing on "Principles of Professional Conduct," "Cultural Differences in the Workplace," "Gender Differences in the Workplace, "Communicating Within a Professional Atmosphere," "Dealing with Conflict at Work," "Dealing with Supervisors and Managers," and "Dealing with Customers," as well as the information in the previous editions on information interviews, information interviews as precursors to job interviews, and employment interviews. A new section on "Being Interviewed" discusses proper behavior, improper behavior, appropriate dress, questions interviewees need to ask, potential

- Group Leadership and Conflict Management

    Chapter 11 is refocused. There are new sections on strategic flexibility, emergent and shared leadership, seeking diversity, and the value of substantive conflict. There is information in the section on the Internet, about setting up or overhauling an online group discussion, and there are fourteen tips for resolving conflicts in online discussion groups.

- Computer-Mediated Communication (CMC)

    This in-text appendix covers computer-mediated communication, how it relates to the communication model, why CMC is chosen over face-to-face communication, how online credibility is developed, virtual communities (including blogs), and how ethics relates to CMC.

- Getting Started in Public Speaking and Finding Speech Material

    Chapters 12 and 13 of the previous edition have been combined and rewritten. There are new sections on "Why Study Public Speaking" and "Knowledge of Public Speaking" and its importance.

- Public Speaking Anxiety

    In Chapter 14, the approach encourages students to adopt a new philosophy—that public speaking requires a communication orientation and not a performance orientation. A new table compares the two approaches. Suggestions for reducing public speaking anxiety are also included.

- The Informative Speech

    There is an expanded section on "Types of Informative Speeches," which includes a discussion of "Overarching Principles." The section on the Internet includes answers to two questions. The first, for speakers, is "When do I have enough information?" and the second, more focused on listeners is "What expectations do listeners have concerning speakers?"

- The Persuasive Speech

    In this chapter there is a "Consider This" box by Sheila Murray Bethel—a professional speaker—who discusses the process she uses to prepare speeches. Also, there is a new caution regarding appeals to logic versus appeals to emotion, and the importance of engaging listeners' critical thinking, allowing them to weigh emotions, and permitting decisions based on whether or not points are sufficiently supported.

- Sample Speeches

    There are two new sample speeches. The first, "Forgetting Everything You've Learned," by Mauricio Raúl Muñoz, is an informative speech, and the second, "Giving Something Back," by Daquisha Lettrell, is a persuasive speech. Both relate well to students and offer memorable and valuable information.

SUPPLEMENTS TO ACCOMPANY COMMUNICATING EFFECTIVELY, EIGHTH EDITION

Communicating Effectively is accompanied by a comprehensive package of resources designed to facilitate both teaching and learning. These include:

Communicating Effectively CD-ROM provides students with creative and effective tools that make learning easier and more engaging. These tools are integrated with the text through the use of CD icons in the text margins that direct students to the appropriate tools. These include:

- *Video:* Includes clips that illustrate basic communication concepts and excerpts of student speeches.
- *Self-Quizzes:* There are fifteen multiple-choice and five true/false questions for each chapter.
- *Assess Yourself:* Provide scaled responses to the end-of-chapter questionnaires and surveys that challenge students to asses themselves.
- *Audio Flash Cards:* Students can use these digital flash cards to hear how key terms are pronounced and to study for exams.
- *PowerPoint Tutorial:* Provides helpful tips on design and implementation of presentation software.
- *Business Document Templates:* Provide a convenient set of forms for creating professional cover letters, resume, agendas, and memos.

Instructor's Manual/Test Bank

This manual is a source of both daily plans and activities for the classroom. Every chapter of the *Instructor's Manual* contains Learning Objectives, Tips for Teaching, Chapter Highlights, Activities, and Essay Questions. Additionally, the *Instructor's Manual* includes sample course outlines, annotated sample speeches, and a users guide to the videos. The Test Bank includes true/false, multiple choice, and short answer questions created by the author of this book.

Online Learning Center www.mhhe.com/hybels8

This free, Web-based supplement for students and instructors features helpful tools for class and exam preparation. Designed specifically to complement each text chapter, the Online Learning Center offers:

- Chapter Objectives, Outline, and Summaries that give students signposts for understanding and recognizing key chapter content while participating in class and while studying on their own or in groups.
- Self Quizzes that provide a place to practice at taking multiple choice and true/false tests for each chapter.
- Glossary Crossword Puzzles that allow students to test their mastery of key concepts when solving these puzzles.
- Self-assessment Tools and Sample Resumes

Instructor's Resource CD-ROM

A source of both daily plans and activities for the classroom, the Instructor's Resource CD-ROM contains for each chapter: Learning Objectives, Tips for Teaching, Chapter Highlights, Activities and Essay Questions. Additionally, the Instructor's Resource CD-ROM includes sample course outlines, annotated sample speeches, and a user's guide to the videos. The Test Bank includes true/false, multiple choice, and short answer questions—all developed by Richard Weaver. The Test Bank is available on the Instructor's Resource CD-ROM as a computerized test bank or as a basic Word document. McGraw-Hill's EZ Test is a flexible and easy-to-use electronic testing program. The program allows instructors to create tests from book specific items. It accommodates a wide range of question types and instructors may add their own questions. Multiple versions of the test can be created and any test can be exported for use with course management systems such as WebCT, BlackBoard, or PageOut. EZ Test Online is a new service and gives you a place to easily administer your EZ Test-created exams and quizzes online. The program is available for Windows and Macintosh environments. PowerPoint Slides include not only standard lecture support for the entire text, but incorporate illustrations and other special features from the text.

PageOut: The Course Web Site Development Center

All online content for this text is supported by WebCT, eCollege.com, Blackboard, and other course management systems. Additionally, McGraw-Hill's PageOut service is available to get you and your course up and running online in a matter of hours, at no cost. PageOut was designed for instructors just beginning to explore Web options. Even the novice computer user can create a course Web site with a template provided by McGraw-Hill (no programming knowledge necessary). To learn more about PageOut, ask your McGraw-Hill representative for details, or fill out the form at www.mhhe.com/pageout.

ACKNOWLEDGMENTS

We would first like to thank all the instructors and teachers who have chosen to use this textbook from among many. We appreciate your choice, and we consider it both a responsibility and a privilege to be working for you. Likewise, we wish to thank all the students. Although we know it wasn't your choice to read this textbook, we recognize your commitment—especially when you read the book—and we have worked hard on your behalf.

My coauthor, Saundra Hybels, died unexpectedly September 18, 1999. A dedication to her is printed in the sixth edition. Although I (Richard) did the work on the seventh and eighth editions, I continue to write as if Saundra is present (in my mind, she is), and we are writing as a team. Her presence is greatly missed.

I would like to thank my colleague and friend of more than 30 years, Howard W. Cotrell. When I met Howard he was a faculty facilitator at Bowling Green State University who worked with a variety of professionals to help them improve their teaching and research. We have coauthored more than 50 articles, and he has been a contributor to my thoughts, feelings, and ruminations on almost every project undertaken. Although his name does not appear on all my published works, he is there in both substance and spirit.

A special thanks to my mother, Florence (Grow) Weaver, who died in 1998. My mother was always interested, encouraging, and supportive. I have dedicated my book on public speaking to her memory. After all, she was the one for whom I delivered my first public speech.

Thanks, too, to Marge and Jim Norris and Marilyn Hulett, my sisters, and Marge's husband. My sisters have been wonderfully supportive, interested, and inquisitive. Many of the stories and anecdotes refer back to the time when we were the nuclear family.

Thanks to Edgar E. and Zella Willis, my in-laws. There is no way I can ever thank them enough for their love and kindness. Edgar's background in teaching and writing in the area of radio, television, and film has always proven instructive and valuable. Thank you, too, to Richard, Betsy, and Frank Willis, and to Frank's friend Kirstin Nielsen. You are all special and important people in my life.

I want to thank my friends for their continuing support and encouragement: Jim and Pat Angel, Gary and Linda (Lyn) Miller, Sharon Knitt, Larry and Sherry Bush, David and Sharon Andersen, and Larry Sr., Mary, Larry Jr., and Becky Spencer. To Randy and Carol Prescott, Richard (and Barbara, now deceased) Bongiovanni, Ron and Nancy Loescher, Richard and Rosemary Kofler, Larry (and Jean, now deceased) Ambs, and Pete and Bev Carpenter, and the great times we shared. The Pondview Drive days and the many gatherings since have etched deep and rich memories that continue to inspire, enlighten, and encourage.

Thank you to MaryJane Hughes, Manager, and Mary M. O'Shea, of The Copy Center of Perrysburg, Ohio, who have helped me duplicate and collate material and who have met deadlines above and beyond the call of duty. It is great having people assist you who are caring, concerned, and committed to doing their best and producing quality work. A big thank you as well to Valerie Pickard, English Centre, University of Hong Kong, for her help in getting information on the Virtual English Centre (VEC), developed by the teachers of the English Centre at the University of Hong Kong, Hong Kong. Thank you, as well, to Sheila Murray Bethel and her husband Bill, for their continuing support and concern. A "Consider This" by Sheila—a professional public speaker—appears in Chapter 16, "The Persuasive Speech," that reveals the way she prepares her speeches. Thanks, Sheila, for your e-mails.

Also, I want to thank my immediate family: Andrea, my wife, and Scott, Jacquie, Anthony, and Joanna have been inspirations to both my writing and life. Thanks to David Smeltzer, Jay Brooks, and Karen Radford Weaver and their families, Dale and Joyce Smeltzer, the late Bud and his wife Betty Brooks, and Terri Radford, our extended families. Thanks to my grandchildren: Madison, Morgan, Mckenzie, Amanda, Lindsay, Austin, Grant, and Bryce. Many of the personal examples I have shared with readers over the years, even though often unattributed, have been drawn from a positive, supportive, close, loving, and productive family life.

A special thank you, of course, to Andrea for her support, contributions, and love. She is always there, willing to help, to share, to give, and make space in her life for my time at the computer. There is no way this book could have reached its eighth edition without the aid and assistance of my wonderful wife and family—both immediate and extended. I do not take them for granted. I am fortunate to have this incredibly valuable support system, and I know and appreciate it.

I would like to thank the following reviewers for their detailed and insightful comments:

- Donna Acerra,
  Northampton Community College
- Barbara Daniel,
  Florida State University
- Randy Duncan,
  Henderson State University
- Leonard M. Edmonds,
  Arizona State University
- Delryn Fleming,
  Brookhaven College
- Tracy Frederick,
  Southwestern College
- Iva Goldman,
  University of Hawaii at Hilo
- Anne Grissom,
  Mountain View College
- Deborah Hefferin,
  Broward Community College
- Linda Hoyer,
  Madonna University
- Rita Ludwig,
  Lindenwood University
- Robert E. Mild, Jr.,
  Fairmont State University
- Ron St. John,
  Maui Community College
- Robert C. Steinmiller,
  Henderson State University
- Mark T. Zeigler,
  Florida State University

Visual Preview

Communicating Effectively Encourages Critical Thinking

Consider This

"Consider This" boxes encourage students to think critically about real-life events.

TOPIC: Knowing Your Relationship Partner

TOPIC: Some Criticism of Tannen's Work

Another Point of View

"Another Point of View" boxes provide students with contrasting opinions, encouraging critical thinking.

TOPIC: Evaluating Information Critically

Thought-provoking examples help students recognize how diversity benefits our lives.

The text helps students recognize and appreciate the ways in which diversity enhances and enriches the quality of our lives and helps them develop sensitivity to various cultural heritages and backgrounds.

The chapter on intercultural communication expands discussions on cross-cultural and intercultural communication that are interwoven throughout the text.

Active, everyday applications help students apply their skills . . .

Assess Yourself

"Assess Yourself" is a chapter-related questionnaire survey or evaluation form that challenges students to examine their assumptions, attitudes, and feelings. Scaled responses are included on the student CD-ROM with additional discussions or explanations.

Assess Yourself

How Effective Will You Be in Small-Group Discussions?

Indicate the degree to which you agree or disagree with each statement using the following scale: 5 = Strongly agree; 4 = Mildly agree; 3 = Agree and disagree equally; 2 = Mildly disagree; 1 = Strongly disagree. Circle your response following each statement.

1. I dislike participating in small-group discussions.   5 4 3 2 1
2. I recognize and respond in an appropriate way to differences in values, class, culture, ethnicity, lifestyle, point of view, and personal characteristics.   5 4 3 2 1
3. People are quite critical of me.   5 4 3 2 1
4. In general, I am comfortable while participating in small-group discussions.   5 4 3 2 1
5. I understand the concept of conflict, and I use strategies for handling it.   5 4 3 2 1
6. I often feel "left out," as if people don't want me around.   5 4 3 2 1
7. I am tense and nervous while participating in group discussions.   5 4 3 2 1
8. I possess effective relationship skills including trust, risk taking, empathy, listening, sharing, responsibility, respect for others, and expression of feelings.   5 4 3 2 1
9. People seem to respect my ideas and opinions about things.   5 4 3 2 1
10. I like to get involved in small-group discussions.   5 4 3 2 1
11. I understand the importance of working effectively with others and the need for courtesy and cooperation to accomplish a task.   5 4 3 2 1
12. People seem to like me.   5 4 3 2 1
13. Engaging in a group discussion with new people makes me tense and nervous.   5 4 3 2 1
14. I am willing to be both an effective and flexible small-group member.   5 4 3 2 1
15. Most people seem to understand how I feel about things.   5 4 3 2 1
16. I am seldom calm and relaxed while participating in group discussions.   5 4 3 2 1

TOTAL POINTS: _____

Before totaling your score, go to the *Communicating Effectively* CD-ROM or the Online Learning Center at www.mhhe.com/hybels8 and follow the directions there.

mhhe.com/hybels8

Sources: For questions 1, 4, 7, 10, and 13, I am indebted to *An Introduction to Rhetorical Communication*, 4th ed., by J. C. McCroskey, 1982, Englewood Cliffs, NJ: Prentice Hall. McCroskey's Personal Report of Communication Apprehension-24 (PRCA-24) scale was published in *Measures of Personality and Social Psychological Attitudes* (pp. 170–173), by J. P. Robinson, P. R. Shaver, and L. S. Wrightsman, 1991, San Diego, CA: Academic Press. For questions 2, 5, 8, 11, and 14, I am indebted to "Group Effectiveness: Interpersonal, Negotiation, Teamwork," ICANS (Integrated Curriculum for Achieving Necessary Skills), Washington State Board for Community and Technical Colleges, Washington State Employment Security, Washington Workforce Training and Education Coordinating Board. Adult Basic and Literacy Educators, P.O. Box 42496, 711 Capitol Blvd., Olympia, WA 98504. Retrieved March 24, 2003, from http://www.literacynet.org/icans/chapter05/groupeffectiveness.html. For questions 3, 6, 9, 12, and 15 I am indebted to "Acceptance by Others and Its Relation to Acceptance of Self and Others: A Reevaluation," by W. F. Fey, 1955, *Journal of Abnormal and Social Psychology*, 50, pp. 274–276. The "Acceptability to Others" scale was published in *Measures of Personality and Social Psychological Attitudes* (pp. 409–411), by J. P. Robinson, P. R. Shaver, and L. S. Wrightsman, 1991, San Diego, CA: Academic Press.

to their current academic, personal, and professional lives.

Strategic Flexibility (SF)

Strategic Flexibility, a new feature, helps students expand their communication repertoire to enable them to use the best skill or behavior available for a particular situation.

SF introduces a six step process (*anticipate, assess, evaluate, select, apply,* and *re-assess and re-evalutate*) to reinforce concepts in the chapter.

Working Together

Working Together boxes provide activities that encourage group learning and discussions of key concepts.

Critically acclaimed public speaking chapters help students prepare and deliver successful speeches.

A Quick Guide to Public Speaking

The handy reference tool summarizes the goals students should strive to achieve in order to prepare and deliver a successful speech.

Communicating Effectively provides annotated examples of student Informative and Persuasive speeches

Informative Speech "Forgetting Everything You Learned"

Persuasive Speech "Giving Something Back"

A continuing goal of this text is to encourage students to use technology for research, speech preparation and presentation.

New appendix on Computer-Mediated Communication covers virtual communities and ethical implications.

New sections at the end of every chapter discuss the impact, implications, advantages, and limitations of Internet use.

Discusses how the Internet bears on self-concept.

Examines types of leadership of online discussion groups.

Communicating Effectively

CHAPTER 1

The Communication Process

OBJECTIVES

After reading this chapter, you should be able to:

- Explain communication needs and relate them to your life.
- Define *strategic flexibility (SF)* and explain where its power lies.
- Define *communication* and explain it as a process.
- Describe the types of communication.
- Define and explain the importance of *intercultural communication*.
- Discuss the principles of ethical communication and the foundation out of which ethical conduct is most likely to grow.
- Discuss the ways you can improve your own communication skills.
- Explain how Internet communication relates to the model of communication and the four characteristics that make it unique from normal face-to-face communication.

THE FOLLOWING ARE THREE EXAMPLES THAT REVEAL THE POSITIVE ROLE speech communication courses can play in the lives of students. For Ashley, Andrew, and Wanda, they served as pivotal points for changing their lives.

When Ashley visited her guidance counselor in high school, Mr. Vernon, she was really on a personal quest to find out more about herself and to get an expert's advice about her college potential. Ashley had goofed around in high school—far more interested in the social whirl than anything academic. After telling Mr. Vernon what she was doing in high school, and after examining her grades, he uttered the excruciating words: "I'm afraid you're not college material." Those six words were the very wake-up call she needed. In a required speech communication course at a small liberal arts college where she was accepted because of her parents' pleading, she discovered what she needed: an instructor who saw her potential, a course that offered specific information and activities that motivated her and reinforced her talents, and a result—a solid A—that proved she definitely had college potential. It was her speech communication instructor who discovered this bright, fun, articulate young woman who could do anything she put her mind to.

My name is Andrew, and I want to tell you this in the first person: I have never acted before, but my friends said I was a natural-born actor. When I came to college, I was sitting in the cafeteria among a horde of talking, milling students. They all seemed so confident, directed, and older. I was hoping no one noticed me sitting there alone. In walking across campus, I saw the "call" posted on a kiosk. The drama department was looking for actors for an upcoming play. Auditions were the following week. I went to the library, checked out a copy of the play, and read it in one sitting. Although terrified, I tried out. My name did not appear on the call-back sheets, but I knew I could do better, and I knew it could happen. I realized at that moment that any knowledge I could gain about effective communication, and any experience I could get, would help me build the confidence and poise I needed. The course in speech communication was essential for me to face myself and the future I wanted.

Don't ever think that majoring in subjects such as philosophy, literature, or speech has little value in our society because they won't help you get a good job. This crass materialism infects too many students, parents, and employers. I (Wanda Jean DuCharme) studied speech communication at a midsized midwestern university because I wanted to polish my communication skills. I went on to get a master's degree in both speech and English, and now I earn a substantial income as a business consultant, and I run my own business. How did my background prepare me for the work I do now? I learned to think and organize ideas. I could discern patterns and form valid conclusions. I could communicate with senior management, workers, and the public alike. I learned to question, listen, and put ideas into words. My philosophy is, "Do what you love, and the money will follow."

EVERYONE NEEDS COMMUNICATION SKILLS

Your success in this world depends on effective communication skills. The problem isn't a lack of ability to communicate; the problem is simply that you have never mastered the skill. Even the very top students from highly competitive schools frequently are unable to write clearly or make persuasive presentations.[1] This is true for two reasons: (1) We take communication for granted. After all, we've been communicating since we were born, with that much practice, why wouldn't we be good at it? (2) We often think we are better at it than we really are.

If you were told that there were skills that are *more important* to your success than a knowledge of computers, more important than any job-specific skills, and more important than your knowledge of any content area or major, would you want to pursue those skills and improve your ability to perform them? Those skills—basic oral and written communication skills—are the most frequently cited factors in aiding graduating college students to both obtain and sustain employment. The list of studies that support this conclusion goes on and on.[2]

What are the benefits? Why should you take a speech communication course seriously? As a result of a speech communication course you will feel more confident about yourself, you will feel more comfortable with others' perceptions of you, you will experience greater ease in reasoning with people, you will use language more appropriately, and you will have improved critical thinking skills.[3]

This author (Richard) decided on a career in medicine in junior high school. All the courses I took targeted me in that direction. In high school I focused primarily on math and science courses—taking all the school offered. During my first two years at the University of Michigan, as a premedicine major, I did the same. Then came the university's required speech course. Not only did I do well in the course, I decided to use my last free elective slot to schedule a second speech course, and I was hooked. I found out what I could do with a speech major, how it both complemented and supplemented any other major, and I pursued it for the rest of my college career—both at the undergraduate and graduate levels.

Here is what I discovered that made me switch from a premed major to speech. First, I discovered that speech communication is the ultimate people-oriented discipline. I had pursued premed because I wanted to be in a people-oriented business. I loved the idea that here was a discipline that would develop my thinking and speaking skills. In speech I could apply my imagination, solve practical problems, and articulate my ideas. I was truly free to be human.

The second factor that made me switch majors was that I wanted to be a leader. I knew what skills were important to this goal. Ask yourself, what skills should leaders possess? They are the very same skills every college graduate should have, and they are the same as those that more than 1,000 faculty members from a cross section of academic disciplines selected: skills in writing, speaking, reading, and listening; interpersonal skills, working in and leading groups; an appreciation of cultural diversity; and the ability to adapt to innovation and change.[4] These are all skills that are developed, discussed, emphasized, and refined in a basic speech communication course. They are the central focus of this textbook.

The third and final ingredient that made me switch majors resulted from my study and experience. I recognized the importance of communication skills to my success. Whether it was oral presentations, time spent in meetings, interpersonal skills, interactions with other employees, or use of multimedia technologies, developing effective communication skills was going to be vital in all areas of my life.

Patrick Combs, author of the book *Major in Success*, includes a chapter titled "Classes Worth Their Weight in Gold." In this chapter he admonishes his readers to "Take a course that includes discussions and practice on delivering persuasive speeches, body language, assertive communications, and audiovisual aids. . . . In our society, shyness is not considered an asset." Combs writes, "A speech course can help you feel confident speaking to one or 1,000. And you can apply this confidence to situations that occur more often than in public speaking: speaking well over the phone; speaking up in class;

making a good impression in an interview; and expressing your ideas in a meeting."[5] Combs then adds this sentence in capital letters: "THE ABILITY TO COMMUNICATE EFFECTIVELY HAS BEEN CONSISTENTLY RANKED THE NUMBER ONE PERFORMANCE FACTOR FOR PROFESSIONAL SUCCESS."

STRATEGIC FLEXIBILITY (SF)

Strategic flexibility (SF) means expanding your communication repertoire (your collection or stock of communication behaviors that can readily be brought into use) to enable you to use the best skill or behavior available for a particular situation. Let's say you're caught in an unfamiliar situation, but you realize that if you can communicate your position effectively, you will free yourself from this uncomfortable position. You suddenly need all of the best skills and behaviors you can call upon. SF is a primary characteristic of successful people, a vital component of excellent relationships at work and at home, a trait of effective group leaders and participants, and the attribute of public speakers who can adapt to changing circumstances or unexpected occurrences.

People who possess SF are happier and more fulfilled because they are not only aware of their own communication skills and deficits, but also they can bring to bear on any situation they encounter a broad range of potentially valuable behaviors. Going into a new situation, they don't always know exactly what will be required, but they realize that their own background, experience, and repertoire will be sufficient to not just meet the new circumstances but to succeed in them as well. The knowledge that SF provides yields confidence and security, and helps reduce any unnecessary and unwanted fear.

Those without SF are those who approach every situation with their own limited resources. Often, this results in knee-jerk responses that depend on nothing more than the same set of behaviors used to approach any and every situation that confronts them. The problem with this approach is that there is no single way to behave in the world. The world is too complex; problems are too complicated; circumstances are too intricate and involved. It's a little like the leader who applies exactly the same set of solutions to every problem saying "You may not like my solutions, but at least you know exactly where I stand." This is discomforting information simply because it shows no recognition of SF. All problems require different sets of solutions that result from study, thought, and the serious application of a wide variety of potential behaviors.

The power of the SF concept is in its application. The six steps of SF make this possible. These steps will allow you to take SF into the world and apply it to the real-life circumstances you encounter daily:

1. **Anticipate** = Think about potential situations and the needs and requirements likely to arise because of them. The key to anticipation is forecasting. Remember Louis Pasteur's famous dictum: "Chance favors only the prepared mind."

2. **Assess** = Take stock of the factors, elements, and conditions of the situations in which you find yourself. The key to assessment is alertness.

3. **Evaluate** = Determine the value and worth of the factors, elements, and conditions to all those involved and how they bear on your own skills and abilities. The key to evaluation is accuracy.

4. **Select** = Carefully select from your repertoire of available skills and behaviors those likely to have the greatest impact on the current (and future) situations.

Consider This

In her book *Letitia Baldrige's New Manners for New Times: A Complete Guide to Etiquette*, the author writes the following as the opening paragraph in a chapter titled "The Key to Good Communication: More Than Electronics":

You can spend your life pressing keys, buttons, and whistles to get your thoughts across electronically, but the ability to use language, to communicate with people in times of joy and sorrow, and to persuade, soothe, enchant, or calm another person, is a great gift. It's also an art. We all can become accomplished in this art, if we just make ourselves aware of how important it is to both our success and happiness.

Source: *Letitia Baldrige's New Manners for New Times: A Complete Guide to Etiquette* (p. 593), by Letitia Baldrige, 2003, New York: Scribner's.

Here, one must also predict and forecast the potential effects of the skills and behaviors that will be used. The key to the selection process is appropriateness.

5. **Apply** = Now, with care, concern, and attention to all the factors that are likely to be affected—including any ethical considerations that may be appropriate—apply the skills and behaviors you have selected. The key to application is relevance.

6. **Reassess and reevaluate** = For every action taken, there is likely to be feedback as well as actions taken by others as a direct result of those taken by you. There will be other effects as well—some immediate that can be observed, some long-range that can only be surmised and anticipated. Reassessment and reevaluation may result in the application of further skills and behaviors needed to clarify, extend, continue, or even terminate the situation. The key to reassessment and reevaluation is accurate, careful observation.

Creativity

Another factor that must be mentioned within the umbrella of SF is the notion of **creativity**—the capacity to synthesize vast amounts of information and wrestle with complex problems. Creativity is not a rare or special power, and it relates directly to communication because every time you open your mouth, the unique combination of words emitted is a creative extension of who you are. Creativity requires this synthetic ability—this capacity to draw together and make sense of vast amounts of information. The more information you have (from whatever sources you can draw upon, including this instructor, this course, and this textbook), the more you have to bring to or bear upon your noticing, remembering, seeing, speaking, hearing, and understanding language and nonverbal communication. Not only are these processes important—a definite understatement—but they also allow you to search and transform the spaces on this earth you occupy. Your creativity frees you to generate possibilities, which of course is the very foundation of SF.

So, what you have is a complementary set of processes that are interwoven and mutually contributing: Creativity offers some of the creative force that drives successful SF, and SF provides the opportunities when you can apply your best creative thinking to a task.

To live, then, is to communicate. To communicate effectively is to enjoy life more fully. Consider this textbook, then, a *guide* for empowering effective communicators—for encouraging both SF and creativity. On the premise that increased knowledge helps you do things better, let's begin with a discussion of how communication works.

COMMUNICATION IS A PROCESS

A Definition of Communication

Communication is any process in which people share information, ideas, and feelings. It involves not only the spoken and written word but also body language, personal mannerisms, and style—anything that adds meaning to a message.

Each of the three opening stories illustrates communication as a process. When we say communication is a process, we mean that it is always changing.[6] When Ashley visited her guidance counselor, she looked for any sign from Mr. Vernon that would encourage her. Instead, she received a negative verbal message of six words: "I'm afraid you're not college material." This message stimulated a number of internal messages of motivation: "I'll show him. I *am* college material. I'll prove it."

The messages Andrew received also show how communication is always changing. Think, first, of the internal messages of lack of confidence, indecision, and immaturity he experienced while sitting in the cafeteria. Think, second, of the cognitive dissonance (mixed internal messages) he experienced trying to reconcile those messages with those from his friend about becoming a great actor. Think, third, of the messages he gave himself when he tried out for the play, saw that he was not on the call-back sheets, knew that he could do better, then pursued a course of action that would build his confidence and poise.

Finally, Wanda Jean DuCharme began her academic career with both direction and focus. Think about how her communication changed as she learned to think, organize ideas, question, listen, and put ideas into words. It changed, too, as her self-confidence and personal strength grew when she discovered she could communicate using her body language, personal allure, and engaging style in communicating with senior management, workers, and the public.

Knowing that communication is a process contributes positively to SF and creativity because it provides a foundation for growth, development, and change. Basically, it supports the kind of changes likely to occur as you read, experience, criticize, and put into practice the ideas, theories, and knowledge gained from a textbook and course in speech communication.

The Elements of Communication

The communication process is made up of various elements; sender-receivers, messages, channels, noise, feedback, and setting. Figure 1-1 shows how all these elements work together. The amoebalike shape of the sender-receiver indicates how this person changes—depending on what he or she is hearing or reacting to.

Sender-Receivers

People get involved in communication because they have information, ideas, and feelings they want to share. This sharing, however, is not a one-way process where one person sends ideas and the other receives them, and then the process is reversed. First, in most communication situations, people are **sender-receivers**—both sending and receiving at the same time. When you are discussing a problem with a close friend, your friend may be talking, but by listening closely, you are acting as a receiver. By paying careful attention, putting your hand on his or her arm, and showing genuine concern you are sending as many messages as you get, even though you may not say a word.

Figure 1-1
The Elements of Communication

Second, in all situations, sender-receivers share meaning. In your discussion with a close friend, both of you share the language and also share understanding of the situation.

Messages

The **message** is made up of the ideas and feelings that sender-receivers want to share. In the situation above, your close friend's message dealt with what had happened to him or her and how he or she was dealing with it, while your message was one of comfort and support. Meaning, however, is *jointly created* between sender and receiver. That is, it isn't just a sender sending a message to a receiver. There is no message at all if there aren't common symbols, like an understanding of each other's language. There is no message—or, perhaps, a very weak one—if there are no common referents, like understanding what the other person is talking about. How often, for example, do you "tune out" teachers if you have no idea where they are coming from?

Notice in Figure 1-1 that the message-feedback circle is exposed behind the amoeba-like sender-receiver shapes. This reveals that your "presence" within a message-feedback situation influences you. More than common symbols and common referents, presence can have powerful emotional, intellectual, physical, and, perhaps, spiritual effects. Think of being in the presence of a message-feedback occurrence between you and the president of the United States; an actor you admire; a priest, rabbi, or minister; or your professor. In these cases, it may not be the setting (to be discussed in a later section), or any other aspect of the message that influences you. It is simply being present within that message-feedback situation.

Ideas and feelings can be communicated only if they are represented by symbols. A **symbol** is something that stands for something else. Our daily lives are full of symbols. We all know that the eagle stands for the United States, the Statue of Liberty equals freedom, and roses express love. Two people walking close and holding hands reflects romance, books represent knowledge, and teachers stand for instruction.

Feedback and nonverbal communication are important when we communicate with others.

All our communication messages are made up of two kinds of symbols: verbal and nonverbal. The words in a language are **verbal symbols** that stand for particular things or ideas. Verbal symbols are limited and complicated. For example, when we use the word *chair*, we agree we are talking about something we sit on. Thus, *chair* is a **concrete symbol,** a symbol that represents an object. However, when we hear the word *chair*, we all might have a different impression: A chair could be a recliner, an easy chair, a beanbag, a lawn chair—the variety is great.

Even more complicated are **abstract symbols,** which stand for ideas. Consider the vast differences in our understanding of words such as *home, hungry,* or *hurt*. How we understand these words will be determined by our experience. Since people's experiences differ to some degree, individuals will assign different meanings to these abstract words.

Nonverbal symbols are ways we communicate without using words; they include facial expressions, gestures, posture, vocal tones, appearance, and so on. As with verbal symbols, we all attach certain meanings to nonverbal symbols. A yawn means we are bored or tired; a furrowed brow indicates confusion; not looking someone in the eye may mean we have something to hide. Like verbal symbols, nonverbal symbols can be misleading. We cannot control most of our nonverbal behavior, and we often send out information of which we are not even aware.

Many nonverbal messages differ from one culture to another just as symbols differ from culture to culture. Black is the color for funerals in Western cultures; in Eastern cultures, that color is white. The crescent moon of male-oriented Islam used to be the symbol for female-oriented worship of the moon mother in ancient Arabia.[7] In one culture, showing the sole of your foot when you cross your legs is an insult. In another culture, respectful behavior is shown with a bow; while in still another, deep respect is shown by touching the other person's feet. Whether or not you are aware of nonverbal messages, they are extremely important in all cultures. Albert Mehrabian, a scholar of nonverbal communication, believes that over 90 percent of the messages sent and received by Americans are nonverbal.[8]

Channels

The **channel** is the route traveled by a message; it is the means a message uses to reach the sender-receivers. In face-to-face communication, the primary channels are sound and sight: We listen to and look at each other. We are familiar with the channels of radio, television, CDs, newspapers, and magazines in the mass media. Other channels communicate nonverbal messages. For example, when DeVon goes to apply for a job, she uses several nonverbal signals to send out a positive message: a firm handshake (touch), appropriate clothing (sight), and respectful voice (sound). The senses are the channels through which she is sending a message.

Feedback

Feedback is the response of the receiver-senders to each other. You tell me a joke and I smile. That's feedback. You make a comment about the weather and I make another one. More feedback.

Strategic flexibility is an important aspect of jointly created messages. The ability to change messages in ways that will increase your chances of obtaining your desired result is exactly what SF is all about, and the need to change underscores the importance of SF in communication. People are infinitely varied in their individual traits, and even though you think you have created a message with common symbols and referents, it may not be true. Using SF, you can adapt, change, adjust, correct, or do whatever is needed to get the result you wish.

Feedback is vital to communication because it lets the participants see whether ideas and feelings have been shared in the way they were intended. For example, when Deletha and Jordan decide to meet on the corner of 45th and Broadway in New York City, it would be good feedback for one of them to ask, "Which corner?" since the four corners at that particular intersection are among the busiest and most crowded in the city.

Sender-receivers who meet face-to-face have the greatest opportunity for feedback, especially if there are no distractions—or little noise. But, often in these situations a limited amount of feedback occurs because rather than being sensitive to the feedback, communicators are busy planning what they are going to say next. **Sensory acuity** means paying attention to all elements in the communication environment. Are you paying attention to what others are saying? Are you aware of how they are saying it? Do their nonverbal messages support or contradict their verbal messages? Are you gaining or losing rapport with the other person? Is your communication bringing you closer to achieving your objective? Are you aware of distractions or noise that can derail your communication? You begin to notice at once the contribution that sensory acuity can play in all six steps of SF.

Noise

Noise is interference that keeps a message from being understood or accurately interpreted. Noise occurs between the sender-receivers, and it comes in three forms: external, internal, and semantic.

External noise comes from the environment and keeps the message from being heard or understood. Your heart-to-heart talk with your roommate can be interrupted by a group of people yelling in the hall, a helicopter passing overhead, or a weed wacker outside the window. External noise does not always come from sound. You could be standing and talking to someone in the hot sun and become so uncomfortable that you can't concentrate. Conversation might also falter at a picnic when you discover you are sitting on an anthill and ants are crawling all over your blanket.

Internal noise occurs in the minds of the sender-receivers when their thoughts or feelings are focused on something other than the communication at hand. A student doesn't hear the lecture because he is thinking about lunch; a wife can't pay attention to her husband because she is upset by a problem at the office. Internal noise may also stem from beliefs or prejudices. Doug, for example, doesn't believe that women should be managers, so when his female boss asks him to do something, he often misses part of her message.

Semantic noise is caused by people's emotional reactions to words. Many people tune out a speaker who uses profanity because the words are offensive to them. Others have negative reactions to people who make ethnic or sexist remarks. Semantic noise, like external noise and internal noise, can interfere with all or part of the message.

Setting

The **setting** is the environment in which the communication occurs. Settings can have a significant influence on communication. Formal settings lend themselves to formal presentations. An auditorium, for example, is good for giving speeches and presentations but not very good for conversation. If people want to converse on a more intimate basis, they will be better off in a smaller, more comfortable room where they can sit facing each other.

In many situations the communication will change when the setting changes. For example, in the town where one of your authors lives there was an ice cream stand just outside the city limits. People parked in front, got out of their cars, and walked up to a window to order their ice cream. On warm evenings, the place attracted many of the area's teenagers. After years of great success, the owner retired and sold the stand. The new owners decided to enclose it and make it more restaurantlike. You still had to order at the window, but because of the new addition at the front of the building, no one could see you anymore. Once you had your ice cream, you could take it to your car or eat it in the restaurant at one of the tables.

The new restaurant was certainly comfortable. You no longer had to stand in the rain, the place was open year-round, and you could sit down at a table and have dinner. However, comfort wasn't the issue: Every teenager deserted the place and headed for the Dairy Queen down the road. Why? So that they could be seen. For them, eating ice cream was secondary to participating in the social ritual of interacting with or being seen by their peers. In other words, the setting was an important part of their communication.

Setting often shows who has power in a relationship. The question "Your place or mine?" implies an equal relationship. However, when the dean asks a faculty member to come to her office, the dean has more power than the faculty member. When a couple meet to work out a divorce agreement, they meet in a lawyer's office, a place that provides a somewhat neutral setting.

Settings can have a significant influence on communication.

Another Point of View

In his book written specifically for college students, Patrick Combs writes in the opening two paragraphs of Chapter 1, "On the Road to Greatness":

Think of the students around you. What personal characteristic do you think will make the difference between those who become great at something and those who never rise above mediocrity? Intelligence? Family background? Confidence?

The answer is surprising. Benjamin Bloom, a professor at the University of Chicago, recently studied 120 outstanding athletes, artists, and scholars. He was looking for the common denominators of greatness and mastery. The study concluded that intelligence and family background were NOT important characteristics for achieving mastery of a desired skill. The only characteristic that the 120 outstanding people had in common was extraordinary drive.

Source: *Major in Success: Make College Easier, Fire Up Your Dreams, and Get a Very Cool Job* (p. 3), by Patrick Combs, 2003, Berkeley, CA: Ten Speed Press.

The arrangement of furniture in a setting can also affect the communication that takes place. For example, at one college, the library was one of the noisiest places on campus. Changing the furniture solved the problem. Instead of having sofas and chairs arranged so that students could sit and talk, the library used study desks—thus creating a quiet place to concentrate.

All communication is made up of sender-receivers, messages, channels, feedback, noise, and setting. Every time people communicate, these elements are somewhat different. They are not the only factors that influence communication, however. Communication is also influenced by what you bring to it. That is the subject of our next section.

COMMUNICATION IS A TRANSACTION

A communication transaction involves not only the physical act of communicating but also a psychological act: Impressions are being formed in the minds of the people who are communicating.[9] What people think and know about one another directly affects their communication.

The Three Principles of Transactional Communication

Communication as a transaction—**transactional communication**—involves three important principles. First, people engaged in communication are sending messages continuously and simultaneously. Second, communication events have a past, present, and future. Third, participants in communication play certain roles. Let's consider each of these principles in turn.

Participation Is Continuous and Simultaneous

Whether or not you are actually talking in a communication situation, you are actively involved in sending and receiving messages. Let's say you are lost, walking in a big city that is not familiar to you. You show others you are confused when you hesitate, look around you, or pull out a map. When you realize you have to ask for directions, you look for someone who might help you. You dismiss two people because they look like they're in a hurry; you don't ask another one because she looks as though she might be lost too. Finally you see a person who looks helpful and you ask for information. As you listen, you give feedback, through both words and body language, as to whether you understand.

As this person talks, you think about how long it will take to walk to your destination, you make note of what landmarks to look for, and you may even create a visual image of what you will see when you get there. You are participating continuously and simultaneously in a communication that is quite complicated.

All Communications Have a Past, a Present, and a Future

You respond to every situation from your own experiences, your own moods, and your own expectations. Such factors complicate the communication situation. When you know someone well, you can make predictions about what to do in the future on the basis of what you know about the past. For example, without having to ask him, Lee knows that his friend Jason will not be willing to try the new Indian restaurant in town. Lee has been out to eat with Jason many times, and Jason always eats the same kind of food, burgers and fries. Lee also knows that Jason doesn't like changes of any kind, so he knows better than to suggest that they go out of town for a concert because he knows that Jason will respond that they should wait until the group comes to their town.

Even when you are meeting someone for the first time, you respond to that person on the basis of your experience. You might respond to physical traits (short, tall, bearded, bald), to occupation (accountant, gym teacher), or even to a name (remember how a boy named Eugene always tormented you and you've mistrusted all Eugenes ever since?). Any of these things you call up from your past might influence how you respond to someone—at least at the beginning.

The future also influences communication. If you want a relationship to continue, you will say and do things in the present to make sure it does ("Thanks for dinner. I always enjoy your cooking"). If you think you will never see a person again, or if you want to limit the nature of your interactions, this also might affect your communication. You might be more businesslike and thus leave the personal aspects of your life out of the communication.

All Communicators Play Roles

Roles are parts you play or ways you behave with others. Defined by society and affected by individual relationships, roles control everything from word choice to body language. For example, one of the roles you play is that of student. Your teachers may consider you to be bright and serious; your peers, who see you in the same role, may think you are too serious. Outside the classroom you play other roles. Your parents might see you as a considerate daughter or son; your best friend might see the fun-loving side of you; and your boss might see you as hardworking and dependable.

Roles do not always stay the same in a relationship. They vary with others' moods or with one's own, with the setting and the noise factor. Communication changes to meet the needs of each of your relationships and situations. For example, even though Eduardo and Heidi have been married for 10 years and have three children, they still try to reserve Saturday night for a romantic date. While they are out, they try not to talk about children and family issues. Instead, they focus on each other and what the other is thinking and feeling. On Sunday morning, their roles change. Eduardo fixes breakfast while Heidi gets the children ready to go to church. Now their roles are children and family centered.

The roles you play—whether established by individual relationships or by society—may be perceived differently by different people. These perceptions affect the communication that results. For example, Tom, in his role of youth director, is well organized and maintains tight control over the activities he directs. The kids who play the games he coaches know they have to behave or they'll be in big trouble. Therefore they speak to him in a respectful voice and stay quiet when they're supposed to. To

Working Together

Working with classmates as a group, create a model of communication as a transaction. Drawing on everything that each person has read and all the information received in class, the group is to develop a complete model of communication as a transaction by following each of these steps:

Step 1: Talk through the process of communication as a transaction, making certain each group member contributes his or her thinking.

Step 2: Create a list of all the elements that need to be included in a model of communication as a transaction. Remember to include, as well, any important subpoints to the major principles.

Step 3: Have each member of the group create the same visual representation of the model in his or her own notebook. Each aspect of the model should be entered simultaneously, only when it is agreed upon by all members.

Step 4: One member of the group should explain the group's model to the entire class.

If there is time before this group exercise is complete, discuss as a group the question, "Why are visual representations effective tools for explaining a theory, idea, or process?"

---

some kids, however, Tom's discipline seems rigid and inflexible. These kids avoid the youth center; they choose not to communicate with him at all.

TYPES OF COMMUNICATION

As you can see in Figure 1-2, there are different kinds of communication. The figure shows four of the kinds most often used: intrapersonal, interpersonal, small-group, and public communication. In this section we will also discuss intercultural and computer-mediated communication.

Intrapersonal Communication

Intrapersonal communication is communication that occurs within you. It involves thoughts, feelings, and the way you look at yourself. Figure 1-3 shows some of the things that make up the self, hence, intrapersonal communication.

Because intrapersonal communication is centered in the self, you are the only sender-receiver. The message is made up of your thoughts and feelings. The channel is your brain, which processes what you are thinking and feeling. There is feedback in the sense that as you talk to yourself, you discard certain ideas and replace them with others.

Even though you are not directly communicating with others in intrapersonal communication, the experiences you have had determine how you "talk" to yourself. For example, think about the intrapersonal communication—all the internal messages—that Andrew (in the second opening example in this chapter) may have been creating while sitting in the cafeteria among a horde of talking, milling students who all seemed so confident, directed, and older: "What am I doing here? I am not like all these people. I don't have their confidence and security. I don't know what I want. I am so young and immature when I compare myself with them."

Interpersonal Communication

Interpersonal communication occurs when you communicate on a one-to-one basis—usually in an informal, unstructured setting. This kind of communication occurs mostly between two people, though it may include more than two.

15

Figure 1-2
Types of Communication

Intrapersonal Communication

Interpersonal Communication and Interviewing

Small-Group Communication

Public Communication

→ Primary Messages
⇢ Secondary Messages

Figure 1-3 Intrapersonal Communication

Your Appearance and Physical and Psychological Condition
Healthy
Good frame of mind
Neat
Clean
Stylish
Etc.

Your Ideal Self
Hopes
Dreams
Wishes
Goals
Desires
Aspirations
Etc.

Your Moods and Feelings
Humor
Anger
Hate
Love
Contentment
Etc.

Your Social Traits
Outgoing
Assertive
Warm
Emphatic
Etc.

Your Self
What you say
What you think
What you feel
How you are

Your Social Roles
Parent
Family provider
Community leader
Professional person
Etc.

Talent You Possess or Lack
Artistic
Musical
Athletic
Writing
Speaking
Etc.

Your Intellectual Capacity
Logical
Reflective
Studious
Speculative
Etc.

Your Strong Beliefs
Religious beliefs
Beliefs about success
Patriotic beliefs
Beliefs about family
Education beliefs
Etc.

Interpersonal communication uses all the elements of the communication process. In a conversation between friends, for example, each brings his or her background and experience to the conversation. During the conversation each functions as a sender-receiver: Their messages consist of both verbal and nonverbal symbols. The channels they use the most are sight and sound. Because interpersonal communication is between two (or a few) people, it offers the greatest opportunity for feedback. Internal noise is likely to be minimal because each person can see whether the other is distracted. The persons involved in the conversation have many chances to check that the message is being perceived correctly. People who want to engage in interpersonal communication usually look for informal and comfortable settings.

Small-Group Communication

Small-group communication occurs when a small number of people meet to solve a problem. The group must be small enough so that each member has a chance to interact with all the other members.

Because small groups are made up of several sender-receivers, the communication process is more complicated than in interpersonal communication. With so many more people sending messages, there are more chances for confusion. Messages are also more structured in small groups because the group is meeting for a specific purpose. Small groups use the same channels as are used in interpersonal communication, however, and there is also a good deal of opportunity for feedback. In keeping with their problem-solving nature, small groups usually meet in a more formal setting than people involved in interpersonal communication.

Computer-Mediated Communication

Computer-mediated communication (CMC) is defined as "a wide range of technologies that facilitate both human communication and the interactive sharing of information through computer networks, including e-mail, discussion group, newsgroups, chat, instant messages, and Web pages."[10] Using this definition alone, CMC is strictly about the variety of channels that serve as conduits for conveying messages and feedback between senders and receivers. However, when CMC is conjoined with digital literacy—"the ability to understand and use information in multiple formats from a wide range of sources when it is presented via computer"—then the combination of CMC and digital literacy fits neatly into the communication model presented earlier in this chapter with few changes except for the type of CMC technology used.[11]

The most important aspects of CMC over face-to-face communication (FtFC) include the fact that CMC occurs over a single channel, it is asynchronous (the time and place for communication is at the discretion of the individual), and the mode of communication can support thought-out prose. CMC also exhibits social leveling (it brings all people, of whatever status they hold in society, to a near-equal footing or level) as the cues to social status are removed. There are a wide variety of reasons—personal, interpersonal, and experimental—why you would choose CMC over FtFC.

Public Communication

In **public communication** the sender-receiver (the speaker) sends a message (the speech) to an audience. The speaker usually delivers a highly structured message, using the same channels as in interpersonal and small-group communication. In public communication, however, the channels are more exaggerated than in interpersonal communication. The voice is louder and the gestures are more expansive because the audience is bigger. The speaker might use additional visual channels, such as slides or the computer program PowerPoint. Generally, the opportunity for verbal feedback in public communication is limited. The audience members may have a chance to ask questions at the end of the speech, but usually they are not free to address the speaker during the speech. However, they can send nonverbal feedback. If they like what the speaker is saying, they may interrupt the speech with applause. If they dislike it, they may fidget a lot or simply stop paying attention. In most public communication, the setting is formal.

Intercultural Communication

There are cultural and technological forces that are now reshaping the world. It is the communication skills—whether of senders or receivers—that determine how well individuals, organizations, industries, and even nations do in acquiring and applying knowledge, thus broadening their chances for success in this information-driven world. The better you are at negotiating the cultural issues in communication, the greater the competitive edge you gain in a global society.

When we talk about **culture,** we mean "the ever-changing values, traditions, social and political relationships, and worldview created and shared by a group of people bound together by a combination of factors (which can include a common history, geographic location, language, social class, and/or religion)."[12] Cultures could include the Amish or Pennsylvania Dutch, groups with a common history. Cultures could include the Japanese or Taiwanese, groups with a common geographic location. Cultures also could include those who speak the French or Islamic languages.

By **co-culture,** we mean people who are part of a larger culture but also belong to a smaller group that has some different values, attitudes, or beliefs. For example, co-cultures could include the socially elite, those in the top 1 percent income bracket, the Baptists, Catholics, Unitarian-Universalists, or Jews—all part of the larger U.S. culture, yet smaller groups possessing some different values, attitudes, and beliefs. African Americans, Native Americans, Hispanic Americans, and Asian Americans make up large co-cultures within the U.S. culture. Within the U.S. culture are co-cultures made up of gay and lesbian people, older people, and people with physical disabilities.

To help people understand each other better, scholars, teachers, and worldwide business leaders have developed the field of **intercultural communication**—the communication that occurs whenever two or more people from different cultures interact. This field studies how differences between people affect their perceptions of the world and, thus, their communication. Of course, there is no way to understand all cultures and co-cultures. There are, however, certain characteristics that occur again and again, and the study of intercultural communication rests on these characteristics.

Why should you be concerned about intercultural communication? What if your job involved coordinating international student services and exchange programs at your university or college campus? What if you were the manager of a biotech com-

Every year the United States becomes more culturally diverse.

pany responsible for leading a diverse team of scientists doing innovative research? What if you were a member of a campus group interested in gathering the support of diverse groups on campus to extend an invitation to a controversial speaker? In each case, to overlook the different cultural backgrounds of those receivers might mean your communication would be less constructive and may result in misunderstandings and breakdowns as well. There are inherent cultural issues associated with any form of communication.

Although people throughout the world have many characteristics in common, there are also many differences. Thus, if people from different cultural or co-cultural groups want to communicate, they must be aware that they may have different systems of knowledge, values, beliefs, customs, and behaviors. For example, crossing your legs in the United States reveals a relaxed attitude, but in Korea it is a social faux pas. In West Africa, the comment "You've put on weight" means you look healthy and prosperous and is a great compliment; in America it is an insult. In Japan, they put business cards in safe places and handle them with great care, because they view them as an extension of the person, in America they are viewed as a business formality and convenience, and Americans are quick to put them away, a behavior insulting to the Japanese.[13] Understanding differences and then utilizing them in the preparation, development, and presentation of your ideas can only help you become a more effective communicator.

ETHICAL COMMUNICATION

Ethical communication, a component of each of the six types of communication, is communication that is honest, fair, and considerate of others' rights. Communication is honest when communicators tell the truth; it is fair and considerate when they consider listeners' feelings. Most people reading this believe that truthfulness, accuracy, honesty, and reason are essential to the integrity of communication, just as it is written in the National Communication Association's (NCA's) Credo for Ethical Communication.[14]

The problem, of course, is neither with what you know to be true nor with what you want to have happen. The problem occurs as you are faced with complex demands (too much being asked of you), limited resources (like time), or the easy access to alternatives to ethical behavior (being handed an exam, paper, or speech)—or what is often likely, the combination of some or all of these. There is always the very human temptation to try to make life easier by nullifying some of your fundamental ethical responsibilities. That, of course, is when your true ethics are revealed.

You have undoubtedly heard numerous excuses for unethical conduct. The most often may be "I didn't know that was considered unethical." Others include "Everyone does it," or "I'm sorry, I just didn't have the time [to be ethical]," "What harm is there in it?" "I've been sick," "I've never done it before," "You know, I'm very busy." It is not surprising that those who engage in unethical behavior have quick and easy excuses for what they do. No excuse, of course, is good enough to justify truly unethical conduct.

Why should you be concerned about ethical communication? It is clearly stated in the NCA's Credo: "Unethical communication threatens the quality of all communication and consequently the well-being of individuals and the society in which we live."[15] As the Credo states in its opening paragraph, ethical communication is "fundamental to responsible thinking, decision making, and the development of relationships and communities within and across contexts, cultures, channels, and media. Ethical communication enhances human worth and respect for self and others."[16] Because of the worldwide publicity given to the unethical practices of large corporations such as Enron, Tyco, WorldCom, and in the mutual funds industry, there is an increasing trend for organizations to integrate a code of ethics into their daily activities.

"Questions of right and wrong arise whenever people communicate," the Credo states, thus, it is important to establish a basic code of ethics as you begin a course in speech communication. As you read the following principles of ethical communication, notice the two ethical communication themes of caring and responsibility. These seven principles have been paraphrased from the Credo:

- Protect freedom of expression, diversity of perspective, and tolerance for dissent.
- Strive to understand and respect others' communications before evaluating and responding to their messages.
- Help promote communication climates of caring and mutual understanding that protect the unique needs and characteristics of individual communicators.
- Condemn communication that degrades individuals and humanity through distortions, intolerance, intimidation, coercion, hatred, or violence.
- Commit yourself to the courageous expression of your personal convictions in pursuit of fairness and justice.
- Accept responsibility for the short- and long-term consequences of your own communication, and expect the same of others.
- Avoid plagiarism—presentation of the work of another person in such a way as to give the impression that the other's work is your own, whether it be:
  - the verbatim use of part of a book or article without using quotation marks and without citing the original source.
  - paraphrasing another's words without noting this is a paraphrase essentially taken from another source.
  - using another person's illustrative material without citing the source and, thus, giving credit where credit is due.

  The basic idea in avoiding plagiarism is simply to give credit when using someone else's ideas. If you have any doubts, give the credit—using a footnote or a reference *during* (as part of) the communication.[17]

Sometimes it is easy to look at what goes on in this world and develop a hardened, insensitive, and unfeeling attitude toward ethics: proper conduct. But if you conduct yourself as an ethical person in your dealings with family, friends, and others, refraining from activities that may be construed as unethical—whether they are governed by written or unwritten codes of personal conduct, rules, or regulations—and if you continue your wholehearted commitment to being a credible, quality person who demonstrates care, consideration, and dedication to values and morals, you will promote ethical thinking and living and be an example to others.

COMMUNICATING EFFECTIVELY

Once you understand the process of communication, you can begin to understand why communication does or doesn't work. In an ideal communication situation the message is perceived in the way it was intended. But when messages don't work, it is useful to ask these questions: Was there a problem with the message? Was the best channel used? Did noise occur? Knowing the right questions to ask is essential to building skills in communication.

Most of us already have considerable communication skills. You have been sending and receiving verbal and nonverbal signals all your life. Nevertheless, you have probably had times when you have not communicated as effectively as you should. If you got a lower grade on a paper than you expected, you unintentionally hurt somebody's feelings, or if the instructor did not understand a question you asked in class, you are not communicating as effectively as you could.

Where to Begin

The information about communication is so vast that most of us could spend a lifetime studying the subject and not learn even a fraction of what there is to know. However, as you begin your study of communication, the following five questions are a good starting point.

Which Communication Skills Am I Most Likely to Need?

Find out what communication skills are important to you. What do you intend to do in your life? What kind of work do you expect to do? What communication skills are required in this work? Which of these skills do you already have? Which ones need improvement? Which ones do you need to acquire?

For example, a career in business requires almost every communication skill. You need interpersonal skills to get along with the people you work with, intercultural communication skills if you are going to work with people from other countries, and public-speaking skills for making presentations. Although you may use some communication skills more than others, at one time or another you are going to need every one we have discussed in this chapter.

Which Communication Skills Am I Most Lacking?

Which kinds of communication are most difficult for you? Intrapersonal? Interpersonal? Intercultural? Small group? Public speaking? What are the symptoms of difficulties in these areas? What problems do you have to overcome before you can perform effectively?

Many people would prefer to avoid, rather than work in, the area that gives them the most trouble. For example, if you are anxious about public speaking, you might feel inclined to avoid any circumstance where you have to give a speech. A better approach, however, would be to get over this fear: You'll be able to offer a wedding toast, give a presentation at a meeting, consider many more job possibilities, and so forth. If you can conquer fear by plunging in and practicing the thing that gives you the most trouble, you will expand the possibilities in your life.

How Can I Get Communication Practice?

Are there situations, other than class, where you can practice communication skills that will be useful to you? Are there groups and organizations you can join that will help you develop these skills? It's always a good idea to take what you have learned in class and try it out on the world. Using new skills helps to develop and refine them.

Where Can I Get Help?

What people do you know who will help you develop communication skills and give you feedback on how you are doing? Are there people you can ask who will give you support when you are trying something new and threatening? Are you willing to ask them to support you? You can usually count on this kind of support from your friends. Don't you have a friend who would be willing to listen to one of your speeches and tell you whether it works and how you might improve it? Also, don't forget your instructors. Many of them sit in their offices during office hours hoping that students will drop by.

What Timetable Should I Set?

Have you set a realistic timetable for improvement? Knowing that it is difficult to learn new skills or break bad habits, are you willing to give yourself enough time? Your speech communication class is going to last for a semester or a quarter, and although you will be making steady progress in your interpersonal communication and public-speaking skills, change will not happen overnight. The act of communicating—whether with a single person or a classroom audience—takes time and effort. The most realistic timetable is one in which you say, "I'm going to keep working at this until I succeed."

THE INTERNET AND THE COMMUNICATION PROCESS

The landscape of the Internet along with all aspects of technology and communication continues to change quickly. The problem with relating the Internet to the communication process is that the Internet contains many different configurations of communication. **Synchronous communication** means talk that occurs at the same time—with no time delay. With respect to senders and receivers, it could be one-to-one, one-to-a few, one-to-many, or even many-to-one. The best examples of synchronous communication are instant messaging (IM) and chat rooms. **Asynchronous communication** does not occur at the same time, such as e-mail messages or when you seek information from Web sites. For those familiar with the Internet, Usenet, electronic bulletin boards, and Listservers are asynchronous. The words *synchronous* and *asynchronous* help categorize Internet communication, but also reveal some of the problems in trying to categorize it.

The point here is not to confuse but to show the role of the Internet in the sender-message-receiver elements of communication pictured in Figure 1-1. Sometimes the elements are configured similar to the model; sometimes they are put into entirely new configurations.

An Internet model of communication must have an active receiver who emits information, interacts with—or has the potential of interacting with—the sender or Web site and selects his or her own information and decodes it according to personal interests. Because of the influence of the Internet and the active character of the public (a mass of active receivers), the Internet has become one of the most important elements of public opinion formation.

Messages can be as simple as conversations between two people, but they can also be traditional journalistic news stories created by a reporter or editor, stories placed on Web logs (blogs) by people with unknown or uncertain credentials, stories created over a long period by many people, or outdated stories that have been stored on a Web site and never updated since their creation years ago—the latter is called Web rot.

Although the channel for the communication may be one computer—or a network of computers—with another, settings can vary from one's home or office to anyplace where one can carry a laptop or gain computer access. You have seen people with laptops in airport terminals, waiting for a bus, or in hospital waiting rooms. Cell phones provide yet another means of access.

If how we communicate is affected by the tools we use to communicate, then it should be clear that the communication we have with others via the computer is significantly different from communication we might have via the telephone, a written letter, or a face-to-face meeting. We will explore some of these differences in the Internet communications sections in every chapter.

Perhaps the major difference the Internet introduces into communication is the removal of face-to-face communication. Face-to-face interactions will increase with direct video links between computers. The Internet's effect on communication has four characteristics that make it unique from normal face-to-face communication. The first is **globalization**—there are no limitations because of borders. The second is **temporality**—there are no limitations because of time. The third is **access to roles.** Whoever has the technical capacity to receive messages with a computer can also send them. Senders and receivers do this without restrictions on their roles, whether it involves being a student, commentator, reporter, businessperson, citizen, politician, or some fabricated identity. The fourth characteristic is **content openness.** There are no limitations on content. Within the obvious boundaries of a computer's capabilities, content can take on any form desired by senders and receivers. Just as a message may be typed, videotaped, audiotaped, or simply visualized, news too can be communicated via text, games, or letters.

These characteristics make audiences more independent of traditional media sources, but they involve a loss of control over source reliability, selection of information, and control over verification. It increases risks because of the loss of traditional journalistic controls—or any controls—over the information market, and, as a result, it raises the responsibility for Internet users to be wise consumers.

The Internet will continue to lead to changes in how people communicate, solve problems, and create knowledge. It will continue to evolve. What we can do is examine, assess, and evaluate the changes and how they affect senders, receivers, messages, feedback, channels, and settings—interpersonally, at work, in groups, and in public-communication settings.

Assess Yourself

Do You Have Strategic Flexibility?

For each question circle the numerical score that best represents your performance, skill, or ability using the following scale; 7 = Outstanding; 6 = Excellent; 5 = Very good; 4 = Average (good); 3 = Fair; 2 = Poor; 1 = Minimal ability; 0 = No ability demonstrated.

1. Do you try to anticipate situations—think about them *before* they occur—to prepare yourself mentally (and physically) for what is likely to happen? 7 6 5 4 3 2 1 0
2. Do you generally look at new situations with an eye toward determining if communication will be needed or required by you? 7 6 5 4 3 2 1 0
3. From your assessment of a situation, is it easy for you to determine *when* communication is necessary? 7 6 5 4 3 2 1 0
4. Do you find it easy to know—once engaged in communication—what the purpose of the communication is? What people hope to accomplish? 7 6 5 4 3 2 1 0
5. When you are with a group of people, can you—from simple, preliminary observations—determine what their needs and assumptions are? 7 6 5 4 3 2 1 0
6. When you are with a group of people, do you automatically know what their relationship is to you? 7 6 5 4 3 2 1 0
7. Do you also know what your relationship to this group of people is? 7 6 5 4 3 2 1 0
8. Are you able to anticipate how an audience would use any communication you shared with them? 7 6 5 4 3 2 1 0
9. When you are talking with another person, or other people, are you able to determine—in advance—what effect your communication *should* have on them? 7 6 5 4 3 2 1 0
10. Can you tell from preliminary assessments what kind of communication might be appropriate in particular situations? 7 6 5 4 3 2 1 0
11. Do you feel you have the breadth of knowledge, experience, and skills to more than effectively meet most of the communication-related situations you encounter? 7 6 5 4 3 2 1 0
12. Do you feel comfortable when you encounter a situation where you know you will have to communicate? 7 6 5 4 3 2 1 0
13. Do you feel confident, secure, and free of nervousness when facing communication situations? 7 6 5 4 3 2 1 0
14. When you have to communicate with others, do you feel as if the behaviors and skills you put into use are the same ones you always use? 7 6 5 4 3 2 1 0
15. When you communicate, do you feel like you use some of the techniques, styles, or behaviors of the other gender? 7 6 5 4 3 2 1 0
16. Do you believe there is a possibility of and value for expanding your range of communication skills and behaviors? 7 6 5 4 3 2 1 0

Go to the *Communicating Effectively* CD-ROM and the Online Learning Center at **www.mhhe.com/hybels8** to see your results and learn how to evaluate your attitudes and feelings.

mhhe.com/hybels8

CHAPTER REVIEW

SUMMARY

Everyone needs good communication skills. Effective communication will help you feel more confident about yourself, more comfortable with others' perceptions of you, greater ease in reasoning with others, better at using language, and improvement in your critical thinking skills. It is the ultimate people-oriented discipline, fundamental to effective leadership, and a key to professional success.

Strategic flexibility (SF) means expanding your communication repertoire to enable you to use the best skill or behavior available for a particular situation. People who possess SF are happier and more fulfilled because they can bring to bear on any situation a broad range of potentially valuable behaviors. The six steps of SF are anticipate, assess, evaluate, select, apply, and reassess and reevaluate.

Creativity is the capacity to synthesize vast amounts of information and wrestle with complex problems. Your creativity frees you to generate possibilities, which of course is the very foundation of SF.

Communication is an ongoing process in which people share ideas and feelings. The elements of communication include sender-receivers, messages, channels, feedback, noise, and setting. The essence of communication is meaning making, and meaning is jointly created between sender and receiver.

Every communication is a transaction. Viewing communication as a transaction focuses on the people who are communicating and the changes that take place in them as they are communicating. It also implies that all participants are involved continuously and simultaneously; that communication events have a past, present, and future; and that the roles the participants play will affect the communication.

Six types of communication are discussed in this book. Intrapersonal communication is communication within oneself. Interpersonal communication is informal communication with one or more other persons. Small-group communication occurs when a small group of people get together to solve a problem. Computer-mediated communication refers to a wide range of technologies that facilitate both human communication and the interactive sharing of information through computer networks. It is discussed in the in-text appendix. Public communication is giving a speech to an audience. Intercultural communication occurs whenever two or more people from different cultures interact.

Ethical communication, a component of each of the six types of communication above, is communication that is honest, fair, and considerate of others' rights. Underlying the seven principles of ethical conduct paraphrased from the National Communication Association's Credo are the themes of caring and responsibility. Proper ethical conduct often grows out of an individual's personal commitment to live an ethical life.

Communication can be improved if you concentrate on several important areas. Find out what communication skills are important to you. Discover the kinds of communication that are most difficult for you and work to improve them. Seek out people who will help you develop these skills and give you support and feedback, and set a realistic timetable for improvement.

The Internet plays with the sender-message-receiver features of the elements of communication. There are four characteristics that make it unique from normal face-to-face communication: globalization, temporality, access to roles, and content openness. The Internet will continue to lead to changes in how people communicate, solve problems, and create knowledge.

CHAPTER REVIEW

KEY TERMS AND CONCEPTS

Use the *Communicating Effectively* CD-ROM and the Online Learning Center at **www.mhhe.com/hybels8** to further your understanding of the following terms.

Abstract symbol 10
Access to roles 24
Anticipate 6
Apply 7
Assess 6
Asynchronous communication 23
Channel 10
Co-culture 19
Communication 8
Computer-mediated communication (CMC) 18
Concrete symbol 10
Content openness 24
Creativity 7

Culture 19
Ethical communication 20
Evaluate 6
External noise 11
Feedback 11
Globalization 24
Intercultural communication 19
Internal noise 11
Interpersonal communication 15
Intrapersonal communication 15
Message 9
Noise 11
Nonverbal symbol 10
Public communication 18

Reassess and reevaluate 7
Roles 14
Select 7
Semantic noise 12
Sensory acuity 11
Sender-receivers 8
Setting 12
Small-group communication 17
Strategic flexibility (SF) 6
Symbol 9
Synchronous communication 23
Temporality 24
Transactional communication 13
Verbal symbol 10

QUESTIONS TO REVIEW

1. What are the most frequently cited factors important to aiding graduating college students both to obtain and sustain employment?
2. What is the meaning of strategic flexibility (SF)?
3. What are the six steps of SF, and what is the key to each step?
4. What is the role of creativity in communication?
5. Why is communication called a process?
6. What is the significance in knowing that meaning is jointly created between sender and receiver?
7. What are the differences between the symbols that make up communication messages?
8. Why is communication called a transaction? What are the three principles of transactional communication?
9. How do intrapersonal and interpersonal communication differ from each other?
10. What is the difference between culture and co-culture?
11. Why should you be concerned about intercultural communication?
12. What are the principles of ethical communication, and what is likely to be the foundation for ethical conduct?
13. What are the four characteristics that make Internet communication distinctive from face-to-face communication?
14. What are the risks involved regarding Internet communication?

Go to the self-quizzes on the *Communicating Effectively* CD-ROM and the Online Learning Center at **www.mhhe.com/hybels8** to test your knowledge of the chapter concepts.

CHAPTER 2

Self, Perception, and Communication

OBJECTIVES

After reading this chapter, you should be able to:

- Explain the role of self and perception in communication.
- Describe self-concept and how it is formed.
- Describe the ways you have to improve a weak or poor self-concept.
- Point out the understandings that Alford Korzybski's theory ("The map is not the territory") clarifies.
- Explain how the Internet relates to the self and communication.
- Explain each of the perceptual steps of selecting, organizing, and interpreting.
- Explain perceptual filters and the ways that they may influence your perceptions.
- Explain the difference between objective reality and a subjective point of view.
- Describe the different ways you have of adjusting to perceptual influences.

RAANI BENAZIR WAS A SHY 17-YEAR-OLD LIVING IN BANGLADESH (FORMERLY known as East Pakistan). Raani lived in a large house with her parents and one younger sister and brother. Although Raani attended private school because her father worked for the government, she knew her chances of attending an American university were slim because very few from her country ever did so and because she was not number one in her graduating class. Having heard of Raani's desire, a friend of her father's gave him a scholarship form for Raani to complete. Raani's computer skills and English fluency came to her aid, and she was accepted. In her first-year student orientation class, she met Cheryl Davis, another new student, who helped her understand U.S. customs, interpret others' behaviors, and clarify perceptions and observations.

Raani, experiencing her first time in the United States, was overwhelmed. Her shyness, being a female from a country where women generally occupy a secondary position (to males), and her newness to the university and to this country all created an environment that, in most cases, would produce a weakened self-concept, distorted perceptions, and hesitating (or ineffectual) communication. For Raani, however, it both challenged and motivated her. It was, after all, her dream, and she was determined to be the best she could be—to fulfill her dream and then some.

THE ROLE OF SELF AND PERCEPTION IN COMMUNICATING EFFECTIVELY AND STRATEGIC FLEXIBILITY

An obvious question when beginning a chapter titled "Self, Perception, and Communication" is "What does this have to do with communication?" Or, perhaps, "Why do I need to know this?" Both self and perception are foundations for effective communication. Your **self-concept** is how you think and feel about yourself. Self-concept and perception are so closely related that they are often difficult to separate. **Perception** is how you look at others and the world around you. Now, here's the connection: How you look at the world depends on what you think of yourself, and what you think of yourself will influence how you look at the world. Thus, your communication—the words and nonverbal cues you use when you talk with others—will be a direct and obvious result of both your self-concept and perceptions. As noted in Chapter 1, your communication is always changing because, in part, your self-concept and perceptions are always changing.

Realize that your self-concept can set limits on your behavioral possibilities. Because of your self-concept, you may consider yourself unlovable, irrational, inadequate, incompetent, worthless, or inferior. If you think of yourself as unlovable, this may cause you to believe you are ineligible for the love of another person. If you think of yourself as irrational, this may cause you to believe that you are ineligible to render logical, well-grounded judgments and decisions.

Another limitation imposed by your self-concept has to do with risk taking. Being who you take yourself to be, some action or experience becomes unthinkable. To take *that* action or have *that* experience would so violate who you are that, should you do it, you could no longer take yourself to be the same person. You would be forced to see yourself as someone different. Think of what it might take, for example, to leave a destructive relationship, defend your rights in an assertive and forceful manner, or take the initiative to lead a group in a dramatic new direction.

A third limitation imposed by your self-concept relates directly to perception, but because of its importance, needs to be restated. You will perceive the world in ways that are in keeping with your self-concept. For you, that will be "just the way the world is." If you, for example, think of yourself as "world's greatest failure," then you might read anyone else's positive comments about you as cases of misunderstanding or praise as ill-motivated, deceitful flattery. To have a self-concept, then, is not just to have a certain appraisal of yourself, it is to live in a certain world.

Imagine, for a moment, Raani's situation. Undoubtedly, how she thinks and feels about herself is determined in part by the role and perception of women in Bangladesh, by the way she was raised by her parents, and by the perceptions and reactions of her friends and teachers. It will take her a while to understand the place that women hold in the United States and how she fits into those roles, the function of students at a university and how active they must be to impact their own education, and the perceptions and reactions of her new friends and instructors.

Because Raani has defined the differences as challenges, and has used her situation to motivate personal growth, development, and change, you can see how readily both her self-concept and perceptions will change and how her communication will change as well. Improvements are likely to be observed in her readiness to ask and answer questions, speak out on her observations and perceptions, and take a more active, assertive role in her relationships with others. If you could stand back and observe Raani's changes, you would likely see a much stronger, more certain, and—definitely—more effective communicator emerge.

How do self-concept and perception fit into the six steps of strategic flexibility? First, with stronger self-confidence, you will have a sturdy base of operations—more strength and confidence in your ability to anticipate, assess, and evaluate communication situations. Second, with more accurate perceptions you will increase your repertoire of available skills and behaviors, thus you will have more from which to select and, likely, more accuracy and precision in their application. Reassessment and reevaluation become more effective as well because the context for all your actions will be broader, more immediate, and relevant.

What is important to know is that it doesn't take much change in your self-concept or in your perceptions to influence your communication. The starting point can be just as soon as you want it to be. Nothing is likely to change if you are closed-minded, reluctant, and hesitant or full of fear, doubt, and concern. Nothing is likely to change either if you think you know everything you need to know, or if you think there is no need or room for improvement. You must be open to change, since change is going to happen. You must be open to new findings and understandings. And you must be open to options, alternatives, and possible new choices. It can be a great journey, but without a commitment from you, there's likely to be no journey at all—just words on a page or ideas that travel in one ear and out the other—if, indeed, they get that far.

SELF-CONCEPT

The case of Raani Benazir reveals that the self is mobile, personal, self-reflexive (causing one to think and reflect), and subject to change. Although she was born into a rigid social structure in her native country of Bangladesh, in the United States she became freer to create her own identity. (The words *self* and *identity* are being used synonymously.) How she thinks and feels about herself is socially constructed as she assumes different roles throughout her lifetime. Her identity is established as a result of mutual recognition from others combined with self-validation. For example, those who had contact with Raani discovered a soft-spoken, intelligent, witty, and incredibly perceptive individual who was more than willing to share her background, history, and insights—mutual recognition. Because of what they discovered and the respect and admiration they revealed, Raani became more outspoken, charming, and humorous—self-validation. Her thoughts of being a second-class citizen (how many women are often viewed in Bangladesh) changed, and she emerged from a self- and culture-imposed shell to become more self-confident, self-assured, and self-reliant.

Just as in Raani's case, your self-concept is based on the values of the culture and the community you come from. Your culture tells you what is competent and moral by defining attitudes and beliefs; the community you belong to tells you what is expected of you. The extent to which you reflect the attitudes and beliefs of your culture and live up to the expectations of your community will determine how you see yourself. If Raani were to spend her life in the town where she grew up, her self-concept would be formed by a very limited group of people. When she moved from Bangladesh to the United States, there were many more influences. If she moved between two or more cultures—which she might do because of her interest in international relations—the influences would be even greater.

Self-concept is made up of three distinct elements: reflected appraisals, social comparisons, and self-perception. Let's look at each of them.

Reflected Appraisals

Remember the story of Tarzan? Although Tarzan was a human, he believed he was an ape because he was brought up by apes and had no human experience. Tarzan's story reminds you that you are not born with an identity—others give it to you. Your parents, your friends, and your teachers all tell you who you are through **reflected appraisals:** messages you get about yourself from others. Most reflected appraisals come from things people say about you. Your college speech communication instructor may say you are a good speaker, your peers may say you are a good friend, and your coach may tell you that you must work harder. All such messages from others help create your self-concept.

Besides being given messages about yourself, you are also given lines to speak.[1] These lines are often so specific that some people refer to them as **scripts.** Some scripts are given to you by your parents, and they contain directions that are just as explicit as any script intended for the stage. You are given your lines ("Say thank you to the nice woman"), your gestures ("Point to the horsie"), and your characterizations ("You're a good girl/boy"). The scripts tell you how to play future scenes ("Everyone in your family has gone to college") and what is expected of you ("I will be so happy when you make us grandparents"). People outside your family also contribute to your scripts. Teachers, coaches, religious leaders, friends, the media, and the Internet all tell you what they expect from you, how you should look, how you should behave, and how you should say your lines. Sometimes you receive the messages directly, and sometimes you get them by observing and then imitating others' behavior.

Writer and radio personality Garrison Keillor gives a list of scripts we get as we are growing up. Have you heard any of them or used them on your own children?

    I. *I don't know what's wrong with you.*
        A. *I never saw a person like you.*
            1. *I wasn't like that.*
            2. *Your cousins don't pull stuff like that.*

    B. It doesn't make sense.
        1. *You have no sense of responsibility at all.*
        2. *We've given you everything we possibly could.*
            a. *Food on the table and a roof over your head.*
            b. *Things we never had when we were your age.*
        3. *And you treat us like dirt under your feet.*
    C. You act as if
        1. *The world owes you a living.*
        2. *You've got a chip on your shoulder.*
        3. *The rules don't apply to you.*

II. Something has got to change and change fast.
    A. *You're driving your mother to a nervous breakdown.*
    B. *I'm not going to put up with this for another minute.*
        1. *You're crazy if you think I am.*
        2. *If you think I am, just try me.*
    C. *You're setting a terrible example for your younger brothers and sisters.*

III. I'm your father and as long as you live in this house, you'll—
    A. *Do as you're told, and when I say "now" I mean "now."*
    B. Pull your own weight.
        1. *Don't expect other people to pick up after you.*
        2. *Don't expect breakfast when you get up at noon.*
        3. *Don't come around asking your mother for spending money.*
    C. *Do something about your disposition.*

IV. If you don't change your tune pretty quick, then you're out of here.
    A. *I mean it.*
    B. Is that understood?
        1. *I can't hear you. Don't mumble.*
        2. *Look at me.*
    C. *I'm not going to tell you this again.*[2]

If you were given positive reflected appraisals when you were young, you probably have a good self-concept; if the appraisals were largely negative, your self-concept may suffer. The messages you receive about yourself can become **self-fulfilling prophecies**—events or actions that occur because you (and other people) have expected them. For example, at the beginning of the semester Professor Farley said to Kevin, "You're going to be a very good student." Because of this expectation, Kevin wanted to be a good student and worked hard to live up to Professor Farley's prophecy. Similarly, negative prophecies can have a negative impact. If someone tells a child that he or she will "never amount to much," there is a good chance the child will not.

Social Comparisons

When you compare yourself with others to see how you measure up, you are making a **social comparison.** Social comparisons are not just important, they are necessary in helping develop an accurate self-perception. An accurate self-perception is crucial for navigating and responding to the social world through effective communication.

If you think about it, you can't evaluate yourself without some form of comparison. You may, for example, compare yourself with your peers. You might ask, "Do I look as good as she does?" or "What grade did you get on your midterm?" or "What kind of car do you drive?" If you are a parent, you might compare your child to your friend's child. "Can he talk yet?" "Did she get a position on the softball team?" In your job, you are likely to ask yourself if you are doing as well as your co-workers. Did you get as big a raise as your colleague got? Does the boss ever notice you and praise your work? The answers to these social comparison questions all contribute to your self-concept.

Social comparisons are pivotal to self-evaluations. They depend less on objective circumstances than on how you judge yourself in relation to others on particular attributes. You prefer to compare yourself to others who are similar for the attribute of concern. For example, the first question in the paragraph above, "Do I look as good as she does?" may refer to body image. Social comparisons also can be employed to gather information about highly valued attributes (personality, money, or success), social expectations (appropriate attire and expected behavior), and norms (rules, laws, and acceptable practices). That is why comparisons are likely to be made to a variety of targets—there is such a broad range of information needed.

Let's focus on a single attribute of concern: body image evaluation. The repeated media images of thin females and muscular males make these forms seemingly the standard of attractiveness. The gender differences in the attributes associated with body image are those that would be expected. Weight is the primary feature predicting body dissatisfaction among women. Height and shoulders—or muscular shape—is the attractiveness concern of males. From where do the standards come? Pressures for the proper body image come from parents, peers, dating partners, as well as the media. They can be direct, such as a parent encouraging a daughter to diet or a son to lift weights, or indirect, such as a peer voicing admiration of a particular model who reveals the attributes. Constant exposure is likely to make both men and women self-conscious about their bodies and make them obsess over and consider their physical appearance a measure of their worth. Of course, this is both a narrow and limited measure.

In a single day, you see many images of how people should look and behave. In a lifetime, you may receive 40 to 50 million commercial messages. Magazines, movies, and videos all contribute to what the "ideal you" should be. Even if you can discount

The way we see ourselves is often a reflection of how we compare ourselves with others.

Working Together

As a group, work together to list as many items as you can think of over which you have direct control. Each should be an item that will help people like those in your group to *appreciate themselves more.* After listing items, arrange them in hierarchical order with the most important items listed first. With the list complete, answer the questions that follow.

In her book *In the Dressing Room with Brenda,* Brenda Kinsel suggests some of the following items:

- the color or curl of your hair
- the shape or form of your body
- how your eyes open every morning and allow you to see life
- how your legs take you to your car or to your classes every day
- how your fingers can soothe a sore muscle

Which of the following plays the most important role in determining which items get listed and why: reflected appraisals, social comparisons, or self-perception? Which of these three is likely to have the most impact on each of the members of your group?

What is the point of this group exercise? Kinsel suggests two points:

1. When you begin practicing appreciation, it gets easier.
2. Self-appreciation has its most direct effect on your self-concept.

Source: *In the Dressing Room with Brenda: A Fun and Practical Guide to Buying Smart and Looking Great,* by Brenda Kinsel, 2001, Berkeley, CA: Wildcat Canyon Press (a division of Circulus Publishing Group, Inc.).

these images as being unrealistic, many of the people around you believe them and judge you and others by what they see and hear.

Self-Perception

You think, feel, speak, and act in accordance with your self-image. The way you see yourself is called **self-perception.** The process of accumulating views of your self is both complex and ongoing. Consciously and subconsciously you weigh whether others' thoughts, attitudes, actions, and reactions will work for you. It is a little like putting pieces of a puzzle together; however, not only does the puzzle picture constantly change, but seldom does anyone have all the pieces that make up the picture. Even when you may have a puzzle piece in your hand, the piece may not fit where you think it goes, or it may not fit the picture you thought it would. Why is this process so confusing?

First, self-perception is made up of so many variables. They include physical, social, intellectual, and spiritual elements such as convictions about principles; basic personal wants and desires; moral, religious, and political feelings; as well as responses to personal freedom, social controls, and oppression of one kind or another. They include, too, how you respond to failings and difficulties (or achievements and successes) as well as mental stress and self-deception.

Second, self-perception depends on the phase of your development, which is constantly changing as well. Often, as one ages, one becomes more open to the ideas of others, okay with being wrong, less attached to particular outcomes, and better listeners.[3] When all is said and done, self-perception is a little like what a state trooper told a woman when he stopped her for speeding: "My measure of your speed is but a momentary picture of what occurs in a fraction of a second. That's all it can be."

Numbers of variables and constant change, however, don't deny the importance or application of self-perception. Accept your self-perception as a momentary picture. What can you do to make it positive? First, make certain you have a positive attitude,

Another Point of View

In his article "Lacking in Self-Esteem? Good for You!," Andrew Sullivan writes that self-esteem isn't all that it's cracked up to be. Drawing on the research performed by Brad Bushman of Iowa State University and Roy Baumeister of Case Western Reserve University, Sullivan writes:

> Self-esteem can also be an educational boomerang. Friends of mine who teach today's college students are constantly complaining about the high self-esteem of their students. When the kids have been told from Day One that they can do no wrong, when every grade in high school is assessed so as to make the kid feel good rather than to give an accurate measure of his work, the student can develop self-worth dangerously unrelated to the objective truth. He can then get deeply offended when he's told he is getting a C grade in college and become demoralized or extremely angry. Weak professors give in to the pressure—hence, grade inflation. Tough professors merely get exhausted trying to bring their students into vague touch with reality.

Questions

1. Have you experienced people who think they are God's gift and who are offended if other people don't treat them that way?
2. Can you see how inflated egos can be substituted for a proper sense of self—that is, how distortion can become reality?
3. What are some ways to enhance the realistic and natural development of self-esteem?

Source: "Lacking in Self-Esteem? Good for You!", by A. Sullivan, *Time*, October 14, 2002, p. 102. © 2002 TIME Inc. Reprinted by permission.

---

because how you think about what you do will affect your persistence, attitudes, and achievements. Second, keep your focus objective. For example, look specifically at what is required to achieve success—the steps, resources, or abilities—and not at subjective elements such as your feelings, reactions, and interpretations of the events, people, or situations. Third, try to focus on small achievements because your ability to perform successfully will have a direct effect on your actual performance. Your state of mind clearly impacts your ultimate performance.[4]

Gender, Sex, and Self-Concept

Several research studies show that men and women gain their self-concept in different ways.[5] Two researchers found that when forming self-concept, men give the most importance to social comparisons, whereas women attach more importance to reflected appraisals. Men put more value on reflected appraisals from their parents, while women give more importance to reflected appraisals from their friends.

Other studies have shown that female self-confidence comes primarily from connections and attachments, while male self-confidence comes primarily from achievement.[6] This relates to research findings about gender and language. (In Chapter 5 we discuss how women's language is tied to social networks, while men's language is tied to competition and achievement.)

Although your family and peers may influence how you act as a male or female, there is some evidence that your sexual identity is established when you are born. Researchers know this because of a terrible accident that occurred to an infant boy when he was eight months old. A surgeon was trying to repair a fused foreskin and accidentally cut off the boy's penis. Because the doctor thought he could never live as a boy, he recommended to the parents that they rear him as a girl. When the parents agreed, his testicles were removed and a vagina was constructed.

From this point on, the parents treated the child as a girl. They got her feminine clothes, gave her toys that girls liked, and even put her in the care of a female psychiatrist to help her adjust.

The child, however, never accepted her female identity. She tore off the dresses, refused the dolls, and looked for male friends. Instead of using makeup like her mother, she imitated her father by shaving and urinating standing up.

When she was 12, the doctors began estrogen treatments that enabled her to grow breasts. She did not like the feminizing effects of the drug and refused to take it. When she was 14, she refused any more treatment to feminize her. By this time she was so unhappy that her father told her what had happened to her, and her first feeling was that of relief.

At this point she went back to being a man. The youth took male hormone shots and had a mastectomy (an operation to remove breasts), and a surgeon began to reconstruct male genitals. Although the surgery was only partially successful, he married and he and his wife adopted children.

From this and other cases involving ambiguous genitals in newborns, many scientists have concluded that an infant with a Y chromosome will be a boy, regardless of his genitalia, and that nothing will ever change this.

Psychological Safety and Risk

Ask some second-semester seniors what they are afraid of. Chances are they will reply that they are very apprehensive about going out into the world. Will they find jobs? Can they survive outside the structure of university life? What is the world like? What is their place in it?

For most of us, **psychological safety**—the approval and support that we get from familiar people, ideas, and situations—is important. However, as the late psychologist Abraham Maslow, who worked in the area of self-fulfillment, pointed out, the needs for safety and growth pull us in opposite directions. Maslow believed that in order to grow, people have to abandon some of the safe areas of their lives and take some psychological risks.[7]

A **psychological risk** involves taking a chance on something new. It could be getting to know someone different from us, trying to understand a different point of view, or even moving to a new place. Taking a psychological risk helps improve one's self-concept. For example, when students go away to college, they must leave the safety of home, friends, and family. This is such a great risk that some first-year students spend a week or two away from home, decide they can't stand it, and drop out of school. The majority who remain, however, discover that they can cope on their own. This new knowledge helps improve their self-concept.

Going away to school involves psychological risks—taking a chance on something new.

New college students take risks not only in leaving home but also in being exposed to new ideas. For example, a student who has heard pro-choice ideas at home or in church will take a big risk if he or she tries to really understand a person who is pro-life, and vice versa. Similarly, it's risky for an athlete or a sports fan to try to understand the point of view that high schools might improve if they dropped competitive sports. The problem with taking the risk of really understanding a different point of view is that you might be changed. If you do change, you face the possibility that your family and friends probably will not change and you won't completely fit in anymore. Inevitably, whenever you take a risk, your circle of safety grows smaller.

Often, your first response to ideas that conflict with your own is to refuse to even listen to them. If you take this course, you choose psychological safety. When you take a psychological risk, you are ready to test your self-concept by considering ideas from another person's vantage point. For example, when you are in college, your religious beliefs might be threatened by a philosophy course or by late-night talks in the dorm with other students. If your beliefs are challenged, you might respond by no longer going to church or, in the extreme, by no longer believing in your church or even in religion. When this happens, you have taken a risk. When you go home, if you tell your parents what has happened, they probably are going to be upset; if you don't tell them, a gulf will grow between you and them as a consequence of your doing something so risky.

CAN YOU IMPROVE YOUR SELF-CONCEPT?

If you have any doubt that we, as a society, are obsessed with self-concept or self-esteem, look in the self-improvement section of any bookstore or library. You will find literally hundreds of books—each guaranteeing that if you read it, you will feel better about yourself and will change your self-esteem from negative to positive. One thing that many self-help books say is that the use of self-affirmations will assist you in raising your self-esteem. William Swann, PhD, of the University of Texas–Austin, suggests that self-affirmations, even when endlessly repeated, don't work and may even leave you more demoralized than before using them.[8]

According to Annie Paul, in her review article on "Self-Help," "The only way to change the final product—your self-esteem—is to change what goes into making it—feedback from other people." Then, she quotes Swann, who says "If you find yourself in bad relationships where your negative self-view is getting reinforced, then either change the way those people treat you by being more assertive, or change who you interact with."[9] In one of the most succinct, profound, and instructive summaries, she writes, "Stand up for yourself. Surround yourself with people who think you're great, and tell you so. Do your best to live up to their high opinions. And be patient. Self-esteem is the sum of your interactions with others over a lifetime, and it's not going to change overnight."[10]

You should know that a positive self-concept may have nothing to do with success. Researchers have found that criminals and juvenile delinquents often have high self-esteem.[11] Even though self-esteem may not be connected to success, a positive sense of who you are is good because it will make you feel happier.

Where Should Change Begin?

What is important to understand as you begin any kind of improvement program is that a poor self-concept is part of many human problems. For example, it could be part of a lack of purpose, inadequate motivation, lack of confidence, sadness and pessimism, lack of assertiveness, self-put-down games, and even the lack of wisdom and equality in selecting a mate. When it is related to sadness, just one of these human problems, it could relate to self-criticism, anger turned inward, guilt, shame, feeling inferior, low self-concept, and pessimism. That is why a poor self-concept isn't an easy problem to overcome. Wouldn't it be great if you could just erect a mental wall that would block out all your previous problems, and begin anew, with a blank slate—much as Raani Benazir did in our opening example?

Where would you start if you could erect a solid barrier between where you are today and where you were yesterday (see Figure 2-1)? First, silence your internal critic, nip negative thoughts in the bud, and stop bullying yourself. Replace criticism with encouragement and treat yourself kindly. Second, stop depending on others for your self-esteem; do your own self-evaluation. Stop letting others dominate your life. Take responsibility for your feelings. Just as you can't make others feel happy, don't expect others to make you feel happy or good about yourself. Third, accentuate your strengths and assets. Fourth, accept yourself—warts and all. Give yourself permission to decide that you're doing the best you can. Fifth, avoid your perfectionistic tendencies—the tyranny of all the "shoulds" in your life. Accept flaws, mistakes, and imperfections as part of being human. Sixth, avoid your overreactions to criticism. You needn't feel guilty about things beyond your control.

There are other areas, too, where you can begin to change. A seventh way to get to where you want to be is to modify your negative traits. Focus on what you *can* do, not

Figure 2-1
How to Begin a Program of Change

From "The 'me' you are" to "The 'me' you want to be":
- Silence your internal critic.
- Stop depending on others for your self-esteem.
- Accentuate your strengths and assets.
- Accept yourself.
- Avoid perfectionistic tendencies.
- Avoid overreactions to criticism.
- Modify your negative traits.
- Feel good and adequate by being so.
- Become a high achiever.
- Learn new skills.

on what you can't. Eighth, feel good and adequate by being good and adequate—behave morally. Ninth, become a high achiever. It is more about doing what is expected of you, and then some, than it is about high intelligence or excessive brilliance. Tenth, learn new skills. Open yourself to new possibilities, areas for potential growth, and new ways to develop positive attributes. Eleventh, don't feel responsible for everything. Don't try to be all things (and do all things) for people. Twelfth, forgive and forget. Avoid hanging on to painful memories and bad feelings. Your past can control you if you don't control it. Finally, begin a program of personal change in specific desired areas by working through the following steps.

What Do You Want to Change about Yourself?

Pick one area in which you would like to improve yourself. See if you can figure out why you have had problems in this area. Were you given a script saying you were inadequate in this area? Are you living out a self-fulfilling prophecy?

Are Your Circumstances Keeping You from Changing?

Are you living in circumstances that are holding you back? Do the people around you support you if you want to do something differently, especially if it involves taking a risk? Sometimes the people you live with try to hold you back—even though they might not be conscious of doing so. For example, one spouse says to the other, "Why do you want to go to Europe? We haven't seen all of the United States yet."

Sometimes you are locked into roles that are uncomfortable for you. Many women feel trapped when their children are small; some people hate their jobs; some students hate school. Are you in a role that you have chosen for yourself, or has someone else chosen it for you? Has someone else defined how you should play this role? Can you play this role in a way that will make it more comfortable for you? Can you change the role so that you can be more like the person you want to be?

Are You Willing to Take Some Chances?

Colleges and universities offer great chances to take some risks. Take a course from a professor who is rumored to be hard but fair. Study a subject you know nothing about. Join a club that sounds interesting—even if you don't know any of its members. Many colleges and universities also offer opportunities to study abroad or to take an internship. Going abroad is especially helpful in building self-confidence.

What Would Be a Realistic Goal?

Too often, people decide they are going to change their behavior overnight. Students who habitually get poor grades will often announce that this semester they are going to get all A's. This is an unrealistic goal. If you are going to try to change your behavior, see if you can break down the problem into steps you can handle. Let's say that you are shy but would like to speak up more in class because you often know the answers. Why not set a goal to speak up once a week in one class? That is probably a goal you can manage. Once you feel comfortable with that, you might increase your goal to speaking up two or even three times a week.

Can You Discipline Yourself?

The old saying "Nothing succeeds like success" applies to a positive self-concept: As soon as you experience success, you start feeling better about yourself. Sometimes people think they are unsuccessful because they are not motivated enough. Typical thinking might be, "If only I could motivate myself, I would get better grades." People who think this way confuse motivation with discipline. There's no way to motivate yourself to take out the garbage, do the dishes, or study your class notes. These jobs can be done only through discipline: You say, "I am going to do this job for one hour—whether or not I want to do it is irrelevant." This sort of discipline is what leads to success, which, in turn, helps you feel better about yourself.

Are There People Who Will Support You?

Whenever we try to bring about a change in ourselves, we need to surround ourselves with people who will support us. These are people who understand how difficult it is to change and who understand our desire to do so. Take the example of speaking up in class. If you are very apprehensive about doing this, you might consider discussing the problem with an instructor you like and trust. Tell him or her that you are occasionally going to try to say something, and ask for his or her support. Also tell a couple of friends in your class what you plan to do. Just having other people know what you are trying to accomplish often provides good moral support. Not all people will support you, and some may even consciously try to defeat you. For them, the possibility that you might change is too threatening.

When you have found some people to support you, it's important that you tell them what you want to do and give them some direction as to how they can help you.

Can You Be More You-Centered?

People who lack self-esteem often spend a lot of time looking inward at their miseries, while people who seem happy and content with themselves seem to spend their time interacting with others. If you look inward all the time, you are probably making yourself more miserable. For a few days, experiment with relating more to the people around you. Just asking someone "How was your day?" or "How is your semester (or quarter) going?" shows that you are interested.

If you have an opportunity to bestow some praise, do it. Look for situations around you in which you can praise people, and express your praise with genuine feeling. Tell your mother that her meatloaf tastes great, tell a professor that her class was really helpful on an internship, tell a friend that she looks wonderful in green. When you act positively toward others, they will act positively toward you, and this, in turn, will make you feel better about yourself.

THE MAP IS NOT THE TERRITORY

It was the father of general semantics, Alford Korzybski, who stated, "A map is not the territory it represents, but if correct, it has a similar structure to the territory, which accounts for its usefulness." You have maps inside your head that describe the things outside your head. The maps inside your head represent the territory outside your head.

Figure 2-2

The Map Is Not the Territory

The more accurate your maps are, the better equipped you are to function within society. The accuracy of your maps is a measure of your sanity. But, remember that nobody has completely accurate maps.

What this means for you is simply that your perception of reality is not reality itself, but it is your own version of it—your "maps." In Figure 2-2, the person is bewildered because from the map being held there was no way to know that the mountains on the horizon even existed. Even a road map doesn't accurately depict the territory it is supposed to represent. Your maps, likewise, are distorted because you jump to conclusions with little or no evidence, ignore parts of the territory, see only what you want to see, see things as black and white rather than in shades of gray, and apply labels to people and situations and then refuse to see beyond the labels.

There are some important understandings that Korzybski's theory clarifies for both self-concept and perception. The first has to do with how your maps are created. There is so much information in the world that you can't take it all in, let alone make sense of it all. So what you do is create internal maps of reality that you can refer to as you navigate through life. Your maps contain countless beliefs, values, generalizations, decisions, and numerous other mental aspects about how you see yourself and your relationship to the world around you. Just as a road map, it is a scaled-down version of reality. And just as a road map, maps don't show everything. As you get more information, your maps change.

Now, imagine what people's maps might look like if they grew up with trauma or abuse? Their maps might be useful for navigation within their family unit, but they wouldn't be accurate when they got out into the world on their own. For example, their maps might tell them that other people will hurt them (not realizing that some will and others may not), and their maps may cause them to miss out on many beautiful parts of life. What happens in your life occurs because of your maps of reality—your mind creating experiences based on your maps.

The second understanding is that you react to the maps inside your head, not the territory outside your head. You react to the maps and not to what the maps represent. For example, if your maps tell you that a certain piece of music is pleasant, you will listen to it. If your maps tell you that the same piece of music is unpleasant, you will not listen to it. It is not the music that you are drawn to, it is your maps of the music. The same occurs in elections. You look not to the candidates when you choose how to vote, you look instead to your maps of the candidates.

The third understanding is that no two people can have exactly the same maps. Problems in communication occur when you try to impose your maps upon another person—or other people. Empathizing with others requires learning to recognize the structure of others' maps—seeing the world through their eyes—thus being able to understand and relate to them respectfully and accurately. It helps to know that their maps are likely to be just as jaundiced by their own interpretations as yours are.

No two people have exactly the same maps because people's upbringing, genes, and values differ. But even more, just because two or more things have the same label, they are unlikely to be identical. One American, for example, is not the same as another American, just because they are both Americans. Also, nothing exists in isolation; everything is affected by surrounding conditions. You might appear ignorant when discussing economics with a professor of that subject, but seem like a genius when discussing it with your friends who know little about economics.

The fourth understanding is that to create personal change requires changing maps. There is a natural and understandable desire to protect old maps. That is because they become comfortable. You know how to navigate with these maps, and replacing them with new ones is a little like trying to find your way around a new supermarket. Not only are maps comfortable, they are habit forming. Even when they may not be as useful as they could be, you depend on them because they are what you have. You know where the bread, milk, and cereal are supposed to be in the supermarket. Letting maps go causes temporary chaos, but reconfiguring, reconstituting, or reorganizing maps at a higher level can result in relief from the problems and limitations of the old maps—new abilities to deal with what was previously stressful, perplexing, or overwhelming. You learn where things are located in the new supermarket, and your trips there become efficient, effective, and satisfying.

The fifth understanding is that your maps of reality are *not* who you are—the map is *not* the territory. Rather, your maps are simply a convenient tool you use to navigate through life. To understand that your maps are not who you are but simply a navigation tool will help you understand that maps need to go through the chaos and reorganization process for personal growth to occur. It will help you understand that map "changes" do not represent you in the process of falling apart. The **map is not the territory.** Trying to hold old maps together creates dysfunctional feelings and behaviors such as fear, depression, anger, anxiety, substance abuse, many physical diseases, and numerous other more serious mental problems.

Knowing that the map is not the territory will help you look forward to map changes. Why? Because new maps are likely to work better. New maps will allow you to be a happier, more peaceful person. New maps are likely to produce positive change. And because of the relationship between self-concept and perception, new maps will allow

STRATEGIC FLEXIBILITY
When you permit changes in your maps of reality, you increase your strategic flexibility because new maps are likely to work better than old maps.

you to come at the world more accurately, see things with greater clarity, and understand events, others, and ideas with increased precision..

THE INTERNET, SELF, AND COMMUNICATION

The Internet presents an opportunity seldom, if ever, offered to the adventurous. When engaged in conversations in chat rooms, posting messages on bulletin boards, or even in the construction of blogs or Web pages, Internet users have the option of presenting their real and authentic self to their Internet audience, or creating their own identity. It is impossible to determine how many Internet users choose one course over the other; however, in chat rooms, most participants—for the sake of anonymity (and often, safety)—select to use a pseudonym or clever descriptor to identify themselves.

Technology allows users to become invisible—at least, their perception of invisibility. Actually, Internet users leave cyberfootprints wherever they go, but despite this reality, the perception of invisibility persists. The fact that many people may be engaged in similar activities leads to this perception of invisibility because, the rationale is, any single person's actions are a mere "drop in the pond" and, thus, are unlikely to be detected.

How does this bear on the self-concept? When people are in the process of developing their self-concept and, at the same time, are active users of the Internet, they are obviously influenced by the lack of tangible feedback and perceptions of invisibility, and it isn't clear how this will affect their development and internalization processes.

What is interesting about the social identities created on the Internet is that, according to some research, it depends on perceptions we have of the Internet. Because it is through our relationships with others that we discover ourselves, it may be that Internet communication, which enables a higher level of self-disclosure because of its relatively anonymous nature, promotes self-discovery for some, better than communication in real life.[12] Some computer-mediated communication (CMC) partners engage in more intimate questions and deeper disclosures than those in ongoing face-to-face relationships.[13]

When the Internet is perceived as a sociable medium, the disclosures on ICQ (instant messaging) tend to be open, personal, intimate, honest, and in great extent about negative feelings and opinions. When people perceive the Internet as a personalized medium, disclosures will be more about themselves. And when the Internet is perceived as sensitive, warm, and active, the disclosures appear more private and intimate but the contents are more negative and undesirable.[14]

There are two important conclusions regarding the Internet, self, and communication. First, people who have more positive self-evaluations have more positive self-disclosures in both the offline world and the cyberworld. To be more specific, the Internet simply provides another channel for the same kind of communication that occurs in the real world. People who gain satisfaction in communication have a more positive self-image and are more eager to disclose themselves on the Internet or in instant messaging.

Second, how people perceive the Internet determines how they use it. Those who perceive it as a warm medium are more likely to disclose private and intimate information including negative or undesirable things about themselves. Just as when trust is developed in a relationship, a warm and safe environment develops at the same time. Perceived as a sociable medium, disclosures are open, personal, intimate, and honest. Perceived as a personalized medium, disclosures are about themselves.

The point is simply that for those who find effectiveness and success in real-life communication, they are likely to find success and effectiveness in Internet communication in the same way—whether it be self-perception, self-development, or self-expression. Much depends on their perception of the Internet; however, those with a positive self-concept are more likely to perceive it as just another channel of communication—an additional way to share knowledge, ideas, and information.

PERCEPTION

Perception, you will recall, is how you look at others and the world around you. Acts of perception are more than simply capturing incoming stimuli. These acts require a form of expectation, of knowing what is about to confront you and preparing for it. These expectations or predispositions to respond are a type of perceptual filter called **psychological sets,** and they have a profound effect on your perceptions. "Without expectations, or constructs through which you perceive your world," writes John Ratey, associate clinical professor of psychiatry at Harvard Medical School, "your surroundings would be what William James called a 'booming, buzzing confusion,' and each experience truly would be a new one, rapidly overwhelming you. You automatically and unconsciously fit your sensations into categories that you have learned, often distorting them in the process."[15]

For example, how you view a new instructor depends on your views of all the instructors you have had in the past. How you think about forming a new romantic relationship depends on the romantic relationships you have had in the past. Your knowledge, background, and experiences form the psychological sets and, thus, provide the matrix—that which gives shape or form to anything—into which any new idea or event is placed

The Perceptual Process

Your perceptions affect more than your direct interactions with people. They also influence your response to all the information around you. Whenever you encounter new information, whether it's from a television program, a newspaper, the Internet, or another person, you go through a three-step perceptual process: You select the information, you organize it, and you interpret it.

We do not all perceive information in the same way. Even when several people have access to the same information, they are likely to select, organize, and interpret it in different ways. Let's say, for example, that three different people read the same newspaper: Omar is a Syrian who is studying in the United States; Caroline is an American who has been an exchange student in Syria; and Jim is an American who has never traveled.

When Omar reads the paper, he looks for (selects) news about Syria. In his mind he organizes the information on the basis of what he already knows. He may

Whenever you encounter new information you go through a three-step perceptual process: You select the information, you organize it, and you interpret it.

interpret it by asking the meaning of certain government actions or by thinking that the reporter has the wrong slant on the story. Caroline goes through a similar process. She has a high interest in stories about Syria because she has been there. She, too, organizes what she reads according to what she knows about the country. However, she may interpret the news stories differently because she doesn't have as much information as Omar. Also, her interpretation will probably be from an American point of view. When Jim reads the newspaper, he skips all the stories about Omar's country. He has never been there and has no immediate plans to go there. In fact, he skips all the news about the world and goes directly to the sports section. These three people are all exposed to the same information, but they all perceive it differently.

Deletions, Distortions, and Generalizations

Any perceptions you have are less than perfect because of deletions, distortions, and generalizations.[16] **Deletions**—blotting out, erasing, or canceling information—must occur first because your physical senses are limited. Your sight, hearing, touch, taste, and smell are the means you use to get information, but those senses focus only on those aspects of the environment that are most important for your survival. Your senses are not capable of perceiving everything in your external environment. Deletions occur, too, because of your beliefs. If you believe something to be true, you have an almost infinite capacity to delete information that contradicts that belief. In addition, if you believe something to be true, you will go through your life searching for information that supports that belief and ignore information that does not.

In addition to deleting information, you also distort much of the information from your environment. **Distortions** involve twisting or bending information out of shape. You distort information, first because you observe only a small part of your external environment. Since what you observe is such a small part of the whole, you must fill in the blanks—specifically add information—to make your information make sense. The other reason you distort information is so that it will support your existing beliefs and values—fit into your psychological sets.

In addition to deleting and distorting information, you draw generalizations based on little substantial information. **Generalizations** involve drawing principles or conclusions from particular evidence or facts. Once you have observed something a few times, you conclude that what has proven true in the past will prove true in the future as well. Generalizations are important to your survival. Getting burned by putting a hand on a hot stove will give you a conclusion about the consequences of putting your hand on a hot stove in the future. If you had several bad experiences with members of the opposite sex, of a different race, of a different culture, or of a particular organization, you might generalize that *all* members of the opposite sex, a different race, a different culture, or a particular organization are bad. Then, all future experiences are filtered through that belief, information that contradicts the belief is deleted, and you distort other information so it will support the belief.

Keep these three activities in mind as you read the next section on perceptual filters. Realize that even before perceptual filters come into play and certainly while they are operating as well, deletion, distortion, and generalization are also influencing the information.[17]

Perceptual Filters

Deletions, distortions, and generalizations are important and affect your perceptions, but perceptual filters can be even more important. **Perceptual filters** are limitations that result from the narrowed lens through which you view the world. For example, your biologic makeup has a significant influence. If your biologic makeup differs from that of the predominant society—if you are obese, short, or unattractive, for example—you may have difficulty securing and maintaining a positive self-concept because of the distortions your senses cause. You automatically see things differently than members of the predominant society.

Other significant influences on your perceptions include your culture, values, and beliefs. You, like most people, find it easier to communicate with members of your own culture. Many of your customs (e.g., Halloween), values (e.g., everything should be clean), and beliefs (all humans are created equal)—as well as your manners, ceremonies, rituals, laws, language, religious beliefs, myths and legends, knowledge, ideals, accepted ways of behaving, and even your concept of self—are culturally determined.

There are numerous other influences, such as the ways you have for coping with and tolerance for stress as well as your conflict resolution strategies.[18] If through your upbringing you have developed inadequate coping patterns to adapt to stress or resolve conflict you narrow your lens, and your perceptions will be distorted. One major influence would be the familial patterns you observed between your parents and between your parents and you or other siblings. For example, some of the patterns you may have observed could include the excessive use of denial, projection of blame and responsibility, hypersensitivity to criticism, and rationalizing of failures. Destructive behaviors may have included overeating, excessive smoking or drinking, the overuse of over-the-counter medications, or illicit drug use. Even high rates of illness as a result of high blood pressure, ulcers, irritable bowel syndrome, frequent headaches or neck aches may also have been influential.

Other influences on your perceptions could include your previous experiences. Many failures rather than successes may create difficulty. If you attribute your successes to luck, chance, or the influence of powerful others rather than to your own personal behavior, this could be a factor. If you have suffered stressful life events such as financial difficulties, problems on a job, change or loss of a job, relationship concerns, sexuality concerns, divorce, or moving, particularly if they have been cumulative, your perceptions could be affected. Illnesses, traumas, and surgery, too, can create alterations in self-esteem, body image, and personal identity and can influence your perceptions. Even your current physiological state can influence your perceptions. Insufficient nutritional food, lack of sleep, or a serious night of drinking and the consequential hangover can be influential.

Our purpose here has not been to cast a negative light on the role of your perceptions in creating and maintaining your self-concept; rather, it is to show how many factors are likely to filter your perceptions. Any changes from the norm—the perceptions of those who make up your predominant society—will influence your perceptions in some manner. Because there are so many influences, and because these influences are likely to combine in unknown ways and even have some cumulative effect, there is no way to predict or know how much effect the influences on your perceptions have nor how your self-concept is altered. What is interesting is that even self-assessments are likely to be distorted, since the self doing the assessing is also subject to the distortions!

Figure 2-3
Perception

Objective Reality (The World As It Is) → Individual's Unique Perceptual Filter (Values, Needs, Goals, Interests, Beliefs, Attitudes, Expectations, Wants, Knowledge, Feelings, Languages, Education) → Subjective View (The World As It Appears)

Adjusting to Perceptual Influences

George A. Miller, the psychologist, said, "Most of our failures in understanding one another have less to do with what is heard than with what is intended and what is inferred." It would be great to believe that there were no such thing as perceptual filters. It would be great to believe that you come at the world straight on and that objective reality is, indeed, your reality. It would be great to believe, because of the truthfulness and honesty with which you conduct your life, that any observation you make is accurate, precise, and correct—that the conclusions you draw conform exactly to truth or to the standard set by the norm of others in your culture. Unfortunately, this is *never* the case. The fact is, your perceptions and the conclusions you draw from them represent, as noted in Figure 2-3, your reality, your subjective view, or the world as it appears to you.

The difference between **objective reality**—the actual territory or external reality everyone experiences—and a **subjective view**—your personal mental maps of the world—is easy to demonstrate. It is the difference between an examination, or the actual written document that contains the questions (objective reality), and your maps of that examination (subjective reality) which are constructed from your beliefs about the need for examinations, your attitudes toward examinations, your expectations regarding this particular examination, your knowledge about what is likely to be on the examination, and your related thoughts regarding your preparation, as well as your feelings (anxiety or apprehension).

If you think about it, if you were affected by any one of the perceptual influences listed in the section on perceptual filters—lack of sleep, for example—you would experience some distortion from the norm. Whether or not you knew the distortion was occurring might depend on the severity of the influence (three nights without sleep), the circumstances in which you found yourself (taking a final exam), or whether you had other comparisons to make; that is, you had a way to compare your sensory data (observations) with that of others. (Others thought the exam was fair; you thought it unfair.) You have drawn a conclusion that is true based on your perceptions.

Stay healthy, get rest, and exercise. Make every effort to come at the world as healthy, well rested, and sufficiently exercised as possible. Because perception depends on your senses, the better condition that your senses are in, the more likely they will respond in proper ways. It is more likely that you will be aware of and adjust to perceptual influences when you have a proper state of mind and body. For example, can you imagine getting physically and emotionally upset with an instructor because of an exam you felt was unfair after three days of no sleep, living on Mountain Dew, isolated in your room, and trying to study a semester's worth of notes in a day and a half?

Avoid hasty conclusions. If you feel it is necessary to publicly announce a conclusion, then state it tentatively rather than as a conclusion. For example, rather than stating that you know that flying saucers exist because you saw strange lights in the sky last night, why not offer your observations in a tentative way that will allow exploration and discussion: "You know, I saw strange lights in the sky last night. Did anyone else see any strange lights?"

Take more time. The third method for adjusting to perceptual influences follows from the last one. Take more time. When it is said patience is a virtue, nothing could be more succinct or accurate. Time has a number of benefits. It allows you to gather more facts. With more facts, it is likely your conclusions will change. Time also allows you to think about your observations and conclusions. For example, you might overhear another conversation about the strange lights in the sky, or read a newspaper article about a meteor shower last night, or the glow from locally launched weather balloons. How often have you discovered that your first impressions were wrong—that, for example, you could not tell what a book was about by its cover alone?

There is an important caution to be aware of as you search for information. As noted previously, when you believe something to be true, you will find information to support that belief. That statement introduces the caution. Your external environment contains ample evidence to support all beliefs about a subject.[19] If you believe that most people are bad and will lie, cheat, steal, and otherwise injure you, you can find plenty of evidence in the news and in your daily encounters with others to support that belief. If you believe that most people are good and will behave in honest, caring, and courageous ways, you can find plenty of evidence to support this belief as well. The point of gathering information is to seek evidence that might suggest your beliefs are in error or that other explanations exist for the conclusions you have reached.

Be available. A fourth method for adjusting to perceptual influences follows from the previous methods. Be available to see the other person's viewpoint. Availability, here, means both physical and psychological openness. How often in the heat of an argument could you not stop long enough to really listen to another person's side? Rather, you were so upset you were framing your own ideas, choosing your own words, defending yourself from attack, and trying to outdo, outmaneuver, and outwit the other person. The advantage of counting to 10 to allow your emotions to calm, or stepping back and taking more time, or just trying to put yourself in the other person's shoes helps you become more available. The question "Did anyone else see strange lights?" reveals availability and openness.

There are two other ways you have to adjust to perceptual influences.

Be committed. Commit yourself to seeking more information. Commit yourself to having additional information before making any judgment. Commit yourself to being as fully informed as you would expect others to be with you before sharing their conclusions. Buy a local paper, for example, and examine it for possible explanations of strange lights in the sky. Listen to a local newscast for information. Go ask or make a call to a local expert who might have an answer. It is this kind of climate—the kind of climate in which educated and informed conversation and dialogue can take place—that is likely to produce additional perspectives, alternatives, and conclusions.

Be prepared to change. If everything has worked thus far, you are likely to get information, hear viewpoints, or gain perspectives, alternatives, or conclusions that you did not originally have. If this is true, you must be prepared to change accordingly. Whatever adjustments are necessary, you must be ready to make them. This is why it is important to avoid making hasty conclusions at the outset. In that way, changes at this point will be unnecessary. You simply adjust internally. If you expressed a hasty conclusion, now you must admit the error or openly reveal the adjustment necessary to accommodate the new information, viewpoint, perspective, alternative, or conclusion, and you can't save face, or protect yourself from embarrassment. Publicly admitting an error is difficult for anyone. As it turned out, the strange lights in the sky were a number of planes returning to the local airport at the same time, having all been at the same air show in another state. From the ground, at night, depending on your position or location, the planes lit up the night sky.

As you take steps to reduce the effect of perceptual influences on you, you will notice changes simply because the information you will get is likely to be more accurate and dependable. It will be better information for use in building a stronger self-concept.

STRATEGIC FLEXIBILITY

When you anticipate, assess, evaluate, and select, be ready to change instantaneously and adjust accordingly because of new viewpoints, perspectives, alternatives, or conclusions.

Assess Yourself

What Do You Think of Your Self?

Please mark each statement in the following way:
If the statement describes how you usually feel, put a check in the column *Like Me*.
If the statement does *not* describe how you usually feel, put a check in the column *Unlike Me*. For this inventory, there are no right or wrong answers.

		Like Me	Unlike Me
1.	I'm pretty sure of myself.	_____	_____
2.	I often wish I were someone else.	_____	_____
3.	I'm easy to like.	_____	_____
4.	I never worry about anything.	_____	_____
5.	I find it very hard to talk in front of a class.	_____	_____
6.	There are lots of things about myself I'd change if I could.	_____	_____
7.	I can make up my mind without too much trouble.	_____	_____
8.	I'm a lot of fun to be with.	_____	_____
9.	I always do the right thing.	_____	_____
10.	I'm proud of the college work that I do.	_____	_____
11.	Someone always has to tell me what to do.	_____	_____
12.	It takes me a long time to get used to anything new.	_____	_____
13.	I'm often sorry for the things I do.	_____	_____
14.	I'm never unhappy.	_____	_____
15.	I'm doing the best work that I can.	_____	_____
16.	I give in very easily.	_____	_____
17.	I'm pretty happy.	_____	_____
18.	I like everyone I know.	_____	_____
19.	I like to be called on in class.	_____	_____
20.	I understand myself.	_____	_____
21.	Things are all mixed up in my life.	_____	_____
22.	I'm not doing as well in college as I'd like to.	_____	_____
23.	I can make up my mind and stick to it.	_____	_____
24.	I have a low opinion of myself.	_____	_____
25.	I don't like to be with other people.	_____	_____
26.	I'm never shy.	_____	_____
27.	I often feel upset in college.	_____	_____
28.	If I have something to say, I usually say it.	_____	_____
29.	I always tell the truth.	_____	_____
30.	Most people are better liked than I am.	_____	_____
31.	I always know what to say to people.	_____	_____
32.	I often get discouraged in college.	_____	_____
33.	Things usually don't bother me.	_____	_____

Go to the *Communicating Effectively* CD-ROM and the Online Learning Center at **www.mhhe.com/hybels8** to see your results and learn how to evaluate your attitudes and feelings.

mhhe.com/hybels8

Source: In J.P. Robinson, P. R. Shaver, & L. S. Wrightsman, *Measures of Personality and Social Psychological Attitudes* (San Diego: Academic Press, 1991), pp. 127–31. Adapted from S. Coopersmith, *The Antecedents of Self-Esteem* (San Francisco: W. H. Freeman and Company, 1967,) Used with permission.

CHAPTER REVIEW

SUMMARY

Both self and perception are foundations for effective communication. Self-concept is how you think about and value yourself. Perception is how you look at others and the world around you. How you look at the world depends on what you think of yourself, and what you think of yourself will influence how you look at the world.

Self-concept comes from three sources: reflected appraisals, social comparisons, and self-perception. Scripts and self-fulfilling prophecies also influence your self-concept. If people are willing to give up some of their psychological safety and take some risks, their self-concepts will become more positive.

Although being accepted by others may be more important than it should be, is a fleeting and temporal circumstance, and is based on their viewpoint alone, the fundamental components start with accepting yourself. It also means accepting who everyone else is and changing your attitude.

Improving your self-concept is not easy because a poor self-concept is part of many human problems. To start, you must silence your internal critic. Then, stop depending on others for your self-esteem, accentuate your strengths and assets, accept yourself, avoid your perfectionistic tendencies, avoid your overreactions to criticism, modify your negative traits, behave morally, become a high achiever, learn new skills, don't feel responsible for everything, and forgive and forget.

To focus on a single area for improving your self-concept, decide what you want to change, consider your circumstances, take some chances, set reasonable goals, use a program of self-discipline, find people who will support you, and act positively toward others.

Alford Korzybski's theory that the map is not the territory means that your perception of reality is not reality itself but only your version of it—your map. Problems in communication occur when you try to impose your map upon another person. To create personal change requires changing your map. Map changes do not represent you in the process of falling apart; often, they work better, create greater happiness, produce positive change, and increase the accuracy and clarity of perceptions.

Those who find success in real-life communication will find success and effectiveness in Internet communication. For the adventurous, Internet users have the option of presenting their real and authentic selves. Those with a positive self-concept will perceive the Internet as just another channel of communication.

The perceptual process includes the steps of selecting, organizing, and interpreting information. Perceptions are less than perfect because of deletions, distortions, and generalizations. Also, numerous perceptual filters will have an effect on your perceptions. Because there are so many influences, and because these influences are likely to combine in unknown ways and even have some cumulative effect, there is no way to predict or know the effect of the influences on your perceptions nor on how your self-concept is altered.

Adjusting to perceptual influences requires that you stay healthy, avoid hasty conclusions, take more time, be available and committed, and be prepared to change. Strategic flexibility—especially the steps of anticipating, assessing, evaluating, and selecting—requires a readiness to change instantaneously and adjust appropriately not just because of new viewpoints, perspectives, alternatives, and conclusions, but because people often come to wrong conclusions. Your interpretations of reality—your mental maps—need to be checked continually to see how accurately they represent the territory, and being prepared to change is part of that process.

CHAPTER REVIEW

KEY TERMS AND CONCEPTS

Use the *Communicating Effectively* CD-ROM and the Online Learning Center at **www.mhhe.com/hybels8** to further your understanding of the following terms.

Deletions 46
Distortions 46
Generalizations 46
Map is not the territory 43
Objective reality 48
Perception 30

Perceptual filters 47
Psychological risk 37
Psychological safety 37
Psychological sets 45
Reflected appraisals 32
Scripts 32

Self-concept 30
Self-fulfilling prophecies 33
Self-perception 35
Social comparisons 33
Subjective view 48

QUESTIONS TO REVIEW

1. What is the role of self and perception in communication?
2. How is the self-concept formed?
3. What are the differences among reflected appraisals, social comparisons, and self-perception? Which one is likely to have the most influence on self-formation?
4. In what specific ways can you make your self-perception more positive?
5. What are the fundamental components of being accepted?
6. What are the ways you can improve a weak or poor self-concept?
7. What is the value of Alford Korzybski's theory (The map is not the territory), and how does it contribute to strategic flexibility?
8. What are the influences of the Internet on self and communication?
9. What are the three steps of the perceptual process?
10. What role do deletions, distortions, and generalizations play in perception? Can you give an example of each?
11. What are some of the perceptual filters that narrow the lens through which you view the world?
12. What is the difference between objective reality and a subjective view, and why is this important in communication?
13. What are some of the ways you can adjust to perceptual influences, and which aspect of adjustment contributes most to strategic flexibility?

Go to the self-quizzes on the *Communicating Effectively* CD-ROM and the Online Learning Center at **www.mhhe.com/hybels8** to test your knowledge of the chapter concepts.

CHAPTER

3

Intercultural Communication

OBJECTIVES

After reading this chapter, you should be able to:

- Define the role intercultural communication plays in communicating effectively and in strategic flexibility.
- Offer a clear definition of *culture* and *co-culture*.
- Explain what it means to possess a cultural identity.
- Relate intercultural communication to the model of communication.
- List and briefly explain six dimensions or frameworks for studying cultural differences.
- Explain the potential barriers to intercultural communication.
- Distinguish among assimilation, accommodation, and separation strategies, and explain their purpose.
- Explain the influence of the Internet on intercultural communication.

MY NAME IS STANLEY MARTINEZ, AND I WAS INTRODUCED TO GANGS, drugs, and violence at an early age. My uncle, a burly man covered in tattoos who was just released from the state penitentiary, taught me the rules of our neighborhood, and those rules, along with drugs and alcohol, served as my school of survival. I grew up fast, and the inner strength gained from my uncle's advice, my ability to watch and listen, and my common sense caused the home boys I ran with to make me their gang leader. Their trust in me not only gave me courage and comfort but it also empowered me. They also broadened my perspective.

All through my life it was as if I were outside myself looking in, and when I lost gang members because of useless deaths on the street, addictions to drugs, and unwanted pregnancies, I realized I had a higher purpose. A member of the Chicano Youth Center (CYC) helped me secure a job, and my employer put me in contact with the Educational Opportunity Program (EOP) which helped me enroll in college. In ethnic studies classes I learned of my heritage, and I didn't just begin to appreciate my culture, I began to proudly share it with others.

For my first speech in my speech communication class, I dressed as a gang member and talked about my life story. Halfway through the speech I took off a layer of clothing to reveal a shirt and tie, and I talked about the biases and prejudices of mainstream society that push down members of our ethnic cultures. It was in my speech communication class that I made a commitment to dedicate my life to breaking down the barriers that prevent home boys and home girls from entering college.

In this chapter we first look at the role of intercultural communication in communicating effectively and in strategic flexibility. Then we look at the word *culture* and the importance of understanding your role as a cultural being. In the next section, we discuss the importance of intercultural communication. Then we relate this topic to the model of communication discussed in Chapter 1. We present six dimensions or frameworks for studying cultural differences. There are four barriers to intercultural communication, and we examine how to deal with the barriers—which includes a discussion of dominant and nondominant cultures. We look at ways for improving intercultural communication, and, finally, we discuss the influence of the Internet.

THE ROLE OF INTERCULTURAL COMMUNICATION IN COMMUNICATING EFFECTIVELY AND STRATEGIC FLEXIBILITY

In Communicating Effectively

What does intercultural communication have to do with communicating effectively? First, we must all agree that it is communication skills—both sending and receiving abilities—that determine how well individuals, organizations, industries, and nations do in both acquiring and applying knowledge. The better the communication, the greater likelihood of success. Second, we must all agree that because of globalization and the importance of information, there is a rising new category in the world known as the **knowledge class.** It is a class supported solely by its participation in the new information industries with little, if any, reliance upon traditional manufacturing, production, or agriculture. The ability of members of this knowledge class to effectively negotiate the inherent cultural issues in communication will give them a competitive edge in a global world.

Closer to where you live, perhaps, the relevance of intercultural communication is no less important. What if it were your job to coordinate international student services and exchange programs on your college campus? What if you were the manager in a biotech company, responsible for leading a diverse team of scientists doing innovative research?

The world today is characterized by an ever-growing number of communications between people with different linguistic and cultural backgrounds. It is likely that you will make such contacts because they occur in the areas of business, military cooperation, science, education, mass media, entertainment, and tourism, and because of immigration brought about by labor shortages and political conflicts—as well as informally in Internet chat rooms and on Internet bulletin boards. Just a quick example will make this point. The U.S. Department of Education found that close to 40 percent of public school students were minorities in 2000, up from close to 30 percent in 1986. Also, the number of students who spoke a language other than English at home rose by 46 percent from 1979 to 1999. Many teachers are faced with teaching a diverse student population.[1] The communication throughout all these contacts needs to be as constructive as possible if misunderstandings and breakdowns are to be avoided.

In Strategic Flexibility

Intercultural communication has a direct and noticeable effect on each step of strategic flexibility. In the first step (anticipate), you will have a new slant or angle from which to think about potential communication situations. The needs and requirements will be different than without this new knowledge, and forecasting may require the introduction of new or different skills and abilities.

In the second step (assess), the factors, elements, and conditions of situations in which you find yourself will be different. Becoming alert to the introduction of these new ingredients will become easier as your experience broadens. In the third step (evaluate), you will more accurately be able to determine the value and worth of the factors, elements, and conditions and how they bear on your own skills and abilities. Because you will have developed more skills and abilities, in the fourth step (select) you will find it easier to select those most likely to affect the situation.

In the fifth step (apply), you will take greater care and concern and give greater attention to the factors that are likely to be affected. You will understand how to judge their relevance with greater accuracy, and when you reassess and reevaluate your actions you will have increased sensitivity to the intercultural demands of communication situations and how you can enhance, nourish, and encourage further communication efforts.

WHAT IS CULTURE?

Culture is not a box but a fluid concept that is an ever-changing, living part of you, reflecting your learned, socially acquired traditions and lifestyles. The following is a useful definition. As you read it, recognize that there are no hard edges; rather, there are phenomena that tend to overlap and mingle. **Culture** is:

> *The ever-changing values, traditions, social and political relationships, and worldview created and shared by a group of people bound together by a combination of factors*

The words you choose reflect your culture because that is where you learned them, and that is where they originated.

(which can include a common history, geographic location, language, social class, and/or religion).[2]

The word **worldview** means an all encompassing set of moral, ethical, and philosophical principles and beliefs that govern the way people live their lives and interact with others. Your worldview governs the way you think, feel, and behave whether you realize it or not and affects in a major way how you view every aspect of life—physical, spiritual, emotional, moral, sociological, and mental.

Culture is significant in your life because it is part of you. It includes your patterned, repetitive ways of thinking, feeling, and acting.[3] Thus, it is not only maintained but often expressed through your communication. When Jonathan left a prominent position at a prestigious company, his best friend, Adam, explained his departure this way: "Voicing concern and choked with emotion, Jonathan was no longer able to step up his efforts, as his American dream turned into a nightmare, his emotional roller coaster came to a full stop. Sending shock waves through family and friends, he said his final good-byes, and called it quits." Not only was Adam's communication full of cliches, but each one—eight in two sentences—was uniquely American. Where do the words you choose come from? They reflect your culture because that is where you learned them, that is where they originated, and they are likely to be all you know!

Because it is part of you, culture not only influences your perception of your self and your perception of others (discussed in the last chapter) but your perception of everything in life with which you have contact. Think about what might be considered true American values and freedom: things like democracy, individualism, property, equality, freedom, community, and justice. The degree to which you accept these as your own values is also the degree to which you measure your sense of self on those same values. For example, you would feel better about yourself if you were actively involved in your democracy (being informed of the positions of political candidates and voting), expressing your individualism (being assertive and sticking up for your rights), and owning property (having a nice car).

YOU ARE A CULTURAL BEING

One desired outcome from reading about *culture* is that you will recognize and accept *yourself* as a cultural being. **Cultural identity,** composed of ethnicity, culture, gender, age, life stage, beliefs, values, and assumptions, is the degree to which you identify with your culture, and it is determined by the values you support. If you were born and raised in the United States, your cultural identity involves the degree to which you identify with being American. But, it doesn't stop there. You have a number of cultural identities—being a member of the student body, a particular race, a specific age group, a religion, and so on. The word **co-culture** represents nonwhites, women, people with disabilities, homosexuals, and those in the lower social classes who have specific patterns of behavior that set them off from other groups within a culture.[4] Which cultural identity is prominent depends on the situation, the people you are with, and the conversational topics.

Stanley Martinez in our earlier example was clearly a member of a gang co-culture. Although that co-culture was distinguished by members who followed the rules of the neighborhood and were often characterized by the use of drugs, alcohol, and violence, he was a member of two other cultures as well. First, he was a Latino American, a large co-cultural group where he lived. He grew up speaking Spanish, living in overcrowded conditions, and suffering extreme social discrimination—having been called lazy, shiftless, lawless, and violent, all unfortunate, negative stereotypes that had a direct effect on his self-concept. Second, he identified with being an American. Born and raised in the United States, his cultural identity involved a very clear identification with the beliefs, values, and assumptions of the dominant culture. The co-cultures of Martinez and their relationship to the dominant culture are depicted in Figure 3-1.

There are three things that you need to understand about possessing a cultural identity. First, cultural identities are learned. You learn the ways of thinking, acting, and feeling from your family first, then from your friends and communities. Second, cultural identities vary in strength. Morgan, for example, had all the speech and language patterns, all the actions and reactions of a typical American student. All were so deeply embedded within her that she wasn't even aware of it until she visited Australia with her debate team.

Third, cultural identities vary in their content. For example, not everyone would define what it means to be an American in the same way, just as students have different ways of defining what it means to be a student. The importance of this point becomes evident when you begin to generalize about cultures. To what extent do you value freedom, pleasure, social recognition, and independence. These are values often

Figure 3-1

Relationship of Co-cultures to Dominant Culture

- U.S. culture made up of numerous co-cultures (Dominant culture)
- Latino-American co-culture
- Latino-American gang co-culture

ascribed to members of the U.S. culture. What if you were a Japanese American and you held cultural identities for both these cultures? The Japanese culture values self-sacrifice, harmony, and accepting traditions—values that, in part, directly contradict those of the U.S. culture.

When you realize all the cultural identities people possess, you also can see the perplexities associated with the *intersection* of issues of race and ethnicity, language, religion, gender and sexual orientation, generation and age, and so forth, as they operate within individuals. These factors interact and come out differently in different people. Understanding cultural identities offers insights into how individuals relate to the many groups to which they belong, but not only that, to understand others, and yourself, you need to realize the variety of groups that create their (and your) cultural identity.[5]

Cultural identity can be a complex issue. For example, a second-generation girl, living in a minority area, whose parents are Korean immigrants, whose friends are Spanish-speaking co-workers, identifies herself as Korean American, a woman, or an American depending on the **context**.

Cultural identity can be a simple issue, too. Some groups create their own co-cultures to isolate themselves from others. In many cities the immigrants still seem to live and work in isolation and resolve to protect their heritage by maintaining all vestiges of their culture and not assimilating. Regarding your perception of others, you might perceive them based on the same set of values—those that you hold dear.

"Culture is a mental set of windows through which all of life is viewed."[6] It is more than an environment or geographical location in which you live, and it is more than any single component of your personality or background, including your race, ethnicity, nationality, language, gender, religion, ability or disability, or socioeconomic status. These components—and certainly the way they combine and interact—affect your social and educational status as well as your family, community, and professional interactions. Culture is the way you make sense of your life.[7]

From this brief discussion of culture it is easier to understand intercultural communication. When a message is created by a member of one culture, and this message needs to be processed by a member of another culture, **intercultural communication** takes place.[8]

THE IMPORTANCE OF STUDYING INTERCULTURAL COMMUNICATION

The chances for contacts with people from other cultures have increased dramatically with changes in the workplace; U.S. businesses expanding into world markets in a process of globalization; people now connected—via answering machines, faxes, e-mail, electronic bulletin boards, and the Internet—to other people whom they have never met face-to-face; the ever-increasing mobility of U.S. families; and the changing demographics within the United States and changing immigration patterns as well.[9] It is precisely this increased contact that makes studying intercultural communication so important. (See Figure 3-2.)

Understanding Your Own Identity. The first reason for studying intercultural communication is to develop a sensitivity to various cultural heritages and backgrounds to better understand your own identity. In her book *Torn Between Two Cultures*, Maryam Qudrat Aseel says, "It was through the experience of living and being raised in the United States that I came to truly appreciate and understand my own religion, heritage, culture, and language."[10] Your decisions about the values you want to adopt or continue

Figure 3-2

The Multicultural Self

The community co-culture may include work, school, friends, and romantic relationship, but these may occur outside the community as well.

(Diagram labels: Self; Work co-culture; School co-culture; Friends co-culture; Romantic relationship co-culture; Family co-culture; Community co-culture; Dominant co-culture; Things outside the community co-culture)

holding, the lifestyles or orientations you wish to pursue, and even the friends you want to have—not to mention the major, occupation, or profession you desire—are affected by racial, cultural, gender, and social-class factors that affect your personal identity, who you are and who you want to be.[11]

Enhancing Personal and Social Interactions. The broader your outlook, the more tolerant and accommodating you become. The chances of having close, personal, interactions with those different from you—whether in age, physical ability, gender, ethnicity, class, religion, race, or nationality—are increasing daily. Such relationships help you learn about the world, break stereotypes, and acquire new skills.[12]

Solving Misunderstandings, Miscommunications, and Mistrust. Until recently our nation has not learned, nor has it needed to learn, to be multiculturally competent.[13] The study of intercultural communication will not just unlock doors closed for generations; it will open those doors and, thus, resolve misunderstandings, miscommunications, and mistrust through honest, open, positive, healthy communication. People not only fear, but they also distrust the unknown. Trust is gained through knowledge and understanding.

Enhancing and Enriching the Quality of Civilization. Recognizing and respecting ethnic and cultural diversity are important steps on the road to valuing the ways in which diversity enhances and enriches the quality of our civilization. According to Carlos Cortes, "many multiculturalists today seem unwilling to deal with the growing factor of intermarriage. Too much of multicultural education is frozen into a kind of group purity paradigm, when in fact, intermarriage is one of the enormous changes that is taking place in America. For example, one-third of all Latinos born in the United States now marry someone who is not Latino.... What will these cultural blends be like?"[14] In

---

STRATEGIC FLEXIBILITY

Strategic flexibility requires learning about the world, breaking down stereotypes, and acquiring new skills. Greater tolerance and accommodation will expand your available skills and behaviors as you anticipate, assess, evaluate, and select from your repertoire. In addition, you will reveal greater care, concern, and attention as you apply those skills.

Working Together

The word *multicultural* means different things to different people. The commonly held view suggests that being multicultural means being tolerant of racial and ethnic minorities, mainly of their dress, language, food, religious beliefs, and other cultural manifestations.

For this activity, allow each member of your group to express his or her ideas and feelings on each of the following questions:

1. Multiculturalism seeks to preserve distinctly different ethnic, racial, and cultural communities (co-cultures) without melting them into a common culture. Is this definition of U.S. society an acceptable one?
2. Can diversity be preserved while also establishing a unifying set of cultural symbols—symbols like language? Should teachers in the United States, despite their background or current geographic location, teach students in English alone?
3. Should the word *multicultural* include—in addition to ethnic, racial, and co-cultures—struggles against sexism, heterosexism, classism, linguisism, and ableism?
4. Does multiculturalism encourage racial and ethnic harmony as well as cross-cultural understanding?

2002 there were 1,674,000 interracial marriages, close to a 40 percent increase in 22 years.[15] When you consider the potential for the new perspectives, cultural insights, and unique wisdom that intermarriages can produce, there is no doubt about the corresponding increase in the quality of our civilization.

Becoming Effective Citizens of Our National Communities. **National communities** are co-cultural groupings within the country. National communities were established from the beginning as "our forefathers acquired the lands of Native Americans, 34 percent of the territory of Mexico in 1848, and the island of Puerto Rico in 1898."[16] Prior to the 1960s, most of the immigrants to the United States came from Europe, but of the million or so immigrants who now enter the United States every year, 90 percent are from Latin America and Asia. A study by the Population Reference Bureau suggests that by 2050 the United States will be a global society in which nearly half of all citizens will be from today's racial and ethnic minorities.[17]

INTERCULTURAL COMMUNICATION AND THE COMMUNICATION MODEL

Using our broad definition of *culture*, and with the clear understanding that much of communication is intercultural, you can also see how much influence intercultural communication has had on the model of communication in Chapter 1.

It Influences Senders and Receivers. If my values, traditions, social and political relationships, and worldview are different from yours, given the same subject to respond to and with everything else in the assignment the same, I will compose a significantly different response. As the differences among communicators become greater, the results in thoughts, feelings, and messages become more divergent as well.

It Influences Messages and Feedback. When my parents taught in Pakistan, they were told that raising a question in the classroom is considered an affront to a respected and esteemed authority: the teacher. Instead of interpreting the lack of student response as indifference or lack of understanding, my parents encouraged students to respond among themselves with the teacher as overseer, guide, and outside resource. Jun Liu, in his book *Asian Students' Classroom Communication Patterns in U.S. Universi-*

ties, attributes silence in Asian cultures to politeness, the pace of the discussion in U.S. classrooms, fear of wasting class time, and face saving with other international students or with the professor.[18]

Both verbal and nonverbal messages are affected by intercultural communication. Most Americans pay attention and show respect in the classroom by maintaining eye contact with teachers. But Navajo students in the classroom show respect by avoiding eye contact.

It Influences the Setting. Setting can refer to the way communication fits into history: past, present, and future. It also describes how communication fits into a relational setting, such as the influences of power and distance, individualism versus collectivism, or femininity versus masculinity. It can refer to gender, ethnicity, or nationality.

Setting, too, can relate to your own position within a speech community. If you are the only person with a physical disability in an otherwise abled environment, or the only gay man or lesbian in a heterosexual environment, you may face specific expectations or have people project their motivations on your communication.[19]

STUDYING CULTURAL DIFFERENCES

There are a number of ways to contrast a group of cultures to another group of cultures.[20] Geert Hofstede examined cultural distinctions based on deeply rooted values and derived five dimensions.[21] A sixth dimension, Edward T. Hall's high context versus low context, follows our discussion of Hofstede's five dimensions.[22]

Cultural differences are manifest in the cultural identities of the people, as the examples within each category will reveal. Cultural identity influences behavior including choices of symbols, heroes and heroines, rituals, and even the values one chooses.

The dimensions discussed here are general tendencies only. They are not always true of a culture, nor true of everyone in a culture. Jackie Low is a good example. Raised in Ohio, she has never been to China, never spoken a word of Chinese, and did not know much about China. Anyone who assumed from her looks that Jackie was Chinese would have been incorrect.

Iris Chang, in her book *The Chinese in America*, verifies Jackie Low's experience when she says about the ethnic Chinese in America: "None can truly get past the distinction of race or entirely shake the perception of being seen as foreigners in their own land."[23]

Power Distance

Power distance is a way of contrasting a group of cultures to another group of cultures by measuring social inequality in each. You will notice power differences in family customs, the relationships between students and teachers, the young and the elderly, language systems, and organizational practices. When Lennie observed Tupac—who was from Africa, a high-power-distance country—he noticed he always did as he was told by their boss, who Lennie thought was authoritarian, dictatorial, and unfair, and wasn't afraid to say so. When he talked to Tupac, he realized most people from Africa consider their boss a benevolent dictator and do as they are told.

Continents with high power distance include Africa, Latin America, and Near Eastern countries. Low-power-distance countries include the United States, Germany, China, and Great Britain.

Our way to contrast a group of cultures to another group of cultures is to use the dimension of power distance—social inequality. The picture reveals potential power distances between students and teacher as well as between the younger and the elderly.

View "Culture and Self," clip #9, on the CD to further understand the value of examining cultural differences.

Individualism versus Collectivism

The degree of integration and orientation of individuals within groups is referred to as **individualism versus collectivism.** When Elaine worked with the Peace Corps in Argentina, she learned about collectivist cultures. Working hand in hand with Eduardo Puerta, a native Argentinian, she realized he had never worked side-by-side with a female and needed to be in control and maintain face. In their discussions, she also came to understand his devotion to his family and preference for government control over the economy and press. Knowing about collectivist cultures helped Elaine not just understand Eduardo, but learn from and respect him as well.

You will notice that people in individualistic cultures such as Great Britain, the United States, Canada, France, and Germany value self-expression, view speaking out as a way to solve problems, and use confrontational strategies to deal with interpersonal problems. In collectivist cultures such as many Arab, African, Asian, and Latin American countries, people have unquestioning loyalty to the group, and when in conflict they use avoidance, intermediaries, and other face-saving techniques.

Femininity versus Masculinity

A way of contrasting a group of cultures to another group of cultures that looks at the division of rules between men and women is called **femininity versus masculinity.**

High-feminine cultures believe women should be nurturant, concerned for the quality of life, and reveal sympathy for the unfortunate. In general, feminine cultures allow cross-gender behaviors. High-masculine cultures believe men should be concerned about wealth, achievement, challenge, ambition, promotion, and that they should be assertive, competitive, tough, and recognize achievements. Masculine cultures are more likely to maintain strictly defined gender roles and, thus, have distinct expectations of male and female roles in society. High-feminine cultures include Africa and the Nordic countries of Europe. High-masculine cultures include Latin America, Great Britain, Japan, and the United States.

Uncertainty Avoidance

Uncertainty avoidance compares tolerance for the unknown when contrasting a group of cultures to another group of cultures. When Amelia entered her math classroom on the first day, she was startled to realize her teaching assistant was from Japan. Because Amelia knew Japan was a low-uncertainty-avoidance country, she was able to put into perspective much of what she learned from Junji Akimoto. Junji behaved quietly without showing aggression or strong emotions. Easy-going and relaxed, he ran an open-ended class.

Cultures that feel threatened by ambiguous and uncertain situations and try to avoid them prefer formal rules to control social behaviors. The best example is China. Low-uncertainty-avoidance cultures need few rules and accept and encourage dissenting views and risk taking. Countries with low uncertainty avoidance include Latin America, Africa, and Japan. The United States is considered "medium" on this dimension—neither high nor low.

Long-Term Orientation

Long-term orientation measures the trade-off between long-term and short-term gratification of needs. This dimension was added by Hofstede as a result of his work with Michael Bond.[24] Bond labeled it Confucian dynamism. Elisha's roommate, Mei Li, explained by example that virtuous behavior in China means acquiring skills and education, working hard, and being frugal, patient, and persevering. Knowing what long-term orientation meant helped Elisha bond with Mei Li and appreciate her industriousness.

Those at one extreme on this dimension—having long-term orientation—admire persistence, ordering relationships by status, thriftiness, and having a sense of shame that emphasizes care for others and being loyal and trustworthy. China, Japan, and other Asian countries have an extraordinary long-term orientation toward life. At the other extreme—with short-term orientation—are countries like Finland, France, Germany, and the United States where people value personal steadiness and stability but do not have as much respect for tradition because it prevents innovation, nor for saving face, which can hinder the flow of business. These countries, too, favor reciprocation of greetings, favors, and gifts as related to social rituals.

High Context versus Low Context

High context versus low context contrasts how much information is carried in the **context** (high) and how much in the code or message (low).[25] In high-context communication most of the information is already in the person; very little information is in the coded, explicit, intentionally transmitted part of the message. For example, in the Japanese, African, Mexican, Asian, and Latin American cultures most of the meaning of a message is either implied by the physical setting or is presumed to be part of the individual's beliefs, values, and norms. Often, in long-term relationships communication is high context because the slightest gesture, quickest glance, or briefest comment is interpretable without explicit statements or extended explanations.

Why? Because most of the information has already been experienced. Few explicit statements or extended explanations are necessary unless new areas of experience or discussion occur. Some people who date a lot tire of it simply because of the time it takes to move from low context to high context—often the preferred mode of communication because it is easier and doesn't require as many explanations and clarifications.

Most Western cultures prefer low-context messages in which the majority of the information is in the communication itself—not in the context. Computer instructions are low context because they require that every space, period, letter, and number be precisely in the right location; there are no exceptions. All the information is in the instruction, or the instruction does not work.

These six dimensions are basic frames of reference to help you appreciate differences. No culture is better than another; no culture is strange; no culture is unusual or foreign. Using these tools will help reduce misunderstandings by encouraging empathy, tolerance, respect, and perhaps, a more accurate interpretation of messages from people of another culture group.

BARRIERS TO INTERCULTURAL COMMUNICATION

Some people do not know about other cultures, and some do not want to know. There is no doubt that both ignorance (lack of knowledge) and naivete (lack of sophistication) can be important barriers to intercultural communication.

In this section, we will briefly consider ethnocentrism, stereotyping, prejudice, and discrimination. These are barriers because each is constructed around a judgment made before any communication takes place that then biases the communication that follows. All communication has a past, present, and future; barriers are part of the past that influence the communication that takes place now and affect all that follows in the future.

Ethnocentrism

When I lectured in Australia, I was told never to show arrogance or in any way to reveal condescension or become patronizing. It was wise advice. My hosts had warned me not to be ethnocentric: a common occurrence, they said, when Americans spoke to Australians.

Ethnocentrism is the belief that one's own cultural group's behaviors, norms, ways of thinking, and ways of being are superior to all other cultural groups. Ethnocentrism is not to be confused with *patriotism,* which is devotion to one's country. Ethnocentrism carries devotion to the extreme point where you cannot believe that another culture's behaviors, norms, ways of thinking, and ways of being are as good or as worthy as your own. It becomes a barrier in intercultural communication when it prevents you from even trying to see another's point of view—that is, when it hampers all attempts at empathy.

Stereotyping

Stereotypes are oversimplified or distorted views of another race, another ethnic group, or even another culture. They are simply ways to categorize and generalize from the overwhelming amount of information we receive daily.

The problem with stereotypes is that whether they are positive or negative, once they are established, it is difficult to remove them. Sometimes they exist in our subconscious; these are even more difficult to discard because we are less aware of them. We tend to pick up information from our environment that supports the stereotypes rather than denies them. This simply embeds them more deeply. To remove them, we must first recognize them, then we must obtain individual information that will counteract them.

Consider This

In her book *The Majesty of the Law*, Supreme Court Justice Sandra Day O'Connor discusses survival in an increasingly multinational environment:

> We live in a world that is constantly shrinking. Cellular phones, fax machines, beepers, e-mail—all of these new forms of communications have made it much easier for us to talk to one another, no matter where we are. We need, however, more than technology to communicate with people from other nations. We need language skills. We need deeper understanding of foreign cultures. We need to know how to survive in an increasingly multinational environment.
>
> Many of our schools recognize this need, and many parents are taking great interest in language training. High schools now offer more than French and Spanish. They are adding Japanese and Russian as well. American businesses have been in the forefront of this move toward what newspapers constantly herald as the "globalization" of trade. There are McDonald's restaurants in Moscow, Kentucky Fried Chicken franchises in Beijing.

Source: *The Majesty of the Law: Reflections of a Supreme Court Justice* (p. 231), by Sandra Day O'Connor, 2003; New York: Random House.

Questions

1. What signs have you noticed that we are now living in an increasingly multinational environment?
2. What implications do these changes hold for you?
3. If you were trying to prepare the next generation for the changes occurring in our culture, what suggestions would you make?

Prejudice

Prejudice is a negative attitude toward a cultural group based on little or no experience.[26] The difference between stereotypes and prejudice should become clear in this example: When Chris was young, his parents told him never to go into the city because Mexican gangs ruled the city streets at night. Chris, of course, then had the preconceived notion that all Mexicans were bad people. From this stereotype Chris formed a prejudice against Mexicans. The stereotype told him what a group (Mexicans) was like; the prejudice told him how to feel about the group. All this changed when Chris worked for the city to help pay his way through college, and almost all his co-workers were Mexicans. Their attitude toward Chris as well as their behavior quickly changed the stereotype and altered his prejudice.

Discrimination

Discrimination is the overt actions one takes to exclude, avoid, or distance oneself from other groups.[27] Discrimination takes stereotypes and prejudice one step further—to action, whether overt or covert. You can discriminate against someone subtly by slightly turning away your body when in a conversation, or by avoiding eye contact with them. You can discriminate against people by hurling verbal insults at them. You can discriminate, too, by using physical violence, systematically eliminating the group from which the individual comes, or even in extreme cases by using genocide, as when autocratic tyrants exterminate racial or national groups. Yet another form of discrimination occurs when you exclude others from jobs or from other economic opportunities.

Obviously, discrimination can be interpersonal when you do it against another person, collective (when a number of individuals or a group perform the discrimination), or institutional (when a business or industry chooses not to serve a particular group of people).

DEALING WITH BARRIERS TO INTERCULTURAL COMMUNICATION

For accurate communication to occur, sender-receivers must be operating from the same perceptual point of view. This is usually not a problem when we are interacting with people from our own race or culture; however, when we communicate with someone from a different race or background, we must realize that this person will be operating from an entirely different point of view.

Communication between Nondominant- and Dominant-Group Members

Much of the literature about communication is written from the point of view of the dominant, or majority, culture. In the United States **dominant culture** includes white people from a European background, while **nondominant culture** includes people of color; women; gays, lesbians, and bisexuals; and those whose socioeconomic background is lower than middle class.

When people are not part of a dominant culture, how do they communicate with people who are? In a tantalizing piece of research, Orbe looked at how people from nondominant groups (people of color; women; gays, lesbians, and bisexuals; and those from lower socioeconomic backgrounds) communicated with people from the dominant group.[28] He found that nondominant members adopted one of three basic strategies when they wanted to confront oppressive dominant structures and achieve success: assimilation, accommodation, and separation.

Assimilation Strategies

When nondominants use **assimilation,** they drop cultural differences and distinctive characteristics that would identify them with the nondominant group. As you can see in Table 3-1, there are three types of **assimilation strategies.**

Nonassertive Assimilation. In this type of assimilation, minority members want to belong to the majority group, but they do not want to use aggression to get there. In order to achieve acceptance, they emphasize what they have in common with the

Table 3-1 Assimilation

Nonassertive	Assertive	Aggressive
Emphasizing what the dominant and nondominant groups have in common	Carefully preparing for meeting dominant-group members	Disassociating from one's own group
Acting positive	Manipulating stereotypes	Copying dominant-group behavior
Censoring remarks that might offend the dominant group	Bargaining	Avoiding interaction with other co-cultural groups
Avoiding controversy		Ridiculing oneself

dominant group and sometimes censor themselves to fit in. However, it often comes at a terrible cost, as you can see in the following passage:

> *I spent the fifties essentially either going to graduate school or beginning my career as a teacher who was very much in the closet—and very much attempting to hide the fact that I was a lesbian. And that meant putting down and holding down a whole part of myself that was really vital to my being. I have these visions of faculty parties or church parties or picnics to which I would oftentimes go with a gay man friend of mine, and we would put on an incredibly good show.*[29]

Assertive Assimilation. In assertive assimilation, people are likely to take a stronger approach to fitting in. They will often carefully prepare for an encounter with the dominant group. They may overcompensate by trying to be twice as smart, twice as witty, and so forth.

African American writer Patricia Raybon, in her book *My First White Friend*, describes her assertive assimilation stage, which occurred when she was a child living in a predominantly white culture:

> *I was reared to smile, to be polite, to say please and thank you and not to act ugly. I was reared to be the cleanest, nicest, smartest, kindest black child I could possibly be. That would make people like me. White people especially.*[30]

Aggressive Assimilation. In this type of assimilation, minority-group members want to fit into the dominant group at any cost. They will imply that there are no differences between the two groups and will be careful to not do or say anything that would indicate their difference, such as speaking in a dialect or making reference to their own group's behavior. They are so eager to be part of the dominant group that they might ridicule the group they belong to.

Accommodation Strategies

The next main category consists of accommodation strategies. **Accommodation** works toward getting the dominant group to reinvent, or at least change, the rules so that they incorporate the life experiences of the nondominant group. The three types of **accommodation strategies** are summarized in Table 3-2.

Nonassertive Accommodation. In nonassertive accommodation, the person does not act in any way that would cause dominant-group members to be defensive or cautious but tries to make people more aware of the group she or he belongs to and tries to change stereotypes they might have. For example, Anna who is Mexican often talks to her co-workers about her friends who are professionals, trying to break the stereotype of Mexicans as manual laborers.

Assertive Accommodation. Those who use this strategy try to achieve a balance between their own group and the dominant group. They try to get their own group's members to know the dominant group by sharing something about their lives; they also attempt to educate others about their group's members. Often they will choose a member of the dominant group as a mentor who can guide, support, and assist them.

They also try to educate the dominant group about their group's culture. Maria, for example, persuades some dominant-group members to go to a Mexican restaurant and guides them through the menu.

Aggressive Accommodation. The strategy in this approach is to get into a dominant group and try to change it, although nondominant-group members may confront

Table 3-2 Accommodation

Nonassertive	Assertive	Aggressive
Increasing visibility	Letting DG members know who they really are	Confronting members of the DG when they violate the rights of others
Avoiding stereotypes	Identifying and working with DG members who have similar goals	Referring to DG oppression of NG
	Identifying members of the DG who can support, guide, and assist	
	Educating others	

Note: DG = dominant group; NG = nondominant group.

dominant-group members to gain an advantage. For example, a woman on a committee that brings international scholars to the university may point out that no women have been chosen. Persons using aggressive accommodation may also warn dominant-group members of their history of oppression.

Separation Strategies

In the third category of strategies, nondominant-group members have given up. In **separation,** nondominants do not want to form a common bond with the dominant culture, so they separate into a group that includes only members like themselves. During the 1960s and 1970s, many African Americans and women, unhappy that power structures were not changing quickly enough, formed separate groups that excluded members of the dominant group as well as nondominant-group members who did not share their views (Black Muslims exclude other blacks as well as whites). Some of these groups still exist today. Table 3-3 outlines the three types of **separation strategies.**

Nonassertive Separation. In this type of separation, the nondominant person avoids the dominant group whenever possible. Although the nondominant may work

Table 3-3 Separation

Nonassertive	Assertive	Aggressive
Maintaining barriers between themselves and the DG	Asserting their voice regardless of the consequences	Making direct attacks on DG members
Keeping away from places where DG members are found	Making references to DG oppression with the goal of gaining advantage	Undermining the DG by not letting its members take advantage of their privileged position

Note DG = dominant group; NG = nondominant group.

with dominant-group members, he or she won't go out to lunch with them or socialize after work. Through verbal and nonverbal cues, the dominant group senses that this person wants to be left alone. For example, when Tom, who is gay, is asked whether he is going to the office Christmas party, he answers no because he knows that the man he lives with would not be welcome.

Some nondominant groups make no attempt to become part of the dominant group. An example is the Hmong people who immigrated to the United States because they were no longer safe in Laos. Anne Fadiman describes them after they had lived for 17 years in the United States:

> *Seventeen years later, Foua and Nao Kao use American appliances but they still speak only Hmong, celebrate only Hmong holidays, practice only Hmong religion, cook only Hmong dishes, sing only Hmong songs, play only Hmong musical instruments, tell only Hmong stories, and know far more about the current political events in Laos and Thailand than about those in the United States. . . . It would be hard to imagine anything further from the vaunted American ideal of assimilation, in which immigrants are expected to submerge their cultural differences in order to embrace a shared national identity.*[31]

Assertive Separation. Persons practicing assertive separation work to form organizations where they can be separate from the dominant group. While in these groups, they work against any dominant-group messages that imply the dominant group is superior and they are inferior. One communication strategy they use is reminding the dominant group of their oppression. Patricia Raybon, whose passage we quoted in the assimilation discussion, describes some of the feelings that led to her assertive separation stage:

> *White people—that relentless, heavy presence. Never benign. Never innocent. "White people" as a category embodied in my view a clear and certain evil—an arrogant malevolence—that had done unspeakable things that I couldn't ignore because I knew the facts of these things. Names and dates and numbers. And the facts haunted me and the numbers justified my hate for all of the evil that I believed white people had done.*[32]

Aggressive Separation. In aggressive separation, people separate from the dominant group and expect their fellow nondominant-group members to do so too. They are very critical of those who practice assimilation or accommodation. It is not uncommon for groups fighting against oppression to separate from the dominant group.

If members of these groups have to have interaction with the dominant group (for example, at work), they will try to undermine the dominants by not letting them take advantage of their privileged positions. For example, an employee would bring legal action against his or her boss for discrimination.

The Consequences of Nondominant- and Dominant-Group Communication

Orbe's research does not lead to a very optimistic picture of American society. If we depict his results on a continuum, as in Figure 3-3, on one end are people who want to belong so much that they are willing to give up or suppress their own cultures, while on the opposite end are people who have decided that they cannot live in the dominant culture of the United States and have gone off on their own. In a country that prides itself on being a place where people from all cultures can live in harmony, nothing on the continuum is acceptable to our vision of what democracy should be.

Figure 3-3
Nondominant Persons' Communication to Dominant Groups

Belongers |——|——|——|——|——|——|——| Separatists

Nonassertive assimilation | Assertive assimilation | Aggressive assimilation | Nonassertive accommodation | Assertive accommodation | Aggressive accommodation | Nonassertive separation | Assertive separation | Aggressive separation

IMPROVING INTERCULTURAL COMMUNICATION

Sometimes in an intercultural-communication situation with a person different from us, we may interpret the other person as *abnormal, weird,* or simply *different*. It is important to learn to control the human tendency to translate "different from me" into "less than me."[33] Rather, we need to raise questions. Are there effective ways of dealing with different kinds of people? Can I develop a repertoire of five or six approaches that will help me reach others in real and meaningful ways?[34]

Pay attention to your words and actions. It is only through your thoughtful communication with others that you become aware of your own thinking patterns, assumptions, perceptions, prejudices, and biases.[35] When students come to Cruz-Janzen's classes expecting to learn how to communicate with nonwhites, she tells them they are first going to study themselves, their gender, racial, ethnic, cultural, socioeconomic, and physical (ability, disability, and appearance) socialization. Cruz-Janzen has a very clear motive in this: "As long as whites continue expecting others to explain themselves, whites are setting themselves as the norm, the normal ones, against whom all others must be judged and measured."[36]

Control your assumptions. An **assumption** is a taking for granted or supposition that something is a fact. You can learn from generalizations about other cultures, but those generalizations turn sour when you use them to stereotype or oversimplify.[37]

- Don't assume that there is one right way (yours) to communicate. Question your assumptions about the "right way" to communicate.
- Don't assume that breakdowns in communication occur because others are on the wrong track. The point isn't "who is to blame for the breakdown?" it is "who can make the communication work?"[38] Remember, ineffective communication can occur for a variety of reasons:
  - You may not have transmitted your message in a way that can be understood.
  - Others may misinterpret what you say.[39]
- Don't assume that the preferred rules of interpersonal relationships you have learned in your culture apply universally across all cultures. They do not.

STRATEGIC FLEXIBILITY
To apply the steps of strategic flexibility may require that you ask questions that help you more accurately anticipate, assess, evaluate, select, and apply your abilities and skills. Questions can also help you demonstrate the care, concern, and attention that may reveal true sensitivity—opening the doors to effective intercultural communication.

Another Point of View

One popular way to educate people who will be entering another culture is to provide them with lists of do's and taboos. The Internet, for example, is good at providing such lists. Here is what Linda Beamer and Iris Varner think of such lists:

The do's and taboos lists are usually accurate, but their helpfulness is limited: One-sentence advice on behavior is like seeing a snapshot from a movie. It is accurate, but without the content of the movie's story line, character development, or even the specific episode, the snapshot's significance may not be understandable. Lists of do's and taboos can't explain why you should or should not behave in a particular way in a particular place. Lists can't possibly be comprehensive. And even if a business traveler were armed with a very long list, who can consult a list for every nuance in every different country? It's no wonder that businesspeople may seem to discard tips on do's and taboos in favor of simply being themselves and acting the same way abroad that they would at home. And yet most businesspeople know that business as usual—doing what they do at home—can be counterproductive when doing business abroad.

Source: *Intercultural Communication in the Global Workplace* (p. 11), by L. Beamer and I. Varner, 2001, New York: McGraw-Hill/Irwin.

Questions

1. Have you ever seen or used a list of do's or taboos? Have you found them helpful?
2. Do you think a list of do's and taboos would serve the purpose when you just don't have time to make a thorough or comprehensive introduction to the new culture?
3. What do you rely on when you have no instructions of any kind and you are in a new culture? How do you behave? How do you know what to do?

- Don't assume that your cultural definitions and successful criteria of conflict management apply universally across all cultures. They do not.[40]
- Don't assume because another's values and beliefs differ from your own that you are being challenged.
- Don't assume that you can learn about intercultural communication by staying in your comfort zone. Even if it is awkward at first, you need to expose yourself to different cultures.[41]
- Don't assume you know what is best for someone else.

Engage in transpection. Instead of assuming—a process most people begin quickly, naturally, and often subconsciously—take a moment to relax and reflect. **Transpection** is the process of empathizing across cultures.[42] "Achieving transpection, trying to see the world exactly as the other person sees it, is a difficult process. It often involves trying to learn foreign beliefs, foreign assumptions, foreign perspectives, and foreign feelings in a foreign context. Transpection, then, can only be achieved by practice and requires structured experience and self-reflection."[43]

Striving *toward* transpection can help you avoid assumptions and move you closer to tolerance, sensitivity, respect, empathic listening, and effective communication responses. Listen carefully to others, understand their feelings, be interested in what they have to say and sensitive to their needs, and try to understand their points of view.[44]

Gain knowledge. The greater your cultural and linguistic knowledge, and the more your beliefs overlap with those from other cultures, the less likelihood for misunderstandings.[45] You need to read, observe, ask questions, and visit places where there are people from different races and ethnic backgrounds.

When Madison found out her new roommate was from Saudi Arabia, she immediately worried because of what she'd heard in the media about Saudi terrorists. She went online to find out more about the country—customs, traditions, religion, and anything else she could discover. The words *Saudi Arabia* produced over 11 million Web sites. Using online resources such as The World Factbook, Saudi Arabia Information

Resource, Saudi newspapers, and the Lonely Planet World Guide, Madison strove toward transpection to help herself avoid assumptions.

Gain experience. You cannot learn how to be a good communicator just by reading, observing, asking questions, or doing research on the Internet. But gaining experience doesn't require making actual visits to foreign countries or foreign cultures. Find an individual of another culture, and ask if the two of you could have a conversation about intercultural communication. With that as your focus, ask some pointed, specific questions designed to help you better understand him or her and others of the same culture. The following 10 questions are designed to get your conversation started:

- How do you, or other members of your culture, cope with and adapt to unfamiliar cultural environments?
- How can members of other cultures begin to communicate with members of your culture?
- What factors can increase our effectiveness in communicating?
- If we had a conflict, what strategies would be successful for managing it?
- What important factors contribute to the development of interpersonal relationships with you or with members of your culture?
- What changes have you noticed in yourself as a consequence of your experiences in a new culture?
- How can I become more *intercultural* as a result of our contact and communication with members of your culture?
- Can we develop community with members of your culture?[46]
- What are some of the worst offenses people outside your culture make in communicating with you or with members of your culture?
- What do you feel are some of the worst offenses you have made as you have become acclimated into this culture?

There are other ways to gain experience in intercultural communication—to obtain a broader worldview. Frequent ethnic restaurants, watch world news in addition to local news, read books written by authors from other countries, learn another language, and when countries with which you are unfamiliar are mentioned, find them on a map. Listen to world music, rent foreign films, and travel—whether in person or through videos. Your local library has dozens of videos on foreign countries. But don't just observe. Converse with people of other cultures. Take part in cultural celebrations that differ from your own. Volunteer to serve on committees, teams, or groups in which members of other cultures will be serving. Listen, engage, and keep asking questions. Take time to understand what people believe about childrearing, educational opportunities, world politics, and life in general.

How you learn about intercultural communication will depend on your willingness to find it out. You will see that the knowledge and understanding you gain is well worth any effort you put forth.

THE INTERNET AND INTERCULTURAL COMMUNICATION

One of the most important influences on intercultural communication is the Internet. We are increasingly linked together across the globe, and we can connect with people on the other side of the world as quickly as we do with friends and family at home.

Assess Yourself

Cultural Awareness Self-Assessment Form

For each statement circle the numerical score that best represents your performance, skill, or ability using the following scale:
7 = Outstanding; 6 = Excellent; 5 = Very good; 4 = Average (good); 3 = Fair; 2 = Poor; 1 = minimal ability; 0 = No ability demonstrated.

1. I listen to people from other cultures when they tell me how my culture affects them.   7 6 5 4 3 2 1 0
2. I realize that people from other cultures have fresh ideas and different points of view to bring to my life and to the workplace.   7 6 5 4 3 2 1 0
3. I give people from other cultures advice on how to succeed in my culture.   7 6 5 4 3 2 1 0
4. I give people my support even when they are rejected by other members of my culture.   7 6 5 4 3 2 1 0
5. I realize that people outside my culture could be offended by my behavior. I've asked people if I have offended them by things I have done or said and have apologized whenever necessary.   7 6 5 4 3 2 1 0
6. I realize that when I am stressed I am likely to make myself and my culture right and another culture wrong.   7 6 5 4 3 2 1 0
7. I respect my superiors (boss, teacher, supervisor, group leader, etc.) regardless of where they are from. I do not go over their heads to talk to someone from my culture to try and get my way.   7 6 5 4 3 2 1 0
8. When I am in mixed company, I mix with everyone. I don't just stay with people from my culture, or only with people from the dominant culture.   7 6 5 4 3 2 1 0
9. I go out of my way to work with, recruit, select, train, and promote people from outside the dominant culture.   7 6 5 4 3 2 1 0
10. When people in my culture make jokes or talk negatively about other cultural groups, I let them know that I don't like it.   7 6 5 4 3 2 1 0

TOTAL POINTS: _____

Go to the *Communicating Effectively* CD-ROM and the Online Learning Center at www.mhhe.com/hybels8 to see your results and learn how to evaluate your attitudes and feelings.

mhhe.com/hybels8

Source: Adapted from *Cultural Awareness Self-Assessment Form 3*, I CANS (Integrated Curriculum for Achieving Necessary Skills), Washington State Board for Community and Technical Colleges, Washington State Employment Security, Washington Workforce Training and Education Coordinating Board, Adult Basic and Literacy Educators, P.O. Box 42496, 711 Capitol Blvd., Olympia, WA 98504. Retrieved March 14, 2003, from http://www.literacynet.org/icans/chapter05/cultural3.html

The Internet serves as a vehicle not only for searching for common values and understanding, but also for hearing and seeing in real-time events that take place thousands of miles away. It can bridge the culture gap among nations of the world. For example, it has helped worldwide organizations function by bringing together people from different physical locations with common interests and goals. More than 45,000 Muslims had joined Naseeb.com by February 2004, after it went online in the fall of 2003. Monis Rahman, who founded Naseeb, said the word means "destiny" in Arabic, Urdu, Persian, Malaysian, Indonesian, Turkish, and Hindi.[47] In fact non-English-language website growth has overtaken English Web site growth, and by 2007 Chinese will be the most common language on the Internet. All those with access to the Internet now have the opportunity to expand their horizons by learning how to communicate, relate, collaborate, and understand their changing world.

CHAPTER REVIEW

SUMMARY

Intercultural understanding increases both sending and receiving abilities, making communication between people with different linguistic and cultural backgrounds as constructive as possible. With broader experience, the care and concern you demonstrate will not just nourish intercultural communication but will encourage further communication efforts as well.

Culture is the ever-changing values, traditions, social and political relationships, and worldview created and shared by a group of people bound together by a combination of factors (which can include a common history, geographic location, language, social class, or religion).

To accept yourself as a cultural being means embracing a cultural identity composed of ethnicity, culture, gender, age, life stage, beliefs, values, and assumptions. A cultural identity is learned, varies in its strength, and varies in its content as well.

Five reasons for studying intercultural communication include (1) better understanding your own identity, (2) enhancing your personal and social interactions, (3) helping solve cultural misunderstandings, miscommunication, and mistrusts, (4) valuing the ways it enriches the quality of our civilization, and (5) becoming effective citizens of our national communities.

Intercultural communication influences the communication model first by its effect on the values, traditions, social and political relationships, and worldview of senders and receivers; second, by its effect on verbal and nonverbal messages; and, third, by the influences it has on the historical setting, relational setting, and a person's position within a speech community.

Power distance relates to social inequality. Individualism versus collectivism relates to the degree of integration and orientation of individuals. Femininity versus masculinity pertains to the division of roles between women and men. Uncertainty avoidance describes the degree of tolerance for the unknown. Long-term orientation relates to trade-offs between long-term and short-term gratification of needs. Finally, high versus low context refers to the amount of information already contained in the person or context versus the amount in the coded, explicit, transmitted part of the message.

The four barriers to intercultural communication include ethnocentrism, stereotyping, prejudice, and discrimination. To deal with barriers, nondominant-group members use one or more of three main strategies to get what they want from dominant-group members: assimilation, accommodation, or separation.

Five ways to improve intercultural communication are: (1) pay attention to your own words and actions; (2) control your assumptions; (3) engage in transpection—the process of empathizing across cultures; (4) gain knowledge; and (5) gain experience.

The Internet offers a vehicle for searching for common values, understandings, and approaches to managing a world of different cultures.

KEY TERMS AND CONCEPTS

Use the *Communicating Effectively* CD-ROM and the Online Learning Center at **www.mhhe.com/hybels8** to further your understanding of the following terms.

Accommodation 69
Accommodation strategies 69
Assimilation 68
Assimilation strategies 68
Assumption 72
Co-culture 59
Context 60
Cultural identity 58
Culture 57
Discrimination 67

Dominant culture 68
Ethnocentrism 66
Femininity versus masculinity 64
High context versus low context 65
Individualism versus collectivism 64
Intercultural communication 60
Knowledge class 56
Long-term orientation 65

National communities 62
Nondominant culture 68
Power distance 63
Prejudice 67
Separation 70
Separation strategies 70
Stereotypes 66
Transpection 73
Uncertainty avoidance 65
Worldview 58

CHAPTER REVIEW

QUESTIONS TO REVIEW

1. What is the role intercultural communication plays in communicating effectively and in strategic flexibility?
2. What are the strengths and weaknesses of the definition of *culture* offered in this textbook?
3. What does it mean to possess a cultural identity?
4. Can you make a case for the study of intercultural communication?
5. What are the likely components of a multicultural self?
6. How does intercultural communication relate to the model of communication?
7. What are the six dimensions that can be used as a framework for studying cultural differences?
8. What are four barriers to intercultural communication, and how do they work? Why are they considered barriers?
9. What are the three ways members of a nondominant group work to get what they want from dominant-group members?
10. What are some ways for improving intercultural communication?
11. What is the process of transpection, and why is it important?
12. What is the influence of the Internet on intercultural communication?

Go to the self-quizzes on the *Communicating Effectively* CD-ROM and the Online Learning Center at www.mhhe.com/hybels8 to test your knowledge of the chapter concepts.

CHAPTER 4

Listening

OBJECTIVES

After reading this chapter, you should be able to:

- Explain the role of listening in strategic flexibility.
- Distinguish among the elements of the Integrative Listening Model (ILM).
- Differentiate and give an example of each of the four listening styles.
- Clarify the effects of culture and gender on listening.
- Differentiate between good listeners and poor listeners.
- Distinguish among and give the key characteristics of active, critical, and empathic listening.
- Explain how you can talk so others will listen.
- Identify the three areas where the Internet is likely to have an effect on listening.

PATRICIA REYES WAS BORN A CHEERLEADER—PRETTY, EXUBERANT, AND communicative. Even before she could talk she would mimic the gestures and sounds of others. As an only child her parents enjoyed the sound of her voice and encouraged and reinforced her, because her voice was music to their ears. Throughout elementary school she was warned by her teachers to "stop talking" and "listen." But Patricia loved talking more than listening. In high school she would often get assignments confused when given orally by teachers because she wouldn't listen closely to the details. She would have to spend more time on assignments because her attention and concentration skills suffered—her mind easily wandered. Patricia had difficulty sustaining relationships with others because she found it difficult to listen to others with attention and care. Seldom did others feel validated or supported by her because of her ineffective listening habits.

It was part of a class in gerontology (the scientific study of the process and phenomena of aging) when Patricia, at last, had to directly confront her "problem." Throughout the class students had to make regular visits to a nursing home, and the instructions were clear: "You are to listen to the patients. Let *them* talk. You may briefly reflect on their comments but only to encourage *them* to talk more." Patricia followed her instructions to the letter, and she discovered a whole new world: that others had valuable ideas, interesting insights, and their own life stories. It was the very wake-up call she needed, and it turned her life around.

The **Integrative Listening Model (ILM)** provides a framework for assessing listening both systematically and developmentally. **Listening** includes the processes of listening preparation, receiving, constructing meaning, responding, and remembering.[1] Each of these processes will be discussed in the next sections, as well as how this framework of listening relates to the framework established in Chapter 1 for strategic flexibility. In addition, the process of remembering is discussed more fully in a separate section.

THE ROLE OF LISTENING IN COMMUNICATING EFFECTIVELY AND STRATEGIC FLEXIBILITY

When you reexamine Figure 1-1, "The Elements of Communication," in Chapter 1, you will notice that there is no element labeled "listening." It is not mentioned there as one of the elements of communication, and yet, you know intuitively that listening is an essential component of effective communication. Now look at Figure 4-1.

When you look closely at the ILM framework for listening previously discussed, you realize that listening—just like strategic flexibility—actually begins *before* the elements contained in the model. **Listening preparation** includes all the physical, mental, and behavioral aspects that create a readiness to listen. These are the same aspects that you bring to any communication situation as you **anticipate** (SF) the various needs and requirements likely to arise.

Second, according to the ILM framework, listening involves the element of receiving. This is where the process of listening begins to relate to the elements in the model of communication. **Receiving** is the process of taking in, acquiring, or accepting. It occurs through the various senses (hearing, seeing, smelling, touching, and tasting) and happens within sender-receivers as they receive all the cues, signals, and impulses. Listening is one part of the whole perceptual process discussed in Chapter 2. It is similar to, but not the same as, the **assessment** stage of strategic flexibility in which all the

Figure 4-1
Listening, Strategic Flexibility, and the Model of Communication

Listening
1. Listening Preparation
2. Receiving
3. Constructing Meaning
4. Responding
5. Remembering

Strategic Flexibility
1. Anticipate
2. Assess
3. Evaluate
4. Select
5. Apply

Setting, Channel, Message-Feedback, Sender-Receiver, Noise, Sender-Receiver, Message-Feedback

---

factors, elements, and conditions of situations are considered. Assessment assumes the receiving process has taken place.

There is an important distinction between hearing and listening that takes place at the receiving portion of the framework. You hear sounds—such as words and the way they are spoken—but when you listen, you respond to much more. Hearing is a physiological process involving the various parts of the ear, whereas listening is a more complicated perceptual process involving your total response to others, including verbal as well as nonverbal communication.

Receiving messages is accomplished with your ears in conjunction with your other four senses, and it involves hearing, *not* listening. It is only when you move to the next part of the framework that listening occurs.

Third, according to the framework, listening involves constructing meaning. **Constructing meaning** is the complicated and unique process of making sense of the cues, signals, and impulses received. It goes on in the brains of sender-receivers. A unique aspect of human beings is the ability to make meaning. Although you often think of listening as connected with hearing alone, it usually requires the full and active use of all the senses. For example, let's say that you are at a crowded party with a potentially romantic partner. Your partner utters the words "I love you," which you hear quite clearly above the sounds of the people and music around you, but you don't fully understand why those words were said in this context, nor what their full meaning might be. You see that your partner may have had too much to drink, you smell the odor of beer, your partner's touch appears to be suggestive, and the kiss revealed the taste of beer. You heard the words, but you can see that only when all the senses come into play can you construct meaning from those words.

One significant part of constructing meaning involves focusing your attention on particular stimuli. In the "I love you" example, notice how the words rang out loud and clear above the sounds of the people and music around you. **Selective attention** is the ability to focus perception. Although you may be able to focus your attention in specific ways, most people's attention spans are very short. Few people, for example, can give full attention to a message for more than 20 seconds.[2] Something in the message reminds you of something else, or you disagree with the message and let your mind wander. Fortunately, you are able to quickly refocus your attention on the message, but every listener and speaker should be aware of just how easily attention can go astray.

As another part of constructing meaning, you must assign meaning to the cues, signals, and impulses—deciding what in the message is relevant and how it relates to what you already know. Assigning meaning is an important process before responding because you must weigh what the speaker has said against the personal beliefs you hold, question the speaker's motives, wonder what has been omitted, or even challenge the validity of the ideas. As in the "I love you" example, you may understand *what* was said, but do you fully understand *how* it was said? When you assign meaning, you give meaning to the speaker's tone of voice, gestures, and facial expressions as much as you do to his or her words.[3]

Constructing meaning involves two steps in the strategic flexibility process as you can see in Figure 4-1. There is no way to make sense of cues, signals, and impulses if **evaluation** (SF)—determining the value and worth of the factors, elements, and conditions—fails to occur at the same time. This is the only way to determine how all those cues, signals, and impulses bear on your own skills and abilities. Constructing meaning also involves **selection** (SF): carefully selecting from your repertoire of available skills and behaviors those likely to have the greatest impact on the current (and future) situations.

Fourth, according to the ILM framework, listening involves responding. **Responding** means using spoken or nonverbal messages to exchange ideas or convey information. In strategic flexibility it is the same as **applying**—with the appropriate care, concern, and attention to all the factors that are likely to be affected, including any ethical considerations that may be appropriate—to apply the skills and behaviors you have selected.

From the "I love you" example think about all the potential nonverbal elements that could affect how you might respond: the clothing or dress of the other person; the gestures made while speaking the words; the body movement, posture, and touch; and, perhaps, most important, the way the words were spoken. An additional element might be the setting in which all of this takes place. What would be the appropriate response? What would you say to the other person who has just said, "I love you"?

The fifth stage of the listening process is **remembering,** as shown in Figure 4-2. A number of strategies that will help ensure that information is being learned well and stored securely in your memory system are discussed in the next section.

In strategic flexibility, the process is complete when the steps of reassessment and reevaluation have taken place. This is just as important in the listening process. You simply need to look back at what has taken place and determine its value, worth, success, effectiveness, or efficiency in light of what you expected.

To review, the listening process has five stages: listening preparation, receiving, constructing meaning, responding, and remembering. Figure 4-2 shows these five stages and offers examples to illustrate how they might occur.

Often, all of these aspects of the framework for listening occur instantaneously, sometimes without conscious effort. Understanding these aspects may help you assess if and where the process breaks down. It may help you slow down the process so that all the information you

Figure 4-2

The Listening Process

1. **Listening Preparation**
Think to yourself: I want to have some fun tonight.

2. **Receiving**
Best friend asks: "Are you hanging out with us tonight?"

3. **Constructing Meaning**
Selective Attention: Does this mean meeting them at the library, at the on-campus center, or just hanging out?
Assign Meaning: Usually they want to hang out.

4. **Responding**
"Sure, if you're all hanging out. Are we meeting at 9?"

5. **Remembering**
"I'm writing it in my daily reminder, so I'll see you then."

need can be obtained. Sometimes, for example, patience allows time for more observation and the collection of more information. It may also help you better understand why others may not understand what you say. A pause, for example, may allow time to reflect on what and how you said something but, too, on the full meaning of the other's response.

REMEMBERING INFORMATION

There are a number of techniques useful for remembering information, but there is no single right way or best way to improve your memory. All techniques require your motivation and dedication to the task, because when you are motivated, you concentrate harder, and concentration makes information easier to remember. Motivation is a key; using mnemonic devices (used for remembering information that is to be memorized, but not necessarily understood) is unlikely to create any long-term effect. Information that is simple, clear, and vivid is more easily remembered as is anything that is unusual, funny, or personal.

There are four major techniques. The first is organization. Find a pattern, structure, order, plan, format, or framework. The second is association. Make the things you want to remember relate to each other or to categories you already understand. Group them, if possible. The third technique is visualization. Picturing what you want to remember creates a strong, vivid memory of it. The fourth is repetition. When you repeat ideas, you burn them into your memory. Reading them into a tape recorder, for example, and listening to them repeatedly implants them by sheer repetition. Other techniques often asssociated with assisting memory include creating rhymes, acronyms, and abbreviations.

Much of the effectiveness of remembering information will depend on the notes you take, because notes will reduce the amount of information. Also, with good notes, it will make it easier to use the memory techniques outlined above.

NOTE-TAKING SKILLS

Just as active listening is essential to effective note taking, effective note taking is essential to remembering information. There are those who recommend that you not take notes so you can focus your attention wholly on what the speaker is saying. If you are blessed with a great memory, this method may work for you. There are others who will tape a lecture so they can give it their full attention while it is occurring, then write notes from the tape. The problem with taping lectures is finding the time to listen to the tapes. Taking notes—whenever you do it—has four benefits. First, it will help you remember the information. Second, it will help you organize what the speaker is saying. Third, it may aid in your understanding of the information. Fourth, it is likely to require you to think.

Having been a large-group lecturer for the basic speech communication course for many years, I (Richard) was often asked how to take notes in my lectures. Here is the essence of my advice:

- Sit where you can easily see and hear the lecturer. Also, sit where you can see the board and any slides or overhead projections that might be shown.
- Do not try to write out everything that is said. Think before you write, but don't get behind. If you get behind, leave a blank where you are (to be filled in later, if possible), and move ahead to where your lecturer is right now.
- Feel free to record the lectures using a small, inconspicuous recorder. If you plan to do this, ask lecturers for their permission before making a recording. If you record, make sure you write down everything on the board or slides in your notes.
- Jot down notes of the main and minor points of the lecture. Often, supporting material can be filled in later.
- Listen carefully for verbal or nonverbal cues that indicate key or essential points.
- Write legibly, and use abbreviations wherever possible. If you cannot write clearly enough so that you can understand your writing later, make certain you allow time to decipher your notes before they grow cold. Reviewing notes later that make no sense can be disheartening.
- If you record the lecture, compare your notes of the main and minor points with the information on the tape, as you listen a second time. Taking notes and recording at the same time will help you remember the information better.
- Fill in any details missed the first time through as you listen to the tape, but do not copy down everything.
- Annotate and highlight any key points or essential information.
- If you did not record the lecture, compare and discuss your comprehension and notes with other students.

- Review your notes shortly after the lecture to reinforce both your memory and understanding of the contents.
- Once you have your notes reduced to the essence of the lecture, review them several times just before the examination.

If you find information particularly difficult or challenging, and you must remember it for an examination, once you have reduced your notes to their essence, read them into a tape recorder, as mentioned in the previous section. Then listen to your notes in your car, at home in your room, or whenever a spare moment occurs. Listening to them over and over will help you learn the material thoroughly. If you think this level of commitment—actually following all these recommendations—is too much for you, it might help you to understand that it all depends on what you want out of college. A college education is what you make of it.

LISTENING STYLES

Most of you have discovered, after being in school for so many years, that there are different ways of learning and different ways of listening. Researchers have identified four different kinds of listening styles.[4] In a **people listening style,** you are concerned with the other person's feelings. You seek out common interests with others and respond to emotions. This listening is common among couples, families, and best friends.

In an **action listening style,** you want precise, error-free presentations, and you are likely to be impatient with disorganization. A boss, for example, might ask for a report from one of the division heads on how the company is doing. She would expect this report to be focused and to the point.

In a **content listening style,** you prefer complex and challenging information. Since this information is generally abstract, you can listen without emotional involvement and then evaluate information before you make a judgment. A doctor might, for example, ask for information from his colleagues on how a particular patient should be treated. Because of his training and experience he will not have difficulty understanding a complex medical explanation.

The final style is **time-style listening.** In this style, you prefer brief and hurried interaction with others and often let others know how much time they have to make the point. Newspeople, getting ready for a television newscast, need to get information quickly and efficiently because they are always working against the clock, so they are likely to be time-style listeners.

For the most part, you do not have just one listening style—although you may prefer one over some of the others. You listen in all the ways discussed here depending on the circumstances. To a roommate, for example, you will use a people style, for a group project you may reveal an action listening style, in a lecture it may be a content listening style, and racing out to run errands in a short amount of time, you may adopt a time-style method of listening before you go.

The most skillful listeners are able to adapt their listening styles to the circumstances. If you haven't learned to do this, you will have a problem in some of your interactions with others. For example, when a person is complaining about a co-worker, she would probably prefer a people-style listener. Yet her boss, who is short of time, wants her to state her problem, listen to his suggestions, and then leave his office—a reaction that will leave her feeling unsatisfied.

When you work with people, it's important that you be aware of their listening styles. For example, if you want some critical reaction to a paper

---

STRATEGIC FLEXIBILITY
Because of your quick ability to anticipate, assess, evaluate, and select from your repertoire of available skills and behaviors, you will be able to adapt your listening style to the circumstances.

you have just written, a content-style listener will be more helpful than a people-style listener because the people listener wouldn't want to hurt your feelings by pointing out your mistakes.

Some research shows that a person's listening style might depend on the culture he or she comes from. One study that compared American, German, and Israeli speakers found that Americans were the most people centered and were likely to pay careful attention to the feelings of the people they were talking to while Israelis concentrated more on the accuracy of the messages. Germans were the most active listeners and often interspersed questions as they listened.[5]

Culture and Listening

More and more, intercultural encounters will become an important part of your everyday life whether it is in casual encounters, business transactions, interviews, or telephone conversations. Much of the misunderstanding in such encounters can be traced to problems in listening, and when experiencing such problems it is essential that you demonstrate both empathy and sensitivity to cultural differences.

As discussed in Chapter 3, intercultural communication often requires that you adjust the ways you approach fundamental aspects of communication—aspects that you may consider normal. For example, you may have to adjust your vocabulary. Both colloquial language and figures of speech often confuse those from other cultures. "The plan was really screwed up," could be restated as "The plan failed completely." Another adjustment might include the elimination of poetic language such as the use of metaphors and literary examples.

There are other adjustments as well. You may need to simplify your grammar. The complex grammar that frequently results from long sentences needs to be altered. Short sentences, for example, and simple grammar can be used instead. Informal communication styles may confuse non-native speakers who learned more formal English in school; thus, choosing a more formal style may help. Referring to culture-specific rituals and activities may be confusing, too.

Intercultural communication interactions are not always marked by misunderstanding, confusion, and hurt feelings. Often, however, varying degrees of misunderstanding, confusion, and hurt feelings do interfere. For example, the British find it rude and manipulative to be asked their full names. Americans, on the other hand, seek others' full names as a way of showing friendship. To be aware of potential misunderstandings is the first step toward adapting and adjusting your communication.

Lack of knowledge, insufficient language, and even lack of sureness about the conventions that underlie the use of language in intercultural situations create difficulty. For example, a convention the Japanese are known for is gracious apologies, even at the slightest mishap, and even when the fault is not theirs. In a New York supermarket, a member of the Japanese culture had her shopping cart bumped by another shopper's cart, and turned immediately to say "Oh, sorry," even though it wasn't her fault.

Willingness to ask questions, seek clarification, admit errors and difficulties, and reveal empathy, will help resolve many intercultural communication problems. Often, you need to understand that using your own cultural rules, even when speaking to someone from a different culture or co-culture, may not just be inappropriate, but it may offend, too. The more you know and the greater your willingness to achieve accurate, effective communication, the better your chance of being both an effective listener and communicator.

Another Point of View

"There is no denying that women have an edge in the listening category," says Audrey Nelson in her book *You Don't Say: Navigating Nonverbal Communication Between the Sexes* (p. 264). However, men have a responsibility as well—"sit face to face, make continuous eye contact, touch (if appropriate), and employ nonfluencies like 'uh huh' and 'umm' to indicate they are listening. They should also eliminate any props or barriers to listening, which means putting away the remote, turning off the game, or setting aside the newspaper," she adds.

> On the other hand, while women appear to be the champions in the listening department, they still have some homework to do! They must be sensitive to a man's level of discomfort when they are actively listening! He may dislike all the attentiveness (face-to-face position, eye contact, touch); in fact, it can cause him to shut down. Women must be patient—involved, but not too intense. They can self-disclose, but shouldn't tell too much, too soon. It may overwhelm the man. Remember, he is wrestling with his own feelings, and he's listening even though he may not be maintaining eye contact. If he really appears distracted and tuned out, ask him, "Is this a good time for you? You seem distant." Giving attention is generally not a man's forte! (p. 265)

Source: *You Don't Say: Navigating Nonverbal Communication Between the Sexes*, by Audrey Nelson, 2004, New York: Prentice Hall/The Berkley Publishing Group (a member of Penguin Group (USA) Inc.).

Questions

1. Why does most of the burden for effective listening—or communication within relationships—fall on the woman's shoulders and not the man's?
2. Why do men have to engage in all this "touchy-feely stuff"? Shouldn't female relationship partners just know that their male partners care about them and what they are saying?
3. Do you think that men and women truly think differently about feelings?
4. When a woman perceives that a man is not listening, could there be a variety of possible explanations? Could it be, for example, that the man is inattentive, unable to "understand" her, or unwilling to empathize with her? How often does not listening have a variety of explanations?

Gender and Listening

Anyone who has had some experience in the world might suspect that men and women listen differently. For example, how often have you heard the complaint, "My boyfriend/husband doesn't listen to me" or "You never listen to me"?

Scholars who have studied communication between men and women have discovered that men and women have different listening styles. In the study of cultural listening styles mentioned above, the researchers found that in all three cultures (American, German, and Israeli) women were more likely to be people listeners than were men.[6]

Deborah Tannen, a linguist whose work is discussed in detail in Chapter 5, maintains that men and women come from different communication cultures: Women are interested in relationships and networking, while men are more interested in competitive communication.[7] This theory explains why a husband does not show much interest when his wife tells him about two people who were quarreling at her work. By the same token, the wife pays little attention when her husband talks about the batting averages of some of the players in the major leagues.

Tannen has also found that when men and women talk, women are more likely to be the listeners. Curious about how long this communication behavior has existed, Tannen went back to the literature of earlier times. She found that little has changed over the ages: In Shakespeare's fifteenth-century *Julius Caesar*, Portia begs Brutus to talk to her and not to keep his secrets from her. Tannen says that the culture of boys is based on status and that to maintain their status boys will hold the center of attention by boasting and telling jokes or fascinating stories; the same thing was true of the hero of *Beowulf*, an eighth-century saga.[8]

Notice in the Another Point of View box by Audrey Nelson the interpersonal adjustments necessary by both men and women to try to accommodate the differences in their listening styles. If you consider listening to be important, then you will not be able to continue listening in the same ways you have in the past, and that is precisely the point Nelson is making.

One problem women have to face when they enter the executive or professional world is getting men to listen to them. When Sandra Day O'Connor, the first female Supreme Court justice, was asked what problems she had in her career, she replied that the greatest problem was not being listened to. Finally she found a technique that made people pay attention to her: "I taught myself early on to speak very slowly—enunciating every word—when I wanted someone's undivided attention."[9] Her strategy makes sense: When we find that someone's attention seems to be fading, we are inclined to talk faster.

Another mistake women are likely to make in a business setting is to smile and wait their turn instead of using the male tactic of jumping into the discussion when they have something to say. Men don't follow the female system of taking turns. Patricia O'Brien advises that if women want to be listened to at work they should sit at the middle of the conference table where they can't be ignored, speak with conviction, avoid disclaimers such as "I might not be right but . . . ," and go directly to the main point, omitting the details.[10]

THE DIFFICULTY OF LISTENING

As discussed in an earlier section, listening preparation includes all the physical, mental, and behavioral aspects that create a readiness to listen. There is far more in that statement than what meets the eye. If listening was as natural, easy, and successful as it appears, there would be no need for a whole chapter on the topic. Physically, mentally, and behaviorally, most people are *not* ready to listen well. Figure 4-3 shows some of the factors that have a bearing on senders and receivers.

Because these aspects are likely to affect any listening you will do, but also how effective that listening is likely to be, let's just list some of the factors. They are listed here in no particular order simply because at any given point in time, any one of them might be the cause (or result) of poor listening. Your attitude (tense, worried, anxious, or troubled), knowledge (comprehension, understanding, or expertise), and abilities or skills (adeptness, talent, or training) will be factors. Your state of mind is also important because listening is hard work. Laziness alone can affect your listening. The setting (environment, location, or position) might have an impact as well as how open-minded (unprejudiced, nonpartisan, neutral, nonjudgmental, nondiscriminatory, objective, broad-minded, or tolerant) you are. Your attention to the stimulus (some people have a very short attention span), empathy with the person or subject being discussed, and respect for the other person could have an effect. Also, your physical well-being matters. Being tired, hung over, or ill might have an effect just as much as if you are rushed, stressed, or tense.

There is an additional factor as well. Speakers speak at approximately 125–250 words per minute. Listeners listen at something greater than 600 words per minute. Some researchers have actually suggested that listening may occur at a rate of 1,000–3,000 words per minute. The point is, no matter whom you are listening to, they are speaking slower than you are listening. What do you do with the difference? What does anyone

Figure 4-3

Some of the Many Factors That Can Be Barriers to Effective Listening

Closed-mindedness, Laziness, Insincerity, Boredom, Opionatedness, Sender-Receiver, Skills and Abilities, Knowledge, Physical well-being, Attention span, Empathy & respect

do with the difference between speech speed and thought speed? What you do with that difference may determine how effective you are as a listener, and suggestions will be provided in this chapter. Any wonder people don't listen well?

Steven Golen did some research on the factors and barriers to effective listening.[11] Out of 23 potentially important factors in listening, the 6 listed in Table 4-1 are the ones that stood out. How these factors turn into barriers are listed as well. When you examine each of the barriers in Table 4-1, are they familiar? How many have you actually experienced?

Four other factors cause difficulty in listening: cognitive dissonance, anxiety, control, and passiveness. **Cognitive dissonance** occurs when you feel conflict because you hold two or more attitudes that are in opposition to each other. For example, when Dr. Roman came into the classroom, you knew you would have difficulty listening because you were fearful, scared, and afraid. You were told he had high standards, a fearless attendance policy, and a tendency to humiliate students not prepared for class. It was Dr. Roman's approach to the class, however, that created the cognitive dissonance. Talking casually with you and your classmates, he defended his grading policy, explained the importance of attending class, and clarified the need to be prepared. His genuine warmth and caring made it difficult for you to listen because it didn't conform to what you had been told.

Anxiety is a disturbance that occurs in your mind regarding some uncertain event, misgiving, or worry. Many college courses create anxiety because so much is uncertain, there are so many misgivings, and the nature and structure of courses and examinations cause worry. It cannot be avoided. Just knowing that you have an exam coming up later in the day can cause you not to listen well in classes or lectures earlier the same day.

Table 4-1 Factors and Barriers to Effective Listening.

Factors	Barriers
Laziness	Avoid listening if the subject is complex or difficult.
	Avoid listening because it takes too much time.
Closed-mindedness	Refuse to maintain a relaxing and agreeable environment.
	Refuse to relate to and benefit from the speaker's ideas.
Opinionatedness	Disagree or argue outwardly or inwardly with the speaker.
	Become emotional or excited when the speaker's views differ from yours.
Insincerity	Avoid eye contact while listening.
	Pay attention only to the speaker's word rather than the speaker's feelings.
Boredom	Lack interest in the speaker's subject.
	Become impatient with the speaker.
	Daydream or become preoccupied with something else when listening.
Inattentiveness	Concentrate on the speaker's mannerisms or delivery rather than on the message.
	Become distracted by noise from office equipment, telephone, other conversation, etc.

Source: Adapted from "A Factor Analysis of Barriers to Effective Listening," by S. Golen, *The Journal of Business Communication*, 27 (Winter 1990), p. 32.

Control is the desire to have governing influence over a situation, and **controlling listeners**—like Patricia Reyes, in our opening example—prefer talking to listening. They seek to control their listeners by looking for ways to talk about themselves and their experiences. Often, they do not notice nonverbal signals from others, ignore signs that their listeners are bored, and even overlook overt verbal comments like "I'd better get going" or "I just noticed how late it is."

Passiveness involves the suspension of the rational functions and the reduction of any physical functions to their lowest possible degree. Passive people believe that listening involves no work. If you believe that you don't have to do anything, that you can just sit back and listening will happen, then you are in serious trouble. To learn—especially in situations where the speaker or the subject is not very interesting—requires a serious and concerted effort. So often students put the responsibility on the instructor: "Make it interesting, and I will listen." Education, however, often demands that students actively participate in the learning (acquisition of knowledge) process.

LEARNING TO LISTEN

You have now read about the role of listening in communicating effectively and in strategic flexibility. You have also read about the effect of culture and gender on the process and the difficulty of listening. Are you aware of how much time you are likely to spend listening? Estimates vary, but some listening researchers estimate that the majority of people spend as much as 60 to 70 percent of their waking hours communicating. About 9 percent is time spent writing, 16 percent is in reading, 30 percent is in speaking, and 45 percent is in listening.[12]

Figure 4-4 shows the average percentage of time people devote to the four communication skills: listening, speaking, reading, and writing. If you spend 70 percent of your waking day engaged in some form of communication, and if you are awake for 16 hours, then you are communicating in some way during 11 of those hours. Of that time, you spend 7 hours listening. You listen more than you do any other human activity except breathe. Although you spend the greatest amount of time listening, it is the skill that is taught the least.

Listening is a skill that can be learned, but like any skill, it has to be practiced. Listening well is habitual, and if the habit of good listening isn't deeply entrenched through constant practice, you are likely to fall back on your ineffective, unproductive, and unprofitable listening patterns.

Michael Purdy, writer and researcher on listening, conducted a study of 900 college and military students aged 17 to 70 which showed the traits of good and poor listeners:

A good listener:

1. Uses eye contact appropriately.
2. Is attentive and alert to a speaker's verbal and nonverbal behavior.
3. Is patient and doesn't interrupt (waits for the speaker to finish).
4. Is responsive, using verbal and nonverbal expressions.
5. Asks questions in a nonthreatening tone.
6. Paraphrases, restates, or summarizes what the speaker says.
7. Provides constructive (verbal or nonverbal) feedback.
8. Is empathic (works to understand the speaker).
9. Shows interest in the speaker as a person.
10. Demonstrates a caring attitude and is willing to listen.
11. Doesn't criticize, is nonjudgmental.
12. Is open-minded.

Figure 4-4

Percentage of Time Devoted to Various Communication Skills

- Listening 45%
- Reading 16%
- Speaking 30%
- Writing 9%

A poor listener:

1. Interrupts the speaker (is impatient).
2. Doesn't give eye contact (eyes wander).
3. Is distracted (fidgeting) and does not pay attention to the speaker.
4. Is not interested in the speaker (doesn't care; daydreaming).
5. Gives the speaker little or no (verbal or nonverbal) feedback.
6. Changes the subject.
7. Is judgmental.
8. Is closed-minded.
9. Talks too much.
10. Is self-preoccupied.
11. Gives unwanted advice.
12. Is too busy to listen.[13]

STRATEGIC FLEXIBILITY

Changing your listening habits will give you more insights, ideas, suggestions, and knowledge on which to base all steps in strategic flexibility. Effective listening—like perception—is bedrock (down to fundamentals or the truth of the matter) in strategic flexibility.

If you wanted to change your listening habits, the Purdy study offers 12 guidelines for change: use good eye contact, be attentive and alert, be patient and don't interrupt, use responsive verbal and nonverbal expressions, ask nonthreatening questions, paraphrase, restate and summarize, offer constructive feedback, reveal empathy, show interest, demonstrate a caring attitude that shows you are willing to listen, and be nonjudgmental and open-minded. If we were to add one additional guideline, it would be to build your vocabulary. The more words you learn, the better listener you will become.

If you avoid those characteristics of a poor listener, and if you are flexible in your listening style (people-, action-, content-, or time-style listening), you are likely to develop a positive, constructive, and worthwhile listening habit that will, through use, become deeply entrenched. You can speed this entrenchment by challenging your listening ability—seeking out situations many try to avoid rather than experience. You must stretch if you want to grow. Force yourself to listen carefully to sermons, political speeches, lectures, debates, and other material that requires concentration. Given today's movies, television, the Internet, and computer games, seldom is such concentration required. It will, however, be rewarded by your gains in insights, ideas, suggestions, and knowledge in general—let alone your increased ability to listen.

THREE KINDS OF LISTENING

Just as you might choose a different style of listening when you are in different situations, there are three different approaches that can be taken in three different kinds of circumstances. In the classroom, or in a lecture hall, you would engage in **active listening**—making a mental outline of important points, thinking up questions or challenges to the points that have been made, and becoming mentally involved with the person talking. This is sometimes referred to as listening for information. **Critical listening** includes all the ingredients for active listening, but it includes, in addition, evaluating and challenging what is heard. Critical listening often occurs when you are being persuaded to do something or when you are exposed to advertising. **Empathic listening** involves trying to understand what others are feeling from their point of view and reflecting those feelings back. This often occurs with friends and family members. Because each of the three kinds of listening requires a different set of skills, we will briefly discuss each one.

Active Listening

Because this is the most common kind of listening that occurs in college, we will devote most of our time to it. We use it, too, to obtain directions, understand others, solve problems, and share interests. In an earlier section, we discussed the difference between speech speed and thought speed, and we asked the question "What do you do with the difference?" It is a crucial question in active listening simply because, if you don't know about the difference, or if you don't know what to do with the extra time, it is easy to become bored, distracted, or otherwise mentally disengaged. There is no speaker who can keep up with the speed of your thinking. So, what do you do with the difference? Here are six suggestions. They are specifically designed to keep your mind focused, connected, and centered.

Our first experiences of learning to listen usually come from our parents.

First, *identify the central idea,* the essential thought that runs through the speech or communication. Once identified, look for **main heads**—the points that reinforce the central idea. Then, once main heads are located, listen for **supporting points:** the material, ideas, and evidence that back up the main heads. This can be a memory tool as well, because when you remember the central idea, the main heads often follow. Main heads without a central idea may look like a number of unrelated points that make no sense and can easily be forgotten. Central ideas tie fragmented ideas together and give them meaning.

Second, *form a* **mental outline**—a preliminary sketch that shows the principal features of the speech or lecture. Often, such an outline gives you clues about the way speakers or lecturers are thinking, what they want you to know, and how they are going to move through their material. When you have a mental outline, it allows you to see the forest, not just the individual trees.

Third, *predict what will come next*. To predict is simply to forecast or to try to make something known beforehand. Why do this? Remember the overall goal: to keep your mind focused. Since attention comes in spurts—as little as 20-second intervals—you must force yourself to concentrate, and prediction is a mind game that can keep you tuned in to what is going on.

Fourth, *relate points to your experience*. Good listeners attempt to relate material to their own experiences. Not only does this add meaning to the information but it also makes the information more memorable. Adults often do well when they go back to school simply because they have more experiences to which to relate the new information they receive.

Fifth, *look for similarities and differences*. How is the information you are receiving similar to or different from what you already know? Sometimes similarities

Working Together

This is a two-pronged activity. In your group you are to answer two questions. Everyone in the group should have an opportunity to answer the first question, and all the responses should be put into hierarchical order with the most important one (voted on by all group members) placed first and the least important answer placed last. Then move to question two, and proceed in the same manner—brainstorming with everyone participating, first, then placing the responses into hierarchical order.

Question 1: Why don't college students ask more questions in class?

Question 2: What *specifically* could be done to get college students to ask more questions?

---

and differences are obvious. For example, you hear that all Chinese people use chopsticks to eat their food. This is an obvious difference from the American or European practice of using forks. A more subtle difference emerges when you examine the natural resources of each of these cultures to see how they might influence the creation of eating utensils. Bamboo, for example, is found throughout China, so it is not surprising to find that many chopsticks are made of bamboo.

Sixth, *ask questions*. When you ask questions of yourself, you challenge, test, stretch, and demand more. This not only is energy producing but is likely to be exciting, stimulating, and inspiring as well. When you find questions you can't answer, write them down or try to remember to ask the speaker or lecturer.

Although it seems likely that college students would ask questions, most of them do not. When researchers studied classes in a variety of subjects, they discovered that over a 30-hour period students asked only 108 questions, or 3.6 per class. Of the 108 questions, 29 were about classroom procedures ("Will this be on the test?"); 27 were information seeking ("What date did that happen?"); 23 were for clarification ("Will you repeat that definition again?"); 13 were confirmation ("Am I correct in thinking that . . . ?"); 13 were asking instructors' opinions; and 3 did not fit into any of these categories.[14]

Critical Listening

Ideally, all communication should be listened to critically. When you are receiving new information, however, it is sometimes difficult to evaluate it critically because you do not know much about the subject—or possibly about the speaker either.

When people are persuading you to do something or believe something, critical listening is vitally important. One way to put yourself in the proper frame of mind is to think of yourself as a reporter. As a journalist, get answers to each of the following questions of who, what, when, where, why, and how. Who benefits? Who gets hurt? What happened? What can I do about it? When did it happen? Where did it happen? Why did it happen? Why is this important? How did it happen? Questions beginning with *who, what, when, where, why,* and *how* can be rephrased in any way that will make sense to you; they simply give you a place to begin your questioning.

There are five jobs you have in connection with critical listening. The first is to *determine the speaker's motives*. With a commercial ad—certainly a persuasive communication—the motive is simply to determine: Who wants to sell you a product or services? With political candidates, the motive may be more complex. They want to be elected, so the most important question is why? Are they after money or power? Do they want to bring about social change? Do they want to keep things the way they are?

Your second job is to *challenge and question ideas*. Where did the speaker get his or her information? Did it come from sources generally regarded as credible? Is the speaker quoting the information accurately or taking it out of context? Does the speaker identify his or her sources of information so that the audience can check them later? Is important information omitted? Is contrary information overlooked?

Your third job is to *distinguish fact from fiction*. A **fact** is something that can be verified in a number of ways, which might include experiments, direct observation, or books by authorities. Everyone who applies the same test or uses the same sources should be able to get the same information. An **opinion** is a personal belief. That cinnamon comes from the bark of a tree is a fact that can be found in any number of books and encyclopedias. That cinnamon is tasty in foods, especially cookies, is an opinion because some people will disagree. During the course of a day you hear many more opinions than facts, so it is important that you, the listener, make the distinction.

Although all facts are equally true, some opinions are more reliable than others. You are, for example, more likely to trust the opinions of speakers who have similar beliefs to your own, who have been right before, who have a high degree of authority or credibility, or whose opinions have been (or are) supported by people you respect.

Your fourth job is to *recognize your own biases*. Sometimes there are messages you don't hear because they contradict your attitudes and beliefs. In some cases, you might not even be aware that you are blocking out messages. One study found that although jurors had heard instructions about the rules of circumstantial evidence, only 40 percent correctly followed the instructions. The authors of the study concluded that this misunderstanding of the law was not merely a matter of poor listening. They believed that jurors were likely to misinterpret the law—to listen to and consider circumstantial evidence—because they didn't believe in the law.[15] The tendency to interpret information in light of your beliefs can lead you to distort the information you hear. As a listener you must be aware of your values and attitudes, especially when you hear information you might resist or disagree with.

Your fifth job in critical listening is to *assess the message*. Assessment can take place as part of listening preparation, the receiving process, constructing meaning, responding, remembering information, or—as in strategic flexibility—in reassessment and reevaluation just after or long after the situation has taken place. To **assess** is to determine the value of something. Basically, it is a critical process: chewing over what you have heard before you swallow it. Ideas that may seem acceptable when you first hear them may not be as palatable when you have had time to think about them. This is especially true for important ideas: It is essential to reflect on them before they become part of you and of your thinking.

The important thing in assessment is to learn to delay taking a position until you receive all the facts and other evidence, until you have had a chance to test them in the marketplace of ideas, and until you have had an opportunity to chew over everything before digestion. Figure 4-5 is a critical listening evaluation checklist for a speech or lecture.

Empathic Listening

Empathy is the process of mentally identifying with the character and experiences of another person. Often, it involves the emotional projection of your self into another's life—or their life as revealed by and through their communication. It is all about feelings. Michael P. Nichols, who has written about listening, points out that when you listen with empathy, you have to suspend your ego and immerse yourself in the other person. Only by doing this will you be able to enter into his or her feelings.[16]

Listening to other people's feelings, as noted in the introduction to this section, is not just a way of giving emotional support, but it is a way of creating intimacy with others as well. To do this effectively, you need to recognize what feelings are involved,

Figure 4-5
Critical Listening Evaluation Checklist for a Speech or Lecture

1. Were you able to make any accurate predictions about what the speaker was going to say? What helped you to do so?

2. What was the speaker's central idea? Was it clearly stated?

3. Do you have any ideas of the speaker's motive for giving this speech? If you know the motive, does it make the speech more or less believable?

4. What kinds of supporting points were used to back up the speaker's ideas? Were these points based on evidence you respect?

5. What questions would you like to ask the speaker? Are they questions that clarify what the speaker has said or questions that ask for more information?

6. Think of one or two ways you would like to challenge the speaker.

7. How would you evaluate this speech? What did the speaker do well? Was there anything the speaker could have done to make the speech better?

---

let speakers tell you what has happened, and then encourage them to find the solution to their problem.

Identify the emotion(s). First, listen to what the other person is *really* saying. If, for example, your roommate comes back to your room and says, "I am going to kill my advisor!" he is obviously not saying that he literally plans to kill her. What is he really saying? In this case, it would be reasonable to assume that your roommate is feeling anger. If you respond with "Boy, you really sound mad," you create the opportunity for your roommate to tell you what has happened.

Listen to the story. Another part of an empathic response is to listen attentively. As the whole story comes out, there is no need to respond with anything very specific. At this point the person just wants to be listened to. You can show your interest and concern if you listen and look sympathetic—not like you are ready to leave for your next class.

Let's go back to your roommate and his problem with his advisor. What happened to make him so angry? He explains that his advisor overlooked one of his requirements, and to fulfill it means he must take an overload, take the course in summer school, or graduate late.

After your roommate has told you the whole story, he is not quite so mad, but he's still pretty upset. As you listen, you discover other feelings in addition to anger. He feels betrayed because he thinks his advisor never really liked him and is doing this on purpose. He feels humiliated because he has told all his friends exactly when he would be graduating and how much coursework he has yet to complete. Usually people do not feel just one emotion—they have a whole assortment of them.

If you can let your roommate talk through the entire problem, without making judgments but by offering support, it is likely that the full range of the problem will be revealed. One way to reach this point is through **paraphrasing:** restating the other person's thoughts or feelings in your own words. If your roommate says "I just feel like giving up," an appropriate paraphrased response might be, "You sound like you are very upset." (You know dropping out of school is not a realistic option, so you don't include it in your paraphrase.) This response not only helps identify the feelings but it also helps find out whether you have been hearing accurately and shows that you are paying attention. A paraphrased response provides a mirror for the other person's remarks.

Finally, *let the person work out the problem*. Sometimes just listening and letting people explain what is upsetting them largely solves the problem. You often hear someone say, "I feel better just because I've talked to you." People frequently want to vent their feelings, and once they have done so, they feel better.

But sometimes merely listening is not enough; your roommate has a problem, and he wants some help in solving it. In such a situation, the best approach is usually to trust the other person and his or her ability to work out the problem. This does not mean, however, that you ignore the problem. Empathic listening includes helping others find a way to solve the problem.

The last step in empathic listening, then, is to give the person a chance to work out the problem. In the case of your roommate, you don't want to say "You should quit!" Let him decide what he wants to do. If the emotion in the situation has died down, it might be appropriate to ask some general questions such as "What are you thinking about doing?" It might also be possible to ask some questions that may lead to a solution the other person has not thought of: "Could you go to the department where the course is offered to see if there is a way to 'place out' of it?" "Do you think your advisor might have made a mistake?" "Would it be possible to get credit for the course because of all the other related courses you have already taken?" "Do you think this course is offered on a campus near your home where you could take it along with your job next summer, and then transfer the credit?"

The important thing to remember at this stage is that you do not have to solve the problem. If you try to solve every problem that people bring you, you will put a heavy burden on yourself. Think of the person with the problem as "owning" that problem. This attitude also will help the other person grow in his or her ability to deal with problems.

When strong emotions are involved, people often need a sounding board. To be there and to utter an occasional "Oh," "Mmmm," or "I see" is often enough. Much comfort and support is derived from just being listened to.

Table 4-2 compares active, critical, and empathic listening. Notice that there are significant differences. A strategically flexible person will be aware of the differences and will respond appropriately.

Table 4-2 Active, Critical, and Empathic Listening Compared

Active Listening	Critical Listening	Empathic Listening
Identify the central idea	Determine motives	Identify the emotion(s)
Form a mental outline	Challenge and question ideas	Listen to the story
Predict what comes next	Distinguish fact from opinion	Let the person work out the problem
Relate points to your own experience	Recognize your biases	
Seek similarities and differences	Assess the message	
Ask questions		

This African American woman shows through her communication that she is an empathic listener.

TALKING SO OTHERS WILL LISTEN

There is a downside to the technology-oriented, information-driven society that you are experiencing, and that is a corresponding reluctance to listen. Whether it is distractions, preoccupations, time limitations, or the difference in the slow rate of others' speaking to you versus the rapid pace of gaining information from the media and from the Internet—how accustomed you've become to having your attention span satisfied by video games, chat room banter, and fast-paced television programs—the fact is, you do not listen well nor does anyone else. Whether this represents a societal change or simply a continuation of a well-documented, ongoing problem is not the point. The point is, what can be done when you realize others are not and will not be listening to you? Is it a hopeless situation?

Although there are numerous techniques for reaching out and grasping the attention of others, the following are some that may work. Often, a combination of techniques works best. We'll briefly discuss assertiveness, getting to the point, being prepared, writing down ideas, being flexible, and changing your vocal style.

First, and perhaps most obvious, you need to be more assertive. In the article "Talking Back to Your Doctor Works," Greider says, "Studies show that doctors remember best the cases of assertive patients. Medical outcomes are also likely to be better."[17] See the Consider This box. These results are likely to apply across communication contexts. It has long been an established research result that assertive behavior tends to be associated with positive outcomes.

Consider This

The doctor–patient relationship represents one significant example where listening is often a problem:

Next time you visit your doctor keep in mind one crucial if little-known rule: catch 23.

The catch works this way: Doctors typically will listen to a patient's "opening statement" little more than 23 seconds before changing the subject or "redirecting" the talk.

That means you, the patient, must talk not only fast, but compellingly, even knowledgeably, to get his or her attention. That's important for your doctor to fully grasp what's bothering you.

Too often doctors don't. In fact, researchers increasingly are finding that one big reason treatments don't work—or aren't prescribed at all—is because of problems in the way doctors and patients communicate.

Or, more precisely, fail to communicate. And when communication fails, the results can be disastrous.

Late last year the National Academy of Sciences (NAS) reported that some 7,000 patients die every year because of medication errors.

Even more alarming, the NAS found medical errors in hospitals cause between 44,000 and 98,000 deaths every year.

Some mistakes can be avoided, experts believe, if doctors and patients do a better job talking to each other.

Questions

1. Have you ever had this happen to you? How have you handled it?
2. Are there other situations—other than doctor–patient relationships—in which you have discovered that effective listening was a problem? Lawyer–client? Salesperson–buyer? Parent–child? Teacher–student?
3. What are the barriers, hurdles, or restrictions that cause you to be reluctant to deal with the other person in such relationships in an effective manner?

Source: "Talking Back to Your Doctor Works," by L. Greider, *AARP Bulletin*, February 2000.

Second, knowing that the other person is likely to be a weak or indifferent listener, avoid idle chit-chat and friendly conversation and get to the point fast. In advance of the conversation, think about what you want to say, how you plan to say it, and what you want from the other person. Then, try to follow your plan. The point isn't to memorize a speech; rather, it is to move rapidly toward your point.

Third, do your homework—that is, know what you are talking about. If some research is necessary to gather facts and relevant information, go to the library or use the Internet to ferret out the facts that will make your case or back up your position. Well-informed people tend to get the ear of others, as opposed to those who either do not know what they are talking about or are simply willing to hear the ideas of others and make no significant contribution of their own.

Fourth, write down your most important points or questions, and prioritize them. A list of ideas has always been associated with a rational, judicious, well-thought-out approach. Even if you do not use your notes, writing them out will assist you in organizing your ideas and phrasing them in the most effective way. When you put your most important ideas first, it is more likely they will be heard or noticed. Otherwise, they may be hidden in the middle or end of your conversation, or they may come too late for the attention span of your listener.

Fifth, have some options in mind, and be willing to listen. You are more likely to get the attention of others when you appear flexible and willing to listen yourself. The old adage "It takes one to know one" suggests that if you want someone to listen to you, you must also be willing to listen to them. But preparation and forethought does not necessarily mean all the alternatives have been considered. Thus, remember that this is a conversation; it is two-way. You must be willing to prepare your ideas and, in turn, listen to the ideas of others.

STRATEGIC FLEXIBILITY

When you assess, evaluate, and select from your repertoire of available skills and behaviors, you must appear flexible. As we say in this paragraph: "You must be willing to prepare your ideas and, in turn, listen to the ideas of others."

Sixth, try to change your vocal style. For some people—as indicated earlier in this chapter—this may mean slowing down your rate of delivery. If your pace tends to be slow already, or plodding, speeding up may be a useful approach. Often, it may simply be a need for variety. A change in volume, either louder or softer depending on the circumstances, may also help.

There are many ways to talk so others will listen. These suggestions will get you started, but overriding any of them are, of course, the courtesy and respect you need to demonstrate. Being assertive, for example, is not an excuse for being aggressive and thoughtless. Avoiding idle chit-chat and friendly conversation is not an excuse for overlooking necessary or important human concerns and connectiveness. You should make all decisions in the context of good judgment, common sense, thoughtfulness, and **propriety**—the character or quality of being proper, especially in accordance with recognized usage, custom, or principles.

Throughout all of this—your use of techniques to get others to listen to you—you need to recognize that there are some people who will not listen to you no matter what you do. Fortunately, these people are likely to be few and far between. You should not be disappointed if the techniques you use fail to work. The bottom line is: Communication involves a large number of factors or variables. No situation is the same as any other. No one has or ever will have control of all the factors or variables; no one has that kind or level of control. The more experience you have, the more practice that you engage in, and the more you believe in yourself and your abilities, the more likely you will be successful. Success is never guaranteed.

THE INTERNET AND LISTENING

There are three areas where the Internet is likely to have an effect on listening. The first has to do with what speakers are likely to bring to their presentations because of the Internet—and, coordinately, what this means for listeners in an Internet-saturated world. The second has to do with the increased amount of information listeners are likely to possess because of Internet accessibility. The third concerns the listening materials available.

The Internet has provided a benchmark for improved communication. It is the dawning of a new era of communication that is listener focused, listener directed, and listener dominated. Why? Because of the ease and accessibility of an overwhelming amount of information. People have no excuse for being uninformed—unless they choose *not* to take advantage of this resource. Thus, they now can focus and direct their information specifically toward their listeners. It is an enormous challenge and an incredible opportunity for speakers to inform, educate, and persuade.

The second issue has to do with what listeners are likely to possess because of the Internet. This issue is closely related to the first, but it removes listening from strictly a public-speaking context. As noted, wide channels of information are now available because of the Internet. With this supply, listeners can expect full disclosure from others. Professionals, for example, are expected to communicate clearly and sensitively. Doctors must listen carefully, notice the body language of patients, show empathy, and offer patients more information. Because of the Internet patients know more about their own illnesses and the treatments for those illnesses. With careful observation and a sensitive, empathic approach, doctors can focus on what is known and, thus, make their assessments, diagnosis, and treatment more complete and more specifically tailored to individual patient needs and knowledge.[18]

Third, and finally, what listening materials are available on the Internet? The word *listening* written into the Google search engine produced 116,000,000 hits (October 18,

Assess Yourself

Are You a Good Listener?

For each statement circle the numerical score that best represents your listening ability using the following scale:

7 = Outstanding; 6 = Excellent; 5 = Very good; 4 = Average (good); 3 = Fair; 2 = Poor; 1 = Minimal ability; 0 = No ability demonstrated.

1. I listen for the other person's feelings, not just to the words he or she says. 7 6 5 4 3 2 1 0
2. I paraphrase what other people say to me. 7 6 5 4 3 2 1 0
3. I don't interrupt. 7 6 5 4 3 2 1 0
4. I am open-minded to ideas, some with which I may not agree. 7 6 5 4 3 2 1 0
5. I remember what people say. 7 6 5 4 3 2 1 0
6. I am willing to express my feelings. 7 6 5 4 3 2 1 0
7. I don't complete other people's sentences even when I think I know what they are going to say next. 7 6 5 4 3 2 1 0
8. I make eye contact. 7 6 5 4 3 2 1 0
9. I don't think of what I'm going to say next while the other person is talking. 7 6 5 4 3 2 1 0
10. I ask the person questions to get more information and show that I am interested in what he or she is saying. 7 6 5 4 3 2 1 0
11. I am comfortable with silence. 7 6 5 4 3 2 1 0
12. I am aware of a person's body language and my own body language. 7 6 5 4 3 2 1 0

TOTAL POINTS: _____

Go to the *Communicating Effectively* CD-ROM and the Online Learning Center at **www.mhhe.com/hybels8** to see your results and learn how to evaluate your attitudes and feelings.

mhhe.com/hybels8

Source: Adapted from *Assessing Your Listening Ability*, I CANS (Integrated Curriculum for Achieving Necessary Skills), Washington State Board for Community and Technical Colleges, Washington State Employment Security, Washington Workforce Training and Education Coordinating Board, Adult Basic and Literary Educators, P.O. Box 42496, 711 Capitol Blvd., Olympia, WA 98504. Retrieved October 18, 2005, from **http://www.literacynet.org/icans/chapter05/assessing.html**

2005). The words *Listening on the Internet* produced 38,500,000 hits, and enclosed in quotation marks, the same three words produced 738 hits. The first site (http://ec.hku.hk/vec/listening/listint.htm) explains that listening material on the Internet use two kinds of software: Real Audio and Shockwave. To use material on the Internet, you will need to check that your computer is capable of running the latest versions of the software.

There are numerous sites listed on the Internet related to listening. Some are specifically designed for English as a Second Language (ESL) students. There is the English Listening Lounge; a BBC site by which you learn English by radio; a Voice of America (VOA) Special English site where the speaking rate is reduced and a simplified vocabulary is used for those learning to speak the English language; and other sites.

The point is that the Internet is making a significant difference in the way it is producing a new breed of listeners, in the additional wide variety of general information that it makes available, and in offering those with difficulty in listening or those with weak comprehension skills a place to go to learn, practice, and improve.

CHAPTER REVIEW

SUMMARY

Of all the communication faults people are accused of, not listening probably ranks as number one. Listening is a skill, and like any other skill it must be learned and practiced.

The Integrative Listening Model (ILM) includes the processes of listening preparation, receiving, constructing meaning, responding, and remembering. It begins before the elements of communication in the model in Chapter 1 with listening preparation, and it continues after the elements depicted there with the process of remembering. Listening, because it is one aspect of the process of perception, is essential to all steps in strategic flexibility.

There are numerous strategies that will help you ensure information is being learned well and stored securely in your memory system. All require conscious effort. Just as active listening is essential to effective note taking, effective note taking is essential to remembering information. Effective note taking requires commitment on your part as well.

Culture has an effect on listening simply because of the potential misunderstandings that can occur. Adjustments in vocabulary, grammar, or informality may need to be made. Gender has an effect because men and women listen differently. Understanding the differences will aid in effective communication.

There are as many factors, or combinations of factors, that cause difficulty in listening as there are listeners. One element is the difference between speech speed and listening speed. In addition to the six factors singled out by Steven Golen, there are the factors of cognitive dissonance, anxiety, control, and passiveness as well.

To be a good listener, you must become actively involved in changing your listening habits. In his study of good and poor listeners, Michael Purdy offers 12 guidelines for change. In addition to building your vocabulary, you need to challenge your listening ability by seeking out situations where concentration and careful listening are required.

There are three kinds of listening discussed in this book: active listening (sometimes referred to as listening for information), critical listening, and empathic listening. Active listening involves identifying a central idea, forming a mental outline, predicting what comes next, relating points to your experience, seeking similarities and differences, and asking questions. Critical listening involves determining motives, challenging and questioning ideas, distinguishing fact from opinion, recognizing your biases, and assessing the message. Empathic listening involves identifying the emotion, listening to the story, and letting the person work out the problem.

When you discover that those you want to listen to you are not listening, the techniques of assertiveness, getting to the point, being prepared, writing down ideas, being flexible, and changing your verbal style are ways—or combinations of ways—for reaching out and grasping attention. Whatever techniques you choose, you need to avoid being aggressive and thoughtless and show courtesy and respect. All decisions should be made using good judgment, common sense, thoughtfulness, and propriety.

The three areas where the Internet may have an effect on listening include what speakers are likely to bring to their presentations because of the Internet; the increased amount of information listeners are likely to possess because of Internet accessibility; and the wide variety of listening materials available on the Internet.

KEY TERMS AND CONCEPTS

Use the *Communicating Effectively* CD-ROM and the Online Learning Center at www.mhhe.com/hybels8 to further your understanding of the following terms.

Action listening style 85
Active listening 92
Anxiety 89
Anticipate 80
Applying 82
Assessment 81
Central idea 93
Cognitive dissonance 89
Content listening style 85
Constructing meaning 81
Control 90
Controlling listeners 90
Critical listening 92
Empathic listening 92
Empathy 95
Evaluation 82
Fact 95
Integrative Listening Model (ILM) 80
Listening 80
Listening preparation 80

CHAPTER REVIEW

Main heads 93
Mental outline 93
Opinion 95
Paraphrasing 96
Passiveness 90
People listening style 85
Propriety 100
Receiving 80
Remembering 82
Responding 82
Selection 82
Selective attention 82
Supporting points 93
Time-style listening 95

QUESTIONS TO REVIEW

1. What is the role that listening plays in strategic flexibility?
2. What are the elements of the Integrative Listening Model (ILM), and how do each of the elements relate to the model of communication discussed and illustrated in Chapter 1?
3. What are the four kinds of listening styles, and why is it helpful to know someone's listening style if you are communicating something important?
4. What effects are culture and gender likely to have on listening?
5. What are the factors that make listening difficult?
6. If you wanted to become a better listener, what are some of the ways you have to improve?
7. What are the strategies you can use to remember information?
8. What skills are involved in effective note taking?
9. How do identifying the central idea, main points, and supporting material, and forming a mental outline contribute to better listening?
10. In addition to listening for information and asking questions, what must be added when you are listening critically?
11. What is empathic listening, and what are some of the circumstances in which you might use it?
12. What are some of the techniques you can use to reach out and grasp the attention of others when you must talk so others will listen?
13. In what areas does the Internet affect listening?

Go to the self-quizzes on the *Communicating Effectively* CD-ROM and the Online Learning Center at **www.mhhe.com/hybels8** to test your knowledge of the chapter contents.

CHAPTER 5

Verbal Communication

OBJECTIVES

After reading this chapter, you should be able to:

- Briefly describe how you acquired your ability to use words.
- Describe the relationship of the Sapir-Whorf hypothesis to strategic flexibility.
- Explain how language is symbolic.
- Explain Hayakawa's ladder of abstraction and why it is important.
- Explain the function of role in a language environment.
- Define *style*.
- Describe differences between women's language and men's language.
- Define *report-talk* and *rapport-talk*.
- Explain differences between standard American English and dialect.
- Describe the ways in which speaking and writing differ.
- Describe some of the ways to make your verbal style clearer, more vivid, and more ethical.
- Describe the four influences of the Internet on verbal communication.

WESLEY COLEMAN DIDN'T KNOW HOW LUCKY HE WAS. He had two parents who cared deeply about him and who were determined to give him a better life. His parents knew that people who communicate clearly, respond quickly, tell interesting stories, and make compelling arguments have a distinct advantage. Those who can't are put at a distinct disadvantage. Even while Wesley was in the womb, his mother would read him stories of adventure, challenge, and risk. In his early years, Wesley loved to be read to, and whenever he visited his grandparents, he would beg to have them sit with him and read. His parents created a ritual of reading Wesley stories before going to bed, and these stories always stimulated his imagination. Soon he was reading to them, and always he was learning new words—building his vocabulary. Wesley loved to write, and he would keep a journal just to record his thoughts on things in this world. He would write short stories and read them to anyone who would listen. Wesley's was a world of words. His friends admired him because he was so verbal and eloquent. Teachers appreciated his class contributions because he had a way with words. It was his verbal acumen, his success in school, and his desire to help others that led him to law school. Wesley went on to become a successful trial lawyer, but he credits his success to parents who took an active interest in his development of language skills.

The flip side to Wesley Coleman's ability in acquiring and using proper languaging skills, as his parents were well aware, can be devastating. In his book *A User's Guide to the Brain,* John Ratey, a clinical professor of psychiatry at Harvard Medical School, states it succinctly: "When people . . . fail to make proper language connections, or do not stop and consider what they are saying, they wind up not only with speaking, reading, or writing problems—which are bad enough—but with difficulty sustaining social relationships, making moral decisions, controlling anger, and even feeling emotions."[1] The potential repercussions of poor language acquisition and use are enormous, to say the least. There is even evidence that a poor command of language may inhibit your ability to imagine and think up new ideas.[2]

So, when you learned to use language in the elementary grades, you did more than master the basic skills. You learned to express feelings and opinions, and, as you matured, to support your opinions with sound arguments and research. You became aware of the many purposes for which language is used and the diversity of forms it can take to appropriately serve these purposes and a variety of audiences. You learned to use the language and forms appropriate for different formal and informal situations—for example, the formal language of debate, the figurative language of poetry, the technical language and formal structures used in report writing. In sum, through your mastery of lan-

Protests and demonstrations will probably have a lot of connotative language.

guage, you have experienced expressive and communicative powers, and you appreciate language as both a source of pleasure and an important medium for recording and communicating ideas and information.

Language is just as important in your personal life. How you use language will affect your relationships with friends and loved ones. Failures in relationships with friends and family are often attributed to a failure of language. Lack of effective communication is often cited as a leading cause of marital breakups.

THE ROLE OF VERBAL COMMUNICATION IN COMMUNICATING EFFECTIVELY AND STRATEGIC FLEXIBILITY

Communicating Effectively

When you look at the model of communication presented in Chapter 1, it may be too obvious to say that the verbal communication component takes place in the message-feedback element of the model—the words that make up both message and feedback. It may be obvious, but that is far more simplistic than what actually occurs. It overlooks the importance of the senders and receivers. For example, how *you* acquired your ability to use words depended on three factors: (1) native architecture, (2) cognitive development, and (3) environmental influences. See Figure 5-1 for some of the elements involved.

With respect to your native architecture, you can thank the presence of the FOXP2 gene—among others—which enabled the emergence of behaviorally modern humans (those with the ability to use language) somewhere between 120,000 and 200,000 years ago. The fact that the FOXP2 gene makes clear is that as a human being, you have inborn language-transmission and language-acquisition devices—native architecture. This nature architecture transforms the surface structure of language, which appears in

Figure 5-1

Verbal Communication and the Communication Model

the model as message-feedback, into an internal deep structure, which appears in the model as sender-receiver, that you readily understand.

Cognitive development is the development of the thinking and organizing systems of your brain. It involves not only language but also mental imagery, reasoning, problem solving, and memory development. It began well before your birth as your brain took in information and created paths to a storage area for each bit of information.

Much of your brain "wiring" resulted from environmental influences that took place as your parents and siblings played with and had conversations with you, explained what was happening as you went through your days, introduced you to new activities and environments, encouraged you to explore and experiment, gave you choices, read to you, were interested in your interests, let you know it was okay to make mistakes, and loved and were proud of you. This was your language-acquisition support system. You were analyzing language content long before you were discovering and understanding grammatical structures.

Just as your communication with others is directly affected by other senders and receivers, the messages and feedback that take place, and the setting and cultural environment in which they occur, these are also the precise elements that affect its development in you, as noted earlier.

Strategic Flexibility

Verbal communication is a key component in strategic flexibility as well. Edward Sapir (1884–1936)[3] and Benjamin Lee Whorf (1897–1941),[4] Sapir's pupil, proposed a theory, the **Sapir-Whorf hypothesis,** that suggests that the language you use to some extent determines or at least influences the way in which you view and think about the world around you. This simply means that your thoughts are affected by or influenced by your language. When you want to talk about how you feel, you are at the mercy of the language you possess. When you are thinking about something that you have perceived, your linguistic habits predispose certain choices of interpretation. When you see automobiles at an intersection, it is what you know about the red, yellow, and green colored lights that helps you understand what is happening and what the choices are.

It is important to underscore the vital connection that exists between oral language and reading, writing, and critical thinking.[5] An increase in any one area results in a direct and proportional increase in ability and skills in the others. The bottom line is this: The better understanding you have of verbal communication, and the more words you have at your disposal, the more complete will be your ability to think about and view the world around you.

One understanding that the Sapir-Whorf hypothesis instills is that it is a two-way process. That is, the kind of language you use is also influenced by the way you see the world. In the strategic flexibility framework, the more you know about verbal communication, and the more words you have at your disposal, the better you will be at thinking about potential situations and the needs and requirements likely to arise (anticipate)—your view of the world and its possibilities; the better you will be at taking stock of the factors, elements, and conditions of situations in which you find yourself (assessment); the better you will be at determining the value and worth of the factors, elements, and conditions (evaluation); the better you will be at selecting from your repertoire of available skills and behaviors those likely to have the greatest impact (selection); the better you will be at applying the skills and behaviors you have selected (application); and, finally, the better you will be at reassessment and reevaluation.

Here, then, is one fascinating interrelationship, and you can see it in Figure 5-1 in the large arrow from setting to sender-receiver labeled "social pressure." The language of a culture and co-culture together with the unique language of a sender-receiver represent a subtly selective view of the world. This combination of languages and pressures tends to support certain kinds of observations and interpretations and to restrict others. Such transformative power—with the strength of being able to alter your very nature—goes largely unnoticed and, often, even when manifest, retreats to transparency. Thus, the influence of language on strategic flexibility is always present, but is likely to be subtle, difficult to perceive, and often transparent.

HOW WORDS WORK

When you say a word, you are vocally representing something—whether that thing is a physical object, such as your biology textbook, or an abstract concept, such as peace. The word is, as noted in Chapter 1, a symbol: It stands for the object or concept that it names. This is what distinguishes a word from a random sound. The sounds that are represented in our language by the letters *c a t* constitute a word because we have agreed that these sounds will stand for a particular domestic animal. The sounds represented by the letters *z a t* do not make up a word because these sounds do not stand for anything. A word that stands for a concrete and emotionally neutral thing—such as the word *mailbox*—can usually be interpreted with good fidelity because most people respond primarily to its **denotative meaning**—that is, its dictionary definition.

Other words stand for abstract concepts that evoke strong feelings. Words such as *freedom* and *love* are easily misunderstood because they carry a lot of **connotative meaning**—the feelings or associations each individual has about a word. For example, when you hear the word *love*, you don't just think about the word; you probably associate it with a person or an experience you have had. The connotative aspect of words may cause problems in communication because a single word may evoke strong and varied feelings in listeners. Think of the many different reactions people have to the phrases *affirmative action* and *axis of evil*. Figure 5-2 illustrates the difference between connotation and denotation. Notice, too, that your thoughts about the tree are influenced by your language, as discussed in the previous section on strategic flexibility.

Although you need abstract connotative words to express ideas, precise denotative words work best when you want to convey information or get things done—like giving directions or following a recipe. Figure 5-3 shows S. I. Hayakawa's "ladder of abstraction" from his book *Language in Thought and Action*.[6] The **ladder of abstraction** is a diagram of how we abstract through language, classifications, types, categories, and so on. It assists communicators in finding the right rung on the ladder with enough detail (e.g., examples and illustrations) for clarity, yet not so much that the detail gets in the way of the communication. It has been adopted and adapted in hundreds of ways to help people think clearly and express meaning.

At the bottom of the ladder in Figure 5-3 are examples and illustrations. Farmer Jones's Bessie is a single example, and because of language, you can classify, categorize, and label Bessie—due to its similarities and dissimilarities in features to other organisms—as a cow. Such a label raises the level of abstraction from a specific example (Bessie) one rung up on the ladder to a category of animals called cows.

You can observe this particular cow in an environment with other animals such as horses and pigs. One step up on the ladder, in a broader, more abstract, less restrictive classification, you can say this cow is part of Farmer Jones's livestock. His livestock exists within an environment with Farmer Jones's buildings and equipment. Taken together, you move one rung up the ladder of abstraction, and you group his livestock,

Figure 5-2
The Difference between Connotation and Denotation

Your view of the tree

dictionary definition of the tree

Connotation

Denotation

Figure 5-3
The Ladder of Abstraction

Abstract

- Wealth
- Farm
- Live-stock
- Cow
- Bessie

Concrete

Concepts, Themes } Multiple meanings

Examples, Illustrations } Fewer meanings

buildings, and equipment using a new category or label that is even more abstract—farm. Finally, this farm contributes to an even more abstract classification that you can call Farmer Jones's wealth.

A level 5 abstraction might be people of the world. Level 4 could be U.S. society; level 3 could be people who are dominant in that society; level 2 could be spoiled children; and level 1 could be your brother Tim. The more level 1 abstraction you use in your communication, the more likely you will be understood by your listeners. For example, if you are trying to describe a woman and you mention that she wore Birkenstocks and a jean skirt, you have evoked a specific image in your listener's mind. If, on the other hand, you said the woman was dressed in casual attire—a level 2 abstraction—the listener's impression is not as specific, and he or she is free to interpret your meaning in ways that you may not intend. The woman could be wearing a bathrobe and slippers because that, for some people, is casual attire. Using the levels of abstraction carefully will help convey meaning to your listeners.

Why else is the ladder of abstraction useful? First, it will help you better analyze your communications, understandings, and misunderstandings. If a friend down the hall shouted to you "Hey, your econ book is on the floor at your door," that says something more specific and meaningful to you than if the friend said, "Hey, part of your education is sitting out in the hallway." Notice in this example the words *econ book* were substituted for *Bessie* in Figure 5-3, and *education* was substituted for *wealth*.

Second, it will help you immunize yourself against political propaganda, advertising, and vacant rhetoric (talk that has no substance behind it). If a politician visiting campus said, "And, if elected, I will centralize educational opportunity and expedite a new system of open access," you would quickly notice his or her operation at a high level of abstraction because the politician's words contain no specifics, only generalized, highly abstract references. Recognizing this, you might inquire, "What exactly do you mean? What do you plan to do?" What the candidate might mean is that he or she plans to eliminate the major you are pursuing (centralize educational opportunity) by moving it to another state campus, and lower standards (expedite a new system of open access) by making the state system open to anyone who wishes to attend college—with no prerequisites and no standardized admission tests. This could, you might quickly discover—once the level of abstracted language is reduced—drastically alter the value of your college diploma.

Third, you will make a number of personal adjustments as you become more aware of your own abstracting. You will better differentiate between what happens, what you sense of what happens, what you describe of what your senses sense, and what you infer (a much higher level of abstraction) from what you describe. Think about it this way: What actually happens (e.g., a car accident) to you is concrete and specific—low on the ladder of abstraction. What you sense of what happens (e.g., an interference in your life) depends on your background and experiences and is likely to be high on the ladder of abstraction (abstract) because of all the multiple meanings you use to make meaning of what actually happens (the concrete). Knowing this, to describe what happens, you must make a switch from the interference (abstract) to the accident itself (concrete). What you infer, at an even higher level of abstraction, could include the interference of alcohol, cell phone usage, young, inexperienced drivers, or lousy road signs. Once you realize this, you begin to respond more conditionally to what happens in your life because things are not always what they seem to be. A simple car accident can be road rage, a way to collect on an insurance policy, a mechanical malfunction, or any of a

STRATEGIC FLEXIBILITY

Here, then, are a number of adjustments you need to make as you anticipate, assess, evaluate, and select. Delay your responses, leap to fewer conclusions, snap to fewer judgments, and make fewer inappropriate assumptions and the care, concern, and attention required as you apply your skills and behaviors will not just increase, but the entire application step will be more accurate and relevant.

dozen possibilities. You will delay more of your responses, leap to fewer conclusions, snap to fewer judgments, and make fewer inappropriate assumptions.

There are situations when abstract language works best. For example, when you want others to know some general information (like about a dying parent, or a crash that killed a close friend), but details would not be necessary. Here is a story that circulated via the Internet with just the sender's name attached, that reveals the power of abstract over concrete language:

> *The Smiths were proud of their family tradition. Their ancestors had come to America on the Mayflower. They had included senators and Wall Street wizards. They decided to compile a family history, a legacy for their children and grandchildren. They hired a fine author. Only one problem arose—how to handle that great-uncle George, who was executed in the electric chair. The author said he could handle the story tactfully. The book appeared. It said, "Great-uncle George occupied a chair of applied electronics at an important government institution, was attached to his position by the strongest of ties, and his death came as a great shock."*[7]

When you study a language, whether it is your native tongue or a foreign one, you must learn what the words stand for; that is, you have to know both their denotative and their connotative meanings. You must also know how to put the words together to make the phrases and sentences that express relationships between the words. This is the *grammar* of a language.

Because the United States has been a one-language nation, many Americans do not understand how language and perception of the world are connected. Americans sometimes complain that immigrants to the United States do not learn and use English. However, if you accept the theory that language influences your world and your perception of it, you see that learning a language is not just a matter of learning a sign system: It is also learning a different way of looking at the world. For example, one of your authors taught a student who had immigrated to the United States when she was a child. Although she was fluent in English, she said she always prayed in Polish; if she used English, the prayer didn't seem real to her.

PEOPLE DETERMINE MEANINGS

For the listener to understand what you intend, you should have something definite in mind. If an idea or impression is vague, the resulting message will be confused and ambiguous. Understanding is the core of meaning, and understanding is a two-way process; that is, you are responsible for presenting the idea clearly, and the listener is responsible for trying to understand it accurately. Meanings are ultimately determined by people, not by words.

When speaking of some subjects, you have to use a very specialized vocabulary. As Mary Boone, in her book *Managing Interactively* says, "The accountants have their language, the marketing people have their language, the businesspeople have their language, the IT people have their language. . . . That's what they've gotten their degrees in."[8] Here is how Keith Moffatt and Ytaka Shimomura, mathematicians, explain the forces at work on a spinning egg: "We may note that a raw egg does not rise when spun, simply because the angular velocity imparted to the shell must diffuse into the fluid interior; this process dissipates most of the initial kinetic energy imparted to the egg, the remaining energy being insufficient for . . . the state of gyroscopic balance to be established."[9]

You have undoubtedly had the experience of going home from college and talking with friends or family members who did not go to college. Often, the difference can be detected in vocabulary alone. Sometimes your friends or family members who did not go to college will be put off by your use of words that you have recently picked up from your psychology or sociology courses, from your political discussions with your college friends, or from lectures, speeches, and your extensive reading of college textbooks and related information. Your use of newly acquired words is healthy because it is only through use that new vocabulary is obtained and exact meanings for those words is applied. Your new vocabulary also will help you access an even greater amount of information, for it makes both reading and listening more comfortable and enjoyable.

New meanings are continually created by all of us as we change our ideas, our feelings, and our activities. As we think, read, travel, make friends, and experience life, the associations and connections that words have for us are changed.

THE LANGUAGE ENVIRONMENT

All language takes place within a particular environment. A minister speaks in the environment of a church; two friends have a conversation in the student center; an instructor gives a lecture in a classroom. Language that is appropriate to one environment might appear meaningless or foolish in another. The language you use in a dormitory, for example, might be completely inappropriate in a classroom or at home.

People, Purposes, and Rules

According to Neil Postman, who writes about language and education, the **language environment** is made up of four elements: people, their purpose, the rules of communication by which they achieve their purpose, and the actual talk used in the situation.[10] To illustrate these elements, let's take the simple example of John and Mary, who greet each other:

Mary: Hi. How are you?

John: Fine. How are you?

Mary: Good.

The rules for this sort of conversation are known to you, since you often participate in it yourself. If John had failed to follow the rules, however, and had stopped to talk for five minutes about how miserable he felt, Mary might have been annoyed. John would have gone beyond the limits of that sort of conversation.

The kind of conversation Mary and John had illustrates language as a ritual. **Ritual language** takes place in environments where a conventionalized response is expected of you.[11] Greetings are a ritual; you briefly respond to someone—usually only half listening to what the other person has said—and then go about your business.

The rituals you use are determined by the language environment. If you are at a baptism or *bris*, you are expected to say how good-looking the child is or how well he or she behaved during the service. At a wedding you wish the couple happiness and tell the bride she looks beautiful.

Every society's language rituals are determined by the cultural values of that society. In rural East Africa, it would be rude to pass a man you know well with a brief "Hello." You are expected to stop and inquire about the person, his home, his livestock, and his health. In some cultures it is appropriate to tell a couple at their wedding that you hope they will have many sons; in American society, such a comment would be considered inappropriate.

You learn ritualized language when you are very young, from your parents or other adults around you. Researchers have found that young children do not automatically make the conventional responses of "Hi," "Good-bye," or "Thanks"—even though they hear adults doing so. If children are going to use these conventional terms, they must be taught.[12]

As children grow older, they begin to learn and use ritual language. Anyone who has handed out candy on Halloween can tell you that although the younger children may have to be prompted, this is no longer necessary with the older children; they offer their thanks spontaneously.

Appropriate Language

For any society to function it must have some sort of understanding about which words are inappropriate. As children grow up, they try out the new words they hear and, from the reactions of the adults around them, learn the words they shouldn't use. Generally, Americans (and probably most cultures) would agree that the following are inappropriate: First are racial or ethnic epithets against members of groups to which you do not belong. For example a white person should never use the word *nigger* to describe an African American. African Americans, however, can use this word within their own culture because in that context it has a different emotional meaning. Second are words that insult others' appearance or behavior. These words may range from *stupid* or *ugly* to *clumsy* or *incompetent.* Third are words that are blasphemous (religious words) or obscene (body-function words). Fourth are aggressive words intended to control others, such as *shut up* or *drop dead.* Words in any of these categories are highly loaded, emotional words that can do serious damage to human relationships.

Sometimes you have to refer to something for which it would be impolite to use the direct word. To do this you use a **euphemism**—an inoffensive word or phrase that is substituted for other words that might be perceived as unpleasant. For example, you ask "Where's your bathroom?" even when you don't intend to take a bath. If somebody has died, you might use the phrase "passed away." In one instance, when a restaurant in Taiwan wanted to serve dog meat, the owners knew that it would offend some people, and so rather than admit what it was, they called it "fragrant meat." Closer to home, you call your own meat "beef," "veal," and "pork" to veil that it is really dead cow, calf, and pig.

Whereas euphemisms are substitutions for unpleasant words, **doublespeak** refers to words deliberately constructed for political purposes—words specifically intended to impose a desirable mental attitude on those using them. Doublespeak and euphemisms are identical except for two things: (1) Doublespeak does not always have to do with unpleasant words, and (2) doublespeak always relates to a political agenda. For example, the military used *aerial ordinance* for bombs and missiles. George W. Bush used *axis of evil* to refer to countries to be attacked (Iran, North Korea, and Syria). The words *collateral damage* have been used to refer to bystander casualties, ecological destruction, and environmental contamination that result from war. *Freedom fighters* are terrorists with whom our government agrees; *rogue nations* are enemies, usually ones that are not aligned with a group of other nations in agreements that regard the conduct of warfare.[13]

You learn appropriate language as you become more sophisticated and mature. By the time you reach late adolescence, you probably know what language to use for a particular language environment. Whether you want to use the prescribed words is largely irrelevant. The language environment dictates the language that is expected of you. If you violate these expectations, you run the risk of having people respond to you negatively.

Specialization

Most language environments have words that are specialized and are used only in those environments. If your plumber tells you that your toilet needs a new sleeve gasket, you probably won't know what that means. You would understand if the plumber told you that the toilet needs a new seal at the bottom to keep the water from leaking out onto

Working Together

Here, now, is an opportunity for your group to make a significant contribution to the whole world. Based on the combined backgrounds and experiences of the members of your group, you are to combine all of your knowledge and expertise to establish a set of rules for members of *your* generation. We will call these rules "Handy Reminders for Comfortable Communication." These are rules that could be distributed to every member of your generation that would absolutely ensure the use of appropriate language.

Come up with as many rules as you can given the amount of time you have. Then, as you have established the fundamental rules, arrange them in the order of most importance, with the most important rules at the top of your list. Brainstorm, first, for rules on which every member of the group can agree. Arrange them only after a set of 5 to 10 rules has been agreed upon.

---

the floor. Most professions and occupations have a language that only its practitioners understand. Professional cooks make a *roux*, teachers write up their *behavioral objectives*, and contractors install *I-beams*. Members of an occupational group must learn their specialized language to master their field.

Some language environments can be specialized even if the communicators are trying to reach a mass audience. For example, if you watch a jewelry show on a home shopping network on television, you soon discover that there are many words for describing jewelry. For example, the clasp used to keep the jewelry on your body may be a *lobster claw clasp*, a *box closure*, or a *snap bar* closure. Do you want a *faceted stone*, an *emerald cut*, or a *diamond cut*? You can't make choices until you learn this language. The language of the Internet is an excellent example of specialization.

Other groups develop a language that is never intended to be understood by outsiders. Car salespersons, for example, have many words for describing customers who are out of earshot. A *tire-kicker* is a person who pretends expertise but has none. A *roach*, *flake*, or *stoker* is a person with a bad credit rating, while a *be-back* is a customer who promises to return but probably won't.[14] Sometimes people create a special language when they feel they don't have as much power as the people around them. Quite often it is a language that those in power do not understand, and it is deliberately used to keep information from them. Students, especially those in high school and college, are one example of special-language groups. They use slang or a special meaning to exclude outsiders or members of the adult establishment. When away from adults, they may also use some of the language the culture considers inappropriate.

When a group has created a special language, you usually cannot step into that group and use its language unless you have some legitimate claim to membership. Students, for example, might secretly make fun of a teacher who tries to talk as they do. How you are expected to speak in a language environment depends on the role you are playing.

Whenever you shift roles, you shift your language environment and your speech as well. Let's say that in a single day you talk to your roommate, you go to class, and you speak to your mother on the telephone. Your role has shifted three times: from peer relating to peer, to student relating to instructor, to child relating to parent. Each circumstance has entailed a different language environment, and you have probably changed your speech accordingly—perhaps without even realizing it.

The important thing to remember about a language environment is that you must choose language that is appropriate to it. The language used in one environment usually does not work in another. When you think about the environment, you need to ask yourself who it is you are going to be talking with and in what context your language is going to be used. If you don't adapt to the environment, your language will not work, and you will lose the chance for effective communication.

STYLE, ROLES, AND GROUP MEMBERSHIPS

The words you use are determined by all your past experiences, by everything in your individual history. Stephen King, in his book *On Writing*, says it this way: "You undoubtedly have your own thoughts, interests, and concerns, and they have arisen, as mine have, from your experiences and adventures as a human being."[15] You learn words to express thoughts, and thought and language develop together, as discussed in the section on cognitive development at the beginning of this chapter. The way you think and the way you talk are unique; they form a distinctive pattern. In a sense, you are what you say because language is the chief means of conveying your thoughts. Neither language nor thought can be viewed in isolation because they are so interrelated. Together, they determine your verbal style.

Sheryl Perlmutter Bowen, a teacher of communication and women's studies at Villanova University, describes her own language and verbal style in this way: "My own speech . . . is often marked by a preference for personal topics, abrupt topic shifts, storytelling (in which the preferred point is the teller's emotional experience), a fast rate of speech, avoidance of inter-turn pauses, quick turn-taking, expressive phonology, pitch and amplitude shifts, marked voice quality, and strategic within-turn pauses. Given these characteristics," she adds, "my complaining and teasing should both be seen as normal interaction strategies."[16]

Style is the result of the way you select and arrange words and sentences. People choose different words to express their thoughts, and every individual has a unique verbal style. Not only do styles vary among people, but each person uses different styles to suit different situations. In the pulpit, a minister usually has a scholarly and formal style. At a church dinner, however, his or her style is likely to be informal and casual. When a football player signs autographs for fans, he speaks to them in the role of athlete—even though he might drop this role when he is with friends and family.

Sometimes style can negate a communicator's other good qualities. You probably know someone who is extremely shy and speaks in a faltering manner. You might also know some people who can never seem to get to the point. If you are critical of these people, it is probably because of their style.

Style, because of its power and influence, is just as important to the acceptance of ideas as all the other aspects of communication. Even if you have the proper information, the right occasion, and a listener interested in your message, what you have to say may be lost if your style is inappropriate.

Impressions of personality are often related to verbal style. When you characterize a person as formal and aloof, your impression is due in part to the way that person talks. Since your style partially determines whether others accept or reject you, it also influences how others receive your messages. Style is so important that it can influence people's opinion of you, win their friendship, lose their respect, or sway them to your ideas.

Like language environment, verbal style is often connected with the roles you play. Professionals, for example, are expected to speak grammatically correct English—both in private and in professional life. A college student is also expected to use correct grammar. Yet if he takes a factory job during summer vacation, using correct grammar might get him into trouble with his fellow workers, for his verbal style could identify him as a "college kid."

Gender and Language

Sociolinguist Deborah Tannen has found that men and women have almost completely different styles of speaking.[17] In fact, she maintains that their languages are so different that they might as well come from different worlds. According to Tannen, when women have conversations, they use the language of **rapport-talk.** This language is designed to lead to intimacy with others, to match experiences, and to establish relationships. Men, however, speak **report-talk.** In this type of speech the speaker's goal is to maintain status, to demonstrate knowledge and skills, and to keep the center-stage position.[18] Because of their different ways of speaking, men and women often have problems when they try to talk to each other, Tannen says. For example, a stock cartoon shows a man and woman at the breakfast table, with the man reading the newspaper and the woman trying to get his attention. The man is using the newspaper as a source of information he needs for future report-talks. The woman, however, is looking for interaction, or rapport-talk.

Tannen also says that men are more likely than women to look at problems in terms of "fixing them." A woman, for example, might tell her husband that someone insulted her. Her husband's reaction is to take revenge as a way of fixing the problem. For the woman, this probably is not a satisfactory solution; she would prefer a statement of understanding or an expression of empathy from him.[19]

Other researchers have also looked at differences between the way men and women interact. They have found that when men and women talk together, men are more likely to interrupt ("Let's go on to the next topic") and give directives ("Why don't you write this down?"). Women use more personal pronouns and more intensive adverbs ("I really like her"). The researchers also found that women use more questions and more justifiers ("The reason I say this . . . ").[20]

Tannen believes that gender differences in language are important considerations in the college classroom. In a typical classroom, she says, male students are likely to say what they know before the whole class and to welcome arguments and challenges from their classmates. They are also likely to reject anecdotal information as unimportant. Female students, on the other hand, do not find much pleasure in verbal conflict and are much more comfortable when they work in small groups and offer personal anecdotes. Since most classrooms are organized on the male model, Tannen believes that many women find the classroom to be a hostile space.[21]

An interesting example of gender differences in language occurred when a teacher asked her students to make up words that described experiences unique to their sex but that did not already exist in English. She found that women's and men's words were in entirely different categories. Women created words that tended to put women into passive roles, such as *perchaphonic* ("waiting for someone to phone you") and *herdastudaphobia* ("fear when passing a group of strange men"). Men, however, created words that focused on competency and the power to change things, such as *gearheaditis* ("making your car the best on the road") and *beer muscles* ("believing you are tough after you have had something to drink").[22]

Where does gender-specific language come from? Tannen believes that it begins in childhood and that children learn it from their peers. She reports that one researcher who observed preschool children found that when the children wanted to do something, the girls would start with, "Let's . . . " while the boys would give direct commands, "Sit down."[23] In looking at videotapes of second-graders, Tannen says that in language and behavior, second-grade girls were more similar to adult women than they were to second-grade boys.[24] When the same second-graders were put in pairs and were asked to talk about "something serious," the girls did so. The boys, however, resisted or mocked authority.[25] Since language behavior starts so young, it's not surprising that it soon becomes automatic.

While some scholars have criticized the emphasis put on differences between male and female language because they feel that those who do the studies often interpret the results in a way that reinforces stereotypes society already holds about men and women, others attempt to explain the female advantage in language aptitude. In her

Another Point of View

Some Criticisms of Tannen's Work

Seems to be based on anecdotes.

Seems to overgeneralize.

Seems to consider only white middle-class women and men.

Seems to focus on heterosexual women and men.

Sees problems in relationships between men and women as based in difference and not dominance.

Seems to ignore political and economic differences between men and women.

Relies on individuals' intentions ("He didn't intend to dominate") rather than on facts and also others' interpretations.

Tries to separate dominance and gendered culture. Doesn't explain why men and women have these different styles.

Questions

1. To what extent does criticism of an author automatically convey truth? How difficult would it be to verify the criticisms of Tannen's work?
2. Does criticism of a work nullify the value of or findings in that work? To what extent do sales of a work or the effect of a work mitigate (cause to become less harsh or harmful) criticism of that work?
3. If you were the author of a criticized work, how would you go about addressing that criticism?

Source: "Language and Gender" (1998) University of Colorado. Retrieved July 27, 2002, from **http://www.colorado.edu/linguistics/sp98/2400/tannen.hyp**

---

book *The War Against Boys,* Christina Hoff Sommers—the W. H. Brady Fellow at the American Enterprise Institute in Washington, DC, who has a PhD in philosophy from Brandeis University and was formerly professor of philosophy at Clark University—offers research to support her contention that physiological sex differences correlate with differences in preferences and aptitudes. She cites the research of Bennett and Sally Shaywitz, neuroscientists at Yale University.[27] Using brain-imaging technologies—specifically functional magnetic resonance imaging (MRI)—to look for sex differences in the brain, they gave 19 men and 19 women volunteer subjects a simple language task. "In both men and women," writes Sommers, "the front of the cortex in the left hemisphere lit up brightly, indicating that to be the area where this task is carried out. But in 11 of the 19 women—and none of the men—an area in the right hemisphere also lit up. If two parts of the female brain focus on language, this might explain the female advantage in this area".[28]

Michael Gurian, in his book *What Could He Be Thinking?*, gives further evidence of the role that gender plays in language. The cerebral cortex is the area of the brain known for transforming emotion into thought. Females use more cortical areas for verbal experience (talking, writing, and reading), and they turn their experiences into emotive verbal responses. "Because the female brain does language in about seven brain centers, whereas the male brain does it in only one or two," Gurian notes, "there is a greater tendency in the female brain to process all of its experience, including emotive experiences, by using words."[29]

Powerful Talk

Powerful talk is talk that comes directly to the point—talk that does not use hesitation or qualifications. People who engage in powerful talk are found to be more credible, more attractive, and more persuasive than those who do not.[30] In the college classroom, teachers who used powerful language are considered by their students to be more believable and to have more status.[31]

Powerful talk is characterized by the *nonexistence* of certain communication behaviors. First, hedges and qualifiers—expressions such as "I guess" and "kind of"—weaken the power of speech. Hesitation forms such as "uh" and "you know" make speakers sound too uncertain. Third, tag questions—comments that start out as statements but end as questions ("It would be nice to go on a picnic, wouldn't it?") make speakers seem less assertive. Finally, disclaimers—words and expressions that excuse or ask listeners to bear with the speaker—weaken communications. Examples are "I know you probably don't agree with me, but . . ." or "I'm really not prepared to speak today."[32]

The number of women in powerful positions is increasing steadily, but it has been a struggle for them. Why has there been a struggle? Supreme Court Justice Sandra Day O'Connor says that "In the past there was a widespread belief—declining today, but certainly still there—that women are unfit for power positions." Whether it has to do with powerful talk or assertiveness, O'Connor says "The image of the aggressive leader does not lie easily with traditional notions of femininity."[33]

Many of us dilute our conversations and speeches with powerless words and expressions. However, the use of these expressions is mainly a matter of habit. Once you recognize your bad habits, you can start to break them.

Besides using powerful language, you can use several other techniques to make your language more lively. A sense of urgency is communicated mainly by verbs—the action words of language. "Judy slapped him" and "The children jumped up and down" are both sentences that sound energetic. Language is also livelier when you put sentences in the active rather than the passive voice. "The boy hit the ball" is more energetic than "The ball was hit by the boy."

Culture and Language

The number of U.S. residents age five and older speaking a language other than English at home jumped from 32 million in 1990 to 47 million in 2000. That means that nearly one in five Americans speak a language other than English at home and the top five languages, excluding English, are Spanish, Chinese, French, German, and Tagalog (Philippines). The difference between those speaking Spanish (28.1 million) and those speaking Chinese (2 million) is enormous. School districts are scrambling to find bilingual instructors, governments are looking for ways to help those who don't speak English well, and more and more companies are diversifying their advertising and marketing campaigns to reach people who speak other languages.[34] Why wouldn't companies want to diversify? African Americans and Latinos/Latinas account for one-quarter of department store sales, according to strategic marketing communications agency Meridian.[35]

Although English is unlikely to become the world's dominant language, it will remain one of its most important languages. For routine language, people will probably switch between two or more languages, but, according to British language expert David Graddol, "English-only speakers may find it difficult to participate in a multilingual society."[36] "In 1995, English trailed Chinese as the most common native language. Native English speakers were 9% of the world. That is expected to fall to 5% by 2050," Graddol said, "as Arabic and Hindi-Urdu overtake English."[37]

Why is an understanding of the impact of culture on language important? The following are stories cited by Marilyn Carlson Nelson, chair and CEO of the Carlson Companies, in her speech "On the Path." She says that Chevrolet tried to launch its Nova car in Latin America where *Nova* in Spanish actually means "no go." The successful "Got Milk?" campaign was almost trashed when the translation for "Got Milk?" was discovered to mean "Are You Lactating?" When the phrase "Pepsi, the choice of a new generation" was translated into Chinese, it came out as "Pepsi, the drink that will awaken your ancestors from the dead." Buick planned to launch its new Lacrosse in Quebec, until it learned that the name was Quebec slang for sexual self-gratification. These examples simply underscore the importance of understanding how culture affects language and language choices.[38]

Dialect

Toward the end of the summer in central Pennsylvania, many cooks begin to fry or preserve "mangoes." Outsiders are always surprised that Pennsylvania cooks are so interested in this tropical fruit. What they don't know is that in that part of the country a mango isn't a fruit at all; it's what everyone else calls a green pepper or a bell pepper. The central Pennsylvanians' use of the word *mango* is an example of dialect.

A **dialect** is the habitual language of a community. It is distinguished by unique grammatical structures, words, and figures of speech. The community members who use the dialect may be identified by region or by such diverse factors as education, social class, or cultural background. Many people will hold on to their dialects because they are a tie to their own community. See Figure 5-4 for some examples of dialects.

When radio and television became widespread, linguists predicted that their popularity might herald the end of dialect because people would imitate the standard American speech they heard on these media. However, it didn't work that way. Linguists have found that dialect is growing stronger, especially in many urban areas.[39]

It is important to understand what a dialect is and is not. Clearly it is *not* Mexican-Americans living in a Mexican-American neighborhood in Dallas, Texas, using a dialect when they speak Spanish to each other. But, what if an American from the south, who learned Spanish in high school, went into this Mexican-American neighborhood in Dallas, Texas, and talked with the Mexican-Americans living there? This American would likely speak his or her high-school learned Spanish using his or her Southern dialect of American English. True to his or her background, this American would *not* have the variations of idiom, vocabulary (or phonemes [units of sound] and morphemes [meaningful units]) peculiar to the Mexican-Americans from the neighborhood. He or she could not. His or her language would quickly reveal itself to the Mexican-Americans from the neighborhood as "off their standard"—an imperfect use of the standard language used by those Mexican-Americans from the neighborhood for whom Spanish is their native language.

Any language (French, German, Spanish, etc.) learned solely in the classroom will retain recognizable elements of the parent language, but it will have distinctive vocabulary, pronunciation, forms, and idiom that will quickly distinguish it as a linguistic branch of—and not the same as—the parent language. It is exactly the same as when the person, above, speaking Spanish using his or her Southern dialect of American English, traveled north in the U.S. and found him- or herself anywhere in the north using the Southern dialect of American English. The Southern dialect would have similar distinctions to his or her Spanish, from people in the north who speak American English.

Although there are no clear-cut rules for where and when it is appropriate to use a dialect, it is possible to make some generalizations. A dialect is appropriate in a group with a strong ethnic identity, but it may be inappropriate in situations where standard English is used. Linguistic scholars agree that some dialects have more prestige than others and that prestige is determined by both the people who speak the dialect and those who hear it. Thus, if you want to be accepted by and identified with people who use a dialect or who use a standard English different from your own, you might have to adapt to their way of speaking. Many people in America have discovered that it is not difficult to speak two "languages," a dialect and standard English. By so doing, they find it possible to keep their ethnic identity as well as function in a world where expectations are different.

Speaking and Writing

We use language in both speaking and writing, but the transactional nature of speaking makes it very different from writing.

Figure 5-4

Some Examples of Dialect in the United States

Standard American English branches to: British dialect, East Tennessee dialect, Southern dialect, New York's Lower East Side dialect, Los Angeles's Back Bay dialect, South Boston dialect, Western dialect, Texas dialect, Midwestern dialect, Arkansas dialect, New England dialect, Fargo, North Dakota dialect, Etc. (all others)

When two people are engaged in conversation, they interact continuously and simultaneously. Both get and give information, form impressions, and respond to each other. On the basis of each other's responses, both can change their comments to explain, backtrack, hurry up, slow down, or do whatever is necessary to be understood.

Sometimes conversation reflects the participants' past knowledge of each other. They can use a kind of shorthand because of the experiences they've had together. If you are in a close relationship or desire one, you know that the words you speak may affect your present and future relationship. If the relationship is more impersonal, the choice of words might not be so important.

You also are able to change your language to reflect the circumstances. When you get negative feedback, you can change language to appease your listeners. You can use simpler words or concepts if listeners don't seem to understand. Spoken language is also accompanied by **paralanguage**—vocal cues, or the way you say your words. For example, your meaning can be influenced by your pitch and rate (high and fast if you are excited), your volume, and how often you pause. This kind of adaptation occurs in every conversation. Whether you are talking to your father, a professor, or a friend, your language will reflect your impression of this person, the kinds of experiences you have had together, and the role you are playing.

In contrast, it's not so easy to change your written language. In fact, writers have an entirely different set of problems than speakers do. When you are speaking, people are reacting to you as the message occurs. For writers, reaction from their audience is unusual, and they have no way of knowing if they have pleased or offended someone, or if they have even communicated their ideas. [This means that their words must be chosen very carefully. Also, they have time to go over their words, polish their phrases, and check their grammar. Their readers have more time too. They can always reread the words if they're not clear the first time.] Writers are more likely to use a larger vocabulary

➡ COMMUNICATION ON THE INTERNET.

than speakers do, and readers can look up the words if they don't understand them. Writers do not have the paralanguage of speakers to add to their meaning. If the words they choose don't work, their attempt at communication fails.

Writers have no way of taking the future effects of their words into account. When an Indian author, Salman Rushdie, wrote *The Satanic Verses,* he could not predict that his words would be seen as blasphemous and would be condemned by an Iranian religious leader, who "gave permission" for any Moslem to kill the author.

WORKING ON YOUR COMMUNICATION

When you set out to communicate verbally, you are more likely to be successful if you use words and ideas that have the same meaning to the person with whom you are communicating as they do to you. Sometimes, although you think you are being clear, the other person might not perceive what you think you have communicated.

Communication can go awry at various stages. Let's look at some of the places where this might happen.

What Do You Want to Say?

In 1938, Orson Welles broadcast *The War of the Worlds,* a radio play about martians invading the United States. You can assume that in writing this play, Welles intended to entertain his audience. Although Welles's intent was clear to him, at least one million people misunderstood it and believed that the play was real. They believed that martians really had landed and that their lives were in peril. By the time the network announced that the broadcast was only a play, many people had already reacted to it by fleeing their homes to find a place of safety.

Although this is an extreme example of intent going astray, most of us have had times when people's responses were different from those we intended. You intend to tell your roommate to meet you at 7:00, but she thinks you said 7:30. You intend to make a joke, but you end up insulting someone. When you are involved in one-to-one communication, you often have a chance to clear up misunderstandings. If you see that the other person looks confused or annoyed or if the response you get indicates that you have not communicated something as precisely as you had intended, you can attempt to clarify what you said.

When you are talking to an audience, however, it is not so easy to clear up misunderstandings. In a public-speaking or mass-communication setting, you may not have a chance to respond to feedback or you may not be able to respond until the communication is over. Therefore, when you are going to communicate to a large audience, you must prepare your words much more carefully than you do in an interpersonal setting.

The first thing you must consider is, What exactly do you want to say? Students who are new to public speaking often do not think through this step clearly enough. Speakers who do not know precisely what they want to say frequently end up confusing their audience. The same may happen if they have not clearly thought out their words.

How Do You Want to Say It?

Although you are often told that you should make careful language choices, you might not know how to go about doing so. Command of language requires years of practice and study. Since it is impossible to lay down strict rules that govern the choice of language for all occasions and for all circumstances, the discussion here is limited to three important aspects of language choice: clarity, vividness, and ethics.

Consider This

What are your perceptions of people who use English that is different from your own? Let's say the person has difficulty speaking the language correctly—as you have come to understand it. In her book *The Opposite of Fate*, Amy Tan talks about the perceptions others have of her mother who uses "broken" or "fractured" English:

> I know this for a fact, because when I was growing up, my mother's "limited" English limited my perception of her. I was ashamed of her English. I believed that her English reflected the quality of what she had to say. That is, because she expressed them imperfectly, her thoughts were imperfect. And I had plenty of empirical evidence to support me: the fact that people in department stores, at banks, and in restaurants did not take her seriously, did not give her good service, pretended not to understand her, or even acted as if they did not hear her.

Source: *The Opposite of Fate: A Book of Musings* (p. 274), by Amy Tan, 2003, New York: Putnam's Sons.

Questions

1. When you speak imperfectly—using improper or broken English—do you think it influences others in negative ways?
2. Do you think there might be a relationship, as indicated in Tan's quote, between ideas expressed imperfectly and imperfect thoughts?
3. What means do people who use imperfect English have to discover that they are using imperfect English? When it is discovered, how can they improve their use of English? Do you think such improvement is advantageous, or do you think people should not worry about it?

Clarity

A pilot died in the crash of a private jet because the instructions on how to open the emergency door were so unclear that she could not get it open. Although a lack of clarity is usually not a matter of life or death, it can lead to frustration and misunderstanding. In most situations, you have to speak as clearly as possible if you want to be understood. **Clarity** is that aspect or characteristic of style by means of which a thought is so presented that it is immediately understood, depending on the precision and simplicity of the language. Clarity is especially important when there is little opportunity for feedback. For example, if you are saying something of special importance, making a formal speech, or being interviewed by the media, clarity is essential since you will probably not get another chance.

Jargon is a language that can be so specialized that it is inappropriate to use it outside the field where it originated. Emanuel Rosen, in his book *The Anatomy of Buzz*, writes this about the use of jargon: "From ancient fortified cities to current gated communities, people have always put walls and other barriers around themselves to keep intruders away to differentiate themselves from others. Networks have their own walls and fences, but instead of wire or bricks, people use dialect, jargon, and acronyms to keep strangers out."[40] Physicians often use a highly specialized language to describe illnesses and injuries. Although doctors can communicate with each other, sometimes they have problems communicating with patients because of the walls and fences. Many newspapers carry a column in which a physician answers questions from readers who do not understand what their own doctors told them—a way to break down the walls and add gates to the fences.

Other language that might not be clear to everyone is slang. Slang has its place when you are talking informally with your friends. However, many slang words have such broad and vague meanings that they could apply to almost anything. If you use the word *cool* to compliment someone's shirt and use it again to describe beautiful scenery, you reduce everything to a common element.

Sometimes people feel that if they have taken the trouble to learn long and complicated words, they should use them whenever they can. On a bottle of fluoride solution, the consumer is advised to "hold the solution in the mouth for one minute and then expectorate." In case the consumer doesn't understand the word *expectorate*, the phrase *spit it out* follows in parentheses. Since the purpose of this message is to communicate with the consumer, the simpler words, *spit it out,* should have been used in the first place.

Use more complicated words only when they help make your meaning clearer. For example, if you want your car painted red, you'll be happier with the final results if you use a more precise description than *red.* What shade do you prefer? Burgundy? Crimson? Vermilion? Garnet?

When you increase your vocabulary, you increase your chances of getting your intended meaning across to your listener. The more words you have at your command, the more precise you will be. This does not mean that you should search for big words; on the contrary, familiar words are often the best.

One of the delights of language is that it offers you many subtleties and shades of meaning. Choosing the same words to express all your ideas is like eating a Big Mac for dinner every night. Language is a marvelous banquet providing you with a vast array of choices for anything and everything you want to say.

Vividness

Remember those ghost stories you heard when you were a child? The best ones were those that filled you with terror—the ones laced with bloodcurdling shrieks, mournful moans, mysterious howling. They were usually set in dark places, with only an occasional eerie light or a streak of lightning. If any smells were mentioned, they were sure to be dank and musty.

The teller of a ghost story usually speaks in the first person. Any narrative told from the point of view of "I was there" or "It happened to me" is particularly vivid. By recreating an experience for your listeners, you can often make them feel what you felt. **Vividness** is the aspect or characteristic of style by which a thought is so presented that it evokes lifelike imagery or suggestion.

Vividness also comes from unique forms of speech. Some people would say that a person who talks too much "chatters like a magpie," a phrase that has become a cliché. To one Southern speaker, however, this person "makes a lot of chin music." When we say that language is vivid, we often mean that someone has found a new way of saying old things. Children often charm us with the uniqueness of their language because they are too young to know all the clichés and overused expressions. Another place to look for vivid language is in poetry and song. Although more words have been written about love than any other subject, many songwriters have given us new expressions and therefore new ways of looking at the experience. Their unique perspectives make an old idea sound original and exciting.

To Whom Are You Talking?

STRATEGIC FLEXIBILITY
Your success in being strategically flexible rests on this aspect: *Know* to whom you are talking. Your sensitivity to other people—along with your awareness of language choice and use—will largely determine your communication effectiveness.

As you talk to people, become conscious of them as particular individuals for whom you need to adapt your message. Note the language environment in which your conversation is taking place, and make the adjustments that are necessary. Also, when you are talking about a particular subject, see if you can find words that are unique to the subject—even if you have to define them. Often, learning about a subject is also learning the vocabulary of the subject. Be conscious of what you are saying. This added consciousness will increase your sensitivity to other people as well as your awareness of language choice and use.

Sometimes people confuse personal authenticity with inflexible language usage, and they equate undisciplined speech with spontaneity. "Telling it like it is" becomes an excuse for allowing the first words that come into your head to spill out in a torrent. Such language choices reflect a kind of self-centered indulgence that says to your listener, "Never mind who you are—listen to me." Adapting your language to the individual with whom you are talking can result in a more satisfying exchange.

What Metamessages Are You Sending?

You probably choose your words carefully when you are making a public presentation. It might not occur to you, however, to be so careful when you are talking to a friend or conversing with a small group of people. Yet you might occasionally have had a conversation that made you feel uneasy—the words all sounded right, but there was something else going on.

In such cases, you need to think about the **metamessage** (sometimes called *subtext*)— the meaning apart from what actual words express. For example, when one spouse tells the other, "We need to talk," he or she really might be saying, "I want to complain."

Metamessages take many forms. At a graduation ceremony, the president of the university introduced everyone on the stage except one of the deans. The dean realized that this was more than a simple oversight, that he might be in serious trouble. He was right: he was fired the next term.

Many metamessages don't involve words at all. Deborah Tannen believes that American men refuse to ask directions because it puts them in an inferior position and the person they ask in a superior position.[41]

Sometimes metamessages are recognizable to people within a specific culture but not to outsiders. A Polish professor complained that when she was in the United States, one of her American colleagues kept saying, "Let's have lunch sometime." When she tried to pin him down, he looked annoyed. What she didn't realize until much later was that this is an expression that some Americans use to terminate a conversation.

Language is filled with metamessages, and you have to listen for this kind of talk and understand its meaning if you are going to have accurate communication. You also should be aware of the metamessages you yourself send. For example, it is not unusual for a student speaker to begin a speech by implying that the speech will not be very good: "I just finished this speech this morning," "I couldn't find any research on this topic," or "You'll have to excuse me because I am feeling sick." If you say anything of this sort, you may be engaging in a metamessage; what you may really be saying is, "I am feeling extremely nervous and anxious about giving this speech."

Ethics

Ray Penn, a communications professor, points out that "a choice of words is a choice of worlds."[42] He reminds us that we can cause considerable damage to others by choosing the wrong words. For example, if you are asked to remember your most painful moment, the response will most likely be something someone said.

Penn asks us to consider whether "our analogies create a self-fulfilling prophecy that will ultimately keep us from relating to others unless we get our way." For example, how often in life do you talk of "winners" and "losers," condemning the losers to permanent failure? On the international scene, does calling Osama bin Laden "another Hitler" create a self-fulfilling prophecy? When political figures in the Middle East refer to the United States as "Satan" or "the devil," does such labeling influence the way we, as a country, react to them?

Penn also reminds us that language choices can influence people's perceptions of themselves. Insulting words, he points out, can reduce an individual to a mere trait ("dyke," "queer"); they can reduce someone to less-than-human status ("pig," "chicken"); or they can tell the person "I know all about you and you have no mystery" by means of labels ("hillbilly," "redneck," "geek").[43]

Penn reminds us that we make moral choices when we choose the language we are going to use. Many of the choices you make not only determine how you present yourself to others but also decide the nature of your relationships in the years to come. For this reason, it is important that you choose your words wisely and well.

THE INTERNET AND VERBAL COMMUNICATION

Besides the globalization and subsequent multilingualization (one-quarter of the world's languages—about 1,500—have some sort of cyberexistence[44]) of the Internet, there are four other clear and distinct influences where the Internet has affected language and language use. The first is the effect of e-mail messages on language. This effect has nothing to do with the obvious Internet characteristics of typing inaccuracies, misspellings, and lack of capitalization and punctuation which are all nonstandard, playful, and highly deviant. It has to do with **framing**—the way in which messages are divided, arranged, shaped, composed, constructed, and put together as a new whole. For example, let's say you receive a message that contains three different points. Instead of responding to the entire message, you can respond to just a single point, and send back the message. Then, you can respond to the second point, and send back the message, and, likewise, with the third. Your respondent can then respond to each point individually, or he or she can choose to dissect the message even further.

The point is, when you get the message back, an issue—with its development and history—is framed on the screen. Issues can go on and on, reply after reply, all unified and with their history intact. Never before in human written communication, says David Crystal, in his book *Language and the Internet,* has this been possible.[45]

The second influence of the Internet on verbal communication occurs on the World Wide Web. One thing that can be said about traditional writing is that it is *permanent*. When you open a book to page 10, close the book, then open it to page 10 again, the same thing appears on the page. *Impermanence* is what occurs on the Web. Pages can change in front of your eyes. Page content can be updated, rearranged, deleted, or presented in entirely new ways. Words not only appear and disappear, but they also arrive in varied sizes, textures, colors, and fonts, and images fade in and out. The Web offers an animated linguistic channel that is more dynamic than traditional writing and more permanent than traditional speech. "It is," says Crystal, "neither speech nor writing. It is a new medium."[46]

The third arena in which a language revolution has occurred is in chat rooms. Not only do you get screen messages from all over the world, but you get messages from a large number of people at the same time (the number is unlimited) on a theme. Often, conversations cluster into a half-dozen or more subconversations. Similar to being at a cocktail party with numerous conversations going on around you, there is no way to pay attention to all of them. Never before in human communication has it been possible to listen to that many people at the same time.

The fourth arena is the blurring of the division between speaking and writing. E-mails are written, as noted, in a much less formal way than is usual in writing. With voice recordings, it is possible to speak to those who are not in the same place or

Assess Yourself

Verbal Communication Self-Evaluation Form

How effective is your verbal communication? For each question circle the numerical score that best represents your verbal communication. Select an event, a situation, a context, and a time when you recently gave a speech or presentation, and analyze it using the following scale: 7 = Outstanding; 6 = Excellent; 5 = Very good; 4 = Average (good); 3 = Fair; 2 = Poor; 1 = Minimal ability; 0 = No ability demonstrated.

1. *Did you use extended conversation?* That is, did you use language that was not highly formal, that was easy for you to use (not a stretch), that seemed like normal conversation, and that revealed a natural, comfortable, relaxed vocabulary and approach?
   7 6 5 4 3 2 1 0

2. *Did you reveal clarity in your word choices?* That is, were your words immediately meaningful? Did they arouse specific and definite meanings? Was there no ambiguity or confusion revealed?
   7 6 5 4 3 2 1 0

3. *Did you reveal simplicity in your word choices?* That is, did you use simple words? Was your vocabulary instantly understandable? Did you avoid using vague and confusing words? Were you sensitive to audience knowledge and background?
   7 6 5 4 3 2 1 0

4. *Did you reveal accuracy in your word choices?* That is, did your words seem to convey exactly what you meant? Did you give your listeners enough, but not too much, information? In your examples, did you give complete details such as names, places, dates, and other facts? When you used an uncommon or technical word, did you accurately define it for your listeners?
   7 6 5 4 3 2 1 0

5. *Did your verbal communication reveal appropriateness?* That is, did the words you chose have a direct relationship to your listeners? Did all your facts, examples, illustrations, opinions, statistics, and personal experiences relate directly to your audience? Did you use personal pronouns such as *you, us, we,* and *our*? Did you ask your listeners questions or use rhetorical questions that did not require an answer but which created the impression of direct audience contact?
   7 6 5 4 3 2 1 0

6. *Did you reveal dynamism in your choice of words?* That is, was your language vivid? Was it impressive? Did your language appear planned and prepared—like you had given it some specific thought? Did your language reveal your own personal imprint?
   7 6 5 4 3 2 1 0

TOTAL POINTS: _____

Go to the *Communicating Effectively* CD-ROM and the Online Learning Center at **www.mhhe.com/hybels8** to see your results and learn how to evaluate your attitudes and feelings.

mhhe .com/hybels8

---

time as you. You can speak or listen in such situations but not interact. Live television broadcasts can include a mixture of recordings, telephone calls, incoming faxes, as well as e-mails. "One effect of this new technology and the modern universality of writing," says Josef Essberger, "has been to raise the status of speaking. Politicians who cannot organize their thoughts and *speak* [Essberger's emphasis] well on television win very few votes."[47]

CHAPTER REVIEW

SUMMARY

Your ability to use words depends on your native architecture, cognitive development, and environmental influences. It is a key component in strategic flexibility because, as the Sapir-Whorf hypothesis emphasizes, it influences the way you view and think about the world around you.

A word is a symbol; it stands for the object or concept it names. For us to understand one another, we must agree on what the particular word symbol stands for—in both its denotative and its connotative meanings. S. I. Hayakawa's ladder of abstraction helps convey meaning accurately to listeners. It helps analyze communications, understandings, and misunderstandings. It helps immunize against political propaganda, advertising, and vacant rhetoric, and it also helps communicators make personal adjustments as they become aware of their own abstracting.

Language is directly linked to your perception of reality and to your thought processes, which begin in earliest childhood. You create meanings for words as ideas, feelings, and activities change. Because you determine meanings, it is important to present ideas as clearly as possible while your listener tries to understand.

For language to be successful, it must be appropriate to the language environment. The language you should use in a particular environment is determined by the role you are playing in that environment. Certain language rituals are predetermined for you by the values of your society (culture and co-cultures). You learn these and other forms of appropriate language during your childhood. When you become an adult and enter the work world, often you must learn a specialized language used by your occupational or professional group.

Style, the way you express yourself, is an important aspect of language. The style that is expected of you often is determined by the roles you play. If you do not modify your language to fit your role, you may speak in ways that are inappropriate for the occasion.

Your gender influences the language style you use. Men are more likely to use report-talk, a language that maintains their status, demonstrates their knowledge and skills, and keeps them at the center of attention. In contrast, women are more likely to use rapport-talk, a language that leads to intimacy with others, establishes relationships, and compares experiences. Powerful talk, too, will influence your effectiveness.

English is losing its place as a dominant world language. One in five Americans speak a language other than English at home. If you belong to an ethnic group, you may use a dialect—the habitual language of your community. The advantage of dialect is that it helps a person fit into an ethnic community; the disadvantage is that it might not have prestige in a community where standard American English is spoken.

There are many differences between writing and speaking. Writing is formal and structured; uses words alone; and is nonimmediate, with delayed feedback. Speaking is informal and less structured; uses words along with facial expressions, gestures, and tone of voice; and is immediate with, for the most part, instant feedback. Knowing these and the other differences will help you increase both the clarity and accuracy of your messages.

When you work on your communication, you have to decide what you want to say and how you want to say it. In choosing how you wish to communicate, you should aim for clarity, vividness, and ethical choices. Then you should ask to whom you are speaking and what metamessages—the meaning apart from the actual words—you are sending.

There are four influences of the Internet on verbal communication. The first is the framing that occurs in e-mail messages. The second is the impermanence and animation of Web pages. The third is the unlimited number of people with whom you can communicate in chat rooms; and the fourth is the blurring of the division between speaking and writing.

CHAPTER REVIEW

KEY TERMS AND CONCEPTS

Use the *Communicating Effectively* CD-ROM and the Online Learning Center at www.mhhe.com/hybels8 to further your understanding of the following terms.

Clarity 123
Cognitive development 108
Connotative meaning 109
Denotative meaning 109
Dialect 120
Doublespeak 114
Euphemism 114
Framing 125
Ladder of abstraction 109
Language environment 113
Metamessage 125
Paralanguage 121
Powerful talk 118
Rapport-talk 116
Report-talk 117
Ritual language 113
Sapir-Whorf hypothesis 108
Style 116
Vividness 124

QUESTIONS TO REVIEW

1. How did you acquire your ability to use words?
2. What is the Sapir-Whorf hypothesis? How does it influence strategic flexibility?
3. What is meant when a word is referred to as a symbol?
4. What is the difference between denotative meaning and connotative meaning?
5. What is the ladder of abstraction, and why is it useful?
6. What are the four elements that make up a language environment?
7. Define *euphemism* and *doublespeak* and give an example of each.
8. What do you mean when you talk about verbal style? How is it developed?
9. What is the difference between report-talk and rapport-talk, and why is it important?
10. How is powerful talk characterized? When people use it, what impression do they make?
11. What cultural changes are having an effect on language?
12. What is dialect, and what does it have to do with one's cultural background?
13. How do speaking and writing differ? What is the benefit of knowing the differences?
14. What is the difference between clarity and vividness, and what would be an appropriate example of each that reflects the difference?
15. What is the difference between paralanguage and metamessage?
16. What are some of the moral choices you should make in choosing the words you use?
17. What influences does the Internet have on verbal communication?

Go to the self-quizzes on the *Communicating Effectively* CD-ROM and the Online Learning Center at www.mhhe.com/hybels8 to test your knowledge of the chapter contents.

CHAPTER 6

Nonverbal Communication

OBJECTIVES

After reading this chapter, you should be able to:

- Frame a clear definition of nonverbal communication and provide examples to reveal its use.
- Explain the role of nonverbal communication in communicating effectively and achieving strategic flexibility.
- Point out differences between verbal and nonverbal communication and the way the brain processes the information from each.
- Describe and provide an example of the various types of nonverbal communication.
- Point out some of the ways culture influences nonverbal communication.
- Explain some of the ways you can become more aware of and improve your use of nonverbal communication.
- Describe the relationships among the Internet, social presence, media richness, and nonverbal communication.

Until the age of 27, Brian Lewis was overweight, unpopular, shy, and depressed. Two years ago he reached a point where he couldn't take it anymore. He started working out, changed his diet, and started talking to new people. After a year, he had reinvented himself as a 100-pound-lighter, in-shape, social, and confident individual.

Toward the end of Brian's transition, he met Angela. She was smart, pretty, athletic, and funny—someone he had never dreamed of even talking to when he was overweight. Angela accepted Brian for who he is and who he was. He wants to spend the rest of his life with her, and Angela feels the same. Angela gave Brian confidence and reinforced his commitment to continue dieting and exercising, but he credits his reinvention of himself to changes in his opportunities, beliefs about himself and others, personality, confidence, social poise, and views of his future.

Nonverbal communication is information communicated without using words. Much of it—like Brian's overweight, unpopular, shy, and depressed personality—is unintentional. People may not be aware they are sending some nonverbal messages. On the other hand, Brian knew that being overweight, unpopular, shy, and depressed conveyed negative stereotypes he did not like, and with a great deal of personal effort and commitment he set out to change them.

THE ROLE OF NONVERBAL COMMUNICATION IN COMMUNICATING EFFECTIVELY AND ACHIEVING STRATEGIC FLEXIBILITY

As much as 93 percent of communication is nonverbal,[1] with 55 percent sent through facial expressions, posture, and gestures and 38 percent through tone of voice.[2] It is essential to understand how nonverbal communication works and how you can communicate better when you use it.

Communicating Effectively

If you look closely at the communication model discussed in Chapter 1, you will *not* find nonverbal communication as one of the elements depicted there. It is however embedded in every element in the model. Think about it. The size or dress of the sender-receiver is information communicated without using words, just as the pace or loudness of the message or the frown on his or her face is feedback to your message. Information could include noise from others talking too loudly and too close to where you are, or it could be a desperate, clinging handshake—the use of touch as an additional channel—to reinforce the urgency of the meeting. It could be the setting, like a cafeteria, that tells you to moderate what you say so others cannot hear; or, finally, it could be the culture, which may dictate conversational decorum or language choices. Now, when you look at the model—see Figure 6-1—you can see information possibilities in every element.

There are four other things you can learn from Figure 6-1. First, nonverbal communication plays an important role in communicating effectively. Second, to be unaware of nonverbal communication is to miss a significant portion of what goes on in any communication situation. Third, as Figure 6-1 indicates, communication is complex; look at the number of factors you take into consideration—some more important or obvious than others—before, during, and after communicating. Fourth,

Figure 6-1

Information from the Elements in the Communication Model

- Culture
  - Values
  - Traditions
  - Social relationships
  - Political relationships
  - Worldview

- Setting
  - Proxemics (space)
  - Chronemics (time)
  - Environment (place)
  - Conditions
  - Technology

- Channel
  - Touch
  - Sight
  - Sound
  - Smell
  - Taste
  - Technology

- Message/feedback
  - Feelings
  - Paralanguage
  - Animation
  - Metamessages

- Noise
  - External
  - Internal
  - Semantic
  - Volume

- Sender/receiver
  - Credibility
  - Personality
  - Purpose
  - Attentiveness
  - Motivation
  - Emotion
  - Interest
  - Thoughts

All elements flow into the Sender-Receiver.

---

no two communications can ever be the same. There are so many elements and so many different ways to interpret them.

Strategic Flexibility

You are aware of all the nonverbal elements that are likely to affect any communication you have with others. Now, think about all the processing procedures that your brain engages in (your unique perceptual filter depicted in Figure 2-3 of Chapter 2) as it takes in all or some of these elements. You make use of them as you anticipate, assess, evaluate, select, apply, then reassess and reevaluate each communication.

If you are attentive to verbal and nonverbal elements, responsive to current usage, and respectful of differential usage, you will probably be able to move into any social setting in your own society. You will be perceptually fluent, rising to all the demands of both verbal and nonverbal communication. It is both language fluency and nonverbal awareness that are most likely to result in strategic flexibility. When you examine the number of nonverbal factors alone (see Figure 6-1), you quickly understand why some people are better communicators than others. They are not just aware of the elements, but they process them and then use them in the strategic flexibility framework. It isn't a mystery; such ability can be learned.

DIFFERENCES BETWEEN VERBAL AND NONVERBAL COMMUNICATION

Most differences between verbal and nonverbal communication are obvious; however, knowing the differences can help you emphasize the one with which you can be most effective. For example, if you want to make certain that your directions are understood, put your emphasis on verbal communication because it follows specific rules of structure and grammar, because words represent specific things like schools, factories, or stop signs, and because verbal communication has culture- and context-bound meanings. On the other hand, if you want to express your feelings to a spouse who has just lost a close friend, words may be insufficient: your spontaneous nonverbal signs of sorrow, hurt, and loss may be far more significant.

One of the most important distinctions between verbal and nonverbal communication is the way the brain processes the information. Verbal information is conveyed linearly, one word after another. In nonverbal communication, however, the brain creates a composite of all the signals given off by a new experience. It is "a holistic phenomenon," says Carlin Flora, "in which clues (mellifluous voice, Rolex watch, soggy handshake, hunched shoulders) hit us all at once and form an impression larger than their sum."[3]

CHARACTERISTICS OF NONVERBAL COMMUNICATION

All forms of nonverbal communication have five characteristics in common. First, much nonverbal communication is unique to the culture or co-culture to which you belong. Second, verbal and nonverbal messages may be in conflict with one another. Third, much nonverbal communication operates at a subconscious level—you are often not aware of it. Fourth, your nonverbal communication shows your feelings and attitudes. Fifth, nonverbal communication varies by gender.

Nonverbal Communication Is Culturally Determined

Your culture affects almost all your communication behaviors. For example, it governs how close you stand while talking with another person, how you use or avoid eye contact, and how you express or suppress powerful emotions such as joy, disapproval, and anger. Your culture determines whether you feel free to express your love of another in public settings by holding hands, hugging, or kissing—what has come to be known as public displays of affection (PDA).

Much nonverbal behavior is learned in childhood, passed on to you by your parents and others with whom you associate. A good deal of it is learned simply through imitation. Growing up in a particular society, you adopt the traits and mannerisms of your cultural group. In Japan bowing shows rank. Slouching is rude in most northern European areas. Putting your hands in your pocket is disrespectful in Turkey.

Your culture governs your body movement. It determines what moves, when it moves, and where it moves, and it imposes restrictions on that movement. For example, your hips may move in sports and dancing, but not in the services of some churches. Children can move their bodies freely in gym class but not in math.

Nonverbal Messages May Conflict with Verbal Messages

Nonverbal communication is so deeply rooted, so unconscious, that you can express a verbal message and directly contradict it with a nonverbal message. For example, Terrence Sejinowski, of the Salk Institute for Biological Studies in La Jolla, California, has developed a computer program that can detect lies by analyzing fleeting facial expressions.[4] The computer is trained to analyze in real time the almost imperceptible expressions like eyelid flutters and strained smiles—the same expressions it used to take Paul Ekman, a psychologist at the University of California–San Francisco, and his team of researchers hours to catalog. With the new computer program, people can be screened for lying without their even knowing it.[5]

Without computer assistance, most people can spot lies little better than half the time. In her study of lying, Maureen O'Sullivan, a University of San Francisco professor, found only 31 people of more than 13,000 who could do better. These so-called wizards read telltale signals such as fidgeting, pressing the lips together, raising the chin, moving the feet, and changing vocal pitch. Researchers warned, however, that such cues are not universal nor even always indicative of a lie.[6]

In **mixed messages** the verbal and the nonverbal contradict each other. The nonverbal communication is often more reliable than the verbal content. You can learn to manipulate words, but you might find it difficult to manipulate your nonverbal communication. You may not be aware of sending it; the message, however, comes through loud and clear.

View "Nonverbal Messages," clip #4, on the CD.

Nonverbal Messages Are Largely Unconscious

You wake up feeling that you might be getting a cold. It's not yet bad enough to stay home, so you go to classes. The minute one of your classmates sees you, she says, "You look like you aren't feeling very well." She is making a nonverbal assessment: You don't have to say a word for her to know how you're feeling.

When you consider the amount and ordinariness of your nonverbal behavior, it is hardly surprising that you are unaware of much of it.

Nonverbal Communication Shows Your Feelings and Attitudes

The feelings and emotions others can detect in your face include happiness, sadness, surprise, fear, anger, interest, contempt, shame, shyness, and guilt.[7] But research shows that other people are as accurate, if not better, at detecting emotions through vocal cues as through facial expression.[8] As a matter of fact, researchers Planalp and her associates have shown that vocal cues are the most recognizable signs of emotions.[9]

Your body is also quite capable of expressing emotions. In her report on communicating emotion in everyday life, Planalp reports that people easily interpret a person's emotional state from cues such as "being physically energetic, bouncy, jumping up and down, clenching hands or fists, making threatening movements, holding the body rigidly, shuffling, or having a slumped, droopy posture, dancing around, and using hand emblems."[10] If you wanted to demonstrate greater warmth and immediacy to another person, you might reveal a happy facial expression, enthusiastic gestures, closer interpersonal distances, and friendly touches.[11]

Nonverbal Communication Varies by Gender

Men and women use and interpret nonverbal communication differently. North American women not only initiate more eye contact during conversations than men, but they are more comfortable returning eye contact as well. Women maintain a gaze longer, but they are less likely than men to stare at someone—they break eye contact more frequently than men. This is not a contradiction; men are simply less likely to *make* the eye contact, but when they do, they often get "locked in" without realizing their eye contact is being returned.[12]

When surveyed, female students felt that they typically use more gestures than males.[13] Some authorities think women use fewer gestures with other women but more with men. Others think the difference is in the types of gestures used, not in their frequency of use. Although you will automatically return a smile if someone smiles at you first, experts agree that women smile more than men. It is also useful to point out that females are more attracted to others who smile.[14]

Although the experts agree that males use more personal space than females, when students were surveyed, 56 percent of the females felt they required more personal space than males.[15] In Edward T. Hall's book *The Hidden Dimension*, spatial zones are drawn closer for women than for men.[16] Hall notes that women tend to approach others more closely and seem to prefer side-by-side conversations. Men, on the other hand, prefer face-to-face conversations.

Men are more likely to initiate touch with others than are women. Women give and receive more touches than men except when initiating courtship and are more likely to associate touch with personal warmth and expressiveness. When students were surveyed, 57.8 percent of the females agreed that they touch others more than males do.[17] Touch is considered a feminine-appropriate behavior and a masculine-inappropriate one. Mothers touch female infants more than male infants, and female children tend to desire and offer more nonaggressive touch than male children.[18]

Which gender is likely to interpret nonverbal cues better? All experts agree on this one: females are better interpreters. When students were surveyed, 73.7 percent of the females agreed with the experts. There are two reasons for this. First, women tend to be more sensitive communicators. Second, women use a number of verbal and nonverbal channels to actively communicate to others the importance of relationships.

TYPES OF NONVERBAL COMMUNICATION

In this section, we will introduce paralanguage, body movement, eye messages, attractiveness, clothing, body adornment, space and distance, touch, smell, and time.

Paralanguage

Verbal communication consists of the words you use to communicate: nonverbal communication has a **paralanguage**—the way in which you say the words. Paralanguage, or paralinguistic cues, exists beside language and interacts with it. For example, a parent tells a child in a mild voice to clean up his room. When the room is still in the same condition two hours later, the parent says, "I thought I told you to clean up your room." This time the parent's voice communicates "If you don't do it soon, you're in big trouble."

One of the pioneers in the study of of nonverbal communication. Ray Birdwhistell shows how important paralanguage can be in its ability to modify everything that is said and place it into context:

> *These cross-referencing signals [paralanguage] amplify, emphasize, or modify the formal constructions, and/or make statements about the context of the message situation. In the latter instance, they help to define the context of the interaction by identifying the actor or his audience, and furthermore, they usually convey information about the larger context in which the interaction takes place.*[19]

An important aspect of paralanguage—and one noted in the quotation above when Birdwhistell says "by identifying the actor"—paralinguistic cues can create distinct impressions of you, the communicator. For example, what characterizes an attractive, influential voice? Researchers suggest that it is resonant and calm, less monotonous, lower pitched (especially for males), less regionally accented, less nasal, less shrill, and more relaxed.[20]

Albert Mehrabian estimates that 39 percent of the meaning in communication is affected by vocal cues—not the words themselves but the way they are said.[21] In languages other than English, this percentage may be even higher.

Rate

The **rate** (speed) at which one speaks can have an effect on the way a message is received.[22] Faster speakers are seen as more competent, credible, and intelligent.[23] But, they are also seen as less honest and trustworthy than slower speakers.[24]

Another aspect of rate is how one person will accommodate or adapt to another's rate. It's called **convergence.** Fast talkers slow down when interacting with slow talkers; slow talkers speed up when talking with fast talkers.[25] People who converge to another's rate are seen as more attractive and persuasive.[26]

Pitch

Pitch is the highness or lowness of the voice. Some people believe that high-pitched voices are not as pleasant as low-pitched voices. However, the same researchers who studied rate of speaking also found that speakers were judged more competent if they used a higher and varied pitch.[27] Lower pitches are more difficult to hear, and people who have low-pitched voices may be perceived as insecure or shy. Pitch can be changed, but it requires working with someone who has had professional training in voice modification.

Volume

The meaning of a message can also be affected by its **volume**—how loudly a person speaks. A loud voice is fine if it's appropriate to the speaker's purpose and is not used all the time. The same is true of a soft voice. Expert teachers know at what points to increase or decrease their volume when they want a class to be quiet.

Quality

The overall **quality** of a voice is made up of all the other vocal characteristics: tempo, resonance, rhythm, and articulation. Voice quality is important because researchers have found that people with attractive voices are seen as more youthful, more competent, and more honest. However, people with immature voices were seen as less competent and powerful but more honest and warm.[28]

Vocal Fillers

A related aspect of paralanguage but not part of it is **vocal fillers**—the sounds you use to fill out your sentences or to cover up or fill pauses. You use many vocal fillers to let others know you are still speaking even though you may not know specifically what to say. They may be nonwords such as *uh*, *um*, and *er*, or they may be words and phrases such as *you know*, *like*, or *whatever*, when used to fill a pause. Although fillers are sometimes words, they are used in these instances as if they have no meaning.

Body Movement

Body movement, also called *kinesics*, comes "from the Greek word for 'movement' and refers to all forms of body movement, excluding physical contact with another's body."[29] Researchers Ekman and Friesen, divide body movement into five categories: emblems, illustrators, regulators, displays of feelings, and adaptors.[30]

Emblems are body movements that directly translate into words. In western society the extended thumb of a hitchhiker is an emblem that means "I want a ride." A circle made with the thumb and index finger can be translated into "OK." Emblems often cannot be carried from one culture to another. Shaking your head back and forth in southern India, for example, means "yes."

Emblems are often used when words are inappropriate. It would be impractical for a hitchhiker to stand on the side of the road and shout, "Please give me a ride!" Sometimes emblems can replace talk. You might cover your face with your hands if you are embarrassed, and you hold up your fingers to show how many of something you want. Subgroups in a society often use emblems that members of the group understand but whose meanings are intentionally kept from outsiders—the secret handshake of a fraternity is an example.

Illustrators accent, emphasize, or reinforce words. If someone asks how big your suitcase is, you will probably describe it with words and illustrate the dimensions with your hands. Illustrators can go beyond gestures. When an instructor underlines something she has written on the board, she is telling you that this point is particularly important.

In her book *Executive Charisma*, Debra A. Benton clearly defines the role that posture plays as an illustrator. "Stand tall and straight summons up visions of someone ethical, courageous, awake, alert, and alive. Good posture," Benton says, "shows confidence, vitality, discipline, and youthfulness. Slumped posture," she adds, "implies fright, insecurity, lack of self-acceptance or self-control, lack of discipline, a loser, sheepishness, shame, and guilt. To stand tall and straight is to have a demeanor that says, 'I expect acceptance.' "[31]

Regulators control the back-and-forth flow of speaking and listening. "They are the 'traffic cops' of conversation."[32] They are made up of hand gestures, shifts in posture, and other body movements that signal the beginning and end of interactions. At a very simple level, a teacher uses a regulator when she points to the person she wants to speak next. On a more subtle level, someone might turn away slightly when you are talking, perhaps indicating "I don't want to continue this conversation."

Displays of feelings show, through facial expressions and body movements, how intensely a person is feeling. If you walk into a professor's office and the professor says, "I can see you are really feeling upset," he or she is responding to nonverbal cues you are giving about your feelings. You could also come in with a body posture indicating

"I'm really going to argue about this grade"—with your clenched hands or stiff body position showing that you are ready for a confrontation.

Displays of feelings vary in different cultures. For example, many Asian cultures suppress facial expression as much as possible. Mediterranean (Latino/Latina and Arabic) cultures freely express grief or sadness while most American men hide grief or sorrow. Some people see animated expressions as a lack of control. Too much smiling is sometimes viewed as a sign of shallowness.

Adaptors are nonverbal ways of adjusting to a communication situation. They are behaviors that satisfy your physical or psychological needs. What do you do when you feel anxious, relaxed, crowded, or defensive? In general, adaptors are habits and are usually not intended to communicate.[33] However, often they convey a great deal of information.

Because people use such a wide variety of adaptors, and because they are so specific to each person's own needs and the individual communication situation, they are difficult to classify or even to describe generally.

For example, some people use adaptors when they are nervous or uncomfortable in a situation. You might play with jewelry, drum on the table, or move around a lot in your seat. Each of these behaviors is an adaptor—a way of helping you cope with the situation. We all use adaptors, but we are generally not aware of them unless someone points them out.

Eye Messages

Eye messages include all information conveyed by the eyes alone. The most important aspect of eye messages is eye contact, and in American culture, meeting another's eyes is a sign of honesty and credibility as well as warmth and involvement. In many cultures, conversing without eye contact can indicate disinterest, inattention, rudeness, shyness, or deception.[34]

When you think about the functions that eye messages can perform, you quickly realize their importance. Eye messages provide turn-taking signals in conversations that regulate interactions. They indicate attentiveness, involvement, immediacy, and connection to others. Prolonged stares, especially with negative facial expressions, can be intimidating. But one of their most delightful and wondrous aspects is their role in flirtation.[35]

Although eye messages have received marginal attention by intercultural scholars,[36] an African proverb says. "The eye is an instrument of aggression."[37] Many Asians and Pacific Islanders would agree. In their countries young people never make eye contact with their elders. In most African countries and many other parts of the world, if a person has more status than you, you should not look him or her in the eye.

Attractiveness

What is attractive to you? **Attractiveness** is having the power or quality of drawing, pleasing, or winning.[38] The importance of physical beauty to males is universal; men in all cultures around the world prefer young, nubile (of suitable age to marry) women. More than that, however, men prefer having a physically attractive mate because it is a sign of status.[39] Females, on the other hand, select men with sufficient resources to care for them and have stronger preferences for intelligent, considerate, and outgoing mates. Like men of all cultures, women are attracted to wealth, power, and status.[40]

Psychologists Sara Gutierres and Douglas Kenrick of Arizona State University have demonstrated that context counts. If you first see a highly attractive person, then you see a person of average attractiveness of the same sex, the average person seems a lot less attractive than he or she actually is. The reverse of this is also true: People of average attractiveness will seem more attractive than they are if they enter a room full of unattractive people of the same sex.[41]

Physical characteristics you can control are called **elective characteristics** and include clothing, makeup, tattoos, and body piercing. **Nonelective characteristics,** things you cannot change, are height, body proportion, coloring, bone structure, and physical disabilities. Many of the nonelective traits influence how you see the world. A six-foot woman, for example, would see life quite differently from her five-foot sister.[42]

There are some obvious benefits of attractiveness. People perceived as beautiful or handsome generally make more money and get more promotions. On the other hand, overweight and obese people face obstacles to fair pay and promotions. A study co-authored by Dan Cable, an associate professor at the University of North Carolina–Chapel Hill's Kenan-Flagler Business School, and Timothy Judge of the University of Florida has demonstrated that the taller you are, the more money you earn. The researchers controlled for gender, weight, and age and found that height was closely related to incomes in all kinds of professions. They showed, too, that each inch of height is worth an astonishing $789 more a year—six inches of height will net you $4,734 in annual income. Tall people get more of everything: notice, positive evaluations, promotions, and attention from the opposite sex. More than anything, these findings reveal our society's biases with respect to weight and height and how appearances rule over brains.[43]

Clothing

Because clothing gives such a strong and immediate impression of its wearer, it is enormously important to nonverbal communication. Besides communicating, however, clothing may serve as protection; communicate sexual attraction, self-assertion, self-denial, concealment, or group identification; and provide indications of status and role.[44] In addition, think of how much information you can gain from a person's clothing: sex, age, nationality, relation to opposite sex, socioeconomic status, group

Clothing projects a message; by choosing particular clothing, wearers commit themselves to the statements clothing makes.

and occupational identification, mood, personality, attitudes, interests, and values.[45] In his book *You Are What You Wear,* William Thourlby suggests that people make 10 decisions about others based on clothing: (1) Economic level, (2) Educational level, (3) Trustworthiness, (4) Social position, (5) Level of sophistication, (6) Economic background, (7) Social background, (8) Educational background, (9) Level of success, and (10) Moral character.[46]

Even though people may appear to dress in similar ways, they don't always see themselves as similar. An Amish woman points out that although Amish women wear dark clothes that cover the body, they are still aware of style. She writes: "Every culture has its own fashion expectations and requirements, and my people are no exception. They are concerned about how they look. They do not all wear black. They have individual color and style preferences. They enjoy shopping. And they talk about styles and fashions among themselves. . . . To these women, high and proper fashion means busy sewing machines, solid-colored, store-bought fabrics, and patterns passed down from generation to generation."[47]

Clothing falls into four categories: uniforms, occupational dress, leisure clothing, and costumes. Each conveys a different nonverbal meaning.

Uniforms identify wearers with particular organizations. They are the most specialized form of clothing. There is little freedom of choice in a uniform. Its wearers are told when to wear it (daytime, summer) and what they can and cannot wear with it (jewelry, medals, hairstyles).

By showing rank, military uniforms tell what positions the wearers hold in the hierarchy and what their relationships are to others in the organization. The uniform also implies that its wearer will follow certain norms.[48]

Occupational dress is clothing that employees are expected to wear, but it is not as precise as a uniform. It is designed to present a specific image of the employes.[49] Unlike wearers of uniforms, employees who wear occupational dress have choices. Flight attendants are required to wear specific pieces of clothing, but they can mix items and accessories to their own preferences. What teachers wear affects student perceptions. In a study of teaching assistants, researchers found that those who dressed the most informally were viewed the most positively by students. In this case, informal dress was faded jeans, T-shirts, and flannel shirts.[50]

Leisure clothing is worn when work is over. Because this kind of clothing is chosen by the individual, some people assert their personal identities through it.[51] However, not everyone sees styles of leisure wear as a choice. Many teenagers will wear only a particular brand of jeans because when their group agrees on a brand, everyone wears it. The mass media have had such a great influence on leisure clothing that it's hard to separate media influence from individual preference.

Costumes are a form of highly individualized dress. By putting on a costume like cowboy boots, bandanna, and hat, the wearer announces, "This is who I want to be." Costumes not only require thought regarding the image they convey but also go against many norms. As one student shrewdly observed as he changed his shoes for a job interview at a supermarket in the Northeast, "I better not wear my cowboy boots. They look too aggressive."

Body Adornment

Body adornment includes any addition to the physical body designed to beautify or decorate. Throughout the world people have found ways of changing the body they were born with. Americans are no exception. Hairstyles, facial hair, and makeup undergo

Another Point of View

In this excerpt the importance of a single piece of clothing, the *hijab*, is described by Maryam Qudrat Aseel—a first-generation Afghan American girl, born and raised in Los Angeles—in her book *Torn Between Two Cultures*. The *hijab* is a simple head scarf—a small piece of fabric—for the hair, and it is "one element of being a true Muslim, and specifically a true Muslim woman" (p. 78). When Aseel wore the Muslim woman's head scarf, people automatically assumed she was some sort of fundamentalist, a terrorist, or a zealot preaching religion (p. 83). It is hard to believe how important a single nonverbal element could be, but here Aseel describes it:

> On the day of my high school graduation, after three years of being looked upon as an outcast and deviant by both American and Afghan societies, I finally took off my hijab, which had caused so much contempt. I simply couldn't handle the scrutiny of my personal life. Even more ridiculous than being treated as a lesser human being because of my physical traits [deep tan skin, bold green eyes, full lips, and strong bone structure] I was being treated that way because of my clothes. And people had somehow assigned me the position of representing the entire religion of Islam. If I were to do one thing wrong or make one human mistake, I would not pay for it alone—so would Islam. If I so much as wore some lip gloss, I would be met with the attitude of "See, and she is supposed to be so religious—they're all just a bunch of hypocrites."

Source: From *Torn Between Two Cultures: An Afghan-American Woman Speaks Out* (p. 82), by Maryam Qudrat Aseel, 2003, Sterling, VA: Capital Books.

Questions

1. Do you expect a person who wears the symbol or uniform of a particular group to represent every other member of that group? Why or why not?
2. Do you expect a leader like a teacher, principal, or guidance counselor to follow a special code of conduct? Why or why not? Can you think of others expected to follow specific codes of conduct?
3. Have you been stereotyped by others because of your appearance or clothes? Do you think these stereotypes are fair? Why or why not?

---

conservative changes that are widely accepted. In fact, it's hard to believe that only about 100 years ago people were shocked when women used makeup and cut their hair short, or, more recently, when men began to wear earrings.

Space and Distance

The study of **space and distance,** called **proxemics,** examines the way people use the space around them as well as the distance they maintain from others. The minute you enter a classroom, you have to decide where to sit. As you can see in Figure 6-2, your choice depends on how much interaction you want to have with the instructor: If you are in the "action zone," you may be indicating that you want to participate in the class.

Territory is the space that a person considers as belonging to him or her—either temporarily or permanently. For example, you would probably be upset if you came into the classroom and found someone sitting in "your" chair.

Sometimes people unwittingly send out a mixed message about their space. Four students who rented a church that had been converted to student housing with four sleeping lofts found that they had little control over their space. Other students dropped in night and day—probably because the building looked more like a public than a private space. The minute their lease ended, they moved into more traditional housing.

Every culture has rules—usually informal—about the use of space and distance. Edward T. Hall, author of two classic books on nonverbal communication, discovered that North Americans use four distance zones when they are communicating with others: intimate distance, personal distance, social distance, and public distance.[52]

Figure 6-2

A Traditional Classroom Arrangement

In such an arrangement, those students occupying the blue seats will account for a large proportion of the total interaction that occurs between teachers and students. Those in the green seats will interact some; those in the white seats will interact very infrequently. The area enclosed in dotted lines has been called the "action zone."

Intimate distance, a range of less than 18 inches apart, places people in direct contact with each other. Look at a parent holding a baby. All our senses are alert when we are this close to someone. The parent can touch the baby, smell him, and hear every little gurgle he makes. People also maintain an intimate distance in love relationships and with close friends. Intimate distance exists whenever you feel free to touch the other person with your whole body.

When your intimate distance is violated by people who have no right to be so close, you feel apprehensive. If you are on a crowded bus, subway, or elevator and people are pressed against you, they are in your intimate distance. By not making eye contact you can protect your intimate distance psychologically, if not physically.

Personal distance, from 18 inches to 4 feet, is the distance you maintain from another person when you are engaged in casual and personal conversations. It is close enough to see the other person's reactions but far enough away not to encroach on intimate distance.

Social distance, from 4 to 12 feet, is the distance you are most likely to maintain when you do not know people very well. Impersonal business, social gatherings, and interviews are examples of situations where you use social distance and interaction becomes more formal.

Public distance, a distance of more than 12 feet, is typically used for public speaking. At this distance, people speak more loudly and use more exaggerated gestures. Communication is even more formal and permits few opportunities for people to be involved with each other.

Figure 6-3 shows the dimensions of the four distance zones. There are wide variations among cultures in the way people handle space and distance in relationships. When visiting another culture, you (as an American) would probably try to keep your "normal" distance between yourself and someone else—a large zone. Your behavior is typical of northern European communities, Scandinavian countries, and Great Britain but could appear "standoffish" in other cultures like Saudi Arabia, Latin America, Italy, France, and Spain, as well as other Middle Eastern countries. People there tend to keep a much closer distance—a small zone. You might view their maintaining nose-to-nose distance as "pushy" simply because their social space equates to our intimate space. You might find yourself backing away trying to regain your social space while an Arab would be pursuing you across the floor trying to maintain his. If you were visiting a friend in the Netherlands, on the other hand, your roles would be reversed. Their personal space equates to our social space; thus, to maintain your normal distance, you would continue trying to get closer to your friend.

Touch

The closer you stand to someone, the more you increase the likelihood of touching. **Touch** is to be in or come into physical contact with another person, and the study of touch is called **haptics.** You are familiar with the use of touch in intimate situations: You kiss babies, hold hands with loved ones, and hug family members. Touch "is a key component in growing, learning, communicating, and living."[53] The importance of

Figure 6-3
The Four Distance Zones

- 12 – 25'
- 4 – 12'
- 1.5 – 4'
- 0 – 1.5'
- Self
- Intimate
- Personal
- Social
- Public

The distance people keep from other people is determined both by culture and occasion. The people in the left picture are Americans waiting in line at an airport. Those in the right picture are Chinese.

touch for babies was shown in a study of premature babies. For them to thrive, they had to be touched, releasing brain chemicals that promote growth. Premature infants who were massaged three times a day for 15 minutes gained weight 47 percent faster than those who were left alone in their incubators and later did much better on tests of mental ability and motor ability.[54]

When and where people touch one another is governed by a strict set of societal rules. Richard Heslin has described five different categories of touch behavior.[55] The first is *functional-professional touch*, in which you are touched for a specific reason, as in a physical examination by a doctor or nurse. This kind of touch is impersonal and businesslike. *Social-polite touch* is used to acknowledge someone else. The handshake is the most common form. Although two people move into an intimate distance to shake hands, they move away from each other when the handshake is over. In close relationships people use the *friendship-warmth touch*. This kind of touch involves hugs and casual kisses between friends. Touching is one way to communicate liking.[56] In more intense relationships the *love-intimacy touch* is common. Parents stroke their children; lovers and spouses kiss and fondle each other. The final touch Heslin describes is *sexual arousal touch*—touch used as an expression of physical attraction.[57]

Touch can quickly become a violation when it is unexpected or out of the message context. The improper touching of children is an obvious violation, and the most serious violation of touch, of course, is in assault and battery.[58] Inappropriate touch is discussed in the following "Consider This" box.

Smell

The study of smell is called **olfactics.** The sense of smell has long remained one of the most baffling of our senses. Richard Axel of the Howard Hughes Medical Institute at Columbia University and Linda Buck of the Fred Hutchinson Cancer Research Center in Seattle split the 2004 Nobel Prize in medicine for discovering how people discern individual odors.

Consider This

There is much uncertainty about appropriate and inappropriate touch, but much of the uncertainty can be dealt with if some general guidelines are followed. Over time, courts will decide cases, and with respect to sexual harassment especially, a clear list of DOs and DON'Ts will emerge. Until then, however, guidelines—along with the common sense and decency of those involved—offer general parameters of acceptability.

- **Consider the context.** The totality of circumstances always must be considered. This includes the frequency and severity of the offending conduct as well as whether it is physically threatening or humiliating. In addition, whether it occurs in a public situation with other people around or in a private, isolated setting makes a significant difference.
- **Be mindful of the role that perception plays.** With respect to whether any behavior (touch included) is appropriate or offensive, it is always assessed only from the perspective of the recipient, not from the perspective of the alleged harasser. The intentions of the alleged harasser are irrelevant; no excuse is legitimate.
- **Know that unwelcome conduct is unacceptable.** For example, uninvited physical contact such as touching, hugging, patting, or pinching is inappropriate. In addition, repeated offensive sexual flirtations, advances, or propositions, displays of sexually suggestive objects or pictures, or sexually related jokes or remarks are improper. Verbal abuse or innuendo of a sexual nature, comments of a sexual nature about an individual's body, prolonged staring or leering, and obscene gestures or suggestive or insulting sounds are included.
- **Think before behaving.** Is the behavior I am about to engage in unwelcome? Is it of a sexual nature? Is it reciprocal or unilateral? Would a reasonable man or woman, under similar circumstances, react or be affected by such behavior? Are you being sensitive to the reactions of others? Are you honoring the other's request to avoid any behavior or discussion that is offensive or embarrassing? If you are a male, would you behave this way toward your mother or daughter?

Questions

1. What is the problem with any given set of rules or guidelines designed to govern, regulate, or control human conduct? What are the circumstances that cause rules to be broken, or guidelines to be ignored? What are some things that can be put into place that would furnish barriers, or hindrances, to rule breaking?
2. What should you do if you felt you had been subjected to inappropriate behavior? (One important point would be not to reciprocate in any way.)
3. Can you see that when it comes to appropriate or inappropriate behavior, that it can have very different meanings? Can you cite any examples?

Much of your sense of taste depends on your sense of smell. Thus, when you hold your nose or have a cold with stuffy nose, you lose much of the flavor of the food you eat. Odor preferences vary around the world, depending on cultural and genetic variations. If you are constantly or repeatedly exposed to an odor, your ability to perceive it will usually decline. This is called adaptation. About 85 percent of people have a childhood memory linked to a particular aroma, and the aroma most commonly mentioned is the fragrance of fresh baked goods.[59]

Time

The study of time is called **chronemics.** To say that time is very important in American culture is a huge understatement; we are obsessed with time. Our daily life is infused with a sense of urgency driven by the desire to beat the clock. Burgoon, Buller, and Woodall write, "Time is seen as a precious resource, a valuable and tangible commodity. We spend time, save it, make it, fill it, and waste it. It is seen almost as a container with defined boundaries. . . . The way we schedule events also reflects the urgent and precise way we deal with time. We expect classes to start on time (within a minute or so), and when they don't we wait only so long (20 minutes at the most) before leaving."[60]

You can use time for psychological effect. The student who is always late may be communicating considerable negative information. He is really not interested in this class or doesn't respect the instructor. You will probably not arrive too early for a date or party because this might make you appear too eager. If you dent the family car, you might wait for the right time to tell your parents about it. Your control of time, then, is an important form of nonverbal communication. The higher your status, the more control you have over your time. A parent can interrupt children's play to have them eat dinner or to make them go to bed far earlier than they want. Professionals in our society often make others wait for them.

Time differs greatly from one culture to another. Figure 6-4 shows what people in the United States regard as fashionably late, but suppose you were invited to a party in Venezuela, and the host said it would begin about 8 P.M. If you arrived at that time, you would be the only one there—the Venezuelans wouldn't arrive until 9 or 10 P.M. When interacting with people from different cultures, simply assume that their sense of time is different from yours.

FUNCTIONS OF NONVERBAL COMMUNICATION

Nonverbal communication has four functions. Nonverbal cues **complement** a verbal message by adding to its meaning. When you are talking to someone with a problem, for example, you might say, "I'm really sorry," and complement the message with a pat on the shoulder or a hug.

Nonverbal cues also **regulate** verbal communication. How would your boss or one of your teachers tell you that it's time for a meeting to end? He or she might do something obvious, like getting out of the chair, or something more subtle, like arranging papers on the desk, to communicate to you that the conversation is over.

Nonverbal messages can also **substitute** for verbal messages. Your instructor looks up, stares specifically at a couple of class members who are talking, then waits a couple

Figure 6-4
What Is Fashionably Late in the United States?

- One hour or more: 8%
- 21–59 minutes: 33%
- 11–20 minutes: 16%
- Less than 10 minutes: 27%
- Shouldn't be late: 1%

of seconds until everyone is quiet before she begins to speak. Her look says, "All right, everyone be quiet now. It's time to begin."

Often, nonverbal messages **accent** what you are saying. The instructor's voice is strong and firm when she tells the class she will accept no late papers; the teenager leans forward while she is trying to persuade her parents that she needs a new dress.

The key to controlling and thus improving your nonverbal communication is self-awareness. When you are fully aware of the signals you send, you have a greater opportunity not just for controlling them but for evaluating them as well. When you notice you are sending signals that aren't what you intend, you can either suppress them or change them. It is like using strategic flexibility on a personal—or intrapersonal—level or taking **control** of your life and your behavior.

One way to begin controlling your nonverbal communication is to control your emotions. Emotions often arise spontaneously and quickly—and produce subconscious (or unconscious) responses. But when you are aware of your emotions, you can begin to produce a counterresponse to mask, control, or subdue your actual reaction. For example, when someone asks you at the last minute how he or she looks, rather than express your surprise at what you consider to be an outrageous outfit, you mask your reaction.

Because you produce your emotions, you can control them. Once you are thinking rather than allowing your behavior to be at the mercy of your spontaneous feelings, you can better evaluate situations and consciously provide the responses you consider to be most appropriate.

STRATEGIC FLEXIBILITY

Thinking before acting (or emoting) is the basis for effective strategic flexibility because it requires thinking to anticipate, assess, evaluate, select, and properly apply your skills and behaviors. It is more likely that your strategies will be effective if you can control your initial emotional responses.

IMPROVING YOUR NONVERBAL COMMUNICATION

Below are some questions to ask about your nonverbal communication.

View "Nonverbal Messages," clip #4, on the CD.

How Do People React to You?

Do people ever react to you in a way that surprises you? You may be sending nonverbal messages that are being interpreted differently from the way you intended. For example, you may intend to tease someone but instead hurt his or her feelings. If you see that the person looks upset, you have a chance to explain what you really meant.

Can Videotapes Help Your Nonverbal Communication?

Videotape can tell you a great deal about behaviors you were not aware of and even some that you want to get rid of. Here are just a few items that you might look for when you see your tape.[61]

Eye contact. Since eye contact signals interest in others, increases credibility, and opens the flow of communication by conveying interest, concern, and warmth, make certain yours is comfortable and natural, but direct.

Facial expressions. Your face transmits happiness, friendliness, warmth, liking, and affiliation; thus, it pays to smile frequently. By smiling you will be perceived as more likable, friendly, warm, and approachable.

Gestures. Being lively and animated captures others' attention, makes your information more interesting, and provides conversational positive reinforcement.

Posture and body orientation. Posture and body orientation includes the way you walk, talk, stand, and sit. By standing erect, but not rigid, and by leaning slightly forward, you will communicate that you are approachable, receptive, and friendly.

Proximity. Cultural norms dictate the distances you need to stand for interacting with others. By increasing your proximity to others when in conversation, but not excessively, you not only make better eye contact, but you become more sensitive to the feedback of others.

Paralinguistics. You need to modulate your voice by changing such features as tone, pitch, rhythm, timbre, loudness, and inflection. Make sure you don't use a dull or boring voice.

Humor. When you reveal a willingness to laugh, you foster an inviting, warm, and friendly conversational environment. Laughter also releases stress and tension.

Is Your Nonverbal Communication Appropriate to the Role You Are Playing?

Like your language, your nonverbal communication should change as you play different roles. Observe other people in their roles. How much of their communication is nonverbal? What kind of nonverbal communication does a good teacher show? Who don't you want to be like? Is it their nonverbal behavior that turns you off? Do you do any of the same things? Can you stop doing them?

How Do You Use Your Space?

What messages are you sending out through the posters on your walls? Through the cuddly animals on your dresser? How tidy is your space? How much space do you occupy? Are you a sprawler; or do you keep your arms close to your body and your legs together? Are you conscious of certain space as "belonging" to you? Is it important that you have some spaces that you can call your own? What does the way you regard space tell others about you?

How Do You Use Time?

Are you on time or always late? Are you a procrastinator, leaving everything until the last minute?

If your use of time creates a bad impression, is it possible for you to change your ways?

When you look at all the things you communicate about yourself nonverbally, you will see that you should give nonverbal communication attention and care. Although nonverbal behavior is difficult to change, it can be done, especially if you are aware of how you use it.

THE INTERNET AND NONVERBAL COMMUNICATION

When you compare face-to face communication with computer-mediated communication (CMC)—with its lack of visual and other nonverbal cues—CMC is extremely low in social presence. **Social presence** is the ability of CMC users to project themselves socially and affectively (with feeling) into a communication event. When you interact with someone else on the Internet, the degree of intimacy and immediacy you perceive with that person or the degree to which you perceive the person to be real determines your level of social presence.

Closely related to social presence is a concept called **media richness**—how much information is carried by a media source. Lean media carry the least amount of information while rich media carry the most. In an online article on media richness, Brian Newberry ranked seven different media types into a hierarchy from richest to leanest. The hierarchy also reveals the degree of social presence likely in each medium—with the most social presence represented at the top of the list and the least at the bottom:

1. Face-to-face
2. Video conferencing
3. Synchronous audio (as in instant messaging)
4. Text-based chat
5. E-mail and asynchronous audio
6. Threaded discussion (as in bulletin boards, usenet newsgroups, mailing lists, Web conferencing, and Web forums)[62]

Forms that are media rich and that represent high levels of social presence include a greater degree and a wider variety of nonverbal cues. Synchronous forms (where interaction is immediate) tend to include more nonverbal cues than asynchronous forms (where interaction is delayed). "Synchronous by its very nature," says Newberry, "requires that all communicating parties be available and attending to the communication activity at the same time."[63]

Such a ranking does not suggest that one form is better than another. Each form has its own advantages and disadvantages and any one is likely to be more appropriate in certain situations than another. Faced with the question of which to choose, you need to consider both efficiency and the best opportunity for the intended message to be conveyed accurately. As Newberry notes, the choice depends on "technology availability, time constraints, familiarity with the technology, task appropriateness of the technology and desired outcomes of the . . . activity."[64]

The choice of form can directly affect the parties' perception, appreciation, participation, or level of satisfaction. Think about the difference between terminating a relationship with another person via e-mail instead of face-to-face, or learning something about your success on an assignment via an instructor's Web site instead of hearing it face-to-face from the instructor. "Environments where participants do not feel they are recognized as individuals, or in which their input does not seem to be valued, may result in a reduced motivation to participate," says Newberry.[65]

Assess Yourself

Are You Aware of Nonverbal Communication?

How nonverbally aware are you? For each statement circle the numerical score that best represents your nonverbal awareness using the following scale: 7 = Outstanding; 6 = Excellent; 5 = Very good; 4 = Average (good); 3 = Fair; 2 = Poor; 1 = Minimal ability; 0 = No ability demonstrated.

1.	I look others directly in the eye when communicating with them.	7 6 5 4 3 2 1 0
2.	I gesture with my hands and arms when communicating.	7 6 5 4 3 2 1 0
3.	I turn my body fully toward the person with whom I am speaking.	7 6 5 4 3 2 1 0
4.	I use a pleasant, appropriate tone of voice when speaking to others.	7 6 5 4 3 2 1 0
5.	I use a vocal volume that is appropriate when speaking to others.	7 6 5 4 3 2 1 0
6.	When listening to others, I notice and respond to their nonverbal responses to me—their vocal tone, eye contact, facial expressions, posture, gestures, and body movement.	7 6 5 4 3 2 1 0
7.	When listening to others, I am quiet when they are talking and allow them to express their ideas without interruption.	7 6 5 4 3 2 1 0
8.	When listening to another person, I smile when the person uses humor, and I nod at appropriate times.	7 6 5 4 3 2 1 0
9.	When listening to another person, I reveal my full support and attention through my nonverbal cues.	7 6 5 4 3 2 1 0
10.	I feel the nonverbal cues I use when speaking, and those I use in responding to others when they are speaking, reveal my comfort, poise, and confidence as an effective communicator.	7 6 5 4 3 2 1 0

TOTAL POINTS: _____

Go to the *Communicating Effectively* CD-ROM and the Online Learning Center at **www.mhhe.com/hybels8** to see your results and learn how to evaluate your attitudes and feelings.

mhhe.com/hybels8

One area where nonverbal cues are important in day-to-day communication is determining credibility. Although we can never be certain about the truth or validity of any communication, with the lack of nonverbal cues in CMC, the truth of claims made on the Internet cannot easily be determined and credibility is instead established in small increments. In their book *Rules of the Net*, Thomas Mandel and Gerard Van der Leun state, "If you show over time that you are someone whose opinions, demeanor, and attitude are worth taking seriously, more people will endow you with their attention."[66]

CHAPTER REVIEW

SUMMARY

Nonverbal communication is information that is communicated without using words. There are nonverbal elements embedded in every element in the communication model. Your degree of fluency in your native language and your level of awareness of nonverbal components are likely to result in greater strategic flexibility.

You send more messages through nonverbal communication than you do through verbal communication, and although they often reinforce each other, there are numerous differences between them. One clear difference is in the way the brain processes the information. In the nonverbal realm, it is a holistic phenomenon in which clues hit you all at once, and you form an impression larger than their sum.

There are five characteristics of nonverbal communication: It is unique to the culture or co-culture to which you belong; verbal and nonverbal communication may be in conflict with one another; much nonverbal communication operates at a subconscious level; your nonverbal communication shows your feelings and attitudes; and nonverbal communication varies by gender.

There are many different types of nonverbal communication. They include paralanguage, body movement, eye messages, attractiveness (which includes body image as well as elective and nonelective characteristics), clothing, body adornment, space and distance, touch, time, and smell. In each case, there are cultural and co-cultural variations in what is acceptable and unacceptable practice.

Nonverbal communication serves important functions. It can complement, regulate, substitute for, or accent a verbal message. The key to controlling your nonverbal communication is self-awareness. One way to begin controlling it is to control your emotions. What you need to do is think before you express your feelings.

One way of evaluating your nonverbal communication is to ask some questions about how you use it: How do people react to you? Can you use videotapes to improve your nonverbal communication? How do you use your space? How do you use time? The answers to these questions will indicate areas in which you can improve.

Communication using most forms of the Internet tend to be low in social presence and lean with respect to media richness. High social presence and media richness are best represented in face-to-face communication. Video conferencing is next, followed by synchronous audio (as in instant messaging), then text-based chat, e-mail, and asynchronous audio, and finally threaded discussion such as bulletin boards, usenet groups, mailing lists, and Web forums.

KEY TERMS AND CONCEPTS

Use the *Communicating Effectively* CD-ROM and the Online Learning Center at www.mhhe.com/hybels8 to further your understanding of the following terms.

Accent 148
Adaptors 139
Attractiveness 139
Body adornment 141
Body movement (kinesics) 138
Chronemics 146
Complement 147
Control 148
Convergence 137
Costumes 141
Displays of feelings 138
Elective characteristics 140
Emblems 138
Eye messages 139

Haptics 144
Illustrators 138
Intimate distance 143
Leisure clothing 141
Media richness 150
Mixed message 135
Nonelective characteristics 140
Nonverbal communication 132
Occupational dress 141
Olfactics 145
Paralanguage 136
Personal distance 143
Pitch 137
Proxemics 142

Public distance 144
Quality (of voice) 137
Rate (of speech) 137
Regulate 147
Regulators 138
Social distance 143
Social presence 149
Space and distance 142
Substitute 147
Territory 142
Touch 144
Uniforms 141
Vocal fillers 138
Volume (of vocal sound) 137

CHAPTER REVIEW

QUESTIONS TO REVIEW

1. What are some of the nonverbal components in each of the elements of the model of communication?
2. In what ways does nonverbal communication contribute to your ability to be strategically flexible?
3. In what ways do verbal and nonverbal communication differ, and of what value is knowing these differences?
4. What are the basic principles that govern nonverbal communication?
5. What is it called when verbal and nonverbal messages conflict? Give an example of this.
6. What are the different types of nonverbal communication, and what is an example of each type that clearly distinguishes it as the type it is designed to reveal?
7. What is paralanguage? What are the vocal qualities that contribute to paralanguage?
8. Can you give an example of nonverbal communication in each of the following body movements: Emblems? Illustrators? Regulators? Displays of feeling? Adaptors?
9. What does clothing communicate about you? How do the following kinds of clothing differ: Uniforms? Occupational dress? Leisure clothing? Costumes?
10. What is the study of space and distance called? What are the four distance zones, and how do they differ?
11. What are the five different categories of touch behavior? Give an example of each.
12. How does the process of smelling occur?
13. Can you give an example of how one's use of time communicates status? How does the use of time differ from culture to culture?
14. What are the functions of nonverbal communication, and how does each one relate to verbal communication?
15. In what ways does one's culture influence his or her nonverbal communication?
16. What ways do you have to control your nonverbal communication?
17. How would you go about improving your nonverbal communication?
18. In using the Internet, what ways do you have to increase your social presence, and what means would you use if you chose an approach designed to increase media richness?

Go to the self-quizzes on the *Communicating Effectively* CD-ROM and the Online Learning Center at www.mhhe.com/hybels8 to test your knowledge of the chapter contents.

CHAPTER 7

Interpersonal Relationships

OBJECTIVES

After reading this chapter, you should be able to:

- Define *interpersonal communication*.
- Explain emotional intelligence and its importance to strategic flexibility.
- Define and explain *interpersonal needs*.
- Discuss how roles influence interpersonal communication.
- Explain how bids contribute to relationship development and some ways to encourage them.
- Define *self-disclosure*, and tell why it is important.
- Describe the four panes of the Johari Window.
- Describe the effect of the Internet on interpersonal relationships.

LESLIE STEVENS' ONLINE DATING SERVICE HAD HER RATE HERSELF AND HER potential mate in categories ranging from sex drive to "socialistic-butterflyosity." An algorithm then calculated her compatibility with a list of matches. Leslie wanted a vegetarian boyfriend who played piano and liked folk music, and she discovered the exact match in Cody Moore—he lived in a dorm on her campus as well. Leslie began sending Cody online messages, and the next thing they knew they were having lunch together and hanging out in real life. Stevens said, "The chances of meeting Moore without the help of an online community were pretty-much nil."

Online dating services have changed the way the college crowd interacts. Instead of getting to know classmates over coffee or through mutual friends, students can now access a goldmine of information about their peers—and potential mates—online.

Interaction with others is called **interpersonal communication**, and it occurs whenever one person interacts with another—usually in an informal setting. You cannot survive in society without interpersonal communication skills. They enable you to function socially and to maintain relationships important to you.

According to Clyde Lindley, Director of the Center for Psychological Services, Silver Springs, Maryland, "Much research shows the importance of interpersonal relationships to well-being, happiness, and satisfaction with life."[1] One study showed that lack of contact with others doubles the chance of getting sick or dying.[2] In a study of college roommates, the researchers discovered that the more roommates disliked each other, the more likely they were to go to the doctor and to come down with colds and the flu. Isolation has more impact on men than on women. Men without close social ties are two to three times more likely to die earlier than men who have them.[3]

This chapter begins by examining the big picture—how you understand and get along with others, who are you attracted to and why—and then discusses the specifics in the next two sections: talking to each other and self-disclosure. The final sections examine the essential elements of good relationships and the Internet's effect on interpersonal relationships.

EMOTIONAL INTELLIGENCE

Anyone who has taught long enough to see students mature can tell you of some who were smart in the classroom but never went anywhere and others who did not do particularly well in school but went on to have successful careers and relationships. Their success is due to what Daniel Goleman calls "emotional intelligence."[4] At its simplest level **emotional intelligence** is the ability to understand and get along with others. Goleman and other researchers see this kind of intelligence as made up of five characteristics: being self-aware, managing emotions, motivating yourself, recognizing emotions in others, and handling relationships. Let's look at each.[5]

Being Self-Aware

Before you can deal with the emotions of others, you need to recognize your own by paying attention to how you feel. Self-awareness requires the ability to get a little distance from the emotion so that you can look at it without being overwhelmed by it or reacting to it too quickly. For example, if you are having an argument with someone and act on your anger, you might tell the other person that you never want to see him or her again. On the other hand, if you can recognize how angry you are feeling, you might be able to say, "Let me think about this some more and talk to you about it later."

Distancing yourself from an emotion does not mean denying it ("I shouldn't feel this way"). Rather, it's a way to articulate to yourself what you are feeling so that you can act on it appropriately.

Managing Emotions

Managing your emotions means expressing them in a manner that is appropriate to the circumstances.[6] You may not be able to do this easily because emotions often come from below the surface of your consciousness. For example, there may have been a time that unexpected tears came to your eyes, or other times when you felt a terrible rage well up inside you.

Another emotion that gets out of control is anxiety.[7] When anxiety is out of control, you feel so worried or so upset that it interferes with the way you function. In a university setting, for instance, most teachers have had students who have been so worried about the right way to do an assignment that they didn't do it at all or did it poorly because they were afraid to take any chances.

Managing your emotions does not mean that you should never feel angry, worried, or anxious. These emotions are all part of being human, and if you don't find a way to express them, they can result in depression or antisocial acts. It's important that you control these emotions rather than letting them control you.

One interesting finding about emotions is that women are better than men at detecting them. In a study where men and women were shown video clips in which someone was having an emotional reaction, 80 percent of the time women were better than men at discerning the emotion.[8]

Motivating Yourself

Motivating yourself is setting a goal and then disciplining yourself to do what you have to do to reach it. Whether you are an athlete or a writer, talent is not enough to make you win the race or get your story published. Both writers and athletes will tell you that they worked hard on many boring activities before they mastered their discipline.

Self-motivation requires resisting impulses. If you are studying for a test, for example, it might be tempting to go to the computer and chat with a friend. If you give in to this impulse, you might become so engrossed in the computer that you completely forget the test.

Some of the most fascinating research on impulse control was done on a group of four-year-old preschoolers.[9] When a child was put into a room with a researcher, he or she was offered a marshmallow. However, the children were told that the researcher had an errand to run and that if they didn't eat the marshmallow, they would get two when the researcher returned. The researcher was gone 15 to 20 minutes—an eternity for a child. The minute he was gone, one-third of the children ate their marshmallows; the remainder found ways to distract themselves: They tried to go to sleep, they talked to themselves, or they engaged in play.

Later these same children were studied when they were teenagers. Those who waited when they were children were much better in social skills, more assertive, and better able to handle themselves in a crisis. Academically, they were far superior as students, and they scored an average of 210 points higher on SAT scores.[10]

Other influences on motivation, according to Goleman, were positive thinking and optimism. Those who had a strong sense of self could bounce back after they had a negative experience. Rather than dwelling on the failure, they looked at ways in which they could improve.[11]

Recognizing Emotions in Others

Empathy, the ability to recognize and share someone else's feelings, is essential to human relationships. It comes from hearing what people are really saying—both by listening to their words and by reading body language such as gestures and facial expressions, and recognizing what they mean by a particular tone of voice. When someone has the same feelings or experiences you have had, it's not difficult to feel empathy. You are really put to the test when you haven't had the other person's feelings or experiences. For example, how can you feel empathy with an African student who hasn't been home for three years and stays in the dorm over Christmas? You can feel sorry for him, and you could tell him that you would feel terrible if you couldn't go home for the holidays. However, these emotions are pity (feeling sorry for him) and sympathy (saying that you'd feel bad too), but they are not empathy because you have not shared his experience. You may go in the direction of empathy if you talk to him for a while, look at the pictures of his brothers and sisters, hear about all the delicious things his mother cooks for Christmas, and so on. Empathy is the extent to which you can sit in his place, see what he sees, and taste what he tastes.

Empathy has a strong moral dimension. Being able to recognize and share someone's distress means that you will not want to hurt him or her. Child molesters and sociopaths, for example, are people lacking in empathy.[12] Sharing empathy with others also means that you are able to reach out and help them because when you can feel as they feel, they are no longer alone.

Handling Relationships

What are some of the characteristics of popular people you know? Chances are that they are people who are largely positive and energetic and that being with them makes you feel positive too. Most likely, they are also the people who organize others (such as the child who suggests a game), negotiate solutions when there is a problem to be solved, and generally connect with others emotionally.[13]

Being popular, however, is not their only goal. People also need a sense of balance; they need to recognize their own needs and know how to fulfill them. For example, you might be popular if you are always willing to stop studying to go to a party. This, however, would not meet your own need to pass your courses.

THE IMPORTANCE OF EMOTIONAL INTELLIGENCE TO STRATEGIC FLEXIBILITY

Self-concept is the way you think about and value yourself. The way you look at others and the world around you, and how well you understand and get along with others, have direct influence on your self-concept, just as the way you think about and value yourself influences both perception and emotional intelligence.

Perception, emotional intelligence, and self-concept have a direct bearing on strategic flexibility simply because they either enhance or impair your ability to anticipate, assess, evaluate, select, and apply your skills and behaviors. The better your perceptive skills, the more likely that your emotional intelligence is high and your self-concept is positive.

Remember the first characteristic of emotional intelligence: self-awareness. Part of maturity is recognizing that just because you have emotions doesn't necessarily mean you must act on them. Not only do you recognize your own emotions, but you understand, too, the triggers that cause them to come to the surface. As you begin to recognize your emotions and their triggers, you will learn how to manage them and to reveal the appropriate ones in given circumstances.

As you become accustomed to using the strategic flexibility framework, you develop self-control through self-discipline. It is as if you are setting mini-goals for yourself. You anticipate situations with the goal of applying the appropriate and relevant skills and behaviors. You achieve success when you maximize your communication, enhance your credibility, and not only support but achieve your intentions.

Listening to others becomes easier when you are secure in your self. Your perceptions become more accurate, and your observations of the nonverbal behavior of others and attempts to really understand them improve. In the end there is a greater chance that you will be able to handle relationships more successfully. Handling relationships is not easy, nor is it automatic. It is learned behavior, and emotional intelligence can help you establish and sustain long-term, meaningful relationships. The problem is simply that emotional intelligence often develops slowly—along with emotional maturity. If you take each of the areas of emotional intelligence, and you make them an issue (see Figure 7-1) before thinking about any serious relationship, you are more likely to take the necessary time.

ATTRACTION TO OTHERS

Sometimes our attraction to others can be measured by individual features, but we are more than the sum of our individual parts. What makes you more is not only what others can see, but what goes on inside you as well—your confidence, your belief in yourself, your unwillingness to put yourself down (or up). Even if you are the world's best looking and brightest, you could still ruin another person's feeling of being special in your presence, by either attacking yourself or bragging.[14]

Every day you encounter scores of people, but most of them recede into a kind of human landscape. Occasionally, however, you think, "Hey, I would really like to get to know this

Figure 7.1
Things Necessary before Entering into a Serious Relationship

- ✓ Self-awareness
- ✓ Manage your emotions
- ✓ Motivate yourself (self-discipline)
- ✓ Empathy
- ✓ Handling relationships

> There are many factors that make up attraction to others. Physical attraction, perceived gain, similarities, differences, and proximity are some of them. What are the likely factors at play here?

person better." Of the scores of people you meet, how do you pick one whom you want to know better? What are the ingredients that make up your attraction to others?

Physical Attraction

We are often attracted to others because of the way they look; we like their style and want to get to know them better. Physical attraction may be sexual attraction. In most cases, however, it goes beyond that. For adults who have had experience in the world, physical attraction usually recedes into the background as they get to know a person. Physical attraction can be a reason for getting to know someone, but it is usually not the basis for a long-term relationship.

Perceived Gain

Often we are attracted to people because we think we have something to gain from associating with them. For example, you join the ski club to get discounted lift tickets. Someone else joins a business management club because it will help her network when she enters the working world.

Although Americans believe they live in a classless society, this is not true. Even colleges and universities have a social hierarchy: Private schools (especially those in the Ivy League) have the most status, while junior and community colleges have the least. Colleges that are supported by a church are in a category of their own. What does this have to do with attraction? People will usually seek out others in their own class. Sometimes, however, they are motivated to move up and they try to blend into a higher class because the perceived awards will be greater.

Similarities

You may be attracted to someone who shares your attitudes and beliefs or seems knowledgeable about topics you find interesting and significant. Your **beliefs** are your convictions; your **attitudes** are the deeply felt beliefs that govern how you behave. When it comes to a strongly felt belief, you probably look for people who believe as you do. For example, in today's world it would be difficult for an Albanian and a Serb to be close friends—their politics have put them in opposing camps.

As adults grow older and meet more and more people, they become aware of the kinds of people they like and dislike, and they recognize the importance of compatibility. **Compatability means** having similar attitudes and personality, and a liking for the same activities.[15] For example, one couple decides to live in the city and focus on their careers rather than have a family. They like drama and excitement in their life—something the city provides. They often attend hockey and basketball games, and they spend their money on trendy clothes and eating out. Because they like the same things, their relationship is likely to last.

Differences

Although two people who have very different beliefs are unlikely to form a strong and lasting relationship, people with different personality characteristics might be attracted to each other. For example, a person who doesn't like making decisions might be attracted to a strong decision maker. Because these characteristics complement each other, they might help strengthen the relationship.

Specific interests may be so similar that they outweigh any differences. An American who runs in the Boston Marathon might have more in common with a runner from Kenya than with someone who spends every Sunday morning reading the newspaper and eating doughnuts. Association with a group might bring people together. Although a Rotary member from Indiana would have a different cultural background than a Rotary member from India, the fact that they both belong to Rotary will create a common ground for some of their interactions.

Proximity

Proximity is the close contact that occurs when people share an experience such as work, play, or school. Even when people might not otherwise have been attracted to each other, they may begin to know and like each other because they are together so much. For example, being in the same study group for a semester, sharing an office, or standing side-by-side on an assembly line are activities that place people in close proximity. Once they begin to share their lives on a day-to-day basis, they may find themselves becoming friends or even forming a romantic relationship.

Sometimes people who are attracted to each other form a strong friendship but lose touch when they no longer have proximity. Typically, friends who move to different cities vow to stay in touch, but it is not unusual for contact to drop to a yearly holiday card. Proximity, then, is important not just for starting relationships but also for keeping them going.

Cyberattraction

When you filter out those aspects of central importance in face-to-face communication—eye contact, self-contact gestures, posture, voice pitch, intensity, stress, rhythm, and volume—the process changes.[16] In cyberattraction, we depend on cues such as language, style, timing, speed of writing, and use of punctuation and emoticons. These form the substance of computer-mediated communication (CMC), discussed in Chapter 1.

CMC gives people an opportunity to interact without the weight of the physical-attractiveness stereotype and gives the smaller number of cues available a greater value. Partners build their stereotypical impressions of each other based on the language content of CMC messages. One researcher has found evidence that CMC groups gradually increase their impression development to a level approaching that of face-to-face groups,[17] but the process takes longer because the cues are fewer.

What are the specific cues of attractiveness in the cyberworld? First, you need to engage in an attentive and sensitive process of negotiation.[18] The negotiation needs to be both intriguing and enticing. Second, you need to simulate proximity by the shared use of a particular tool such as a chat room or newsgroup, and frequent contact is essential. Third, because people are attracted to someone they believe has attitudes similar to their own, because it is difficult and time consuming to learn how people think about multiple issues online, and because there is no way to compare someone's attitudes with their self-presentation (what people can see for themselves), there must be, according to one researcher, a strategic management of the similarity of perceptions.[19]

The fourth cue of attractiveness in the cyberworld is that you need to attract attention and show interest, usually with flatteries and verbal or multimedia compliments, such as virtual flowers. The fifth cue is humor. Humor is easily expressed in typed text, and those who excel at it increase their score on the interpersonal attraction scale.[20]

One of the most important cues to online attractiveness, the sixth, is a certain level of intimacy, or self-disclosure. Because you have no nonverbal cues on which to rely, and because online partners may be relative strangers, the degree of self-disclosure depends on inferring how the other person feels and how to pursue the relationship further. Anonymity often allows, even encourages, less inhibited behavior and opening oneself to another with little, or no fear of losing face.

MOTIVES FOR INTERPERSONAL COMMUNICATION

Everyone has needs that will vary with personality and moods. When you seek out others, you are trying to meet one or more of the following interpersonal needs: pleasure, affection, inclusion, escape, relaxation, control, health, and cybermotivation.[21]

Pleasure

We engage in a lot of interpersonal communication because it's fun. You chat online or gossip on the telephone with your best friend; you sit around and argue about sports teams with your buddies; you stop at the student center to have coffee, but also in the hope of meeting someone you know.

Affection

Whether it is expressed nonverbally (hugging, touching) or verbally ("I'm really glad you called me today"), affection is important to human happiness.

Unlike inclusion, affection is a one-to-one emotion.

Inclusion

Inclusion—involvement with others—is one of the most powerful human needs. Although nearly everyone has had the experience of being excluded, most people have had more experiences of being included. You may eat with a certain group at the cafeteria, go to parties at friends' houses, or join a club at the university. Belonging in this way is important to everyone's sense of well-being.

Escape

At one time or another, we all engage in interpersonal communication to try to avoid the jobs we are supposed to do. For example, before you begin writing your term paper, you decide to wander down the hall of your dorm to talk to a friend. A new form of escape is escape by computer. Chat rooms, e-mail, and surfing the Internet are particularly popular and enable you to escape without even going anywhere.

Relaxation

You often talk to your friends or families to relax and unwind from the activities of the day. You might sit with co-workers during a break, spend a few minutes with your spouse after work, or go out with a group of friends on the weekend.

Control

In a broad sense control means being able to make choices.

In the best relationships, the persons try to share control, which may change due to circumstances. For example, a couple we know moved to a new place where the wife had to commute two hours a day. This meant that she was not home to cook the evening meal, so her husband had to do it. He took control by reorganizing the kitchen to his liking—a legitimate action since he was now the main cook.

Researchers have found that people who have control over their own lives are healthier both mentally and physically.[22] Students learn better when teachers give them some independence, and workers feel better about their jobs when they can make some decisions about how their work should be done.[23] People who have the sense that they are in control of their lives are meeting one of their deepest needs.

Health

Research shows that people with strong social ties live longer than those who are isolated.[24] If you have a romantic partner, frequent contact with friends and family, or involvement with volunteer or religious organizations, the social support systems you form assist you in keeping heart rate, hypertension, and stress hormones under control. Lonely people often view the world as threatening, and although they want to be connected, they both expect negative responses and engage in self-protective behaviors that are self-defeating. Experts advise lonely people to join a local club or organization just because of the health-protective effects.

Cybermotivation

In computer-mediated communication, there is often considerably less anxiety than in real-life interactions. There is usually increased motivation because engaging in CMC is entertaining and exciting. In addition, CMC can bolster self-esteem, and you can self-disclose with little possibility of losing face. There is anonymity if you want it, and an opportunity to be who you want to be as well. The high levels of affiliation and trust often result in higher levels of self-disclosure, associated with our having a heightened sense of who we are when communicating via CMC.

TALKING TO EACH OTHER

Roles, Relationships, and Communication

All relationships are governed by the roles that the participants expect each other to play. Sometimes these roles are tightly defined; other times the participants have the flexibility to define them.

Often the roles you know best are those that are the most traditionally defined such as teachers and parents. Even though the people who work in these roles might want more flexibility than is allowed by traditional definitions, they often feel social pressure to conform to traditional roles and thus to traditional behavior.

Usually at the beginning of a relationship with someone your own age, you can choose the roles you want to play. Friends, for example, often decide on the role they will play within a friendship. Once the relationship is established, role expectations become fixed and friends expect each other to react in certain ways.

A critical question in a marriage is whether you want to play the role your father or mother played. If you don't, how will you set out to define your own role? Sherod Miller, a psychologist, says that once the partners give up old roles—the ones that were based on gender—they have to work out new ones: a process that leads to negotiating every aspect of their lives, especially when the first baby arrives.[25]

Other psychologists who have studied marriage found that the most successful marriages are ones where the male partners listen to their female partners rather than reacting defensively to complaints and criticism. A husband's willingness to listen shows that he understands and respects his wife's needs, and when this occurs, there is a much better chance of marital stability.[26]

As well as roles for your intimate relationships, there are roles for all aspects of your life and communication that work best in each of them. Your job is to find out which communication works best for all the roles you play. You will see, then, that much of your success in playing a role will depend on how well you communicate in that role.

Beginning Conversations: The Art of Small Talk

Have you ever felt nervous about entering a classroom where you didn't know any of the students? In many new social situations you might feel uneasy. You may wonder whether you will be able to begin a conversation and whether you will find people you like and, just as important, people who like you. The uncertainty you are feeling will probably be shared by other people in the room. How do you go about reducing it?

When most people begin conversations, they engage in **small talk**—social conversation about unimportant topics that allows a person to maintain contact without making a deep commitment. There are all sorts of conventions in small talk. Scholars who have studied conversation have found that it follows a routine that varies only slightly. Figure 7-2 shows this conversation pattern.

As you can see in this figure, many of the conversational responses are based on questions, some to find out information, others to establish common ground. Other questions are asked just to fill time or to be sociable. Since most people like answering questions about themselves, they are flattered when someone shows interest in them.

Dianna Booher, a business communications consultant, offers the following tips for beginning conversations:

Figure 7-2 How People Begin Conversations

If you follow this figure from top to bottom, you will see how conversations begin, progress, and end. In the sections that are numbered, there is some variation: people may speak about one or more of these topics.

1. Greeting
   Introduction
   Health — 2
3. Present Situation
   Reason for Presence
   Weather
   Where Live
   Hometown
   Persons Known in Common
   What Do You Do?
   Education
   Occupation — 4
5. Social Relations
   Compliments
   Interests
   Family
   Sports
   Near Future Activities
   Evaluation of Encounter
   Plan Future Meeting — 6
   Positive Evaluation of Person
   Until Later
7. Reason for Terminating
   Good-bye

- *Introduce yourself in a way that gives the other person a way to respond to you.* This approach will uncover what the two of you have in common, and it will probably lead to subjects for conversation. Here, for example, is how a person who was much younger than most of the guests at the university president's party introduced himself: "Hi, I'm Jim Dolan, and I'm the student member of the Board of Trustees at the university."
- *Give people a way to remember your name.* The author of this text whose last name is Hybels told people that it rhymes with *bibles*. Not only did people learn how to pronounce her name, but often they remembered it when they met her again.
- *Personalize your greeting.* If you know something about the person, try to work it into your greeting. For example, "I liked the presentation you made in class last week."[27]

Booher also suggests that when you end the conversation, you do it as gracefully as possible. "Excuse me, I've enjoyed talking to you" is a short and graceful ending.

Because small-talk topics and questions are socially sanctioned, they create a safe meeting ground. They provide you with a chance to establish who you are with others. They also permit you to find out more about yourself through the eyes of others. Although you don't give away a lot of personal information in small talk, the image you give to others and the image you receive of them will let you know whether you want to see them again.

Bids and the Bidding Process

If you knew specifically what it was that holds relationships together, and you knew that it was within your control, would you change the way you conducted yourself in your interpersonal relationships? What holds relationships together are bids and the bidding process. A **bid**, according to John Gottman and his team of relationship researchers, "can be a question, a gesture, a look, a touch—any single expression that says, 'I want to feel connected to you.' A **response to a bid** is just that—a positive or negative answer to somebody's request for emotional connection." See Figure 7-3.[28]

What Determines Your Ability to Bid and to Respond to Bids?

Some people are likely to be better at bids and responses than others. There are three major influences at work. First, it may be a function of the way people's brains process feelings. Second, it may be a function of the way emotions were handled in the homes where people grew up. And third, it may be a function of people's emotional communication skills. These

Figure 7-3

Bids and Responses to Bids

Questions, gestures, looks, or touches that say, "I want to feel connected to you."

Bid

Response to Bid

A positive or negative answer to someone's request for emotional connection.

three influences can be complex, interacting variables. Despite their influence, however, sometimes just knowing what ingredients can influence a relationship, or just knowing specifically what you can do to make a relationship you cherish a success, is enough. Placing bids and responding to bids is a skill that can be learned, practiced, and mastered.[29]

How Do Bids Contribute to Relationship Development?

In successful relationships, bids for emotional connection are responded to positively. Bids from either relationship partner are neither ignored nor dismissed, whether they are simple or mundane. It is the simple and mundane bids that weave the fabric that forms the backdrop for all future bids. Many come nonverbally and include vocalizing, affiliating gestures (like opening a door or offering a place to sit), playful touching, facial expressions, or affectionate touching.[30] Sure, some bids may be unseen, unheard, or overlooked just as some may be sent in a subtle, camouflaged, confused, or nonspecific manner. It is the overall pattern of behavior that is important, not necessarily any single, solitary bid. Remember, in most positive relationships thousands of bids take place daily.

Each encounter in a relationship is made up of many smaller exchanges—bids and responses to those bids. These exchanges of emotional information will either strengthen or weaken the connections between people, and these connections form the fabric we referred to earlier. Here, in the first example, the response to the bid is negative. In the next, the response is positive:

> Hey, Chris. Did you get that class report finished?
> Would you stop nagging at me? You sound just like my mother!
>
> Would you get me a soda while you're up?
> No problem. Do you want anything else?

The point is not the content, and the point has nothing to do with timing or circumstances. The point is that a positive response to a bid typically leads to continued interaction, and the chances for a successful relationship become better and better. And the reverse is just as clear. Negative responses to bids will shut down communication. Bids cease, and the relationship terminates.

How Can You Encourage Bids?

How can you make certain you respond positively to the bids of others if you choose to do so? Gottman and his researchers discuss six common sense ways to encourage and reinforce the bids of others. These are outlined in Figure 7-4.

Owned Messages

An **owned message** (also known as an I-message, as coined by Thomas Gordon[31]) is "an acknowledgment of subjectivity by a message-sender through the use of first-person-singular terms (I, me, my, mine). 'Responsible' communicators are those who 'own' their thoughts and feelings by employing these pronouns."[32]

Owned messages tend to provoke less interpersonal defensiveness than you-messages, and they are useful for conveying negative information. Some simple examples of owned and unowned messages will demonstrate the difference. To say "You make me mad" is an example of an unowned message (a you-message) and, as is obvious, has the potential for creating defensiveness in another person. To say "I'm feeling angry" is an example of owning a message and is less likely to create defensiveness.

Gordon said owned messages can be called "responsibility messages" because those who send them are taking responsibility for their own inner condition (listening to *themselves*) and

Figure 7-4
How to Encourage Bids

- Focus on the people around you.
- Set a positive tone in conversations.
- Avoid harmful criticism.
- Avoid becoming physically or emotionally overwhelmed.
- Create a climate of praise and gratitude.
- Self-disclose and connect.

assuming responsibility for being open enough to share their assessment of themselves with others. In addition, they leave the responsibility for the other person's behavior with them.[33]

What does an I-message look like? Gordon suggests a behavior/feelings/effects formula for constructing I-messages.

1. A description by the one concerned of the other's unacceptable (disruptive) behavior.
2. The feelings of the one concerned in reaction to the other's unacceptable behavior.
3. An explanation of how the other's behavior interferes with the one concerned's ability to answer his or her own needs.

Example: "Jennifer, when you leave things everywhere (1) I get frustrated (2) because I cannot do what I have to do (3)."

Remember as you use owned messages, any given behavior can be an asset or a liability, depending on the goal or situation. Interpersonal skills are competent when communicators employ them sensitively and sensibly according to the requirements of a particular social setting. Using owned messages is a skill that is generally perceived to be competent across contexts. It can increase your sense of control and responsibility, and control and responsibility are issues that are basic and paramount to interpersonal competence.[34]

SELF-DISCLOSURE: IMPORTANT TALK

To communicate who you are to other people, you have to engage in **self-disclosure**—a process in which one person tells another person something he or she would not reveal to just anyone.

The Importance of Self-Disclosure

Social penetration is the process of increasing both disclosure and intimacy in a relationship, and it is one of the most widely studied processes in relational development.[35] The theory is that relationships become more intimate over time as partners disclose more

Working Together

In a group, discuss bids and responses to bids by answering the following questions one at a time around the group:

1. In what way have you made bids for connection with important people in your life today?
2. How did you feel about the way people responded to your bids?
3. Did you notice anyone responding positively to your bids? In what ways?
4. Did you notice anyone turning away from your bids? In what ways?
5. Did you notice anyone turning against your bids? What did your behavior look like?
6. How have you responded today to other people's bids for connection?
7. Did you respond positively? How?
8. Did you turn away? How?
9. Did you turn against any bids for connection? How and why?
10. Do you think bids and responding to bids is an accurate way to assess the quality of interpersonal relationships?

Source: *The Relationship Cure: A Five-Step Guide for Building Better Connections with Family, Friends, and Lovers* (p. 15), by J. M. Gottman and J. DeClaire, 2001, New York: Crown Publishers.

---

and more information about themselves. When partners in a relationship are motivated, and when they exert the extra effort necessary not just to continue their relationship but to permit its growth, the relationship necessarily undergoes certain qualitative changes. Partners experience an additional sense of connectedness. At the same time, writes one researcher, "communicative transactions become increasingly interpersonal."[36]

Whether you want to encourage a relationship, hold it at the same level, or back off often depends on the information you get during the process of self-disclosure. Gerald Miller and his communication-research colleagues state that there are three kinds of information.[37] The first kind is **cultural information** which tells us about a person's most generally shared cultural attributes such as language, shared values, beliefs, and ideologies. Information at this level is as shallow and impersonal as is a greeting or good-bye. Knowing it allows you to perform acceptably in most social situations, but it is not very helpful when it comes to relationships.

The second kind of information is **sociological** and tells you something about others' social groups and roles. This level of communication allows you to be successful communicating with your doctor, dentist, lawyer, or hair stylist. You know something about their roles and affiliations, but you know relatively little about the person separate from his or her role.

The third kind of information is **psychological**, which is the most specific and intimate because it allows you to know individual traits, feelings, attitudes, and important personal data. This is the type of information on which most of your predictions about relationships will be based.

It is through self-disclosure, then, that you meet someone who believes the way you do—that you discover a common interest, for example, which you can pursue in greater depth because both of you have some background and information to share. Such a partner is likely to react to situations and events the way you would, and you trust him or her enough to reveal even more about yourself. The Assess Yourself box at the end of this chapter is on trusting others, because trust is an important part of the self-disclosure process.

Self-disclosure is important to relationships in other ways as well. You use it in the process of reciprocity: When someone discloses with you, your tendency is to self-disclose in return. You use self-disclosure for self-clarification—to clarify beliefs, opinions, thoughts, attitudes, and problems: "I thought you understood I was only kidding." You

169

Telling a secret might be one form of self-disclosure.

use it for identity management in attempts to make yourself more attractive: "I'm using a new fragrance; did you notice?" You use it for social control when revealing information may increase your control over the situation or a person: "I was given the authority to lead this group, and I think we should all stick to our agenda."

The Process of Self-Disclosure

One way to look at how the self-disclosure process operates was developed by Joseph Luft and Harry Ingham. Combining their first names, they labeled their model the **Johari Window** (see Figure 7-5).[38]

The "Free to self and others" area—the ***open pane***—includes information about yourself that you are willing to communicate, as well as information you are unable to hide (such as a blush when you are embarrassed). When students meet for the first time in a class, they follow the instructor's suggestion and introduce themselves. Most of them stick to bare essentials: their names, where they come from, and their majors. When people do not know one another very well, the open pane is smaller than when they have become better acquainted.

The area labeled "Blind to self, seen by others"—the ***blind pane***—is a kind of accidental disclosure area: There are certain things you do not know about yourself that others know about you. For example, a husband complains that every time his wife comes home from work, she looks mad—something she didn't realize until he pointed it out.

The ***hidden pane***—self-knowledge hidden from others—is a deliberate nondisclosure area; there are certain things you know about yourself that you do not want known, so you deliberately conceal them from others. Most people hide things that might evoke disapproval from those they love and admire: "I was a teenage shoplifter"; "I don't know how to read very well." Others keep certain areas hidden from one person but open to another: A young woman tells her best friend, but not her mother, that her grades are low because she seldom studies.

Figure 7-5 The Johari Window

	Known to Self	Unknown to Self
Known to Others (Disclosure areas)	Open Pane (Free to self and others)	Blind Pane (Blind to self, seen by others)
Unknown to Others (Nondisclosure areas)	Hidden Pane (Open to self, hidden from others)	Unknown Pane (Unknown to self and others)

The **unknown pane** is a nondisclosure area; it provides no possibility of disclosure because it is unknown to the self or to others. This pane represents all the parts of you that are not yet revealed. You might think that you are very brave, but you really don't know how you will react when you are faced with personal danger.

The disclosure and nondisclosure areas vary from one relationship to another, and they change all the time in the same relationship. Figure 7-6 shows how the Johari Window might look in a close relationship. The open pane becomes much larger because a person is likely to disclose more. When disclosure increases, people not only reveal more information about themselves but also are likely to discover things about themselves that they had not known before. If you apply the Johari Window to each of your relationships, you will find that the panes are different sizes in each one. In other words, you are likely to be more self-disclosing in some relationships than you are in others.

Self-Disclosure and Intimacy: Rewards and Fears

Self-disclosure is the most rewarding when it leads to greater intimacy. Only intimate relationships give you a chance to really be yourself, to share who you are with another person. This kind of intimacy can be found in romantic relationships and among family members and close friends. One study has found that both men and women are willing to self-disclose to about the same degree.[39]

Although in this chapter we take the position that self-disclosure is very important if you are going to have deep and satisfying relationships, we also acknowledge that many people fear the consequences of revealing themselves to another.

Figure 7-6
The Johari Window after a Relationship Has Developed

[Diagram showing four panes: Open Pane (large, green), Blind Pane (medium, orange), Hidden Pane (medium, light green), Unknown Pane (small, blue)]

Fear of Having Your Faults Exposed

Self-disclosure in a relationship may lead to communicating that you are not perfect and exposing things from your past that you would rather keep hidden. Once your fears, anxieties, or weaknesses are known to another person, that person could tell them to others or use them against you.

Fear That Your Partner Will Become Your Critic

By telling someone you are vulnerable, you open yourself to attack. A wife, for example, tells her husband how bad she felt when she wasn't invited to the senior prom. One day when they are having a fight, he says, "Don't tell me how much people like you. You didn't even get invited to the prom!"

Fear of Losing Your Individuality

Some people feel that if they reveal too much, they lose their sense of self, that there are private things that only they should know. This might be especially true during the years when teenagers are trying to gain autonomy from their families. Part of being autonomous is making decisions on your own and not telling everything to your parents.

Fear of Being Abandoned

Sometimes one partner is afraid that if the other knows something about him or her, he or she will be abandoned. For example, someone might not want to tell another about his struggle with alcoholism for fear that the other person will no longer love, accept, or want him.

When Should Self-Disclosure Occur?

Disclosure should occur only in relationships that are important to you. People who do not know you very well are likely to feel uncomfortable if you tell them too much about yourself too soon. Wait until you have some signs that a relationship has the possibility of developing further. For example, if someone seeks you out to invite you to go out with him or her, after three or four times this is a sign that the person wants the relationship to develop.

For disclosure to work, both parties must be involved in it. If one person does all the disclosing and the other party just sits back and listens, disclosure is not likely to continue. Remember that disclosure means taking a risk. You will never know how another person will respond to your openness until you give it a try. To avoid getting hurt, try testing the water before you plunge in. One way of doing this is to talk about a subject in general terms and see how the other person reacts before you talk about your own experience with it.

Finally, examine your own motives for self-disclosure. Why do you want the other person to know this information? Will it really enhance the relationship, or can it do harm? All of us have some secrets that we should probably keep to ourselves. Sharing them may cause injury or make the other person lose trust in us. Although some secrets are a burden to keep, it may serve the interest of the relationship to do so. Those in relationships who believe in full and complete disclosure with partners risk the possibility of damage and even loss.

> **STRATEGIC FLEXIBILITY**
> Because of the risks, knowing when to self-disclose requires that you think about potential situations (anticipate); take stock of the factors, elements, and conditions of the situation (assess); determine the value and worth of the factors, elements, and conditions (evaluate); and carefully select the skills and behaviors that are likely to be appropriate (select) before engaging in self-disclosure.

ESSENTIAL ELEMENTS OF GOOD RELATIONSHIPS

Once you have begun using bids, owned messages, and self-disclosure, a relationship has truly begun and you need to "grow" it. Here, we will look at elements that draw people together: verbal skills, emotional expressiveness, conversational focus, nonverbal analysis, conversational encouragement, care and appreciation, commitment, and adaptation.

Verbal Skills

Partners in good relationships must have ongoing conversations, or dialogues, about the relationship itself. They must be able to search together for ways of reducing conflict, to discuss expectations they have of each other, and to explore anything else that might affect the relationship. In her article "Finding Real Love," Cary Barbor ends by saying, "Learning how best to communicate with each other and treat one another will help us enjoy loving, lasting relationships."[40]

Not only do females begin talking earlier than males, on most national assessment tests they score well ahead of males in reading and writing, and many more major in English, comparative literature, and foreign languages than men.[41] To make certain the playing field remains level, males may need to apply themselves more when it comes to verbal skills, because for partners to continue in a relationship, they must find mutually beneficial ways of communicating. Also, males need to alter their perception of relationships as stable, static commodities that never need discussion or reexamination.

Emotional Expressiveness

Gottman noted that your ability to bid and to respond to bids depends on the way your brain processes feelings, the way emotions were handled in your home, and your emotional communication skills.[42] Christina Hoff Sommers claims that females' verbal skills "may be responsible for their superior emotional expressiveness."[43] Her claim is supported by Daniel Goleman in *Emotional Intelligence* who says, "Because girls develop language more quickly than do boys, this leads them to be more experienced at articulating their feelings and more skilled than boys at using words to explore and substitute for emotional reactions such as physical fights."[44] Not only are females more expressive and responsive to others, they "invite others into conversations."[45] Once again, to level the playing field, males need to improve their ability at emotional expressiveness.

Achieving emotional expressiveness may require discussing points of conflict. This is particularly important if relationships are to be successful. Some people are conditioned to stay away from conflict. Childhood messages such as "Hold your tongue" and "I don't ever want to hear you talk that way again" lead us to believe that it's wrong to say words that other people do not want to hear. As adults, however, we have to recondition ourselves to discuss areas of conflict: Withdrawing from or avoiding conflict is too harmful to relationships.

Conversational Focus

A third factor likely to affect your ability to handle relationships is what you choose to talk about. Sommers claims that "Males, whether young or old, are less interested than females in talking about feelings and personal relationships."[46] Researchers at Northwestern University analyzed the conversational focus of college students gathered around a cafeteria table.[47] They discovered that 56 percent of the women's targets were intimates, close friends, boyfriends, and family members, but only 25 percent of the conversational focus of men was friends and relatives.[48] When researchers simultaneously presented male and female college students with two images on a stereoscope, one of an object, the other of a person, male subjects more often saw the object while female subjects more often saw the person.[49] Males need to increase their focus on feelings and relationships—to not only make their feelings known, but to make other people, especially their relationship partner, know how they feel about them and about their relationship.

What are some of the obvious elements of good relationships being revealed in this group?

Nonverbal Analysis

A fourth factor that will affect your ability to handle relationships is your ability to read between the lines, to analyze the nonverbal cues of the other person. Dozens of experiments confirm "that women are much better than men at judging emotions based on the expression on a stranger's face."[50] Not only are women better at observing the nonverbal cues of others, they also "tend to give obvious visual and vocal clues to signal they are following what others say and are interested in it."[51] Clues might include nodding their heads, smiling, establishing eye contact, and offering responsive gestures.[52] Males need to increase their sensitivity to nonverbal cues. Because they are not conditioned to be as observant in this area, they need to be especially vigilant and aware.

Conversational Encouragement

Often, men listen to others without showing their feelings; they keep their responses and feelings to themselves, as noted in the section on emotional expressiveness. This can be interpreted as an unwillingness to listen or lack of interest.[53] Women, on the other hand, encourage others to continue talking using listening noises such as "um, hmmm," "yes," "that's interesting," "so," "and," and so forth. They are encouragers, and these vocalizations not only reveal they are listening and interested, but they also prompt others to continue talking and to elaborate on their ideas.[54]

Roger Axtell, in his book *Do's and Taboos Around the World for Women in Business*, quotes Kathi Seifert, group president of North American personal care products for the Kimberly-Clark Corporation, who says "Women are naturally more caring, nurturing, and better listeners. They like to help and to respond to people's needs."[55] Shmuley Boteach, dean of the L'Chaim Society, which hosts world figures and diplomats and concentrates on values-based leadership, says women "when speaking to their husbands, . . . stop talking in midsentence because they know they are not being listened to. They feel like a piece of furniture, and this experience of being ignored is a denial of their value. Their spirit is crushed."[56] Fein and Schneider, in *The Rules for Marriage*, write "Learn how to listen without interrupting or offering advice, so that you can understand your spouse's perspective on things."[57] Men need to open up more, show their feelings, listen better, and reveal their responses. It may help, too, if men view conversations as Mary Boone describes them: "The purpose of a conversation is not to *agree* with each other, it's to learn from each other on both an intellectual and emotional level."[58]

Care and Appreciation

Scholars have found that people consistently use ways to communicate whether they want to have a relationship with a person or whether they want to avoid him or her.[59] The approach people use most often to foster a relationship is expressing *caring and appreciation* for the other person. Typical remarks might be, "We had such a good time last night, I would like to see you again," or "I am so glad that we are friends"—bids expressing "I want to feel connected to you." The second most used technique is giving *compliments*: "That was such a funny joke you told last night," or "You look great today"—more bids seeking connection. The third technique they use is engaging in *self-disclosure*—(also a bid) telling someone something about themselves that they wouldn't tell most people: "I felt so bad when I failed the test," or "I really like her: I wish she would pay some attention to me."

Commitment

All relationships need **commitment**—a strong desire by both parties for the relationship to continue and a willingness on both parties to take responsibility for the problems that occur in the relationship. Trying to force a partner to make a commitment, however, is a waste of time, claims Adrienne Burgess, in an article "I Vow to Thee" in the *Guardian*. She says, "Not only does it (commitment) provide no guarantees, but it also causes resentment and hostility, which undermines any loving feelings. In relationships with a real future, therefore, commitment usually develops at much the same rate on both sides. But promises of commitment are meaningless in the long-term, too—commitment isn't an act of will (while we can promise to stay with someone physically, we can't promise the same emotionally), and isn't something we do in any active sense. Commitment is a spin-off from other things: how satisfied we are with our relationship; whether we see a viable alternative to it; and whether moving on would cause us to lose important investments (time, money, shared property, and children)."[60]

All relationships have some kind of commitment as their foundation, but sometimes the partners to the commitment have different expectations. *Unconditional* commitments are those in which you commit yourself to another regardless of what may happen. Marriage vows are often cited as examples of unconditional commitments; however, with divorce rates hovering around 50 percent, it is clear that nearly one out of every two couples who accept the unconditional commitment do not fulfill it. *Conditional* commitments set forth the conditions of the commitment and carry with them the implication of "only if." "I will commit to you only if I do not find something better in the meantime," or "I will commit to you only if something extraordinary doesn't happen."

Although commitments are important and reassuring, it is perhaps better to accept them for what they are worth, based on the trust and faith in the person making the commitment and with hope for a positive future. However, it is best to prepare for the fact that most commitments are conditional, and it is unlikely that all conditions will be, or even could be, revealed or even known. Of course marriage should be an unconditional commitment, but we live in a transient society where planned obsolescence, endless technological advances, and instant millionaires guarantee a rapid and regular turnover of products, information, and fortunes; why should we expect relationships, including marriages, to be anything other than of short duration? Dreams, faith, optimism, visualizations, and confidence are all fine, but they really don't prepare you for a realistic conditional future. Only you can do that.

Adaptation

The time and effort dedicated to supporting, encouraging, and nurturing relationships—even well-established ones—must be spent in both introspection (the act of contemplating one's mental processes and emotional state in the relationship) and communication. Introspection and communication within relationships are foreign to conventional masculinity.[61]

Verbal skills, emotional expressiveness, conversational focus, nonverbal analysis, conversational encouragement, care and appreciation, and commitment are tools that help hold relationships together. You need to speak, listen, negotiate, stay on course, and hold your relationship in warm regard.[62] But if you can't adapt and adjust your skills and behaviors to the changes that occur, as introspection and communication will help you to do, these tools are use-

---

STRATEGIC FLEXIBILITY

Adapting and adjusting your behaviors and skills to changing circumstances is the foundation of strategic flexibility. Having all the tools in your toolbox is important, but even more important in strategic flexibility is carefully selecting exactly those tools likely to have the greatest impact and applying them with care and concern.

less. "After years of research," says one writer, "it turns out that what makes for highly adaptive people is their capacity to adapt."[63]

THE INTERNET AND INTERPERSONAL RELATIONSHIPS

People in virtual communities use the words they type on screens to:

> *exchange pleasantries and argue, engage in intellectual discourse, conduct commerce, exchange knowledge, share emotional support, make plans, brainstorm, gossip, feud, fall in love, find friends and lose them, play games, flirt, create a little high art and a lot of idle talk.*[64]

Leslie Stevens and Cody Moore (from our opening example) are a small testament to both the success and nature of the Internet. What has now become dramatically and emphatically clear is that the Internet is more a social creation than a technical one.

There have been numerous studies on the Internet's effect on users, and just as there have been dire predictions about the erosion of language, there were similar predictions about the Internet's effect on interpersonal relationships—that the Internet promotes social disengagement (less voting, going to church, and discussing government with neighbors; fewer voluntary organizations and dinner parties; and less getting together for civic and social purposes). *Time* magazine reported that the amount of time the average U.S. Internet user spends online is 3 hours each day, and that each hour of Internet use reduces face-to-face contact with family members by 23.5 minutes.[65]

Internet addiction also is a problem. John Douglas and Stephen Singular, in their book *Anyone You Want Me to Be*, write that "Surfing the Net for love can easily become a minor hobby that evolves into a major pastime that turns into an addiction that can be almost as demanding and consuming as a full-time job."[66] Dr. Kimberly S. Young, assistant professor of psychology at the University of Pittsburgh–at Bradford, has stated that those most vulnerable to Internet addiction are those who are lonely, bored, depressed, or introverted or who lack self-esteem or have a history of addictions.

In his speech "Avoiding Trends That Deprive Us of Humanity," D. Stanley Eitzen, professor emeritus in the Department of Sociology at Colorado State University, states:

> *We are becoming a society that finds it easier, and even preferable to hide behind our computer screens and chat with a faceless, nameless stream of words from across the country or across the globe rather than deal with people face to face and all the complexities, good and bad, of the human relationship.*[67]

For those raised in an Internet world, it is just another form of relating, a form that is different from other forms, to be sure, but one that provides valuable, important, and worthwhile benefits. For many Americans, e-mail and instant messaging have become essential features of social life. Overall, because of its ease of use, efficiency, and ubiquity, the Internet has made a dramatic increase in the number of interpersonal relationships we are likely to have.

The benefits of Internet communication are too numerous to mention; however, here are a few:

- It promotes healthy communication and interaction.
- It offers a strong support system for interpersonal relationships.
- It allows otherwise marginalized people to be integrated into society (it removes all barriers that shy people never get past in person).

- It reduces the costs of communicating with geographically distant acquaintances and strangers.
- It increases social contacts beyond family and close friends.
- It offers opportunities for communicating on an international level, for meeting those who identify with us, and who aid us in gaining perspective from them and from their backgrounds.
- It loosens the social restrictions that have traditionally protected morality and manners.

Online dating alone is a fixture of single life for adults of all ages, backgrounds, and interests. The extent of its use is staggering. Rachel Greenwald, in her book *Find a Husband After 35*, lists the benefits: (1) You can reach far more interested parties than by any other means; (2) it is fast; (3) it is inexpensive; (4) it is convenient; (5) it gives you the opportunity to tap into new groups of people outside your regular social circle; (6) you can really get to know each other first; thus, physical appearance is not a barrier to learning what really counts about one another; and (7) it is anonymous—you decide whether you want to reply, what you want to reveal, whether you want to meet, and when and where.[68] We discuss pitfalls of online dating in the next chapter.

The Internet has proven its value in interpersonal relationships. Look at the benefit that cell phones and computers with e-mail and instant messaging capabilities provide in keeping families and friends in touch, even though spread over wide geographical areas. The Internet also can affirm, reinforce, and assist in maintaining good relationships.

Assess Yourself

Trusting Others Scale

Indicate the degree to which you agree or disagree with each statement using the following scale: 1 = Strongly agree; 2 = Mildly agree; 3 = Agree and disagree equally; 4 = Mildly disagree; 5 = Strongly disagree. Circle your response following each statement.

1. Most people in my life are reliable and dependable.   5 4 3 2 1 0
2. In general, when there is a task to be done, I prefer doing it myself rather than asking someone else to do it.   5 4 3 2 1 0
3. Other people, in general, possess what I consider to be core (essential) skills and abilities.   5 4 3 2 1 0
4. In general, people share relevant information with me.   5 4 3 2 1 0
5. I get overly anxious when an important job that directly affects me and that I could do is carried out by someone else.   5 4 3 2 1 0
6. In general, the actions others take live up to the values they claim to live by.   5 4 3 2 1 0
7. Sometimes I feel I am being taken advantage of when someone else is taking actions that directly affect me, and yet I have no control over those actions.   5 4 3 2 1 0
8. In general, other people have a benevolent attitude toward me.   5 4 3 2 1 0
9. When in a group, I prefer working independently rather than as part of the group.   5 4 3 2 1 0
10. People tell white lies.   5 4 3 2 1 0
11. I have confidence in the integrity, ability, character, and truth of most other people.   5 4 3 2 1 0
12. In general, when others promise they will do something, I believe it will be done.   5 4 3 2 1 0
13. When others perform actions that directly affect me, I expect positive outcomes to occur.   5 4 3 2 1 0
14. In general, other people are open and honest with me, sharing all of their information, not just selected facts or opinions.   5 4 3 2 1 0
15. Other people voluntarily share their information with me.   5 4 3 2 1 0
16. I prefer to let those around me work independently, even if their work directly affects me.   5 4 3 2 1 0
17. Other people listen to me and to my ideas.   5 4 3 2 1 0
18. In general, others do not do what they say they will do.   5 4 3 2 1 0
19. I prefer situations where people with whom I am working have full opportunities for mutual influence—me influencing them and they influencing me.   5 4 3 2 1 0
20. In general, people are considerate of the ideas and feelings of others.   5 4 3 2 1 0
21. I prefer to monitor the behavior of others when I know their actions will affect me in some way.   5 4 3 2 1 0
22. I am willing to allow others to take actions that are important to and directly affect me, even though I have no control over how those actions will be done.   5 4 3 2 1 0
23. In general, other people are not as important as I am.   5 4 3 2 1 0
24. In general, I prefer to work with others to obtain a mutually acceptable outcome rather than to work alone.   5 4 3 2 1 0
25. In general most people meet my expectations.   5 4 3 2 1 0

TOTAL POINTS: _____

Before totaling your score, go to the *Communicating Effectively* CD-ROM or the Online Learning Center at www.mhhe.com/hybels8 and follow the directions there.

mhhe.com/hybels8

Source: See "Tools for Personal Growth: Building Trust. Coping.org Tools for Coping with Life's Stressors" (provided as a public service), by J. J. Messina and C. M. Messina, 2002. Retrieved October 20, 2005, from http://www.coping.org/growth/trust.htm. I have quoted from their Web page, and I have refrained from using quotation marks simply because quotation marks form a minor barrier to the case of reading the information.

CHAPTER REVIEW

SUMMARY

Interpersonal communication, or one-to-one communication, is necessary for you to function in society. It helps you connect with others and develop empathy, and it contributes to your mental and physical health. Emotional intelligence is made up of being aware of your feelings, managing your emotions, motivating yourself, recognizing emotions in others, and handling relationships. All these have a direct bearing on strategic flexibility.

Strategic flexibility benefits from the contributions of perception, self-concept, and emotional intelligence because together these factors promote self-control, assist in managing emotions, and foster effective listening. They help you maximize your communication, enhance your credibility, and accomplish your intentions—all factors that make your use of the strategic flexibility format both more likely and more effective.

The ingredients that make up your attraction to others include physical attraction, perceived gain, similarities, differences, and proximity. In cyberattraction, those communicating depend on cues such as language, style, timing, speed of writing, and use of punctuation and emoticons.

The motives for seeking out interpersonal relationships are pleasure, affection (warm emotional attachments with others), inclusion (involvement with others), escape, relaxation, control (getting others to do as you want them to or being able to make choices in your life), health, and cybermotivation. Cybermotivation involves less anxiety, entertainment, excitement, unwinding, forgetting about daily problems such as school and work, privacy, complete availability, relieving boredom, bolstering self-esteem, anonymity if you want it, and high levels of self-disclosure.

Relationships with others are governed by the roles you are expected to play. Small talk is an instrument of communication that renders people attractive. To engage in small talk plan ahead, ask open-ended questions, share feelings and information, and reconnect via your past.

Bids and the bidding process are the glue that holds relationships together. Bids can be questions, gestures, looks, or touches, and responses to bids are positive or negative answers to somebody's request for emotional connection. Owned messages are acknowledgments of subjectivity by message senders through the use of first-person singular terms. Their value is that they provoke less interpersonal defensiveness than you-messages.

Self-disclosure is the process of communicating oneself to another person, telling another who you are and what you are feeling. It can be understood through the Johari Window, which has four panes: open, blind, hidden, and unknown. As relationships develop and disclosure increases, the open pane gets larger.

The essential elements of good relationships include verbal skills, emotional expressiveness, conversational focus, nonverbal analysis, conversational encouragement, care and appreciation, commitment, and adaptation.

For many, the Internet serves as a valuable, important, and worthwhile form of communication because it promotes healthy communication and interaction; allows a strong support system; facilitates the social integration of otherwise marginalized people; reduces the costs of communication; increases the numbers of social contacts; offers opportunities for communication on an international level; and loosens social restrictions. The Internet affirms, reinforces, and assists in maintaining effective interpersonal relationships.

KEY TERMS AND CONCEPTS

Use the *Communicating Effectively* CD-ROM and the Online Learning Center at www.mhhe.com/hybels8 to further your understanding of the following terms.

Attitudes 160
Beliefs 160
Bid 166
Blind pane 170
Commitment 176
Compatibility 161
Cultural information 169
Emotional intelligence 156

Empathy 158
Hidden pane 170
Interpersonal communication 156
Johari Window 170
Open pane 170
Owned message 167
Proximity 161
Psychological information 169

Response to a bid 166
Self-disclosure 168
Small talk 164
Social penetration 168
Sociological information 169
Unknown pane 170

CHAPTER REVIEW

QUESTIONS TO REVIEW

1. How is *interpersonal communication* defined, and when do you use it?
2. What role does emotional intelligence play in strategic flexibility?
3. How and why are you attracted to other people?
4. In what ways do your roles and relationships influence your communication? Provide specific examples to support your explanation.
5. What specific health benefits are likely to occur because of interpersonal relationships?
6. Why is small talk important, and what kind of environment supports small talk?
7. What is a bid, what is the bidding process, and how do bids contribute to interpersonal relationships?
8. What are the parts of an owned message, and how do they support both the bidding process and conflict reduction?
9. What contribution does self-disclosure make to nurturing and developing relationships?
10. What is the Johari Window, what are its four panes, and which pane is likely to grow in size along with a developing relationship? Why?
11. What are the essential elements of good relationships that tend to draw people together?
12. What is the effect of the Internet on interpersonal relationships?

Go to the self-quizzes on the *Communicating Effectively* CD-ROM and the Online Learning Center at **www.mhhe.com/hybels8** to test your knowledge of the chapter contents.

CHAPTER 8

Evaluating and Improving Relationships

OBJECTIVES

After reading this chapter, you should be able to:

- Summarize the stages of a relationship in coming together and coming apart.
- Explain extrinsic, intrinsic, and instrumental rewards and costs and show why they are important.
- Define *aggressive talk* and *indirect aggression* and explain how to deal with them.
- Define *regrettable words* and explain how people respond to them and how they affect relationships.
- Distinguish between good and bad criticism.
- Describe the precautions for delivering criticism.
- List and explain the steps in conflict resolution.
- Summarize the precautions necessary to ensure safety and security in online relationships and in those online relationships that transfer to the real world.

WHEN VICKI VANCE LEFT FOR SCHOOL, SHE THOUGHT SHE HAD found the love of her life. Kent was popular, good looking, athletic, and deeply in love with her. Everyone who knew them, knew they were meant to be together—a "match made in heaven" they would say.

Vicki wanted to pursue politics, and she needed a political science major with a communication minor to make it possible. She was looking forward to her undergraduate education because she thought the challenge would be both inspiring and exciting.

Kent did not want to go to college; he didn't do well in high school, and he found reading, studying, and learning dull and boring. His close friends were not planning to further their education, and he liked hanging out with his friends and working at the local department store.

Things between Vicki and Kent were great when Vicki first left for college, but staying in touch with Kent was tough because he didn't like using the Internet, never called just to say "hi," and didn't believe in writing letters. Kent was jealous of Vicki and all the male contacts she had made at school. He resented her continued education, and the tension was magnified when she discussed her classes, assignments, professors, and campus activities. Every time Vicki went home she noticed the distance between them had widened; consequently she went home less and less.

Vicki met Mark in her first political science class, when she had to borrow a pen from him to take notes. Mark would walk her from class, wait for her before class, and always select a seat next to hers in lecture. Soon they were hanging out together, and through their many discussions they discovered they had several similar interests and goals.

Vicki was feeling torn. She had known Kent for nearly four years. They were close, and she knew it would hurt him deeply if she even talked about Mark, much less told Kent they should try to cool their relationship. She felt she had to keep quiet, hope that things would change in some way, and wait for Kent either to find someone else or realize that their relationship was over. Vicki didn't like her decision. She had no guts, and she didn't like that. But she didn't want to hurt Kent.

It would be wonderful if, once relationships were formed, they remained healthy, happy, and rewarding for both partners. Unfortunately, this is not true. If you look at the divorce statistics alone you realize that many relationships don't last, but the fact that 50 percent of marriages end in divorce is *not* true either. By the 5th year of marriage, 10 percent end in divorce; by the 10th year, another 10 percent (or 20 percent cumulatively) end in divorce; another 10 percent end in divorce by the 18th-year (30 percent cumulatively), and by 50 years, another 10 percent (or 40 percent cumulatively). These statistics vary by state, by region within states, and by religious affiliation, race, culture, and co-culture, too. Most marriages that fail, however, do so before the partners reach their mid-40s.

Partners often cite a number of reasons for their failed marriages, and these relate to failed relationships of any kind: poor communication, financial problems, lack of commitment, a dramatic change in priorities, and infidelity. Other reasons include failed expectations or unmet needs; addictions and substance abuse; physical, sexual, or emotional abuse; and lack of conflict resolution skills.

Five factors destroy relationships between young people:

1. The partners fail to anticipate differences resulting from diverse cultural backgrounds, family experiences, and gender.
2. They buy into the notion of a "fifty-fifty" relationship, honestly expecting their partner to meet them halfway.
3. They have been taught that humankind is basically good; therefore they fail to anticipate the conflict that will occur when either of two self-centered partners demands his or her own way.
4. They fail to cope with life's trials. Instead of standing together through hard times, they blame each other or think something is wrong with their partner and the way he or she handles difficulties.
5. They have a fantasy view of love. They quickly feel stuck with an unloving partner and become deceived into believing the next one will be better.

The purpose of this chapter is to discuss some of the ways to evaluate and improve relationships. We will first look at the stages of a relationship—both coming together and coming apart—which will help you better understand where a relationship is, especially if it is in one of the declining stages. We discuss some of the questions that need to be asked in evaluating relationships: questions to ask about yourself, your partner, rewards and costs, and relationship roles. In the section titled "Improving Relationships," we look at aggressive talk, regrettable talk, criticism and complaints, avoidance, defensive communication, resolving conflicts, and the communication strategies you can use in each case. We end the chapter by assessing and evaluating relationships established on the Internet.

Not all relationships are positive and should be saved. Some are highly resistant to any kind of alteration; thus, sometimes any kind of change that either partner attempts will fail.

Just one clarifying comment on the notion of a fifty-fifty relationship mentioned earlier: Often, couples honestly expect their relationship partner to meet them halfway. This is a fantasy. If you have no intention of committing yourself 100 percent to a relationship—on both an initial and an ongoing level—it is unlikely you will be successful. Fifty-fifty is unrealistic simply because when either partner cannot or fails to hold up his or her end of the bargain—which often happens when *any* other commitments come into play (like work or children)—the relationship fails.

THE STAGES OF A RELATIONSHIP

All relationships go through predictable stages as they grow and develop whether they are between romantic couples, friends, business partners, or roommates. Identifying the stages of a relationship and the attributes, stumbling blocks, and joys of each stage can help you negotiate it and the future with more success. The information is useful both to evaluation—do you like where you are, and is it bringing the rewards you want?—and to improvement—what can I do differently to achieve the goals I want?

Most relationships begin with superficial communication; then, if the people like each other, they take steps to see each other again. Mark L. Knapp, a writer and researcher who focuses on relationships, has found that relationships develop along rather predictable lines. He describes five stages in which relationships come together and another five in which they fall apart. Each stage is characterized by certain kinds of communication.[1] Let's begin with a relationship that is coming together, using the example of Vicki and Kent.

Coming Together

Stage 1: Initiating

There are numerous stumbling blocks when people want to initiate a relationship. The *initiating stage is characterized by nervousness, caution, and a degree of hesitation*,[2] but these are healthy stumbling blocks since engaging in the initiating stage bears some risks, the primary one being rejection. The specific suggestions in the last chapter regarding small talk, conversation starters, and bids and responses to bids should be of some help at this early stage.

The joys of entering the initiating stage are enormous. It is like beginning any new adventure where the outcome is unknown, but the trip can make it all worthwhile. Joys, of course, include happiness or just finding a friend (companion, soulmate, intimate, confidante, playmate, kindred spirit, buddy, pal, chum, homeboy, homegirl, or colleague). Sometimes just the boost to your self-esteem is sufficient.

Michael Leviric and Hara Estroff Marano, in an article titled "Why I Hate Beauty," explain the importance of beauty in the initiating stage. They claim that "In the world of abstract logic, marriage is looked on as a basic matching problem with statistical underpinnings in game theory." They state, "Logic says that everybody wants to do as well as they possibly can in selecting a life partner. And when people apply varied criteria for choosing a mate, everybody ends up with a partner with whom they are more or less satisfied. Not everybody gets his or her No. 1 choice, but everybody winds up reasonably content."[3]

Vicki and Kent were introduced by friends on both sides who not only knew they were perfect for each other but told them so. The buildup was so great, both knew the reality couldn't match the hype. Although Vicki didn't like Kent at first (she thought he was a showoff), he was a great dancer, and having a male friend who loved to dance was something Vicki found attractive. Often, first impressions tell you whether the other person is interesting enough for you to pursue a relationship. For Vicki and Kent, it was all the small talk and the bids and responses to bids that started to draw them together—even though the first impression may not have predicted movement to the next stage.

STRATEGIC FLEXIBILITY

It is precisely when you find yourself in the initiating and experimenting stages of coming together when you can really flex your strategic muscles. The environment is right, the stage is set, and everything depends on your ability to be alert and make the accurate, appropriate, and relevant moves.

Stage 2: Experimenting

In the *experimenting stage,* people make a conscious effort to seek out common interests and experiences. They experiment by expressing their ideas, attitudes, and values and seeing how the other person reacts. For example, someone with strong feelings about the equality of all races might express an opinion to see whether the other person agrees or disagrees.

The stumbling blocks in stage 2 are fewer. Perhaps the biggest one is the length of time experimenting can take. Talking with someone superficially at school, work, church, or in a chat room can last for years. This is healthy because so many people do not take the time to get to really know another person, and decisions about moving to the next stage often occur without sufficient knowledge and understanding. Thus, it is good to draw out this stage. Most relationships never go beyond this stage and, it seems, many that did perhaps should not have—especially when no foundation for proceeding had been established.

The joy of stage 2 is that everything is generally pleasant, relaxed, and uncritical, although still a bit uncertain.[4] Stage 2 is rewarding, too, if you like getting to know someone else: seeking common ground, testing the waters with self-disclosure, and providing personal histories. Vicki went through this stage with Kent, and it went on and on simply because dancing and talking together served their purposes early in the relationship, and, particularly, because Vicki was not especially impressed with him early on. Kent would tell Vicki about his family, upbringing, interests, and hobbies, but Vicki was reluctant to open up as much for some time.

Between Vicki and Mark, things were quite different. When Mark waited after class to walk her across campus, the two of them covered more territory getting to know each other in that first meeting than Vicki and Kent did in weeks. They not only found they had common interests and values, but they both decided they wanted to talk even more. Vicki and Mark engaged in an equal amount of self-disclosure. The connectedness and comfort they experienced with each other led them to going for coffee after class, meeting outside class to eat together, and going to campus events together. It was as if stage 1, initiating, was defined and completed when Vicki asked Mark for a pen, and Mark gave her his extra one.

Many relationships stay at this particular stage—the participants enjoy the level of the relationship but show no desire to pursue it further.

Stage 3: Intensifying

There are many joys associated with the *intensifying stage*. Vicki and Mark have discovered that they like each other quite a lot. They spend more time with each other because they are happy, loving, and warm. They swap DVDs and CDs and spend free time together. Not only do they enjoy each other's company, but closeness is both wanted and needed, so they hold hands, kiss, and hug. They start to open up to each other—telling each other private things about their families and friends. They talk about their moral values. They also begin to share their frustrations, imperfections, and prejudices.

Other things happen in the relationship. Vicki and Mark call each other by nicknames; they develop a "shorthand" way of speaking; they have jokes that no one else understands. Their conversations begin to reveal shared assumptions and expectations. Trust becomes important. They believe that if either one tells the other a secret, it will stay between them. They start to make expressions of commitment such as making plans together: "Let's go to Ocean City to work next summer." Expressions of commitment include buying gifts for each other or doing favors without being asked.[5] They also start engaging in some gentle challenges of each other: "Do you really believe that, or are you just saying it?" Openness has its risks in the intensifying stage. Self-disclosure makes the relationship strong, but it also makes the participants more vulnerable to each other.

This is likely to be the only stumbling block—vulnerability. The key here is trust, and it underscores the value of the "getting-to-know-you" stages of initiating and experimenting. Trust often takes time to develop. When trust is secure, there is less chance of being wounded, injured, or attacked because of a breach of trust. Lack of fidelity, lying, or the sharing of personal information with others outside the relationship are breaches of trust and can cause deep wounds that are difficult to overcome.

Stage 4: Integrating

Vicki and Mark have reached the *integrating stage*—the point at which their individual personalities are beginning to merge. People expect to see them together, and they are unhappy when apart.[6] If people see just one of them, they ask about the other. The friendship has taken on a specialness. They do most things together and reflect about their common experiences—the things they do together. They go to the same parties and have a lot of the same friends; their friends assume that if they invite one, they should invite the other. Each of them is able to predict and explain the behavior of the other. They feel like one person.

This is where the problem occurred between Vicki and Kent. Their relationship had already reached stage 4, integrating, before she left for college and before she met Mark. She and Kent had developed a deep and important relationship and suddenly, without warning, Mark entered the picture. Vicki and Mark have not reached this stage; however, given what has already occurred in their relationship, it seems like it won't be very long. Those who reach this stage are usually best friends, couples, or parents and children. It is at this stage—if it hasn't happened before—that partners meet one another's family and friends.

Stage 5: Bonding

The last coming-together stage of a relationship is *bonding*. At this point, the participants make some sort of commitment that announces their relationship to those around them. An announcement of an engagement or marriage would be an example of bonding. In other cases, such as those between friends, the bonding agreement might be less formal—for example, agreeing to room together. Whatever form it takes, bonding makes it more difficult for either party to break away from the relationship. Therefore, it is a step taken when the participants have some sort of long-term commitment to their relationship.

Bonding occurs in nonromantic relationships as well. For example, good friends become best friends often because of some especially meaningful (good or bad) "bonding" experience. Dorm roommates are often randomly assigned, but nonromantic apartment mates, who must depend on each other for bill paying, housekeeping, amenities, and the like, are more likely to be successful if they've reached a bonded relationship before moving in together. Partners in business, in the police, or in the military—where success, reputation, and even survival depend on close bonding with and trusting of each other—each know exactly what to expect from the other in critical situations. This same kind of bonding can occur between dancers and ice skaters as well. Although there are times when you may want to believe it isn't so, sex on its own, or a "one-night stand" with a virtual stranger, is not bonding.

Advancing from Stage 1 to Stage 5

The five coming-together stages build on one another (see Figure 8-1). For a relationship to advance to the next stage, both parties must want the change to occur. Because most of us have only limited time and energy for intense relationships, we are willing to let most of our relationships remain at the second or third stage. The first three stages permit us to become involved in friendships and to carry out normal social activities. The fourth and fifth stages, integrating and bonding, demand much more energy and commitment—they are reserved for very special relationships.

Notice that, for the most part, in the coming-together stages, the joys both partners experience outweigh the stumbling blocks that occur. In all stages you have five

At the bonding stage, participants make a formal commitment that announces their relationship to those around them.

Chapter 8 Evaluating and Improving Relationships 189

Figure 8-1
The Stages of a Relationship

Coming together →
Coming apart →

1 = Initiating
2 = Experimenting
3 = Intensifying
4 = Integrating
5 = Bonding

1 = Differentiating
2 = Circumscribing
3 = Stagnating
4 = Avoiding
5 = Terminating

choices: to continue moving forward, to stagnate, to slow down, to go backward, or to exit.[7] Since stage 3 is the first in which there is self-disclosure, moving from stage 2 to stage 3 is particularly sensitive. If one person opens up too quickly, the other might feel so uncomfortable that he or she will be unwilling to go on to a new stage in the relationship.

Coming Apart

For a relationship to continue, the participants must grow and change together. If they cannot do this in ways that are satisfying to both of them, the relationship will come apart. Although it is more satisfying to look at relationships coming together, we all know that relationships also fail. Relationships that are failing can also be described in five stages—stages that reverse the process of coming together. Notice as you read about each stage that stumbling blocks have eliminated any joy that was there.

Stage 1: Differentiating

Time has passed, and Vicki and Mark have been married for over a year. The first months were a little rocky, but now serious problems are beginning to emerge. Vicki likes to go out several nights each week; Mark wants to stay home. Mark likes to cook new and exotic food; Vicki wants to eat meat and potatoes. Even their love for movies is causing conflict: Vicki wants to see them as soon as they open; Mark wants to wait until they are released as DVDs so that they can watch them at home.

Vicki and Mark have entered the *differentiating stage*. The interdependence of their courting stage is no longer so attractive. Now they are beginning to focus on how different they are, and much of their conversation is about their differences rather than their similarities. There is noticeable arguing, with talk about being incompatible.[8]

STRATEGIC FLEXIBILITY

If you are going to use strategic flexibility effectively—especially with respect to the coming-together stages—it requires great sensitivity. One measure that can be used to help you know what to do is your comfort level. When you evaluate factors, elements, and conditions, how comfortable are you with your assessment?

To some extent, the differentiating stage is a healthy phase that most couples experience. Many work out their differences by being autonomous sometimes and interdependent other times. For example, Vicki and Mark go together to family gatherings and to parties. However, when Mark goes hunting, Vicki goes shopping.

The differences the two recognized and tolerated during the stages of coming together become focal points for discussion and argument. They can be worked out if they are not too great.

The most visible sign of differentiating is conflict. But differentiating can take place without conflict. Even if nothing specific is bothering the couple, they may discover, as they mature and find new interests, that they have less and less to talk about. Vicki, for example, reads the newspaper every day and follows world events. Mark, on the other hand, gets his news from the Internet and finds it too depressing to talk about. Each experiences slight loneliness because the two of them are no longer as close as a couple, and regarding the relationship itself, there is some confusion and inadequacy creeping in.[9] Where is the relationship going? How long can it go on like this? Am I at fault? These are a few of the questions that one or the other partner may be considering; usually they are internalized and never expressed at this stage.

Stage 2: Circumscribing

When a relationship begins to fall apart, less and less information is exchanged. It seems better to stay away from points of conflict in the relationship in order to avoid a full-scale fight. Thus this is called the *circumscribing stage*.

Now conversation is superficial; everyday matters are discussed: "Your mail is on the desk." "Did I get any telephone calls?" "Do you want some popcorn?" The number of interactions is decreased, the depth of discussions is reduced, and the duration of each conversation is shortened. Because communication is constricted, the relationship is constricted.

Most people who find themselves in this stage try to resolve their problems by discussing the relationship itself. In response, the negative turn in the relationship might change. For example, Mark could go out to a movie with Vicki, and Vicki could agree to try some different food. In other cases, discussion about the relationship might reveal greater differences between the participants. In such cases, discussion about the relationship leads to even more conflict, so the participants limit discussion to "safe" topics. Vicki and Mark, for instance, stay away from the topic of having children because they know they will fight about it.

Often, people at this stage pursue different activities. Sometimes, too, they act aloof from each other. These experiences reveal coldness and distance. With respect to each other, partners are uncaring, and one or the other may become depressed or frustrated, feeling unloved and misunderstood.[10]

Persons who are in this stage often cover up their relationship problems. Although they might reveal problems to very close friends, in social situations they give the appearance of being committed to each other. They create a social or public face—in essence, a mask.

Stage 3: Stagnating

The *stagnating stage* is a time of inactivity. The relationship has no chance to grow, and when the partners communicate, they talk like strangers. The subject of the relationship itself is now off limits. Rather than try to resolve the conflict, the partners are more likely to think, "Why bother to talk? We'll just fight, and things will get even worse"; thus, for self-protection, they give short answers to questions.

How long this stage lasts depends on many things. If Vicki and Mark lead busy lives and just come home to sleep, they might go on in this stage for months or even years. However, if Mark stays home and broods about the relationship, he may look for some kind of resolution to their conflict. Most couples whose relationship reaches this stage feel a lot of pain. The partners may find it hard to separate and may hold on to the hope that they can still work things out. Either partner at this stage may feel unwanted, scared, bored, and sentimental.[11]

Stage 4: Avoiding

The *avoiding stage* involves physical separation. The parties avoid face-to-face interaction. They are not interested in spending time together, in building any kind of relationship, or in establishing any communication channels.

This stage is usually characterized by unfriendliness, hostility, and antagonism. Sometimes the cues are subtle: "I only have a minute. I have an appointment." They can also be direct and forceful: "Don't call me anymore" or "I'm sorry, I just don't want to see you." Often, responses are "I don't care" and "I don't know." If communication occurs, it covers general matters only; there is no talk about the relationship.

In relationships where physical separation is impossible, the participants may act as if the other person does not exist. Partners eat in silence, stay busy, and, if possible, spend a lot of time away.[12] Each one carries on his or her activities in a separate room and avoids any kind of interaction. In the case of Vicki and Mark, Vicki might sleep in the bedroom and Mark on the living room couch. Often, partners feel some sense of nervousness, as well as helplessness and annoyance.[13]

Stage 5: Terminating

In the *terminating stage*, the participants find a way to bring the relationship to an end. Differences are emphasized, and communication is difficult and awkward. Each party is preparing for life without the other. They may talk about staying in touch and discuss what went wrong. A goal at this stage may be to divide up their belongings. There are feelings of unhappiness, but these are accompanied by a sense of relief. Often one partner is lonely or scared because of having to face life alone again.[14]

Some relationships cannot be entirely terminated. Partners who have children might terminate their relationship with each other as marriage partners but decide to continue in some kind of relationship as parents to the children. The more amicably this can be done, the better it is for the children involved. Partners might set down a list of rules that will govern the new relationship.[15] When the termination is a divorce, the court is the one that establishes the rules.

Sociologist Diane Vaughan has studied the patterns that occur when a relationship is about to end. She says that one member of the couple, realizing he or she is unhappy, begins the process of ending the relationship. This person typically begins by finding alternatives—often in the form of a transitional person. Although the transitional person might be a romantic interest, the person could also be a minister, a therapist, or a good friend. When one partner begins to find satisfaction elsewhere, the couple's relationship becomes less endurable. At this point the dissatisfied person lets the other know of his or her discontent through body language and words.[16]

Finally the time comes when the dissatisfied person lets the partner know that he or she wants to end the relationship. The partner typically feels betrayed, hurt, and shocked—and is often unprepared. Vaughan says that during the breakup, both partners suffer emotional pain and go through the same stages of disengagement: the process just happens at different times for each of them.[17]

EVALUATING RELATIONSHIPS: ASKING THE RIGHT QUESTIONS

One reason many relationships fail is simply that people seldom take the time to ask the essential questions—especially the questions that should be asked *before* embarking on a serious relationship. It is true, of course, that some of us begin a relationship with no intention of its becoming serious and then discover it has evolved to that level without a decision ever being made. Perhaps some of the questions in this section will help you if this happens.

Our purpose is not to destroy spontaneity, surprise, and discovery, but to deal with some of the broad issues that often lead relationships to fail. When these are resolved to your satisfaction, and you have taken all the necessary precautions that would predict a satisfactory future partner, there will be plenty of room for spontaneity, surprise, and discovery.

Ask Yourself Questions

There are three questions to ask yourself.[18] The first has to do with fear of commitment. Are you concerned about the idea of forever? Do you fear you could make a mistake in the person you choose? Do you fear a loss of your freedom or autonomy? Are you afraid of a bad marriage—like your parents, for instance? Do you fear you would be a bad mate?

Antoinette Coleman, in her online newsletter *The Art of Intimacy*, states that "If you answered yes to any of these, it would be a good idea to begin working to understand where these feelings come from. Once you understand them better, you can choose to address them."[19] It may simply be that you are not ready to make any long-term commitment, and you know at this point in your life that you just need more time, or more emotional growth.

The second question is about fear of forming a relationship with another person. How many dating experiences have you had? Do you tend to rush into relationships, or do you move them along with thought and careful decision making? Can you live without a partner? Can you envision yourself in the immediate future with a partner? Do you really know and like yourself? Do you believe you could have a successful relationship?

The third question asks about making a commitment to *this* particular relationship and to *this* particular person. Is there a genuine connection? Do you have a vague feeling that something is missing? What is the quality of your intimate relating—*not* how often or how good the sex is, but how open, sharing, and real your interactions are with each other. Does it seem like the two of you are just killing time? Does your partner want what you want? Do you seem to be inconsistent in your level of contact and affection? Is your partner still not over a past relationship? Do you (and does your partner) really know what you want?

Ask Questions about Your Partner

Let's say that through frequent contact and increased levels of self-disclosure you have discovered a potential relationship partner, but you don't know whether this partner is even ready for a relationship. What questions should you ask yourself to determine a partner's readiness? Six are absolutely essential:

1. Is this person able to communicate with you openly and honestly?
2. Does this person appear to have a strong self-concept?
3. Is this person aware of the time and effort required to have a long-term, loving relationship?

4. Is this person willing to put forth the necessary time and effort along with you to make a long-term, loving relationship possible?
5. Does this person see the commitment necessary for a long-term, loving relationship as *more than simply fifty-fifty?*
6. Is this person prepared—as you are—to make a relationship partner his or her *first* priority, after himself or herself, in life?[20]

If the answer to any of these questions is "no," then this partner is probably not for you.

Here is a key point: Entering into a relationship hoping that the other person will change, or thinking that you will change the other person, "is not a solid foundation for a loving, committed relationship. In most cases, with rare exceptions, you are wasting your time."[21] Instead, get into the habit of looking for what you can love and appreciate about your partner, rather than how he or she needs to change or be fixed, and it will change the whole dynamic of your relationship.

Ask Questions about Rewards and Costs

In Chapter 7 we introduced a small portion of Altman and Taylor's social penetration theory. Their theory is based on social exchange—the idea that relationships are sustained when they are relatively rewarding and discontinued when they are relatively costly.[22] **Rewards** are the pleasures that result from being in a relationship. **Costs** are the problems. The essential question is, "Do the rewards outweigh the costs?" or, phrased a bit differently, "Are you willing to live with the costs considering the strength of the rewards?" When you know your relationship partner well—see the Consider This box—it is easier to weigh rewards and costs.

Altman and Taylor listed three types of rewards and costs: extrinsic, intrinsic, and instrumental. **Extrinsic** means outside the relationship. **Intrinsic** means within the relationship. **Instrumental** refers to the basic exchange of goods and services. To make sense of these, let's put them into the context of a relationship you have that has not yet progressed to the level of sexual intimacy. Whether or not you want to take it to that level depends on weighing the rewards and costs.

Extrinsic rewards: You like the people your partner has introduced you to and the friends he or she hangs out with.

Intrinsic rewards: You appreciate the attention, warmth, and affection you gain from being in the relationship.

Instrumental rewards: You know that if you decide to raise the current level of intimacy, one of the rewards when you move in with your partner (which you have already discussed) is you will share both the rent and the furniture.

Extrinsic costs: You are not going to have as much time for your friends, and you are going to have to share them with your partner.

Intrinsic costs: Not only will you feel obligated to return the attention, warmth, and affection you are receiving—probably at an increased level if the level of intimacy increased—but you will also spend time listening, communicating, and self-disclosing.

Instrumental costs: You will have to share your belongings.

Now it is up to you. Often, it is good to actually list the rewards and costs honestly not just so you can compare them but so that you can think about them specifically and over time.

Mira Kirshenbaum, a therapist who works with families and couples, holds that since the dynamics of a relationship are constantly shifting, it is better to ask questions about the relationship that go right to the heart of it. For example, she maintains that

Consider This

Know Your Relationship Partner

Test the strength of your relationship by taking this quiz prepared especially for *Newsweek* by John Gottman. Happy couples have a deep understanding of their partner's psyche.

		True	False
1.	I can name my partner's best friends.	____	____
2.	I can tell you what stresses my partner is currently facing.	____	____
3.	I know the names of some of the people who have been irritating my partner lately.	____	____
4.	I can tell you some of my partner's life dreams.	____	____
5.	I can tell you about my partner's basic philosophy of life.	____	____
6.	I can list the relatives my partner likes the least.	____	____
7.	I feel that my partner knows me pretty well.	____	____
8.	When we are apart, I often think fondly of my partner.	____	____
9.	I often touch or kiss my partner affectionately.	____	____
10.	My partner really respects me.	____	____
11.	There is fire and passion in this relationship.	____	____
12.	Romance is definitely still a part of our relationship.	____	____
13.	My partner appreciates the things I do in this relationship.	____	____
14.	My partner generally likes my personality.	____	____
15.	Our sex life is mostly satisfying.	____	____
16.	At the end of the day my partner is glad to see me.	____	____
17.	My partner is one of my best friends.	____	____
18.	We just love talking to each other.	____	____
19.	There is lots of give and take (both people have influence) in our discussions.	____	____
20.	My partner listens respectfully, even when we disagree.	____	____
21.	My partner is usually a great help as a problem solver.	____	____
22.	We generally mesh well on basic values and goals in life.	____	____

Score your results: Give yourself one point for each "True" answer. Above 12: You have a lot of strength in your relationship. Congratulations. Below 12: Your relationship can stand some improvement and will probably benefit from some work on the basics, such as improving communication.

Source: *Newsweek*, by B. Kantrowitz and P. Wingert, "The Science of a Good Marriage," April 19, 1999, pp. 52–57. Although the survey was intended for married partners since that is the focus of the entire article, it seems to work as well for most established relationships.

the answer to a question like the following will tell a lot about a relationship: "Does it seem to you that your partner generally and consistently blocks your attempts to bring up topics or raise questions, particularly about things you care about?"[23]

Ask Questions about Roles

Roles are important simply because to be happy and content in a relationship, both parties must be satisfied with the roles and expectations. Roles may evolve naturally and spontaneously for males, but for females, they must be discussed and negotiated.

One of the questions we asked students in interpersonal-communication classes had to do with relationship expectations: "What role do you expect to play in any future intimate relationship you have?" Sometimes students referred to the roles their parents played, sometimes they offered a politically correct response such as, "That would have to be worked out with my future partner," and sometimes a few would take the traditional stance that males were the breadwinners and females the homemaker raising the kids. Most female students wanted to play a role equal to that of their partner and have an equal say in how roles would be determined.

In successful relationships, the participants have usually worked out their roles and expectations. But circumstances change through the course of a relationship, and if the communication channels are not available and open, unexpected problems can occur down the road.

Consider an example. Doug and Rita had never directly discussed roles; things were essentially equal. Then unexpectedly Rita found herself pregnant, but Doug and Rita never stopped to talk about how their roles would change once the baby was born. Who was going to take care of the baby during the day? Were there going to be any changes in school commitments or workloads, and who was going to make changes if necessary? Who was going to get up at night when the baby cried? Who would adjust his or her schedule if the baby became sick?

There is no way to ask all the questions that will prepare you for changes likely to occur in relationships. There are, however, some questions you could ask while dating that might give you important information about how your partner views relationship roles. For example, "What do you want in a wife (or husband)?"[24] Many women think males want a maid—a wife who stays home, cooks, cleans, and isn't too smart; however, many males *say* they want, more than anything else, a capable, assertive, happy partner, not just a housekeeper. On the other hand, some men think women want a partner who is a big, burly, hairy, handsome "he-man" with money. Most women, however, want a loving, gentle, warm, caring, intelligent, capable, self-confident man who is willing to stand up for his beliefs.

Some other key questions might be, "Who do you think should be responsible for financially supporting the family?" or, a related question, "Who do you think should be responsible for caring for the house and family?" "If you were the husband of a working woman, would you be willing to do an equal share of the housework and child care?" "What determines who will be the boss in a marriage?" "Do you think it's necessary for a couple to be roughly equal in ability in love, in neediness, and in education to have an egalitarian [equal] relationship?"[25]

Both men and women are likely to know how their partner would want them to respond. In the period of infatuation and, often in the early stages of a loving relationship, partners want to please each other. That is sufficient grounds for observing the behaviors of possible future partners to see whether what they say is supported by activities with which you agree—that is, that there are no mixed messages.

Can you ask "too many questions"? Never. Just don't act like it's an interview. Spread them out over a sufficient amount of time, and work them in among other thoughts and feelings, and remember a key point: Often men do not want to open up, share feelings, or even communicate. Accept this as a signal. Do you want to have a long-term relationship in which there is little or no communication?

IMPROVING RELATIONSHIPS: USING COMMUNICATION STRATEGIES

Negative influences are a natural and expected part of relationships. It is *not* the frequency of their occurrence; it is how carefully, delicately, and respectfully they are resolved to *both* partners' satisfaction that is important. All the motivation and willingness to communicate, assertiveness training, owned messages, and listening and communication skills in the world cannot prevent relationships from becoming fertile ground for silence and stonewalling, for anger and frustration, or for just plain hard times. No speech, article, book, or expert can protect you from the range of painful emotions that make you human.[26] The greater the number of skills and behaviors you have in your toolbox, however, the greater the likelihood that you will be able to face and resolve all the negative influences that come your way. This is where your ability in and use of strategic flexibility has its real payoffs—not just in holding your relationships together (the big picture), but in satisfactorily resolving all those daily, nuisance-type issues that seem to provoke and keep you in a negative frame of mind.

In this section we will look at six of the big issues: aggressive talk and aggression, regrettable talk, criticism and complaints, avoidance, and defensive communication. In the final sections of this chapter we will focus on resolving conflicts and the role of the Internet.

Aggressive Talk and Aggression

Aggressive talk is talk that attacks a person's self-concept with the intent of inflicting psychological pain.[27] This kind of talk includes disparaging words such as *nigger*, *faggot*, and *slut*, and phrases such as "You are so stupid," or "You are an inconsiderate idiot." Aggressive talk makes recipients feel inadequate, embarrassed, or angry, and because of the impact it has on receivers, it is seldom justified. Not only does aggression breed aggression, but it can escalate, and verbal aggression can quickly lead to physical aggression. People who can control verbal aggression are those who can recognize their anger and control it when it occurs—usually by giving themselves a cooling-off period.

When aggressive talk leads to aggression—an unprovoked attack—in relationships, often the relationship is doomed. People tempted to use verbal aggression should be aware that such actions can destroy relationships.

A more subtle act, and one we are often not aware of committing, is **indirect aggression** (sometimes called *passive aggression*)—when aggression is a mental act (usually characterized by manipulation, scheming, cunning, deviousness, or conniving). People who use this form of communication often feel powerless, and they respond in the only way they can, by doing something to thwart the person in power. For example, if your mother asked you to clean the kitchen, and you did a poor job so that she would never ask you again, you are using passive aggression. Or, if you were forced to go to college, and you flunked all your courses just to show your parents their decision was wrong.

It is difficult to deal with those who are aggressive, and if the acts of aggression are excessive, uncontrolled, or frequent, it may be necessary to seek professional assistance—for you, your partner, or the two of you together.

If your goal is to deal with the aggressive talk of a partner, your first step is to make every effort to see the situation *from his or her point of view*: with empathy. When the time is appropriate—usually *not* immediately after the aggressive talk has occurred because emotions have been triggered and normal conversation may not take place—you might begin a conversation by asking your partner to explain his or her point of view. Encourage him or her to talk about underlying assumptions, beliefs, or background factors that may have led to the behavior you are upset about. Summarize the person's words and *emotions* from his or her point of view (so that he or she agrees you understand it). Understanding the other's situation, point of view, and reasons for beliefs and behavior is usually the major task to accomplish.

If it is impossible to have this kind of conversation, it might be helpful for you to imagine a scenario that will allow you to defuse your anger. Or you may interpret your partner's aggressive talk as a legitimate need to take care of himself or herself. If you can focus on evidence from the present or past that proves he or she loves you and is not trying to hurt you, it is easier to forgive the behavior, forget about it, and move on.

Regrettable Talk

Regrettable talk is talk you regretted after saying it. You invited someone to help you move into a new place, and he tells you he has just been diagnosed with cancer and will be in the hospital. Of course you couldn't have known that, but you are now embarrassed for having asked him. Regrettable talk might have hurt someone, or it may have shared a secret you were not supposed to tell.

Mark Knapp, Laura Stafford, and John Daly, all communication researchers, studied regrettable words. They discovered that 75 percent of regrettable words fell into five categories. The most common was the blunder—forgetting someone's name or getting it wrong, or asking "How's your mother?" and hearing the reply "She died." The next category was direct attack—a generalized criticism of the other person or of his or her family or friends. The third was negative group references, which often contained racial or ethnic slurs. The fourth involved direct and specific criticism, such as "You never clean house," or "Don't go out with that guy; he's a sleazeball!" The fifth category—revealing or explaining too much—included telling secrets or reporting hurtful things said by others.

When people were asked why they had made the remark in the first place, the most common response was, "I was stupid. I just wasn't thinking." Some said their remarks were selfish—intended to meet their own needs rather than the other person's. Others admitted to having bad intentions. They deliberately set out to harm the other person. On a less negative level, people said that they were trying to be nice but the words just slipped out. Some people said that they were trying to be funny or to tease the other person, and the words were taken in the wrong way.

How did the people who were the objects of the regrettable words respond? Most often they felt hurt. Many got angry or made a sarcastic reply. Some hung up the phone, walked away, or changed the subject. Others were able to dismiss the statement or to laugh about it. When the speaker acknowledged the error, the listener often helped to "cover" the incident by offering an explanation or justification.

One of the most interesting aspects of this study addressed whether regrettable words had a negative impact on the relationship. Of the respondents, 30 percent said there was a long-term negative change, 39 percent said there was no change in the relationship at all, and 16 percent said that the change was positive—for example, "In the long run, I think our relationship is stronger since it happened."

Criticism and Complaints

Most people experience anger from time to time in close relationships. Anger does not have to destroy a relationship: University of Michigan researchers found that the average couple has one serious fight a month and several small ones.[28] John Gottman, psychologist at the University of Washington, found that anger is not the most destructive emotion in a marriage, since both happy and miserable couples fight. He calls the real demons "the Four Horsemen of the Apocalypse"—criticism, contempt, defensiveness, and stonewalling.[29]

Experts agree that it's *how* partners fight that makes the difference. The most effective kind of anger is that which expresses one's own feelings while conveying concern for one's partner.[30] Since most anger begins with a complaint or criticism, let's look at the most effective way to express it.

Criticism is a negative evaluation of a person for something he or she has done or the way he or she is. In more distant relationships, criticism usually originates from a higher status person and is directed toward one with lower status.[31] If the participants are equals, such as friends or a couple, criticism could come from either partner.

> Most people experience anger from time to time in close relationships. Anger doesn't have to destroy relationships. It is *how* people fight that makes the difference.

Researchers have discovered that criticism has five targets: appearance (body, clothing, smell, posture, and accessories); performance (carrying out a motor, intellectual, or creative skill); personhood (personality, goodness, or general ability); relationship style (dealing with others); and decisions and attitudes (opinions, plans, or lifestyle). They found that the target of most criticism is performance, followed by relationship style, appearance, and general personhood.[32]

The researchers also looked at what the recipients perceived as "good" and "bad" criticism. Most of the study's respondents believed that those who did not know them very well didn't have the right to criticize them. They were much more likely to identify criticism as bad if it was given in front of others rather than privately.

Criticism was labeled "bad" if it contained negative language (profanity or judgmental labels such as "stupid jerk") or if it was stated harshly by screaming or yelling. It was better received if it was specific and gave details on how to improve ("If you are going to be home after midnight, please call and let me know where you are"). Criticism was considered good if the person who made it also offered to assist in making the change or if its receiver could see how it would be in his or her best interest to change ("If you called me when you are going to be late, I wouldn't be so upset once you got home"). Finally, good criticism places negative remarks into a broad positive context ("If you called, it would reduce a lot of tension and anxiety in our relationship").

A **complaint** is an expression of dissatisfaction with some behavior, attitude, belief, or characteristic of a partner or of someone else. A complaint differs from criticism in that it is not necessarily directed at any specific person.

In studies of complaints between partners, researchers found that, as with criticism, some responses to complaints were more useful than others.[33] First, when complaints are trivial, they can probably be ignored. "This spaghetti is overcooked," or "Why do I have to be the only one to shovel the snow?" are trivial complaints. Second, a complaint should not be directed at anyone specifically. When you say, "Why doesn't anyone ever close doors?" you are not pointing to any one person, so the guilty party can change his or her behavior without losing face. Third, a complaint should be softened or toned down so that

Another Point of View

In her book *The Dance of Connection*, Harriet Lerner writes about some of the advantages of anger:

> My point is not that you should deny your anger or ignore its sources. On the contrary, anger is an important signal that something is wrong. It always deserves our attention and respect. Anger can sharpen our passion and clarity and inspire us to speak honestly and truly. It can motivate us to say no to the demands and expectations of others, and yes to the dictates of our inner self. Our anger can help us clarify where we stand, what we believe, and what we will and won't do. Our anger tells us when the other person has crossed a line that shouldn't be crossed. In all these ways, our anger preserves the very dignity and integrity of our voice. If we didn't have our anger to motivate us, our fear might lock us into passivity, silence, and accommodation.

Questions

1. Do you have any personal examples of the positive expression of your own anger?
2. Do you think anger when expressed tends to be more positive than negative? Do you think when anger is expressed, it is more frequently negative than positive?
3. Taking the opposite point of view, what are some negative things that occur because of anger?
4. How can the negative outcomes of anger be changed to positive by our own efforts? In a relationship, what can you do specifically to help encourage anger to become positive and not negative?

Source: From *The Dance of Connection: How to Talk to Someone When You're Mad, Hurt, Scared, Frustrated, Insulted, Betrayed, or Desperate*, by H. Lerner, 2001, New York: HarperCollins.

---

the complainer can express his or her frustration or dissatisfaction without provoking a big argument. Fourth, if the complaint is serious, the partners should discuss it and try to arrive at a solution or a compromise before the complaint turns into a serious conflict.

The most useful communication strategy for dealing with criticism is to use owned messages, as discussed in Chapter 7. Rebecca Cline and Bonnie Johnson's research emphasized the importance of making the careful language choices that owned messages require.[34] People react negatively and defensively when conversation is filled with you-messages such as "You always blame others for your problems," or "You need to have the last word, don't you?"

Avoidance

Many people who are in unsatisfying relationships try to dodge any discussion of their problems. Some people use silence; others change the subject if their partners try to begin a discussion. Often people who refrain from discussing relationships are trying to avoid any kind of conflict. The downside of **avoidance**—refusing to deal with conflict or painful issues—is that unless the problem is discussed, it probably will not go away.

The best communication strategy to use with respect to avoidance is a combination of owned messages—"I need to deal with the conflict we're having. I cannot continue avoiding talking about it, because it eats away at me and makes me angry"—and assertiveness. **Assertiveness** is taking the responsibility of expressing needs, thoughts, and feelings in a direct, clear manner. "I know you think that if we don't talk about it, it will just go away, but I know it's going to come up again. I want to talk about it right now [assertiveness]."

STRATEGIC FLEXIBILITY

Plan what you want to say before you say it! This is exactly what strategic flexibility demands: To anticipate, assess, evaluate, and select *requires advanced thought*, so that when you assert yourself you do it with care, concern, and attention.

Defensive Communication

Defensive communication occurs when one partner tries to defend himself or herself against the remarks or behavior of the other. The problem with defensive communication is that we are so busy defending ourselves that we cannot listen to what the other

199

For an example of defensive communication, view clip #1, "Defensive Communication."

person is saying. Also, defending ourselves is dealing with past behavior; it gives us no chance to think about resolving the problem.

How can we avoid defensive communication? A researcher, in a classic article, came up with six categories of defensive communication and supportive strategies to counter each of them[35] (see Table 8.1). Consider the supportive response in each instance, as communication strategies.

Evaluation versus Description

Evaluative statements involve a judgment. If the judgment is negative, the person you are speaking to is likely to react defensively. If you tell your roommate, "It is inconsiderate of you to slam the door when I am trying to sleep," he might respond, "It's inconsiderate of you to snore every night when I am trying to sleep." On the other hand, if you tell your roommate, "I had trouble sleeping last night because I woke up when I heard the door slam," he is much more likely to do something about the problem. Since you have merely described the problem, the message is not as threatening.

Control versus Problem Solving

People who consistently attempt to exert control believe that they are always right and that no other opinion (or even fact) is worth listening to.

Others tend to respond negatively if they think someone is trying to control them. For example, if you are working on a class project with a classmate and you begin by taking charge and telling him or her what to do, you will probably be resented. A better approach is for you and your classmate to engage in problem solving together. The same applies to close relationships. If conflict arises and you decide what should be done ("I'll take the car and you take the bicycle"), your partner is not likely to respond positively. It is better to discuss the options together.

Strategy versus Spontaneity

Often strategy is little more than manipulation. Rather than openly asking people to do something, you try to manipulate them into doing what you want by using strategies such as making them feel guilty or ashamed. A statement that begins "If you love me, you will . . . " is always manipulative. A better approach is to express your honest feelings spontaneously: "I am feeling overwhelmed with all the planning I have to do for the party. Will you help me out today?"

Neutrality versus Empathy

If you receive a low grade on a paper and are feeling bad about it, you don't want your friend to say, "Maybe the teacher was right. Let's look at both sides." When feelings are high, no one wants a neutral, objective response. What is needed is for the other person to show **empathy**—the ability to recognize and identify with our feelings. An empathic response to a poor grade in a course might be, "You must feel bad. You studied hard for that class."

Superiority versus Equality

People who always take charge of situations seem to imply that they are the only ones qualified to do so. Even if we have a position that is superior to someone else's, people will react less defensively if we do not communicate this

Table 8-1 **Categories of Defensive and Supportive Behavior**

Defensive Climate	Supportive Climate
1. Evaluation	1. Description
2. Control	2. Problem solving
3. Strategy	3. Spontaneity
4. Neutrality	4. Empathy
5. Superiority	5. Equality
6. Certainty	6. Provisionalism

Working Together

Imagine that you have caught your relationship partner in a bald-faced lie, and it is clear that he or she cannot deny it, explain it away, or otherwise retreat from the situation. Go around your group, and have each member supply first a defensive statement and then a supportive statement of the same level—or a supportive statement designed to offset, dispel, or otherwise ameliorate the defensive one. For example, the first person in the group supplies an evaluative statement: "You really annoy me when you lie to me like that. We agreed that is unacceptable behavior." The next person will supply a descriptive statement. The next student will offer a controlling statement, and the next a problem-solving one. The next student will offer a manipulative statement, the next a spontaneous one. The next student will offer a neutral statement followed by the next student with an empathic one. A superior statement is offered and then an equal one. And, finally, the next-to-the-last student offers a statement of certainty, and the final one a provisional comment.

---

superiority. An attitude of equality—"Let's tackle this problem together"—produces much less defensive behavior.

Certainty versus Provisionalism

Don't confuse people who are confident and secure with people who think they are always right. Confident and secure people may hold strong opinions; they are likely, however, to make many provisional statements that permit another point of view to be expressed. For example, someone might say, "I feel strongly on this subject, but I would be interested in hearing what you have to say."

Avoiding Defensive Communication: A Practical Example

Although we have discussed each of the six defensive categories separately, in most communication situations several of them appear simultaneously. You can see how this works in the following situations:

A Defensive Dialogue

Boss: You're an hour late. If you're going to work here, you have to be on time. (superiority, control)

Employee: My car wouldn't start.

Boss: That's no reason to be late. (certainty, evaluation) You should have called. (evaluation)

Employee: I tried, but . . .

Boss: When work starts at 8 A.M., you must be here at 8 A.M. (superiority, control) If you can't make it, you should look for another job. (superiority, control, certainty) If you're late again, don't bother coming to work. (superiority, control, strategy)

This dialogue leaves the employee feeling defensive, angry, and unable to say anything. Let's take a look at how it might have gone if the boss had been more willing to listen:

A Supportive Dialogue

Boss: You're an hour late. What happened? (description, equality)

Employee: My car wouldn't start.

Boss: Weren't you near a phone? (still no evaluation)

201

> *Employee:* Every time I tried to call, the line was busy. I finally decided that it would be faster to walk here than to keep trying to call.
>
> *Boss:* When people don't get here on time, I always worry that we're going to fall behind schedule. (spontaneity) Wasn't there any way of letting me know what happened? (problem solving)
>
> *Employee:* Yeah. I guess I panicked. I should have asked my sister to keep trying to call to let you know what happened. If it ever happens again, that's what I'll do.
>
> *Boss:* Good. Now let's get to work. There's a lot of catching up to do.

RESOLVING CONFLICT

When two people are in conflict and have decided that nothing will be served by avoidance or aggression, the option left open to them is **conflict resolution**—negotiation to find a solution to the conflict. Conflict arises because two individuals do not have compatible goals. Through the negotiation process, the two try to find out how they can both reach their goals. For the negotiation to be considered successful, both sides must be satisfied and feel that they have come out ahead. This is often referred to as *win-win negotiating*.

Deborah Wieder-Hatfield, a researcher in this area, has suggested a useful model for resolving conflict. In this model, each individual looks at the conflict intrapersonally. Then the partners get together to work out the problem.[36]

In the first stage, *intrapersonal evaluation*, each person analyzes the problem alone. This analysis is accomplished through a series of questions: How do I feel about this problem? How can I describe the other person's behavior? What are the facts?

In the second stage, the parties in the conflict get together to work out an *interpersonal definition* of the problem. It is important that both parties believe there is a problem and can define what it is. In this stage, it is important that each person listen carefully and check the accuracy of what he or she has heard by paraphrasing what was said. The same is true for feelings. At the end of this stage, both partners should agree on the facts of the problem.

In the third stage, the partners should discuss *shared goals*. Still focusing on the problem, the individuals should ask, "What are my needs and desires?" and "What are your needs and desires?" Then they should work to see whether their needs and goals overlap.

At the fourth stage, the partners must come up with *possible solutions* to the problem. Here it is useful to create as long a list as possible. Then each individual can eliminate solutions he or she considers unacceptable.

In the fifth stage, the partners move on to *weighing goals against solutions*. Some compromises are inevitable at this stage. The solutions may not be entirely satisfactory to either party, but they are a compromise that both hope they can live with. Negotiators would label this a win-win solution.

Since all resolutions are easier to make than to keep, the last stage of the process is to *evaluate the solution* after some time has passed. Did the solution work? Does it need to be changed? Should it be discussed again at a later date? As we mentioned earlier, it is not easy to change human behavior. When partners work to resolve conflict, even when they come up with good solutions there is likely to be some backsliding. It therefore makes good sense to give partners a chance to live up to their resolutions. Letting time pass before both negotiators are held accountable helps achieve this goal.

Gottman, from all of his research on couples, says that happy couples have a different way of relating to each other during disputes. Partners make frequent "repair attempts," reaching out to each other in an effort to prevent negativity from getting out of control in the midst of conflict. Humor, too, is often part of a successful repair attempt. If partners can work together and appreciate the best in each other, they learn to cope with the problems that are part of every relationship. Partners must learn to love each other not just for what they have in common but for things that make them complementary as well.[37]

The Bottom Line

The Institute for American Values conducted a study whose results bear directly on the discussions in this chapter.[38] Their research countered what they labeled the "divorce assumption"—that most people assume that a person stuck in a bad marriage has two choices: stay married and miserable or get a divorce and become happier. The study found no evidence that unhappily married adults who divorced were typically any happier than unhappily married people who stayed married.[39]

Two-thirds of unhappily married spouses who stayed married reported that their marriages were happy five years later. Those in the most unhappy marriages reported the most dramatic turnarounds. These unhappy partners had endured serious problems, including alcoholism, infidelity, verbal abuse, emotional neglect, depression, illness, and work and money troubles. The study found three principal techniques for their recovery; those in unhappy unions of any kind can learn something about what it takes to improve relationships.

The first technique is *endurance*. Many couples, the study found, did not so much solve their problems as transcend them—they simply and stubbornly outlasted their problems. By taking one day at a time and pushing through their difficulties, the unhappy spouses said in their focus groups, many sources of conflict and distress eased—whether it was financial problems, job reversals, depression, child problems, even infidelity.

The second technique is *work ethic*. Unhappy spouses actively worked to solve problems, change behavior, and improve communication. They tackled their problems by arranging for more private time with one another, seeking counseling, receiving help from in-laws or other relatives, consulting clergy or secular counselors, and even by threatening divorce and consulting divorce attorneys.

The third technique was *personal happiness*. In these cases, the unhappy partners found other ways to improve their overall contentment, even if they could not markedly improve their marital happiness. That is, they improved their own happiness and built, for themselves, a good and happy life, despite a mediocre marriage.

The bottom line to improving relationship happiness proved to be *commitment*—having a positive attitude toward the relationship. Unhappy partners minimized the importance of difficulties they couldn't resolve, and they actively worked to belittle and downplay the attractiveness of alternatives to their current relationship.

THE INTERNET AND EVALUATING AND IMPROVING RELATIONSHIPS

When you are using the Internet, and when your goal is to evaluate an online relationship, the key is to move slowly. The potential for lies, deceit, half-truths, hidden agendas, and misunderstandings is real, and they are more likely to reveal themselves over time simply because people have difficulty being on their best behavior for a long period. What are the red flags to look for?

Does the other person avoid direct answers to questions about issues that are important to you?

Does the other person make demeaning or disrespectful comments about you or other people?

Is there any inconsistency in basic information? For example, do the answers about marital status, children, employment, and location appear consistent? How about the information on age, appearance, education, and career?

Is the other person pushing too quickly for an in-person meeting or avoiding phone contact?

Is he or she engaging in overly sexy conversation right from the start?

Is the other person asking for money?

Ask direct questions when you find an inconsistency. Do the answers make sense? If you don't get direct answers, how are the questions declined? If you attempt to dig deeper, which is your right, mature people may respectfully ask you to back off, tell you that you are frightening them, or let you know that your questions are premature. These responses let you know the other person knows, first, how to be respectful and, second, how to take care of himself or herself.

There are seven tips for making the transition from virtual to real world smooth and safe:

1. *Don't give out personal information.* If someone asks for a phone number, get theirs, and call back from a pay phone. Don't tell where you live or work, or what you do.

    Gather as much information about the other person as possible, but stop communicating with anyone who pressures you for personal information or who in any way attempts to trick you into revealing it.

2. *Move slowly.* This not only helps you assess the other person by looking for odd behavior or inconsistencies, but it also allows you to find out whether the other person is indeed who he or she says. One of the problems with online communication is the ease of self-disclosure. You share too much of yourself too quickly, thinking it will make you close, but intimacy is cultivated over time.

3. *Use caution.* Careful, thoughtful decisions yield better relationship results. Trust builds gradually. Pay attention, and look for the red flags.

4. *Be honest.* If you are realistic about your own claims, you will have little anxiety about trying to control and manage your information. Exaggeration is often difficult to explain if you decide to meet later. Be yourself.

5. *Request a photo.* Request photos, not just a single photo. Not only does this give you an idea of a person's appearance, but when you have several images in several settings—like casual, formal, indoor, and outdoors—you have contexts in which to place verbal comments. When you hear excuses about why you can't see photos, consider that the person may have something to hide.

6. *Chat on the phone.* After using the Internet—or along with it—the telephone is the next step. It is another way to find out about a person's communication and social skills, and with the addition of all the vocal cues—volume, pitch, rate, tone, and quality—and the elements of enthusiasm, force, and variety, you begin to form a better, bigger picture of the other person.

7. *Meet only when you are ready.* When you are ready, you can choose whether to pursue the relationship in the offline world. No matter what level of online intimacy was attained, you can still decide not to meet offline. Even if you decide to arrange a meeting, you have the right to change your mind.

If you should decide to meet in person, meet in daylight in a safe, public place where other people will be present. Always tell a friend where you are going and when you will return, and provide your own transportation. If you feel unsafe or uncomfortable, leave.

Assess Yourself

Relationship Survey

The statements below refer to people in a close relationship (e.g., a relationship between two partners in an intimate relationship). For each statement decide to what extent it is characteristic of your feelings and behaviors using the following scale: A = Not at all characteristic of me; B = Slightly characteristic of me; C = Somewhat characteristic of me; D = Moderately characteristic of me; E = Very characteristic of me. Write the letter for the answer in each blank.

_____ 1. I am a good partner for an intimate relationship.
_____ 2. I am depressed about the relationship aspects of my life.
_____ 3. I am better at intimate relationships than most other people.
_____ 4. I feel good about myself as an intimate partner.
_____ 5. I sometimes have doubts about my relationship competence.
_____ 6. I am disappointed about the quality of my close relationship.
_____ 7. I am not very sure of myself in close relationships.
_____ 8. I cannot seem to be happy in intimate relationships.
_____ 9. I tend to be preoccupied with close relationships.
_____ 10. I think of myself as an excellent intimate partner.
_____ 11. I am less than happy with my ability to sustain an intimate relationship.
_____ 12. I would rate myself as a "poor" partner for a close relationship.
_____ 13. I feel down about myself as an intimate partner.
_____ 14. I am confident about myself as a relationship partner.
_____ 15. I feel unhappy about my interpersonal relationships.
_____ 16. I am not very confident about my potential as an intimate partner.
_____ 17. I feel pleased with my love relationships.
_____ 18. I sometimes doubt my ability to maintain a close relationship.
_____ 19. I feel sad when I think about my intimate experiences.
_____ 20. I have few doubts about my capacity to relate to an intimate partner.
_____ 21. I am not discouraged about myself as a loving partner.

Go to the *Communicating Effectively* CD-ROM and the Online Learning Center at **www.mhhe.com/hybels8** to see your results and learn how to evaluate your attitudes and feelings.

Source: Adapted from *The Relational Assessment Questionnaire (RAQ)*, by W. E. Snell, Jr., Department of Psychology, Southeast Missouri State University, September 11, 1999. Retrieved January 10, 2005, from http://www4.semo.edu/snell/scales/RAQ.htm

CHAPTER REVIEW

SUMMARY

The most important relationships in our lives go through five stages as they are coming together: initiating, experimenting, intensifying, integrating, and bonding. Relationships that remain superficial go through only the first or second stage. When relationships come apart, they also go through five stages: differentiating, circumscribing, stagnating, avoiding, and terminating.

In evaluating relationships, ask yourself questions about commitment, forming a relationship with another person, and making a commitment to a specific relationship and particular person. Next, you need to ask yourself questions about your partner. Following that, ask yourself questions about rewards and costs and, finally, ask yourself questions about roles.

To improve relationships you are likely to have to deal with aggressive talk and aggression, regrettable talk, criticism and complaints, avoidance, defensive communication, and conflict. There are no universal, all-encompassing, always successful ways for dealing with each of these areas; however, it should be clear that the better you are at applying the strategic flexibility framework, the better you will be at revealing empathy, using owned messages, and displaying assertiveness when necessary.

The bottom line was revealed in a study by the Institute for American Values and the techniques the survey uncovered that unhappy couples use to recover. The first is endurance; simply outlast the problems. The second is work ethic; put forth effort to solve problems, change behavior, and improve communication. The third is personal happiness; find other ways to improve your overall contentment. All of these techniques require commitment—a positive attitude toward relationships.

There are several ways to evaluate online relationships. We looked at red flags, tips for making the transition from online to real life smooth and safe, and suggestions for meeting in person.

KEY TERMS AND CONCEPTS

Use the *Communicating Effectively* CD-ROM and the Online Learning Center at www.mhhe.com/hybels8 to further your understanding of the following terms.

Aggressive talk 196
Assertiveness 199
Avoidance 199
Complaint 198
Conflict resolution 202
Costs 193
Criticism 197
Defensive communication 199
Empathy 200
Evaluative statements 200
Extrinsic costs 193
Extrinsic rewards 193
Indirect aggression 196
Intrinsic costs 193
Intrinsic rewards 193
Instrumental costs 193
Instrumental rewards 193
Regrettable talk 197
Rewards 193

CHAPTER REVIEW

QUESTIONS TO REVIEW

1. When a relationship comes together, it goes through five stages: initiating, experimenting, intensifying, integrating, and bonding. What happens in each stage?
2. When a relationship is in the process of breaking down, it goes through the following stages: differentiating, circumscribing, stagnating, avoiding, and terminating. What happens in each of these stages?
3. When engaged in the process of evaluating relationships, what are the categories of questions you need to ask? Provide a sample question for each category.
4. What are the differences among extrinsic, intrinsic, and instrumental rewards and costs? Give an example of each.
5. What methods are suggested for diffusing aggressive talk and aggression?
6. What is regrettable talk and what can you do about it?
7. What are the guidelines for delivering criticism?
8. What are the six types of defensive communication, and how can each one be changed to supportive communication?
9. What are the six stages of conflict resolution?
10. When it comes to relationships, what are the three techniques unhappy partners can use to recover from an unhappy union?
11. What are red flags when it comes to online communication? What are some examples of red flag comments?
12. What are some of the essential tips that will help online communicators transition to the real world?

Go to the self-quizzes on the *Communicating Effectively* CD-ROM and the Online Learning Center at **www.mhhe.com/hybels8** to test your knowledge of the chapter contents.

CHAPTER 9

Communicating at Work: Professional Communication

OBJECTIVES

After reading this chapter, you should be able to:

- Define *professional communication*.
- Describe the ways information interviews are used.
- Explain the steps in preparing for the information interview.
- Outline the process of preparing for employment interviews.
- Identify cultural and gender differences in the workplace and show how to cope with them.
- Describe the important ingredients of communicating within a professional atmosphere.
- Demonstrate the process of dealing with conflict at work.
- Explain the strengths and weaknesses of the Internet in professional communication.

KYLIE BEGAN COLLEGE BY ENROLLING IN THE SCHOOL OF BUSINESS WITH an emphasis in sales and sales management and a minor in communication. She knew that a high grade point average (GPA) and a degree would not guarantee her career success; therefore, she wanted to do everything she could to develop and support her skills.

Her undergraduate courses in the principles of selling, sales management, and advanced professional selling convinced her that selling was her specialty. She filled her résumé with evidence that she had the skills employers value: work ethic, communication, information-gathering, and people skills. She took courses that reinforced her analytical and problem-solving skills—skills she knew would be important to future employers as well.

To help support herself, Kylie took on part-time jobs, and she kept a journal that included the dates she worked at each, employers she met, names of potential employers and other contacts, and her impressions of them. She joined business and communication clubs, attended community meetings, volunteered whenever opportunities arose, and visited places of business to find out about potential jobs and to make new contacts. Kylie developed poise and self-confidence and learned to speak and think positively about herself and her abilities.

Kylie had great personal assets she knew would support her interest in sales. In addition, she was a happy person with lots of energy, and in her communication, she was open, honest, and direct.

This chapter focuses on **professional communication**—communication that relates to, engages in, is appropriate for, or conforms to business professions or occupations. We begin the chapter looking at principles of professional conduct as both an umbrella and a touchstone for all the other subjects discussed in the chapter. Second, we look at interviewing because, without a successful interview, it is unlikely that you will enter into the professional realm of business. We next discuss cultural and gender differences in the workplace. Then we examine communicating within a professional atmosphere and dealing with conflict at work, particularly with supervisors or managers and customers. The final section looks at the role of the Internet in professional communication. The Assess Yourself survey for this chapter allows you to measure your professionalism.

PRINCIPLES OF PROFESSIONAL CONDUCT

Every business expects you to conduct yourself professionally and to follow a line of conduct that suggests you are competent. Adhering to professional norms will win you active and supportive cooperation from others, professional success, and promotions, career advancement, and other opportunities. Unprofessional behavior generally results in lost collegiality, contracts, advancement, and jobs.

Following is a list of universal principles of conduct. Each area of business will likely adhere to additional principles or specific codes of acceptable behavior. Often, new employees must sign a code of ethical conduct along with their employment contract.

- **Integrity** is uprightness of character and honesty. Synonyms for integrity leave no question about its meaning: *honor, good character, righteousness, morality, virtue, decency, fairness, truthfulness,* and *trustworthiness*. These qualities are essential in providing a basis for trust, and they go to the core of what is expected from business professionals.

- **Respect** conveys regard and appreciation of the worth, honor, dignity, and esteem of all people. Relationships must be based on mutual respect and civility. Respect means that you will not engage in harassment or discriminate in any way on the basis of race, color, religion, gender, age, national or ethnic origin, political beliefs, marital status, disability, or social or family background.
- **Openness** means the free exchange of ideas within the bounds of reasonable behavior. When all members are receptive to exchanging ideas in an open and free manner, they will likely be amenable to reason, thoughtful consideration, and ideas that are supported by facts, evidence, and other forms of proof.
- **Responsibility** refers to your ability to meet your obligations or to act without superior authority or guidance, to discharge your duty, while perceiving the distinctions necessary between right and wrong, and with proper ethical discrimination. It relies on common sense, maturity, and dependability.
- **Teamwork** is unity of action by a group of workers to further the success of the business or organization while giving and receiving constructive criticism.
- **Self-improvement** means seeking all means available to maintain and enhance your professional competence by improving your knowledge and proficiency. There is a direct, positive correlation between success in your personal life and success on the job.
- **Ethics** is a set of standards that guides behavior in accordance with principles defined by your culture, your community, or your profession. You will not engage in fraud or make any false, misleading, disparaging, or defamatory comments, and your behavior will be in compliance with the rules and guidelines set forth by the business as well as with federal, state, and local laws.

There are a number of other issues involved in professional conduct. For example, it is expected that you will promote the aims of the business and conduct yourself to reflect positively on the business and your profession. You will use all proper means to maintain the standards of the business and your profession to extend its usefulness and sphere of influence, respect any confidence gained in your professional capacity, avoid unwarranted statements that reflect upon the character or integrity of other members of the business or profession, recognize your responsibility for the professional guidance of subordinates under your immediate control, and recognize your responsibility toward the environment and toward other employees.

> **STRATEGIC FLEXIBILITY**
>
> When the principles of professional conduct are a natural and automatic part of your entire skills and behaviors repertoire, then making ethical decisions as you anticipate, assess, evaluate, select, and apply your skills and behaviors becomes spontaneous and habitual.

INTERVIEWS

An **interview** is a series of questions and answers, usually exchanged between two people, that has the purpose of getting and understanding information about a particular subject or topic. Thus, when you ask a professor about a low grade you received on a paper, you are engaged in interviewing. You go in with a purpose—to find out why you received a low grade—and your conversation with the professor is a series of questions and answers.

What makes an interview different from interpersonal communication is that it is task oriented—it has the goal of finding out specific information. You interview someone for information you need to put together a speech, or you go into a job interview with the goal of presenting yourself so well that the interviewer will want to hire you.

Consider This

Key Steps for Successful Interviewing

Step One: Be prepared. Adequate preparation and practice are essential to demonstrate that you are a knowledgeable and credible person.

1. Know the purpose and objectives of the interview.
2. Make certain the setting and time are satisfactory.
3. Remove any barriers that might interfere with a successful interview.
4. Make certain you have communicated effectively with the other interview participant or participants.
5. Dress appropriately.
6. Practice. Immediate impressions will be formed from your verbal and nonverbal communication; thus, make certain your self-confidence, personality, and speech habits convey a positive impression.

Step Two: Have an interview plan, but be adaptable and flexible. Even though the interview may not unfold exactly as you anticipate, a plan shows that you are thoughtful, knowledgeable, and organized. If there is dead space during the interview, your plan will help provide a way to move forward. If the interview drifts far afield from where it should be, having a plan will help you refocus and redirect the interview. Help make certain that the interview efficiently and effectively fulfills its primary purpose and objectives.

Step Three: Follow up. Any commitment to an interview requires both time and effort, and all who participate require a minimum of a thank-you. If they have provided you important information, taken time away from their regular job, or given you an employment interview, a formal thank you in the form of a short, timely letter of appreciation is important and further reinforces and underscores your credibility and thoughtfulness.

The interviews we are most likely to participate in are information interviews and job interviews. Of course, interviewers may discard the regular interview and opt for a phone or e-mail interview or even lunch.

One thing all interviewers will look for, despite the type or format of the interview, is communication skills. "Improved communication is a key to retaining employees."[1] Sherry Morreale, associate director of the National Communication Association, cites a study, "Three Out of Four Say Better Communication Equals Greater Employee Retention," that reports the results of a survey of 4,000 human resource professionals conducted by KnowledgePoint. Seventy-one percent of the respondents cited solid communication skills as the major reason to retain employees. To foster a culture of communication, interviewers will seek people who reveal effective communication skills.

The Information Interview

An **information interview** is an interview in which the goal is to gather facts and opinions from someone with expertise and experience in a specific field. Types of information interviews include the **appraisal interview,** where a supervisor makes a valuation by estimating and judging the quality or worth of an employee's performance and then interviews the employee in connection with the appraisal. A **disciplinary interview** concerns a sensitive area. The manager hears the employee's side of the story and, depending on the outcome, may institute disciplinary action. An **exit interview** occurs at the termination of an employee's employment and is designed to resolve any outstanding concerns of employers and employees. Some exit interviews occur by questionnaire only. A final kind of informative interview is a **stress interview,** which is sometimes part of the job search. A stress interview is

> The goal of the information interview is to gather facts and opinions from someone with expertise and experience in a specific field.

designed to see how you act under pressure—to give interviewers a realistic sense of your response to difficult situations.

Interviews are a flexible means of information gathering. We can credit technology for expanding the media through which they are conducted; thus, often they are carried on in electronic chat rooms, in teleconferences, or via e-mail. The information interview is a useful tool when you are collecting information for a speech, a group discussion, or a paper. Also, it can serve as a way to get answers to questions you may have about a certain occupation, a career field, education, training, or work conditions.

Information interviews help us to get the most up-to-date information. Reporters, for example, make extensive use of information interviews. They interview the mayor of the town about her plans for increasing taxes. They talk to the governor of the state about his plans for reelection. On campus, an interview is the most effective way of getting information from members of the college community. A student interviews the vice president of administration about whether tuition will increase next year; another interviews a department head about the new requirements for a major.

One of the greatest advantages of the information interview is that it allows an opportunity for feedback and follow-up. If you don't understand something, you will have a chance to ask questions. An interview also permits you to explore interesting points of information as they arise—points you may not have been aware of beforehand. For example, if you are interviewing a member of the college administration about a tuition increase, she might mention that electricity costs have gone up this year. You can explore this area: Have they gone up because the utility company has raised its rates or because of greater electricity use on campus?

Preparing for the Interview

Preparation is one of the essential keys to success in most interviewing situations. It has three important benefits. First, it means you are less likely to waste the time of the interviewee because you will be able to focus on just the information you need. Second, with focused questions and pertinent follow-up questions, you are likely to gain a depth of understanding not available otherwise. (These benefits depend, of course, on your choosing the right person to interview.)

Finally, by preparing for the interview you will increase your credibility. If the people you are interviewing see that you have taken time to prepare, they are much more likely to be willing to spend their time with you. If you start out with such questions as "How do you spell your name?" or "I don't know much about this topic; do you have any ideas for questions?" you will not inspire confidence in your skills. On the other hand, if you show that you know something about the interviewee and about the topic, you will likely find much more willingness to discuss the topic seriously, and you will get better and more specific information.

Gathering Background Information.
Typical information you should have before the interview includes the proper spelling of the subject's name and his or her title. If the person is well known, you might be able to discover some biographical information before the interview. *Who's Who in America* contains biographical information about prominent Americans. Don't forget to check out the specialized editions, such as *Who's Who in the South*, *Who's Who in American Women*, and so on. If you are going to talk to someone who works for the college or university, the public relations office is likely to have some biographical information about the person.

You should also have background information on the topic of your interview. The purpose of an interview is not to give you a crash course on a particular topic; it is to give you information that is not commonly known or new insight into an old topic. For example, if you're going to interview someone about using the Internet, you should have some experience in actually using it so that you can speak with some authority.

Deciding on the Format.
Open-format interviews are relatively unstructured. As interviewer, you take note of or record the participant's statements but do not exert a great deal of control. In open-format interviews, you may ask interviewees to respond to a general topic or concern, and they determine the direction of the interview as they react to the points raised.

Closed-format interviews are highly structured. They are as formal, buttoned-down, and structured as the open format is freewheeling. As interviewer, you know exactly what you want to ask, and you work to keep your interviewee on track by asking one of your standardized questions and recording the respondent's answers to each one before moving on to the next question. Although this is an efficient technique for getting information because it is highly scripted, it doesn't allow much spontaneous information to emerge.

Semiopen format interviews occur when you have a core set of standardized questions that you ask in a standard manner and carefully record. However, this format allows you to deviate from the script with spontaneous follow-up questions if they are germane to the interview.

The best way to interview is to ask a variety of different kinds of questions, many of which emerge as the interview progresses. Thus, for most information interviews, our position is that the semiopen format works best because it most successfully accommodates this approach—requiring effective listening on the part of the interviewer and flexibility in adapting to what happens.

Preparing Questions.
In this section we will look at primary, follow-up, open-ended, closed, neutral, and leading questions.

Primary Questions.
Primary questions are designed to cover the subject comprehensively, and should be based on your background research. They often come first. Let's

say you are interviewing a member of your counseling staff about depression. Some of the primary questions you might ask are:

- What is the clinical definition of depression?
- How does depression differ from being in a bad mood?
- What are the signs of a serious depression?
- Where can a student go to get help?
- How is depression treated?

Follow-Up Questions. As the interview proceeds, you will think of other questions based on the answers given by your interviewee. These **follow-up questions** are useful when you want to go into a subject in greater depth. They also enable you to pursue an area that might be new to you or to clarify something you don't understand. Often the answers lead into such interesting areas that interviewers get information they hadn't planned on.

Open-Ended Questions. **Open-ended questions** permit the person being interviewed to expand on his or her answers. They lead to explanations, elaboration, and reflection. Most in-depth questions are open-ended.

Closed Questions. Questions worded in ways that restrict their answers are **closed questions**. "Do you plan to stay in this job?" "Are you going to graduate from school?" Other closed questions require only a short answer; for example: "Do you work better at home or in your office?" "What city would you most like to live in?" Closed questions have some advantages. They are designed to get a lot of information quickly, and they are good for eliciting facts.

When you prepare your interview's primary questions, they should be a mixture of closed and open-ended questions.

Neutral Questions versus Leading Questions. Questions that do not show how the interviewer feels about the subject are **neutral questions**. For example, a reporter interviewing the mayor about a tax increase might ask this neutral question: "Many people think this tax increase will create a hardship for people who live in the city. What do you think?"

Leading questions point the interviewee in a particular direction. If you were to ask the dean, "When is the college going to stop exploiting women?" you would be implying that the college is currently exploiting women. A more neutral way of phrasing this question would be, "Do you think men and women have equal opportunities at this college?" or, if you want to get more specific, "Men's intramural sports are allotted twice as much money as women's. Why is that?"

Leading questions often show the bias of the interviewer, and if there is a negative bias, it might arouse hostility in the person being interviewed. Sometimes, however, leading questions can be used effectively. If you are interviewing a member of Alcoholics Anonymous, it might be appropriate to ask, "How did AA improve your relationships in your family?" Sometimes interviewers use a leading question to get a strong emotional reaction from the person being interviewed. Reporters and talk-show hosts often ask persons they are interviewing provocative questions like "How do you deal with the kind of negative comments being made about you?" or "What is it like to be known for your bad temper and rudeness?"

It's important to know when to ask leading questions. Since some questions can lead to hostility, especially when feelings run high, the inexperienced interviewer should leave them for the end of the interview and concentrate on neutral questions at the beginning. You should also remember that some leading questions can result in explosive replies, and so you should not ask them if you are not prepared for the answers they might evoke.

Working Together

Working with others as a group, come up with follow-up questions to these answers from an interview:

1. The people I hate most are drunken drivers. Ever since our family suffered such a tragic loss, I have been determined to devote my efforts to getting them off the roads.
2. The United States government is taking care of Native Americans through the reservation system.
3. People who live in earthquake-prone areas should take some basic safety precautions.
4. Once the United States has invaded a country, it has an obligation to stay and help the country become stable and functioning again.
5. The harmful chemicals and wastes that are discharged into the air and water of our nation not only make us sick but cause death as well.
6. Burnout, which is stress caused by the inability to cope and adjust to the demands of certain situations, causes irritability, fatigue, and low motivation.

Now the group should create several more statements that will lead to follow-up questions. Pass them along to another group so that they can come up with follow-up questions.

Using Tape or Notes? Before you conduct an interview, decide whether you want to record it on audio or videotape. The main advantage of taping is that it allows you to record the interview without taking notes. You can concentrate on listening and pay more attention to nonverbal cues. Taping also permits you to get precise quotations. This is particularly useful if the topic is controversial. If you are looking only for background information, however, exact quotations might not be your goal. Note taking has advantages of its own. You don't have to worry about equipment, and it is easier to review notes to find what you want than it is to go through a recording cassette. One advantage of conducting an online interview is that you can print out an exact copy of what occurred.

If you are taping, remember that your credibility is as affected by your professional handling of the equipment as it is by your conduct of the interview itself. Get your subject's permission beforehand to record the interview. Make certain you have a long-enough videotape to cover the entire interview and more, and check the lighting and sound conditions.

Sometimes tape recorders or video cameras make people feel self-conscious, and some of the spontaneous nature of an interview can be lost. A very controversial interviewee might not want to be pinned down to his or her exact words. Another disadvantage of taping is that if you have a very long interview, you will find it time consuming to watch or listen to the tape and pick out the main points.

If you decide to take notes instead of making an audio or video recording, it is useful to devise your own form of shorthand. After the interview is over, you should immediately write out your notes in greater detail while the comments are still fresh in your mind.

Conducting the Interview

Whenever you conduct an interview, the most important thing you can do is know what you are talking about. Most people will be pleased if you let them know you have been researching the topic of the interview and have taken the time to find out something about it.

People who are not accustomed to being interviewed might feel nervous, so it is important to help them feel at ease. You can best do this by thanking them for agreeing to the interview and expressing your interest in the topic you will be talking about. If you are taping the interview, try to put the recorder in an unobtrusive place so that it will not make the interviewee feel self-conscious.

Once you begin asking questions and listening to answers, don't be afraid to ask for clarification. Sometimes interviewers do not do this because they are afraid of appearing ignorant. If the person you are interviewing, for example, mentions a Supreme Court case you have never heard of, you should immediately ask for background information on the case.

It is important that you, as interviewer, keep control of the situation. As you ask your questions, you should set the tone for the interview and establish your authority, the course the interview will take, and your relationship to the interviewee.[2] When you are talking to people in their own area of expertise, quite often they will digress or tell you more than you want to know. If you have scheduled a half-hour interview and after the first 10 minutes you are still on your first question, you are losing control of the interview and won't have time to pose all the questions you want to ask. If this happens, the only thing you can do is interrupt. This can be done with such statements as "This is really very interesting and I would like to talk more about it, but I want to ask you a few more questions."

Watch for nonverbal cues. If the issue is sensitive, is the interviewee giving you cues that he or she is dodging the questions? Is he or she avoiding eye contact? Tapping a pen nervously on the desk? Nonverbal cues can often tell you whether to follow up on a point or to steer away from it.

If you are interviewing someone who is on a tight schedule, don't run beyond the time you have scheduled. If you need more time, ask for it at the interviewee's convenience or call back to tie up the loose ends over the telephone. Occasionally, when you listen to your tape or read your notes, you will discover something you missed or something that needs clarifying. The telephone is a good way to get this information after the interview is over.

Once the interview is complete, thank the interviewee. If it was a good interview, don't be afraid to say so. Even people who are interviewed frequently are pleased to hear they have been helpful. Also, let the person know how you plan to use the interview.

STRATEGIC FLEXIBILITY
A key part of strategic flexibility is the word *flexibility*. When you are truly anticipating, assessing, evaluating, and selecting, you will be sensitive to the changes in direction that interviews take, and you will be able to adapt and apply appropriately the skills and behaviors best suited to the situation.

Analyzing the Interview

When the interview is over, spend some time thinking about how you did. Your success can be measured by how the interviewee responded to you and whether you got the information you needed.

You can tell whether your questions were well worded by the way the person answered them. If he or she never quite dealt with the points you raised, the problem may have been with the questions. If he or she asked for clarification, that is another indication your questions weren't well structured.

Looking at your notes will tell you whether you covered the subject thoroughly and listened carefully. Are your notes confusing? Are there gaps in them? Finally, did you conduct the interview in a professional manner? Did you arrange the questions in a logical order beforehand? Had you researched the topic of your interview? Did you know how to run the equipment? The main measure of your professionalism is whether your interviewee took you and your questions seriously.

Information Interviews as Precursors to Job Interviews

Information interviews can help clarify and define career goals, introduce potential employers, and establish a network of contacts that could lead to future employment. Unlike job interviews, information interviews do not require that you sell yourself to employers. They are arranged with individuals who are most likely to provide information directly or who can refer you to persons with information. The best feature of information interviews as precursors to job interviews is that they are a way of exploring your possibilities—choosing academic majors, making career choices, changing careers, or beginning a job hunt.

To use information interviews as precursors to job interviews, analyze your skills, scrutinize your interests, and clarify your career goals. Next, you need to research the world of work. Select occupational fields that fit your career interests and needs, and research them. Then write a résumé.

Now, locate appropriate people to interview. The first and most immediate source of information consists of friends, family, neighbors, colleagues, former employers, and anyone else you know who might either supply an information interview or offer you a referral. Think, too, about contacting faculty, career center personnel, staff at other university offices, alumni, and any employer contacts the career center can provide. Other sources are community service agencies and trade and professional organizations such as the chamber of commerce, women's organizations, or the Information Management Association. You might also scan the *Yellow Pages* and articles in newspapers, magazines, and journals. Consider, as well, attending local, state, regional, or national meetings for professional associations in your career-interest field.

Once you locate someone to interview, prepare a variety of questions in different categories. Tailor your list of questions specifically to the individual and his or her organization. Background questions might include "Tell me about how you got started in this field," and "What educational background or related experience might be helpful in entering this field?" Work-environment questions might include "What do you do during a typical workday or workweek?" "What skills are most essential for effectiveness in this job?" and "What are the most difficult or challenging elements to the job?" Questions on career preparation might include "What kinds of prior experiences are absolutely essential?" and "What kind of lifestyle does your job permit?" You can also ask about current and future job availability and potential job advancement, any personal advice, and referrals to others to whom you could talk.

Setting up appointments requires that you be resourceful and sincere and, above all, show interest in what your target person does. Most people enjoy the opportunity to discuss their work. If they are too busy to meet you during their office hours, explore the possibility of meeting over lunch or after work. If a person cannot meet with you, ask whether you can ask her or him a few quick questions over the telephone.

Here are some final reminders for conducting information interviews as precursors to job interviews:

1. Remember that this is not a job interview. Your purpose is to acquire information. Nevertheless, dress as if it were an actual job interview. First impressions are always important.
2. Get to your appointment a few minutes early, and be courteous to everyone you meet.
3. Take the initiative in conducting the interview. The ball is in your court; you ask the questions.
4. Indicate your strengths and interests at appropriate times.
5. Do not exceed your requested time, but be prepared to stay longer in case the contact indicates a willingness to talk longer.

6. Before you leave, ask your contact if he or she could refer you to others in the same career. By doing this, you can establish a referral list and build a job-search network.
7. Write a thank-you note. Thank the person for his or her time and interest and cite any conclusions or decisions resulting from the interview.
8. Keep a record of each organization you visit. Record the information you obtained, too: names, comments, and new referrals for future reference.

The Employment Interview

The **employment interview** is an interview used by an employer to determine whether someone is suitable for a job. In an employment interview you have two goals: to distinguish yourself in some way from the other applicants, and to make a good impression in a very short time. The key to reaching both these goals is careful preparation.

A **résumé** is a summary of your professional life written for potential employers. It should give an idea of your career direction, present your achievements, and cite examples of your skills. The career center on your campus can provide you with sample résumés. A faster way of obtaining free advice, samples, and different options is to consult the Internet. "How to write a résumé" entered into the Google search engine (October 24, 2005) produced 19,700,000 hits; electronic résumés produced 4,450,000; cover letters, 79,400,000, and "how to write cover letters" produced 23,000,000 hits. The phrase "how to write application letters" produced 18,900,000 Web sites. There is no shortage of information available at your fingertips.

The employment interview is a structured form of communication.

The Interview

The actual interview—when you are sitting face-to-face with a potential employer or his or her representative—is the great equalizer. No matter what your GPA is, no matter how much background and experience you have, and no matter how much you know, if you cannot interview successfully, you will not get the job.

The key to reducing anxiety and trepidation about the interview is being well prepared. Career experts have made it clear that you should spend three, four, or even more hours preparing for the job interview. The best way to start researching a company is simply to type its name into any major search engine. Search for the answers to these types of questions:

- How old is the company?
- What are its products or services?
- Who are its customers?
- Who are its major competitors?
- What is its reputation or industry standing?
- What are its new products or services?
- How large is the company?
- What are its short- and long-term goals?
- How has the company resolved its problems?
- Have there been recent employee layoffs?
- Where is the company located?
- What are the backgrounds of its managers?
- What training programs are offered?
- What is the company philosophy?

Next decide exactly how your skills will benefit the company. Be able to answer simple interview questions like "Why do you want to work for us?" "What do you know about our company?" and "How can you benefit our company?"

Interview Questions. Most employment interviews follow a predictable line of questioning. Spend time practicing your answers in the following areas.

Job Expectations. The interviewer will want to find out whether what you are looking for in a job is compatible with the job the company has to offer. You will be asked what you want in a job, what kind of job you are looking for, and whether you would be content in this particular job. The best way to prepare for such questions is to study the job description carefully and see whether your qualifications and expectations match the job description.

Academic Background. The interviewer will want to know whether you have had enough education to do the job. To find this out, he or she will ask you questions about the schools you attended, the degrees you have, and your grades. This is a good time to mention extracurricular activities that might be pertinent to the job.

Knowledge of the Organization. All interviewers assume that if you are interested enough in the job, you will have taken the trouble to find out something about the employer. Sometimes you will be asked a direct question: "Why do you want to work for this company?" An answer might be, "I know several people who work here, and they like the company very much," or "I am impressed by your management training program."

You should be prepared to ask some questions yourself about the company or organization. For example, "Is it a new position?" "To what extent does the company promote from within versus hiring from the outside?"

Work Experience. The interviewer will want to know about other jobs you have had and whether anything in your work experience might relate to the job you are applying for. Even though your work experience might not be directly related to the job at hand, don't assume it is necessarily irrelevant. Let's say you are applying for a job as manager of a local store and your only job experience has been taking junior high students on canoe trips every summer. Although this summer job might not be directly relevant, it would certainly show that you are a responsible person—a characteristic an employer will be looking for in a manager.

Career Goals. *Short-term goals* concern what you want to do in the next year or so. *Long-term goals* are directed to a lifetime plan. Interviewers want to discover whether you are thinking about your future, to gauge your ambition, and to see whether you will fit into the company's long-term goals. If you are interviewing for a management trainee position in a bank, for example, the interviewer will try to find out whether you can foresee a long-term career with the bank and whether the bank is justified in putting you in its training program.

Strengths and Weaknesses. Most interviewers will want to find out whether hiring you will enhance their organization. To this end you might be asked directly "What do you see as your greatest strength?" or "What is your greatest weakness?" Think about both these points in relation to the job being offered before you go to an interview. Even if you are not asked directly about your strengths, you should be prepared to sell yourself on your good points during the interview. If on your last job you reorganized a department and improved its efficiency by 50 percent, now is the time to mention it. Be honest if you are asked about your weaknesses. If you are doing something about them, mention what it is. For example, "I am not always as well organized as I could be, but I am working on setting priorities and that seems to help" lets the interviewer know you are working on the problem.

Being Interviewed
Proper Behavior. There are some very clear and well-established norms for the face-to-face interview.

- Plan to arrive 10–15 minutes early. Lateness, whatever the reason, is never excusable.
- Treat all people you encounter with professionalism and kindness—including the receptionist, secretary, and maintenance people.
- Maintain a professional image no matter what happens, even if your interviewer takes a casual approach.
- Wait until you are offered a chair before sitting. Sit upright, look alert, and show interest at all times. Be both an effective listener and an effective communicator.
- Always look your prospective employer in the eye while speaking.

- Follow your interviewer's leads and don't interrupt, but try to get him or her to describe the position and duties early in the interview, so you can apply your background, skills, and accomplishments to the position.
- Always conduct yourself as if you are determined to get the job. Never close the door on opportunity.
- Show enthusiasm.

Improper Behavior. Do not smoke, smell like smoke, chew gum, or lie. Do not over-answer questions, and if the interview moves into politics or controversial issues, listen more than speak. Do not answer questions with a simple "yes" or "no"; explain whenever possible. Don't criticize your present or former employers, and never inquire about salary, vacations, bonuses, or retirement in the initial interview unless you are certain the employer is interested in hiring you. If asked about the salary you want, indicate what you've earned, but make it clear that you're more interested in opportunity than a specific salary.

Appropriate Dress. Dress makes up a great deal of the first impression you make. Your attire should be both professional and comfortable. If you are a woman, wear a straightforward business suit, sensible pumps, and simple jewelry. Your hair and fingernails should be well groomed, and your makeup and perfume moderate.

If you are a man, wear a clean, ironed shirt with a conservative tie, a simple jacket and pants or business suit, and polished shoes. Your face should be clean-shaven, facial hair neatly trimmed, and hair and fingernails well groomed, and you should use cologne or aftershave sparingly.

After Your Interview. Make notes immediately so you don't forget any critical details. Send a short thank-you letter to the interviewer without delay. If several people interviewed you, send each a thank-you note. Restate your interest in the position and the confidence you have in your qualification. Do not call the employer back immediately, but if he or she said a decision would be made in a week, you may call back in a week. Again, thank him or her for the interview and, once again, reiterate your interest.

If you receive word that another candidate was chosen for the position you interviewed for, send a follow-up letter to the employer. Thank him or her for the opportunity to interview for the position. Let him or her know, too, that should another similar position open up in the future, you would love to have the opportunity to interview again.

CULTURAL DIFFERENCES IN THE WORKPLACE

Cultural differences, in the broadest sense, include not just obvious differences among people from other countries, but also "differences based upon income, regional origins, dress code and grooming standards, music preferences, and political affiliation."[3] An understanding of cultural differences may not only facilitate communication, but it can also avoid potentially embarrassing or even insulting situations.

Employers take diversity seriously and are willing to invest to establish and maintain it. Remember the principles of professional conduct, and make certain all your actions take place within that framework. First, treat others with respect and fairness as individuals, as if their opinion matters to you. Give others a chance to explain themselves and to "get things off their chests." Second, approach all others with an open mind. Third, put yourself in their place, and try to understand how others think and why they say and do what they do. Fourth, prepare yourself. If you need more information about others such as cultural attributes, religions, or ethnic differences and expectations, use the library or Internet. If co-workers are from another culture, learn about their culture's beliefs and values. Be conscious of things such as the amount of physical space between people who are talking with each other, the amount of eye contact that is appropriate, the significance of voice inflections when asking questions, or the purpose, if any, of head movements and other body language during conversations. Fifth, remember that you can be easily deceived by generalities and stereotypes. Just as there are significant differences among people from your neighborhood, home town, city, or state, there are equally significant differences among people from different countries or religions.[4]

GENDER DIFFERENCES IN THE WORKPLACE

A series of surveys of men and women at five U.S. companies discovered that men in the business world are driven by personal concerns such as career development and professional or financial rewards. Women are driven by the desire to increase communication, expand relationships in the workplace, or improve the quality and focus of customer service.[5] Basic characteristics like these not only drive but underscore many of the gender differences explained in this section.

The gender differences you notice in everyday life are apparent in the workplace. For example, as discussed in Chapter 5, men tend to use a **report style** of language (called report-talk) designed to preserve their independence and negotiate and maintain status. Women use a **rapport style** (rapport-talk) designed to establish connections and negotiate relationships. When both are asked to make a decision, in traditional circumstances men will make it without consultation. Men often believe that seeking input is unnecessary, and when put in charge of making the decision, they do it. Women, on the other hand, may discuss the decision with others and seek their input and feedback. They think it is important that everyone feels they have contributed to the decision in order to support it.[6]

Another report–rapport difference is in goal setting. Men are task oriented and focus on the end result and will move at once, often independently, to achieve it. Women are more concerned about the process and will connect with and involve others as they move toward their goals. Also, when achieving goals involves competition, men generally thrive because they enjoy it. Women, instead, thrive in arenas that involve collaboration.

Yet another result of the report–rapport difference is in giving feedback to others. Because women are more relationship oriented, they tend to use tact and sensitivity and reveal genuine concern about the other's feelings. Men, on the other hand, will be more direct, blunt, and to the point—a straightforward report style. In giving orders, too, men are direct. Women, disposed to maintain harmony, will give an order but follow it up with "If you don't mind," or "If it's okay with you."

Obviously, this is not a complete list of gender differences, nor do these differences apply universally to all men and all women. How these differences play out in actual business circumstances will vary greatly, but this discussion should give you a basic understanding of some of the differences that occur in the business environment and a premise for beginning to resolve differences and misunderstandings.

COMMUNICATING WITHIN A PROFESSIONAL ATMOSPHERE

Much of your success within any business environment will be based on your ability to communicate. Ineffective communication often results in poor cooperation and coordination, lower productivity, undercurrents of tension, gossip and rumors, and increased turnover and absenteeism. What can you do to ensure accurate, clear, and effective communication? Begin by showing concern about both the quality and quantity of your communication.

1. Give more attention to face-to-face communication with co-workers as well as superiors. Do not rely mainly on bulletin boards, memos, e-mail, or other written forms of communication. Trust is built better and faster when conversation is face-to-face.

2. Remember that the key to good communication is effective listening. Show respect for others when they speak. Don't interrupt; give them time to communicate; summarize and repeat what they just said; don't plan your response while the other person is talking; avoid checking your e-mail or shuffling paperwork while you're listening; and make an effort to look the other person in the eye.

3. Speak clearly and use good diction. People may miss your point if you are hard to understand. Be especially clear about deadlines and expectations.
   Rephrase thoughts and repeat what is being said to you back to those who are speaking. This ensures not only that you understood what they said but more importantly what they meant.

4. Maintain a positive attitude. People will be more interested in what you say.

5. Give and receive feedback. Everyone needs to know when they are doing a good job and when they need to make improvements. Give feedback in person, and always keep the criticism focused on the work and not on the individual.

6. If you get angry or upset, calm down before responding. Take a break, count to 10, go for a walk. Do whatever you need to do to cool off. Then sit down and think through how you want to approach the situation before taking any action.

7. Build your credibility. Demonstrate by both your messages and your actions that you subscribe to the principles of professional conduct discussed in the opening section of this chapter. They create a climate of trust and openness with others.

STRATEGIC FLEXIBILITY
The work environment reinforces the importance of strategic flexibility—especially when you are angry or upset. After you have taken a break and cooled down, you need to sit down and anticipate the coming situation, assess all elements, carefully evaluate everything, and select with sensitivity and care before you apply.

DEALING WITH CONFLICT AT WORK

Effective communication is the key to dealing with conflict at work. You can support effective communication with a well-thought-out, reasoned approach. This suggests that your emotions will not be engaged. How can you keep control in a potentially volatile situation? It isn't easy, of course, but the key is "emotional disengaging," according to Florence M. Stone of the American Management Association (AMA).[7] Stone says "it entails turning off your emotions to a situation and examining it as a scenario in a play or plot in a book—that is, objectively."

Some people, when facing conflict on the job, will put on gloves and come out swinging. Some will put on blinders and ignore the problem. But others will seek productive solutions, and the following steps will guide you through that process.[8]

First, *plan, prepare, and rehearse.* You must have a clear idea of your message, and to obtain this clear idea, you must do your homework and review the facts. It may even help to write out the problem. The better command you have of all the facts, the stronger your foundation throughout the process.

Second, *set an appropriate climate.* Anticipate your meeting with the other person by scheduling an uninterrupted time to work through the issues. Make your meeting private so nobody else will witness or overhear your conversation. Set the tone for the entire process by treating the other person as respectfully as you yourself would want to be treated.

Third, *adopt a constructive attitude.* Examine your motives and feelings carefully before delivering difficult or critical feedback. Emotions that reflect anger, frustration, and lack of respect will be quickly detected, as will awkwardness and discomfort. People will more likely be open to critical feedback if they are confident in, feel respected by, and trust the messenger.

Fourth, *assertively state the message.* Assertiveness is neither pushy, obnoxious, aggressive, nor confrontational. It means being open and straightforward about a situation, speaking calmly about what happened and keeping your emotions under control. This is where owned messages come into play. Instead of saying "You did this . . . " say "I was surprised when I heard . . . "

Fifth, *allow your message to sink in.* Stay quiet while your receiver processes your remarks. You do not need to elaborate, justify, or expand on your message at this point. You will have a better discussion if your receiver is allowed time to think and compose himself or herself.

Sixth, *listen carefully to the response.* Do *not* interrupt. Give your receiver an opportunity to express his or her reaction and response, even if this means some emotion is shown. Reveal your understanding and empathy by paraphrasing the remarks, if appropriate, and acknowledge his or her feelings.

Seventh, *restate, clarify, and recycle.* Work with your receiver until he or she has a clear understanding of your position. Encourage discussion to explore the issues, but stay on track. This is not an opportunity to debate and argue the issues. You may elaborate now in response to questions for clarification, but actively acknowledge both the reactions and viewpoints of your receiver as you do. Your active listening skills, accurate paraphrasing skills, and obvious respect for your receiver will help build the trust that forms the foundation for constructive problem solving.

Eighth, *focus on solutions, not personalities.* This is when you both need to offer solutions. It may require a compromise—not a complete adoption of one solution or another—to ensure there is closure to the conflict. It is not about one person winning and another losing; but rather, about both parties finding a way to resolve the conflict.

Ninth, *plan to evaluate solutions.* Schedule a time to meet after a solution has been put into practice, when both parties should be free to discuss it. Did it work? Can we make changes so it will work better?

Some people will never be able to get along with one another no matter what efforts are made. Rather than looking for issues to be upset about, you are more likely to work

---

STRATEGIC FLEXIBILITY

Dealing with conflict requires a thoughtful, rational approach to problem solving. If you apply the strategic flexibility framework at each stage of the problem–solution process, you are more likely to select just the right set of skills and behaviors that, when applied, will help move the problem toward a solution.

with such co-workers if you resolve to take the high road. You will be able to work in a more positive manner and environment if you think about the purpose of the work, the long-range goals of the company, and your individual contribution rather than co-worker problems and personality clashes.

THE INTERNET AND PROFESSIONAL COMMUNICATION

The Internet is the job market of the twenty-first century. Why go online? There are five reasons. (1) You can access current information at all hours of the day or night. (2) You can reach deeper into your local area as well as take your search far beyond your regular boundaries. (3) Using the Internet in your search demonstrates leading-edge skills. (4) The Internet lets you meet new people and initiate new relationships with others in your profession or region. (5) The Internet can help you explore career alternatives and options that you maybe haven't considered.[9]

Searching the Internet specifically for jobs, employment, and careers will bring up numerous results pertinent to you. A high-quality career Web site will include frequently updated job postings. Good sites update their listings several times a week at the minimum, adding new jobs and deleting old or already filled ones as soon as new information is available. The two technologies you should be sure to utilize during your online job search are searchable job databases and résumé databases.

High-quality career Web sites will include free, confidential résumé posting. Most sites offer free résumé posting with registration, but there is no shortage of less reputable sites that may try to trick you. A good one will offer a "private posting" option. This allows you to limit who has access to personal information such as your address, detailed work history, and salary information.

Résumé databases give job seekers additional exposure to recruiters who may search such databases to find candidates for their openings. To make your résumé fit numerous queries, supplement your résumé with industry buzz terms in line with your experiences and qualifications. Customize your résumé for each job. After sending a résumé electronically, mail a hard copy and call the hiring manager to follow up.

Finally, you need to be able to make contacts with people who can help you find information or secure you an interview. Most Web sites, career oriented or otherwise, feature message boards where users can post questions, comments, or the like. Message boards can be another great resource for industry information, as well as for making contacts with people in your area of expertise. Although the Internet is changing almost everything about finding a job, who you know still matters.

Assess Yourself

Measure Your Professionalism

How professional are you? Read the following statements. Then use the following scale to rate your level of agreement:

1	2	3	4	5	6	7
Not at all true			Moderately true			Absolutely true

_____ 1. I am considered a person of good character.

_____ 2. I convey regard and appreciation for the worth, honor, dignity, and esteem of all people.

_____ 3. I fully support and demonstrate the free exchange of ideas within the bounds of reasonable behavior.

_____ 4. I am amenable to changing my position based on the reasoned and thoughtful exchange of ideas when they are supported by facts, evidence, and other forms of proof.

_____ 5. I always meet my obligations and act independently without superior authority or guidance.

_____ 6. I am considered a good team player who knows the value of teams in developing creative solutions to challenges.

_____ 7. I accept constructive criticism well and recognize its value in improving myself.

_____ 8. I seek all available means to improving my professionalism and expertise.

_____ 9. I always act in accordance with right principles of conduct.

_____ 10. I never maliciously or intentionally make false, misleading, disparaging, or defamatory comments about others.

TOTAL POINTS: _____

Go to the *Communicating Effectively* CD-ROM and the Online Learning Center at **www.mhhe.com/hybels8** to see your results and learn how to evaluate your attitudes and feelings.

mhhe.com/hybels8

CHAPTER REVIEW

SUMMARY

Professional communication is that which in some way relates to business professions or occupations. Every business expects you to conduct yourself professionally and to follow a line of conduct that suggests you are competent. Universal principles of professional conduct include integrity, respect, openness, responsibility, teamwork, self-improvement, and ethics. When your skills and behaviors are anchored by these principles, then making the right, moral, honest, lawful, and ethical decisions becomes spontaneous, routine, and habitual.

An interview is a series of questions and answers, usually between two people, for the purpose of getting and understanding information about a particular subject. Interviews can be used for a wide variety of purposes including speeches, group projects, and research papers. Careful preparation is essential.

Information interviews will help you get the most up-to-date information and feedback; they are the most personal way of getting information. Preparation should include deciding on the angle you want to take, the format you plan to use, the kind of questions that will be most appropriate, and whether to use tape or notes.

Before you go to an employment interview, research the organization offering the job. Be prepared to talk about your job expectations, your academic and work backgrounds, your knowledge of the organization, your career goals, and your strengths and weaknesses as a potential employee. Your manner of dress, the kind of questions you ask, and your awareness of potential negative factors will affect the outcome. After the interview, write a follow-up letter or call the interviewer indicating that you are still interested in working for the organization.

There are cultural differences in the workplace, and an understanding of cultural differences may not only facilitate communication but also avoid potentially embarrassing or even insulting situations. To deal with cultural differences, follow the principles of professional conduct, approach others with an open mind, use empathy, prepare yourself, and avoid generalities and stereotypes about others.

Gender differences in the workplace often stem from the differences between men's report style and women's rapport style. This difference affects whom people choose to work with, goal setting, giving feedback, expressing feelings, handling problems, and asking questions.

Communicating within a professional atmosphere should place an emphasis on ensuring accurate, clear, and effective communication. You can do this by giving more attention to face-to-face communication, revealing effective listening, speaking clearly, sharing your ideas, giving and receiving feedback, calming down before responding, building your credibility, and being ethical.

The best way for dealing with conflict is to plan, prepare, and rehearse. You will need to set an appropriate climate; adopt a constructive attitude; assertively state your message; allow your message to sink in; listen carefully to the response; restate, clarify, and recycle; focus on solutions; and, finally, plan to evaluate the solutions adopted.

The Internet has become the job market of the twenty-first century. Two important technologies include searchable job databases and résumé databases. Make certain you use the private posting option when you post your résumé and remember the importance of personal contacts.

CHAPTER REVIEW

KEY TERMS AND CONCEPTS

Use the *Communicating Effectively* CD-ROM and the Online Learning Center at www.mhhe.com/hybels8 to further your understanding of the following terms.

Appraisal interview 212
Closed-format (interview) 214
Closed questions 215
Cultural differences 222
Disciplinary interview 212
Employment interview 219
Ethics 211
Exit interview 212
Follow-up questions 215
Information interview 212

Integrity 210
Interview 211
Leading questions 215
Neutral questions 215
Open-ended questions 215
Open-format (interview) 214
Openness 211
Primary questions 214
Professional communication 210
Rapport style 223

Report style 223
Respect 211
Responsibility 211
Résumé 219
Self-improvement 211
Semiopen format (interview) 214
Stress interview 212
Teamwork 211

QUESTIONS TO REVIEW

1. What are the principles of professional conduct?
2. What is an information interview, and when do you use it?
3. What kind of information should you know before you go to an interview?
4. What are the differences among open-format, closed-format, and semiopen format interviews?
5. What are the differences among primary, follow-up, open-ended, closed, neutral, and leading questions? Give an example of each.
6. What preliminary planning must take place before you conduct information interviews that are precursors to job interviews?
7. What are some of the typical questions asked in job interviews?
8. When being interviewed, what are examples of proper and improper behavior?
9. What are some of the questions you should be prepared to ask in job interviews?
10. What are specific things you can do to reveal your sensitivity to cultural differences in the workplace?
11. What gender differences are likely to show up in the workplace?
12. What are some of the key guidelines for communicating within a professional atmosphere?
13. What are the basic strategies for dealing with conflict at work?
14. What contribution does the Internet make to professional communication?

Go to the self-quizzes on the *Communicating Effectively* CD-ROM and the Online Learning Center at **www.mhhe.com/hybels8** to test your knowledge of the chapter contents.

CHAPTER 10

Small-Group Participation

OBJECTIVES

After reading this chapter, you should be able to:

- List the characteristics of a small group.
- Distinguish among different types of groups.
- Describe the factors that often determine small-group effectiveness.
- Explain how a group becomes cohesive.
- Define *groupthink* and list the indicators that groupthink may be occurring.
- List and explain the steps in group problem solving.
- Identify types of online discussion groups, the differences between online discussion groups and face-to-face discussions, and the keys to success in online groups.

WHEN SAMANTHA RECEIVED HER INSTRUCTIONS, THEY READ AS follows:

1. Introduce yourself to the other members.
2. Keep your messages brief.
3. Stay on the topic being discussed.
4. Emphasize the positive aspects of communication. (Thank others for their messages.)
5. Acknowledge where your ideas came from.
6. Keep your own perspective.
7. Encourage interaction by inviting comments on your work or by asking open questions about an issue.
8. Give and receive feedback. Give people feedback when they respond inappropriately.[1]

As one of the requirements for the small-group segment of her basic course, Samantha had to participate in an online group discussion, and these (the above list) were the guidelines she received—netiquette for online discussions. Netiquette (or Net etiquette) includes the common practices, customs, conventions, and expectations expected of individuals using the Internet.[2] Samantha was about to join thousands of others online who were experiencing online learning—"the ability to discuss topics with other students."[3]

In assigning Samantha to participate in an online group discussion, Samantha's course instructor was aware of the popularity of interest groups. "Global communities of interest have been assembled through use of mailing lists, electronic bulletin boards, chat lines, discussion forums, Internet Usenet or Bitnet Newsgroups, and so on. Traditional communities of geographic proximity are augmented by these communities of interest, where hobbies, medical conditions, professions, athletic and sporting news, automobiles, movie and video heroes, and virtually any other subjects of interest are discussed and debated with worldwide perspective and participation. A posting in an Internet Newsgroup, for example, may be read within a few hours by tens or even hundreds of thousands of individuals from among the 888 million (or more) Internet subscribers.[4] These communities of interest are formed without regard to geographic proximity or political boundaries. And in the foreseeable future, if costs continue to decline and accessibility continues to expand, the only limits will be the levels of interest themselves. The associations thus formed are without precedent for humanity and promise great potential for cooperative problem solving, skills exchange, and unified action. These dynamic communities of interest may be long term or short term because associations are formed to meet particular needs, and dissolved when they are no longer pertinent."[5]

To show you the popularity of groups on the Internet, your authors entered the following words into the Google search engine and came up with the number of Web pages indicated: The word groups had 911,000,000 hits, the word discussion had 694,000,000, and the words group discussion had 285,000,000 (October 24, 2005); the words online group discussions had 49,100,000 hits and e-mail group discussion had 87,400,000 (October 24, 2005). Although the information in this chapter involves face-to-face interactions, much of the material relates directly to online group discussion as well. There are three reasons for beginning this chapter with an example of online discussion rather than face-to-face discussion:

1. It reveals the popularity of discussion as a process.
2. It emphasizes the direction that discussion has taken—away from face-to-face groups and toward Internet opportunities. (This has to do with the time it takes to meet with people, the availability of Internet discussion groups, and the number of people actually taking advantage of online discussion groups.)
3. It reveals the similarities between online discussion and face-to-face discussion.

In preparing for face-to-face group discussion, Internet groups can help you discover a topic, access experts, find current issues, examine opposing issues, discover current trends, and answer questions about your topic.

Small groups are gatherings of 3 to 13 members who meet to do a job, solve a problem, or maintain relationships. Small groups are essential in helping society function efficiently, and many of you—especially those with Internet access—spend several hours each week communicating in such groups. Not only do you participate in chat rooms, mailing lists, newsgroups, Web forums, and other interest groups, you might also take part in a seminar discussion, talk with a group of co-workers about improving job conditions, discuss with family members how to make the household run more efficiently, or discuss a variety of topics and issues with a group of friends. You may even surf the Net just looking for a place where you can express yourself on any number of ideas. Many of you, too, belong to service or professional groups. Often these groups involve both the completion of tasks and social life. Some are singularly social. Whatever groups you belong to, you want them to function efficiently if they are task oriented groups, and you want them to be enjoyable and satisfying if they are social. If a group is task oriented, participation should be pleasurable, but you want to meet, get on with the job, and then spend some time socializing with other group members.

This chapter and the next one discuss how groups work. In this chapter, we note the characteristics of small groups, how such groups go about solving problems, and the process of participating in them. We recognize and acknowledge groups such as marriage-encounter workshops, counseling groups, and growth groups that, in general, have no real collective goal. Also, we recognize groups that exist solely to satisfy the social needs of their participants. Most of these—including the social groups formed in online chat rooms—are informal and seldom have an agenda except enjoyment or friendship. In Chapter 11 we concentrate on both effective leadership and conflict management.

WHY LEARN ABOUT SMALL GROUPS?

You have undoubtedly heard all the stories. As one goes, a camel is just a horse put together by a committee. Another observation is that a committee is a group that keeps minutes but wastes hours. Still a third was reported by a committee member who said, "To be effective, a committee should be made up of three people. But to get anything done, one member should be sick, and another absent."[6] Many people dread group work. Fortunately, there are many who look forward to solving problems, making decisions, and accomplishing tasks while working with others.

Effectiveness in small groups is essential to your career success.[7] Of the nine skills required for career success identified by Whetten and Cameron, more than half of them are either directly related to or can be acquired in small groups. The nine skills are developing self-awareness, managing personal stress, solving problems creatively, establishing supportive communication, gaining power and influence, improving employee performance through motivation, delegating and decision making, managing conflict, and conducting effective group meetings.[8] If we were to add one item it would be achieving strategic flexibility.

Effectiveness in small groups will save you time and money. You are going to spend a significant amount of your time working in groups, whether they involve family, friends, fraternities, sororities, religious groups, work groups, social groups, educational groups, or therapy groups. The better you are at understanding them and developing efficiency in them, the better you will like them and make use of them in developing and obtaining your goals and the goals of the organization. Few leaders can succeed today on their own without the aid of competent, committed team members.

Effectiveness in small groups will help you in college. Students who study in small groups learn more effectively than those who don't, and there is a positive correlation between small-group study experiences and overall satisfaction in college.[9] Small-group work will increase the amount of your participation, the amount you will learn from each other, the motivation you have toward tasks, the responsibility you take for your own learning, and the quality of the solutions you discover.[10]

Effectiveness in groups will help you personally. The better you are in groups, the more likely you will accomplish your own goals and projects, and the more of those goals and projects you complete, the better you will feel about yourself.[11] You will feel better about yourself, too, for the contributions you can make to the success of any group you join. Because of your knowledge, background, and experience, you will be better able to predict what happens when people communicate in small groups and, then, to intervene on behalf of better group decision making and more successful participation by all group members. In addition, because of working closely with others in these contexts, you will expand your understanding of yourself.

It won't take you long as you begin having small-group experiences to understand why the stories shared in the first paragraph of this section are often true. Many groups are not run effectively, skillfully, or diplomatically.[12] With just the knowledge shared in these two chapters on small groups, and with experience in applying what you learn, you will quickly stand out as a valuable member of groups to which you belong. You won't need to announce your superior knowledge nor use heavy-handed approaches. Using the strategic flexibility framework—anticipating, assessing, evaluating, selecting, and then applying your skills and behaviors with care, concern, and attention to all the factors that are likely to be affected—you will be able to subtly and helpfully nudge the group into functioning effectively.[13]

CHARACTERISTICS OF SMALL GROUPS

All small groups have common characteristics. These groups reflect the culture in which they function; they have norms—expectations that group members have of how other members will behave; and they have rules—formal and structured directions for behavior.

Cultural Values

When Americans think they should solve a problem at work or in the community, their first instinct is to form a group. Once the group begins to function, everyone is more or less equal. If someone wants to talk, he or she is given a chance. If all in the group cannot agree on a solution, the group takes a vote and the majority decides.

This kind of group-forming and group-operating behavior seems so natural that we don't think twice about it: It is part of our culture. We should not assume, however, that other cultures work the same way. When one of our authors asked a Polish friend why the Poles didn't organize child care cooperatives, her friend replied, "In Poland, we never work in groups."

Most societies have a dominant problem-solving mechanism, but it may differ greatly from culture to culture. In many countries men are much more likely than women to make decisions about workplace and community issues. In many of these same countries, only elder members of the group can participate in decision making.

Seventy percent of the world lives in a *collectivist* society—a society whose loyalties are to the family or, more broadly, to the clan, the tribe, or the caste.[14] In such groups, problem solving and decision making are most likely to occur within the family or the clan. If a group is formed that includes members from different clans or families, the way the participants work to solve a problem would depend on their perception of how the solution would affect their own families or clans.

Americans who join a group in another country cannot assume that the group will function in the same way that an American group does. In a campus setting, when American students work with international students, they should also be sensitive to the different ways the work of the group may be perceived. In some cases it might be appropriate to explain at the start how American groups work.

Group Norms

Norms are the expectations group members have of how other members will behave, think, and participate. Norms are informal—they are not written down. Members assume that others understand the norms and will follow them.

A daily staff meeting of the editors of a college newspaper shows how norms operate. All the editors (associate, managing, and city editors, as well as editors of the opinion, campus, and sports sections) look to the editor-in-chief not only to set the agenda for the meeting but to begin it, to recognize participants, and to maintain control throughout the meeting. The editor-in-chief assumes that all editors will attend each meeting, be on time, bring the necessary information that pertains to their areas, and generally act in a polite and responsible manner. In other words, they will follow the norms of behavior for their daily staff meeting. The editor's manner and demeanor set the tone for all meetings.

In familiar settings, we take group norms for granted. But if we join a group where the norms are not so obvious, we might sit back and listen until we figure out what the group norms are. For example, a new person joining an online discussion group should sit back and read to try to get a sense of how the group operates before he or she participates. Different chat rooms, user groups, newsgroups, and Web forums each have their own group norms of how people using those interest groups should behave.

Norms are important because they give a group some structure. If members know how to behave, the group will function more efficiently. Also, outsiders can look at the group's norms to see whether they want to join the group. If, for example, you feel comfortable only in informal settings, you will probably not want to join a group that has numerous rituals and ceremonies.

Group norms also govern how participants communicate with each other. This may be especially true in male–female interactions. It is important that group members be treated equally and that all members be given sufficient consideration and concern by all others. Any differences in the way people are treated should be based on their needs or roles in the group and not on gender.

Group Rules

Unlike norms, **rules** are formal and structured directions for behavior. Rules may dictate what jobs group members should do, how meetings should be conducted, how motions should be introduced, and so on. The rules help a meeting to progress and ensure that everyone can be heard but that no one person will monopolize the floor. Sometimes, when order and decorum are especially important, a group will appoint a parliamentarian to see that the rules are properly interpreted and followed.

Not all groups have rules. Informal groups such as book clubs have norms such as meeting at different homes, providing food, and being prepared to discuss a particular book. A community group such as the Junior League, on the other hand, has rules, bylaws, voting, minutes to approve, and even penalties for not attending regularly. These distinctions between groups are likely to be based on the degree of informality or formality or perhaps on size. Formal and large groups generally have both norms and rules. Small and informal groups usually have norms but few rules.

TYPES OF GROUPS

View "Small Group Communication," clip #6, to see a task-oriented group in action.

From your own experience, you can probably distinguish several different kinds of groups. For example, you are probably a member of informal social groups. **Social groups** are groups designed to serve the social needs of their participants. When you were young, you went to school with members of a social group of friends, you met and socialized with friends at work, and you frequently saw friends from your place of worship. All these were social groups; all had norms associated with belonging, but there were few, if any, rules. These are informal groups.

Many groups are **task oriented**—that is, they serve to get something specific accomplished. Task-oriented groups often have problem-solving or decision-making goals. *Problem solving* involves using some specific procedure—such as the one we discuss later in this chapter—to resolve the difficulty (problem) under consideration. *Decision making,* of course, occurs within the process of problem solving whenever alternatives emerge and choices must be made. When a group is designated as a "decision-making group," its task is recommending action—making clear choices among several possibilities.

A task-oriented problem-solving group in the workplace might be designated to solving the problem that smoking presents. That is, what should be done to protect nonsmokers and yet protect the rights of smokers as well? A task-oriented decision-making group might be charged with presenting a variety of possible alternatives to management, yet this group does not solve the problem. That is left to management.

Many decision-making groups operate in our society. Juries are one example. Groups can be delegated to decide who is to receive an award, who might be a guest speaker, or what kind of activities the group might like to support. A classroom professor experienced the operation of a decision-making group when students in one class met and recommended to him that the date of an examination be changed from the day after homecoming weekend to any of three possibilities the group presented. He presented the three alternatives to the class, and a vote determined the new date.

There is another important kind of group meeting as well. The **information-sharing group** can be found in corporations, schools, churches, families, and service clubs, in social fraternities and sororities, and among faculty in departments on campus. Whenever people meet to be informed and to inform others, to express themselves and to listen to others, to get or give assistance, to clarify or hear clarification of goals, or to establish or maintain working relationships, information sharing becomes the purpose. Such groups are necessary when people plan to do business together over a long period.

In either task-oriented or information-sharing groups, there is a closely interrelated social dimension as well. The degree to which members concern themselves with the task or with information sharing affects the social interaction of the group. Likewise, the degree to which members show concern for relationships within the group has a direct effect on task accomplishment or information sharing. In some faculty meetings, department members converse, tell jokes, and communicate informally before the formal agenda begins. This behavior establishes an effective social climate before the information sharing takes place.

Yet another type of group—not discussed in detail in this chapter—is the **learning group,** in which the purpose is to increase the knowledge or skill of participants. While the most obvious is the study group, reading clubs, the League of Women Voters, and Bible study groups are also learning groups. A group of scuba divers or skiers and an investment club are examples of skill-development learning groups.

> **STRATEGIC FLEXIBILITY**
> Determining when and how much social interaction is necessary in task-oriented or information-sharing groups requires strategic flexibility—especially the ability to anticipate, assess, and evaluate the social climate of the group.

SMALL-GROUP EFFECTIVENESS

Why do some groups succeed and others fail? Why do some come up with creative solutions for problems while others fall short? Why do some groups have members who get along and other groups have members who are always fighting?

Research shows that effective small groups have certain characteristics in common: a sense of solidarity, an ability to focus on their task, and a task that is appropriate for their particular group.[15]

Solidarity can come from members' sharing common interests (baseball trivia, exercising), knowing one another at work, or sharing some social time together before and after group meetings.

Focus comes from a leader or member who tries to keep the group directed toward its subject. This is the person who says, "That's an interesting point, but our problem is to . . . "

Appropriateness exists when a group and its task are well matched. For example, a student group cannot solve the problem of a deficit in the university budget. However, it might be able to solve a problem like screening strangers who enter dormitories or finding a better way to publicize elections for student senators.

In addition to having solidarity, focus, and task appropriateness, a truly effective group must be of a workable size, must meet in appropriate surroundings with suitable seating arrangements, and must inspire its members to feel cohesiveness and commitment.

Workable Size

A group works best when all its members can communicate and interact with one another. For a group to be effective, it should have from 3 to 13 members. Research indicates that an ideal size for a group is five members.[16] If a group has too many members, it cannot work effectively to solve problems or do the job at hand. It should be broken up into smaller groups—each with its own job to do. The student government, for example, is usually divided into committees: the social committee, the food advisory committee, the constitutional revision committee, and so on. The committees then study the issues and make recommendations to the larger body.

A group may be too large for all its members to participate in group discussions, decisions, and actions. When this occurs, it is time to break the group into still smaller units. With the student social committee, for example, some members could check out the availability of certain musical groups, while other members could conduct a poll to see which musicians the students would like to have on campus.

Groups can also be too small. When there is a lot of information to gather, or when the task requires specialized skill or knowledge from its members, it is important to have enough members to do the job. For example, if a department is completely computerized, it may be faced with many decisions. Some people might be assigned to find the best kind of computer software—or the best available software for updating what the department already has. Then the question may be how to get everyone to use the system or to check their e-mail. Others might be assigned to establish computerized networks with other departments or programs on campus or to develop instructions for getting onto electronic bulletin boards. If there are enough members to investigate each of these areas, no single person will have too much to do.

An Appropriate Meeting Place

The place where a group meets often influences the general atmosphere of the meeting. A group that meets in a classroom or a conference room will probably be more formal than a group that meets in someone's room or apartment.

The meeting place can be chosen on the basis of who the group members are and what they want to accomplish. Members who know each other well might want to meet in someone's home; when members do not know each other well or if the group wants to attract new participants, it would be better for the group to meet in a public place.

Sometimes the meeting place will be determined by what the group wants to accomplish. A parents' group seeking citywide support for a tax increase in order to add new classrooms to the high school might meet in the high school cafeteria. Travel Abroad, a group of interested citizens who enjoy sharing slides and talks about their travels, might gather in the meeting room of the local public library.

Suitable Seating Arrangements

Seating of group members should not be left to chance, with each member choosing a chair. Donald C. Stone, a professor of public service, believes that a seating plan is important if people are to pay attention at meetings.[17] For small groups, Stone recommends seating people where they can all see one another's faces. A circular table would serve this function, as would classroom desks or small tables placed in a circle. For larger groups, Stone recommends a U-shaped arrangement of tables. In this arrangement people should sit only on the outside of the U. Otherwise, they will have their backs to one another.

Stone also makes recommendations about chairs. The perfect chair, he says, is one that has a little padding on the seat. If the chairs have hard seats, people will not be comfortable in them for very long; if the seats are too soft, group members might be tempted to doze off.

Circular tables facilitate discussion because group members can see one another's faces.

Cohesiveness and Commitment

As a positive force, **cohesiveness** is the feeling of attraction that group members have toward one another.[18] It is the members' ability to stick together, to work together as a group, and to help one another. **Commitment** is the willingness of members to work together to complete the group's task. When members are committed, the group is likely to be cohesive. There are few more powerful and satisfactory feelings than the feelings of belonging to a group and of being loyal to that group.

Although cohesiveness is often a matter of group chemistry, an effective group leader can help cohesiveness develop the first few times the group meets. A good leader will make certain that all members are introduced and, if appropriate, given a chance to say something about themselves. Cohesiveness will also be helped if members have a chance to do a little socializing before and after the meetings. Finally, during the discussions, a good leader will try to draw out the quieter members. The more everyone participates, the better the chance for group unity to develop.

Groupthink

Workable size, appropriate meeting place, suitable seating arrangements, and cohesiveness and commitment are positive aspects of small-group effectiveness. Groupthink is a negative aspect. Social psychologist Irving Janis, having made a careful study of groups, found that cohesive groups can become victims of **groupthink,** a group dysfunction in which the preservation of harmony becomes more important than the critical examination of ideas.[19] Janis's point is simply that groups can bring out the worst as well as the best in people.[20] Because groupthink can limit group effectiveness, group members need to be sensitive to its operation.

Working Together

Working with others in a group, answer the following questions about groups:

1. Why is it that some groups succeed and others fail?
2. What are the specific factors about groups that succeed that make them succeed?
3. What are the specific factors about groups that fail that make them fail?

Divide your group answers into two columns, one labeled "Strengths" and one labeled "Weaknesses." List as many items as you can. When your lists are complete, arrange the items in each list so that the most important items are listed first and the least influential items are listed last.

There is a potential cultural element involved in groupthink. In a culturally diverse group, it could be that cultural norms may be silencing dissenters.[21] "For example," writes Leonard Greenhalgh in his book *Managing Strategic Relationships*, "Asian cultures emphasize interpersonal harmony. In such cultures, it's considered impolite to contradict what someone has just said. Saying 'I disagree' risks loss of face for the person you're disagreeing with."[22] The point is that someone who is interculturally insensitive may misinterpret silence in a diverse group for indifference, and the silent person may be ignored. That's why it is so important to draw out the views of all group members in culturally sensitive ways.

The key indicators that groupthink may be occurring include situations when the group is examining few alternatives, not being critical of each other's ideas, not examining early alternatives, not seeking expert opinion, being highly selective in gathering information, and not having any contingency plans. These are likely to occur in groups when they have an illusion of invulnerability, when they rationalize poor decisions, believe in the group's morality, exercise direct pressure on members to go along, maintain the illusion of unanimity, and use mindguards—information control—to protect the group from negative information.[23] Mindguards are similar to what happens when juries are sequestered and forbidden to talk to those not on the jury, read any newspapers, listen to anything on television or radio, and refrain from Internet access.

There are a number of examples in our history when groupthink influenced decisions, and the decisions resulted in disaster. The Vietnam War, the Bay of Pigs, the *Challenger* disaster, the Iraq War are four. Knowing about groupthink will allow you to see, listen, and evaluate the methods used to sway public opinion on major policies. Watch, for example, as certain words are repeated, specific phrases such as "we're running out of money" or "we're running out of time" are used as a threat, and the coordination of spokespersons who stay focused and "on message" until change occurs are organized and orchestrated until a specific policy or idea is adopted.

Although our society depends on groups to make decisions, and we spend more and more time in groups, not all group decisions are superior. Group decisions can be just or unjust, fair or discriminatory, sensitive or insensitive to the needs of others; they can be responsible or irresponsible, respectful of or in violation of people's rights. In a dormitory, for example, students on one floor decided unanimously to designate a lounge area as a permanent "no-talk study area" where students could go at any time if they needed total quiet for study. When the ruling was put into effect, students found they had eliminated the meeting place of a number of important campus groups that could find no other convenient place to meet.

STRATEGIC FLEXIBILITY

Groupthink—a subjective process—can be detected only when an objective and rationale point of view is used. If you think about the situation (anticipate), take stock of the factors, elements, and conditions (assess), and truly weigh and consider the value and worth of those factors, elements, and conditions (evaluate), you are most likely to recognize and expose the key indicators of groupthink.

240

Two students on the dorm floor knew beforehand about the groups that met in the lounge. Because of the high cohesiveness, solidarity, and loyalty of the deciding group, however, these students chose not to speak up. Their decision to remain silent was a direct result of groupthink.

The essential point about groupthink is that it helps us understand why some groups do not exhibit the kind of critical thinking essential to ethical and responsible problem solving and decision making. It should be clear, too, that groupthink can occur in groups of all kinds. Although our example is a dormitory group, such actions can occur in clubs, committees, boards, teams, or work units. Groupthink is sometimes hard to detect, but detection is worth the effort. When you are part of a group, you want that group to be the best. Groupthink can hinder a group's best efforts.

Teams versus Groups

The term *group* tends to be more general than the word *team;* however, often the two terms are used interchangeably. That interchangeability occurs, too, because a team is a type of group. In their book *Teamwork,* Larson and LaFasto say a **team** has three specific characteristics: (1) two or more people, (2) a specific goal to be attained, and (3) coordination of activity among the members to the goal.[24] Dyer, in his book *Team Building,* places emphasis on the third part, the need for some degree of collaboration to achieve common goals. Teams often demonstrate closeness as well as cooperation.[25]

The following requirements—or ideal conditions—apply to each member of a team. Mutual trust means that team members can state their views and differences openly without fear of ridicule or retaliation. Mutual support means team members can get help from others on the team and give help to them without being concerned about secret agendas. Communication means team members can say what they feel knowing the rest of the team is not only listening but will work hard to understand them. Team objectives are clearly understood by all members. Conflicts are not only necessary, but they are desirable, too. They are not suppressed or overlooked. Team members work through conflicts as a team and all believe they make the team a stronger unit. The team uses all the individual abilities, knowledge, and experiences of team members, and the team accepts and gives advice, counsel, and support to team members while recognizing each member's individual accountability and specialization. Finally, team members work hard at keeping the team climate free, open, and supportive of each team member.[26]

In her article "Teams in the Workplace," Sara Barnett states that "One of the most important aspects of an effective team is to have goals that are clearly defined and challenging."[27] These goals require, she says, equivalent contributions from all team members, that they can be measured so progress toward them can be monitored and results confirmed, and that they be both challenging and attainable. Team members must have individual goals linked to the team's goals so members work together to achieve goals, but, in the end, only the team performs; individual members contribute.[28]

DISCUSSION IN GROUPS

Most groups that work efficiently have a process they typically follow for discussing a problem. Different procedures can work equally well; what is important is that the steps help the group focus on the problem. Many groups use a sequence of steps similar to the one shown in Figure 10-1. Let's look at each of these steps in some detail.

Figure 10-1
Solving a Problem

1. Choose a Topic
2. Identify the Problem
3. Analyze the Problem
4. Find and Evaluate Solutions
5. Choose a Solution
6. Re-evaluate the Solution after Time Passes

Choosing a Topic

If you are in a class, you may be required to pick a topic your group can discuss. How do you choose a topic? How do you find a subject that all group members will find interesting enough to work on?

Your first approach might be to look at your own school. Are there any problems or improvements your group might like to tackle? How's the housing? Does registration run smoothly? Does the bookstore have fair prices? Are computers available to all students 24/7? Any of these questions might lead to an interesting discussion.

Take a look at the community. Are there any problems there? How do students get along with the townspeople? Are students good neighbors? Do the banks cash out-of-town checks without adding a service charge? Do the local merchants realize how important students are to the economy of the town? Are there issues in the city council or county commissioners' office that might affect the school?

If your group is interested in attacking a broader social issue, the supply is almost limitless. World peace, foreign policy in the post–cold war era, abortion, and attacking the federal deficit are all issues that are hotly debated and will continue to be debated in the future. Discussing one of these topics in your group might be a good way for everyone to become informed about an important issue.

When a group cannot find a topic that all members consider interesting, it should try brainstorming. In **brainstorming** all members of the group suggest ideas—however far out they might seem. The goal of brainstorming is for the group to be as creative as possible. No one should make judgments about the ideas suggested during the brainstorming session. If members fear that their ideas might be condemned, they will be less willing to share some of their wilder thoughts (see Table 10-1).

Once the group runs out of ideas, it's time to stop brainstorming and take a look at the topics that were generated. Sometimes one idea is so good that everyone says, "That's it." More commonly, however, the group will have to evaluate the ideas. Each topic should be assessed in terms of whether all members are willing to work on it and whether it can be narrowed enough to permit comprehensive research. For example, taking on the problems of the country's landfills (garbage dumps) is too big

Table 10-1 Brainstorming Guidelines

Have someone record all ideas.
Keep your mind open to all ideas.
Let all ideas flow freely.
Do not belittle any ideas.
Only when your team has exhausted *all* ideas, you should stop generating and recording.
Start evaluating which ideas should be discarded.
Consider how even extreme ideas might be interpreted in other ways.
End up with a manageable number of alternative solutions (3–5).
Make sure everyone is encouraged to participate.

Source: *Brainstorming Guidelines*, by J. Fritz, August 2001. Retrieved January 20, 2005, from http://www.os2cs.unb.ca/profs/fritz/cs3503/storm35.htm

a job. However, the group might be able to research and discuss the problems with the local landfill.

Identifying the Problem

Once the group has a topic, its members can work toward identifying a specific problem. At this point, much of the work focuses on narrowing the problem so that it can be covered thoroughly. For example, let's say a group of students want to work on reducing crime. They narrow the problem to crime on their campus. They narrow it even further to rape, and they then identify the specific problem: getting the campus administration to accept the need for additional lighting on campus. Notice that through this process of narrowing and focusing, the group has come up with a topic it will be able to handle and discuss in the time it has.

The most important thing the group can do in this stage is identify a problem that is manageable. One of the biggest mistakes groups make is choosing a problem that is so broad that it cannot be adequately covered.

Analyzing the Problem

Asking the First Questions

Groups can take several approaches to analyzing problems. Sometimes it is useful to know what has caused the problem; other times it's enough to acknowledge that the problem exists. For example, a group that wanted to raise student awareness about donating blood did not need to explore why the American Red Cross needs blood. The problem was that students were not donating blood. Another group became interested in establishing a pregnancy crisis center because several local newspaper articles indicated that pregnant students had nowhere on campus to turn for assistance. This group, too, acknowledged that a problem existed.

Before making a final choice of topics, a group might want to find out how extensive the problem is and how many people are affected by it. For instance, citizens in one community wanted to establish an exchange of guns for toys. However, a neighborhood survey discovered that few people owned guns. In checking with the local police, the citizens discovered that few gun-related deaths occurred in their community. The group discovered that guns affected so few people in its area that it did not pursue its plan.

The group should also ask whether anyone else is trying to solve the problem now or has tried to solve it in the past. For example, a group that wants to solve the problem of poor student preparation for college should check with local school administrators to see if someone has been, is, or will be working on this problem—as well as whether or not administrators consider it a problem. Perhaps the group can add to the work that other people have already done or are in the process of doing.

Once the group has gone through this initial analysis, it should decide whether to proceed or to find a new topic. If it decides to proceed, it's ready to begin defining terms.

Defining Terms

The group should define any terms related to its problem that might be vague or ambiguous. For example, a classroom group decided that the campus mail-room took too long to deliver mail. Since individual members in the group defined "too long" in various ways, the group had to arrive at a precise meaning for the term. After some discussion they agreed that "too long" was anything over 24 hours. A community group that wanted to start a program to teach illiterate persons how to read and write first had to define "illiterate." Did it apply only to people who could not read or write? What about a person who could do some reading and writing but not enough to function in ordinary society? From a practical point of view, was this person also illiterate?

Seeking Out Information

To understand a problem fully, a group will need to seek outside information. The kind of information will vary depending on the problem or task. To get information, individual members may each investigate a different aspect of the problem. First they might decide to interview people who have had experience with the problem. For example, if they were trying to find out why library hours had been cut, one group member could interview the director of the library and others could interview students or faculty to see if they were affected by the reduced hours.

Many subjects require research that extends beyond personal experience. A group that is discussing the problem of harmful household products being dumped in landfills would find it useful to interview an expert, such as a chemistry professor. Groups can also find background information on their subjects in the library and on the Internet.

A group will work more efficiently if every member prepares for each meeting. Then when the group meets, all members will be ready for discussion and able to move on to the next task.

Wording the Final Question

Once the problem is analyzed, the next step is to phrase it as a question. A well-worded question should summarize the group's problem; it should be simply and clearly worded; and it should focus on a single central idea. It should use neutral terminology and present a specific problem for the group to solve. Depending on the topic, it should take the form of a question of fact, a question of value, or a question of policy.

Questions of fact deal with what is true and what is false. Examples of these questions are the following: How can we protect the drinking water supplies of our largest cities? In what ways can we reduce gun-related deaths in our nation? What are the methods necessary for making our homeland secure? Does sexism affect our lives? What are note-taking skills?

Questions of value are questions of whether something is good or bad, desirable or undesirable: Is recycling a beneficial activity? To what extent is the violence depicted on television and in video games harmful to people in our society? Is fraternity or sorority membership worthwhile?

Questions of policy are questions about actions that might be taken in the future. Such questions are often asked in institutional settings, such as schools, businesses, or organizations, and they usually include the word *should*: Should colleges increase the number of required courses? To what extent should business and industry assume the responsibility for cleaning up the environment? Should all students be required to have real-world work experience as part of their college education? Should businesses be required to be environmentally responsible?

Finding and Evaluating Solutions

Most problems do not have a single easy solution. Sometimes there are a number of alternatives, and the way a group looks at these alternatives is an important factor in the group's effectiveness. Not only must a group suggest alternatives that are realistic and acceptable, but it must also look at both the negative and the positive consequences of all the alternatives.

At other times a group may have difficulty finding appropriate solutions. If members cannot come up with good solutions when they work together, they may find it helpful to work separately for a while, with each member coming up with two or three solutions to present at the next meeting. Some research has shown that when people work alone, they often come up with more innovative ideas than they would in a group.

Sometimes a group can think of several solutions, but some will have to be discarded because they are impractical. In a group that wanted to teach adults to read and write, for example, someone suggested that unemployed elementary schoolteachers should be hired to teach illiterate adults. Although everyone agreed this was a good idea, no one could think of a way to get the money to pay the teachers.

To see if proposed solutions are practical, the group should list each one along with its advantages and disadvantages. Some of the questions a group can ask about proposed solutions include these: Will the solution solve the problem? Is it practical? Is permission necessary to put the solution into effect? Who will implement the solution? How much money will it cost? How much time will it take? If a solution doesn't pass such scrutiny, the group will have to keep working until it finds one that does.

To see if decisions are practical, the group should consider the same types of questions raised regarding solutions. Solutions and decisions are similar because they are both group products or outcomes. Some questions regarding a group's decisions might be the following: What are their relative merits and demerits? What is the best decision the group can support? How will the group's decision be put into effect? To what extent does it satisfy the *Critic-Analyzers*. **Critic-analyzers** are individuals who look at the good and bad points in the information the group has gathered. These people see the points that need more elaboration, and they discover information that has been left out.

Consider This

Sample Problem-Solving Outline

I. Choose a topic.
   A. Look at your immediate situation.
   B. Examine your community.
   C. Look at broader social issues.
   D. Use brainstorming as a way to creatively generate ideas.

II. Identify the problem.
   A. Narrow the topic so that it can be covered thoroughly.
   B. Identify a problem that the group can manage.

III. Analyze the problem.
   A. Use any of the following approaches:
     1. Does a problem exist?
     2. What has caused the problem?
     3. How extensive is the problem?
     4. How many people are affected by the problem?
     5. Is there anyone else who is trying to solve the problem now or has tried to solve it in the past?
   B. Define vague or ambiguous terms.
   C. Seek information.

IV. Find and evaluate solutions.
   A. Most problems have a number of solutions.
   B. Discard solutions that are impractical.
   C. List each solution along with its advantages and disadvantages.

V. Choose a solution
   A. Ideally, groups should work toward consensus—the point at which all group members agree.
   B. If gaining consensus is impossible, group members may have to choose their solutions by putting ideas to a vote, with the majority determining the outcome.

Reevaluating Solutions

It is true that in in-class discussions, it is impossible to reevaluate the solutions groups devise simply because finding and evaluating solutions is the final goal, the solutions are seldom, if ever, implemented, and the discussion groups that originate the solutions are soon terminated, never to meet again. Group members, for the most part, have no long-range, permanent commitment to the solutions. We offer this final step in group discussion work because in business and organizations—as well as in many group discussions that occur in private life—solutions are implemented, and their effectiveness in resolving the problems they are designed to solve becomes not just important but sometimes vital, as when a relationship's survival is dependent on a solution working.

    There are two important ideas when it comes to reevaluation. The first is to set a future time when some formal or informal reevaluation can take place. The second is to ask the essential questions that will help guide or frame the future. Because conditions change and new information arises, solutions may need to be honed, polished, or tweaked to add clarity or accuracy. Solutions may be too broad or too limiting; they may need to be redesigned or changed dramatically; or they may not work at all and may need to be dropped. Questions that might be asked include: Is the solution working? What conditions or information have changed that may make alterations to our solution necessary? Are there things we can do to make the solution work better? As we look down the road now, are there any additional things we can do that will anticipate potential changes that we see occurring in the future? Should we establish another time, now, when we can meet to make another assessment of our solution?

Another Point of View

There are people who feel totally unsuited to small-group experiences. Here is how Anita Diamant, in a section "Meeting Adjourned" from her book *Pitching My Tent*, explains her feelings about group meetings:

> When asked to serve on the board of directors I declined, explaining, "I lack the meeting gene." I am grateful to those who are congenitally able to plan, discuss, hash out, mull, and deliberate, because I can't.
>
> I am not a slacker. I bake cookies, I write brochures, but meetings transform me into a seething misanthrope with violent tendencies. I want to punch anyone who talks too much, even if I agree with what he's saying. I want to shout obscenities at the chair, even if she's my best friend. I do not like the person I become in meetings, which is why I'm so good at saying no when asked to do anything that requires attendance at them.

Source: from *Pitching My Tent: On Marriage, Motherhood, Friendship, and Other Leaps of Faith* (pp. 204–205), by Anita Diamant, 2003, New York: Scribner's.

Questions

1. Do you empathize with Diamant's feelings? Do you know others who feel as she does? From where do you think such intense feelings come?
2. If you found yourself in a meeting with someone who has these same feelings—as those of Anita Diamant—what could you do as either a member or leader to try to make her feel more comfortable and to make certain she knew she was an important and valued member of the group?
3. Knowing that she has such intense feelings regarding meetings, Diamant's first objective is likely to be avoidance; however, given the fact that meetings can hardly be avoided in our meeting-hungry society, what could she do—besides avoid them—to try to make herself more comfortable with them? What suggestions can you provide?

PARTICIPATING IN GROUP DISCUSSION

Groups, like individuals, can be defined as mature or immature. Often an immature group is a new one. It is overly dependent on its leader and, in the beginning, is often passive and unorganized. As the group matures, it is able to function independently of its leader, and its members become actively involved and capable of organizing their discussions.[29]

Although most groups have a specified leader, the leader does not have total responsibility for giving the discussion a direction or for moving the group along. In most groups, an individual member may temporarily take over the leadership from time to time. For example, a member who temporarily leads a group may have more information or experience in a certain area than the usual leader.

Individual group members continue to play the same roles in groups as they do in any other communication. A person who likes to take charge is likely to want the role of group leader, while a person who is shy will be as hesitant in a group as in any other kind of communication. In addition to the roles we play in life, however, some roles are specific to small-group communication. Kenneth Benne and Paul Sheats, pioneers in the classification of functional roles in groups, have identified the various behaviors associated with leadership in organizations and groups. For people interested in improving their skill in functional leadership, the task and/or maintenance roles Benne and Sheats describe offer a variety of different possibilities.[30]

To see an example of the importance of task roles, view "Small Group Communication," clip #6 on the CD.

Task Roles

Task roles are roles that help get the job done. Persons who play these roles help the group come up with new ideas, aid in collecting and organizing information, and analyze the information that exists. Task roles are not limited to any one individual; they may be interchanged among the members as the group goes about its job (see Table 10-2). Following are some of the common task roles.

Initiator-Expediters. Members who act as **initiator-expediters**—by suggesting new ideas, goals, solutions, and approaches—are often the most creative and energetic of the group. When the group gets bogged down, they are likely to make such statements as "What if we tried . . . " or "I wonder if . . . would solve our problem."

Initiator-expediters often can suggest a new direction or can prevent the group from losing sight of its objectives. They are not afraid to jump in and give assistance when the group is in trouble. Often, too, they are the ones who hold the light so that others can see the path.

Information Givers and Seekers. Individual members may both seek information and give it. Since lots of information will lead to better discussion, many members will play the roles of **information givers and seekers.** Information givers are often the best informed members of the group. They might have had more experience with the subject or even be experts on it.

The more complex the subject, the greater the group's need for information seekers. These are people who are willing to go out and research the subject. They might agree to interview experts, go to the library, or initiate an Internet investigation. If the group has very little information on a subject, it might be necessary for several members to play the role of information seeker.

The roles of information giver and seeker are the most important in any group. The information the group gets provides the foundation for the entire discussion. The more group members who play these roles, the better the quality of group discussion.

Critic-Analyzers. **Critic-Analyzers** are individuals who look at the good and bad points in the information the group has gathered. These people see the points that need more elaboration, and they discover information that has been left out.

STRATEGIC FLEXIBILITY

Those whose behaviors exhibit well-honed strategic flexibility skills are likely to be among the best critic-analyzers simply because they often look at the total picture and see how everything fits together. It is part of the process of anticipating, assessing, evaluating, selecting, and applying.

Table 10-2 Group Roles

Task Roles	Maintenance Roles	Dysfunctional Roles
Initiator-Expediters	Encouragers	Aggressor
Information Givers and Seekers	Harmonizer-Compromisers	Blocker
Critic-Analyzers	Regulators	Recognition-seeker
	Observers	Self-confessor
		Playboy
		Dominator
		Help-seeker
		Special-interest pleader

Can you detect those group members who may be playing task, maintenance, and even dysfunctional roles here? Which roles would need to be played to get all members back on a single track?

The critic-analyzer is able to look at the total picture and see how everything fits together. People who play this role usually have an excellent sense of organization. Often they can help keep the group on track: "We have mentioned this point twice. Maybe we need to discuss it in more depth." "Maybe we should go back and look at this information again. Something seems to be missing."

Maintenance Roles

People who play **maintenance roles** focus on the emotional tone of the meeting. Since no one wants to spend his or her entire time being logical, gathering information, and doing the job, it is important that some emotional needs be met. People who play maintenance roles meet these needs by encouraging, harmonizing, regulating, and observing.

Encouragers. **Encouragers** praise and commend contributions and group achievements: "You really did a good job of gathering this information. Now we can dig in and work."

The best encouragers are active listeners. They help in rephrasing points to achieve greater clarity. They do not make negative judgments about other members or their opinions. Encouragers make people feel good about themselves and their contributions.

Harmonizer-Compromisers. Members who help to resolve conflict in the group, who settle arguments and disagreements through mediation, are the harmonizer-compromisers. People who play this role are skillful at discovering solutions acceptable to everyone. **Harmonizer-compromisers** are especially effective when they remind group members that group goals are more important than individual needs: "I know you would like the library open on Sunday morning, but we have to find the times that are best for everybody."

Regulators. As their name implies, **regulators** help regulate group discussion by gently reminding members of the agenda or of the point they were discussing when they digressed: "We seem to be wandering a little. Now, we were discussing . . ."

Good regulators also find ways to give everyone a chance to speak: "Vilma, you haven't said anything. Do you have any feelings on this subject?" Sometimes the regulator has to stop someone who has been talking too much: "Roberto, you have made several interesting points. Let's see what some of the others think of them." A regulator who is too authoritarian, however, might find that others resent him or her. In this role, it is important to word statements or questions tactfully.

Observers. **Observers** aid in the group's cohesiveness. They are sensitive to the needs of each member: "I think we have ignored the point that John just made. Maybe we should take some time to discuss it."

Dysfunctional Roles

Occasionally, things in a group do not proceed as planned. There may be many reasons for weak discussions. One may be that a person or persons in the group are playing "individual" or dysfunctional roles. Recognizing these roles will help both leaders and members suppress, control, or compensate for their influence. **Dysfunctional, or individual, roles** include the following:

- The *aggressor* may work in many ways—deflating the status of others; expressing disapproval of the values, acts, or feelings of others; attacking the group or the problem it is working on; joking aggressively; showing envy toward another's contribution by trying to take credit for it; and so on.
- The *blocker* tends to be negativistic and stubbornly resistant, disagreeing and opposing without or beyond "reason" and attempting to maintain or bring back an issue after the group has rejected or bypassed it.
- The *recognition-seeker* works in various ways to call attention to himself or herself, whether through boasting, reporting on personal achievements, acting in unusual ways, struggling to prevent his or her being placed in an "inferior" position, and so on.
- The *self-confessor* uses the audience opportunity which the group setting provides to express personal, non–group-oriented, "feeling," "insight," "ideology," and so on.
- The *playboy* makes a display of his or her lack of involvement in the group's processes. This may take the form of cynicism, nonchalance, horseplay, and other more or less studied forms of "out of field" behavior.
- The *dominator* tries to assert authority or superiority by manipulating the group or certain members of the group. This domination may take the form of flattering others, asserting a superior status or right to attention, giving directions authoritatively, interrupting the contributions of others, and so on.
- The *help-seeker* attempts to call forth a "sympathy" response from other group members or from the whole group, whether through expressions of insecurity, personal confusion, or depreciation of himself or herself beyond "reason."
- The *special-interest pleader* speaks for the "small-business man," the "grassroots" community, the "housewife," "labor," and the like, usually cloaking his or her own prejudices or biases in the stereotype that best fits his or her individual need.[31]

Just one cautionary note regarding a group's move to suppress individuals playing any of these roles: By suppressing such action, a group may also inhibit, restrict, or suppress comments, suggestions, or input from some of the group's best participants. Participants who play a dysfunctional role at one point may play highly constructive, contributing roles at other points.

If members find themselves playing any of these dysfunctional, or individual, roles and they realize such role playing is not in the best interests of the group as a whole, self-discipline is one of the best ways to control the influence. Consider the good of the whole as more important than the good of any individual part of that whole.

THE INTERNET AND SMALL-GROUP PARTICIPATION

Online discussion groups (ODGs) such as e-mail lists, mailing lists or listservs, Usenet newsgroups, and Web-based bulletin-board-style forums generate a significant portion of online content. They are great places to talk with others interested in whatever you are or just to lurk and learn. These groups provide places to get suggestions and feedback, ask questions, test ideas, or just observe conversations by others around a particular topic. Some consider them to be "the most important and engaging type of content available online."[32]

Synchronous communication, as you recall, occurs in real time, and participants are present at the same time but most likely not in the same location. Types of synchronous communication include text-based chats, instant messaging, audio- and videoconferencing, and virtual whiteboard applications.[33] There are chat rooms on proprietary services such as America Online (AOL), Internet-based chat tools (such as IRC, ICQ, and AOL Instant Messenger). Also, there are hosted online chats where a featured guest responds to questions.

E-mail lists or **mailing lists** are group discussions that are completely passive. The discussion arrives through e-mail. Because it is passive, you can respond to the e-mail message you receive at any time you wish. This is called **asynchronous communication** because members do not have to be virtually present to participate and participants do not communicate at the same time. One advantage of asynchronous communication is that participants have the opportunity to consider and respond to messages posted by others. You must subscribe to a newsgroup first, but once you subscribe, the discussions come to you via e-mail. Mailing lists are automated electronic mail programs that take a message sent to it and send that message to all subscribers' e-mail boxes. Anyone with an e-mail address can belong to a mailing list.

Usenet newsgroups (often referred to just as Usenet) are group discussions that handle individual messages sorted by broad subject areas. They use standardized protocols. Because messages can be replicated around the world, Usenet newsgroups are not useful for private discussions. Because their functions have been integrated into Web browsers, you subscribe to newsgroups through your Internet or corporate network host provider, and the provider decides what newsgroups it will allow on its system. Therefore, you have access to only the newsgroups that your provider subscribes to. The main distinction between a newsgroup and a mailing list is that you go to the newsgroup site to which you subscribe to read the discussions.

Bulletin boards are group discussions originally designed for swapping files and posting notices. Each message is treated independently and is not linked to others of the same topic. Although classified as a form of group discussion by some, bulletin boards are not well adapted to discussion. They require the use of special software for participation. Examples are Spinnaker and Webline, neither of which is free.

Web conferencing or **Web forums** are group discussions that use text messages (and sometimes images) stored on a computer as the communication medium. Participants type messages for others to read instead of speaking them. Unlike the case with face-to-face discussions, messages that are typed into the computer software are recorded. In online group discussions, participants have the opportunity to consider and respond to messages posted by others.

Most participants who try ODGs experience them as ongoing conversations. It is as if people are sitting in a room, talking. "The tone of discourse generally is informal and conversational. Participants tend to be fairly tolerant of occasional typos and other editorial gaffes than the audience of a publication or web site probably would be."[34] Ronald Legon, provost of the University of Baltimore, makes this comment regarding those people who might be shy in face-to-face situations: "Asynchronous online discussions to which students contribute at moments of their own choosing help them overcome shyness and give students time to mull over responses."[35]

There are some important differences between ODGs and face-to-face discussions:

1. You must be able to quickly tell which messages to read and which to ignore.
2. A *thread* is when someone posts a message, and various other people respond to that message. Some have a clear beginning and end; more commonly they meander, split off into subthreads, and evolve.
3. In ODGs you must be able to follow distinct threads of conversation.
4. Often there are several simultaneous threads, which can get confusing. The order in which threads are received does not indicate which thread they belong to.
5. Many ODGs maintain some kind of archive where everything posted remains available, usually indefinitely. This gets confusing when someone revives a past thread but does not immediately make this obvious to other participants.

Whichever you choose to use—asynchronous or synchronous—and however you choose to use them, ODGs are as real as a physical neighborhood or an audience at a workshop, and they offer many benefits.

The keys to the success of ODGs are the same as for those of face-to-face discussion groups. They require a focus and goals, they must appeal to the tastes, interests, and needs of the community that they serve, and they do not make posting a message appear unacceptably risky. These keys need not be as academic or formal as they sound. For example, the goals of ODGs can be as nebulous as creating a sense of community and camaraderie, just having fun, or blowing off steam. Many ODGs, as their primary goal, simply offer a place for those of similar backgrounds or interests to meet and discuss.

Assess Yourself

How Effective Will You Be in Small-Group Discussions?

Indicate the degree to which you agree or disagree with each statement using the following scale: 5 = Strongly agree; 4 = Mildly agree; 3 = Agree and disagree equally; 2 = Mildly disagree; 1 = Strongly disagree. Circle your response following each statement.

1. I dislike participating in small-group discussions.	5 4 3 2 1
2. I recognize and respond in an appropriate way to differences in values, class, culture, ethnicity, lifestyle, point of view, and personal characteristics.	5 4 3 2 1
3. People are quite critical of me.	5 4 3 2 1
4. In general, I am comfortable while participating in small-group discussions.	5 4 3 2 1
5. I understand the concept of conflict, and I use strategies for handling it.	5 4 3 2 1
6. I often feel "left out," as if people don't want me around.	5 4 3 2 1
7. I am tense and nervous while participating in group discussions.	5 4 3 2 1
8. I possess effective relationship skills including trust, risk taking, empathy, listening, sharing, responsibility, respect for others, and expression of feelings.	5 4 3 2 1
9. People seem to respect my ideas and opinions about things.	5 4 3 2 1
10. I like to get involved in small-group discussions.	5 4 3 2 1
11. I understand the importance of working effectively with others and the need for courtesy and cooperation to accomplish a task.	5 4 3 2 1
12. People seem to like me.	5 4 3 2 1
13. Engaging in a group discussion with new people makes me tense and nervous.	5 4 3 2 1
14. I am willing to be both an effective and flexible small-group member.	5 4 3 2 1
15. Most people seem to understand how I feel about things.	5 4 3 2 1
16. I am seldom calm and relaxed while participating in group discussions.	5 4 3 2 1

TOTAL POINTS: _____

Before totaling your score, go to the *Communicating Effectively* CD-ROM or the Online Learning Center at **www.mhhe.com/hybels8** and follow the directions there.

mhhe.com/hybels8

Sources: For questions 1, 4, 7, 10, and 13, I am indebted to *An Introduction to Rhetorical Communication*, 4th ed., by J. C. McCroskey, 1982, Englewood Cliffs, NJ: Prentice Hall. McCroskey's Personal Report of Communication Apprehension-24 (PRCA-24) scale was published in *Measures of Personality and Social Psychological Attitudes* (pp. 170–173), by J. P. Robinson, P. R. Shaver, and L. S. Wrightsman, 1991, San Diego, CA: Academic Press. For questions 2, 5, 8, 11, and 14, I am indebted to "Group Effectiveness: Interpersonal, Negotiation, Teamwork," ICANS (Integrated Curriculum for Achieving Necessary Skills), Washington State Board for Community and Technical Colleges, Washington State Employment Security, Washington Workforce Training and Education Coordinating Board, Adult Basic and Literacy Educators, P.O. Box 42496, 711 Capitol Blvd., Olympia, WA 98504. Retrieved March 24, 2003, from **http://www.literacynet.org/icans/chapter05/groupeffectiveness.html**. For questions 3, 6, 9, 12, and 15 I am indebted to "Acceptance by Others and Its Relation to Acceptance of Self and Others: A Reevaluation," by W. F. Fey, 1955, *Journal of Abnormal and Social Psychology, 50,* pp. 274–276. The "Acceptability to Others" scale was published in *Measures of Personality and Social Psychological Attitudes* (pp. 409–411), by J. P. Robinson, P. R. Shaver, and L. S. Wrightsman, 1991, San Diego, CA: Academic Press.

CHAPTER REVIEW

SUMMARY

A small group is made up of 3 to 13 people who get together to do a job, solve a problem, or maintain relationships. Effectiveness in small groups is essential to your career success, will save you time and money, will help you in college, and will help you personally to accomplish your own goals and projects.

Small groups vary from one culture to another, subscribe to norms, and have rules. The different types of groups vary from social groups, to task-oriented, information-sharing, and learning groups.

For small groups to be effective, they must have a workable size, an appropriate meeting place, suitable seating arrangements, and cohesiveness and commitment, and they must guard against groupthink—when members start to think too much alike. A team is a type of group that has two or more people, a specific goal to be attained, and a coordination of activity among the members is required for the attainment of the goal.

Most groups that meet together to solve problems use a problem-solving sequence to structure their work. A common sequence is that the group chooses a topic, identifies the problem, analyzes the problem, finds and evaluates solutions, and chooses the best solution. Small groups beyond those in the speech communication classroom also reevaluate solutions after some time has passed.

Participating in group discussion involves the use of both task and maintenance roles. Recognizing dysfunctional, or individual, roles will help both leaders and members suppress, control, or compensate for their influence.

Online discussion groups such as e-mail lists or mailing lists, Usenet newsgroups, bulletin boards, or Web conferencing and Web forums provide places to get suggestions and feedback, ask questions, test ideas, or just observe conversations by others around a particular topic. They require a focus and goals; must appeal to the tastes, interests, and needs of the community that they serve; and often, simply offer a place for people with similar backgrounds and interests to meet and discuss.

KEY TERMS AND CONCEPTS

Use the *Communicating Effectively* CD-ROM and the Online Learning Center at www.mhhe.com/hybels8 to further your understanding of the following terms.

Asynchronous communication 251
Brainstorming 242
Bulletin boards 251
Cohesiveness 239
Commitment 239
Critic-analyzers 245
Dysfunctional (individual) roles 250
E-mail lists 251
Encouragers 249
Groupthink 239
Harmonizer-compromisers 249

Information givers 248
Information seekers 248
Information-sharing group 236
Initiator-expediters 248
Learning group 237
Mailing lists 251
Maintenance roles 249
Netiquette 232
Norms 235
Observers 250
Questions of fact 245
Questions of policy 245

Questions of value 245
Regulators 250
Rules 236
Small groups 233
Social group 236
Synchronous communication 251
Task-oriented group 236
Task roles 248
Team 241
Usenet newsgroups 251
Web conferencing 252
Web forums 252

CHAPTER REVIEW

QUESTIONS TO REVIEW

1. Why learn about small groups? How does effectiveness in them affect you?
2. What are the common characteristics that all groups possess?
3. What are the differences among types of groups?
4. From your own experience, what are the traits most likely to contribute to small-group effectiveness?
5. When it comes to an appropriate meeting place and suitable seating arrangements, what are the criteria that contribute the most to a group's success?
6. What is groupthink, what are some key indicators that it may be occurring, and when is it most likely to take place?
7. What is the process most groups follow for discussing a problem?
8. How do teams differ from groups, and what are the ideal conditions for teams to operate well?
9. What step or steps are likely to cause the most difficulty in effectively completing the problem-solving outline?
10. When participating in group discussion, distinguish among task, maintenance, and dysfunctional roles, and explain which behaviors are most associated with progress in problem-solving groups.
11. What are the differences among various online discussion groups, and what benefits do online discussion groups offer members?
12. What are the specific differences between online discussion groups and face-to-face discussions?

Go to the self-quizzes on the *Communicating Effectively* CD-ROM and the Online Learning Center at **www.mhhe.com/hybels8** to test your knowledge of the chapter contents.

CHAPTER 11

Group Leadership and Conflict Management

OBJECTIVES

After reading this chapter, you should be able to:

- Explain the ways in which leaders can influence followers.
- Describe the three elements likely to make people leaders.
- Distinguish among the three traditional leadership styles of authoritarian, democratic, and laissez-faire.
- Explain what is meant by, what is the point of, and what are the advantages of situational leadership.
- Explain the role of strategic flexibility in leading groups.
- Describe other elements important to leading groups effectively.
- Explain how conflict arises, the value it can have, and the ways it can be managed in groups.
- Describe the effect of the Internet on leadership in online discussion groups.
- Explain how to resolve conflicts online and why effort, care, and thoughtfulness are important.

258 Part 3 Communicating in Groups

TRENTON WAS WALKING ACROSS CAMPUS ONE DAY WHEN HE SAW A poster on one of the kiosk bulletin boards. "Sophomore Leadership Series," the headline on the poster exclaimed in large letters. Trenton read on: "This is a leadership development opportunity for sophomores who are interested in learning more about themselves as leaders and as contributing members of teams. The goals of the series are to:

- Provide you with an understanding of teamwork.
- Expose you to leadership concepts.
- Challenge you by choice.
- Demonstrate effectiveness as a team member.

Trenton wrote down the necessary meeting information in his day book.

Although he did not like meetings, this one turned out to be different. Briana began the meeting exactly on time, and she began by dispelling Trenton's major concern: "Nobody likes meetings," Briana said, "most of all me." And with that comment, she turned on a slide that outlined her agenda.

"This is our agenda for all the meetings we will have, and you can hold us to it. We are responsible," Briana said. "Our goal is to make the most of the time we have together, and to always give you valuable information and insights that will make our meetings productive and useful. We will begin by looking at what leaders are made of."

And that is precisely how this chapter begins as well. We begin our discussion answering the question, what is a leader? We then look at how leaders influence followers, how people become leaders, and approaches to leadership. Our final three sections cover leading the group, conflict in groups, and how the Internet impacts group leadership and conflict management.

WHAT IS A LEADER?

Some people hold recognized leadership positions: the president of the United States, a state senator, the principal of our elementary school. Others do not have formal leadership positions but are leaders because a group acknowledges them as such: the student who organizes a study group to prepare for an examination, the employee who puts together a car pool, the friend who gets people together to purchase tickets for a group to attend a rock concert. The characteristic these leaders have in common is that they exert some kind of influence. A **leader,** then, is a person who influences the behavior of one or more people.

Why is one person more influential than another? Why are some people leaders and others followers?

HOW LEADERS INFLUENCE FOLLOWERS

Some leaders influence their followers through sheer force of personality. Others wield influence because they are in a position of power in an organization and the people they lead are their subordinates. Most often, however, leadership is a combination of factors. Researchers have identified five sources of influence for leaders: reward power, coercive power, legitimate power, expert power, and referent power.[1]

For an example of leadership in a group, view "Small Group Communication," clip #6 on the CD.

Reward Power

A leader can have influence if he or she can reward followers; this is known as **reward power.** In an organization, rewards can take such forms as promotions or pay raises. If the leader is liked and admired, he or she can reward followers by praising them, giving them approval, recognizing them, or giving them attention.

Coercive Power

Coercive power is the power to punish. In an organization the leader can punish followers by demoting them or refusing to raise their pay or, more drastically, by firing them. Leaders can also exercise coercive power by criticizing their followers or refusing to pay attention to them. For example, an employee who is not willing to work on a weekend might not get new projects.

Legitimate Power

In a formal organization, a leader is influential because he or she is "the boss." The people who report to the leader must comply because of the organizational hierarchy and its rules. This constitutes **legitimate power.** In the military, for example, the lower ranks must always defer to the higher ranks; ability and personality are not factors.

Expert Power

Expert power denotes the influence and power an expert has because he or she knows more than anyone else. For example, Shin and Nikisha have formed a group of international students to study the problem of not having a common meeting place on campus. Although the group has six other members, Shin and Nikisha lead the group because they have done the most research on the problem.

Referent Power

Leaders with **referent power** enjoy influence because of personality. Members look up to them, want their approval, and try to emulate them. For example, a student who writes a humor column for the campus newspaper is greatly admired and many students defer to her judgments on a variety of subjects.

Figure 11-1 shows whether these five sources of influence come from organizations or from personality and where they overlap.

HOW PEOPLE BECOME LEADERS

What makes a person a leader? Some people are truly motivated to serve others. These people are known as **servant leaders,** people who "work for the well-being and growth of all employees and are committed to creating a sense of community and sharing power in decision making."[2]

In this sections, however, we will discuss other factors like personality and the group situation.

Figure 11-1
Sources of Influence

Organizational → Legitimate Power

Organizational / Personality → Reward Power, Coercive Power

Personality → Referent Power, Expert Power

Personality Traits

Leaders are rarely (if ever) born, and no single set of traits consistently distinguishes leaders from followers. Research suggested that leaders would exhibit higher levels of extroversion, agreeableness, and conscientiousness than nonleaders.[3] But in a study of 99 undergraduates (36 leaders and 63 nonleaders), results did not show significant relationships between leadership and either extroversion or agreeableness.

Some traits do increase the probability that certain leaders will lead their followers successfully. Author Warren Bennis lists self-knowledge, openness to feedback, eagerness to improve, curiosity and risk taking, concentration and persistence, readiness to learn from adversity, a regard for tradition and stability as well as the need for revision and change, and openness of style. Leaders also work well with the system and serve as a model or mentor for others.[4]

Situational Factors

In many situations people emerge as leaders because they have the competence and the skill to solve the problem at hand. The person who emerges as leader is the one who is best able to meet a specific group's needs. These characteristics are *external* in that they depend on the situation and on the kind of skill or expertise needed to solve the problem. For example, if a group of students is assigned to make a videotape and only one student knows how to run a video camera, he or she will be the leader—at least until everyone else has learned.

Although a person may become a leader solely on the basis of outstanding personality or skills, most people become leaders when their personalities or skills are appropriate for a particular circumstance or when they can fulfill a need of the group. Hence the name *functional leadership*—suitability of a leader's personality, skills, or knowledge to the needs of a group.

Strategic Flexibility

Those people who are strategically flexible are more likely to become leaders. Why? First, they are likely to be more perceptive since they are accustomed to anticipating and assessing situations already. Second, they are likely to be well adjusted since it

> In this on-site situation, which leadership style is likely to be the best one? On what factor is leadership style likely to depend in this situation?

requires psychological maturity to deal with anything they are required to face. Third, they have already added bricks and mortar to a solid foundation of communication skills and behaviors; thus, they have more to bring to any situation they face.

Strategically flexible people are also empathic, enthusiastic, and intuitive, all of which supports leaders in reaching their goals. Put into the context of leadership, **strategic flexibility** also will reinforce your self-confidence and help you become more assertive in thinking and dealing with others.

APPROACHES TO LEADERSHIP

There are many approaches to leadership. First, we examine three traditional but somewhat incomplete styles: authoritarian, democratic, and laissez-faire. **Leadership style** is simply the manner in which a leader exerts control over a group. No one leadership style is best for all situations; that is precisely why strategic flexibility is so important in filling leadership roles.

Traditional Leadership Styles

Traditional leadership styles offer a useful reference point for examining today's leadership needs. Here, we will look briefly at authoritarian, democratic, and laissez-faire leaders.

Authoritarian Leaders

The **authoritarian leader** holds the greatest control over a group. He or she takes charge by deciding what should be talked about and who should talk. This leader approves some ideas and discards others. Most of the discussion in the group is directed to the leader for approval.

Often an authoritarian leader gains the leadership position because he or she is the only group member with expertise. Sometimes a group starts out with an authoritarian leader but later operates more democratically.

An authoritarian leader is often the best type of leader when a group must do a job very quickly. For example, a group is meeting to write a grant proposal that is due in two days. One person takes charge of the project and appoints other members to do various tasks. This is the most efficient way to get the job done in the available time.

Democratic Leaders

A **democratic leader** is one who lets all points of view be heard. Rather than decide things personally, he or she will offer ideas and let the group react to them. The group is never told what to do, though the leader may suggest a direction to take. Leadership in a democratic group is often functional: It may vary with the task and may even move from one individual to another when the group finds this appropriate. Democratic groups work best when members are equal in status and experience and when there is sufficient time to solve the problem.

Laissez-Faire Leaders

The **laissez-faire leader** does very little actual leading. He or she might call the group together, but that's about it. Such a leader neither suggests any direction nor imposes any order on the group. Support groups, such as groups for people with cancer or for people who were abused as children, might feel uncomfortable with an acknowledged leader since the members attend for the purpose of helping one another.

STRATEGIC FLEXIBILITY
Effectiveness as a functional leader focuses on your ability to use strategic flexibility—being adaptive, persuasive, aware, sensitive, and responsible. The key may be found in the question, "What skills do I have that will help move the group forward?"

Functional Leadership

We tend to place too much responsibility on the leader of a group and too little on participants. Every member of a group should be a leader in some area. We call this sharing of expertise, when leadership varies with the task of the group and moves from one individual to another as the group finds it suitable, **functional leadership.**

The advantage of functional leadership is that the group's concern is no longer the "property" of any one individual; it belongs to the group as a whole. What matters is whether group needs and goals are being satisfied. This means that leadership is active and changing, that the focus of participants is on the group rather than on an individual leader, and that the importance of sharing and member involvement is emphasized.

To be ready to be leaders at any moment requires that members be persuasive and adaptive; be able to convince the group they can contribute to the direction of the group; foster agreement, cooperation, or understanding; or influence the group's success in any capacity. Functional leaders must be responsible.

Shared Leadership

The best way to view shared leadership is to contrast it to the command-and-control style of authoritarian leadership. **Shared leadership** occurs when all group or team members assume both decision-making authority and responsibility for the team's results. It is similar to democratic leadership, but it does not reside in a single person.

A supportive and encouraging climate for shared leadership is one in which there is a commitment among group members to each other; a trust level where members take what others say in good faith; respect and mutual regard despite large differences among members; a valuing among members of the unique qualities each brings to the group; mutual empathy in which there is a true attempt to understand and feel with; and for those taking part, hope that the conversation holds the possibility that all will gain or learn from the process.[5]

Although shared leadership is an ideal leadership style, there are four potential pitfalls. First, attention to process—maintaining a climate of conversation—can take attention away from the desired product or outcome. The second potential pitfall is the possibility that gifted individuals with unique contributions who might have risen to a leadership role in a functional or emergent situation will not do so in a shared leadership condition.

The third pitfall is that the commitments, understandings, and practices of shared leadership are sophisticated, and for this reason, many may shy away from it. Finally, like all models of leadership, it is culturally specific. What may be viewed as appropriate in one society or group, may not be so in another.[6]

Situational Leadership

In the simplest terms, a **situational leader** can adopt different leadership styles depending on the situation.[7] In his book *E-Leader*, Robert Hargrove recommends a "balanced" leadership style, by which he means one that can be shifted in various situations by asking, "Who do I need to be in this matter?"[8] Leaders may need to be directive, empowering, collaborative, facilitative, or whatever and he makes it clear that there is no one right way to manage. The point of situational leadership is that the talented leader employs the most appropriate style based on the context—which is a combination of task, situation, and group. This is demonstrated in Figure 11-2.

The first situational leadership style (square 1) is labeled **telling** in which the leader is focused more on the task and less on the group (high task–low group). It is similar to the authoritarian style in which the leader states the problem, takes charge of the task, and tells group members what to do. If you were concerned about your grade, placed in

Figure 11-2
Situational Leadership Styles

A 2x2 matrix with Group Orientation (LOW to HIGH) on the vertical axis and Task Orientation (LOW to HIGH) on the horizontal axis:
- Participating (3): High group, Low task
- Selling (2): High group, High task
- Delegating (4): Low group, Low task
- Telling (1): Low group, High task

STRATEGIC FLEXIBILITY

Situational leadership offers the best opportunities to flex your strategic muscles because it capitalizes not just on your own personality factors but synergistically (with the combined and correlated forces) of task factors, group factors, and situational factors as well.

a task-oriented group in which other members did not appear willing or able to complete the task if left alone, you might resort to manipulation or even coercion to get the job done.

The second situational leadership style (square 2) is labeled **selling.** In this style, leaders state the problem and decide what to do, but they sell the other group members on the idea to gain majority support. Selling is high task–high group. Leaders must explain how the idea will benefit the group and then persuade others to go along. The major differences between telling and selling are:

Telling	Selling
• One-way communication	• Two-way communication
• Use of manipulation and coercion for control	• Use of persuasion and explanation for group support
• Negative environment	• Positive reinforcement

The third situational leadership style (square 3) is **participating.** Using this style, leaders state the problem but immediately consult with group members. Participating is low task–high group. With all group members participating, leaders offer support and the group determines the best thing to do only after hearing all members' ideas and reactions. Notice in this style the increased focus by the leader on the group and the corresponding diminished focus on the task.

The fourth situational leadership style (square 4) is **delegating.** Delegating is low task–low group. Leaders hang back and let members plan and execute the job. This style of leadership is utilized in more mature, established groups where members can run their own show—much like the case in shared leadership.

LEADING THE GROUP

Leaders can help groups work better when they are strategically flexible. That is why we begin this section with listening.

Listening

Many of the functions effective leaders must perform in leading the group depend on effective listening. Effective listening helps create an atmosphere of acceptance and understanding in which others can then explore problems and determine solutions. It helps in managing conflicts, developing employees, and tapping into the key issues that drive others. Good leadership involves modesty, empathy, and reflective listening.[9] Some writers believe that listening is "the most important of all leadership skills."[10]

Listening, as you will recall from Chapter 4, is an essential foundation for strategic flexibility. It is the way to obtain the essential messages and information you need to be able to properly anticipate, assess, evaluate, select, and apply your skills and behaviors. Listening also can counter the natural tendency of leaders to give orders, directions, and provide information and answers. It allows others to contribute their ideas and opinions, permits open dialogue to occur, reveals the trust you have in others to provide valuable input, and gives you time to think about whether you should respond at all, and how.

Working Together

Come to some conclusions regarding the following questions:

1. Which of the styles of leadership discussed in this section do you think is the most effective and why?
2. What specific behaviors do the different styles of leadership discussed in this section require of leaders?
3. Are there leadership behaviors that you consider inappropriate under any circumstance? Why or why not?
4. If you were in a situation in which a leader was using a leadership style you considered inappropriate or ineffective, what could you do, as a member of the group, to try to change the situation?

Maintaining Neutrality and Objectivity

Since the point of view of group leaders can affect all group procedures, if they suspend judgment and encourage full consideration of all viewpoints, they are likely to appear neutral. **Neutrality** means not taking sides but allowing the weight of members' evidence to determine the outcome of group decision making. Members prefer open-mindedness and give high marks to leaders who encourage evaluation, examination, and differing interpretations.

A second point of view of leaders that can affect group procedures is **objectivity**, basing conclusions on facts and evidence rather than on emotion or opinions. If the goal of groups is to investigate problems systematically and realistically, then leaders' objectivity can make a difference.

Neutrality and objectivity are important principles that can guide and direct group activity. Without them, groups cannot achieve their greatest potential.

Establishing Procedures

Every formal small-group meeting should be conducted according to a plan that organizes the group's work. An **agenda** is a list of all the items that will be discussed during the meeting. It is often constructed with the cooperation of key participants. The leader should distribute the agenda a few days in advance of the meeting to remind people of the meeting and allow them to prepare. It also ensures that important business will not be overlooked.

Start and end on time, and stick to the agenda. Get all points of view and ideas. Encourage feedback. Make sure minutes are kept of the meeting for future reference.

Finding Solutions

If you are part of a problem-solving group, you will need to follow the steps in decision making (see Figure 11-3). Begin by defining the problem and making certain there is just one problem to solve. You can do this by clearly defining and separating the issues. With this as a base, ask members for alternatives. As members offer suggestions, make certain they are accepted without criticism from the group. What is important is for group members to explore the pros and cons of each idea by asking, in each case, "What are the advantages and disadvantages of this alternative?"

Consider This

What is the history and derivation of situational leadership? Here David L. Dotlich and Peter C. Cairo, in their book *Unnatural Leadership*, offer a historical snapshot:

> In 1989, business management expert and author Ken Blanchard brought together two streams of leadership—task-oriented leadership and people-oriented leadership—and noted that the combination of emphasis between task and people depended on the situation. He concluded that there is no one ideal leadership style; instead, the best leadership varies from situation to situation. On the battlefield and in emergencies, he maintained, the best leadership style is directive. In day-to-day operations among professionals, the best style might be more consultative. In strategic planning requiring the buy-in of many people, participative leadership would be more appropriate. And in situations where direct reports were mature and capable of carrying out their own responsibilities, delegation would be the most appropriate leadership behavior.

Source: From *Unnatural Leadership: Going against Intuition and Experience to Develop Ten New Leadership Instincts* (pp. ix–x), by David L. Dotlich and Peter C. Cairo, 2002, San Francisco: Jossey-Bass.

Questions

1. Do you think leaders today must lead from the inside out—that is, must they understand themselves and accept their own strengths and weaknesses?
2. Why is it important to know what those leaders believe in and what they stand for? What constraints or restrictions does society impose on leaders who have little regard for how objectives are achieved?

When you have investigated the strengths and weaknesses, you will need to choose a solution. A solution can draw from several alternatives, or can be one suggested that stands alone. Sometimes solutions need to be modified to satisfy all members. The important part here is to make certain that all members of the group have had the opportunity to participate in the decision making. Once action has been implemented, the outcome will have to be evaluated. This can be done through discussion, or it can be handled through a report by one member.

Figure 11-3
A Brief Problem-Solving Guide

Define the problem.
Ask for alternatives.
Explore the pros and cons of each idea.
Choose a solution.
Modify it to satisfy all members.
Evaluate the outcome.

Problem → Solution

Helping the Group to Progress

Leaders must be willing to interject themselves and enforce the group's agenda. This requires some discretion and diplomacy because group members do not like to be bossed. A leader might say, for example, "Excuse me for interrupting you, Sabrina, but I wonder if we might hear what some of the others are thinking."

Summarizing is one good way to help the group progress. Doing so alerts the group to where it has been, what it has accomplished, where it is now, and where it is going. A final summary and a statement of goals for the next meeting is also a good way to close each group meeting, "Today we had a disagreement over whether we should lease our equipment to outsiders or permit only our own students to use it. At our next meeting. I think we should work to resolve this issue."

Hidden agendas can interfere with the group's process. **Hidden agendas** are unannounced goals, subjects, or issues that are important to individual members or subgroups but are not on the group's public or stated agenda. For example, in a classroom group one member is more interested in social life than in the topic the group is supposed to be discussing. This person often asks questions about dorm life, football games, or other weekend activities. Most hidden agendas lose their force when recognized by a tactful reminder to the group as a whole to stay on topic.

> **STRATEGIC FLEXIBILITY**
> Helping the group move along requires strategic flexibility—the ability to anticipate group needs, assess what is going on and where the group needs to go, evaluate the information presented and its value, select from your own skills and behaviors and, with discretion and diplomacy, decide to intervene on behalf of group progress.

Seeking Diversity

We've seen that diversity describes the many differences and similarities that exist among people, such as age, race, gender, or ethnicity. Sexual orientation and some physical abilities or qualities may not be apparent. Diversity also includes less obvious differences such as religious and moral values, education, social status, age, political views, or thinking style.

Why should leaders seek diversity? With diversity, group discussions are likely to be livelier, more spirited, and simply more enlightening and interesting.[11] Diversity also promotes broad understanding and knowledge. It prevents minorities from feeling isolated or like spokespersons for their minority, and it creates a vibrant atmosphere that challenges and breaks down stereotypes. When everyone in the group is accepted and feels important, leaders can build a group whose members will work together to learn, interact, and produce better results.

Raising Questions

One of the ways a leader can be most helpful is by raising pertinent questions. Sometimes, during discussion, it is easy for a group to lose sight of its original goal. A group of students, for example, might be discussing the issue of date rape and get diverted to the subject of unfriendly law enforcement officials. If the group leader says. "Is this directly related to the problem?" the group will realize that it is not and will get back on the subject.

Sometimes a group will try to discuss a subject but will lack sufficient information. A group discussing faculty and student parking might realize that it doesn't know how many parking places are assigned to each category. The leader may ask someone to find this information.

Focusing on Answers

Focusing on answers means evaluating alternatives by considering their advantages and disadvantages. A useful leadership role is played by members who ask such questions as these: What consequences are likely to occur? What are the costs going to be? What barriers have to be overcome? How serious are the barriers?

Sometimes solutions call for a plan of action. If your group decides that the only solution to its problem is to demonstrate against the administration, members would be faced with making plans for that demonstration. How are you going to publicize your grievances, get recruits, and carry out the protest? Effective leadership helps a group plan carefully for the action it has decided to take.

Delegating Responsibility

Some people see a leader as the one who does all the work. This should not be true in any group. A good leader should be able to delegate responsibility to the group's members. If a group is going to do research, for example, the leader could assign some members to go to the library, some to interview experts, and others to coordinate and present the information to the group.

Some leaders do not delegate because they believe they are the only ones who can do the job right. If you are one of these people, you should consider taking a risk and letting some of the other people do some of the work. You might be surprised how well they do it. Also, sharing the work makes participants feel more involved and committed.

Encouraging Social Interaction

Social interaction occurs in a group when people feel recognized and accepted by other members. The more friendliness, mutual trust, and respect exhibited, the more likely the members are to find pleasure in the group and work hard to accomplish its goals. Further, group discussions are more likely to be of high quality when group members participate fully in the process. The group leader can also strengthen social interaction by encouraging shy members to speak, by complimenting worthwhile contributions, and by praising the overall accomplishments of the group.

Sharing a Vision

When leaders describe a great leader, the first characteristic on their list is "a creative visionary."[12] Leaders with **vision** are able to anticipate and make provision for future events. They have foresight, insight, and imagination.

Why is having a vision important? First, organizations advance when a clear, widely understood vision creates tension between the real and the ideal; people work together to reduce the gap. Second, a vision motivates as it draws people together to accomplish a common purpose or reach a common goal. Third, a vision will increase support, inside and outside the group. Here is what Rudolph Giuliani, former mayor of New York City, says about vision in his book *Leadership:* "A leader must not only set direction, but communicate that direction. He usually cannot simply impose his will—and even if he could it's not the best way to lead. He must bring people aboard, excite them about his vision, and earn their support. They in turn will inspire those around them, and soon everyone will be focusing on the same goal."[13]

How do you judge a vision? First, ask yourself how clearly it is articulated. Second, does it address the primary concerns of members? Third, does it translate into practical and specific strategies, methods, and techniques that can be used to attain it?

CONFLICT IN GROUPS

When individuals meet in groups to solve problems, conflicts are likely to occur. By **conflict** we mean the expressed struggle between at least two individuals who perceive incompatible goals or interference from others in achieving their goals. One reason there is likely to be conflict has to do with perceptual differences that influence people's responses to any situation. Let's examine some of the obvious perceptual differences.

Culture, race, and ethnicity create perceptual differences because our varying cultural backgrounds influence us to hold certain beliefs about the social structure of our world and the role of conflict in that experience.

Gender and sexuality create differences in perception as a result of different experiences in the world that relate to power and privilege.

Knowledge influences approaches to conflict because it forms the base from which you operate. Whether or not you understand what is going on in *this* case (situation-specific knowledge), and whether or not you have read about or heard about this type of situation before (general knowledge) will influence your willingness to engage in and manage conflict.

In addition to perceptual differences, group conflict generally occurs because of procedure, power, or work distribution.

- *Procedure.* The first source of conflict, and perhaps the easiest to eliminate, is differing views on procedure. How often should the group meet? What form should the minutes take? To keep such conflict from occurring, the group members should discuss and resolve issues of procedure at the first meeting.
- *Power.* Research has found that in business and corporate settings a group often becomes a focal point for power struggles.[14] However, power struggles are not so common in classroom groups. If one person wants power, the problem is often solved by making him or her the chair. If this doesn't solve the problem and members continue their power struggle, the group will probably not work very efficiently.
- *Work distribution.* The third source of conflict, and one of the greatest in classroom groups, is that some members work harder than others. Like power struggles, this kind of conflict is difficult to resolve. Since few students are willing to tell the instructor about such inequality, the harder workers' only hope is to confront the group members who are not working and use peer pressure to persuade them to change.

Although these three kinds of conflict can interfere with group work, not all conflict is harmful. The fourth kind of conflict, conflict about substantive issues, can be rewarding.

The Value of Substantive Conflict

Substantive conflict occurs when people have different reactions to an idea. It is likely to occur when any important and controversial idea is being discussed. As in all exchanges of ideas, people's opinions and perceptions are influenced by their culture, upbringing, education, and experience. These perceptions cause them to react differently to ideas and can create conflict in a group.

Many people believe that conflict is abnormal or bad. There is no doubt that conflict can (and often does) have negative effects. Conflict is destructive when it diverts energy from more important issues and tasks. It is destructive when it deepens differences in values, polarizes groups so that cooperation is reduced, destroys the morale of people or reinforces their already poor self-concepts.

Conflict can however be constructive.[15] It is essential for both healthy relationships and groups if it allows people to grow and change, adapt to new situations, or invent new approaches to problems. There is value in conflict when it opens up issues of importance and, therefore, results in issue clarification—a heightened awareness that a problem exists that needs to be solved.

There is value in conflict, too, when it causes reassessment by allowing for the examination of procedures or actions. Other values include greater quantity and quality of achievement, and creative problem solving. Constructive conflict results, too, in healthier cognitive, social, and psychological development which means those involved are better able to deal with stress and cope with unforeseen adversities. When conflict is avoided or suppressed, all these positive results cannot take place.

The difference between productive and destructive conflict can be seen in their focus. Productive conflict focuses on substantive issues of disagreement, and the goal is to resolve the disagreement. Destructive conflict focuses on the defeat or destruction of the opponent, and it is often characterized by force, aggression, and coercion. Inflexibility is a mark of destructive conflict.

Managing Group Conflict

There are times when conflict can slow down a group or even bring it to a screeching halt. When conflict arises, the group leader has to step in and try to help group members resolve it. The approach the leader takes should depend on the seriousness of the conflict. Robert Blake and Jane Mouton, who have written about ways to resolve conflict, suggest five ways of managing it.[16] Table 11-1 explains the objectives, supporting rationale, and likely outcomes for each of the following approaches.

Conflict in groups can occur over perceptual differences such as culture, race, ethnicity, gender, sexuality, knowledge, or previous experiences. Although conflict can be destructive, there can be great value in it as well.

Table 11-1 Conflict Management Approaches, Objectives, Rationales, and Outcomes

Approach	Objective and Typical Responses	Supporting Rationale	Likely Outcome
Avoiding	Avoid having to deal with conflict. "I'm neutral on that issue. Let me think about it."	Disagreements are inherently bad because they create tension.	Interpersonal problems don't get resolved. They can cause long-term frustration which will be manifested in a variety of ways.
Accommodating	Don't upset the other person. "How can I help you feel good about this? My position isn't important enough to risk bad feelings between us."	Maintaining harmonious relationships should be our top priority.	Other person is likely to take advantage of you.
Competing	Get your way. "I know what's right. Don't question my judgment or authority."	Better to risk causing a few hard feelings than to abandon a position you're committed to.	You will feel vindicated, and the other party will feel defeated and possibly humiliated.
Collaborating	Solve the problem together. "This is my position. What's yours? I'm committed to finding the best possible solution."	Positions of both parties are equally important. Equal emphasis should be placed on quality of outcome and fairness of decision-making process.	The problem will most likely be resolved. Both parties will be committed to the solution and satisfied that they have been treated fairly.
Compromising	Reach an agreement quickly. "Let's search for a mutually agreeable solution."	Prolonged conflicts distract people from their work, take time, and engender bitter feelings.	Participants become conditioned to seek expedient rather than effective long-term solutions.

Source: Reprinted by permission of Harvard Business School Press. From "Managing interpersonal conflict" by J. Ware & L. Barnes. Boston, MA. 1985, pp. 53-62. Copyright © 1985 by the Harvard Business School Publishing Corporation, all rights reserved. In L. A. Mainiero & C.L. Tromley, *Developing Managerial Skills of Organizational Behavior*, © 1994, p. 92. Reprinted by permission of Pearson Education, Inc., Upper Saddle River, NJ. Adapted from Inls 180: Communication Processes: Notes on Conflict Management. Spring 1998. Retrieved October 25, 2005 from www.ils.unc.edu/daniel/180/conflict.html.

Avoidance

Sometimes groups argue over points that are so minor they are not worth the time they take up. If the leader sees this happening, she or he should suggest that the issue doesn't seem very important and that the group should move to another topic.

Accommodation

Accommodation occurs when people on one side of an issue give in to those on the other side. If a leader sees accommodation as a possibility, he or she should attempt to find out how strongly people feel about the sides they have taken. If the issue is not really important to one side, the leader might suggest that that side give in.

Competition

Competition occurs when members on one side care more about winning than about the other members' feelings. When a leader sees competition rising, she or he should try to deflect it before members get entrenched in their positions. Sometimes individual members feel competitive with one another, and they use the group sessions to work out their feelings. If this is happening, the leader might point out to each member privately that the conflict is keeping the group from working together.

Collaboration

In *collaboration*, conflicting parties try to work together to meet each other's needs. Collaborators do not attack one another; instead, they try to understand opposing points of view and work hard to stay away from anything that might harm the group's relationships.

Compromise

In *compromise* each side has to give up something to get what it wants. Compromise will work only when each side believes that what it gets is fair and that it has gained at least a partial victory.

THE INTERNET, GROUP LEADERSHIP, AND CONFLICT MANAGEMENT

There are two extremes regarding the leadership of online discussion groups (ODGs). The first is the unled—often referred to as the unmanaged—group. In this case, someone sets up the mechanism for an online discussion, and then lets it run itself.[17] The success of such groups often depends on the composition of the participant community as well as the group's focus and goals. Such *autopilot* approaches may work fine, or, at least, they may work well enough—especially in groups where functional, shared, or situational leadership occurs.

The other extreme is the fully led (or fully moderated) ODG. In these examples, leaders examine and then approve or exclude every posting before it is published. The advantage of this approach is a highly focused, discussion that is on-topic.

Here are some suggestions for resolving conflicts that occur online.[18]

1. Don't respond right away.
2. Read the post again later.
3. Discuss the situation with someone who knows you.
4. Choose whether or not you want to respond.
5. Assume that people mean well, unless they have a history or pattern of aggression.
6. Clarify what was meant.
7. Think about what you want to accomplish by your communication.
8. Verbalize what you want to accomplish.
9. Use "I" statements when sharing your feelings or thoughts.
10. Use strictly *feeling* statements.
11. Choose your words carefully and thoughtfully, particularly when you're upset.
12. Place yourself in the other person's shoes.

13. Use emoticons to express your tone.
14. Start and end your post with positive, affirming, and validating statements.

The Internet is an ideal place to practice communication. Besides the entertainment value of chat rooms and other forms of online small groups, it is an ideal place for learning and for the stimulation of critical thinking. The Internet also offers opportunities to practice leadership skills and apply conflict-management skills. It can free you to try new and more positive communication and leadership styles, and in asynchronous communication, you can take the time to reflect, structure, and develop your responses.

Assess Yourself

Do You Have What It Takes to Be a Leader?

Indicate the degree to which you agree or disagree with each statement using the following scale: 5 = Strongly agree; 4 = Mildly agree; 3 = Agree and disagree equally; 2 = Mildly disagree; 1 = Strongly disagree. Circle your response following each statement.

1. I easily and comfortably question others' ideas and opinions.   5 4 3 2 1
2. I strive to find out and meet the needs of other group members.   5 4 3 2 1
3. I feel good when I measure the results of my hard work, rather than counting the time it took.   5 4 3 2 1
4. I feel comfortable thinking of others' needs.   5 4 3 2 1
5. I readily listen to the opinions of others.   5 4 3 2 1
6. I feel comfortable sharing power and control.   5 4 3 2 1
7. I seek out and move on to new opportunities.   5 4 3 2 1
8. I express my feelings easily to others.   5 4 3 2 1
9. I am able to easily share my accomplishments with others.   5 4 3 2 1
10. I am aware of my own strengths and weaknesses.   5 4 3 2 1
11. I feel comfortable with conflict.   5 4 3 2 1
12. I feel comfortable with change and making change.   5 4 3 2 1
13. I make goals.   5 4 3 2 1
14. I am able to motivate others.   5 4 3 2 1
15. I am constantly looking for ways to improve.   5 4 3 2 1
16. I feel comfortable knowing people look at me as a model for what is good.   5 4 3 2 1
17. In general I am a confident person.   5 4 3 2 1

TOTAL POINTS: _____

Before totaling your score, go to the *Communicating Effectively* CD-ROM or the Online Learning Center at **www.mhhe.com/hybels8** and follow the directions there.

mhhe.com/hybels8

Source: Adapted from "Leadership Self-Assessment," ICANS (Integrated Curriculum for Achieving Necessary Skills), Washington State Board for Community and Technical Colleges, Washington State Employment Security, Washington Workforce Training and Education Coordinating Board, Adult Basic and Literacy Educators, P.O. Box 42496, 711 Capitol Blvd., Olympia, WA 98504. Retrieved October 25, 2005, from http://www.literacynet.org/icans/chapter05/leadership.html

CHAPTER REVIEW

SUMMARY

One characteristic that all leaders have in common is that they exert influence; thus, a leader is a person who influences the behavior of one or more people by rewarding them, threatening to punish them, using their position of power, knowing more than anyone else, or having a particular personality. One theory of leadership is that people become leaders because of their personalities and the situations in which they find themselves.

The three traditional leadership styles include authoritarian leaders who take charge of a group, democratic leaders who give everyone a chance to participate in decision making, and laissez-faire leaders who do little leading.

Functional leadership occurs when leadership varies with the task of the group and moves from one individual to another as the group finds it suitable. Shared leadership occurs when all group or team members assume both decision-making authority and responsibility for the team's results.

Situational leaders can adopt different leadership styles depending on the situation. Using the telling style, they focus more on the task and less on the group. In the selling style, leaders state the problem and decide what to do, then sell the other group members on the idea. Using the participating style, they state the problem but immediately consult with group members. In the delegating style, they hang back and let members plan and execute the job.

In leading groups, leaders have a number of responsibilities. These include listening, maintaining neutrality and objectivity, establishing procedures, helping the group to progress, seeking diversity, raising questions, focusing on answers, delegating responsibility, encouraging social interaction, and sharing a vision.

Conflict in groups is likely to occur because of perceptual differences, procedure, power, and work distribution. Although substantive conflict in groups can be disruptive, its values in allowing people to grow and change, adapt to new situations, and invent new approaches to problems far outweigh most of the difficulties it creates. One important task of group leaders is to manage conflict. They should determine how serious the conflict is and take one of the following approaches: avoidance, accommodation, competition, collaboration, or compromise.

Because of the popularity of online discussion groups (ODGs), the Internet has become a major player in group discussion. Resolving conflict online requires a great deal of care and deliberation.

KEY TERMS AND CONCEPTS

Use the *Communicating Effectively* CD-ROM and the Online Learning Center at www.mhhe.com/hybels8 to further your understanding of the following terms.

Agenda 265
Authoritarian leaders 261
Coercive power 259
Conflict 269
Delegating 264
Democratic leader 262
Expert power 259
Functional leadership 262
Hidden agenda 267
Laissez-faire leader 262
Leader 258
Leadership style 261
Legitimate power 259
Neutrality 265
Objectivity 265
Participating 264
Referent power 259
Reward power 259
Selling 264
Servant leaders 259
Shared leadership 262
Situational leader 263
Strategic flexibility 261
Substantive conflict 269
Telling 263
Vision 268

CHAPTER REVIEW

QUESTIONS TO REVIEW

1. What are the five sources of influences for leaders?
2. How do people become leaders?
3. What is the contribution strategic flexibility makes in people becoming leaders?
4. What are the strengths and weaknesses of the three traditional approaches to leadership (authoritarian, democratic, and laissez-faire)?
5. What are the differences among functional, shared, and situational approaches to leadership?
6. What are the main differences between classical or authoritarian leadership and shared leadership?
7. What are the distinctions among the four styles of situational leadership: telling, selling, participating, and delegating?
8. What are the differences among leadership factors, group factors, and situational factors when it comes to deciding on a leadership approach? Which are likely to have the greatest influence on deciding which situational leadership style to use?
9. With respect to actually leading a group discussion, what aspects would be the most troublesome for you to accomplish? Why?
10. When it comes to seeking diversity, what would a diverse group look like and what might be its advantages?
11. When it comes to sharing a vision, why is having a vision even important in leadership?
12. What are the likely sources of conflicts in groups?
13. What values does conflict bring to groups?
14. In managing group conflict, which approach looks most promising and why?
15. How should leaders of online discussion groups resolve conflicts that occur there?

Go to the self-quizzes on the *Communicating Effectively* CD-ROM and the Online Learning Center at **www.mhhe.com/hybels8** to test your knowledge of the chapter contents.

APPENDIX A

Computer-Mediated Communication (CMC)

OBJECTIVES

After reading this appendix, you should be able to:

- Define and explain the importance of *Computer-Mediated Communication (CMC)*.
- Relate CMC to the communication model.
- Explain why you might choose CMC over face-to-face communication (FtFC).
- Explain how online credibility is developed and why it is important.
- Demonstrate the value of virtual communities and blogs.
- Apply ethical standards to CMC.

PATRICIA RAMPERSAD IS TOTALLY WIRED. HER CELL PHONE IS PART OF her anatomy. When she's not working independently on assignments, she's downloading songs on her iPod, IM-ing friends, text-messaging her boyfriend, keeping up with her classes through online discussions, researching her papers online, and shopping online. Patricia's world revolves around computer-mediated communication (CMC), and she uses it for interpersonal communication, information seeking, and entertainment.

In this appendix we examine how important CMC is and how it relates to the model of communication in Chapter 1, compare it with face-to-face communication (FtFC), and explain why we sometimes choose CMC over FtFC. We'll also look at credibility and blogs.

CMC AND LITERACY

Now that 75 percent of the U.S. population has access to it, the use of the Internet has displaced television watching and a range of other activities, including socializing with friends, and even sleeping.[1] Any factor that does that must be considered significant.[2]

"The Internet is not about technology, it is not about information, it is about communication—people talking with each other, and people exchanging e-mail.... The Internet is mass participation in fully bi-directional, uncensored mass communication. Communication is the basis, the foundation.... The Internet is a community of chronic communicators."[3]

We will build toward a complete understanding of CMC by looking first at media literacy, and then at CMC specifically.

Media literacy is the ability to access, analyze, evaluate, and communicate information in all its forms—both print and nonprint.[4] Thus, media literacy provides important communication skills for today and tomorrow. To be literate within this definition means that you must learn to receive, comprehend, analyze, and evaluate media messages as well as use technology to create messages. Assumed within this definition, but perhaps not obvious, is a basic understanding about the nature and power of interactivity itself.[5]

Computer-mediated communication, or CMC, is all about the range of technologies that facilitate human communication. But when discussing CMC it is useful to narrow our focus just to information presented via computers. This is **digital literacy.** Digital literacy includes the knowledge and understanding necessary to make full, active, and informed use of all relevant formats from any of the wide range of sources presented via computers.

CMC AND THE COMMUNICATION MODEL

CMC is represented in the communication model by the word **channel**—the route a message travels or the means it uses to reach the sender-receivers. Let us expand the definition a little to include the actual sending and receiving via the computer and make a broad comparison with face-to-face communication.

Figure A-1 is a one-to-one comparison of face-to-face (FtF) groups and electronic groups. **Synchronous communication** occurs when people are directly connected, as in a telephone conversation, an FtF encounter, or a real-time, online group format such as instant messaging (IM). In **asynchronous communication** people are not directly connected with each other at the same time, such as in e-mail and bulletin boards (online discussions). Most of the exchanges between people on the Internet consist of asynchronous communication.

Many differences between the channels of communication are obvious, but the differences in the social cues to communication—especially the social leveling and the differences in turn taking—are important. The computer could easily be labeled "the great leveler." It is precisely because of this that source validation for information gained from the Internet becomes so important. *Anyone can be a publisher on the Internet.* Another aspect of leveling, too, is that often in FtFC the assertive, highly confident individual may have an edge with respect to credibility or gaining an audience for his

Figure A-1 Communication in Face-to-Face and Electronic Groups

Face-to-face group	Electronic group
Channels of communication	
Uses a variety of channels: words, intonation, posture, etc. to convey meaning and emotion	A single channel: textual. This is why some see electronic groups as cold and impersonal. Emotion can be conveyed by symbols or smileys: :) happy : (sad/frown
Synchronous: all are physically gathered in a given place at a given time.	Asynchronous: time and place for communication is at the discretion of individuals.
Essentially verbal, but with a great deal of nonverbal cues like intonation, posture, facial expressions and hand movements.	The mode of communication is a mixture between verbal and written text. This is now known as interactive writing. E-mail texts can be spontaneous and can tolerate misspellings and grammatical errors as with spoken texts. E-mail can also support thought-out prose as in written texts.
Social cues to communication	
Members of a face-to-face group are aware of social cues to status in their environment and with their group leader.	Electronic groups experience a social leveling, as many of the cues to social status are removed.
You need to wait your turn in a face-to-face group and you may even miss the opportunity to say something.	There is no need to wait your turn in electronic groups; you contribute when you feel like it with either a spontaneous or a thought-out response.

or her ideas—even, perhaps, at having greater opportunities (turns) for talking. On the Internet, assertiveness traits are often not detected, so shy, nonassertive individuals have an equal opportunity for self-expression.

The fact that the Internet is two-way also is important. Media such as radio, television, and newspapers are one-way, with restricted access, meaning that not everyone owns a radio station, television station, or newspaper with which to communicate his or her ideas. But on the Internet you can communicate with many senders, and they with you.

In one study that compared the Internet and FtFC, Lisa Flaherty, Kevin Pearce, and Rebecca Rubin found that use of the Internet as a communication channel is not perceived by users as a functional alternative to FtFC. "The FtF channel," they found, "has more social presence than the Internet; the possibility of immediate feedback with FtF interaction conveys greater personal closeness."[6]

One final thought about a similarity between FtFC and CMC: facial expression, eye contact, gestures, and body movement are missing from CMC, but the mind plays a role in completing the interpersonal picture. We may mentally supply even vocal tone and emphasis because of what we know of others' uses of words, phrases, or expressions.

WHY CHOOSE CMC OVER FtFC

CMC and FtFC are different. Neither is better than the other, but one may be superior to the other for a specific purpose. Given the differences, why might you choose CMC rather than FtFC? We have separated our answer into three categories: (1) fulfilling personal needs, (2) fulfilling interpersonal needs, and (3) experimenting with interpersonal skills and behaviors.

Personal Needs

Using CMC to fulfill personal needs may include impression management, social reticence, security, equalizing of experience, control, intentionality, and escape.

Impression Management

Whether consciously or subconsciously, you work to regulate what information about yourself is known and not known by others. Because it is missing visual and aural information, CMC offers you an opportunity to manage the impression others have of you.[7]

Social Reticence

"CMC enables socially reticent individuals to develop interpersonal skills because it removes the social pressure of immediate FtF reactions from others."[8] Mazur, Burns, and Emmers-Somway discovered that people who are apprehensive about interpersonal communication perceive greater success and comfort levels with online partners.[9]

Security

CMC gives you more time to think about how you want to express yourself—the thought-out response; thus, you have more control over your message. There is greater security when your response is more rational than emotional.

Equalizing of Experience

Online, status is not an issue unless it is made so by participants. Not only does CMC allow the shy to be bold and the socially reticent to become gregarious,[10] it allows people to share a safe harbor from the socially aggressive, the arrogant, and the dominant.

Control

You can initiate communication, govern the pace at which it occurs and the topics that are discussed, and even terminate conversations at will.

Intentionality

Because in CMC you are not distracted by nonverbal elements, and you are not forced to make an impromptu, spontaneous response, you can concentrate on both the social and task dimensions of communication. Messages sent in asynchronous CMC are likely to be carefully crafted because there is more opportunity to reflect, edit, and select the information and cues you transmit to receivers.

Escape

CMC can serve for entertainment, for play, and for relief of boredom.

It is likely that when people choose to use CMC, they are not just fulfilling personal needs, fulfilling interpersonal needs, or experimenting with interpersonal skills and behaviors, instead, they are likely to be doing some of each.

Interpersonal Needs

CMC also plays a significant role—different from that of FtFC—in fulfilling interpersonal needs for contact and information. Many of these are so obvious that they do not require discussion. Making contact with and keeping in touch with others, for instance, are the most frequently used functions of CMC.

Hyperpersonal CMC

When the levels of affection and emotion developed through CMC equal or surpass FtF relationships, the phenomenon is called **hyperpersonal CMC.** One writer said this about his own hyperpersonal CMC experience:

> *This quality of anonymity in friendship, however, is a totally new experience. I find myself trying to picture what each of these people looks like, what the sound of their*

voice might be . . . . While gaining the benefit of their words, their thoughts and advice, I lose that subliminal interaction so important to friendship. On the other hand, were it not for CMC I might not know these people at all.[11]

CMC's Value to Business

When it comes to business, interpersonal needs and information flow intersect. In CMC, decisions can be reached quickly and efficiently because layers of management in the organizational hierarchy are eliminated, information flows faster, and time and travel expenses are reduced to zero.[12]

Experimentation

Whether it is role-playing, games, fantasy, or virtual reality experimentation, what makes CMC such a fascinating tool is how it can be used to experiment with your self-identity. CMC provides more freedom than FtFC for regulating the nature, amount, and timing of information shared.[13]

STRATEGIC FLEXIBILITY

When it comes to strategic flexibility, Susan B. Barnes, in her book on CMC, states it accurately: "Individuals select communication tools based on the benefit and cost of how each tool can be used to meet communication goals."[14] Weighing benefits and costs is embedded in the process of anticipating, assessing, evaluating, and selecting from your repertoire of skills and behaviors.

CMC AND DEVELOPING ONLINE CREDIBILITY

Credibility, the believability of a person based on his or her expertise, dynamism, trustworthiness, and ethics, is an important aspect of developing an identity both online and offline.[15]

The Importance of Language

In CMC you develop your reputation based on your use of language. Obvious errors such as bad spelling, improper grammar, excessive punctuation, and illiterate prose make a poor impression.[16] In chat rooms and online discussions, you will quickly discover that some writers are responded to and others are ignored. The reason is clear: People reading messages online need to believe that you are a reliable source of information, a source to consider, and a source to justify the time they spend reading your messages.

Essential Criteria

What are the essential criteria for developing online credibility?

1. Use common sense in judging what is acceptable and unacceptable behavior.
2. Know what has been going on previously if you choose to contribute to an ongoing online discussion. Acknowledging the ideas of others will increase your own credibility and will make others more willing to listen to your ideas.
3. Limit how much you write so that it is conveniently and easily read by others. Lengthy passages are considered boring, and often they are not read closely; miscommunication can result.
4. Whenever you give statements of fact, try to include references and sources to back them up and add additional credible information. Your credibility will depend in part on the credibility of the sources of information you supply.
5. Allow others sufficient time to respond to your ideas. In addition, read carefully all they have to say before answering them.

6. Respect your readers. Avoid profanity, confrontational behavior, and ad hominem attacks (attacks on the person, not on his or her ideas). Avoid **flaming**—the sending of rude or hostile messages.
7. Recognize that CMC is not private communication. Let good sense and self-protection guide what you say, how you say it, when you say it, and where you say it.[17]

VIRTUAL COMMUNITIES

Credibility in Virtual Communities

Howard Rheingold, in his book *The Virtual Community*, stated "my direct observations of online behavior around the world over the past ten years have led me to conclude that whenever CMC technology becomes available to people anywhere, they inevitably build virtual communities with it."[18] Rheingold defines a **virtual community** as "a group of people who may or may not meet one another face to face, and who exchange words and ideas through the mediation of computer bulletin boards, and networks."[19] Barnes clarifies Rheingold's definition by adding that virtual communities are "informational and emotional support groups."[20] Having credibility in virtual communities allows you to take advantage of the friendships that can be developed there.

Values of Virtual Communities

There are many reasons why virtual communities serve as gathering points for people with common interests, beliefs, and ideas. They include "shared personal, recreational, and professional interests, such as a hobby, role-playing games, providing mutual support for addiction or medical problems, exchanging computer information, and talking about popular television programs or recording artists," says Barnes.[21] Race, gender, age, national origin, and physical appearance are not readily apparent. People with physical disabilities who may have trouble forming new friendships FtF, find that in virtual communities, they are treated as if their disability does not exist.[22]

Blogs as Virtual Communities

A **Web log** (or **blog**) is a spontaneous public online journal (or diary) in which Internet users share their lives and their opinions. Readers are free to respond to blog posts.

Blogs

Blogs are significant because of their extent and rapid growth. Internet users under 25 are the most enthusiastic about creating content and most likely to have blogs. One study suggested that as many as 7 percent of users have created Web diaries,[23] even though those are not regularly updated. Anyone who can fill out a form can have an online journal or blog.[24]

Blogs are significant, too, because they are strangely addictive and can eat up enormous amounts of time. For example, "for isolated individuals, blogs can be a lifeline to a larger community."[25] For the writer (or blog creator) they are not only cathartic—a way to express and channel one's emotions—but often a lifeline. One blogger says it this way: "Throughout all my adult life computers and the online world have been the only real outlets I've had. In a very real way, they've kept me alive."[26]

Who Reads Blogs?

According to the Pew Internet and American Life Project, the number of Americans reading blogs jumped 58 percent in 2004 to an estimated 32 million people, with about 11 million looking to political blogs for news during the presidential campaign.[27]

Do Blogs Have Impact?

Blogs *do* have impact. For example, CNN reserves a special section on its site for blog assessments. However, the exposure of flaws in CBS's *60 Minutes* episode about President Bush's National Guard service and the premature exit poll results that led many to believe John Kerry was winning the presidential election on Election Day illustrate why you must be careful about believing everything written on blogs. Remember, *anyone can be a publisher on the Internet.* The best advice to readers of blogs is "let the buyer beware."

HOW DO ETHICS RELATE TO CMC?

As a CMC user, you will be considered ethical if you reflect competence, integrity, responsibility, and respect for others' rights and diversity.

Before You Write or Post

When you are faced with making an ethical decision online, what questions should you ask yourself?

- Have I reviewed the facts carefully?
- Have I thought carefully about my options?
- Have I used all the resources available?
- Have I discussed the issues and decision options with others (peers, friends, or supervisors)?
- What are the consequences of my decision?
- Will my decision stand the test of time?

If you are unsure, get the advice and guidance you need.

Before You Read

The best guideline for evaluating what you read online is simply to be wary of how much you trust. All CMC is subject to human error and biases. Use the kinds of assessment criteria outlined in Chapter 12 to assess the reliability, authority, currency, objectivity, and validity of the messages you receive. The application of your intuition is a valuable part of ethical assessment, too.

Assess Yourself

Are You CMC Literate?

For each question answer Y for *yes*, N for *no*, and O for *I don't know*.

_____ 1. Do you understand how CMC works? (CMC includes e-mail, bulletin boards or discussion forums, MUDs [multiuse domains], MOOs [multiuser domain, object-oriented], IM (instant messaging), the Internet, and the World Wide Web.)

_____ 2. Are you electronically literate? (Can you use e-mail, word processing, the Web, spreadsheets, as well as informed information retrieval?)

_____ 3. Do you have effective reading and writing strategies to deal with the conventions of word-processing packages, computer systems, and networks?

_____ 4. Are you aware of and responsive to the changing nature of CMC in our society?

_____ 5. Do you know the basic conventions of the various CMC technologies? (Conventions are the rules, principles, forms, and techniques of conduct attached to each of the technologies listed in question 1.)

_____ 6. Can you read, analyze, evaluate, create, produce, and communicate using a variety of CMC technologies?

_____ 7. Do you use information gained from CMC technologies accurately and creatively? (Can you organize and integrate information and apply it to decision making, problem solving, critical thinking, and creative expression?)

_____ 8. Do you have the critical thinking skills necessary for questioning, interpreting, analyzing, and evaluating both the informational and emotional content derived from CMC?

_____ 9. Are you willing to weigh information you gain from CMC technologies carefully and wisely to determine its quality (i.e., its relevance, accuracy, validity, completeness, and impartiality)?

_____ 10. Do you exhibit ethical qualities and practice ethical behavior with regard to information and information technology?

Go to the *Communicating Effectively* CD-ROM and the Online Learning Center at **www.mhhe.com/hybels8** to see your results and learn how to evaluate your attitudes and feelings.

mhhe.com/hybels8

CHAPTER REVIEW

SUMMARY

Seventy-five percent of the population has access to the Internet, and computer-mediated communication (CMC) has changed the way governments, businesses, commerce, and educational systems perform.

CMC includes the idea of digital literacy—the ability to understand and use information in multiple formats. Thus, CMC fits our basic communication model, although there are differences in the channels and in the social cues to communication.

People choose CMC over face-to-face communication (FtFC) for the fulfillment of personal needs, interpersonal needs, and for experimentation. Personal needs include impression management, social reticence, security, equalizing of experience, control, intentionality, and escape. Interpersonal needs include making contact with and getting information from others, hyperpersonal CMC, and business goals. In experimentation, users can act out their fantasies, challenge social norms, and exercise aspects of their personality.

Online credibility is important if you expect to be a "considered" source online. You develop your online reputation through your use of language.

Virtual communities are valuable for developing friendships and serve as gathering points for people with common interests, beliefs, and ideas. Blogs or online journals can create virtual communities significant because of their extensiveness and influence, but readers of blogs must be cautious about believing what they find there.

To be ethical online, ask appropriate questions and remember the caution, "Let the reader beware."

KEY TERMS AND CONCEPTS

Use the *Communicating Effectively* CD-ROM and the Online Learning Center at www.mhhe.com/hybels8 to further your understanding of the following terms.

Asynchronous communication 277
Channel 277
Credibility 281
Digital literacy 277
Flaming 282
Hyperpersonal CMC 280
Media literacy 277
Synchronous communication 277
Virtual community 282
Web log (or blog) 282

QUESTIONS TO REVIEW

1. What is CMC, and why is it important?
2. Why would you choose to use CMC over FtFC?
3. When might CMC be a better way of getting to know others than FtF?
4. Why is online credibility important?
5. What guidelines will help you in developing online credibility?
6. What values do virtual communities fulfill?
7. Why are blogs significant, and why can they be considered virtual communities?
8. What are the cautions readers of blogs need to take and why?
9. What does ethical conduct in CMC entail?

Go to the self-quizzes on the *Communicating Effectively* CD-ROM and the Online Learning Center at www.mhhe.com/hybels8 to test your knowledge of the chapter contents.

APPENDIX B

A Quick Guide to Public Speaking

PREPARATION

- ***Focus on your audience.*** The focus of all public speaking is the listeners—to gain a response from the audience. If you can get them to think, feel, or act in a certain way, you have achieved a measure of success. To accomplish this, you need to discover as much as you can about them and adapt your speech to their specific needs and interests.

- ***Find a good topic.*** Select a topic that interests both you and your listeners and one on which you can complete some research.

- ***Choose your purpose and central idea.*** Choose your general purpose (to inform, to persuade, etc.), your specific purpose (what you want to achieve with your listeners), and your central idea (a one-sentence statement of your message) with your specific audience in mind.

- ***Carefully organize your speech.*** Devise two or three main points you want to explain and develop that will support your central idea.

- ***Find strong support.*** Use personal experience, examples, facts, expert opinions, and statistics to develop each main point.

- ***Use transitions.*** Smooth bridges are needed to help listeners know where you have been in the speech, where you are, and where you are going. Anytime you jump to a new point, it is helpful to have a signpost indicate the move: "My second reason is . . ."

- ***Create an effective introduction.*** Begin your speech with information that will grasp listener attention and make them want to listen to the rest of your speech. Fascinating stories, intriguing questions, interesting facts and statistics, or engaging quotations are great attention-getters.

- **Use an outline.** Put all parts of the speech (introduction, main points, transitions, and conclusion) into an outline. Everything in the outline should explain, illustrate, or prove your central idea.
- **Prepare a speaking outline.** From your complete outline, prepare a keyword outline that you will use when you deliver your speech.
- **Practice until you feel comfortable.** Go over your speech using your keyword outline only. Speak your ideas differently each time you give your speech. Don't memorize it word-for-word.

DELIVERY

- **Reveal self-confidence.** Strength comes from knowing your material, feeling you have something to share with your listeners, and having a positive attitude about yourself.
- **Channel your nervousness.** Use it as a source of energy. Take a few deep breaths on the way to the lectern, pause before beginning your speech, and strive to be vital, enthusiastic, and involved.
- **Begin your speech confidently.** Walk confidently to the lectern. Arrange your notes, get your first sentence firmly in your mind, look directly at your listeners, and begin your speech. Throughout your speech maintain eye contact, be expressive, and speak clearly.
- **Use your notes sparingly.** Notes should never be a crutch. Avoid reading them or staring at them absentmindedly. Use them occasionally to pick up your next point.
- **End your speech with strength.** After your conclusion, pause a few moments and, if appropriate, ask if there are any questions. The impressions you give as you move away from the lectern contribute to the overall effectiveness of you and your message.

CHAPTER

12

Getting Started and Finding Speech Material

OBJECTIVES

After reading this chapter, you should be able to:
- Develop a procedure for narrowing a topic.
- Distinguish between an informative speech and a persuasive speech.
- State a specific purpose and a central idea for a speech.
- Know what you need to know about your listeners.
- Describe the process of researching a topic in preparation for giving a speech.
- Ask the questions necessary to judge the quality of Internet information.
- Select and use the various kinds of supporting materials.

HEIDI REALLY WANTED TO BE AN ACTRESS AND MAJORED IN THEATER and Speech Communication in college. She knew she had to conquer her speech phobia. She tried and tried to confront her fears by speaking up in certain classes. Her determination to overcome stage fright also motivated her to prepare carefully for small parts in plays. Later she had a chance to appear on the campus radio as a news announcer. She was scared, but she did it.

Eventually, as a senior, Heidi became one of the anchorpersons on the campus TV news, and she gained confidence. A few months after she graduated, she found work as an on-camera reporter for a small TV station. Two years later she was coanchor of the local evening news. As she became more experienced, she noticed an interesting thing happening—she became less and less uptight while performing, but she remained very anxious and disorganized before going on the air. There was almost a panic reaction, difficulty concentrating, dry mouth, and an upset stomach as she prepared to read the news. When it was airtime, she settled down. It surprised her to discover that many seasoned professionals experience intense stress prior to performing.[1]

WHY STUDY PUBLIC SPEAKING?

Public speaking is a vital area of personal development and a crucial factor in your professional success as well. Being able to speak with integrity, in a style that both engages and motivates listeners, is one of the most important traits employers look for in new employees and will allow you to accomplish just about anything you want. It can open doors, reduce barriers, and build connections between you and others.

KNOWLEDGE OF PUBLIC SPEAKING

If you do not know very much about public speaking, it is easy to believe that success in doing it is simply a knack. But few people who are truly accomplished public speakers would tell you that. As in so many areas, public speaking knowledge is the foundation on which skill depends. Then, as your knowledge expands and your skill develops through repeated experiences, and you have opportunities to both test your knowledge and customize and individualize it, your expertise grows along with your confidence and competence.[2]

PUBLIC SPEAKING AND THE ELEMENTS OF COMMUNICATION

Public speaking relies on the same elements as other forms of communication: sender-receivers, a message, a channel, and feedback. The speaker is the main sender-receiver, although audience members also respond as sender-receivers by providing nonverbal feedback or asking questions. The message in public speaking is the most structured of all communication. The speaker works on the message beforehand, planning what he or she will say. The usual channel is the voice and gestures, but some speakers enhance the channel by using graphics such as computer-generated visuals, posters, or slides. Feedback to a speech usually comes from the entire audience rather than from one or a few individuals. Typical feedback would be applause, laughter, or slight verbal or nonverbal expressions of agreement or disagreement.

Chapter 12 Getting Started and Finding Speech Material 291

PREPARATION FOR PUBLIC SPEAKING

You have heard the aphorism "If you fail to prepare—you prepare to fail." It is the purpose of this section of the chapter to give you the basics of preparation: finding a topic, narrowing it, selecting a purpose and central idea, analyzing the audience and occasion, doing research, gathering supporting material, and organizing and outlining what you discover.

Finding a Topic

Before you find a topic, be sure to know the purpose of your speech. Is it to inform, to persuade, or to entertain? The general purpose of your speech will help guide you in finding a topic. Any great speech begins with a great topic. One obvious place to begin is by making a personal inventory. A **personal inventory** is an assessment of your own resources. What are you interested in? What are you passionate about? Would your interests make a good speech? See Figure 12-1.

Why is it important that passion drive your search for a topic? In addition to improving your delivery, passion will make it easier for you to do the appropriate research and gather the necessary supporting material. There is no question that passion will buttress the delivery of your speech by eliminating some of your anxiety, creating a sense of desire, generating some of your animation, and framing a sense of purpose and determination. You will feel better at every step in the process.

Beyond the Personal Inventory

In addition to making your personal inventory, begin brainstorming for topics and develop as long a list of ideas as possible. Listen to the radio and television, check the Internet, and read magazines and newspapers extensively to keep up with current news and stories

Things to Ponder

- Hobbies you enjoy
- Teachers who stand out
- Things you want to accomplish
- Values you cherish
- The life you want to lead
- Interests you have
- Jobs you've held
- Experiences you've had
- Books you've read
- Traveling you've done
- Personal concerns
- Views you hold
- What you want to do with your life
- Your family life
- Things you feel are wrong in this world
- Things you feel are right in this world
- Friendships you value
- The job that you want to hold
- Presents you've received
- Lessons that you've learned
- Personal convictions

Figure 12.1
Making a Personal Inventory

of interest. Remember that your goal will be to present and clarify a subject so that your audience will not only understand and recall the information you share, but use the information as well. If your general purpose is persuasion, in addition to clarifying the subject your goal will be to change the way your listeners think or feel about your topic, or to get them to do something about it. To do that, you need to be informed.

Keep your audience in mind as well as your own interests as you search for a topic. If the topic concerns your health, happiness, or security, it is likely to affect theirs as well. If it offers a solution to an obvious problem that disturbs or unsettles you, it is likely to trouble them as well. If the topic generates controversy or conflict of opinion when you mention it to others, you can be sure it will generate some disagreement among your listeners. And, if it offers information about a misunderstood, mistaken, or misinterpreted issue, it is likely to have interest for your audience for the same reasons it caught your attention.

If you are still having difficulty locating a topic for your speech, we recommend looking at the *Topic Selection Helper* at the Maui Community College Speech Department–University of Hawaii Web site, **http://www.hawaii.edu/mauispeech/html/infotopichelp.html**. Entering these keywords into a search engine may produce a similar site.

Narrowing the Topic

A common mistake made by beginning speakers is trying to cover a topic that is too broad. Look at the topic of music in Figure 12-2 and all the possible subtopics there. Each subtopic would include more than enough information for many a speech. On any subtopic in the figure you would discover so much relevant and interesting material that you would not even be able to read it all, let alone cover it in a single speech. But, you can see, too, that if you chose to cover the entire topic—music—your treatment would be so superficial that your speech would not be very meaningful.

How do you narrow a topic? First, for any topic you select, brainstorm some narrower aspects of it. Write down those ideas. Second, choose one of the narrower topics

---

Figure 12-2
Possible Speech Topics under the Heading "Music"

Source: *Analyzing Your Topic*, December 17, 2004. Research Tutorial for Freshman and Transfer Seminars—Webster University. Retrieved October 5, 2005, from **http://library.webster.edu/freshman/fseminar.topic.html**

Types of music
- Rap
- Country
- Jazz
- Classical
- Rock
- Blues

Technology
- CD software
- MP3 acoustics

Music education
- Primary/secondary
- College music major
- Private lessons

Famous artists
- Individual performers
- Bands
- Songwriters

Social issues
- Censorship
- Violence
- Copyright
- Sex
- Drugs

Careers in music
- Music teacher
- Performer
- Reviewer
- Composer

that you find interesting. Third, ask the following four questions about the narrowed topic:

- Will this narrowed topic be of interest to my audience?
- Will this narrowed topic be understood by my listeners?
- What are the specifics of the assignment, and will this topic fit into those specifics?
- How long do I have to cover the topic?

The broader the topic, the more superficial the speech. Remember that your time allotment will have a great deal to do with how much information you can cover.

Selecting a Purpose

Whenever you give a speech, having a purpose will help you look for materials, organize and outline your speech, and adapt to the needs and interests of your audience.

There are three stages in working out the **purpose** for your speech: (1) selecting the general purpose, (2) selecting the specific purpose, and (3) stating the central idea.

The General Purpose

When you state your **general purpose,** you should determine whether you intend to inform or persuade. **Informative speeches** generally concentrate on explaining—telling how something works, what something means, or how to do something. A speaker who gives an informative speech usually tries to give his or her audience information without taking sides, even when the issue is controversial. For example, if you are giving an informative speech about using animals for research, you will not state whether you are for or against doing so; you will let members of the audience make up their own minds.

Many of the important decisions in speechmaking require that speakers answer questions they ask themselves.

In a **persuasive speech** the speaker takes a particular position and tries to get the audience to accept and support that position. For example, student fees should be incorporated into college tuition, or free music downloads should be legal.

Often the same subject can lead to either an informative or a persuasive speech—depending on your wording of the topic and your approach. "Technology has added a whole new dimension to student cheating," is clearly an informative topic. But "The university must take greater strides to prevent student cheating" is persuasive. Even more strongly persuasive, because it places the responsibility on the shoulders of listeners, is, "Each of us has a responsibility to help prevent cheating in college."

Sometimes it's difficult to fit a speech firmly into an informative or a persuasive slot. In a persuasive speech, informative material often plays an important role. If you are speaking in favor of political candidates, it is natural to use information about their backgrounds and voting records. In an informative speech, even when you try to present both sides, one side might seem more persuasive than the other to some audience members.

The Specific Purpose

After you have decided whether the general purpose of your speech is to inform or persuade, you must then decide on a **specific purpose**—a single phrase that indicates precisely what you expect to achieve in your speech. For example, "To inform my audience of the methods the university uses to protect the safety of its students." Your specific purpose statement is used in the development of your speech; you don't actually say it in your speech. There are five guidelines for constructing your specific purpose:

1. *Make it a clear, complete, infinitive statement,* not a sentence fragment, and not a question:

    To inform listeners of the value of home schooling.

    To persuade listeners to become educated consumers.

2. *Phrase it in terms of the effect you want to have on listeners:*

    To inform listeners of ways they can help people with disabilities.

    To persuade listeners of the negative effects of binge drinking.

    You should also be able to rephrase your specific purpose from a listener's vantage point. At the end of your speech, listeners will refrain from binge drinking or be able to explain specific ways they can help people with disabilities.

3. *Limit the statement to one distinct idea only.* For example, a specific purpose that reads "To inform my audience about the value of daydreams and how to use them to escape and relax" would need to be rephrased to focus on either their value or on how to use them to escape and relax.

4. *Use specific language:*

    To inform listeners of the negative effects of alcohol on the body.

    To persuade listeners that they should help control drunk driving.

5. *Make certain your purpose meets the interests, expectations, and levels of knowledge of your listeners.*

If your audience will be students, use yourself as a gauge: does your specific purpose meet your own interests, expectations, and levels of knowledge?

Once you have determined your statement of purpose, you should subject it to some tests. Does it meet the assignment? You might discover, for example, that your opinions on a subject are so strong that you are unable to talk about it without favoring one side over the other. This means your subject is better for a persuasive speech than for an informative one. If you have been assigned an informative speech, you should keep this subject for a later time.

Another important test is to ask whether you can accomplish your purpose within the time limits of the speech. If your speech purpose is too broad to fit into the allotted time, you will have to either narrow the topic further or find a new topic. One speaker discovered, for example, that her purpose, "to inform my audience about physical fitness," was too broad; too many issues were involved. She rephrased her purpose: "to inform audience members about how low-impact aerobics can improve their health."

The Central Idea

Whereas the specific purpose expresses what you want to accomplish when you give the speech, stating the **central idea** establishes the main thrust of the speech. The central idea is much like the thesis statement you learn about in writing courses. Everything in the speech relates to the central idea. In an informative speech, the central idea

Working Together

Discuss the ethical implications of the following speech topics. To what extent should speakers pay attention to the values implied in their topic choices? Are the following topics appropriate for speeches?

- How to break into "secure" sites on the Internet.
- How to get out of paying a speeding ticket.
- How to make a bomb.
- How to shoplift without being detected.
- How to destroy others' credit ratings.
- How to get into an athletic event without paying.
- How to lie without being detected.
- How to cheat on college examinations.
- How to get out of paying income taxes.
- How to make a false ID card.

---

contains the information you want the audience to remember; in a persuasive speech, it tells audience members what you want them to do.

The difference between a specific purpose and a central-idea statement is illustrated in the following examples. Notice that the central idea, though a first draft, explains the why or the how of the specific purpose:

Specific purpose: To persuade audience members to protect themselves against unsuccessful and unhappy marriages.

Draft of central idea: Unsuccessful and unhappy marriages occur because people do not take the time to become friends first, communicate honestly with each other, resolve conflicts constructively, learn to work around problems, discover an enduring attraction, contribute equally to the relationship, trust each other, and take their commitment seriously.

When the central idea was stated, it encompassed too many points to cover in a single speech. So the speaker rephrased it in such a way that the ideas could be grouped:

Central idea: Unhappy marriages occur because of poor communication.

The central idea should be stated in a full sentence, should contain one idea, and should use precise language. Sometimes it is not possible to come up with a central-idea statement until you have finished organizing and outlining the speech. When you start working on your speech, you should have a tentative central idea in mind; when you have finished organizing and outlining, you can refine it.

It is important to have a specific purpose and central idea to guide your research and investigation, but you must not let them bind you unnecessarily. Part of the process of research is being flexible and responsive to what you discover. If you are actively engaged in research, you never know what you are going to find.

Analyzing the Audience

Audience analysis means finding out what your audience members know about your subject, what they might be interested in, and what their attitudes and beliefs are. The very next step in audience analysis is adapting your speech to their interests, level of understanding, attitudes, and beliefs. Audience analysis has two important benefits: First, it will improve your effectiveness since your

STRATEGIC FLEXIBILITY

As you research, think about your potential speech situation and the needs and requirements likely to arise because of it. Take stock of all the factors, elements, and conditions that you are likely to find yourself in. As you select the material you will use, remain open and flexible to the possibility of making changes in your specific purpose and central idea so that they reflect exactly what you plan to accomplish in your speech.

presentation will be created and delivered with listeners' specific needs in mind. Second, when you focus on what matters most to your listeners, it will help you accomplish your objectives.

Strategic flexibility is important in audience analysis. What choices are likely to make you the most strategically flexible? First, choose your target audience. A **target audience** is a subgroup of the whole audience that you must reach to accomplish your goal. It is on this subgroup that you are likely to have your greatest impact.

The second choice is to do your homework. Go to the library, work on the Internet, use surveys, interviews, or informal conversations to gain as much information as you can about your target audience. If you are asked to speak before an organization, talk extensively about the group to the person who arranged the speaking engagement or the one who invited you. Doing your homework will also help you avoid stereotyping—using preconceived notions about your listeners and, thus, neglecting individual differences.

The third choice likely to make you the most strategically flexible in audience analysis is to continue to analyze your audience even after you begin speaking. Here is what to look for as you gain feedback from your audience:

- Do your listeners look confused? Have you overestimated their knowledge of the topic? Take the time to clarify terms to offer them the necessary background.
- Do your listeners look bored? Are there ways to spice your speech with more examples, greater audience involvement, more animation, or a higher degree of excitement?

Audience Knowledge

One important aspect of audience analysis is taking into account how much the audience is likely to know about a subject. If you are talking to a lay audience and pick a topic related to a specialized field of knowledge, you will have to explain and define some basic terminology before going into the subject in any depth. For example, when Sam spoke to his class about dietary fat, he had to explain such terms as *saturated, polyunsaturated, hydrogenated,* and *trans* fats before he could talk about anything else.

Using only the information you have from these pictures, what do you know about these audiences—their interests, attitudes, and beliefs? How might this knowledge help you shape a speech you intend to give them?

Speakers should realize that although people have general information about many subjects, they usually don't know the specifics. Most people know, for example, that the Constitution guarantees us the right to free speech. Yet if you were to ask them what *free speech* means, they would probably be a little fuzzy on a definition or on what is encompassed by the term. Would they know, for example, that the courts regard ringing a bell or burning a flag as a form of free speech?

Audience Attitudes and Beliefs

When planning your speech, you also need to consider your audience's attitudes and beliefs about your subject. **Attitudes** are beliefs that cause people to respond in some way to a particular object or situation—like the topic of your speech. **Beliefs** are statements of knowledge, opinion, and faith: convictions about what one thinks is right and wrong or true and false. You will have a much better chance of having an impact on your audience when you already know how they feel about your topic. This is where strategic flexibility can play a major role in your preparation as you anticipate, assess, and evaluate your potential speech situation and the needs and requirements likely to arise because of it.

If you discover—through informal conversation, a show of hands, or even a brief survey—that listeners hold positive views about your topic and your message, you can use your speech to focus chiefly on reinforcing those views.

If you discover that listeners hold negative views, you will have to plan your speech carefully. Anticipate their objections and prepare your responses—even build those responses into your speech. You may have to limit what you ask of them, or you may have to start your speech with points you know will get agreement from them and move to more controversial points only after you have their agreement on acceptable issues. You might even begin your presentation by listing opposing arguments before explaining your own position.

Since people's attitudes and beliefs will affect how your speech is received, it is absolutely essential to consider them when you are planning your speech. You can find important clues to people's attitudes and beliefs through audience demographics.

Audience Demographics

Even if you have no specific information about your audience's knowledge, interest level, and attitude toward your subject, certain factual information about the audience members can tell you a great deal. **Demographic analysis** reveals data about the characteristics of a group of people, including such things as age, gender, education, occupation, race/nationality/ethnic origin, geographic location, and group affiliation.

When you work with demographic information, you generalize about the entire audience; your generalizations might not be true of individual members. For example, on the basis of demographic data you have gathered, you might generalize that the ages of your speech class audience are between 18 and 27—even though one member is in his 50s. On the basis of such generalizations, you can make some predictions about what might interest the people in this audience and what they might be knowledgeable about.

Age. As a speaker, you need to have a sense of the age range of your audience because interests differ with age. College-age people are usually interested in school, future jobs, music, and interpersonal relationships. Young parents are often interested in subjects that might affect their children, such as school bus safety and school board policy. However, computers, elections, and world and national news have interest for most age groups because they affect everyone.

Another Point of View

Here is some advice found in a college public-speaking textbook published in the mid-1960s:

Generally, women are more interested than men in subjects related to the feminine gender, such as women's clothing, cosmetics, housework, the rearing of children, the local ladies' aid society, home decoration, etc. On the other hand, men show strong masculine interests in rough competitive sports like football. More than women, men tend to enjoy technical and scientific subjects, particularly those related to mechanics, electronics, and engineering. Since more men than women serve as chief breadwinners for their families, they are more apt to be interested in matters pertaining to occupations and professions—but remember the possible exceptions.

Questions

1. Is any of the advice from this 1965 textbook relevant today? Why or why not?
2. What problems will you encounter if you stereotype listeners according to their gender?
3. Are there topics today that are more appropriate for one gender than for the other? What are they?
4. In what ways can speakers make topics relevant to both sexes?

Source: *The Art of Public Address* (p. 25), by Win Kelley, 1965, Dubuque, IA: Brown.

It is sometimes difficult to generalize with respect to age. Look, for example, at "college-age" people. The average age of college students is no longer about 20. It is now around 26, and it is likely to go higher with more adults going back to school. We need to be sensitive to age differences to avoid stereotyping in your speeches.

Gender. In a speech that's open to the public, you will probably have both men and women in your audience. If you deliver a speech to a mixed audience but do not acknowledge the presence, and appeal to the needs, of both genders, not only will you miss the mark, but your speech may even seem sexist and inappropriate.

Education. The audience's level of education gives you some idea of the group's knowledge and experience. We can assume that the more education people have, the more specialized their knowledge. Lawyers, doctors, and PhDs all have specialized knowledge; however, they might have little information about subjects other than their own. Your main consideration when you prepare a speech is whether your audience has the same knowledge you have or whether you will have to start with the basics.

Occupation. Sometimes occupation indicates an area of specialized knowledge: Paramedics and nurses know about the human body; lawyers know about legal rights; social workers know about social problems. A person's occupation can also indicate interest in a subject. Most professional groups would probably be interested in a speech about ethics in their profession. If you are speaking to an occupational group, try to adapt your speech to that audience's job interests.

Race/Nationality/Ethnic Origin. When politicians speak to whole audiences made up of a single racial or ethnic group, they try to identify with the listeners' goals and aspirations.

If you are speaking to a group with members from diverse backgrounds, you should be particularly careful in your use of language. If your audience includes foreign students, they may have problems understanding slang and colloquial expressions. Not everyone has gone to summer camp, and not everyone has eaten *kim chi*.

Consider This

Here is a brief survey you can use to gather information about your audience. Although this survey is designed primarily for classroom use, you can easily adapt it to a broader audience by changing some questions and adding others. Have students circle the correct response or add a response in the blank labeled "Other."

1. I am:
   A. Female
   B. Male

2. My approximate age is:
   A. 18–22
   B. 23–29
   C. 30–39
   D. Over 40

3. My primary ethnic background is:
   A. Anglo
   B. African American
   C. Hispanic
   D. Native American
   E. Asian
   F. Other _____

4. My marital status is:
   A. Single
   B. Married
   C. Divorced
   D. Other _____

5. I live:
   A. In my parents' home
   B. In my own apartment or house
   C. In a dormitory
   D. In a fraternity or sorority

6. I am involved in: *(Circle all that apply.)*
   A. Athletics
   B. Student government
   C. A fraternity or sorority
   D. Intramural activities
   E. An honor society
   F. Other _____

7. I currently:
   A. Go to school full time
   B. Go to school full time and work part time
   C. Go to school part time and work part time
   D. Go to school part time and work full time
   E. Other _____

8. To what extent are you liberal or conservative in your religious orientation? *(Circle the number that most closely reflects your attitude.)*
   Liberal 5 4 3 2 1 Conservative

9. To what extent are you liberal or conservative in your political orientation? *(Circle the number that most closely reflects your attitude.)*
   Liberal 5 4 3 2 1 Conservative

10. How involved or committed are you on this issue?

    _____
    (Write the topic of your speech here.)
    Highly involved 5 4 3 2 1 Not involved

11. How informed are you on this issue?

    _____
    (Write the topic of your speech here.)
    Well informed 5 4 3 2 1 Poorly informed

12. How interested are you in this issue?

    _____
    (Write the topic of your speech here.)
    Very interested 5 4 3 2 1 Not interested

Geographic Location. Your audience's geographic location may affect the content and approach of your speech. If the federal government is giving money to improve airport runways, find out if some of this money is coming to the local airport. If the nation has been hit with a crime wave (or a heat wave), has this been a problem in your local area? If you have a chance to speak in a town or city other than your own, the audience will be pleased if you know something about its area.

Group Affiliation. Knowing the clubs, organizations, or associations that audience members belong to can be useful because people usually identify with the goals and interests of their own organizations. If you speak to a group, you should be aware of what it stands for and adapt your speech accordingly. Some groups have particular issues or themes for the year, and they look for speakers who can tie their speeches into these themes.

Respecting Your Audience

Whenever you are the speaker, no matter what the situation or occasion, the audience has certain expectations of you, and to be effective, you must fulfill these minimal requirements:

- You must not waste their time.
- You must have practiced your speech until your delivery is polished.
- You must be knowledgeable about your topic.
- You must present what you know in an interesting way.
- You must be sincere and enthusiastic about your desire to share your thoughts.
- You must have analyzed your audience.
- You must be aware of your time limit.

The better you are at fulfilling these requirements, the better the impression you will leave on your listeners, the more successful you will be in attaining your goal, and the better you will feel about the situation afterward.

Analyzing the Occasion

Your analysis of the occasion should go hand-in-hand with your assessment of the audience. Let's look at the questions you need to ask about the occasion for speeches outside the classroom.

Time

Three facets of time matter: time frame for the speech, time of day, and the length of time of your speech. First, time frame for your speech refers to the events leading up to a speech event—even long-term historical forces. If something recent bears directly on your subject, you need to mention it in your speech to (1) put your topic into the proper framework, (2) let audience members know that you are aware of the event and its relationship to your speech, and (3) help your credibility.

Second, time of day has a direct bearing on speech effectiveness. Audiences are less alert in the early morning and late afternoon. Giving a speech at either of those times requires you to make special efforts to hold their interest. An interesting topic, or a topic handled in an interesting way, can get the attention of even a sluggish audience.

Finally, respect the length of time you have been given for your speech. Stick to the time limit. Listeners will get restless if you go on too long and be disappointed if you run short.

Place

Place refers to the physical stage for the speech and the interaction with the audience. If you are not familiar with the room, make sure you take a look at it before you speak. Is the temperature comfortable? Is the lectern where you want it? Are the chairs arranged the way you want them? How big is the room? Do you need a public address system?

Channel

What **channel** of communication links you and your audience: Is it closed-circuit television? Is the address on the radio? Is the transfer made over an Internet connection? The channel could be the sound system in a large auditorium. When technology is involved in any way, it is important that it works, but you need to know what to do if it doesn't.

Researching Your Topic: Where to Look

Once you have decided on the topic, specific purpose, and central idea of your speech, it is time to begin looking for useful information. The four most common sources you can draw on for relevant material are your own personal experience and observation, interviews, the library, and the Internet. Because there is an enormous amount of information to be obtained from the Internet, it is accessible 24/7, it is a comfortable and easy way to access information, it is cost effective, and it is the resource of choice for finding information, you are likely to devote most of your time to Internet research. Check with your instructor to determine the research expectations for your speeches.

STRATEGIC FLEXIBILITY

In Chapter 1 a connection was made between strategic flexibility and creativity. As you anticipate, assess, evaluate, and select appropriate supporting material for your speech bring all your creative powers to bear on the decisions you make.

Drawing on Personal Experience and Observation

If you have chosen a topic in which you have a strong interest, the first thing you should ask yourself is whether you have had any direct experience with the subject. Your own experience can provide interesting and valuable material.

Let your topic be the stimulus for freeing your thoughts and prompting your creativity. **Creativity** is the ability both to have new thoughts *and* to rearrange old ideas in a new way. As your creative juices begin to flow, make certain you record your ideas, whether on notecards, a PDA, a tape recorder, a notepad, or the back of an envelope.

Before you discard any ideas, remember that sometimes we do not put enough value on personal experience; we think that if something happened to us, it can't be important. Relating personal experiences to the subject of your speech can provide the most interesting material you use. On the other hand, sometimes we rely on it too much and exclude other sources of information. Reach a balance.

Interviewing

When you can talk directly to decision makers, conducting interviews is one of the best ways to gather up-to-date information from experts. If the subject is complicated, you can ask questions about points you don't understand.

One advantage of the Internet is that it provides contact with authorities and others around the world on a 24-hour basis. Using interest groups such as mailing lists, newsgroups, live chat groups, and Web forums, you can ask questions, share ideas, sound off, and just plain converse with others on almost any topic.

Using the Library

Any library—whether large or small—has millions of pieces of information. Fortunately for users, all libraries organize their information in essentially the same way, so when you learn how to use one library, you can use this skill in any library. Today, most library resources can also be found on the Internet.

Using Computer Databases

Literary, musical, artistic, reference materials, and periodical and newspaper collections are all stored in **computer (or online) databases**—which are collections of information organized for easy access via the computer. Databases vary in their content as well as in their arrangements and protocols. The reason is that there are many database producers and vendors, and each of them has its own corresponding software. For most classroom speeches, computer databases will supply most of the necessary resources.

Computer databases put an immense amount of information at your fingertips 24 hours a day, 7 days a week.

Using the Internet

There are a number of useful steps for engaging in research on the Internet. Just as in doing any research, it is best to begin by defining and understanding your problem. Having a general purpose, a specific purpose, and a central idea can be a big help. Here are steps for doing research using the Internet.

1. *Define your goals.* Be specific about the information you need. Breaking a topic into its component parts will make your information search clear and easier to conduct.

2. *Determine the types of information you need.* Knowing the kinds of information you want will help you choose the resources and tools that will best meet your needs. For example, are you looking for statistics, in-depth books, magazine articles, expert comments, or biographies?

3. *Identify keywords, phrases, and subject categories.* Play with your search terms; use synonyms; try distinctive terms; apply alternative spellings. Search by topic, subtopic, company, product, a person's name, and so on.

4. *Read the instructions, tips, and techniques for using the search tools you have chosen.* If you understand the types of information each tool covers and the kinds of search options you have available, you will expedite your search.

5. *Use more than one source and search tool.* Although there is duplication among sources on sites, queries performed on different search engines usually produce different results.

6. *Practice netiquette.* Be considerate of others in doing your research.

7. *Review your progress.* Look at some of the most promising records, and see if there are other terms that you can use to sharpen or widen your search. Compare what you've learned with what you decided you wanted to learn in step 1. Make adjustments or redirect your focus if necessary.

8. *Practice critical thinking!* Evaluate the information you find. Don't accept what you read as the truth; get confirming sources, ask questions, talk to experts, probe for motivations, and use your intuition. If something just doesn't sound right, check it out further.

Evaluating Information on the Internet. The fact that something is on the Internet does not make it credible, valid, or worthwhile. Just as in any library, along with all the good information there is plenty of bad information as well.

The stature of researchers can be measured not in the quantity of information they amass but in its quality. To ensure that you are gathering material of high quality use the following six criteria.

1. *Reliability.* What is the source of the information? Did the information come from an academic, government, or commercial site? An educational institution is likely to offer information designed to teach or help learners, whereas a commercial organization is likely to offer information designed to sell or market a product. We would tend to ask about information posted at a commercial site, "What's in it for them?" or "What is their agenda?"; we would be less inclined to ask the same question regarding information posted at an educational site.

   The essential question you need to ask to find reliable material is, "What sources are likely to be fair, objective, lacking hidden motives, and showing quality control?" Investigate the source before you print the information. With so many sources to choose from in a typical Internet search, there is no reason to settle for unreliable material.

2. *Authority.* Who sponsors the site, who manages it, and what are their credentials? The sponsors should clearly have some expertise in the subject area of their site or in the subject area being written about.

   If no credentials are offered, enter the name of the author into a search engine such as Google. Often, you will find that the author has a home page that can be quickly accessed, and in many cases the necessary credentials appear on that page. If no credentials are available, you need to reserve judgment about the value of the information you have discovered. There is no need to discredit an unknown source, but you should, at the very least, make your listeners aware of the situation.

3. *Currency.* How up to date is the site? Has it been updated recently? The most recent date should be clearly listed somewhere on the site. But the fact that a Web site is recent doesn't mean the information contained there is recent—it could be reprinted from somewhere else. You need to discover, if you can, how old the information is and when it was first published.

4. *Objectivity.* What is the purpose of the organization sponsoring the document or information? Is the purpose purely to collect and publish data? Are there political, ideological, or other agendas? Is the information presented objectively, or does it represent the biases of its author? Is there evidence to support the conclusions? Is the coverage thorough? If you have questions about the data, are you able to call the provider and ask for the identification of the original source of the data? Can you ask about data-collection techniques?[3]

5. *Validity.* Is the information at the site confirmed by information at other sites? One way to make certain that information is sound is to find it repeated at a number of different Web sites or in other sources. Does the work update other sources or add new information? A goal of researchers is to ensure that their information compels serious attention and acceptance; thus, it must be supported by generally accepted authorities.[4]

6. *Intuition.* Think clearly about the Web site you have chosen and the information found there. Web sites are rarely refereed or reviewed; thus, you must be the judge. Avoid information from sources, for example, that use citations poorly. If sites are unsigned or badly written, this may be a sign that you should not use the information. Is the source too elementary, too technical, too advanced, or just right for your needs? Remember, even children publish on the Web. Does the information strongly or directly contradict other information you have found? Are there relevant and appropriate links to additional sites? Have you checked them out?

Citing Your Sources in Your Speech

Do not waste your research by failing to cite it in your speech. If you have done the research, citing it makes you and your information credible. There are several important ingredients of any verbal citation:

- The name of the person being quoted, or who wrote the article, or who authored the book, or who you interviewed.
- The qualifications of the person or author. What is it that makes him or her an expert? Why did you choose to quote this person in your speech?
- The name of the article, book, magazine, or journal.
- The date of the quotation or the piece being cited, or the date the interview took place.

For example, "Jane Smith, surgeon general of the United States, in her article on "The Health of American Citizens," said in last week's *Time* magazine, ..." If you are citing an Internet Web site you might say, "Robin Converse, author of the 2005 best-selling book *It's a Matter of Time*, said this on her Web page that is updated daily. . . . " Such citations give your listeners an opportunity to weigh and consider your sources, but probably even more important, they let your listeners know that you have done your homework. Obviously you need to record all relevant information about your sources as you go along.

Supporting Material: What to Look For

Once you know where to look, your next task is to begin searching for useful material. **Supporting material** is information that backs up your main point and provides the essential content of your speech. Four important guidelines should help direct your search. First, return to the specific purpose of your speech, and let that keep you focused and directed in your search. Second, keep your audience in mind. Find supporting material that you know will interest them. Third, try to find material that you know will hold listener attention. The better it is at holding attention, the easier your job of delivering your speech will be. Fourth, consider the short attention spans of your listeners. Use short narratives; much variety; little history; short explanations; clear, uncomplicated information—nothing that requires deep concentration; startling information that holds attention easily; a minimal amount of numbers; and numerous transitions and internal summaries.

Every speech you put together should have supporting material for the main content. In the sections that follow, we discuss types of supporting material: comparison, contrast, definition, examples, statistics, testimony, and polls.

STRATEGIC FLEXIBILITY

As you use your specific purpose for guidance, keep your audience in mind, find material that will hold listener attention, and realize listeners have short attention spans. Remain strategically flexible because it is your unique combination of material that will make your speech not only unique, but potentially outstanding.

Comparison

Comparisons point out the similarities between two or more things. For example, Kalyani, who spoke about the use of peer evaluation in one of her classes, used this comparison:

> *Think of peer evaluation as a reflection of real life. Like real life, it includes people who take it seriously and those who do not; opportunities to assist friends and hurt enemies; and even a wide range of possible, and often contradictory, viewpoints.*

Sometimes a comparison can show us a new way of looking at something. Mario Cuomo, in a graduation speech at Iona College, used a comparison he borrowed from the president of his alma mater, Father Flynn. Cuomo said he asked Flynn how he should approach his graduation speech:

> "Commencement speakers," said Father Flynn, "should think of themselves as the body at an old-fashioned Irish wake. They need you in order to have the party, but nobody expects you to say very much."[5]

Contrast

Contrasts point out the differences between two or more things. A contrast might reveal how using the Internet is different from using the library or how online medical advice is different from medical advice from one's private-practice, real-life doctor. Here, Avery Austin uses contrast in his classroom speech to show how blogs are different from anything that previously existed:

> Blogs are vehicles for any of us to share ideas with others, and there are no magazine or newspaper editors to scrutinize or judge what is printable—where I can be my own editor and make these judgments myself.

Definition

A **definition** is a brief explanation of what a word or phrase means. Use definitions whenever you suspect that some people in your audience might not know what you are talking about. After you define something, it also might be appropriate to give an example. In the speech excerpt below, the student gives a definition followed by an example:

> Fatigue is decreased ability of an organism to perform because of prolonged exertion. Have you ever studied and studied for a tough examination only to go into the examination completely tired out and exhausted?

Examples

An **example** is a short illustration that clarifies a point. Commonly used in speeches, examples can come from personal experience, from research, or from imagination.

Gary Selnow, executive director of WiRED (World Internet Resources for Education and Development), in his speech "The Internet: The Soul of Democracy," used this personal example:

> I wish you could have seen the 15-year-old Kosovar girl who asked if I could help her find a cousin who had fled before the war. The two best friends hadn't heard from each other in nearly two years. A Web search turned up a possibility in London, and the teenager e-mailed a message, hoping this note-in-a-cyber-bottle would find the girl she sought. The next day, she logged onto her Hotmail account and screeched at the sight of the "You Have Mail" message from her cousin. Before I left, she asked me to take her picture with my digital camera. Then she e-mailed it to London. A 15-year-old looks much different from the 13-year-old, and she wanted her cousin to notice. What do you think this e-mail episode said to these kids about a free exchange of information and about an open society?[6]

Sometimes speakers use **hypothetical examples**—examples that are made up—to illustrate a point. A speaker should always tell the audience if an example is hypothetical. The words *imagine yourself* cue the audience that the example is hypothetical:

> Imagine yourself at the beach in the summer—the sand, the glistening water, and the sun beating down on you. As you sit up from your beach towel, you scan the

> No matter the general or specific purpose of the speech, no matter the subject matter or occasion, and no matter the formality or informality of the presentation, examples are one of the best means for arousing interest and keeping attention.

beach and notice a sign that reads "Save the Whales!" That sign should also read "Save Your Skin!" Although the effects of tanning may not show up for 10 to 20 years, the health risks and problems that tanning causes can be serious.

Statistics

Statistics—facts in numerical form—have many uses in a speech. Being factual material, they are a convincing form of evidence. Quite often, a speaker who uses statistics is seen as someone who has done his or her homework.

Using the Internet, statistics are easy to find. There are numerous statistical sources available and most computer databases supported by your campus library, or libraries that make their information available to the public online, include statistical databases in their lists of reference works. Often, however, you don't have to make a special search for statistics; the sources you use for your speech will have figures you can use.

Rules for Using Statistics. *Know Who Generated the Numbers and How.* Notice that when you read or hear statistics, the first thing you usually find out is who, or what company, institution, or business, generated the numbers. It is helpful to know not only who produced them but how they were created. For example, results from a sampling of 10 students do not carry as much weight or significance as from a sampling of a thousand. If those thousand students are distributed across the nation, the weight and significance increases again.

Use the Best Possible Sources. The headline "World's Food Supply Failing to Keep Pace" will be much more believable if it comes from *The New York Times* than from one of the tabloid newspapers by the checkout stand in your local supermarket. Get your statistics from well-respected sources.

Make Sure the Information Is Up to Date. Figures on military spending in 1996 are useless—unless you want to compare them with figures for the current year. If you do this, you must account for inflation.

Use Statistics That Show Trends. We can often tell what is happening to an institution or even a country if we have information from one year to another. There is even a Trends Research Institute, based in Rhinebeck, New York, with its own *Trends Journal*, designed to follow major trends in every area of life.[7]

Emily Asher quoted an online publication of the Harvard School of Public Health to show that when prevention efforts are in place, college binge drinking can be kept at a stable level—even though the rate of college binge drinking remains high.

> The 2001 Harvard School of Public Health College Alcohol Study surveyed students at 119 4-year colleges that participated in the 1993, 1997, and 1999 studies. Responses in the four survey years were compared to determine trends in heavy alcohol use, alcohol-related problems, and encounters with college and community prevention efforts. In 2001, approximately two in five (44.4 percent) college students reported binge drinking, a rate almost identical to rates in the previous three surveys. Very little change in overall binge drinking occurred at the individual college level.[8]

Use Concrete Images. When your numbers are large and may be hard to comprehend, using concrete images is helpful. William Franklin,[9] president of Franklin International, Ltd., speaking to members of the Graduate School of Business at the Japan Business Association and International Business Society in New York, reduced demographic information he had to the following:

> If we shrink the world's 5.7 billion population to a village of 100 people—with all existing human ratios remaining the same—here is the resulting profile.
> Of these 100 people, 57 are Asian, 21 European, 14 from North and South America, and eight from Africa.
> 51 female, 49 male
> 80 live in substandard housing.
> 70 cannot read.
> Half suffer from malnutrition.
> 75 have never made a phone call.
> Less than one is on the Internet.
> Half the entire village's wealth would be in the hands of 6 people.
> Only one of the hundred has a college education.
> You are in a very elite group of only 1 percent who have a college education.[10]

Testimony

When you cite **testimony,** you use another person's statements or actions to give authority to what you are saying. Experts are the best sources of testimony. Suppose you are planning to speak about NCAA violations and you get some information from the athletic director of your school. When you use this information in your speech, tell your audience where it came from. Because the information is from an expert, your speech will have more authority and be more convincing than it would be if you presented only your own opinions.

Testimony can also be used to show that people who are prominent and admired believe and support your ideas. For example, if you want to persuade your audience to take up swimming for fitness, it might be useful to mention some famous athletes who swim to stay fit. If you want people to sign your petition to build a new city park, mention other citizens who are also supporting the park.

If you use quotations keep them short and to the point. If they are too lengthy, your speech could end up sounding like everyone but yourself. If you have quotations that are long and wordy, put them into your own words. Whether you quote or paraphrase, always give credit to your source. In her speech "We, The People: Prize and Embrace What Is America," Farah M. Walters, president and CEO of University Hospitals Health System and University Hospitals of Cleveland, used the words of Eleanor Roosevelt, who said, "As individuals, we live cooperatively and, to the best of our ability, serve the community in which we live. Our own success, to be real, must contribute to the success of others. When you cease to make a contribution, you die."[11]

Polls

Polls are surveys of people's attitudes, beliefs, and behavior. Quite often they are conducted on controversial subjects. If you want to know how the U.S. public feels about Social Security, abortion, or the war on terrorism, you can probably find a poll that tells you. National polls can also provide useful information about what particular segments of the population think or know about an issue.

A single poll may yield far more information than is necessary for a speech. You must decide how much or how little to use. Try to select responses that will appeal precisely to your listeners' ages and socioeconomic circumstances.

When your statistics come from a survey, it is important to find out how many and what kinds of people were questioned. For example, if you discovered survey results saying that 30 percent of the U.S. public eats with chopsticks, you might find the statistic fairly startling and be tempted to use it—until you note that the survey included only 100 people and that many of them were Chinese immigrants.

Spend Time Pondering What You Have Uncovered

At the end of your investigation you are likely to end up with far more material than you can possibly use in a single speech. Using the strategic flexibility framework, you have probably already anticipated, assessed, and evaluated as you moved through the research phase of your preparation. Now comes the selection process.

The more you have to select from, the more precise you can be. Take time to think first, and then decide: (1) What material will best meet your specific purpose? (2) What material do you know for sure will interest listeners? (3) What material will hold their attention? (4) In what ways can you appeal to your stimulation-saturated listeners?

THE INTERNET AND GETTING STARTED

The Internet has increased the research burden that falls on speakers' shoulders. Never before has so much information been so readily available and accessible. Speakers must also evaluate the information they discover and plan to share with their listeners. Speakers, thus, are a crucial ethical and judgmental link between Internet information and audiences; they cannot just present information and expect listeners to make those assessments themselves. Most online sources are available to everyone; thus listeners must be given enough information not only to check out the Internet sites for themselves, but to know that your investigation ranged widely among available online resources. It is helpful, as you generate information for your speech, to record the appropriate URL for each piece of information you plan to use. How you choose to share it is up to you; writing it on the board, providing a handout, or giving URLs orally are three methods.

Computers have greatly changed the methods we use to do research. In using the Internet, you have developed your own methods for organizing, facilitating, and expediting searches as well as taking notes on what you discover. The important thing now is to make certain you spend time evaluating the information you gather.

Assess Yourself

Do You Have Confidence as a Speaker?

For each statement circle the answer that best represents your feelings about your *most recent* speech, either "True" or "False." Work quickly and don't spend much time on any statement. We want your *first impression* on this survey.

1. I look forward to an opportunity to speak in public. — True / False
2. My hands tremble when I try to handle objects on the lectern. — True / False
3. I am in constant fear of forgetting my speech. — True / False
4. Audiences seem friendly when I address them. — True / False
5. While preparing a speech I am in a constant state of anxiety. — True / False
6. At the conclusion of a speech I feel that I have had a pleasant experience. — True / False
7. I dislike using my body and voice expressively. — True / False
8. My thoughts become confused and jumbled when I speak before an audience. — True / False
9. I have no fear of facing an audience. — True / False
10. Although I am nervous just before getting up to speak I soon forget my fears and enjoy the experience. — True / False
11. I face the prospect of making a speech with complete confidence. — True / False
12. I feel that I am in complete possession of myself while speaking. — True / False
13. I prefer to have notes on the platform in case I forget my speech. — True / False
14. I like to observe the reactions of my audience to my speech. — True / False
15. Although I talk fluently with friends I am at a loss for words on the platform. — True / False
16. I feel relaxed and comfortable while speaking. — True / False
17. Although I do not enjoy speaking in public I do not particularly dread it. — True / False
18. I always avoid speaking in public if possible. — True / False
19. The faces of my audience members are blurred when I look at them. — True / False
20. I feel disgusted with myself after trying to address a group of people. — True / False
21. I enjoy preparing a talk. — True / False
22. My mind is clear when I face an audience. — True / False
23. I am fairly fluent. — True / False
24. I perspire and tremble just before getting up to speak. — True / False
25. My posture feels strained and unnatural. — True / False
26. I am fearful and tense all the while I am speaking before a group of people. — True / False
27. I find the prospect of speaking mildly pleasant. — True / False
28. It is difficult for me to search my mind calmly for the right words to express my thoughts. — True / False
29. I am terrified at the thought of speaking before a group of people. — True / False
30. I have a feeling of alertness in facing an audience. — True / False

Go to the *Communicating Effectively* CD-ROM and the Online Learning Center at **www.mhhe.com/hybels8** to see your results and learn how to evaluate your attitudes and feelings.

mhhe.com/hybels8

Source: *Insight vs. Desensitization in Psychotheraphy*, by G.L. Paul, in *Measures of Personality and Social Psychological Attitudes* (pp. 188–190), by J. P. Robinson, P. R. Shaver, and L. S. Wrightsmen (Ed.), 1991, San Diego, CA: Academic Press.

CHAPTER REVIEW

SUMMARY

To be an effective public speaker, you need knowledge, preparation, and delivery. It is important that everything you do as a public speaker is rooted in knowledge because practicing skill without knowledge is a fruitless endeavor.

After knowledge, preparation is the second major component of effective public speaking. Whenever you are scheduled to make a speech it is important to find a topic that interests you. Begin your search by making a personal inventory and consult newspapers, books, magazines, interviews with others, and indices to magazines and journals, along with the Internet.

Narrow your topic by brainstorming narrower aspects, writing down those ideas, then asking which ones will be of interest to and understood by your audience. Consider also what your assignment requires and how long you have to cover your topic.

Every speech should have a general purpose, a specific purpose, and a central idea. The general purpose relates to whether the speech is informative or persuasive. The specific purpose focuses on what you want to inform or persuade your audience about—or what you want your listeners to achieve as a result of your effort. The central idea captures the main idea of the speech—the specific idea you want listeners to retain after your speech.

Audience analysis is the process of finding out what your listeners know about your subject, what they might be interested in, what their attitudes and beliefs are, and what kinds of people are likely to be present. Useful demographic information about your audience includes age, gender, education, occupation, race/nationality/ethnic origin, geographic location, and group affiliations.

Analysis of the occasion should accompany your assessment of the audience. Time involves the time frame for the speech, time of day, and the length of time of your speech. Place refers to the physical stage for your speech and your interaction with your listeners. Channel is the route traveled by your signal as it moves from one location to another. Purpose refers to your specific purpose, that statement that tells precisely what you want to accomplish.

When you are putting together material for your speech, you should consider drawing on four areas: your personal experience and observations, interviews with others, the library, and the Internet. Always evaluate the quality of Internet information on the basis of reliability, authority, currency, objectivity, validity, and your own intuition.

Supporting material includes comparisons, contrasts, definitions, examples, statistics, testimony, and polls. Once you have gathered all your supporting material, you need to spend time pondering what you've uncovered.

The Internet has increased the research burden that falls on speakers' shoulders because of the amount of information available and the need to evaluate it. Speakers are a crucial ethical and judgmental link between their Internet information and their listeners.

KEY TERMS AND CONCEPTS

Use the *Communicating Effectively* CD-ROM and the Online Learning Center at **www.mhhe.com/hybels8** to further your understanding of the following terms.

Attitudes 297
Audience analysis 295
Beliefs 297
Central idea 294
Channel 300
Computer (online) databases 301
Contrast 305
Creativity 301
Definition 305
Demographic analysis 297
Example 305
General purpose 293
Hypothetical examples 305
Informative speech 293
Personal inventory 291
Persuasive speech 293
Polls 308
Purpose 293
Specific purpose 294
Statistics 306
Supporting material 304
Target audience 296
Testimony 307

CHAPTER REVIEW

QUESTIONS TO REVIEW

1. What justifications are there for studying public speaking?
2. Why is having knowledge about public speaking so important to growth, development, and change in developing public-speaking skills?
3. What are the elements that need to be considered in selecting a topic for a speech?
4. What is it that distinguishes among general purpose, specific purpose, and central idea?
5. What contribution does strategic flexibility make to analyzing the audience?
6. What are the most effective ways to gain knowledge about your listeners?
7. What must be discovered about your audience? Is it clear to you why information about your listeners is so important in the planning and preparation of your speech?
8. When you analyze a speech occasion, what are the most important factors to consider?
9. In researching your topic, what are the places you have available to you for looking for information?
10. What are some of the ways you can use to jump-start your creative spirit?
11. What are the specific questions you need to ask to make certain the information you get from the Internet is of high quality?
12. Why should you cite your research sources in your speech? How should you do this?
13. What are the four guidelines that should help direct your search for supporting material for your speech?
14. What are the differences among comparison, contrast, examples, statistics, testimony, and polls? What are the benefits of using a variety of different kinds of supporting material for a speech?
15. What is the nature of the research burden speakers must assume because of the Internet?
16. Why do speakers have an ethical responsibility to evaluate the information they discover on the Internet?

Go to the self-quizzes on the *Communicating Effectively* CD-ROM and the Online Learning Center at **www.mhhe.com/hybels8** to test your knowledge of the chapter contents.

CHAPTER

13

Organizing and Outlining the Speech

OBJECTIVES

After reading this chapter, you should be able to:
- Organize and outline your speech.
- Identify the six patterns of organization for a speech, and choose the best one for your purpose.
- Explain the function of an introduction and be able to write one.
- Explain the function of a conclusion and be able to write one.
- Explain the function of transitions and be able to write them.
- Use both full-sentence and keyword formats to outline a speech.
- Write a reference list for your speech.

SOFIA DECIDED THAT EACH MAIN HEAD IN THE BODY OF HER SPEECH ABOUT reducing test anxiety would be one phase in dealing with anxiety, and within that phase she would mention a number of methods. Although her single bold point would be that there are specific, simple ways for dealing with anxiety, she also knew that one of the best methods was to start early and maintain both your mental and physical health.

Sofia decided to deal with three phases: (1) long-range planning, (2) short-range planning, and (3) the day of the test. Given her time limit (five minutes), she decided she would have to keep the information under each main point brief, but she would try to deal with some methods she could illustrate with a personal experience or an example—to maintain listener interest.

Sofia separated her information into three piles. As she was dividing up the information, she discovered some that would work for the introduction and conclusion to her speech, and she labeled it at once so she wouldn't forget. Because she was working at her computer, Sofia began typing a rough draft of her outline. She knew it was early, but having an outline allowed her to discard information that was not relevant, focus specifically and intently on information she wanted to include, and organize her thinking at this early stage.

    I. There is an important long-range approach for dealing with test anxiety.
       A. Maintain your physical health through exercise, diet, and rest.[1]
       B. Sustain your mental health by focusing on past testing successes and engaging in positive self-talk.[2]
       C. Bolster your confidence by believing you will do well, knowing the information backward and forward, taking self-tests, and having another student quiz you.[3] Not one Web site I visited failed to mention the importance of good study habits.

    II. The short-range approach for dealing with test anxiety is more familiar to us all.
       A. "Preparation is the best way to minimize anxiety."[4]
       B. Create a study plan by determining how much time you have and how much you have to study. How much material will you cover in each session? When are the review sessions?[5]
       C. Try to anticipate the test by asking yourself what questions may be asked and answering them by integrating ideas from your lectures, notes, texts, and supplementary readings.[6]
       D. Begin a program of positive self-talk: "I am smart enough." "I am capable." "I am ready and I can perform well." Use such statements to block out negative and self-defeating comments.[7]

    III. There are important last-minute activities you can engage in to relieve test anxiety on the day of and at the test.
       A. Be rested and comfortable; you must be psychologically and physically alert to perform well.[8]
       B. Know what to expect. Learn ahead of time the kind of test it will be, where and when it will be held, and what materials to bring. This helps eliminate the element of surprise.[9]
       C. Relax as much as you can by using deep-breathing exercises, imagery, visualization, and muscle relaxation techniques to increase your focus and concentration.[10]

D. Avoid contact with others—especially worried test takers. Test anxiety is contagious and unproductive.[11]

E. Read the test instructions carefully; *make sure your copy of the test is complete* (that there are no pages missing); answer the easiest questions first; read each question carefully; review the test questions and your answers to them before you turn in your test.[12]

Sofia filled in the details of her outline, and wrote it out completely for her instructor. She condensed the outline to just keywords and put them on several 3 × 5-inch cards. She began practicing her speech using the cards. Because she had been so thorough in her research, she was so familiar with her material, and she had chosen an important and relevant topic, she could speak on it conversationally and comfortably without having to rely on her note cards (see Figure 13-1).

When the time came to give her speech, her delivery was smooth. Sofia felt strong and in control. The structure of her speech was easy for her to remember and instantly intelligible to her listeners. After the speech, several classmates told her she had done a terrific job.

Figure 13-1

Sofia's Keyword Outline

Notice two things: (1) her entire outline of the body of her speech would fit on three 3 × 5-inch cards, and (2) she has placed her sources on the card too, so she doesn't forget to cite them in the verbal portion of her speech.

I. Long-range
   A. Exercise, diet, and rest (Mann & Lash, 2004)
   B. Past testing successes (Probert, 2003)
   C. Believe, know info, take self-tests, be quizzed (Muskingum Center for Advancement of Learning)

II. Short-range
   A. Preparation (SUNY Potsdam Counseling Center)
   B. Study plan (Penn. State University)
   C. Anticipate test (SUNY Potsdam)
   D. Self-talk (Probert, 2003)

III. Last-minute
   A. Psych. & Phys. alert (Mann & Lash, 2004)
   B. Elim. surprise. (Academic Services. Southwestern University)
   C. Deep-breathing, imagery, vis. (Mann & Lash, 2004)
   D. Avoid Contact (U. of IL Counseling Center)
   E. Read inst., copy complete, answer easy ques., read ques., review (U. of FL Counseling)

PRINCIPLES OF ORGANIZATION

Relate Points to Your Specific Purpose and Central Idea

The points you make in your speech should relate directly to your specific purpose and central idea. In this outline of a speech titled "The Challenge to Excel," notice that all the main points do this:

Specific purpose: To inform my classmates about the four things required to excel.

Central idea: No matter what people's abilities are, there are four things they can do to excel.

Main ideas:
I. Learn self-discipline.
II. Build a knowledge base.
III. Develop special skills.
IV. Bounce back from defeat.

For help in outlining your material, use the computerized "Outline Tutor" on the CD.

Distinguish between Main and Minor Points

When organizing your speech, distinguish between main points and minor points. If you do this, the speech will flow more naturally and will seem logical to your listeners. The **main points** are all the broad, general ideas and information that support your central idea; the **minor points** are the specific ideas and information that support the main points. Say that the purpose of your speech is to persuade audience members to learn to incorporate computer-generated graphics into their research papers. The central idea of your speech is that they can illustrate their ideas better and more efficiently by using a computer. Your main point would have this broad, general idea: "Computers help you draw faster, revise drawings more easily, and produce a better-looking, better-illustrated paper." Your minor points will explain the main point in more specific terms: (1) most people do not draw very well; (2) a computer enables you to draw like a professional, even if you don't have drawing skills; and (3) revising and changing drawings is easy and efficient. All these minor points help explain the ways in which the computer is more effective and efficient for illustrating ideas.

If you have difficulty distinguishing between major and minor points, write each of the points you want to make on a separate index card. Then spread out all the cards in front of you and organize them by main points, with minor points coming under them. If one arrangement doesn't work, try another.

Phrase All Points in Full Sentences

Writing all your points in full sentences will help you think out your ideas more fully. Once your ideas are set out in this detailed way, you will be able to discover problems in organization that might need more work.

Working Together

For each of the following sets of sentences, identify the main point with an *M* and the minor or supporting point(s) with an *S*:

1. _____ There are thousands of different kinds of dolls.
2. _____ Nesting dolls is the term for dolls that fit inside each other.
3. _____ Baby dolls resemble infants.

1. _____ Don't wear anything that glitters.
2. _____ Don't wear all-black or all-white clothing.
3. _____ If you are appearing on television, be careful what you wear.

1. _____ The amount of agricultural land under cultivation does not support the population.
2. _____ Famine can occur for many reasons.
3. _____ Population exceeds the food sources.
4. _____ Unusual weather, such as drought, occurs.

In each of the next sets there are two main points. Find them and match them with the correct minor points.

1. _____ Certain signs indicate that your pet is too fat.
2. _____ Cut back food by one-third.
3. _____ It tires easily after a little exercise.
4. _____ Put your pet on a diet.
5. _____ Use low-calorie fillers such as rice or cottage cheese.
6. _____ It looks fat (or everyone calls it "Butterball").

1. _____ Some studies indicate that people who drink coffee in large amounts are more prone to heart disease.
2. _____ Caffeine can cause birth defects such as cleft palate and bone abnormalities.
3. _____ Decaffeinated coffee is a good alternative to coffee with caffeine.
4. _____ If you want to break the caffeine habit, cut down by a cup or two a day.
5. _____ People who drink large quantities of coffee may be endangering their health.
6. _____ You can break the coffee–caffeine habit.

Answers: The main points are:
- There are thousands of different kinds of dolls.
- If you are appearing on television, be careful what you wear.
- Famine can occur for many reasons.
- Certain signs indicate that your pet is too fat.
- Put your pet on a diet.
- People who drink large quantities of coffee may be endangering their health.
- You can break the coffee–caffeine habit.

Give All Points a Parallel Structure

Parallel structure means that each of your points will be in the same grammatical form. For example, on a speech about alcohol, the speaker started each suggestion with the words *what alcohol* followed by a verb.

What alcohol is.
What alcohol feels like.
What alcohol does to your body.

In his speech "Sustainability," Richard Lamm, former governor of Colorado, used parallel structure in this manner:

> *Our globe is warming, our forests are shrinking, our water tables are falling, our icecaps are melting, our coral is dying, and our fisheries are collapsing. Our soils are eroding, our wetlands are disappearing, our deserts are encroaching, and our finite water is more and more in demand. I suspect these to be the early warning signs of a world approaching its carrying capacity. We cannot call upon the lessons of history to*

317

help us evaluate the seriousness of these problems because it is an entirely new paradigm. Ecologically we are sailing on uncharted waters while moving at unprecedented speed. We have lost our anchor and our navigational instruments are out of date.[13]

PATTERNS OF ORGANIZATION

Once you have researched your speech, decided on a specific purpose, and listed the main points, you are ready to choose an organizational pattern. This organizational pattern will mainly affect the **body**—the main part of the speech. (Introductions and conclusions are discussed later in the chapter.)

The body of the speech is made up of your main points. Most classroom speeches should not have more than four or five main points, and many will have no more than two or three. If you want to cover a topic in depth, use fewer main points. If you want to give a broad, general view, you might want to use four or five main points.

In this section we discuss six possible arrangements of main points: time order, spatial order, cause-and-effect order, problem–solution order, motivated sequence, and topical order.

Time Order

Time order, or *chronological order,* is used to show development over time. This pattern works particularly well when you want to use a historical approach. For example, in a speech about what to do if you are the victim of a crime, the speaker arranged her main points in chronological order:

Specific purpose: To inform my audience members about what to do if they are victims of a crime.

Central idea: If you become a victim of a crime, there are some things you should do.

STRATEGIC FLEXIBILITY

Although strategic flexibility is important throughout the organizing and outlining process, there are several key points when it becomes crucial. Selecting the method you choose to use to arrange the main points in your speech is certainly one of them.

The "Speech Preparation Checklist" on your CD can help you prepare your speeches.

The speech topic, the audience, and the amount of time available are factors to consider when determining your pattern of organization.

Another Point of View

Throughout this chapter, and you will see it again and again in this textbook, your authors stress the need to let your listeners know where you are going in your speech. Here is another point of view, written by C. M. McKinney (2002) at the Advanced Public Speaking Institute:

> I suppose most of my readers know by now that when I'm speaking in public I push the limits most of the time to make sure my audience stays awake. It should be no surprise to you then that I will attack another common old style snoozer technique (and I know I will get letters from educational theory folks, but that is OK) . . . that is, telling the participants what you are going to cover during your presentation. I SAY LET 'EM FIGURE IT OUT AS YOU GO. If they think they know where you are going during a public speaking engagement, then it is easy for them to "zone out" since they "think" they know what you are going to say. The way I do it is to make them wonder, "What in the heck is he going to do next?" which forces them to stay alert to find out.

Questions

1. Do you think McKinney has a valid point? Can you be well organized and still leave your listeners wondering what you're going to do next?
2. Are there other ways to keep listeners alert and awake besides keeping your organizational scheme a secret? What techniques could you, as a speaker use, to make certain your listeners stayed alert, and yet reveal your method of organization to them—or, at least let them know where you are going?

Source: "Public Speaking: Make 'Em Wonder" (p. 1), by C. M. McKinney, 2002, Advanced Public Speaking Institute, Box 2630, Landover Hills, MD 20784. Retrieved October 26, 2005, from http://www.public-speaking.org/public-speaking-letemwonder-article.htm

Main points:
I. Try not to panic.
II. Attract attention; scream or yell "Fire!"
III. Protect your own safety; if there is a weapon or you don't know whether there is, don't resist. If there is no weapon, fight back, kick, or run.
IV. Report all crimes immediately to the police; don't disturb any evidence.

Spatial Order

When you use **spatial order,** you refer to a physical or geographical layout to help your audience see how the parts make up the whole. To help your audience visualize your subject, you explain it by going from left to right or from top to bottom, or in any direction that best suits your subject.

For example, a student decided that spatial order is the best way to explain how speakers should "stage" their presentations to include the use of visuals such as slides, overheads, movies, or computer displays. She organized her speech around three aspects of a speaker's presentational environment.

Specific purpose: To inform audience members about how to be fully effective by staging their presentations.

Central idea: Speakers need to approach their environment from three angles: space, lighting, and mechanics.

Main points:	I. Speakers should control the space as much as possible (location of speaker, screen, and visuals).
	II. Speakers must have control over the lighting, since proper lighting is important to relaxed viewing.
	III. Speakers must have control over the mechanics of how projection systems work and where controls are located.

Notice how the speaker moved from the largest aspect of presentational concern—space—to the next smaller concern—lighting—to the smallest or most defined concern—location of the mechanics of controlling the equipment. This is a well-thought-out spatial order.

Cause-and-Effect Order

A speaker who uses **cause-and-effect order** divides a speech into two major parts: cause (why something is happening) and effect (what impact it is having). Notice the cause-and-effect order revealed in items I and II under "main points" in the following outline:

Specific purpose:	To inform my audience about the possible effects of tattoos and body piercings.
Central idea:	Everyone needs to be aware of the health risks posed by such body modification practices, including physical disfigurement, bacterial and viral infections, along with blood-borne pathogens like HIV and the C and B forms of the hepatitis virus.
Main points:	I. Tattoos and body piercings have become so common that they hardly attract notice. One recent study of 7,960 college students in Texas found that one in five had at least one tattoo or piercing of a body part other than the earlobe.
	II. Dr. Scott Hammer, professor of medicine at Columbia College of Physicians and Surgeons, estimated that 1 piercing in 10 becomes infected. Staphylococcus bacteria, which can live on the skin and in the nose, is a frequent cause.[14]

Problem–Solution Order

Like speakers who use a cause-and-effect arrangement, a speaker who uses a **problem–solution order** also divides a speech into two sections. In this case, one part deals with the problem and the other deals with the solution. For example, look at this outline for a speech titled "Lose Weight Fast":

Specific purpose:	To inform audience members that by eating a high-fiber diet, moving around, and pumping iron, they can lose weight fast.
Central idea:	You don't have to starve yourself, become a competitive athlete, or engage in other extraordinary measures in order to drop unwanted weight.
Main points:	I. When I asked how many in here would like to shed 10 pounds fast, you all raised your hands, but unfortunately there are too many highly hyped, too-good-to-be-true

Consider This

In their scholarly book *Blessing for a Long Time: The Sacred Pole of the Omaha Tribe*, Robin Ridington and Dennis Hastings discuss the *uki'te*, a term used to designate the form or order in which the tribal organization ceremonially camped, in which each one of the villages, or clans, had its definite place.

In regard to the accompanying figure, the authors explain that the "*hu'thuga* [or dwelling place] was divided into halves or moieties that corresponded to the two 'grand divisions' of the tribe. The Sky people camped in the northern half of the *hu'thuga*. The Earth people camped in the southern half. The entrance of the *hu'thuga* faced east when the tribe had stopped to conduct its ceremonies."

Questions

1. If you were giving an informative speech about the camps of the Omaha tribe, can you see how easy it would be to arrange the speech in a spatial pattern?
2. By using just the information provided in this figure, suggest what other kinds of patterns of arrangement could form the basis for a speech.

Source: *Blessing for a Long Time: The Sacred Pole of the Omaha Tribe* (p. 112), by Robin Ridington and Dennis Hastings (In'aska), 1997, Lincoln: University of Nebraska Press.

The Beauty of an Indian Camp

- a - Sacred Tent of War
- b - Tent of Sacred Pole
- c - Tent of Sacred White Buffalo Hide
- ⦿ - Location of Pole during He'dewach

---

diets and fads that are unsafe. Some diets are safe and reputable; others are not.

II. You can eat as much as you want of vegetables, fresh fruits, grains, and unrefined starches. Rather than taking special programs in aerobics or dancing, you need to make movement, such as increased walking, a regular and habitual part of your daily activities. You need to change fat into muscle by regular (20-minute) strength-training routines.

Motivated Sequence

The **motivated sequence,** developed by Professor Alan H. Monroe in the 1930s,[15] is also a problem-solving pattern of arrangement. The sequence is designed to persuade listeners to accept a point of view and then motivate them to take action. The full pattern has five steps:

1. *Attention:* The speaker calls attention to the topic or situation.
2. *Need:* The speaker develops the need for a change and explains related audience needs. This is the problem-development portion of the speech.
3. *Satisfaction:* The speaker presents his or her solution and shows how it meets (satisfies) the needs mentioned.
4. *Visualization:* The speaker shows what will result when the solution is put into effect.
5. *Action:* The speaker indicates what kind of action is necessary to bring about the desired change.

Any persuasive problem-solving speech can be adapted to the motivated sequence. Notice how the speaker uses this pattern in "To Cheat or Not to Cheat: That Is the Question":

Specific purpose: To persuade my listeners that they should take a strong stand to eliminate academic dishonesty.

Central idea: Unless you are willing to take a strong stand to eliminate academic dishonesty, cheating is likely to continue and will hurt us all.

Main points:
I. Attention. The decision to cheat or not can be difficult to make—especially when you are under a lot of pressure.
II. Need. Often students face the temptation to be academically dishonest daily, whether it be cheating or helping others to cheat.
III. Satisfaction. Students need to focus on the value of honesty, the importance of integrity in academic matters, and the privilege of a college education.
IV. Visualization. Academic honesty is important to educational growth: Aim for learning, grades that represent solid effort, feelings of self-worth and integrity, and a clear conscience about never having helped others to cheat.
V. Action. Think about academic honesty. If you have ever cheated, don't do it again. If you haven't, don't start. Being honest in your work makes you feel better about yourself.

Topical Order

You can use a **topical order** whenever your subject can be grouped logically into subtopics. Here are some examples: four ways to save money for college, inexpensive ways to travel abroad, five foods that help you live longer.

In the next sample, a student uses a topical order in a speech titled "Native Americans."

Specific purpose: To inform my audience about the importance of family in Native American culture.

Central idea: To protect their values, continue their traditions, and maintain their families, Native American tribes are trying to keep children from being adopted by outsiders.

Main points:
I. Native American tribes have values that are different from those of mainstream American society.
II. Native Americans believe their traditions will die out if their children are adopted by outsiders.
III. Native Americans want to maintain their families, for values and traditions must be taught to children while they are young.

THE SPEECH INTRODUCTION

The **introduction** is the opening statement of your speech. It gives the audience members their first impression of you, it introduces them to the topic, and it motivates them to listen. If you don't hook audience members in the beginning, you might never get their attention.

Outlining an introduction would be especially valuable to beginning speakers who want to make certain everything important is included. If you have a wonderful idea for one, use it. If you need some guidance, try to use some or all of the following techniques in your introduction:

Get attention.
Announce your topic.
Preview your central idea and main points.
Establish your credibility.

> **STRATEGIC FLEXIBILITY**
> Another key point when strategic flexibility becomes crucial in the organizing and outlining of your speech is when you construct your speech introduction. Your introduction sets the tone for your entire speech; thus, you must bring all your skills to the task of carefully planning and preparing it.

State Your Purpose, Central Idea, and Main Points

By the time you reach the end of your introduction, your audience should know what you intend to accomplish and the central idea of your speech. For example:

The physical abuse of children is a serious problem in this country, and today I want to talk about how bad the problem is and some of the things we can do about it.

In your introduction, you might also want to use **initial partition**—to preview your main points at the outset. Not only does this give members of the audience a sense of your direction, but it also helps them to follow your speech more easily. The student speaking on the physical abuse of children previewed her main points this way:

Since this problem covers such a broad expanse, I would like to limit my talk to three areas: parental abuse of children, social agencies that deal with abuse, and what the ordinary citizen can do when he or she suspects a child is being abused.

Get Attention

In addition to telling your audience what you are going to talk about, your introduction should arouse attention and interest. Gaining attention is not just a matter of getting audience members to listen to your first words—they would probably do that anyway.

Rather, it is a matter of creating interest in your subject. You want your listeners to think, "This really sounds like an interesting subject" or "I am going to enjoy listening to this speech."

Notice in the following example how Sofia Mena began her speech "Dealing with Test Anxiety." She designed her introduction to get the attention of her listeners:

> *I have heard it over and over again until I am getting sick of it. "It's just not fair. I didn't ask to be here. I don't deserve this kind of treatment." Have you heard students saying things like this? Although my speech today is titled "Dealing with Test Anxiety," it could just as well be called "Taking Responsibility for Your Life." Throughout my speech today, I want you all to keep one thought in the back of your mind: You are responsible for your own learning.*

Certain techniques are proven attention getters. Let's look at others and at the functions they serve. Note that sometimes a speaker might use more than one of these techniques.

Use Humor

Research shows that speeches with some humor produce a more favorable reaction to the speaker.[16] Often a speaker will use humor in his or her introduction. Notice how Garrison Keillor, no stranger to humor himself as the creator and host of *A Prairie Home Companion*—the radio program centered on the events of the fictional town of Lake Wobegon, Minnesota—began his commencement address to Gettysburg College:

Getting the attention of your audience is a matter of creating interest in your topic.

> *I bring you greetings from Lake Wobegon, to all of you in the German branch of the Lutheran Church—we pray for you daily without ceasing. It's a great pleasure for all of us on this platform to be part of your day—the Class of '87. And to be here as witnesses at this grave and solemn moment in your lives.*
>
> *When I graduated from college, I sat about where you are and watched a candidate for summa cum laude honors walk up the stairs to be recognized, and step on the inside hem of his gown. And walk all the way up the inside of it. It was something that we all remembered, who saw it, as an object lesson in how talent and intelligence might fare in this world. And some of us had tears in our eyes as we saw it.*[17]

Use an Example

Short examples often work quite well in introductions. They may be personal examples, or they could have happened to someone else. A student used this example to spark interest in her speech:

> *Gilbert is 42 years old. He has three children, ages 17, 10, and 4. Gilbert never read to his two oldest children or helped them with their schoolwork. If they asked for help with reading, Gilbert's reply was, "Ask your mother." Last week everything changed. Gilbert*

read The Cat in the Hat *to his four-year-old. It was the first time Gilbert had ever read to one of his children. In fact, it was the first time Gilbert had read anything aloud at all.*

Gilbert had been illiterate. For the past four months he has been learning to read through a program in the literacy council. I am Gilbert's teacher.

Refer to the Occasion

If you are asked to speak for a special occasion or if a special occasion falls on the day you are speaking, make a reference to it, as when a speaker said, "I am very honored to have been asked to give a speech for Founders' Day."

Because the introduction to your speech is so important, it is worthwhile to spend extra time trying to find something unique or unusual. This is especially true when the speech is a traditional one, like a commencement speech, and the attention of audience members is likely to be seriously divided between the speaker and many potential diversions. Here is how Robert L. Dilenschneider, president and CEO, The Dilenschneider Group, chose to face the challenge in his commencement address at Muskingum College, New Concord, Ohio:

Thank you very much. Muskingum is a great place. I am privileged to be here. And I am thrilled that you asked me to speak today. Thank you. When I took suggestions on what to say here today, two pieces of advice stuck with me.

First, my two sons, 15-year-old Geoffrey, and 11-year-old Peter, said, "Keep it short, crisp, and to the point." They reminded me of Robert DeNiro's talk at New York University several years ago when the actor stood up and told several thousand students, faculty, and parents, "Break a leg."

And then DeNiro sat down.

The second thought came from a friend in Ireland who said, "The students have been lectured to for four years. Don't give them another lecture. They want to get on with the day and their lives."[18]

Show the Importance of the Subject

Showing audience members that the subject is important to their own lives is a good way of getting and keeping attention. In the example below, not only does the student let her listeners know how important the subject is to them, but she also keeps their attention by building suspense:

If I asked you right now, how many of you have done what I am going to talk about today, every one of you would raise your hand. This is a topic that affects everyone. Sometimes it nags at us day in and day out. Often it creates a negative spiral of fear of failure, self-doubt, feelings of inadequacy, anxiety over the expectations others have of us, and even feelings of being overwhelmed—that tasks seem unmanageable and that we are overextended—by trying to manage too much. All this takes a serious toll on us physically, mentally, and emotionally. We even have some wonderful mental self-seductions for tolerating the discomfort: "I'll do it tomorrow," "What's the harm of a half-hour of TV now? I've still got time," or "I deserve some time for myself." What is this thing that makes us feel we have lost control over our day-to-day routine? It is procrastination.

Use Startling Information

Using information that startles or surprises your audience is a good device for gaining attention. The only caution is that you do not overdo it because it will lose its effect.

A student began her speech using startling information in this way:

How often have you said "I'm stressed out," or "I'm under way too much stress"? It really doesn't matter whether it's too much to do, not enough sleep, a poor diet, or having to give a speech. Of course, it could just as easily be about money, a loved one's illness, failing an exam. If any of this fits you, realize that if it is or becomes prolonged, according to Sora Song, "The Price of Pressure," in Time magazine, July 19, 2004, you are twice as likely to get sick from a cold or flu, you are likely to experience an increase in your blood pressure, your heart rate, your respiration, your metabolism, and even the blood flow to your muscles. Subjects exposed to stress, according to some Internet Web sites I'll introduce you to momentarily, showed increases in infection rates from 74 percent to 90 percent and clinical colds rose from 27 percent to 47 percent.

Use Personal Examples

Don't be afraid to refer to your own life when you can tie examples from it into your subject. Personal examples make a speech stronger because they are a way of showing that you know what you're talking about. In the next example, the speaker used an example from his own experience to begin a speech about dropping out of school:

> Seven years ago I was a teenage dropout. I went away to college because my parents wanted me to. I moved into a dorm, made lots of friends, and began to have a wonderful time—a time that was so wonderful that I only occasionally went to class or studied for an exam. The college, realizing that first-year students take time to adjust, put me on probation for the first year. In the second year, however, I had to settle down.
>
> I tried to study, but I didn't have any idea of what I was studying for. I didn't have a major, and I had no idea of what I wanted to do with my life. Finally I asked myself, "What am I doing here?" I could come up with no answer. So after finishing the first semester of my sophomore year, I dropped out. It was the second-best decision I ever made. The first-best was to come back to school—at the grand old age of 27.

Use a Quotation

Sometimes you can find a quotation that will get your speech off to a good start. A well chosen quotation can also give credibility to your speech. For instance, a political candidate giving a campaign address about the need to raise taxes might begin by quoting Franklin D. Roosevelt:

> Taxes, after all, are the dues that we pay for the privileges of membership in an organized society.

Additional Tips for Introductions

When writing an introduction to a speech, remember the following points as well:

1. Although you might want to build curiosity about your speech topic, don't draw out the suspense for too long. The audience will get annoyed if it has to wait to find out what you're going to talk about.

2. Keep your introduction short. The body of your speech contains the main content, and you shouldn't wait too long to get there.

3. Be ready to adapt. Was there anything in the situation that you did not anticipate and need to adapt to? For example, did someone introduce you in a particularly flattering way? Do you want to acknowledge this? Did your audience brave bad weather to come and hear you talk? Do you want to thank them?

THE SPEECH CONCLUSION

A good **conclusion** should tie a speech together and give the audience the feeling that the speech is complete. It should not introduce any new ideas.

If you have not had very much experience in public speaking, it is especially important that you plan your conclusion carefully. No feeling is worse than knowing that you have said all you have to say but do not know how to stop. If you plan your conclusion, this won't happen to you.

In preparing a conclusion, it may be helpful to follow a model. A conclusion should:

- Signal the end of your speech. (You could say, "The last thing I would like to say . . ." or "Finally . . ." Please note that the phrase "In conclusion I would just like to say that . . . " is overused. Try to find an original signal.)
- Summarize your main points.
- Make a memorable final statement.

> **STRATEGIC FLEXIBILITY**
> The third key point when strategic flexibility becomes crucial in the organizing and outlining of your speech is when you construct your speech conclusion. It is the final thing listeners hear you say, and it must not just make a lasting impression, but should make the audience want to hear from you again as well.

This model is designed to show beginning students what to work toward as they prepare their conclusions. Try not to let the model stifle your creativity or imagination. Give your conclusion an inspirational quality. Make the audience members feel that the speech was terrific and that they would like to hear you speak again.

Here are some approaches to concluding your speech.

Summarize Your Main Ideas

If you want your audience to remember your main points, it helps to go back and summarize them in the conclusion of your speech. The student whose topic was "Five Tips for Improving Term Papers" concluded her speech this way:

> *Let me briefly summarize what you should do whenever you write a term paper. Use interviews as well as the Internet, show enthusiasm about the subject, paraphrase quotations, don't pad your paper, have your paper printed on a quality printer, and proofread your paper before you hand it in. If you follow these hints, you are certain to do better on the next paper you write.*

Include a Quotation

If you can find a quotation that fits your subject, the conclusion is a good place to use it. A quotation gives added authority to everything you have said, and it can often help sum up your main ideas. In his speech to persuade the audience not to make political choices on the basis of television commercials, the student used a closing quotation to reinforce his point:

> *An executive in the television industry once wrote, "Television programming is designed to be understood by and to appeal to the average 12-year-old." Since none of us are 12-year-old viewers, I would suggest that we fight back. There is only one way to do that. Turn off the television set.*

Inspire Your Audience to Action

When you give a speech, especially a persuasive one, your goal is often to inspire the audience to some course of action. If this is the goal of your speech, you can use your conclusion to tell audience members precisely what they should do. Notice how Carole McKenna closed the farewell speech she gave to participants in one of her five-day self-improvement seminars:

> *The certificate we will give you singles you out as someone who has been part of a unique opportunity. You found skills to practice, knowledge to digest, and feelings to understand. Also, you found each other. Most importantly, I trust, you found yourself. I hope you will now put to use all that you have discovered. You now recognize the truth in the statement "The greatest distance you have yet to cover still lies within you." Use this seminar as the beginning of competition, knowing that the most rewarding competition is with yourself, to improve yourself. Take charge of your life. Good luck to all of you.*

Additional Tips for Conclusions

When writing a conclusion for a speech, keep these additional points in mind:

1. Work on your conclusion until you feel you can deliver it without notes. If you feel confident about your conclusion, you will feel more confident about your speech.
2. If you tell your audience you are going to conclude, do so! Don't set up the expectation that you are finished and then go on talking for several more minutes.
3. Don't let the words "Thank you" or "Are there any questions?" take the place of a conclusion.
4. Give your conclusion and leave the speaking area if appropriate. If you don't do this, you will ruin the impact of your conclusion and perhaps even your entire speech. (Leaving the speaking area may not be appropriate if there is a question period following the speech.)

SPEECH TRANSITIONS

The final element to work into your speech is **transitions**—comments that lead from one point to another to tell your audience where you have been and where you are going. Transitions are a means of smoothing the flow from one point to another. For example, if you are going to show how alcohol and tobacco combine to become more powerful than either acting alone, you might say:

> *We all know, then, that cigarette smoking is hazardous to our health and we all know that alcohol abuse can kill, but do you know what can happen when the two are combined? Let me show you how these two substances act synergistically—each one making the other more powerful and dangerous than either would be alone.*

Now you are set to speak about their combined effect.

Tips for Transitions

In writing transitions, you should pay attention to these points:

1. Use a transition to introduce main heads and to indicate their order: "First . . . Second . . . Third . . . "; "The first matter we shall discuss . . . "; "In the first place . . . "; "The first step . . . "; "Let us first consider . . . "; and the like.

2. Write out your transitions and include them in your speech outline. A transition that is written out and rehearsed is more likely to be used.
3. If in doubt about whether to use a transition, use it. Since a speech is a onetime event, listeners cannot go back and refer to previously mentioned material. Do everything you can to make the job of listening easier and more accurate.

PREPARING AN OUTLINE

An **outline** is a way of organizing material so you can see all the parts and how they relate to the whole. Outlining your speech will help you organize your thoughts and discover where your presentation might cause problems in structure.

The Outline Format

Your speech will be organized into an introduction, a body, and a conclusion (with transitions connecting them). Since the introduction and the conclusion deal with so few points, they are usually not outlined, although some people prefer to outline them. As previously noted, outlining can help you see whether all essential parts are included. This is especially important for beginning speakers. We use Roman numerals to designate the main points of the body of the speech, as demonstrated in the examples of speech organization.

Main and Supporting Points

The outline sets forth the major portion of the speech—the body—and shows the content's organization into main and supporting (minor) points. Remember that the broad, general statements are the main points; the minor points contain the more specific information that elaborates on and supports the main points.

Standard Symbols and Indentation

All outlines use the same system of symbols. The main points are numbered with Roman numerals (I, II, III) and capital letters (A, B, C). Minor, more specific points are numbered with Arabic numerals (1, 2, 3) and lowercase letters (a, b, c). The most important material is always closest to the left-hand margin; as material gets less important, it moves to the right. Note, then, that the outline format moves information from the general to the more specific through the use of numbers, letters, and indentation:

    I. *University*
        A. *College of Arts and Sciences*
            1. *English*
            2. *History*
            3. *Mathematics*
            4. *Psychology*
            5. *Science*
        B. *College of Business Administration*
            1. *Accounting*
            2. *Economics*
            3. *Finance*
            4. *General Business*

  C. *College of Education*
   1. *Early Childhood Education*
   2. *Elementary Education*
   3. *Secondary Education*
   4. *Special Education*

 Another thing you should note about the outline format is that there should always be at least two points of the same level. That is, you can't have just an A and no B; you can't have just a 1 and no 2. The only exception to this is that in a one-point speech, you would have only one main point.

Full-Sentence and Keyword Outlines

There are two major types of outlines: full-sentence and keyword. A **full-sentence outline** is a complete map of what the speech will look like. All the ideas are stated in full sentences. In a full-sentence outline it is easy to spot problem areas and weaknesses in the structure, support, and flow of ideas. This type of outline is useful as you plan and develop your speech.

 Keyword outlines give only the important words and phrases; their main function is to remind the speaker of his or her ideas when delivering the speech. Sometimes speakers will add statistics, quotations or sources to keyword outlines when such information is too long or too complicated to memorize or they simply need reminders. Some speakers prepare a full-sentence outline on the left and a keyword outline on the right, as in the following example. The keyword outline enables the speaker to avoid having to look at his or her notes all the time.

Produce should be carefully washed before you eat it.	Wash produce
Breads without preservatives should be refrigerated.	Refrigerate bread
Meat should not be eaten raw.	No raw meat

 The main points (whether presented in full sentences or by keywords) are sometimes put onto cards—one to a card. We discuss the reasons for this in Chapter 14.

THE REFERENCE LIST

At the end of your outline you should have a **reference list** of all the material you have used—and only that which you have used—in preparing your speech. This reference list should include everything you have employed in your speech (books, newspapers, magazines, and Internet resources) as well as all the people you have interviewed. At the end of this chapter, after the sample outline, you will find a speech reference list.

 There are a couple of things to remember about reference lists. First, adopt a style and be consistent. For example, every book you cite should be recorded using exactly the same style. Every magazine should be recorded using the same style for magazines, and every Internet citation should be consistent as well. Because there are so many different kinds of Internet resources besides Web sites, if you need reference-list style guidelines for other resources such as e-mail, newsgroups, Internet books (sometimes referred to as e-books), and online magazines (often referred to as e-zines), use the sources mentioned in Figure 13-2 or, as an alternative, enter "citing Internet resources" in your search engine. Google produced 15,500,000 Web sites (without quotation marks, October 26, 2005; with quotation marks 27,000). Instructors may have a preferred style they want you to follow, so check, first, to see what the assignment calls for.

The second point is to keep careful notes along the way. If you look at the style requirements *before* you begin gathering information, you will have all the data necessary when you begin to put together your reference list. Trying to piece together—if not locate—information at the last minute is both frustrating and time consuming.

Rather than viewing the requirement of submitting a reference list as a chore—or, as some students would label it, "busywork"—think of it as a useful, productive exercise. How? Look at your reference list to make sure you have secured information for your speech from a wide range of sources. This not only helps validate the data you are using but lets listeners know, too, that your viewpoints are more credible.

When you have assembled your entire reference list, look at the sources you have accumulated. Do they look like credible sources when you examine the expertise of the authors or the credibility of the Web sites? Using credible sources, of course, adds to your own credibility. Just as important—and maybe more—using poor material, or sites with no credibility can destroy your credibility in an instant.

THE INTERNET AND ORGANIZING AND OUTLINING THE SPEECH

There is no shortage of good information on organizing and outlining oral presentations online. Some Web sites include complete explanations; however, most are outlines only with brief explanations. The sites that follow are arranged in alphabetical order. Most have no author and, because the information does not go out of date, there are no dates listed. Be aware, however, that sites are changed, and material gets reorganized.

- [No author]. (no date). *Designing effective oral presentations*, Riceowl—The Rice. On-Line.Writing.Lab. Retrieved October 26, 2005, from **http://www.ruf.rice.edu/~riceowl/oralpres.html**. At this site, the following topics are covered: "Understand the context of your presentation," "Analyze your audience," "Understand and articulate your presentation's purpose," "Choose and shape your presentation's content," "Organize your presentation," "Choose an appropriate speaking style," "Practice an effective delivery style," "Select and use visual aids effectively."

- [No author]. (no date). *Developing an outline*. Purdue University Online Writing Lab. Retrieved October 26, 2005, from **http:owl.english.purdue.edu/handouts/general/gl outlin.html**. At this Web site the topics covered are "Developing an Outline," "Purpose," "Process," "Theory" ("Parallelism," "Coordination," "Subordination," and "Division"), and "Form."

- [No author]. (no date). *Oral presentations*. College Success Seminars. Retrieved October 27, 2005, from **http://www.wmich.edu/asc/College%20Success%20Seminars/OralPresentations.htm**. Here in three pages you will find "Questions to Ask Yourself," "Presentation Styles," "Organization of Speech" ("Beginning the Presentation," "During the Presentation," and "After the Speech Is Over"), and "To Relieve Your Anxiety and Improve General Speaking Quality" (a section that contains 13 specific suggestions).

Figure 13-2

Cite the sources you use in your speech in your references section at the end of your speech material. With the exception of the citations for books, magazines, and newspapers, the information in this figure is adapted from: *Citing Internet Resources*, 2004, Connected Teacher-Classroom Connect. A Harcourt Education Company. Retrieved October 27, 2005, from **http://www.classroom.com/community/connection/howto/citeresources.jhtml**

The important thing in citing your sources is to choose a citation style and use that style consistently throughout your references section.

E-Mail
Structure:
Sender of e-mail message <sender's e-mail address>. Subject line of the message. Date of message (day, month, year). E-mail recipient <recipient's e-mail address>.

Example:
Meredith, Paige **<pmeredith@classroom.com>**. "RE: Museums in Paris." 17 August 2001. Christine Borror **<chrissyborror@yahoo.com>**.

World Wide Web
Structure:
Author or originator. Title of item. [Online] Date of document or download (day, month, year). URL **<http://address/filename>**.

Example:
U.S. Census Bureau. "American FactFinder. Facts About My Community." [Online] 17 August 2001. **<http://factfinder.census.gov/servlet/BasicFactsServlet>**.

Online Images
Structure:
Author or originator. Description or title of image. [Online image] Date of document or download (day, month, year). URL **<http://address/filename>**.

Example:
USGS. "Map. Major Volcanoes in Ecuador." [Online image] 17 August 2001. **<http://vulcan.wr.usgs.gov/Volcanoes/Ecuador/Maps/map_ecuador_volcanoes.html>**.

Online Sounds
Structure:
Author or originator. Description or title of sound. [Online sound] Date of document or download (day, month, year). URL **<http://address/filename>**.

Example:
Jussi Bjorling Home Page. "Di quella pira," aria from *II Travatore*, by Guiseppe Verdi. [Online sound] 30 November 1999. **<http://www.geocities.com/Vienna/Strasse/3468/bjorling.htm>**.

Online Video Clips
Structure:
Author or originator. Description or title of video clip. [Online video clip] Date of document or download (day, month, year). URL **<http://address/filename>**.

Example:
Zoological Society of San Diego. "Indian Rhino Calf Born at Park," e-zoo videos, San Diego Zoo. [Online video clip] 17 August 2001. **<http://www.sandiegozoo.com/virtualzoo/videos/index.html>**.

FTP (File Transfer Protocol)
Structure:
Author or originator. Title of item. [Online] Date of document or download (day, month, year). URL **<http://address/filename>**.

Example:
Oppenheimer, Frank. "Exhibit Collection and Design at the San Francisco Exploratorium Museum." [Online] 1 December 1999. **<ftp://ftp.exploratorium.edu/pub/publications/Exhibit_Conception_And_Design>**.

Usenet Newsgroups
Structure:
Author or originator. Title of item. [Online] Date of document or download (day, month, year). URL **<http://address/filename>**.

Example:
Google Groups. "Plato's Real Name." [Online] 17 August 2001. **<http://groups.google.com/groups?hl=en&safe=off&th=e19ab821b99e42ee,6>**.

Citation Sources
American Psychological Association. "APA Style of Citation: Electronic

(continued)

Figure 13-2 *Continued*

Sources." [Online] 16. August 2001. <http://www.apastyle.org/elecref.html>.

Gibaldi, Joseph. *MLA Handbook for Writers of Research Papers*. 5th ed. New York: Modern Language Association, 1999. <http://www.mla.org>

McCullen, Carolyn. "The Electronic Thread," *Middle Ground* Oct. 1999: 7–9 and 52. <http://www.nmsa.org>.

Books
Structure:
Author. Title. Place of publication: Publisher, date.

Example:
Safier, Rachel. *Mr. right now: When dating is better than saying 'I do.'* San Francisco, CA: Jossey-Bass, 2004.

Magazines
Structure:
Author. Title of article. Name of magazine. Date of issue. Page number.

Example:
Underwood, Anne, and Jerry Adler. Diet and genes. *Newsweek*, January 17, 2005, 40–48.

Newspapers
Structure:
Author. Title of article. Name of newspaper. Date of issue. Page number.

Example:
Alboher, Marci. Don't speak the language? Live with the locals. *The New York Times*, February 1, 2005, 7C.

- [No author]. (2003). *Organizing and integrating information*. Learning Skills Program, Counseling Services, University of Victoria. Retrieved October 27, 2005, from **http://www.coun.uvic.ca/learn/organize.html**. In this two-page Web site there are "Guidelines and Tips," but five links to additional "Organizational Practice," and one to "Concept Mapping." It is these additional links that make this site especially valuable.

- Sawyer, T. M. (2000). *2 Organizing a speech or oral presentation*. College of Engineering, University of Michigan. Retrieved October 27, 2005, from **http://www.engin.umich.edu/dept/techcomm/resources/orals-TMS/2-organizing.html**. In this four-step, six-page site the material begins with "First, Make It Short," "Second, Make the Organization Obvious," "Third, Make the Ideas Simple and Vivid," and "Fourth, Summarize and Be Prepared for Questions." There is a great deal of explanation and numerous examples of each of these points, and three references are listed.

Sample Outline

To help you create your outline, here is a sample speech titled "Fearless Public Speaking" by Deirdre Chong-Reed, done in outline form. The topical outline works well for this particular speech because all the main points aid speakers in limiting their fear of speaking in public.

General purpose: To persuade.
Specific purpose: To persuade my listeners that through education, experience, and expression you can limit your fear of speaking in public.
Central idea: I want my audience to know how to deal with the fear of public speaking so that they, too, can turn their fear into fearlessness.

Fearless Public Speaking

Introduction

Undoubtedly you all already know that the fear of public speaking ranks number one in the minds of a majority of people (Wallechinsky & Wallace, 1993). Far above the fear of death and disease comes the fear of standing, just like this, in front of an audience. The fear is so great it prompted Jerry Seinfeld, in his comedy routine, to remark, "Studies show that fear of public speaking ranks higher than the fear of dying. I guess this means that most people at a funeral would rather be in the coffin than delivering the eulogy" (Ragsdale, 2000). Well, you can't count me among those who fear it. True, you could have, but not now. Not now—because I know too much. In the past two weeks or so I have had one of the best educations I could ask for—an education in how to deal with the fear of speaking in public. And now I am fearless, and I want to help you become fearless, too.

There are some excellent ways to deal with the fear of speaking in public. I'm going to label them education, experience, and expression. When I was very young, I wanted to be a movie star, but I was terrified of the spotlight. My first public humiliation came in the third grade, when, as a top-heavy apple tree in the play "Johnny Appleseed," I fell off the stage. I hid for weeks. Kids can be so cruel. One of them said to me, "You sure made it easier for ole' Johnny to pick your apples." How could I ever be a whole human being again? I might as well have died.

Well, I had other humiliating experiences connected with public speaking, and if you want to know the truth, it is really amazing—at least to me—that I can stand here before you today and say, "I have really gotten this fear under control!" But how it has happened is what I want to talk about today.

Transition: Almost all of us have experienced the sweaty palms, the stomach wretching, the queasy

---

Deirdre first acknowledges what her audience already knows: then she adds the quotation from Jerry Seinfeld—just in case some members of her audience had not yet heard his joke.

Deirdre's personal experience serves as a tie between her topic and herself and establishes her credibility on the topic by stating how long she has spent researching it.

After giving her central idea—helping listeners become fearless—and the three divisions of her speech—education, experience, and expression—she relates a personal experience to provide humor, get attention, and connect her with her listeners.

She ends her introduction with a direct confession and a lead-in to her speech.

Her first transition acknowledges the physical traits of public-speaking anxiety and the reasons why it feeling, and the quivering voice. And most of us, too, do not like making ourselves so vulnerable to others. Getting up here like this is not only intimidating, but it opens us up to criticism—and who would ever choose that? (Ragsdale, 2000) But whether we like it or not, we're going to have to do it, so we might as well learn how to limit the fear. I will be talking about education, experience, and expression.

Body
I. With *education* you can limit your fear of public speaking. This is a broad area and can cover a variety of topics. I will cover three: knowledge of yourself, knowledge of the problem, and knowledge of your topic.
   A. Knowing yourself is important to limiting your fear of public speaking.
      1. Are you focusing on yourself? Often, it is your own fear of failure, exposure, or judgment that causes a fear of speaking in public. Remember: Fear is normal, and you are not alone.
      2. Focus on your audience. According to Morton C. Orman (2002), a medical doctor who writes on "Conquering Public Speaking Fear," this will not only remove the spotlight from you, but it places the emphasis on the very essence of public speaking—giving listeners something of value.
   B. Knowing about the problem of the fears connected to public speaking is helpful to limiting your fear because there is so much helpful information. I want to recommend two terrific Web sites for you to examine.
      1. The first is the medical doctor I referred to earlier: M. C. Orman "How to Conquer Public Speaking Fear," 2002, **http://www.stresscure.com/jobstress/speak.html**. The reason for recommending this site is Orman's nine principles—the first of which is "Speaking in public is **not** inherently stressful." He has eight more just as good.
      2. The second site is: D. Ullius (1997). "Crossing a Bridge of Shyness: Public Speaking for Communicators." Editorial Eye, EEI Press, Georgetown University. **http://www.eeicom.com/eye/shyness.html**. In addition to advice, Ullius offers numerous sources for novice speakers.

Transition: Two of the benefits of examining different Web sites on "The Fear of Public Speaking" are, first, the fear affects people in different ways, and so how you read the information may be completely different from how someone else reads it. But, second,

occurs and then reminds listeners of her three main points.

With the first main head, she uses parallel structure and partitions her three subheads as well—knowledge of yourself, the problem, and your topic.

Her two sub-subpoints (1 and 2) relate to each other. The first suggests that you should not focus on yourself, and the second offers the solution: Focus on your audience.

Notice that in subpoints A, B, and C Deirdre also uses parallel structure in the statement of the idea, but the second thing she does is relate that knowledge to her goal: limiting listeners' fears of public speaking.

The two sub-subpoints for subpoint B (1 and 2) give listeners specific Web sources for further information. Deirdre wrote these on the chalkboard and covered them with poster board until using them in her speech. In addition to these specific references, Deirdre also gives her Web references throughout the speech—wherever a citation occurs in the outline.

Deirdre's second transition is from subpoint B to subpoint C because she feels listeners would have forgotten where she was after uncovering her two references on the chalkboard. Here, she is simply trying to reorient the audience before continuing.

(continued)

Sample Outline (continued)

there is so much advice. The advice best for you is likely to be a combination or synthesis of what you read, and, once again, everyone is different.

We've talked about knowing yourself, and we've talked about knowing about the problem of fearing public speaking. Here, I want to talk about knowing your topic.

    C. Knowing your topic is important to limiting your fear of public speaking.
        1. Most of the sources you will read mention proper and thorough preparation as the key to limiting the fear (Laskowski, n.d.). Laskowski, a professional speaker, suggests that proper presentation and rehearsal reduce the fear of speaking in public by 75 percent.
        2. You will know your topic better if you select one with which you are already familiar—or one that you know will help you in some way. I selected this one for a reason unknown to any of you right now: As president of my sorority, I have to give an address to our regional conference in about a month or so. I want to do my best.

Transition: Know yourself; know the problem; and know your topic—all aspects of becoming educated about the fear of speaking in public. But there is another element needed, and that is experience.

  II. With *experience* you can limit your fear of public speaking. You have heard the old axiom, "Practice makes perfect" (Ragsdale, n.d.). True, you don't need to be perfect, but practice certainly helps to reduce the fear.
    A. Think about what you want to achieve and what you can reasonably achieve in the allotted time (Price, 1998). Cover only what you have time for.
        1. As you practice, keep your listeners in mind: organize carefully so that audience members have both a structure and a framework. Illustrate so that listeners can visualize your information (Nordgren, 1996). Keep audience focused.
        2. Practice in front of a mirror or in front of someone else. If you use notes, watch yourself to see how much you are relying on them. "Most people find the more they practice, the more at ease they feel when they give their presentation" (Brown, n.d.). Visualize yourself speaking.
    B. Seek opportunities to speak. Whether it's in other classes, in clubs and organizations, in your community, or on the job, the more

---

Notice that the end of the transition gives both sub-points A and B and then gives C, too, which Deirdre repeats—to drive the point home.

In these two sub-subpoints, Deirdre first cites an authority (Laskowski) and a statistic he provides. In the second sub-subpoint, she offers another personal experience to support her point—not that you should select a topic with which you are already familiar, but that you should select one that may help you in some way.

Her third transition in the speech repeats subpoints A, B, and C, relates them to main head I—education—and moves listeners immediately to the second main head—experience.

She begins main head II using the same parallel structure as in main head I.

In sub-subpoints 1 and 2, Deirdre talks about the importance of practice, and she gives specific audience-centered ideas for practicing speeches. Also, Deirdre cites Molly Brown, the author of the quotation in sub-subpoint 2.

Subpoint B offers listeners further practical suggestions for limiting the fear of public speaking. Also, at the end of subpoint B, Deirdre uses a phrase she often you are in front of people delivering messages, the easier it will become (Ullius, 1997). With increasing competence comes greater confidence (Orman, 2002).

Transition: I have talked about the importance of both education and experience in limiting your fear of public speaking. Now, I want to talk about the importance of expression.

III. With *expression* you can limit your fear of public speaking. The first part of expression may be less familiar to you than the last part.
   A. The first part of expression has to do with mental preparation—the pep talk you give yourself. Give yourself the four C's for speech success. Tell yourself over and over: "I am capable; I am confident; I am in control; and I want to communicate" (Gater, 1996).
   B. The second part of expression has to do with physical preparation.
      1. Can you practice your speech in the same location where it will be given?
      2. Can you check to make sure all elements in the physical environment in which you will speak are set up and in order? (McGavern, 2002, p. 9)
   C. The third part of expression has to do with emotional preparation—the commitment to your ideas.
      1. "A speech that conveys genuine emotions resonates with listeners" (Ullius, 1997, p. 3).
      2. "Be yourself. Your audience will forgive your nervousness, but they will be turned off by false modesty or bravado" (Public Speaking, 1999).
      3. Maintain eye contact; use natural hand gestures; keep body movement quiet and natural; maintain appropriate voice volume; and maintain a constant rate of speech (Brown, n.d.) . . . And if you make a mistake, keep going. Don't stumble. Pretend it was intended (Ragsdale, n.d.).
      4. Turn nervousness into positive energy by harnessing it and transforming it into vitality and enthusiasm (Laskowski, p. 3).

Transition: There are three parts of expression: mental, physical, and emotional preparation. The final aspect, emotional preparation, has to do with conveying emotions, being yourself, connecting with your listeners, and turning your nervousness into positive energy.

developed during her research: "With increasing competence comes greater confidence."

Notice how simple and straightforward her transition from main head II to III is. Once again, the topic—expression—was repeated to drive the point home.

Deirdre does not give away her subpoints in her statement of main head III; however, notice, once again, the parallel structure in the statement of subpoints A, B, and C: The first part . . . , the second part . . . , and the third part. . . .

Also, notice how Deirdre uses a convenient method for subdividing the three parts of main head III: mental, physical, and emotional preparation.

Her point about emotional preparation is especially important because all these ideas relate to speakers' being themselves, being natural, and maintaining a comfortable and relaxed connection with listeners. Not only is a commitment to the ideas essential, but the commitment often has these effects.

In the transition from the body of the speech to the conclusion, she first reviews subpoints A, B, and C—mental, physical, and emotional preparation of main head III—and then her most recent point—emotional preparation: conveying emotions, being yourself, connecting with listeners, and turning nervousness into positive energy.

(continued)

Sample Outline (continued)

Conclusion

What is interesting here is that you will discover that some nervousness is good! Nerves can empower you. They can help you think of details you might otherwise forget (Eggleston, 1997). They can get you excited about sharing ideas with your listeners. And they can add energy and dynamism to those ideas. You don't want to eliminate your fear of public speaking, you just want to get it under control—to limit it. What's scary is that the fear of public speaking could even cause you to prepare more! And, as you think about these ideas, remember the old saying, "The person who fails to prepare is preparing for failure." So, prepare, prepare, prepare. In that way, you can turn fear into fearlessness.

As she begins her conclusion, she first tells listeners some of the benefits of nervousness. She chooses to use another well-known quotation here, "The person who fails to prepare is preparing for failure," but she uses it to emphasize the importance of preparing. Then she ends by referring once again to the title of her speech "Fearless Public Speaking."

Speech Reference List

Brown, M. (n.d.). "Presentations." The Writing Center, Sage Laboratory, Rensselaer Polytechnic Institute, Troy, NY. Retrieved June 15, 2002, from **http://www.rpi.edu/web/writingcenter/text/present.htm**

Eggleston, S. (1997, August 12). "Fear of public speaking: Stories, myths and magic." Trial by Fire. Retrieved June 15, 2002, from **http://www.access.digex.net/,nuance//fearspkl.html**

Gater, J. (1996, October 7). "Notes on public speaking." Retrieved June 15, 2002, from **http://www.cyberus.ca/csbruce/shyness/pubspeak.html**

Laskowski, L. (n.d.) "Overcoming speaking anxiety in meetings & presentations." LJL Seminars, Newington, CT. Retrieved June 15, 2002, from **http://www.ljlseminars.com/anxiety.htm**

Nordgren, L. (1996, September 23). "Designing presentation visuals." Media Services, Robert A. L. Mortvedt Library, Pacific Lutheran University. Retrieved June 15, 2002, from **http://www.plu.edu/libr/media/designing_visuals.html** (Jan. 31, 2000).

Orman, M. C. (2002). "How to conquer public speaking fear." Retrieved June 15, 2002, from **http://www.stresscure.com/jobstress/speak.html**

Price, R. M. (1998, April 29). "Technical presentations: Hints & suggestions." University of Mississippi. Retrieved June 15, 2002, from **http://home.olemiss.edu/cmprice/lectures/badpres.html**

[No author]. (n.d.). "Public speaking." Canadian Association of Student Activity Advisors. Retrieved June 15, 2002, from **http://www.sentex.net/casaa/resources/sourcebook/acquiring-leadership-skills/public-speaking.htm**

Ragsdale, L. (n.d.). "Solutions." Retrieved June 15, 2002, from **http://www.geocities.com/BourbonStreet/6411/solutions.html**

— (n.d.). "What is the one thing you fear most?" Retrieved June 15, 2002, from **http://www.geocities.com/BourbonStreet/6411/target1.html** (Jan. 31, 2000).

— (n.d.). "Why do we fear public speaking?" Retrieved June 15, 2002, from **http://www.geocities.com/BourbonStreet/6411/fears.html**

Ullius, D. (1997). "Crossing a bridge of shyness: Public speaking for communicators." *Editorial Eye*, Georgetown University. Retrieved June 15, 2002, from **http://www.eeicom.com/eye/shyness.html**

Wallechinsky, D., & Wallace, A. (1993). *The book of lists*. New York: Bantam.

Assess Yourself

How Much Do You Know about Organizing a Speech?

For each question circle the letter of the best answer.

1. What is the primary reason for organizing a speech? A well-organized speech:
   A. promotes clear communication.
   B. is an easier way to prepare any speech.
   C. provides more of a challenge for listeners.
   D. allows for the preparation of an outline of the speech.

2. What is one of the advantages of organizing your speech? Organizing it will give you:
   A. believability.
   B. a point of view.
   C. total comprehension.
   D. an emotional advantage.

3. Once you have written your general and specific purposes, what are the next three levels on which you can organize your speech?
   A. Main head and first two subpoints.
   B. Introduction, main heads, and conclusion.
   C. Evidence, attention factors, and transitions.
   D. Central idea, main points, and supporting material.

4. Which of the following pieces of advice relates to refining your main points?
   A. Restrict each one to no more than two ideas.
   B. Always limit your number of main heads to three.
   C. Make sure all your main points develop your central idea.
   D. Determine your main points by the quantity and quality of your supporting material.

5. If you arranged your main points in a time sequence—for example, dealing with periods of time in history—you would be using which of the following organizational patterns?
   A. Causal.
   B. Topical.
   C. Spatial.
   D. Chronological.

6. Which of the following is the cardinal rule for using supporting material? They must:
   A. hold attention.
   B. enliven your speech.
   C. be easy to remember.
   D. support, explain, illustrate, or reinforce your central idea.

7. Why is it important to make your organization obvious to your listeners?
   A. This isn't important; you should not make it obvious.
   B. Because organization—whatever the topic—convinces.
   C. Because a listening audience can't stop the speech and go back over it.
   D. If you have spent the time on it, the audience should notice your efforts.

8. Why is it important to time your speech in practice?
   A. Speaking is different from reading.
   B. To help you memorize your words.
   C. So you know where to place your emphasis.
   D. To help you better phrase the main heads of your speech.

9. What is the key to effectiveness in presenting your well-organized ideas to your listeners?
   A. Be conversational.
   B. Elevate your language and approach.
   C. Speak slightly below your audience's level of understanding.
   D. Try to talk to your audience as if you are talking entirely to yourself.

10. In the conclusion of your speech—with respect to the organizational pattern you have selected—you should do what?
    A. Repeat your main heads.
    B. Offer listeners new evidence for your position.
    C. Tell them if it was topical, spatial, causal, or chronological.
    D. Be totally spontaneous, natural, relaxed, and comfortable as you think of any additional ideas that may help them understand your speech better.

Go to the *Communicating Effectively* CD-ROM and the Online Learning Center at **www.mhhe.com/hybels8** to see your results and learn how to evaluate your attitudes and feelings.

CHAPTER REVIEW

SUMMARY

The principles of organization include selecting information that relates to the specific purpose and central idea; distinguishing among the introduction, body, and conclusion of the speech; distinguishing between main and minor points; and phrasing all points in full sentences with parallel structure.

Six patterns of organization work well for organizing speeches: time order, using a chronological sequence; spatial order, moving from left to right, top to bottom, or in any direction that will make the subject clear; cause-and-effect order, showing why something is happening and what impact it is having; problem–solution order, explaining a problem and giving a solution; motivated sequence, following the steps of attention, need, satisfaction, visualization, and action; and topical order, arranging the speech into subtopics.

The purpose of the introduction is to set the tone for the speech, introduce the topic, and get the audience's attention. Some attention-getting devices are using humor, giving personal examples, referring to the occasion, showing the importance of the subject, telling startling information, asking questions, and using quotations.

The speech conclusion should signal the audience that the speech is over and should tie all the ideas together. In their conclusions, speakers often summarize main ideas, use quotations, and inspire the audience to take further action.

Speech transitions help an audience follow where a speaker is going. They introduce main heads and may be written into the speech outline.

An outline is a way of organizing material to highlight all the parts and how they relate to the whole. In most cases, the body of the speech is what is outlined—the introduction and conclusion are handled separately.

The outline shows the organization as main and minor points through the use of standard symbols and indentation. Many speakers like to construct two outlines: a full-sentence outline for organizing the speech and a keyword outline to summarize the main ideas and to function as notes during delivery of the speech.

Your outline should be followed by a bibliography—a list of all the material from other sources that you have used in your speech. All the items should be presented in a standard bibliographical form.

The Internet is a source of a great deal of information on organizing and outlining oral presentations.

KEY TERMS AND CONCEPTS

Use the *Communicating Effectively* CD-ROM and the Online Learning Center at www.mhhe.com/hybels8 to further your understanding of the following terms.

Body (of speech) 318
Cause-and-effect order 320
Conclusion (of speech) 327
Full-sentence outline 330
Initial partition 323
Introduction (of speech) 323

Keyword outlines 330
Main points 316
Minor points 316
Motivated sequence 322
Outline 329
Problem–solution order 320

Reference list 330
Spatial order 319
Time order 318
Topical order 322
Transitions 328

CHAPTER REVIEW

QUESTIONS TO REVIEW

1. Can you tell the difference between an organized speech, presentation, lecture, or report and one that is not organized? What difference does this make in your attentiveness to the speaker? In your understanding of the information? In your overall evaluation of the effort?

2. Is organizing ideas difficult for you? Why or why not?

3. Which pattern of organization was most appealing to you? Why? Which seems to be the most difficult? Why?

4. How important are introductions in speeches? What purposes do they serve?

5. Is it true that if you grab the attention of listeners in the introduction to your speech, you will have their attention throughout the speech? Why or why not?

6. How are transitions used in a speech?

7. Have you ever been moved by a speech? What was it about the speech that moved you?

8. Do you think most speakers follow the examples set in the sample speech regarding outlining and organizing their ideas? Why or why not? What are the barriers or hindrances that restrain people from organizing their speech efforts as well as they could?

9. Faced with an upcoming speech that you have to prepare, do you ever feel overwhelmed with ideas and suggestions? What do you do in situations like that? Do you just go on and prepare in your own way? Or do you actually take and use as many new ideas and suggestions as you can, given the time you have to prepare your speech?

Go to the self-quizzes on the *Communicating Effectively* CD-ROM and the Online Learning Center at **www.mhhe.com/hybels8** to test your knowledge of the chapter contents.

CHAPTER 14

Delivering the Speech

OBJECTIVES

After reading this chapter, you should be able to:

- Distinguish among the four types of delivery.
- Use appearance, body movement, eye contact, facial expressions, and gestures to enhance your speech.
- Identify the elements that affect how you sound, and adjust them to improve your delivery.
- Use visual support for your speech.
- Apply the guidelines for constructing PowerPoint visual support for your speech.
- Place public-speaking anxiety in its proper perspective, and employ techniques to reduce or control it.
- Outline the steps to follow in rehearsing your speech.

TINA USED TO WAKE UP IN THE MIDDLE OF THE NIGHT WITH HER HEAD SPINNING with thoughts about a speech, book report, or presentation she had to give. She knew she was missing opportunities for personal advancement and achievement, but she had begun fleeing public speaking at an early age. By now her fears out-weighed any potential advantages.

She worried about possible failure, being asked a question she couldn't answer, or forgetting her place in her speech. She would awaken at night racked with apprehension about what might happen.

When Tina started to use specific techniques to help reduce her anxiety and fear, she gradually became much more relaxed and at ease. As a result, not only has she been able to sleep more peacefully, but when sudden fear wells up, she can now release that fear and anxiety and go back to sleep. But most important, she has been able to focus on the positive which has resulted in constructive improvement in her speaking preparation and delivery.

There is no magic formula for effectively delivering your speech. From your own observations of speakers, you know that the most effective ones often are those who use their natural gestures and idiosyncracies to their best advantage. Delivery is a highly personal matter, and because there is no standard form, the best advice is for speakers to tailor their speech to their own personal strengths and weaknesses. How do you discover your own personal strengths and weaknesses? Four ways will work: (1) gain experience; (2) engage in self-critiques; (3) listen to the advice, criticism, and suggestions of others; and (4) experiment and be willing to make the changes necessary to increase your effectiveness. Remember, only you control what works and what doesn't; use your control to your best advantage.

The United States Marine Corps has a wonderful saying that applies here: "Proper prior planning prevents poor performance." Just because there is no formula and no standard for effectively delivering your speech doesn't mean you shouldn't plan. First, rehearsal will certainly reduce anxiety and improve your performance. Second, there are always things you can do to enhance your message. And, third, don't forget that *how* you present is as important as *what* you present. If you have devoted yourself to the task of preparing an effective speech, as discussed in Chapter 12, then surely you will want to give the same attention to the way you present that information to your listeners.

STRATEGIC FLEXIBILITY

This is an opportunity to turn strategic flexibility toward your own natural talents and abilities and try to forecast, with as much accuracy, alertness, and appropriateness as possible, the skills and behaviors you need to call upon, with reference to specific speech occasions, to express yourself in the most advantageous, useful, powerful, and potent manner you can.

CHARACTERISTICS OF GOOD DELIVERY

A good speech can bring even more satisfaction to speakers than to listeners. There is nothing quite like the experience of communicating your ideas effectively, having them understood clearly, and feeling an entire audience respond to you in a positive way. Successful speakers love the "rush" they get from compelling performances.

Speaking to audiences is a skill you can learn if you are willing to discover and develop your personal strengths and weaknesses. Success in delivering a speech, however, cannot be defined as simply getting from the beginning to the end without suffering any major catastrophes. The key question is: "Does your delivery effectively do what it is intended to do?"

- Did you increase your listeners' understanding of your ideas?
- Did you successfully change the way they felt about an idea?

- Did you change their beliefs?
- Did you move them to action?

These are your goals, and all aspects of your delivery should contribute to achieving them.

Some potentially distracting elements can be controlled. For example, speakers who pace, pound the lectern, or jingle coins in their pockets draw the focus onto themselves rather than to their message. When his attention was brought to the strength of his accent and its effect on his Sunday messages, a newly hired interim pastor immediately sought help from a speech and language tutor, and, with the tutor's help, began to speak more slowly and more carefully articulated his words.

In the following section, the characteristics we will discuss include conversational quality, attentiveness, immediacy, and directness. Sections that follow consider other important elements as well such as how you look and how you sound. It is important to note at the outset that effective delivery does not rest in a single element. Effective delivery is a composite—a blend, mixture, or synthesis of all the elements combined into one impression.

Conversational Quality

When speakers are attentive, immediate, and direct, in most cases they will sound conversational. When you have a **conversational quality,** you talk to your audience in much the same way that you talk when you are having a conversation with another person. The value of sounding conversational in speaking is that you give the impression that you are talking *with* the audience rather than *at* it. In the next excerpt, notice how the speaker uses conversational language and the word *you* to involve his audience:

> *Have you ever felt embarrassed—I mean really embarrassed—where you never wanted to show your face in public again? Has your face ever turned red when lots of people were watching you? I would guess that you've had this experience once or twice in your life—I know I have. But—don't you ever wonder what happens to our bodies when we're embarrassed?*

How do you achieve a conversational tone in speaking? The most useful way, right from the planning stage, is to imagine giving your speech to one person or to a small group of people. Have a mental picture of this person or persons, and try to talk directly with him, her, or them in a normal, conversational manner. This will help you achieve the right tone.

There is an important caution, however: A conversational tone doesn't mean being casual. A speech occasion is more formal than most conversations. Even though you are aiming for a conversational tone, you shouldn't allow long pauses or use such conversational fillers as "OK" or "you know." You should also avoid some of the slang and "in" jokes or expressions you would use in casual conversation. Here are a few additional hints on how to achieve a conversational quality:

- Use contractions such as *don't, can't, isn't,* and *weren't.* They are more conversational than their two-word counterparts.
- Use words everyone will understand.
- Use an outline rather than writing out your speech word for word.

Attentiveness

You might wonder how a speaker could be inattentive to his or her own speech. Yet it's quite possible to be present and functioning as a body while not being there in spirit. You are so overcome with the mechanics and anxiety of giving a speech that you forget that doing so is basically a human encounter between a speaker and listeners.

Attentiveness means focusing on the moment, being aware of and responding to your listeners' needs. To ensure that you will be attentive to your audience, you can do a number of things:

1. *Pick a topic that is important to you.* If you are speaking on something of great interest and importance to you, it is likely that you will communicate your interest and enthusiasm to your audience. Also, if you can get involved in your subject, you are likely to feel less anxiety about giving your speech.

2. *Do all the work necessary to prepare the best speech possible.* If you work on your speech—organize and practice it—you will be much more confident about it and will feel less anxious when the time comes to give it. Then you will be able to concentrate on delivering your speech.

3. *Individualize your audience members.* Try to think of your audience as individual human beings rather than as a mass of people. As you give the speech, think: "I am going to talk to Kristen, who sits in the second row. Gabriel always looks like he is going to sleep. I am going to give a speech that will wake him up."

4. *Focus on the audience rather than on yourself.* As you speak, look for audience feedback and try to respond to it. The more you focus on the audience members and their needs, the less likely you are to feel anxiety.

Alberta followed these four guidelines when she gave her speech. She selected a topic, "Foster Care for Problem Kids," that was important to her; she did the work necessary to prepare the best speech she could; she looked at individual audience members as she delivered her speech; and she focused on listeners rather than on herself. At one point, noting some restlessness in her audience, she even added an unplanned anecdote to her speech.

Immediacy

Immediacy occurs when the communicator is completely focused on the communication situation. Assess the difference between the following two excerpts from student speeches. Which one appears more immediate, and why?

> *The way humans express themselves sexually is learned at a very young age, and throughout our lives we use very similar, if not the same, reoccurring patterns to express ourselves sexually. However, sexual expression is learned behavior, and it may not mean the same for everyone. To improve people's understanding of each other, it will help us to know how we develop sexual knowledge, feelings, and behaviors.*

This is the second excerpt, and it deals with a similar topic:

> *If you and I are like the average population, sexual activity among all of us here has occurred much earlier than ever before. There has been more pressure placed on us to have sex. You know that you and I can blame our peers, and we can blame the media as well. It doesn't really matter who or what is to blame, the fact is that along with this sexual activity, you and I must accept responsibility for our sexual behavior.*

Both excerpts are about the same length, and they both are about a topic that relates to listeners. But the first speaker uses the pronouns *we* and *our* and the word *people*. These choices are removed from listeners and noninvolving. The excerpt is abstract and lacks immediacy. The second speaker began and ended with *you and I* and even included it in the middle of this quotation; this closes the gap between speaker and audience. Notice, too, the second speaker's use of *here,* which reinforces the speaker's sense of the present. From just a casual reading of both excerpts, the second is more immediate, lively, and likely to hold audience attention.

Directness

Closely aligned with both attentiveness and immediacy is directness. **Directness** means being natural and straightforward. Your writing teachers have probably told you that you shouldn't choose big words if a small word says the same thing—that your goal is to communicate with readers, not to dazzle them with your vocabulary and knowledge of complicated grammatical structure. The same is true for a speech, only more so. Your audience is going to hear this speech only one time, so you have to be as specific and direct as possible.

The second goal in trying to achieve directness is to be straightforward. Being straightforward means selecting an effective specific purpose and a strong central idea. Then make all your points and examples relate to them.

Sometimes you come up with a wonderful idea or example, but you find that you can't relate it directly to the main point. One of the hardest things to do in speaking (or in writing) is to get rid of material that is fascinating or wonderful but doesn't work. However, it has to be dropped if it interferes with your directness. (Put it in a file folder and use it for something else another day.)

TYPES OF DELIVERY

There are essentially four methods of delivery: making impromptu remarks, speaking from a manuscript, memorizing the speech, and speaking extemporaneously from notes.

Impromptu Speaking

Impromptu speaking is the giving of a speech on the spur of the moment. Usually there is little or no time for preparation. Sometimes your instructor might ask you to give an impromptu speech in class. Other times you might be asked to give a toast or offer a prayer at a gathering, or you may make a few remarks at a meeting.

If you are asked to give an impromptu speech, the most important thing is not to panic. Your main goal is to think of a topic and organize it quickly in your head before you start to speak.

In finding a topic, look around you and consider the occasion. Is there anything you can refer to? Decorations? A friend? A photo that recalls a time together? Formal occasions usually honor someone or something, and the person or thing being honored can provide a focus for your speech: "I am delighted to be at this yearly meeting of documentary filmmakers. Documentary filmmaking is one of the noblest professions." Other times you might want to refer to the place or the people: "I am happy to be here in Akron again. The last time I was here . . ." or "I am very touched by the warm reception you have all given me."

In impromptu speaking it's essential to keep your remarks brief. No one expects you to speak for more than a minute or two. The audience knows that you are in a tight spot, and it doesn't expect a long and well-polished speech.

> If you are asked to give an impromptu speech, the most important thing is not to panic.

Speaking from a Manuscript

Speaking from a manuscript involves writing out the entire speech and reading it to the audience. When you read a speech, you can get a clear idea of how long it is, so manuscript speaking is a good method when exact timing is necessary. Because a manuscript also offers planned wording, political leaders often favor this method when they speak on sensitive issues and want control over what they say. When Louisa, for example, decided to run for president of the student government, she prepared a five-minute speech in manuscript form for her appearance on the campus television station with the other candidates. Louisa knew that having a manuscript would help her stay within her time limit and would also help her say exactly what she wanted to say. However, she knew that she had to be very familiar with the manuscript so that she could break away from it to look directly at the camera.

There are other reasons why some speakers feel it necessary to give a manuscript speech. For example, Lutie Eugenia Sterns, as reported by Brenda Knight, had a bad stammer, but she cared so much about the public library system, that she traveled the state of Wisconsin by train, buggy, and sleigh preaching about public libraries. Sterns wrote out her speeches to avoid the letters she had trouble with, but she was so effective that before she retired to campaign for women's suffrage she had established 101 free libraries and 1,480 traveling libraries—all this in the late nineteenth century.[1]

Speakers find that it is difficult to sound spontaneous when using a manuscript; if listeners think they are being read to, they are more likely to lose interest. Experienced speakers who use manuscripts are often so skilled at delivery that the audience is not aware the speech is being read. Beginning speakers, however, have difficulty making a manuscript speech sound spontaneous and natural.

Feedback is another problem in speaking from a manuscript. If the audience becomes bored and inattentive, it is difficult to respond and modify the speech; the speaker is bound to the manuscript. A manuscript also confines a speaker to the lectern—because that's where the manuscript is.

Speaking from Memory

Speaking from memory means writing out the entire speech and then committing it to memory word for word. It has the same advantages for speakers as the manuscript method: Exact wording can be planned, phrases and sentences can be crafted, and potential problems in language can be eliminated. Also, a memorized speech can be adapted to a set, inflexible time limit. Francisco, who was running against Louisa in the student election, decided to memorize his speech. He felt this was a good idea because he wanted exact wording, but he also wanted the freedom to move around. Feedback was not a problem to Francisco because he was speaking to a television audience via the campus's closed-circuit television station. In other situations, however, responding to feedback can be a problem because it is difficult for the speaker to get away from what he or she has memorized. A speaker who gets off track or is distracted may forget parts of the speech or lose his or her place.

A memorized speech can create considerable pressure. Not only does the speaker have to spend the time memorizing the speech, but he or she is also likely to worry about forgetting it. In addition, making a memorized speech sound natural and spontaneous requires considerable acting talent.

Extemporaneous Speaking

In the **extemporaneous speaking** method, a speaker delivers a speech from notes. The speaker might commit the main ideas of the speech to memory—possibly also the introduction and conclusion—but will rely on notes to remember most of the speech.

Extemporaneous speaking has several advantages. It permits flexibility so that a speaker can adjust to the feedback of listeners. For example, if a speaker sees that several audience members do not understand something, he or she can stop and explain. If the audience looks bored, the speaker can try moving around or using a visual aid earlier than planned. Extemporaneous speaking is the one method of delivery that comes closest to good conversation because a speaker can be natural and responsive to the audience.

One disadvantage of the extemporaneous method is that the speaker may stumble over or grope for words. However, much of this problem can be overcome by rehearsing the speech beforehand. Sometimes speakers want to use exact words or phrases. Although in extemporaneous speaking the speech as a whole is not memorized, there is nothing wrong with memorizing a particularly important sentence or having it written down and reading it from a note card.

For the beginning speaker, speaking extemporaneously is the best method of delivery. In addition to eliminating heavy burdens for the speaker (writing out or memorizing the speech), it enables a natural and spontaneous style of speaking. It also makes the listeners a central element in the speech, for the speaker is more free to respond to them.

STRATEGIC FLEXIBILITY
It is the extemporaneous type of delivery that makes the best use of on-the-spot strategic flexibility when you can use all the immediate, available, and obvious audience and situational cues to assess, evaluate, and select the skills and behaviors likely to have the greatest immediate impact on your listeners and apply them at once as you adjust, tailor, enhance, and fine-tune your communication.

HOW YOU LOOK

Appearance

As you rise from your chair and walk to the lectern to give your speech, the audience's first impression of you will come from how you look. Audience members will notice how you are dressed, if you walk to the lectern with confidence, and whether you look interested in giving this speech.

On days when you are going to make a speech, it is a good idea to look your best. Not only does looking good give the audience a positive impression of you, but it also gives you a psychological boost. Deanna D. Sellnow and Kristen P. Treinen, in a research article "The Role of Gender in Perceived Speaker Competence," discovered that being sloppily dressed had a greater negative impact on audiences than being casually or formally dressed had a positive one.[2]

Try to stay away from clothing that might distract from your speech. For example, avoid T-shirts with writing on them and accessories you might be tempted to play with.

If it's a formal occasion, wear dress-up clothing; if it's informal, wear what you think everyone else will wear. If you don't know what others will be wearing, ask the person who has invited you to speak.

Body Language

A speaker who uses some movement is likely to attract more attention than a speaker who stands absolutely still. Of course, this does not mean that all movement is good. To be effective, your movement should be carefully coordinated with your speech. For example, if you want to stress your most important point, you might indicate this nonverbally by moving closer to your audience. If you want to create intimacy between you and your audience as you are telling a personal story, you could sit on the edge of the desk for a brief period.

Avoid movement that might be distracting. Probably you have seen a speaker (or teacher) who paces back and forth in front of the room. This movement is not motivated by anything other than habit or nervousness: as a result, it's ineffective.

Eye Contact

In North American culture it is considered extremely important to look into the eyes of the person you are talking to. If you don't, you are at risk of being considered dishonest or of being seen as having something to hide. However, there are sharp differences between cultures. Eye behavior varies according to the environment in which it is learned.

Careful audience analysis may uncover differences in other areas of nonverbal communication, language, rules of social situations, social relationships, and even motivation.[3] Be sensitive to these, and when you are an audience member be careful about judging speakers from other cultures by standards that they have not learned and to which they do not personally subscribe.

Facial Expression

Because speakers are their own most important visual support, listeners have every reason to expect an expressive face and voice. By using a mirror or videotape, you have a chance to see your own face and to know what you are expressing. If you don't look like someone you would like to listen to, obviously facial expression is an area you would need to work on. Since facial expressions often mirror attitude, perhaps you need to change your attitude. Rather than thinking of giving the speech as an assignment, a chore, or more busywork, think of it as a legitimate opportunity to share some important information with people who really care. If you think such a change in attitude doesn't matter, you may be surprised by a negative listener reaction.

Gestures

When we speak, we usually use hand and arm gestures to express or emphasize ideas or emotions. The best way to add more gestures to your speech is to practice in front of a mirror. Always aim for gestures that look spontaneous and that feel natural to you.

Posture

The way you sit in your seat, rise and walk to the lectern, and return to your seat after the speech, can leave as much of an impression as the posture you use during your speech. Because we don't have a very good sense of how we look to others, a speech class is a great opportunity to get some feedback. Try to listen to critical remarks from your instructor and classmates without feeling defensive. If you can learn from your mistakes, you will improve every time you give a speech.

HOW YOU SOUND

When members of a speech class have a chance to see themselves on videotape, most of them react more negatively to the way they sound than to the way they look. Few people really like their own voices.

Our voices reveal things about us that might be far more important than the words we speak.[4] How loud, how fast, how clear and distinct the message—all are part of the information we send about ourselves.

The voice is also a powerful instrument of communication. Because it is so flexible, you can vary it to get the effect you want. You can speak in a loud voice and then drop to a mere whisper. You can go through basic information quickly and then slow down to make a new and important point. You can even use your voice to bring about a change of character. Notice how your favorite actor or comedian uses many different voices.

Volume

You probably need to speak in a louder voice than you feel comfortable with. Always check out the back row to see whether people can hear you. Generally you can tell if they are straining to hear you, and often they will give you some nonverbal sign (like leaning forward or cupping a hand behind an ear) that you need to speak louder. If the place in which you are speaking is unusually large, ask whether people in the back can hear. If people have to strain to hear you, they probably will not make the effort unless you have something extraordinary to say.

Using a Microphone

The rules for using microphones are simple: Make sure they are turned on, and don't blow into them to see if they work. If the microphone is a stationary one, make certain it is adjusted to your height, and stand 8 to 12 inches away from it while you speak. You should not have to lean down or over to speak into it. If you have attached a small microphone to your clothing, you will want to test it first to see whether everyone can hear you. Also, in one auditorium, whenever the speaker moved in front of one of the side speakers, there was a loud reverberation. This is another reason for checking out the facilities and equipment before giving a speech.

Pace

Like volume, pace is easy to vary. **Pace** refers to how fast or how slowly a person speaks. If you speak too fast, you may be difficult to understand. If you speak too slowly, you risk losing the attention of your audience. If audience attention seems to be drifting away, try picking up your pace. Usually speakers don't know that they have been going too fast until someone tells them so after the speech is over.

Ideally a speaker varies his or her pace. Speaking fast and then slowing down helps keep the attention of the audience. Also, don't forget the benefits of pausing. Making a pause before or after a dramatic moment is a highly effective technique. The next time you are watching a comedian on television, notice how he or she uses pauses.

Pitch and Inflection

As we noted in Chapter 6, pitch is the range of tones used in speaking. **Inflection** is a related concept. It refers to the change in pitch used to emphasize certain words and phrases. A person who never varies his or her speaking voice is said to speak in a **monotone.**

If you listen to professional newscasters or sportscasters, you will discover that they use a lot of inflection. By emphasizing certain words and phrases, they help direct listeners' attention to what is important.

Try reading the following sentence, emphasizing a different word each time you read it; you should be able to read it in at least eight different ways:

You mean I have to be there at seven tomorrow?

The best way to get inflection in your voice is to stress certain words deliberately—even to the point of exaggeration. Try taping something in your normal voice and then in your "exaggerated" voice. You might be surprised to find that the exaggerated voice is more interesting.

Enunciation

Enunciation is made up of articulation and pronunciation. **Articulation** is the ability to pronounce the letters in a word correctly; **pronunciation** is the ability to pronounce the whole word. Not only does good enunciation enable people to understand us, but it is also the mark of an educated person.

Three common causes of articulation problems are sound substitution, omission of sounds, and slurring. Sound substitution is very common. Many people say "dere," "dem," and "dose" for *there, them,* and *those.* In this case a *d* is substituted for the more difficult *th* sound. The substitution of a *d* for a *t* in the middle of a word is widespread in American English. If you need any proof, try pronouncing these words as you usually do: *water, butter, thirty, bottle.* Unless you have very good articulation, you probably said "wader," "budder," "thirdy," and "boddle."

Some people believe they have a speech defect that prevents them from producing certain sounds. This can be easily checked. For example, if you always say "dere" for *there,* make a special effort to make the *th* sound. If you are able to make it, you have a bad habit, not a speech defect.

People also commonly omit sounds. For example, some people say "libary" for *library,* and some frequently omit sounds that occur at the ends of words, saying "goin" for *going* and "doin" for *doing.*

Slurring is caused by running words together, as in such phrases as "Yawanna go?" and "I'll meecha there." Slurring, as with other articulation problems, is usually a matter of bad speech habits, and it can be overcome with some effort and practice.

Once you are aware of a particular articulation habit, you can try to change it. Sometimes it helps to drill, using lists of words that give you trouble. It also helps to have a friend remind you when you mispronounce a word. If you are in doubt about how to pronounce a word, look it up in the dictionary. The Internet offers pronunciating dictionaries where you can hear the proper pronunciation.

USING VISUAL SUPPORT

Visual support includes devices such as charts, graphs, slides, and computer-generated images that help illustrate the key points in a speech. Visual support serves four functions: It helps hold the attention of listeners, it provides information in the visual channel, it helps audience members remember what speakers have said, and it helps speakers in several ways. Visual support often helps speakers by:

1. providing another means for supporting or illustrating content.
2. adding an attention-grasping element to the speech.
3. giving them a chance to move around or demonstrate.
4. offering them assistance in remembering their information.

According to one study, if audience members are given only verbal information, after three days they remember a mere 10 percent of what they were told. If they are shown material without verbal communication, they remember 35 percent of what they see. However, if both verbal and visual information is provided, listeners remember 65 percent after three days. But just because you have visual support does not mean that audience members will automatically give you their attention. Poorly designed or inappropriate visual materials will not keep listeners' attention.

Types of Visual Support

Your visual material should help make your topic lively and interesting to the audience. There are numerous types of visual support to choose from. In making your choice, ask yourself which kind of visual material would best illustrate your topic and appeal to your listeners.

The Chalkboard (or Whiteboard)

Since a chalkboard (or whiteboard) exists in every classroom, it is the most accessible visual support. It works particularly well for writing keywords or phrases, drawing very simple diagrams, and giving URLs (Web addresses) for speech material.

When you use the board, it's important that you write quickly to avoid having your back to the audience any longer than necessary. Once you have the word or diagram on the board, turn around, stand next to it, and as you explain, point to it with your hand. Make sure that your writing is large and clear enough for the entire audience to read.

The Actual Object

Sometimes it is useful to use the thing you are talking about as visual support. Audience members like to see what you are talking about, especially if the object is not familiar to them. One student brought a violin and a viola to class to demonstrate the differences in the sounds and the looks of the two instruments. Another, explaining how to make minor adjustments on one's car, brought a carburetor. Still another borrowed a skeleton from the biology department to illustrate a speech on osteoporosis, a bone disease.

Models

A **model** is a replica of an actual object that is used when the object itself is too large to be displayed (a building), too small to be seen (a cell), or inaccessible to the eye (the human heart). A model can be very effective visual support because it shows exactly how something looks. It is better than a picture because it is three-dimensional. A student who was discussing airplanes used in warfare brought in models of planes he had constructed.

Posters, Diagrams, and Charts

A poster consists of lettering or pictures, or both. The purpose of a poster is to enhance the speaker's subject. For example, when speaking about the style of electric cars, a student used a poster showing pictures of one make to show how the batteries had been incorporated into the overall design of the car. A poster may also be used to emphasize the keywords or important thoughts in a speech. A student who spoke on how to save money on clothes used a poster to list the following points:

- Decide on a basic color.
- Buy basics at one store.
- Buy accessories at sales.

Not only did the poster provide the audience with a way to remember the points, but it also gave, in visual form, the general outline of the speech.

A diagram may range from a simple organizational chart to a complex rendering of a three-dimensional object. Diagrams are particularly valuable in showing how something works. For example, in a speech about storing toxic wastes, a student used the diagram in Figure 14-1 to show how waste can be stored in a salt cavern. Including a drawing of the Empire State Building was particularly useful because it gave the viewer an idea of the depth of the mine.

An **organizational chart** shows the relationships among the elements of an organization, such as the departments of a company, the branches of federal or state government, or the committees of the student government. Note how a speaker used the organizational chart in Figure 14-2 to show how the academic side of a university is organized and how a student wishing to express dissatisfaction should approach people in a specific order, beginning with a faculty member.

A **flip chart** is a series of pictures, words, diagrams, and so forth. It's called a "flip chart" because it is made up of several pages that you flip through. A flip chart is best used when you have a complicated subject that needs several illustrations or when you want to emphasize several points in your speech.

Tables and Graphs

Tables and graphs are easy to prepare and can condense a lot of information into a useful, understandable form. Perhaps most important, anyone can make this visual support because no special skills are required. With the use of a computer, creating tables, putting information into the tables, changing the tables, and creating titles for the tables can be accomplished through the click of a mouse.

Figure 14-1
One Cavern's Size

Tables are columns of figures arranged in an order that enables the viewer to easily pick out the information needed. For example, when Rosa Amin spoke to her class on the topic "Living Alone," she used a simple table to illustrate problems associated with creating a budget. She said, "My monthly budget is divided into these things" and pointed to the table (see Table 14-1). "This represents costs of $1,360 a month," said Rosa. "I work 30 hours a week at the library for $8 an hour, for which I receive $960 a month. I am fortunate to receive an allowance from my parents of $100 a week, or $400 a month—while I am in school—which brings my monthly income to $1,360. So, if I can stick to my very strict budget, I am able to just break even each month. Often, I can cut corners on food, clothing, school supplies, and entertainment— and then I can sometimes realize a monthly savings," Rosa said.

Figure 14-2
Organizational Chart

Faculty Member → Department Head → Dean → Vice President for Academic Affairs

Table 14-1 — **Rosa's Budget: Expenses**

Rent	$ 300
Car payment	250
Food	300
Utilities	100
Clothing	100
Books/school supplies	100
Entertainment	100
Savings	60
Miscellaneous	50
Total	$1,360

Graphs are used to present statistical material in a visual form that helps viewers see similarities, differences, relationships, or trends. There are three commonly used types of graphs: bar, pie, and line. If you want to see a variety of the graphs available, look in any issue of *USA Today*. The bar graph in Figure 14-3—as the source notes—is from one of these graphs.

A line graph is particularly useful for showing trends over a period of time or for making comparisons. For example, Figure 14-4 shows how many people were online as of February 2002; however, the source notes that "The art of estimating how many are online throughout the world is an inexact one at best. Surveys abound, using all sorts of measurement parameters."[5] So, how did ComputerScope Ltd. get its results? "From observing many of the published surveys over the last two years, here is an 'educated guess' as to how many are online worldwide."[6]

Figure 14-3

List of Things That People Fear

Source: "Snakes Scarier than Public Speaking" (USA TODAY Snapshots), *USA Today*, March 26, 2001, p. 1. From a Gallup Poll of 1,016 adults February 19–21, 2001; margin of error +/– 3 percentage points.

Category	Percent
Snakes	51%
Public Speaking	40%
Heights	35%
Being closed in small spaces	34%
Spiders and insects	25%
Needles and getting shots	21%
Mice	19%
Flying on an airplane	17%

Figure 14-4

More than 606 Million Internet Users in Year 2005

Source: *How Many Online?* ComputerScope, Ltd., Scope Communications Group, Prospect House, 3 Prospect Road, Dublin 9, Ireland. Retrieved October 28, 2005, from http://www.nua.ie/surveys/how_many_online/

In a speech titled "Let's All Read," Martin used the pie graph in Figure 14-5 to illustrate the fact that nearly half the nation's population doesn't buy books, much less read them.

Computer Graphics

The computer offers numerous options to speakers. The phrase **computer-generated graphics** refers to any images created or manipulated via computer—art, drawings, representations of objects, pictures, and the like. If you want to create a graph or some other piece of visual support, a computer with a graphics program can generate it. Computers are best for processing numerical data and then converting that data into bar, line, or pie graphs. Having a computer-generated graph enlarged is a relatively simple, inexpensive process; photocopiers can enlarge images, sometimes to 200 percent of the original size.

The average computer user may not yet have the capacity to produce visuals like those seen on television—which often cost thousands of dollars to produce—but well-thought-out visuals, projected on a screen or a computer, can give your presentation a professional and sophisticated look. And the computer software available today can make even the simplest attempt at slide production extremely professional looking.

Perhaps the most important advice regarding your slides is to make them readable. Follow the "6 × 6 rule." Use no more than six words horizontally, and use no more than

Nearly Half the Nation Doesn't Buy Books

- No Books: 48%
- 1–10 Books: 38.2%
- 11–24 Books: 9%
- 25 Plus Books: 4.1%

Figure 14-5
Pie Graph

six items on a page—less than that, if possible. This will result in a slide that conveys its meaning readily, and it will help ensure that the slide can be seen by the people farthest away. Here, we'll apply the 6 × 6 rule in a bulleted list:

- Keep text larger than 18 points.
- 44 points = titles; 32 = text; 28 = subtext.
- Use no more than three fonts.
- Use dark background and bright text.
- Overheads need light background, dark text.
- Insert tables and graphs when appropriate.

One essential element in any slide presentation is visual variety. How do you obtain variety? You can use diagrams, flowcharts, and graphs to illustrate your ideas. Most software packages offer opportunities to obtain variety. There are clip-art packages that allow you to insert professional-quality graphics into your slides. There are numerous Internet sources where clip art can be downloaded free. With a scanner, you can add cartoons, magazine and newspaper headlines, and photographs. To keep the focus of listener attention on you, not the slides, occasionally intersperse a slide without words or pictures to give audience members a chance to refocus their attention, and concentrate on your textual message.

You can get additional visual variety through the use of **multimedia**—various media (sound, graphics, and animation, as well as text) used to deliver information. You can liven up your message with pictures and music, but you need to be cautious, especially if you are a beginner. Aim for just enough graphics, sound, and animation to support, elaborate, and focus the point of your message without risk of obscuring or overwhelming your point.

The techniques combining CDs with television and computers and computer-generated graphics with video cameras bring sophisticated capabilities to the nonprofessional as well as the professional speaker: Many of these resources are already being used in high-quality workplace speeches and sales presentations. Check to see if you have access to such technology.

PowerPoint

One of the most widely used software programs is Microsoft's PowerPoint (PP). Its popularity results from three benefits: (1) It provides tools for creative multimedia presentations that combine text, graphics, video, and sound; (2) it lends itself to a wide variety of speech applications; and (3) it is easy to use.

The most important guideline for the successful use of PP is to treat it as an aid, or, as one component of a speech. A great PP presentation should enhance your information, *never* take its place. Thus, when you use PP, you should:

- Use bullets, not numbers. (Never include full paragraphs of text.)
- Put no more than one topic on a slide.
- Use the 6 × 6 rule already discussed.
- Select a readable typeface and size. Use a minimum 36-point font for titles, and 24 points for the other information. Avoid using all caps; it makes it look like you're shouting.
- Use the same colors consistently throughout the presentation. Always choose light letters on a dark background.

The key to an effective PowerPoint presentation is to plan for simplicity and clarity.

- Keep the background simple and allow plenty of space around words and images.
- Include a combination of words, pictures, and graphics. It is this kind of variety that keeps the presentation interesting.

Remember, computer-generated graphics and multimedia are props that should support and enhance your main ideas, not take their place. It is you—the main actor, speaker, and focus of the speech—who must engage your listeners.

Videos

If you decide to use a video to support your speech, you have two choices: You can use one made by other people, or you can make your own. If you are making a long speech, a preprogrammed video can be a very good visual reinforcement of what you are saying. A student who gave a speech on how applicants are propagandized by college admission tapes followed her speech with the college's own admissions video. The students were amazed at the difference between their perception of the college and the tape's portrayal of it.

If you have access to your own video camera, you can make your own tape and customize it to match your subject and your audience. One student made a videotape illustrating four basic karate moves for his speech. Because video is so easy to work with, he was able to stop the tape, talk about each move, and then go on to the next one.

Handouts

When material is complex or when there is a lot of it, audience members may need a handout. For example, a student who spoke about the calories in fast foods gave audience members a handout showing the caloric values of specific foods. Other times a handout is useful to reinforce the points you are making in your speech. A student who spoke about 10 ways to recycle made a handout of her main points and distributed it at the end of her speech.

If you use handouts, choose the best time to pass them out. If you distribute your handouts too early, the audience will read them and ignore you. Also, most people dislike having a handout read to them. If your handout repeats the points you are making, give it out when your speech is over.

Rules for Using Visual Support

- *Use visual support to supplement, not replace, the speech.* The visual support should not become the whole show. It should be a useful addition to reinforce the speech.
- *Show the visual support only when you are ready for it.* Put the visual in an inconspicuous place; then, when you are ready to use it, take it out. When you are finished with it, put it away. You don't want it to compete with you for attention.
- *Before your speech, check the room to see if your visual support can be easily displayed.* If you are using projection equipment, find the electric outlets and see if the room has blackout shades or curtains. If you are hanging a chart, decide how to hang it. Are you going to need tape or thumbtacks?
- *Practice with your visual support before the speech.* Practice using equipment until you can operate it quickly and easily. Check to see how much time your visual support takes. If it is going to take too much time, decide how you will cut back.
- *Talk to the audience, not to the visual.* You may need to look at your visual occasionally, but remember to maintain eye contact with the audience.

PUBLIC SPEAKING ANXIETY

Public-speaking anxiety is a disturbance of mind regarding a forthcoming public-speaking event for which you are the speaker. The fear is nearly universal, yet it obviously does not prevent successful speeches. There are a number of things to remember when coping with public-speaking anxiety.

Experienced public speakers get nervous before a presentation. There are stories of extreme public-speaking anxiety among some of our most successful and experienced politicians, evangelists, and entertainers including Franklin Roosevelt, Ronald Reagan, Billy Graham, Jane Fonda, Lily Tomlin, Barbra Streisand, Cher, Donald Sutherland, and Donny Osmond. Winston Churchill, one of the most famous diplomats and orators of the twentieth century, fainted the first time he gave a speech.

Nerves do not need to be your enemy. Being nervous can work to your advantage. It can give you the added boost of energy that animates you and helps give your message assurance and enthusiasm.

No matter how nervous you are, you are probably the only one who knows it.

As long as you act like you are confident and play the role of a secure and knowledgeable speaker, you will be in command of the public-speaking situation.

A Good Place to Begin

An important philosophy to help you deliver your ideas with confidence is to focus on your speech as a communication *task, not* a performance.[7] (See Table 14-2.) "Most speakers with stage fright view speeches as *performances*."[8]

"The goals, attitudes, and behaviors that make for effective public speaking are in fact more like those of ordinary communication encounters than of public performances."[9] Mentally connecting public speaking with daily communication episodes, *not* performances, has several advantages. First, it means that all those negative past public

Table 14-2 Speaker-Perceived Differences between a Communication Orientation and a Performance Orientation

Communication Orientation	Performance Orientation
Goal: to share ideas with an audience	Goal: to satisfy an audience of critics
Audience interested in what the speaker has to say	Audience interested in analyzing and criticizing your performance
Similar to everyday conversation	Formal talk
Normal, natural behavior	Put-on, artificial behavior
Common, ordinary, average	Extraordinary, exceptional, unusual
Familiar circumstances	Unfamiliar circumstances
Reveals genuine and true expression of self	Must follow proper behaviors to be correct
Results depend on whether or not you shared your message	Results depend on polish, eloquence, and refinement

performances you may have had—from elementary school through high school—can be deleted from your memory.

Second, you do not have to memorize your material. Performances create anxiety because of the fear of forgetting words, thoughts, or your place in the speech. Seldom do you have memory blocks during conversations with others. Third, you can focus on your *real* purpose in speaking to your audience—getting your listeners to accept and understand your information or change their attitude or actions. "The typical speech audience," says Motley, "is more interested in hearing what you have to say than in evaluating your performance skills."[10]

Figure 14-6 will help you achieve a conversational orientation. A performance orientation causes an emphasis on put-on, artificial behavior (undue emphasis on self), whereas in conversations, you are seldom looking at yourself at all.

Other Strategies for Reducing Anxiety

There is no single, surefire formula that reduces every person's anxiety before a speech. Here are a few more suggestions.

- *Dress in comfortable clothes.* Wear clothes you feel at ease in—but clothes that show you have made some kind of special effort for the speech. Psychologically, it is important to feel confident and in control.
- *Practice positive self-talk.* Whenever a negative idea appears ("I'll never get through this speech"), replace it with a positive one ("I'm feeling nervous, but that won't stop me from doing a good job"). Don't give yourself any negative messages. Don't say, "I know I'm going to blow it" or "I'm so nervous I'll lose my voice."

STRATEGIC FLEXIBILITY

The change from a performance orientation to a communication orientation can have a significant effect on the strategic flexibility framework. When you anticipate, assess, and evaluate the factors, elements, and conditions of situations, the behaviors that are likely to have the greatest impact should have as their goal sharing ideas with listeners in normal, natural, common, ordinary ways that reveal the genuine and true expression of your self.

Figure 14-6
To Help Prevent Last-Minute Choking

Stop looking in at yourself.

Quiet your mind by reducing the amount of self-chatter.

Stop defending your ego against failure and criticism. (Threats to your ego have no real implications.)

Practice self-compassion. When failures, setbacks, and losses occur, be gentle with yourself.

Don't overfeed the self by chronically setting and pursuing goals.

Stop being preoccupied with yourself.

Sources: Based on Leary, Mark (2004, July/August), "Get Over Yourself!" by Mark Leary, July/August 2004, *Psychology Today*, p. 65. The information in this figure comes from a column within this article, titled "Quieting the Self." (Dr. Leary is the chair of the psychology department at Wake Forest University.)

- *Be well prepared.* Do not wait until the last moment to put your speech together.
- *Concentrate on your message.* Think about really communicating with your listeners about your important message. The point is to take your focus from yourself and aim it at the message and toward your listeners.
- *Picture yourself doing well.* If you can imagine yourself walking to the front of the room, speaking to a responsive audience, hearing your words flow without hesitation, and receiving a positive response from listeners, you have a visual image of success.
- *If your anxiety is high, ask your instructor if you can speak first or second.* Being among the first to speak means you have less time to worry.
- *Take several deep breaths on the way to the front of the room.* An increased respiratory rate because of nervousness can cause you to feel short of breath. Taking several deep breaths can break this cycle and have a calming effect.
- *Remember that your audience is made up of people just like you.* They want you to do well; they are supportive.
- *If possible, move around.* Moving releases nervous energy and restores a feeling of calm. Try to gesture and move when you use transitions and personal examples.
- *Pick out friendly faces, and make eye contact with these people.* An encouraging, supportive expression on a listener's face can do wonders to promote confidence and reassure speakers.
- *Give yourself a reward after your speech, and congratulate yourself for having succeeded.* Even though your speech may not have been perfect, remind yourself that you were able to do it. Remember, you're human, and humans aren't perfect.

REHEARSING YOUR SPEECH

You may be hesitant to rehearse because you feel silly talking to an empty room. Yet if you go into a store to buy a new piece of clothing, you probably spend a lot of time in the dressing room looking at it from several angles. By rehearsing a speech, you are doing the same thing: You are trying it on to see if it fits; if it doesn't, you will have time to make the necessary alterations.

How can you rehearse delivery so that you will feel comfortable with the content and language of your speech and yet not get so locked in that your words sound memorized or mechanical? Below is a plan that seems to work well for most speakers.

Preparing Your Speech

Before you give your speech in a rehearsal session, you should do the following:

1. Prepare the content thoroughly. Your speech will be no better than the effort you've put into it. Do you have a clear statement of purpose? Do the materials you have collected support this statement of purpose? Have you done enough research to provide support for each of your main points?
2. Organize your content into a full-sentence outline. Have you made the proper distinction between main idea and supporting points? Does your outline flow clearly and logically? Are you quite clear about what you are going to say in your introduction and conclusion? Is your conclusion worded in such a way that you can end the speech and sit down without feeling awkward?

3. From your full-sentence outline, prepare a keyword or short-phrase outline that you can use while you rehearse and also while you give your speech. Put your keyword outline on a series of 3 × 5-inch cards using one side only. Can you follow the speech from this outline? Have you written out phrases, quotations, or sources that you want to quote precisely? Can you read the cards easily?

Trying Out Your Speech

STRATEGIC FLEXIBILITY

Trying out your speech is an opportunity to put the entire strategic flexibility framework into action as you anticipate your forthcoming speech situation; assess its factors, elements, and conditions; evaluate them, then carefully select from your repertoire of available skills and behaviors those likely to have the greatest impact; apply those in your rehearsal sessions; then reassess, reevaluate, and *make any adjustments* before you come before your listeners.

During the tryout sessions, focus on the content of the speech and whether it is working the way you imagined it would. Actually say the words—stop to clear up imprecise language, maybe add a transition, try out the conclusion. It will take you a while to get through the speech because you will be making corrections as you go along—especially the very first time.

Daniel Schacter, in his book *The Seven Sins of Memory*, states that "Everyday experience and laboratory studies reveal that emotionally charged incidents are better remembered than nonemotional events."[11] This means that if you have selected a subject that you care about or one you can become emotional about, you are far more likely to remember your ideas. As you are trying out your speech, give the content and the way you have structured and phrased your ideas your special attention.

One other technique to use when trying out your speech is visualization—the deliberate attempt to see your successful performance in your mind's eye.[12] Charles Manz and Henry Sims, Jr. state, "Visualization may be particularly useful the next time you make a speech or deliver a briefing. Try to engage in a mental rehearsal by visualizing yourself delivering the speech in a very effective manner."[13]

Rehearsing Actual Delivery

The next stage is to actually deliver the speech. As you practice your delivery, try to imagine an audience. If you videotape your rehearsal you will be able to evaluate your performance using the Assess Yourself at the end of this chapter.

1. Stand against one wall and look over your "audience." Remember to establish eye contact with people in all parts of the room.

2. Check your starting time. In this practice session you want to find out how long your speech is.

3. Deliver the speech all the way through without stopping. As you speak, remember to look at your audience.

4. When the speech is over, check your ending time.

5. Analyze your performance: Did any parts of the speech give you difficulty? Did the speech seem clearly organized? Check your outline. In giving the speech, did you leave anything out? Was your outline clear and easy to follow? How about time? Do you need to add or delete any material to make the speech the proper length?

6. Make the necessary changes, and rehearse the speech again.

Consider This

Many speakers think their work is done after they say the final words of their conclusion. However, some of the most valuable work begins *after* the speech is over. This is the time to ask whether you reached your goal and to discover what effect you had on your listeners. Here are some questions that you need to ask yourself after you give a speech:

1. Did I follow the plan for my speech? Did I stick to my outline and cover the material I wanted to cover? Did I keep my central idea in mind?
2. Was my speech completed in the time allotted? If it was too long, did I go too slowly or did I have too much material? If it was too short, did I talk too fast or did I have too little material?
3. Did I pay attention to my audience? Do I have a sense of how audience members responded to my speech? If they started losing interest, did I do anything to try to reengage them?
4. Did I make eye contact with the audience? Was I conscious of using appropriate gestures to make certain points?
5. Did I have a well-defined conclusion? Did I communicate to my audience that the speech was finished?
6. The next time I speak, what things should I change?

Your answers to these questions should help you improve every time you get up to speak. Remember, the goal of your speech communication class is to make you an effective communicator. Reaching this goal involves having the information that will help you improve, but it also involves your putting this information to work for you.

You should rehearse delivering the speech until you feel comfortable with it. As you rehearse, try to use wording that sounds natural to you. Every time you speak, your wording should be a little bit different—otherwise, your speech will sound mechanical. Also, as you rehearse, you should become less and less dependent on your notes. Try to consult them as little as possible.

If you think you will need a lot of time to feel comfortable with your speech, it is better not to rehearse it all at once. Put the speech away for a few hours or even overnight. The next time you approach it, you may be surprised to find fresh ideas or ways of solving problems that hadn't occurred to you before.

THE INTERNET AND DELIVERING THE SPEECH

It won't take you long to discover how much material about speech delivery you can find in the Internet. The following four sources will provide you with examples of the range available.

- [No author]. (n.d.). *Fastfacts: Managing nervousness during oral presentations*. The Learning Commons, University of Guelph, Ontario, Canada. Retrieved October 28, 2005, from **http://www.learningcommons.uoguelph.ca/ByTopic/Learning/Learning General/LearningGeneralLearningFastfacts/Fastfacts-ManagingNervousness.html.** Topics include "Nervousness: Causes and Cures," "Choosing a Topic," "Preparation," "Rehearsal," "Performance Strategies," and "Your Best Resource."

- St. John, Ron. (2002). *Preparing speeches*. Speech Department, the University of Hawaii at Maui, Community College. Retrieved October 28, 2005, from **http: www.hawaii.edu/mauispeech/utml/preparing_speeches.html.** This is one of the most complete Web sites on speech preparation available on the Internet. There are also a number of sample speeches that you can both look at and listen to.

- Tracy, Larry. (2003). *How "fear of speaking" can make you a better speaker*. Web-Source.net. Retrieved October 28, 2005, from **http://www.web-source. net/web_development/public_speaking.htm.** This is an excellent site full of support and encouragement.

- [No author]. (n.d.). *Visual support.* University of Pennsylvania. Retrieved October 28, 2005, from **http://www.sas.upenn.edu/cwic/docs/vs1.doc.** Though it is brief, this is one of the most complete explanations of visual support found on the Web.

Here are two Web sites helpful in managing stress.

- [No author]. (n.d.). *Stress management.* Counseling Center, University of Illinois, at Urbana–Champaign. Retrieved October 28, 2005, from **http://www.couns.uiuc.edu/Brochurse/stress.htm.** This site tells you what stress is, how you can eliminate it, and how you can manage it better through the use of six areas of influence.

- [No author]. (2005, September 6). *Stress management techniques.* Self Help Counseling Center, Texas Woman's University. Retrieved October 28, 2005, from **http://www.twu.edu/o-sl/counseling/SH009.html.** This is a straightforward listing of 52 strategies for managing stress.

Assess Yourself

Delivery Self-Evaluation Form

How effective is your delivery? For each question write the numerical score that best represents your delivery using the following criteria: 7 = Outstanding; 6 = Excellent; 5 = Very good; 4 = Average (good); 3 = Fair; 2 = Poor; 1 = Minimal ability; 0 = No ability demonstrated. Use this form as you assess, evaluate, and critique the rehearsal you videotape for your speech.

1. Did you demonstrate a conversational quality? _____
2. Did you focus on the moment by being aware of and focusing on your listeners' needs? _____
3. Were you completely focused on the communication situation? _____
4. Were you natural and straightforward? _____
5. Did you deliver your speech extemporaneously—showing your natural responsiveness to your listeners without depending on your notes? _____
6. Did you appear spontaneous and not rehearsed or reading your notes? _____
7. Was your attire appropriate for the occasion? _____
8. Were your body movements appropriate and not distracting? _____
9. Did you look into the eyes of individual audience members? _____
10. Did your face appear expressive and yet natural? _____
11. Did your gestures appear natural, comfortable, and spontaneous? _____
12. Did your posture help reinforce a positive, alert impression? _____
13. Did you speak loudly enough, and yet not too loud? _____
14. Was your pace or rate of speaking varied and, thus, not monotonous? _____
15. Did your voice and inflection reveal emphasis and variety when needed? _____
16. Did you reveal proper and effective enunciation (both articulation and pronunciation)? _____

TOTAL POINTS: _____

Go to the *Communicating Effectively* CD-ROM and the Online Learning Center at www.mhhe.com/hybels8 to see your results and learn how to evaluate your attitudes and feelings.

mhhe.com/hybels8

CHAPTER REVIEW

SUMMARY

To achieve effective delivery, speakers need to tailor their speech to their own strengths and weaknesses by gaining experience, engaging in self-critiques, listening to the advice of others, and experimenting and making the necessary changes.

Good delivery involves, first and foremost, achieving a conversational quality. But, the bottom line is, "Does your delivery effectively do what you intend it to do?"

The four ways of delivering a speech are speaking impromptu, with very little preparation; speaking from a manuscript; speaking from memory; and speaking extemporaneously, from notes.

Speakers should concentrate on what they wear and on their body movement, eye contact, gestures, and posture so that they appear at their very best and, thus, their appearance does not distract in any way from their message. Speakers should also pay special attention to volume, pace, pitch and inflection, and enunciation.

Visuals help hold attention and clarify information. Common types of visual support include the actual object, models, chalkboards and whiteboards, posters, diagrams, charts, tables, graphs, computer-generated graphics, PowerPoint presentations, videos, and handouts. When using visual support, make sure that it can be easily seen, enhances the speech rather than overpowers it, and never takes the place of the speaker but reinforces and underscores the content of the message.

One key to reducing nervousness is to think of delivering your speech as a communication task, *not* as a performance. Other ways include dressing in comfortable clothes, practicing positive self-talk, being well prepared, concentrating on your message, picturing yourself doing well, and remembering your audience is composed of people like you.

The final step in getting ready to deliver a speech is to rehearse it. Your rehearsal should include saying the speech out loud, imagining an actual audience, checking the speech for clarity and organization, and checking its length.

The Internet offers a wide range of practical information about both delivery and stress management.

KEY TERMS AND CONCEPTS

Use the *Communicating Effectively* CD-ROM and the Online Learning Center at www.mhhe.com/hybels8 to further your understanding of the following terms.

Articulation 352
Attentiveness 346
Computer-generated graphics 357
Conversational quality 345
Directness 347
Enunciation 352
Extemporaneous speaking 349

Flip chart 354
Immediacy 346
Impromptu speaking 347
Inflection 352
Manuscript (speaking from) 348
Memory (speaking from) 348
Model 354

Monotone 352
Multimedia 359
Organizational chart 354
Pace 352
Pronunciation 352
Public-speaking anxiety 351
Visual support 353

CHAPTER REVIEW

QUESTIONS TO REVIEW

1. What is at the heart of effective speech delivery?
2. To what extent should the focus of your listeners be on delivery aspects of your speech?
3. Which is the most important characteristic of an effective delivery style?
4. Of the different types of delivery (impromptu, manuscript, memory, and extemporaneous), with which style are you most comfortable? Why? Which do you find most difficult? Why?
5. If you were motivated to improve your speaking ability, which of the different types of delivery would you concentrate on, and why?
6. Weigh the value of how you look when it comes to giving speeches. How important is it? How important is the way you sound?
7. What visual support is best for your speech? Why? Will it simplify, clarify, and enhance your speech? In what ways?
8. What is the most important guideline when it comes to PowerPoint presentations? Explain.
9. What is the philosophical approach recommended for reducing public-speaking anxiety, and what are its strengths?
10. What are some other strategies that you can see would help those who experience public-speaking anxiety and who need assistance in controlling their nervousness?
11. What method do you use for practicing your speeches?

Go to the self-quizzes on the *Communicating Effectively* CD-ROM and the Online Learning Center at www.mhhe.com/hybels8 to test your knowledge of the chapter contents.

CHAPTER 15

The Informative Speech

OBJECTIVES

After reading this chapter, you should be able to:

- Distinguish the four types of informative speeches: speeches about objects, processes, events, and concepts.
- Use the strategies for defining ideas: etymology, example, comparison and contrast, and function.
- Use the strategies for describing ideas: size or quantity, shape, weight, color, composition, and fit.
- Use the strategies for explaining ideas: using numbers, connecting the known with the unknown, and repeating and reinforcing ideas.
- Get your listeners interested and involved in your speech.
- Help listeners remember your main points.
- Describe your preparation for a presentation.

IN DOING INITIAL RESEARCH FOR A SPEECH THAT HE NEEDED TO WRITE FOR A speech communication class Louis discovered some information claiming that half the marriages in the United States fail—that is, that there is a 50 percent chance that a marriage won't make it. The statistic was cited by an infidelity support group, in the promotion for a book on divorce, and by a men's counseling center in California. With further research, however, Louis discovered that pollster Louis Harris wrote, "The idea that half of American marriages are doomed is one of the most specious pieces of statistical nonsense ever perpetuated in modern times."[1] Louis knew that he had a unique angle on a topic that would not just interest the class but teach them something as well, because everyone wants a successful marriage and wants to know how to attain it.

Having developed an informative speech topic, Louis began his research. With the tentative title "Until Death Do Us Part," he talked to two divorce lawyers, consulted a number of online statistical sources for current information and statistics, and examined three books: Debbie Ford's *Spiritual Divorce: Divorce As a Catalyst for an Extraordinary Life* (HarperSanFrancisco, 2002), Stephanie Staal's *The Love They Lost: Living with the Legacy of Our Parents' Divorce* (Dell, 2000), and Edward Baiamonte and Ted Baiamonte's *The 91% Factor: Why Women Initiate 91% of Divorce, End Most Relationships, and What Can Be Done About It* (American Political Press, 1999). After framing a thesis and devising points that would support it, Louis organized his evidence around each of the points and refined them as he continued. The visual aid he planned to use would *refute* America's most-often-cited statistic: "Fifty percent of marriages will end in divorce." Louis ended his content preparation by writing out his conclusion in full, then, finally, his introduction. As Louis practiced his delivery and presentation skills, he not only visualized his audience before him, but he also kept his goal of creating understanding in his listeners at the forefront of his mind.

The purpose of an informative speech is to provide listeners with information that will help them make decisions as individuals and as citizens. The need for high-quality information demands skill in our ability to produce and deliver it. Although some of this information is delivered in written form, much of it is oral: The teacher before the class, the radio or television reporter broadcasting to an audience, the professional sharing ideas with colleagues, the employer explaining policies to employees, the politician clarifying issues or defining approaches to problems—all of them need oral skills to convey information.

The **informative speech**—one that defines, clarifies, instructs, and explains—is a common phenomenon in our society. If we are going to prosper in the information society, the ability to give an informative speech is a necessary skill. The need to increase understanding is a universal one.

You are likely to encounter informative speeches in a variety of contexts. You're probably familiar with the *lecture,* which is simply an informative talk given before a class audience. One is unlikely to escape college or university without experiencing a number of lectures, since the lecture remains the most common form of class presentation. The next is a *lecture/demonstration,* an informative talk that shows listeners how to do something or how something works. Teachers show how to prepare an assignment; sales representatives show how their products work; supervisors show employees how to do their jobs. The last is an *explanation* of ideas or policies. Mauricio Raúl Muñoz's speech, "Forgetting Everything You've Learned," which appears at the end of this chapter, is an example of a speech

Table 15-1 Guidelines for Selecting Your Informative Topic

Audience knowledge	Relate your topic to your audience	Work on your topic
• Be clear. • Maintain their interest. • Keep it simple (not too technical).	• Why does your audience want to hear this? • What does your topic have to do with them? • How can you elicit audience involvement? • What familiar and relevant information can you use?	• Make it real. • Avoid abstractions. • Use detailed descriptions. • Use comparisons, metaphors, similes, and analogies.

of explanation. Most of the examples in this chapter, too, come from speeches of explanation.

Table 15-1 is a useful place to begin work on your informative speech. It draws together valuable information from previous chapters.

GOALS OF AN INFORMATIVE SPEAKER

With so much information available, it's surprising that listeners don't buckle under from information overload. When listeners are so swamped with information, we face a serious problem as speakers. We have to ask ourselves, "How can I, as an informative speaker, make my information stand out?"

Increasing Understanding

Since the goal of an informative speech is to give the audience new or in-depth information on a subject, it is particularly important that a speaker put together a speech that audience members will understand. Several things will help understanding: language choice, organization, and illustrations and examples.

Language Choice

In our highly technological world, many of us speak a specialized language that is understood only by people in the same field. If you are giving a speech that uses technical or specialized vocabulary, you must take the time to define your terms, or consider whether you can avoid technical terms altogether.

Organization

A good organizational pattern will show how ideas relate to one another and will help listeners move from one idea to another. As a listener you probably know that your attention will wander if the speaker is rambling or you have trouble finding the main points of the speech.

Illustrations and Examples

If you are going to explain a principle that might be unfamiliar to your audience, use an example to show what it is or how it works. For example, a student who was explaining three basic body types held up pictures to illustrate each type. When he held up a picture of a thin, lightly muscled person, the meaning of the term *ectomorph* was immediately clear.

Getting Attention

The first goal of a speaker is to get the attention of audience members. In most public-speaking situations there are many distractions: People come in late; the air-conditioner fan turns on and off; a fly buzzes around the room; the microphone gives off feedback.

The best way to get and keep attention is to create in your audience a strong desire to listen to your material. Ask yourself whether your material is relevant. Does it apply to the people in your audience? If it doesn't, how can it be adapted to their needs?

If the audience perceives the information as new, it is more likely to pay attention. "New" doesn't necessarily mean a subject no one has ever heard about—you might present a new perspective or a new angle. Certain topics are going to provoke a "ho-hum" reaction from the audience. You don't want your audience to think "Not another speech about jogging" (or dieting and nutrition, or getting organized). When Richard Lamm, from the Center for Public Policy and Contemporary Issues at the University of Denver, was asked to deliver an address to the 1998 World Future Society, he chose a title that might—just from hearing it—put many listeners to sleep: "Unexamined Assumptions: Destiny, Political Institutions, Democracy, and Population." So he planned an introduction that ran counter to both his title and his topic, one that he knew would get the attention of his audience. He began:

> *A priest was riding in a subway when a man staggered toward him, smelling like a brewery, with lipstick on his collar. He sat in the seat right next to the priest and started reading the newspaper. After a few minutes, the man turned to the priest and asked "Excuse me, Father, what causes arthritis?"*

The goal of an informative speech is to give listeners new or in-depth information on a subject.

>*The priest, tired of smelling the liquor and saddened by the lifestyle, said roughly "Loose living, drink, dissipation, contempt for your fellow man and being with cheap and wicked women!"*
>
>*"That's amazing," said the drunk and returned to his newspaper. Awhile later, the priest, feeling a bit guilty, turned to the man and asked nicely, "How long have you had arthritis?"*
>
>*"Oh," said the man, "I don't have arthritis, I was just reading that the Pope did." The parable, of course, is a lesson on assumptions.*[2]

When you want people to remember certain points, it is useful to give these points special emphasis. Sometimes this can be done with verbal cues: "This is my most important point" or "If you remember only one thing I said today, remember this." Sometimes you can use a cue after a point: "Now let me show you how important what I just said can be to you." A point can be emphasized, too, by repeating it, by changing your rate of speech, or by pausing just before you say it.[3]

Helping Retention

There are other ways to help retention. Whenever possible, use several brief examples and illustrations for each concept you are introducing, and vary them as much as possible. Realize that some of your listeners will respond better to verbal explanations, some to graphs and charts, and some to video and so on. The more variety you supply, the greater the likelihood you will tap into methods your listeners use to stimulate their recall.

Yet another effective way to help retention is by using visual support. "Presentation research shows that really 'a picture is worth a thousand words'—with message retention being increased over words by a factor of five."[4] A study by the Wharton School of Business found that "on average, people retain about 10 percent of a presentation communicated through words alone, whereas the effective use of visual aids increases retention up to 50 percent."[5]

TYPES OF INFORMATIVE SPEECHES

As you read about the following types of informative speeches, keep in mind that to be successful, you must never overestimate the information your audience has nor underestimate their intelligence.

Objects

Speeches about objects are about things, people, places, animals, and products. Because of the time limits placed on the length of your speech, you cannot discuss any topic completely. This means you must focus your attention on some aspect of your topic. Instead of focusing on body adornment, for example, you might choose tattoos.

Processes

Speeches about processes deal with patterns of action. One type of speech about processes is the **demonstration speech,** a speech that teaches people how to perform a process. A speech on how to research the job market might discuss the process of evaluating online job sites. The important thing to remember is that you need to limit your information to just what can be explained clearly and completely in the time you are allowed.

Events

Speeches about events focus on things that happened, are happening, or will happen. They need to go one step further than mere history and show listeners how they can use the information. One student, who traveled to Washington, DC, to become part of a nationwide protest, talked about the kinds of students she met, but also showed her listeners how they could organize an effective protest movement—things she learned from her trip.

Concepts

Speeches about concepts deal with theories, ideas, beliefs, and other abstract principles. Here it's important to be both clear and understandable. For example, Nadia chose the topic "the empowerment of women." Because her definition and approach were abstract, she then focused on units on her own campus where imbalance was clear: faculty, administration, and female representation on important committees and boards.

Notice how easily Nadia could turn her speech into a persuasive one—especially considering the reason she pursued the topic in the first place: the imbalances she heard about and observed on her campus. Nadia kept her speech informative by doing two things: providing unbiased information and refraining from making arguments.

Overarching Principles

No matter which of the general types of informative speeches you choose, the principles that make a good speech remain the same. Strive for clarity, strong organization, and vivid language. Don't try to cover too many points, clarify the relationship between your main points, and keep your speech moving forward according to a well-developed plan. Define your terms and use examples. Restate and paraphrase, and use numerous transitions. Involve your audience, offer clear supporting material, and conclude your speech with impact. In all cases, avoid becoming too technical. The test of a good speaker is to communicate even the most complex ideas clearly and simply.

STRATEGIC FLEXIBILITY
The process of determining which type of strategy for presenting material in informative speeches is dependent on your effective use of strategic flexibility—thinking about potential situations and the needs and requirements likely to arise because of them. The key for speakers here is forecasting.

STRATEGIES FOR INFORMATIVE SPEECHES

There are different types of strategies for presenting material in informative speeches. Each type requires a special skill. Sometimes all of these types can be found in a single speech; usually at least two will be used.

View clip #7, an excerpt from an informative student speech, "Indian Weddings, by Preeti Vilku."

Defining

A **definition**—an explanation of the meaning of a word or phrase—can often make a critical difference in whether your audience understands your speech. Sometimes a dictionary definition is sufficient; other times you must expand on it by using your own words or those of others.

Definition can also go beyond explaining words or phrases. Four useful ways to define concepts in a speech are by etymology, example, comparison and contrast, and function.

Etymology

Etymology, the study of the origin and development of words, can be used as a basis for definition. For example, when discussing romantic love and the intense feelings that occur, one speaker pointed out that the word *ecstasy*, which is a common label for emotions during the time of romantic love, is derived from a Greek word meaning "deranged"—a state beyond all reason and self-control.[6] She went on to show that the word *deranged* accurately describes the state of mind that exists early in romantic relationships. The *Oxford English Dictionary* is the best source for word etymologies.

Example

An example illustrates a point. When using an example, a speaker often either points to an actual thing or points out something verbally.

In this excerpt, Christina Burton talks to her class about her addiction:

Choices of strategies for presenting material in informative speeches depend on the unique combination of speaker, topic, audience, and situation.

> *I am an addict, and I admit it. But I'm not alone because I know that many of you are too. When my roommate gets out of bed, the first thing she does is turn on her four-cupper for a cup-a-joe to jumpstart her day. She's one of 167 million coffee drinkers in the United States, and together we consumed nearly 6.3 billion gallons last year alone.*[7]

Comparison and Contrast

Comparisons point out the similarities between two or more things. When Dwight Cushenberry, who grew up in a rural farming community, gave his class speech "Auctions, 24/7," he not only had numerous experiences with farm auctions and found them exciting, but in his speech, he could compare those with the excitement and thrill of using eBay:

> *eBay has brought the excitement of participating in an auction to millions. It revved up the old auction spirit in me as well. Just like an old farm auction, you're likely to find almost anything on eBay; just like a farm auction, too, when you use eBay you are part of a community of members. And just like an old farm auction, you are likely to get carried away with the excitement and overpay for something. For me, eBay has been a godsend because it captures all the excitement of an old farm auction, but the real thrill is that you can enjoy the excitement 24/7.*

Contrasts point out the differences between two or more things. In her class speech "Girls Get a Grip," Lenore Ashley used contrast when she talked about the way males and females express their anger:

> *Now, you all know how guys express their anger because first, it's obvious, and second, it's consistent. When that bubbling cauldron of hormone-laden emotion explodes, guys will express their anger physically. They'll shove someone's face into a toilet, or they'll push them up against a car. The reason you don't always see females express their anger is that it's more subtle. That doesn't mean it's less effective, and if you're ever on the receiving end of a female's anger, you already know how effective it can be. Females express their anger in nonphysical, indirect, covert forms: backbiting, exclusion, rumors, name-calling, and manipulation.*

Working Together

For each of the following ideas, decide which kinds of definitions would work in a speech—etymology, function, example, or comparison and contrast—and have each member of the group offer an example of each one.

- an incomparable experience
- awesome dreams
- ethical actions
- free speech
- independence
- great instructor
- recession
- unbeatable bargain
- war
- well done

Function

With certain topics it's useful to define by function—showing how a thing performs or how it can be used. Speakers may stress an object's usefulness, advantages, benefits, convenience, or service. Eugene Finerman, a satirist and professional speechwriter, began his speech on humor, "Humor and Speeches: A Stand-Up History," by defining the function of humor:

> *A plumber, a jockey and a rabbi walk into a pet store . . . What a cheap trick to get your attention, but that is the charm—and the power—of humor. Humor can engage, entice, coax and persuade. It can ridicule, vilify, agitate and incite. Humor can warm an audience or inflame it. The effective speaker and the astute speechwriter know the value of and place for humor. It is a natural means of communication, and it has served the public speaker for as long as there have been speeches.*[8]

Describing

To describe is to provide a mental image of something experienced, such as a scene, a person, or a sensation. Many times your audience will be able to visualize what you are talking about if you create a picture for them.

Size or Quantity

Size is the measurement or extent of a thing when compared with some standard. Notice how Kellie, a student, described a spider's web in her speech:

> *Not only did it stretch from the ground to the lower limbs of one tree, close to six feet off the ground, but several dew-covered fibers—only one-millionth of an inch in diameter each—secured the hundreds of other radiating and evenly spaced fibers between trees as well. This spider's strong and elastic web silk—its stretched strength second only to that of fused quartz—was a geometric orb the size of the front door of our house with the spider sitting motionless in the central hub.*

Shape

Shape is the outward form, configuration, or contour of a thing. In a speech on insect control in gardening, one student used the following description of a cabbage worm:

> *It looks like a brilliant yellow-green caterpillar that begins at a length of an inch or so with about the circumference of your little finger. It has antennae coming from its head with numerous short pudgy feet. As it chomps away at garden cabbage throughout the summer, it extends its length from two to three inches, and it grows in circumference to about the size of the large part of your thumb.*

Weight

Weight is the heaviness of a mass, object, or thing. Since people have a hard time visualizing large numbers, speakers need to relate them to something from the listeners' own experience. One speaker was trying to impress her listeners with how much a million was. She said that a class in Des Moines, Iowa, collected 1 million bottle caps. How much did they weigh? According to the speaker, these caps weighed 21½ tons: "They were put into 200 bags and the bags were so heavy it required a moving van to take them away."

Color

Color is an obvious component of description and serves quickly to call up mental pictures. Here, Aaron Roberts uses the importance of color in Web site design in his speech "Color My Web":

> *What do you first think about when you see the color red? How about blue? And yellow? Which of these colors best represents you—who you are? How many of you have Web sites? Do you realize that your Web site is the window through which the world can catch its first glimpse of you? Because the Web is for the world, you must take the time and effort to choose colors that best present you to the world.*

Composition

Composition, a description of the makeup of a thing, can be a useful part of description. Notice here how Jeremiah Stamler, in a speech called "Internet Snake Oil," discussed what the composition of a good Web site is—especially important if you happen to be surfing the Internet for medical sites for information about treatment and rehabilitation:

> *Do you know what the composition of a good Web site is? Well, no site is perfect, but the best ones share five important qualities. First, they are upfront about who they are and what their mission is. Second, the advertising on reputable Web sites is always clearly separated from the editorial content. Third, both the original source of the information and the date it was posted or reviewed are marked. Fourth, online experts are identified by name, credentials, and institution. And, fifth, confidentiality is treated as more than a technicality.*

Explaining

We were not born knowing how to do such things as cook or play volleyball—someone told us how to do them. Explaining is the process of making something clear.

For example, in a speech on how to make a toasted cheese sandwich with an iron, the speaker used the following steps:

1. Gather what you need: bread, cheese, margarine, aluminum foil, and an iron.
2. Heat the iron to medium-high.
3. Make a sandwich from the cheese and bread. Butter both sides of the bread on the outside.
4. Wrap the sandwich in aluminum foil.
5. Place the iron on each side for about 20 seconds. (Check to see if you need more time.)

Using Numbers

Few people can visualize large quantities, such as millions or billions. When you work with numbers, follow these suggestions.

- If numbers are unusual or surprising, explain why.
- Round off large numbers.
- If you have a lot of numbers, try to convert them to percentages.
- Look for opportunities to replace numbers with words. For example, it's easier to understand "More than half the people said . . ." or "A majority believed . . ." than "More than 370 people said . . ."
- Try to relate numbers to something familiar. For example, say "The number of people killed in the earthquake was equal to the entire student body of this college."
- If possible, try to compare numbers. For example, "Forty-five percent of the seniors but only 3 percent of the first-year students believed . . ."
- Use graphs and other visual aids to make numbers more concrete.

Connecting the Known with the Unknown

When listeners are unfamiliar with a subject, a speaker can help them understand it by connecting the new idea to something they already know. For example, when a British student wanted to explain the game of cricket to her American classmates, she started by listing the ways that cricket was similar to baseball.

Repeating and Reinforcing Ideas

Repetition in a speech is important because it helps listeners remember key points. However, if it is overdone, speakers run the risk of boring listeners. Let's look at a format that will enable you to spread out the repetition and reinforcement in a speech.

Whether you are using numbers, connecting the known with the unknown, or repeating and reinforcing ideas, when you are explaining, your main goal is making something clear.

In your introduction, tell your listeners what you plan to tell them in the body of your speech. In the introduction to her speech "Becoming a Smart Buyer," Heather listed her main points: "Today I want to talk about the four steps to becoming a smart buyer. These steps are: find out price, get a receipt, examine service and repair, and read contracts carefully."

In the body of your speech, tell your listeners your full message (explain your points). In Bishetta's speech, she explained each of her steps:

The first step in dealing with difficult bosses is to understand them. To find out what makes them tick will allow you to speak their language.

The second step is to reveal loyalty. Most bosses will give you the freedom to solve problems in your own way as long as they are convinced of your loyalty.

The third step in dealing with difficult bosses is to establish strong communication channels. With good rapport, problems can be discussed openly and directly, facts and discoveries can be given, and information that might prove valuable can be shared.

In your conclusion, tell your listeners *what you told them* in the body of the speech. This is the place to summarize your main ideas. Bishetta concluded her speech by saying:

Now you can see how you can go about dealing with difficult bosses. You need to understand them, show loyalty, and establish strong communication channels.

AROUSING INTEREST IN YOUR TOPIC

Besides arousing curiosity, presenting anecdotes, building anticipation, and building suspense, there are numerous other techniques you can use for holding attention throughout a speech. One of the keys is to think specifically about holding listener attention at every point during your speech preparation.

Arouse Curiosity

One way to make sure that you will be listened to is to create a desire to learn about your subject by stimulating your listeners' curiosity. For example, one speaker began his speech with "Do you know how to stop procrastinating?" Another stated "Before this speech is over, I plan to share with you a message that has the potential of changing your life forever."

Present Anecdotes

An **anecdote** is a short, interesting story based on your own or someone else's experience. Although some speakers use them in their introductions, anecdotes are particularly useful in the body of your speech because they can get audience attention back if it is wandering.

Nicole Gant, a mother who home-schooled both a daughter and a son before returning to school herself, used this anecdote in her speech to her class:

The Internet kept not only me, but both my children as well, connected to the rest of the world—to libraries, research institutes, and other students and families with similar interests. My kids dissected virtual frogs, worked through a set of college-level genetics problems offered by MIT, checked in on a vocabulary-building site that sprinkled their

STRATEGIC FLEXIBILITY
Note that one of the keys to holding listener attention is thinking about it at every point during speech preparation. If you make it part of the entire strategic flexibility process, it will be one of the factors, elements, or conditions to which you continually respond.

dialogue with SAT–worthy words, and researched the life of Georg Philipp Telemann, who composed the baroque trio that my son, a flutist, plays with friends in an afternoon group. When I look at the moldering set of World Books that formed the intellectual basis for my early education, I just laugh out loud.

Build Anticipation

One way to build anticipation is to preview your points in the introduction. Gwendolyn Haas, for example, said that she was going to talk about what makes Olympic champions. Then she said in a speech titled "Olympic Inspiration":

The qualities I want to talk about not only make Olympic champions; they are invaluable, too, in school, in the home, or on the job. First, champions anticipate. They have a dream of themselves as a champion. They aim high, because often they don't just meet their goals but surpass them. Second, champions motivate. They are driven not just to be the best but to do their best as well. They never quit because they know the satisfaction of completing a difficult task against the odds. Third, champions activate. They make their own luck because they know luck strikes those best prepared to capitalize on it.

The audience is now more likely to listen for each of her points: (1) anticipate, (2) motivate, (3) activate. Notice the way Gwendolyn kept them parallel. Framed in the same way, they were easier for listeners to remember.

Build Suspense

Building suspense is one of the best ways of keeping attention. Esteban Estrada decided to speak on drunk driving, and he began his speech with a personal experience:

There was no way I could anticipate what would happen. My girlfriend, Angelica, and I were coming home from dinner out and a movie. We were on State Street, one of the main streets of my hometown, when suddenly we were sideswiped by a car. Not knowing what was going on, and thinking it was inadvertent, we continued driving. Suddenly, the car sideswiped us again. We were about seven blocks from the police station, so we drove there fast. But the car that had been following us disappeared. We waited almost 20 minutes, and thinking it safe, we decided to continue toward Angelica's house. Suddenly, out of nowhere, it was behind us again. We made it to Angelica's and ran inside. The car squealed past, but forgetting the curve leading into the court where Angelica lived, the outlaw car missed the turn, ran one wheel in the gutter and another up a driveway, and broke the front axle. The police were called; all three teenage boys had been drinking.

Other Techniques for Getting Attention

Most of these ideas have been discussed elsewhere; they are gathered here to highlight the way they can help get attention in informative speeches. Don't forget that it is a combination of elements working together that holds listeners' attention.

Content

When thinking about the *content* of your speech, tie old ideas to new ones. One student talking about food additives (an old idea), for example, tied it to chemicals found naturally in foods that cut the risk of cancer and heart attack (a new idea).

Evidence

Speakers can use *evidence* to hold attention when they select their information with listeners in mind. Mauricio Raúl Muñoz's speech on "Forgetting Everything You've Learned" at the end of this chapter demonstrates this well. Notice, for example, that Muñoz begins with a dramatic quotation about college being "one of the worst possible environments in which to retain anything we've learned." Knowing that his listeners would need serious evidence to support his points, he mentions PhDs and MDs, then researchers at Boston's Beth Israel Deaconess Medical Center under main point one. In addition to personal experience, he used statistics from Tufts University, an opinion from a researcher at Stanford University, and two from the National Institute of Aging for main point number two. He cites the Harvard College Alcohol Study and researchers from the University of North Carolina's Bowles Center for Alcohol Studies for main point three.

Immediacy

Choosing examples that are immediate is another way to hold attention. *Immediacy* means closeness or nearness in time or space. Shelly gave a speech on the importance of psychological counseling, and she scheduled an interview with an on-campus psychologist before her speech to make her example more immediate. In this way she could talk not only about how to go about making such appointments and where and when the services were provided but also about what topics are of most concern to students on her campus. Thus, the subject of psychological counseling became immediate.

Organization

Organization is so important that we spent a whole chapter discussing it. When speakers use transitions and internal summaries, and relate their material to their central idea, it helps listeners follow the speech. When listeners can't follow a speech, their minds will tend to wander. Making only a few points and using some repetition also help sustain interest throughout a speech.

Style

Content, evidence, and organization are important, but so is *style* or language, as you learned in Chapter 5 on verbal communication. We suggest rereading that chapter before you give your speech.

Delivery

Finally, speakers can get attention through their *delivery*. Take an active role in motivating and getting your audience involved. When you are the fifth speaker in an 8 A.M. class on a Monday, people aren't going to listen to you just because you are there.

GETTING LISTENERS INVOLVED

Before we discuss three external ways to get the audience involved, let's review the methods for getting audience involvement that are within the speech:

1. Choose a topic that is inherently interesting—one that is both significant and relevant and has attention-holding value in and of itself.
2. Select examples, personal experiences, and stories that are interesting and relevant to listeners.

> **STRATEGIC FLEXIBILITY**
>
> Here, we reinforce the importance of making certain that all judgments and decisions regarding speech material are made with listeners in mind. Once again, if you make it part of the entire strategic flexibility process, it will be one of the factors, elements, or conditions that you continually include in your decision making.

3. Use an organization scheme that is simple, clear, and easy for listeners to follow.
4. Incorporate transitions that guide listeners to what has been said, what is going to be said, and the purpose or central idea of the speech.
5. Make certain that all judgments and decisions regarding speech material are made with listeners in mind.

Now we look at getting the audience to participate, asking rhetorical questions, and soliciting questions from the audience.

Get the Audience to Participate

As every magician knows, choosing someone from the audience to participate in an act is a good technique for keeping attention. In a speech on first aid, the speaker called for a volunteer from the audience so that she could point to pressure points. Getting everyone to participate works too. In a speech on self-defense, the speaker had the class practice a few simple moves.

Ask Rhetorical Questions

Some speakers use **rhetorical questions**—questions audience members answer mentally rather than out loud. Meredith Carey used rhetorical questions in her speech "Recover, Refocus, Regenerate":

> *I was there when they lowered my grandmother into the ground; I was very close to my grandmother, and it hurt deeply knowing she was gone forever. I knew that the fights between my parents were leading to separation, but their divorce was devastating for me because I loved them both so much, and even the idea of divorce really shocked me. And going away to college—leaving my friends, the town and home where I grew up, and my boyfriend all the way through high school—almost ripped me apart. Have changes like these shaken you to the core? Have there been other changes in your lives that have freaked you out? What do you do with all your feelings of rage? Hurt? Sorrow? What do you do when you feel like you are drowning in a sea of anger? Or in an ocean of despair? Are you a person who likes regularity in your life? Predictability? Can you cope with all these changes? Are you prepared for even more changes in your lives?*

Solicit Questions from the Audience

A question-and-answer session encourages listeners to get involved. You might even tell your listeners at the beginning that you will take questions when you finish, which may encourage them to pay attention in preparation for asking questions.

Here are some useful guidelines if you plan to solicit questions from your audience: First, make sure you listen to the full question before answering it. Second, if a question is confusing, ask the questioner to rephrase it. If you are still confused, rephrase it yourself before answering it. For example, say, "Let me make sure I have heard you right; what you are asking is . . . . Am I right?" Finally, in responding to questions, try to keep your answers brief and to the point. This is no time for another speech. As a final check, it's also a good idea to ask, "Does that answer your question?"

PRESENTATIONS

A wide variety of people are called upon to make presentations, explain concepts, communicate complex data, make recommendations, or persuade and motivate others. A **presentation** is created to communicate ideas in a compelling and graphic manner. Presentations may be informative or persuasive. One of the major differences between speeches and presentations is the presentation's emphasis on visual support. Still, there are many similarities between speeches and presentations.

Why do presentations deserve special attention? First, they require a different emphasis and a different approach. Second, with the ready availability of and access to high-quality computer-generated graphics, and the ease of use and popularity of PowerPoint, compelling presentations are within the reach of everyone.

The most important guiding principle that governs all aspects of presentations is the requirement for careful planning—not unlike the advice offered throughout the public-speaking chapters of this book. There are three ingredients of successful presentations: (1) thorough preparation, (2) natural delivery, and (3) effective visuals.

Thorough Preparation

Before they do anything else, presenters must know the constraints under which they are operating. Audience size and arrangement, room size, and the equipment provided are important considerations. Because presenters often have so much material they could present, they also must decide what they want to achieve and can achieve in the time frame given.

Audience analysis is challenging when delivering presentations, especially when communicating to diverse audiences. If audience knowledge of technical expertise is

> The biggest difference between a presentation and a speech is the degree of visual support used and expected in presentations.

STRATEGIC FLEXIBILITY

Presenters must carefully appraise their audiences—this could be an underlying theme of this chapter. When it is part of the entire strategic flexibility process, it is one of the factors, elements, or conditions that is included in all aspects of the decision making that goes into communicating effectively.

slim, it might require more definitions, a gradual development of the ideas, simplified charts and graphs, and, perhaps, the elimination of some of the more technical or sophisticated information.

Presenters must establish a clear central idea, sometimes referred to as the thesis, goal, objective, or purpose. Every element of the presentation should support the central idea, and any element that detracts in any way must be eliminated or minimized. To accomplish this, presenters need to determine (1) what is to be done, (2) how it will be done, and (3) what will be its significance. When they know this, presenters should also know how they want their listeners to respond.

Natural Delivery

Natural delivery is the collection of speech and actions that best represents your true self—that is free from artificiality, affectation, and constraint. It requires using an extemporaneous style: carefully preparing your thoughts, but not deciding on your words in advance or reading a script. If your thoughts are so cloudy, foggy, or murky that they need to be written and read, you are not ready to make a presentation. How do you prepare for an extemporaneous presentation?[9]

- Develop a key-idea outline, not a complete-sentence outline. (Do not write out the speech or commit any substantial portion of it to memory.)
- Use the key-idea outline as the basis for practice and for preparing your visual support. Fit your words and your visual support to your ideas.
- Present your talk, working from your outline, in front of friends, family, or anyone else you can get to listen. You are ready to give your presentation when you can go through all your material without faltering. (This does not require memorization; it requires extreme familiarity with your key ideas.)

Presentations require a high degree of professionalism. Refrain from being sarcastic, cute, flippant, or entertaining. Keep focused on the central idea. As one writer advises, "Sell steak, not sizzle."[10]

One author lists the top 10 negative nonverbal cues (before, during, and after a presentation): A weak handshake is number one; sloppy clothes are number two. These are followed by too much jewelry, inappropriate hairstyle, slouching, staring at your notes, bad breath, dirty fingernails, repeated hand mannerisms, and general bad manners. The final category includes having poor eye contact, arriving late, using crude language, rubbing an ear, or taking more time for the presentation than allotted.[11]

A variety of outline patterns are recommended by authors writing about presentations. One suggestion is to give the presentation in the form of a story by creating a clear beginning, middle, and end.[12] Another suggestion is to use an introduction, giving the results of the investigation, discussing the results and suggesting future work, and offering conclusions.[13] Still another suggestion is to use the inverted pyramid approach: Present your conclusions first, then the general supporting background information, and finally the detailed support.[14] If you have a great deal of theory or a substantial amount of data to present, this is the approach we support. If your presentation is a report on scientific research, we suggest you follow the normal organizational pattern of published research.[15] Whatever pattern presenters select, an essential requirement is that they don't switch patterns midway through the presentation. Consistency is crucial.

Effective Visuals

Perhaps the biggest difference between a presentation and a speech, as noted earlier, is the degree of visual support used and expected in presentations. Visual support must reinforce and expand the message, focus listener attention on key ideas, and clarify meaning.

One author writing about presentation graphics suggests using the acronym **PETAL** to conceptualize every presentation.[16] Develop *pertinent* materials, choose an *engaging* format, present your materials in a *timely* manner, satisfy yourself that they are *appropriate* to the audience, and ensure that everything is *legible*. Everything in the presentation should be pertinent to the topic; no element should be added just for effect. An engaging format results from the judicious use of color, a consistent, uncluttered design format, and relatively limited text. The word *timely* refers to the placement of visuals. They should be placed where they are needed in the presentation, not before and not after their oral complement has been delivered. And they must be legible: large enough and clear enough to be seen by everyone.

Practice with the equipment—whether it is a computer, projection system, screen, lighting, installed software, or microphone. Have backups if you are unsure of the situation. The room should not be totally darkened; this allows you to share the platform with the visuals and still maintain eye contact with listeners.

Presenters, too, need to use transition statements between visuals. One writer suggests following the words represented by the acronym **RDAT:** *Read* the visual, *describe* its meaning or significance, *amplify* it with an explanation or illustration, and, finally, make a *transition* to the next slide.[17]

Remember that just because you can prepare an elaborate slide presentation doesn't mean you should. As we saw in the discussion about creating a PowerPoint presentation (Chapter 14), which you should review, the rule of 6, simplicity, and consistent colors work best.

For guidance in creating PowerPoint presentations, see "PowerPoint Tutorial" on the CD.

THE INTERNET AND THE INFORMATIVE SPEECH

The Web has presented users with huge amounts of information. You can find out virtually anything about any person, place, thing, fact, problem, and more. A key decision when preparing an informative speech using the Internet is therefore "When do I have enough?" To answer, ask yourself:

- Is the information I am finding repeating what I have already discovered?
- Do I have a sufficient number of credible sources supporting the points I want to make in my speech?
- Have I uncovered sources besides those on the Internet that confirm the information I found there?
- Do I have a sufficient variety of sources so that I will be credible and able to hold the audience's attention?

Note the role that strategic flexibility plays here in anticipating, assessing, evaluating, and selecting.

Do not ask yourself, "Do I have enough information to fill the time limit for my speech?" This question is irrelevant to the proper development of your topic. It is also irrelevant to the accumulation of solid, credible information. *The key to information management is focusing on the quality of the data you receive*. The questions you need to ask to judge the credibility of information were discussed in Chapter 12. Remember: Don't waste your time. Don't waste the time of your listeners. Don't waste the time of your instructor. Take the time to establish your specific purpose and central ideas—the main points of your speech—with reliable, valid information.

Blogs, unless they have been constructed by experts who have credentials in specific subject areas, are opportunities for all to express their opinions on the Web. For the most part, they do not provide credible information for speeches. While your opinions may be important, they too carry little weight when you are trying to support the points of your informative speech.

How does the Internet influence the expectation listeners have of speakers?

- Speakers must be well informed. With the Internet available 24/7, there is no excuse for being poorly informed.
- Speakers must tell us something we don't already know.
- Speakers must share only credible information. They must have done their homework, evaluating and assessing information.
- Speakers must supply their sources and demonstrate their credibility.

These expectations are not new or unusual, but the Internet imposes on speakers a larger burden of responsibility for meeting them.

Sample Speech

In this speech by Mauricio Raúl Muñoz, notice several things. First, notice how well organized his speech is and how he has incorporated transitions to help his listeners. Second, notice how he has incorporated his sources into his speech both to help his listeners find sources on the topic and to add to his own credibility. Third, notice how he has used his own personal experiences to hold listener attention.

General purpose: To inform.

Specific purpose: To inform my class about the devastating effects that lack of sleep, poor diet, and alcohol can have on learning and memory.

Central idea: To show that the place we all go to get an education may be one of the worst possible environments in which to retain anything we've learned.

Forgetting Everything You've Learned

Introduction

What I am going to say here may not come as a shock to any of you, but each of you—if you are a typical college student—is doing everything you can to defeat the very purpose of education. In a recent article, "The Perils of Higher Education," Steven Kotler writes, "It turns out that the exact place we go to get an education may in fact be one of the worst possible environments in which to retain anything we've learned."[1] I'm not excusing myself here, but my roommate is a perfect example of what I am talking about. First, he goes without or with very little sleep for most of the week, and then crashes on the weekends. His diet consists of Coke, pizza, macaroni and cheese, hot dogs, donuts, spam, and Twinkies, and for variety he simply rotates the items so he doesn't have each one every day. Third, I don't want to suggest that my roommate is a drinker, but he's given a new meaning to the definition of binge drinking.

Notice how Muñoz begins his speech with a rather shocking statement to arouse attention, about everyone doing everything they can to defeat the very purpose of education. He follows it with an impressive quotation to back it up. For his third introductory item, he uses his roommate as his example. With this example, he provides the initial three divisions of his speech: lack of sleep, poor diet, and overdrinking.

Transition: Today, I want to look at these three areas—sleep, diet, and drinking—and show you the devastating effects they have on learning and memory.

Muñoz follows his introduction with a transition into the body of his speech and provides listeners with his specific purpose about the devastating effects.

Body

I. There is a price to be paid for losing sleep.[2]
   A. Robert Stickgold, PhD, John Winkelman, MD, PhD, and Peter Wehrwein, in an article on sleep for *Newsweek*, write: "Research now suggests that regular, ample sleep is one of those indispensables, ranking right up there with eating right and exercising."[3]
   B. Stickgold, Winkelman, and Wehrwein write that lack of sleep makes us more vulnerable to infection, to many important diseases such as diabetes, high blood pressure, obesity, and, in addition, may increase your risk of having a heart attack.

Muñoz divides his first main point into three subpoints, suggesting that loss of sleep is one of the indispensables, that loss of sleep makes us more vulnerable to infection and diseases, and then drives his point home by talking about the effect of loss of sleep on students—under subpoint C.

Sample Speech (continued)

    C. But here is the price that we students pay for losing sleep:
        1. Sleep is crucial to declarative memory—the kind that helps us remember facts and dates.[4]
        2. Sleep is essential for procedural memory—the kind that helps us write a five-paragraph essay.[5] Robert Stickgold and Matthew Walker, at Boston's Beth Israel Deaconess Medical Center, found that if you learned to type a sequence of numbers in the evening, then were retested following a night's sleep, your improvement would be 15 percent to 20 percent faster and 30 percent to 40 percent more accurate than those who learned the sequence in the morning and were retested without sleep, 12 hours later.[6]
        3. And listen to this, "if someone goes without sleep for 24 hours after acquiring a new skill, a week later they will have lost it completely."[7] What this means for all of us is very simple: If we pull an all-nighter during exam week, sure, we might do fine on our tests, but we may not remember any of the material by next semester.

Muñoz has offered listeners a well-balanced outline with three points under his first main head, then three points, too, under subpoint C where he talks about sleep being essential for declarative memory, procedural memory, and permanent memory as well.

Transition: There is a price to pay for your lack of sleep, but there is another price as well.

  II. We pay a price for the diets we follow.
    A. Today, I walked over to the cafeteria and there I found a smorgasbord of French fries, greasy pizza, burgers, potato chips, and the like. I wasn't at McDonald's, Burger King, or Wendy's. These foods are easy alternatives, and a Tufts University survey "found that 50% of students eat too much fat, and 70 to 80% eat too much saturated fat."[8]
    B. And here's a connection I'll bet most of you have never heard before: According to sleep researcher Emmanuel Mignot of Stanford University, one reason college students pack on the pounds is because sleep deprivation increases levels of a hunger hormone that causes overeating and weight gain. Getting enough shut-eye is a critical component in weight control.[9]
    C. But the important point is that college students are eating themselves stupid. Fast foods are full of trans fat because it extends the shelf life of foods, and, according to Kumar Madala Halagaapa and Mark Mattson of the National Institute on Aging, "people who eat high-fat diets and high-fat/high-sugar diets are not only

This is a brief transition, but it works well between main point one and main point two.
Under main point two, once again Muñoz divides his main head into three subpoints, and he uses powerful evidence to support each of his three subpoints: a Tufts University survey, a sleep researcher from Stanford University, and two researchers from the National Institute of Aging.

damaging their ability to learn and remember new information, but also putting themselves at much greater risk for all sorts of neurodegenerative disorders like Alzheimer's."[10]

Transition: You've seen, then, how we pay a price because of our lack of sleep, and you've seen how we pay a price because of our high-fat diets, but we pay an additional price as well.

III. We pay a price for our alcoholic foolishness.
   A. According to a report, 1,400 campus deaths and 500,000 injuries are attributable each year to binge drinking—often defined as having four or more alcoholic beverages at one sitting.[11]
   B. Here is what was uncovered by the Harvard College Alcohol Study of 10,000 students at 119 colleges, which reports that fraternities, sororities, and intercollegiate sports are at the center of binge drinking:
      1. Seventy-five percent of fraternity and sorority house residents binge drink.
      2. Fifty-seven percent of male and 48 percent of female athletes are binge drinkers.
      3. Forty-eight percent of all the alcohol college students drink is consumed by those below the legal drinking age.[12]
   C. Ask most students and they will simply reply that their booze-induced foolishness wears off once their hangover is gone. But that isn't what researchers have found. Kimberly Nixon and Fulton Crews at the University of North Carolina's Bowles Center for Alcohol Studies have found that "alcohol not only inhibits the birth of new cells but also inhibits the ones that survive."[13] What does this mean for all of us?
      1. Studies show that we consume far more alcohol than anyone previously suspected.
      2. According to the Harvard study I referred to earlier, 44 percent of us drink enough to be classified as binge drinkers.
      3. If we follow a weekend of heavy drinking with a week of heavy studying—the normal pattern—we might not forget everything we learn, but we're likely to struggle come test time.[14]

Transition: So, you see the price we pay for our lack of sleep, for our poor diets, and for our binge drinking.

Conclusion
Let me leave you with three quotes. About sleeping, in an article called "Night Life," Hara Estroff Marano says, "What we do at night affects everything we do during the day—our ability to learn, our skills, our

The transition picks up main point one and main point two, and it forecasts main point three.

Notice how in each of the main heads, Muñoz mentions the price we pay—to keep the main points parallel. You can see, too, that he is providing readers a topical outline, with the topics sleep, diet, and drinking.

Another thing Muñoz has maintained throughout his outline is his use of three subpoints. Notice that main point three has an A, B, and C, and both subpoints B and C have three sub-subpoints as well.

Also notice, under main point three, his use of evidence. He cites the Harvard College Alcohol Study and the University of North Carolina's Bowles Center for Alcohol Studies. Throughout his speech Muñoz has used first-class, high-level, effective evidence to support his points.

In this final transition, Muñoz briefly summarizes each of his three main points, and then he proceeds directly into his conclusion.
Muñoz summarizes each of his main points with a quote from an expert on each. He adds a touch of humor when he says, "Just imagine what would happen to GPAs . . ." When Muñoz says "that is not the point of this speech," he makes it clear

Sample Speech (continued)

memory, stamina, health and safety."[15] About diet, it was Emmanuel Mignot of Stanford University who said, "Sleep-deprived people eat more because they're hungrier, they're awake longer and may be tempted by foods everywhere they go."[16] And about binge drinking, Robert Davis, writing about five binge-drinking deaths, in a newspaper article says, "In some college towns, drink specials at bars and loose enforcement of liquor laws make it easier and cheaper for students to get drunk than to go to a movie."[17] Just imagine what would happen to GPAs at a vegetarian university with a 10 P.M. curfew! Now, I know I'm not going to change my roommate's habits with facts like these, and I know I won't change yours—that is not the point of this speech. But, I do know I've put in too much time and too much effort, and that as a result of *my* college experience I *don't* want to forget everything I've learned!

that his is a speech to inform, *not* a speech to persuade and that he knows the difference.

Speech Reference List

1. Kotler, S. (2005, March/April). The perils of higher education. *Psychology Today*, 66.
2. Stickgold, R. A., J. W. Winkelman, & P. Wehrwein. (2004, January 19). You will start to feel very sleepy . . . *Newsweek*, 58.
3. Ibid.
4. Kotler, The perils of higher education, 66.
5. Ibid.
6. Gorman, C. (2004, December 20). Why we sleep. (Science) *Time*, 49.
7. Kotler, The perils of higher education, 66.
8. Kotler, The perils of higher education, 68.
9. Hellmich, N. (2004, December 7). Healthy weight might rest with diet, exercise and sleep-linked hormones. *USA Today*, 1D.
10. Kotler, The perils of higher education, 70.
11. [No author]. (2004, September 26). Drinking to death. *The (Toledo) Blade*, 4B.
12. [No author]. (2002, August 10). Binge drinking can ruin student's life. (Annie's Mailbox). *The (Toledo) Blade*, 2D.
13. Kotler, The perils of higher education, 70.
14. Ibid.
15. Marano, H. E. (2003, November/December). Night life. *Psychology Today*, 43.
16. Hellmich, N. (2004, December 7). Sleep loss may equal weight gain. *USA Today*, 2D.
17. Davis, R. (2004, October 7). Five binge-drinking deaths "just the tip of the iceberg." *USA Today*, 11D.

Overall, Muñoz has used nine sources in his speech: two from *Psychology Today*, one from *Time*, one from *Newsweek*, two from *The (Toledo) Blade*, and three from *USA Today*. Because his topic is current and shares recent studies and opinions with his listeners, he has used no books to support his topic.

Assess Yourself

Have You Followed a Complete Program for Speech Preparation?

The assumption underlying this evaluation form is that you have selected an outstanding subject, developed a specific purpose and central idea for your speech, created main points that support your central idea, done sufficient research and investigation to discover supporting material that supports your main points, organized your speech effectively, and prepared an outline for your speech—all prior to using this form.

Answer Y for yes, N for no.

_____ 1. Have you prepared an outline for your speech at least three days before you plan to give the speech?

_____ 2. Have you converted the key parts of the outline to note cards?

_____ 3. Have you read through your outline several times to become familiar with the structure and flow of your ideas?

_____ 4. As you began to rehearse the delivery of your speech, did you check the time?

_____ 5. Using your notes, did you begin speaking and not stop until you completed your speech?

_____ 6. Did you check the time once again to see how long your speech took?

_____ 7. Once you completed your first complete run-through of the speech, did you go back and look at your outline to analyze your effort?
   _____ A. Were any key ideas omitted?
   _____ B. Were some ideas discussed too long or too briefly?
   _____ C. Did all your ideas receive proper and appropriate clarification and support?
   _____ D. Did both your introduction and conclusion flow smoothly?
   _____ E. Were you able to feel the presence of your future audience?

_____ 8. Did you make certain your notes were an effective tool for you?
   _____ A. Did you put too many notes on a single card?
   _____ B. Did you record just key ideas or keywords?
   _____ C. Are your notes written large enough for you to see them from a distance?
   _____ D. Did you record brief quotations or important statistics on your notes?
   _____ E. Did you write on one side of the cards only?
   _____ F. Did you clearly number each of your cards so that the order is easy to determine?

_____ 9. Did you continue rehearsing the speech using your notes as you will in the final speech?

_____ 10. Are you saying the speech differently each time you rehearse it, letting your ideas trigger your words?

_____ 11. Have you rehearsed using all the props or visual support that you will be using in your speech?

_____ 12. Have you visited the exact location where you will be giving your speech? Are you certain all the props and visual support will work as you intend them to in the location?

_____ 13. Did you review your notes quickly, one last time, before going before your audience to give the speech—checking, of course, to see that all your notes are in order?

_____ 14. Do you feel relaxed, confident, and in control of your information?

Go to the *Communicating Effectively* CD-ROM and the Online Learning Center at **www.mhhe.com/hybels8** to see your results and learn how to evaluate your attitudes and feelings.

mhhe.com/hybels8

CHAPTER REVIEW

SUMMARY

The informative speaker should increase understanding through careful language choices, coherent organization, and illustrations and examples. The speaker should hold attention with narratives, select subjects with which listeners can identify, and use visual support to help listeners retain information.

The principles that make a good speech remain the same for all four types of informative speeches: speeches about objects, about processes, about events, and about concepts.

Definitions can use etymology, example, comparison or contrast, or function. Descriptions include size, shape, weight, color, or composition. Explanations can rely on numbers, connecting the known with the unknown, and repeating and reinforcing ideas.

Creating interest in your topic is a matter of presenting anecdotes, building anticipation or suspense, and using a variety of other techniques. A speaker can involve the audience by selecting an interesting topic and examples, choosing a simple and clear organizational pattern, and using transitions. Three other methods are inviting volunteers to participate in the speech, asking rhetorical questions, and soliciting questions from the audience.

Presentations are popular because the means for providing the visual support they require is readily available and easy to use. As a presenter you must thoroughly prepare, demonstrate natural delivery, and use effective visuals.

The Internet has reinforced two essential questions: "When do I have enough information?" and "What expectations do listeners have concerning speakers?" Listeners expect speakers to be well informed, tell them something they don't already know, share only credible information, and supply sources and demonstrate their credibility.

KEY TERMS AND CONCEPTS

Use the *Communicating Effectively* CD-ROM and the Online Learning Center at www.mhhe.com/hybels8 to further your understanding of the following terms:

Anecdote 381
Comparisons 377
Composition 379
Contrasts 377
Definition 376

Demonstration speech 375
Etymology 376
Informative speech 372
Natural delivery 386
PETAL 387

Presentation 385
RDAT 387
Rhetorical questions 384

CHAPTER REVIEW

QUESTIONS TO REVIEW

1. How many informative speeches have you heard in the past week? In what contexts have most of them been delivered? Were most of them effective? What made them effective or ineffective?
2. What are the biggest challenges that giving an informative speech presents to you?
3. What specific techniques can you use to increase listener understanding? Get the attention of listeners? Assist listener retention?
4. What are the differences among the four types of informative speeches—speeches about objects, processes, events, and concepts?
5. What principles govern the creation of any informative speech?
6. What are the different strategies you can use if you need to define your ideas?
7. What strategies can you select if your goal is to describe your ideas?
8. Of the different strategies for informative speeches, which ones do you feel most comfortable using and why?
9. What are the best methods for arousing your interest in a speaker's topic? What is likely to grab your attention?
10. If you were making suggestions to a person who needed to make a forthcoming presentation, based on your reading, what suggestions would you make?
11. What effects does the Internet have on informative speaking?
12. Do you think Mauricio Raúl Muñoz's speech "Forgetting Everything You've Learned" was effective? Why or why not? Do you think he used too many sources? Why do you think he chose to use so many?

Go to the self-quizzes on the *Communicating Effectively* CD-ROM and the Online Learning Center at **www.mhhe.com/hybels8** to test your knowledge of the chapter contents.

CHAPTER

16

The Persuasive Speech

OBJECTIVES

After reading this chapter, you should be able to:
- Explain how persuasion relates to the communication model.
- Define *persuasion* and describe its purpose.
- Distinguish among values, beliefs, and attitudes, and explain the purpose of each.
- Explain what makes persuasion difficult.
- Describe each of the strategies persuaders can use.
- Describe specific techniques for building your credibility.
- Briefly outline the seven ethical standards persuaders should follow.

IN CONNECTION WITH HER COMMUNITY SERVICE AT UNITED WAY, LENA discovered the Louman Center, a community gathering place on the east side of town. The Louman Center focuses on youth activities, and as term projects for both a sociology and a speech communication class, Lena created a packet of information designed to convince the board of the Louman Center to institute an after-school leadership program. The information packet was buttressed by a persuasive speech designed to outline such a program, convince the board of the need for such a program, and offer specific methods for implementation. Looking forward to her capstone project for the minor she was pursuing, Lena mentioned her availability the following term to actually put such a program in place and get it started.

Because of her persuasive speech, the board of the Louman Center accepted her proposal in its entirety, and Lena looked at it as a great way to pursue her goal to help others. As part of her capstone project, Lena not only gave persuasive speeches about the value of the after-school leadership program to other service organizations around the community; she also gave "recruitment" type speeches in all the schools in the community as well, seeking a wide diversity of students who had an interest in becoming leaders.

Lena is engaged in **persuasion**—the process of trying to get others to change their attitudes or behavior. Most likely, you are involved in some sort of persuasion every day of your life. You try to persuade someone to join you for lunch or to join your study group. Others are involved in trying to persuade you: Radio commercials exhort you to buy, professors try to persuade you to turn in your papers on time, candidates for student and local government try to persuade you to vote for them, and the Internet offers a constant barrage of persuasive messages.

Since persuasion runs through every aspect of our society, you need to study how it works. Understanding persuasion will help you evaluate the persuasive techniques of others and develop your own persuasive messages in the most effective way possible.

PERSUASION AND THE COMMUNICATION MODEL

Often when we think of persuasion, we think of a communicator having an influence on a listener or on many listeners, such as a salesperson on a purchaser or a politician on a group of potential voters. This view emphasizes the source of the communication as the main influence in the persuasion process. However, sometimes when we think of persuasion, we think of people buying products ("Okay, I'll buy the larger TV with the clearer picture"), changing their attitudes ("Maybe Paula is the better candidate"), or altering their beliefs ("All right, maybe student demonstrations can make a difference"). This view emphasizes the receivers of persuasive messages as the main part of the persuasion process. When we emphasize the message in a persuasive situation, we might say, "That is a powerful statement" or "What a great speech!"

And yet the focus of persuasion should not be on the sender, the receiver, or the message. All share in the persuasive process, even though one may play a more important role than the other two. Only when all three combine successfully does effective persuasion occur.

WHAT IS PERSUASION, AND WHAT IS ITS PURPOSE?

Listing all the persuasive messages that have affected you over the past 12 hours is a difficult task. Advertisers have tried to get you to buy their products; a friend may have asked for a loan; your family may have tried to get you to come home for the weekend; a newspaper editorial may have convinced you to support a charitable cause; your friends may have persuaded you to go downtown with them; an instructor may have told you to keep up with your reading; a partner in a chat room may have asked you to continue conversing.

It is impossible to escape persuasive speaking, and persuasion has consequences. Change can occur when persuasion takes place. *Persuasion* is the process that occurs when a communicator (sender) influences the values, beliefs, attitudes, or behaviors of another person (receiver).

The key to understanding persuasion is influence. **Influence** refers to the power of a person or thing to affect others—to produce effects without the presence of physical force. For example, an instructor could have changed your habits by getting you to read regularly rather than cramming at exam time. Influence implies a degree of control over the thinking, emotions, and actions of others. *Social influence* is what occurs when a person's values, beliefs, attitudes, or behaviors are changed because of the behavior or presence of a person, individuals, a group or groups, or society.

Persuasion thus depends on influence, but you are unlikely to do something just because someone else affects you in some way. That is where motivation comes in. **Motivation** is the stimulation or inducement that causes you to act. For example, let's say you decide to go downtown with your friends to avoid their pestering if you don't go. Maybe you decide to keep up with your reading because doing so will help you do better in a course. Thus, in addition to being open to influence, we must also be motivated to do what we do.

Persuasion, influence, and motivation are closely linked. As persuaders, if we can relate our goals to things that persuade, influence, or motivate our listeners because they lead to desirable outcomes, we are far more likely to be successful. But if persuasion were truly this simple, people would be pulled and pushed so often that a numbing effect might eventually block out persuasive efforts.

Any persuasive effort has ethical implications. Sometimes ethical choices are clear from common knowledge and good judgment alone. Sometimes they are not. When making decisions about persuasion that may be questionable, you should consult other people if possible.

There is no doubt that persuasion plays a significant role in people's lives, and it does have consequences. Before we discuss specific strategies that persuaders can use to influence and motivate others, we need to look at values, beliefs, and attitudes because these are precisely what persuaders are trying to influence.

VALUES, BELIEFS, AND ATTITUDES

When a persuasive message taps into our values, beliefs, and attitudes, not only are we more responsive, but we are more likely to accept the sender. For example, we tend to respond positively to people who share our values. If you believe in the importance of recycling, you are more likely to be receptive to a speaker who advocates recycling. Thus, persuaders who have investigated audience values, beliefs, and attitudes

If a persuasive speaker can tap into our values, beliefs, and attitudes, we are more likely to respond to his or her message.

are more likely to be effective if—and this is the big "if"—they can adapt to them and use them effectively in their presentations.

Marcus, as he was thinking about subjects for a persuasive speech, considered talking to his class on the topics of welfare, Medicare, and the graduated income tax. As he used the information he gained from his own classroom audience analysis, he came up with an entirely different set of subjects; topics more closely tied to students' values, beliefs, and attitudes included suicide, racism, and political indifference.

Values

Values are the ideas we have about what is good and what is bad and how things should be. They are general guiding principles, standards, or judgments about how we should behave or about some final goal that may or may not be worth attaining.[1] These general guiding principles divide into two types: (1) *instrumental values*, which guide people's day-to-day behavior, and (2) *terminal values* or final goals that are or are not worth attaining.

Instrumental and terminal values are fairly easy to distinguish. Values that guide day-to-day behavior are loyalty, honesty, friendliness, courage, kindness, cleanliness, thrift, and responsibility. Terminal values may vary, but some are shared by all human beings: freedom, world peace, family security. Other enduring values include inner harmony, happiness, safety, personal security, achievement, progress, enlightenment (the value of the scientific method and rationality), and patriotism.

There are two points to think about when considering terminal values. First, they are not likely to change because of one brief, persuasive speech; they change only over time. Second, the degree to which you can tie your approach or appeal into widely accepted terminal values may help determine whether you achieve your goals. If you can show that your approach is consistent with or reinforces the values your audience members hold, they are more likely to accept it as a natural outgrowth of the values they already support. For example, Marcus chose racism as his topic because he could relate it to so many terminal values his classmates support: freedom, equality, friendship, inner harmony, and happiness.

Beliefs

Often, it is values that determine and anchor beliefs. For example, if one of our values is patriotism, we might believe in a capitalistic economy, a democratic form of government, and a public education system.

Beliefs are statements of knowledge, opinion, and faith. A statement of knowledge is "I believe [know] that if I let go of this book, it will drop to the floor." A statement of opinion is "I believe [have an opinion] that vitamin supplements help keep us healthy." A statement of faith is "I believe [have faith] that there is a God."

Beliefs can come to us from a variety of sources. Besides our own observations, we depend on the observations of our parents, teachers, religious leaders, and friends—especially as we grow up. As adults, we depend more on the observations of professionals, scientists, and journalists. We seldom develop beliefs in isolation. Our interactions have much to do with what we observe, how we observe it, and the conclusions we draw from our observations.

If you compare values with beliefs, you realize that beliefs are, in general, easier to change than values. Values are central; they are more securely anchored. The fact that beliefs are easier to change does not necessarily mean they can and will be changed. While statements of knowledge can be changed with more knowledge and statements of opinion can be changed in the same way, statements of faith are less likely to be changed—at least by a brief persuasive speech.

Attitudes

Attitudes are predispositions to respond favorably or unfavorably toward a person, subject, or situation. A favorable attitude toward honesty in your educational experiences would cause you to respond in some way: to speak out in favor of doing your own work, to discourage friends or classmates from being dishonest, or, depending on the strength of the attitude, to report cheating or plagiarism that you observe.

WHY PERSUASION IS CHALLENGING

One obvious difficulty is the sheer amount of persuasion that occurs. To say that we are besieged by persuasive messages is an understatement. Your persuasive message is likely to be received as just another persuasive message unless you take special care to make it stand out from others.

A second challenge is that persuasion tends to work slowly, over time. For example, how often have you gone out and bought a product after hearing or seeing just one advertisement for it? Persuasive speakers, however, ordinarily do not have the luxury of repeated efforts.

A third difficulty is that the value, belief, or attitude you are trying to change may be deeply entrenched. It's unusual for a single speech to shake or change our strongest feelings.

Another challenge is laziness. Getting people to do something can be difficult, let alone getting them to change an established way of doing things or of thinking. The routine is easier and perhaps more rewarding.

Finally, a threat to freedom, like a persuasive appeal that seems coercive—"Do things my way"—causes people to react, maybe even to reject, the appeal. Some people respond

To make a persuasive message stand out it must be made special or unique.

Consider This

Dr. Sheila Murray Bethel, best-selling author of *Making a Difference*, now in its 21st printing (and translated into five languages), is a professional speaker. She was inducted into the Speaker Hall of Fame in 1986 and has been recognized as one of the "Twenty-one Top Speakers for the 21st Century" by *Successful Meetings* Magazine. She has given over 2,500 presentations to more than two million people in 17 countries. Here, she shares the steps she takes when preparing a speech:

When I prepare for a speech I imagine a blank canvas on which I will paint word pictures to persuade, entertain, and inform my audience. There are several steps I take to begin:

First, determine what the theme of the presentation will be. This is my umbrella. I confer with my client to establish their needs and goals for the event to which I will be speaking. In the professional speaking business we refer to this as a "needs assessment." Without it you will never truly engage the audience.

Second, I ask myself if I have only 30 seconds to leave one vital message on this topic (theme) with the audience, what would it be? I follow that thought pattern until I have six or more central ideas in descending order of importance. This allows me to be flexible with the time frame of the presentation. Many times a speech is cut short because of an event at the venue that is out of my control.

My speeches are hydraulic. If I have the allotted time then I can deliver all of my main points; if not, the most important won't get lost in the cutting. That does not mean that the speech dwindles to a low key ending. It means I know where I can cut at the last minute. Each main point then has a story, anecdote, quote, or statistic assigned to it to help paint the picture and persuade.

At this point, I design a powerful opening and closing. Laughter and/or pathos are the quickest way to your listener's heart and mind.

I usually have a short "cheat sheet" of the key points to put near the lectern as I am speaking. When you give several speeches a month to different groups with different agendas, there is no way you can truly "tailor" the presentation and remember all the little important items for each audience. People often think you have to memorize the speech. Not so. Every speech given by a U.S. President, or leader in any field is on a Teleprompter, monitor, or actual notes.

I do not use PowerPoint or audio/video clips or special effects. I can't compete with the movie makers. Audiences are so sophisticated in their viewing habits that if I try to compete I'll fail. And, I believe a good story told with passion, humor, and conviction will paint a more powerful picture in the listener's mind than all the external resources you can use.

In the end, if I have done all this to the best of my ability, I remind myself that no matter how good I am, 50% of the responsibility of my message being well received lies with the audience. I do my best, and the rest is up to them.

Source: From Dr. Sheila Murray Bethel. She shared these steps with the author in a personal e-mail dated May 18, 2004. Her e-mail address is located on the Web site **http://www.bethelinstitute.com**. Telephone: 760-346-3525. Her lecture topics include leadership, branding, customer service, and communications. A free video is available at **http://www.speakerstreams.com/murraybethel/**

View clip #8, an excerpt from a persuasive student speech, "Living Wills, by Susan Hrabar."

negatively to a persuasive appeal even when the point of view expressed is similar to their own.

Many other factors can affect the receptiveness of your audience. Time of day may affect how awake or responsive people feel. Educational level could affect how much your listeners understand, how complex your argument can get, or how technical your language can be. Socioeconomic level might affect the kinds of subjects to which your audience responds. For example, you might speak to an audience of young people about how to get a job or how to impress an employer or talk to a group of retirees about investments and exotic travel opportunities.

Speakers can turn such difficulties into strengths by carefully analyzing their audiences and using this information in their research and other preparation—in selecting their organizational schemes, choosing their language, and presenting their messages. Persuasion requires all three elements—sender, message, and receiver—working together.

STRATEGIES OF PERSUASION

In persuasion, just as in any other from of communication, there are no guarantees. No strategy is foolproof. The best approach is to use all the available strategies to meet the demands of the audience. Obviously, different audiences will require different approaches, so the more strategies you can use, the better.

Determine Your Purpose

Subtracting a purpose from a persuasive effort is like pulling out the main rod of an umbrella. Without the rod, the whole umbrella collapses. Your purpose should be a highly specific and attainable persuasive goal.

When you begin planning a persuasive speech, one of the first questions you should ask yourself is what you want your audience to think or do. As we have noted in previous chapters, this is called your *specific purpose*. Here are some specific-purpose statements for persuasive speeches:

> **STRATEGIC FLEXIBILITY**
> It is when you face choices—which strategies are likely to be best for this audience?—that your strategic flexibility will be revealed. The more knowledge and experience you have, the larger the repertoire of available skills and behaviors you will have from which to select.

To Get Audience Members to Believe a Certain Way

- To persuade audience members that state lotteries exploit poor people.
- To persuade audience members that their college theater program is worthwhile.

To Get Audience Members to Act

- To persuade audience members to eat more fresh fruit and vegetables.
- To persuade audience members to write to their congressional representatives in support of stronger gun-control legislation.

If you keep your specific purpose in mind, it will be easier to generate main points for support. As you find support for your purpose, remember that you will want your audience members to respond in one or more of the five following ways:

1. *To change or reinforce beliefs.* A speaker wants to persuade the audience to change a belief or way of thinking or to reinforce a belief and take action. For example, a speaker who wants to convince listeners that state lotteries exploit the poor will provide evidence that poor people are the most likely to spend money on lotteries and that lotteries serve no constructive purpose.

2. *To take action.* For example, a speaker who wants the audience to eat more fresh fruits and vegetables or write to congressional representatives will try to motivate listeners by outlining probable results.

3. *To continue doing what they are already doing.* Some audience members might already be doing what you are asking them to do. For example, if several members of the class are taking theater classes, they might find a speech on supporting the college theater program interesting because it reinforces what they already believe.

4. *To avoid doing something.* The speaker might want audience members to stop buying or wearing fur, to stop watching a particular television program, or to get their legislators to prohibit personal firearms or abolish capital punishment.

5. *To continue not doing something.* This goal is slightly different from the second goal. It works best if audience members are considering taking action that you are

against. For example, if they're thinking about playing the lottery (because the payoff has become so large), you might be able to persuade them not to do so.

Any audience is likely to represent every possible point of view on your subject. When you're planning your speech, you should consider all of them.

Analyze Your Audience

Whether you use your own observations, surveys, interviews, or research, you need to get good information about your audience—as we discussed in Chapter 12 in order to appeal to your audience's values, beliefs, and attitudes whenever possible.

The second reason to analyze your audience is to predict its response to your persuasive effort. For example, even when speaking about day care to a group of working mothers—who share a common desire to find good day care for their children—you will find big differences in age, socioeconomic background, and even marital status. It might be helpful to select a target audience.

Your **target audience** is a subgroup of the whole audience that you must persuade in order to reach your goal. You aim your speech mostly at the individuals in this subgroup, knowing that some members of your audience are opposed to your message, some agree with it, some are uncommitted or undecided, and some find it irrelevant.

Politicians always go after a target audience because their success often depends on how many different constituencies they can appeal to. When uncommitted or undecided individuals are targeted, the reason is that they are the ones most likely to be influenced by persuasion.

Appeal to Your Audience Using Logic

One of the most important theorists in the history of the speech communication discipline, Aristotle, thought that effective persuasion consisted of three parts: a source's credibility (*ethos*), emotional appeals (*pathos*), and logical appeals (*logos*). We consider these in reverse order, beginning with logical appeals.

A **logical appeal** is one that addresses listeners' reasoning ability. Evidence in the form of statistics or any other supporting material will help persuade the audience. Chapter 12 explains in detail the kinds of supporting material you can use in a logical appeal.

A logical appeal may be argued in several ways: through deductive reasoning, inductive reasoning, causal reasoning, or reasoning by analogy. These appeals are developed and supported within the body of your speech. Causal reasoning and reasoning by analogy are both forms of inductive reasoning, but because of their importance, we will discuss them briefly in separate sections.

Deductive Reasoning

Deductive reasoning moves from the general to the specific. Here is a deductive argument used by one student:

> Acid rain is a problem throughout the entire northeastern United States.
>
> Pennsylvania is a northeastern state.
>
> Pennsylvania has a problem with acid rain.

Care is needed, however, with this pattern of reasoning. Have you ever heard someone say, "It's dangerous to generalize"? A faulty premise really is faulty deductive thinking, as in this example:

All college students procrastinate.

Mary is a college student.

Therefore, Mary procrastinates.

Deductive reasoning can form the structure for an entire speech, for just a single part, or for several parts. In his commencement address "The New Entrepreneurship" to the Olin School of Business, Boston College, Wellesley, Massachusetts, Peter Bell, CEO of Storage Network, Inc., used deductive reasoning for each of the three qualities that entrepreneurs share:

> *Take the first quality—resilience. You won't find successful entrepreneurs blaming others for their own failure—because they actually use failure as a lesson.*
>
> *I've suffered a number of complete failures—and they hurt. Like when I was unable to raise enough capital to launch a venture—which eventually caused the company to close its doors. Or when I was unable to turn around a company.*
>
> *I really hate to fail. I know that there are some people in the world who actually derive pleasure when others fail. But I've learned from my failures. My failures made me work ten times harder. And they've given me valuable experience.*
>
> *The second quality of successful entrepreneurs is initiative. They don't hide. They're out front. Consider this analogy from baseball. If you look at the fielding percentages of some shortstops, you could be misled by the number of errors they make. That's because some of the greatest shortstops in history put themselves on the line. They go after groundballs and pop-ups that their less driven counterparts don't even attempt. The great shortstops aren't afraid of being visible—even if it means they fail. And entrepreneurs can't afford to be afraid either.*
>
> *The third quality of successful entrepreneurs is an enormous capacity for perseverance and determination.*
>
> *I think Ellen Hancock, the CEO of Exodus Communications, is a great example. After 29 years at IBM, where Ellen became the most senior female executive in the company, reporting to the CEO—she left. She joined Apple and Apple fired her. Then she went to National Semiconductor and they fired her, too. But instead of hanging it up, she went to Exodus—a small company with fewer than 20 employees at the time. And she built Exodus into the largest web-hosting company in the world.*
>
> *I believe Ellen's success story is a terrific illustration of how successful entrepreneurs never quit.*[2]

Inductive Reasoning

Another logical technique is **inductive reasoning**—reasoning from the specific to the general. Usually when we use inductive reasoning, we move from a number of facts to a conclusion. The facts, in this case, could be developed within the body of the speech, with the conclusion offered at the end, in the speech's conclusion. Here is how a student used inductive reasoning to persuade her audience that the college should require everyone to take a foreign language:

In some parts of the United States, you need to understand Spanish to get by.

Americans are traveling more and more to countries where a language other than English is spoken.

The mark of an educated person is that he or she can speak, write, and read at least one other language.

Conclusion: Everyone should learn another language.

In her speech to her class, "I Lived to Tell about It," Adrienne Bower used inductive reasoning to arrive at the action step of her speech. She believed that her listeners might reject her conclusions if they heard them first, so she built her case slowly with statistics, facts, opinions, and a personal example. Here is some of the information she provided her audience:

1. *According to the Core Institute at Southern Illinois University, cited in an article in* USA Today, *by Michael P. Haines, the director of the National Social Norms Resource Center at Northern Illinois University, the average number of alcoholic drinks consumed weekly by freshmen in 2000 was 8.5 for males, 3.7 for females. For sophomores, it was 9.1 for males, and 3.8 for females.[3] Yet, at one institution, the Core Institute reported that 58 percent of students surveyed had consumed five or more drinks at one sitting in the previous two weeks.[4] The average, according to the Core Institute, across campuses is 46.5 percent who had consumed five or more drinks at one sitting in the previous two weeks.[5]*

2. *"Half the students age 10 to 24 questioned in a 1999 study by the Centers for Disease Control said they had consumed alcohol in the preceding month" reported Jeffrey Kluger in an article "How to Manage Teen Drinking (The Smart Way)" in* Time *magazine.[6] The Core Institute, which surveys 30,000 to 60,000 college students annually, reports that heaviest drinkers are males in fraternities or on athletic teams followed closely by female students in sororities.[7]*

3. *"College students are young and irresponsible, and drinking is part of their culture," says Rob Waldron in an article "Students Are Dying; Colleges Can Do More," for* Newsweek.[8] *Another article in* Time, *"Women on a Binge," by Jodie Morse includes the line "More college women regularly get drunk," as part of her headline.[9] Morse also includes the statistic, "Since 1993, women's colleges have seen a 125 percent increase in frequent binge drinking."[10]*

4. *Last year, I was drinking hard lemonade and bottled mixed drinks with friends in the parking lot of Burger King. I didn't know how much my friend Stephanie had to drink, and I thought she was being careful, but she crashed the car on the way back to our sorority. The tree hit the driver's side of the car, and Stephanie died in the hospital of her injuries. You probably read about it last year. Three of my sorority sisters and I lived to tell about it, but it was a harrowing experience I never want to relive.*

   Now, my point is not to try to eliminate drinking from college campuses. "Prohibition didn't work for the nation in the 1920s, and it's a failure on college campuses today," says Michael P. Haines.[11] It isn't going to happen. My point, too, isn't to develop terror campaigns designed to scare students about the hazards of drinking too much. This is another approach that hasn't worked well.[12]

   My solution has five parts, and it is based on one common assumption: College-age kids are going to drink: (1) Lower the national drinking age to 18 so that drinking takes place in the open where it can be supervised by police, security guards, and health-care workers.[13] (2) Get out the information that heavy drinkers are not in the majority, that most students who drink "do so responsibly, according to a study funded by the U.S. Department of Education."[14] "When students are armed with the truth about the moderate and responsible drinking habits of the majority of their peers," says Haines, "they tend to consume less themselves."[15] (3) Widely promote a designated-driver program whereby all local bars give free soft drinks to the nondrinker in any group.[16] (4) Establish a university policy whereby all college students are sent a birthday card to arrive the day before they become eligible to drink, which wishes them a happy birthday but reminds them to drink responsibly. (5) Drink responsibly. Take full responsibility for yourselves, knowing that moderate drinking habits are "a powerful way to help create a healthier, safer campus culture."[17]

Sometimes it will work best to give the facts and then draw the conclusion (induction); in other cases you might want to start with the conclusion and then support it with facts (deduction).

Causal Reasoning

Another way to reason is causally. **Causal reasoning** is a logical appeal that pertains to, constitutes, involves, or expresses a cause and therefore uses the word *because*, which is either implicitly or explicitly stated. For example, "I failed the class because I didn't complete the assignments," or "The basketball team is losing because it has an incompetent coach." The latter example points out some of the problems of causal reasoning. That the coach is incompetent may be a matter of opinion. The team might be losing because it doesn't have good players or because the other teams have taller players or because there is no way of recruiting good players. The causal pattern can be used for presenting evidence as well as for organizing an entire speech. The cause-and-effect pattern is one of the ways to organize a speech that is discussed in Chapter 13.

Reasoning by Analogy

Finally, you can reason by **analogy.** In this case you compare two similar cases and conclude that if something is true for one, it must also be true for the other. Casey used analogy to try to get his listeners to understand the value of new electronic gadgets. He said, "Think of these as tools to make your life easier. These are just like the tools you've been using all along. The only difference is that these electronic tools are faster, smaller, and more adaptable to your specific needs."

Often speeches of policy use analogy. Advocates of a policy look to see if the policy has succeeded elsewhere. For example, Katrina Paschalis was trying to get her listeners to understand that a better lifestyle will help prevent cancer. Her goal was to get her listeners to take an active part in their own preventive health care:

> You all know the threat that cancer holds on your life. It is a pervasive threat, but it needn't be scary. It is something you can handle. Think of living a healthy lifestyle as similar to owning a new automobile. Just as you want to keep the inside clean, you want to avoid smoking to keep your own insides clean. Just as you want to make sure all the fuel and other liquids you put into your car are exactly what the manufacturer's warranty requires, you, too, want to make certain you only take in drinks and foods known to be good for you. And just as you want to drive your car with care, you, too, want to use proper physical activity. If you take care of the insides, what you put into it, and how you drive it, you can keep your car in new condition. If you avoid smoking, a poor diet, and physical inactivity, you can prevent half of all the cancers in the USA and, thus, live your life as if in new condition.

Logical Fallacies in Argument

Fallacy is an improper conclusion drawn from the premise. A **premise** includes the reasons given in support of a conclusion.

- **Naturalistic fallacy** occurs when something is identified as being good or desirable because it appears to be a natural characteristic. ("Everyone wants to be wealthy so systems should be designed on the basis of economic incentives.")

- *Fallacy of* **sweeping generalization** occurs when a general rule is applied to a specific case to which the rule is not applicable because of special features of the case. ("Everyone has a right to his or her own property; therefore, even though Jones has been declared insane, he should keep his machine gun.")
- *Fallacy of* **hasty generalization** occurs when an isolated or exceptional case is used as the basis for a general conclusion that is unwarranted. ("I had a bad relationship with the first person I ever dated. I'm sure all relationships are bad.")
- *Fallacy of* **bifurcation** occurs when one presumes that a distinction is exclusive and exhaustive, but other alternatives exist. ("America—love it or leave it." "Companies can either make a profit or be socially responsible.")
- *Fallacy of* **begging the question** occurs when an argument, instead of offering proof for its conclusion, simply reasserts the conclusion in another form. ("God exists because the Bible says so. I know the Bible is true because it is the work of God.")
- *Fallacy of* **question-begging epithets** occurs when slanted language is used to reaffirm what we wish to prove but have not proved yet. ("No right-thinking American could support this measure, a cunning plot hatched in backrooms by corrupt politicians.")
- *Fallacy of* **false analogy** occurs when a comparison between an obscure or difficult set of facts and one that is already known and understood, and to which it bears a significant resemblance, is erroneous and distorts the facts of the case being argued. ("Why should we sentimentalize over a few hundred Native Americans who were ruined when our great civilization was being built? It may be that they suffered injustices, but, after all, you can't make an omelet without breaking a few eggs.")
- *Fallacy of* **false cause** occurs when events are causally connected but in fact no such causal connection has been established. ("Most of the company's managers before the bailout were Caucasians. Therefore, the government should demand that more minorities be in upper management before it provides any guaranteed loan.")
- *Fallacy of* **ad hominem** occurs when an argument diverts attention away from the question being argued by focusing instead on those arguing it. ("The candidate used drugs; thus we shouldn't trust his views on drug control.")
- *Fallacy of* **appeal to authority** occurs whenever an idea is justified by citing some source of expertise as a reason for holding that idea. ("Of course there shouldn't be government intervention; after all, Adam Smith and Milton Friedman are opposed to government intervention.")
- *Fallacy of* **mob appeal** occurs when an appeal is made to emotions, particularly to powerful feelings that can sway people in large crowds. ("I [a candidate for public office] almost died of cancer; therefore, you can trust me to be a good president.")
- *Fallacy of* **appeal to ignorance** occurs when an argument is based on an opponent's inability to disprove a conclusion as proof of the conclusion's correctness. ("I know that God doesn't exist because nobody has yet been able to prove God's existence.")

In their book *How to Persuade People Who Don't Want to Be Persuaded*, Joel Bauer and Mark Levy report the results of a study published in the *Harvard Business*

Review showing messages that caught the attention of executives had four characteristics: (1) they were personalized, (2) they evoked an emotional response, (3) they came from a trustworthy or respected sender, and (4) they were concise. But Thomas Davenport and John Beck, who conducted the study with 60 executives, concluded that "The messages that both evoked emotion and were personalized were more than twice as likely to be attended to as the messages without those attributes."[18] Bauer and Levy summarized the findings by driving the main point home to their readers even more dramatically: "To get attention, to be remembered, to change the moment, you must make your messages personal and evoke emotion in your listener."[19]

Appeal to Your Audience Using Emotion

An **emotional appeal** focuses on listeners' needs, wants, desires, and wishes. Recent research shows that the people who are most successful at persuasion are those who can understand others' motives and desires—even when these motives and desires are not stated.

In a public-speaking situation it is impossible to appeal to each individual's motives and desires, so it helps to know about basic needs we all have.

Psychologist Abraham Maslow proposed a model that arranges people's needs from relatively low-level physical needs to higher level psychological ones. This model, referred to as a **hierarchy of needs,** is shown in Figure 16-1.

As you can see at the bottom of the figure, the first needs all human beings have are *physiological needs.* Starving people do not care about freedom; their need for food is so great that it outweighs all other needs. Therefore, physiological needs must be taken care of before other needs can be met. Since we usually assume that basic needs are taken care of, they are generally not a basis for a persuasive speech, although politicians, clergy, and educators may try to persuade citizens to address the unmet basic needs of the poor.

Figure 16-1

Maslow's Hierarchy of Needs

Self-Actualization Needs
(Genuine fulfillment, realization of potential)

Self-Esteem Needs
(Recognition, respect from others, self-respect)

Belongingness and Love Needs
(Friendship, giving and receiving love, affection)

Safety Needs
(Stability, freedom from violence, freedom from disease, security, structure, order, law)

Physiological Needs
(Food, water, sleep, and physical comfort)

Safety needs are next in the hierarchy. The whole area of safety needs can be useful in persuasion, since all of us have these needs in varying degrees. In the excerpt below, notice how the speaker appeals to the student audience's need for safety:

> *In the last three months there have been six assaults on this campus. Where have they occurred? All in parking lots with no lights. When? At night, after evening classes. Does this mean that you can't take any more evening classes without fearing for your life? Should you leave your car at home so you can avoid the campus parking lots?*

Belongingness and love needs, the next level, also have a potent appeal. If you doubt this, turn on your television set and note how many commercials make a direct pitch to the need to be loved.

Here is how one student used the need to belong to urge new students to join the Campus Fellowship—a student social group on campus:

> *The first year is the hardest year of college. You are in a new environment and are faced with a bewildering array of choices. I felt this way in my first year. Then I met someone from "The Campus Fellowship" who invited me to one of its meetings. The minute I walked in the door several people met me and made me feel welcome. Today some of these people are my best friends.*

Self-esteem needs stem from our need to feel good about ourselves. We see a lot of persuasion based on these needs in self-help books. Typical themes are that you'll feel good about yourself if you change your fashion style, learn how to climb mountains, practice meditation, and so on. One student appealed to self-esteem needs when she gave a speech called "Try Something New:"

> *I have a friend who, at the age of 35, decided to learn how to play the flute. She had never played an instrument before, but she loved music and thought it would be interesting to give it a try. Now that she has been studying for two years, she told me, "I will never be a great player but this has been a wonderful experience. I enjoy my CDs even more because I know what the musicians are doing. I understand so much more about music. It's wonderful to try something new." I am here today to urge you to try something new yourself. To see what you can discover about yourself.*

At the top of his hierarchy, Maslow puts *self-actualization needs*—the need to realize one's potential and attain fulfillment, to do our best with what we have. An admissions director for a community college made this statement in a speech to a group of older students in an attempt to persuade them to go to college:

> *I'm sure that many of you look back at your high school days and think "I was a pretty good writer; I wonder if I still could write," or "I*

How many different emotions or needs are being tapped to get results like these?

really liked my business courses; I would like to try my hand at bookkeeping again." I believe one of the saddest things that can happen to us is not to be able to try out things that we are good at, things that we have always wanted to do. Our new college program for returning adults will give you a chance to do just that—try out the things you are good at.

You have the best chance of choosing the right emotional appeal if you have done a thorough job of researching your audience. For instance, safety needs tend to be important to families, especially those with young children. On the other hand, younger audiences, such as college students, generally focus more on belonging, love, and self-esteem needs. If you focused on safety needs to encourage a college audience to buy savings bonds, the students probably wouldn't find your speech very interesting. Self-actualization needs probably appeal most to older audiences. Adults who are approaching midlife are the most likely to ask themselves whether they have made the right choices for their lives and whether they should make some changes. Age, of course, is only one factor to consider in assessing needs. The more information you have about your audience, the better your chance of selecting the right emotional appeals.

Although emotional appeals can be powerful, they can also be very personal, and if you are faced with a decision of whether to use an appeal to logic or an appeal to emotion—especially with an audience you are not totally familiar with—your best bet is likely to be to use logic and to depend on your listeners' critical thinking skills.

STRATEGIC FLEXIBILITY

The key to selecting and applying the right emotional appeal is based on strategic flexibility, but how you anticipate, assess, and evaluate the factors, elements, and conditions depends on the foundation you have established as a result of researching your audience.

Use Research to Prove Your Points

No matter how you plan to appeal to your listeners—whether by logic or emotion—a crucial element in the persuasion process is your research. Larry Tracy, a professional speaker, in a speech to a chapter of the National Speakers Association titled "Taming Hostile Audiences," said it succinctly: "Emotions do indeed play an important role with any audience, but it is still verifiable, factual data that persuades reasonable people to come to your side."[20]

When doing your research for your speech, look for a variety of sources. An opinion from an expert may be your best piece of evidence, but an additional fact might drive the point home. Don't forget to include your own personal experience with your topic.

A variety of research is more likely to hold the attention of your listeners, too. Just as a series of statistics (numbers) is likely to bore your audience, a series of similar examples or opinions can do the same thing.

There is no overall guide to how much evidence you need to prove a point to your listeners, but ask yourself: "What would it take to convince me?" A second guideline is to ask yourself: "How much time do I have?" For most short, in-class speeches you might want to follow the "rule of three": three main heads, three subpoints for each, and three brief pieces of evidence to support each subpoint. Although the rule of three generally applies to most speeches, some evidence takes time to relate—like examples, illustrations, and personal experience—and some points require more evidence and some less. These are judgment calls, and because you are in charge, you will need to make the decisions.

Choose Your Language Carefully

Remember, people are not inclined to think or act the way you want them to unless they are motivated. Try to keep language in mind as you select supporting material. You want to stimulate the emotions of your listeners with special words. And you want to create emotional pictures that will make people feel what you are talking about.

Look at the images created by the language in Lance R. Odden's speech "Talk to Your Children about the Tough Stuff":

> *Remember that the innocent freshman pledge who died at MIT last year had been told to drink a beer and a bottle of bourbon. Remember the three students who died in the Virginia college system with no one learning from the previous experience. Remember the deaths of the students at LSU. Remember the rape, which was alcohol induced, at a local high school party. Note that just last Tuesday, in Denver, an 18-year-old girl died after having consumed over a liter of tequila.*[21]

Appeal to Your Audience Using Your Credibility

Why are some people more persuasive than others? Research on persuasion says you are more likely to be effective as a persuader if listeners consider you to be credible. **Credibility**, or believability, consists of four qualities: expertise, dynamism, trustworthiness, and ethics. Aristotle, as you will recall, labeled this ethos. Let's look at each of them.

Expertise

Someone who has **expertise** possesses special ability, skill, or knowledge. That is, he or she is an expert. A speaker who is perceived as an expert on his or her subject gains much credibility. For example, let's say that on the news one night you see a woman talking about the effects of long-term exercise on health. The anchorperson introduces her as a doctor from Johns Hopkins Medical School who has been studying the effects of exercise. The next day you hear a student give a persuasive speech about the value of exercise. Some of his comments, however, contradict some of what you heard on the evening news. Which speaker do you believe? In this case there isn't much doubt. You believe the physician because she is an expert.

Expertise Based on Personal Experience

When you are a speaker trying to persuade an audience, it will help your credibility if you can show some expertise about your subject. Expertise does not depend only on book learning or specialized training; you can be an expert because of your personal experience. Nancy, for example, speaks of her own experience with alcoholism:

> *One night I went to a party. I remember the early part of the evening but that's about all. The next thing I remember was waking up in my own bed. I didn't remember the end of the party or how I got home. When I woke up that morning and realized I didn't remember anything, I knew I was in serious trouble.*

You don't always have to relate such a dramatic experience as Nancy's. One student who had donated blood with the Red Cross persuaded classmates to donate blood as well.

Expertise Based on Commitment

Another way to show expertise is to establish your commitment to your topic. Listeners are more inclined to believe speakers who have taken actions that support their positions. If you can show that you have contributed to a charity, you are more likely to persuade others to contribute.

Expertise through Research

You can develop expertise through research. By interviewing and by reading articles and books, you can quote acknowledged experts, thereby making your speech more credible. When you are using information derived from experts, make that clear in your speech with such references as:

> According to Dr. Jessica Smith, a noted authority in this area . . . From Ronald Jones's best-selling book, *The Growing Years* . . .

Dynamism

Speakers with **dynamism,** another aspect of credibility, show a great deal of enthusiasm and energy for their subjects. For example, when a student tried to get his classmates to become more politically active, he spoke of his own work in a local politician's primary campaign as one of the most exciting times of his life. He described his experience so vividly that the audience was able to feel his excitement.

Much of the dynamism in a speech will be created nonverbally. A speaker who stands up straight, projects his or her voice to the back of the room, and doesn't hesitate will be seen by the audience as more dynamic than one who doesn't do these things. Watch for the most dynamic speakers in your class, and make some mental notes on how they convey their energy and enthusiasm nonverbally.

Trustworthiness

A speaker with **trustworthiness** is perceived as reliable and dependable. Sometimes we have no way of knowing whether a speaker is trustworthy unless he or she does something unreliable, such as showing up an hour late for a speech. In a speech communication class, however, after a month or so, most students can identify classmates who are reliable and dependable. These are people who come on time for class, give their speeches on time, pull their weight in a group, and give evidence that they have spent time preparing for a speech. They are perceived as trustworthy and therefore worth listening to.

Because so much of persuasion depends on the person doing the persuading, compare these two pictures. Make a judgment. Which person is likely to be more persuasive because of expertise, dynamism, trustworthiness, and ethics—and why?

Working Together

Apply the ethical principles you have just read about to each of the following situations:

1. Is it ethical to give a speech advocating a position with which you disagree?
2. Is it ethical to present a speech just to fulfill an assignment—a speech that you feel no commitment to or responsibility for?
3. Why are student speakers under obligation to provide listeners with ideas that are logically developed and well supported?
4. Why are student speakers responsible for being fully knowledgeable about their topics?
5. Should student speakers concern themselves with the consequences of their speaking? Why or why not?

Ethics

Ethics are a matter of conforming to acceptable and fair standards of conduct. Ethics are particularly important to persuasion because you are trying to change people—often in a significant way. If your audience doesn't perceive you as ethical, your speech will fail. Here are some ethical principles that are particularly useful in persuasive speaking:

1. Treat your audience with respect. Assume that audience members are intelligent and mature and will respond to a well-reasoned and well-organized appeal.
2. Take care not to distort or exaggerate your facts. Find the best facts you can, and let them stand on their own.
3. Avoid lying or name calling. Even if you think that the opposing side is stupid or vicious, it's unacceptable to say so. Show that your ideas are better.
4. Avoid suppressing key information. If you discover important information that doesn't support your view, include it but find a way of refuting it.
5. If you have something to gain personally from your persuasive speech, tell your audience what it is.

STRUCTURE YOUR MATERIAL EFFECTIVELY

How you decide to structure your material may depend on the material itself; it may depend on your own interests or intentions; or it may depend on the situation or assignment. The most important consideration, however, is your listeners' attitude, or how you expect your audience to react.

STRATEGIC FLEXIBILITY

As you draw together the information you have discovered on your own interests and intentions, on the situation and assignment, and, of course, on your listeners' attitudes and how you expect them to react, these factors become the foundation for strategic flexibility.

Questions of Fact, Value, and Policy

Chapter 10 discussed using questions of fact, value, and policy in group discussions. Now let's see how these questions can be used for persuasive speeches.

Questions of Fact

A *question of fact* deals with what is true or false. Brandon Adams used a question of fact when he spoke on the topic "Do Most Students in Our Society Run Late?" Here is how he set up his speech:

Specific purpose: To persuade my audience that most students run late.

Central idea: Running late is a habit that can be broken.

Main points:
I. Most students are unaware of the feelings and habits that surround their lateness.

II. Running late can cause problems such as lost school credits, jobs, friendships, romantic relationships, even marriages.

III. To break the pattern, late people must identify the psychological forces that underlie their habit and reprogram the way they think.

Questions of Value

A *question of value* is concerned with some aspect of a moral issue: whether something is good or bad, right or wrong, beneficial or detrimental, and so on. Note how a student used a question of value to discuss the topic of plagiarism:

Specific purpose: To persuade my audience that plagiarism of any kind is unacceptable.

Central idea: Plagiarism may have short-term gains, but it does long-term harm.

Main points:
I. People's professional careers have been ruined when it was revealed that they had cheated in college.

II. People who plagiarize deny themselves the opportunity to learn new skills.

III. Plagiarism is theft; rather than take someone's possessions, you steal his or her ideas and work.

Questions of Policy

A *question of policy* deals with specific courses of action and usually contains such words as *should, ought,* or *must*. Here are the main points for a speech based on a question of policy:

Specific purpose: To persuade my audience that all students should be granted a one-term work-experience opportunity as part of their college education.

Central idea: A work experience will give students a realistic understanding of the workplace before they graduate.

Main points:
I. Work experiences are an effective way to give students real-world college.

II. Work experiences provide students with useful contacts outside college.

III. Work experiences offer students a better base for understanding their education.

IV. Work experiences develop skills that may not be developed in college.

One-Sided versus Two-Sided Arguments

Should persuaders present one side or both sides of an issue? When you know your listeners basically support your ideas, one side may be sufficient. For example, a student knew that she didn't have to persuade her audience of the pros and cons of speed dating. Instead, she came up with some unique ideas for how her listeners could find dates.

There are occasions, however, when speakers should present both sides of the picture. Often the presentation of both sides will boost credibility: The speaker is likely to be perceived as fairer and more rational. When an issue of public importance is controversial, it's a good idea to present both sides, since most people will probably have heard something about each side. When a student spoke on gun control, he presented both sides because he knew there were strong feelings for and against.

Research results seem to indicate that (1) a two-sided speech is more effective when the listeners have at least a high school education; (2) the two-sided speech is especially effective if the evidence clearly supports the thesis; and (3) the two-sided presentation is more effective when listeners oppose the speaker's position, but the one-sided approach is more effective when listeners already support the thesis.[22]

Ethical considerations should sometimes be taken into account when deciding whether to present two sides. For example, if presenting only one side will suppress key information, then presenting two sides is essential, but you may need to refute the side you don't agree with.

Order of Presentation

The organizational schemes most commonly used in persuasive speeches—covered previously in Chapter 13—are the cause-and-effect order, problem–solution order, and the motivated sequence. The cause-and-effect order has two parts. The first part of the body develops the cause of a problem, and the second discusses its effects. For example, the first part could talk about the time pressures and convenience that drives people to fast food. The second, the effects, could discuss the unhealthy results—including obesity.

In the problem–solution order the first part of the body of the speech develops the problem, and the second part of the body of the speech gives a solution. A speaker, for example, could talk about negative emotions and chronic pessimism as risk factors for heart disease, smoking, excessive drinking, and poor eating habits—the problem. In the solution half, the speaker could support the benefits of optimism—the body of evidence that well-adjusted, socially stable, well-integrated people have a lower risk of disease, premature death, and even lower blood cholesterol levels[23]—and how to develop an optimistic point of view.

The third pattern of organization, motivated sequence, is a time-tested adaptation of the problem–solution order. The motivated sequence includes five steps: attention, need, satisfaction, visualization, and action. Often, the attention step is handled in the introduction, and the action step is treated in the conclusion, while the three middle steps become the main points of the body of your speech. It could be, too, that all five steps take place in the body of the speech, and the introduction and conclusion introduce the topics and summarize their development.

- **Attention**—Call the attention of your listeners to the problem. You can do this in the introduction to your speech.
- **Need**—Support your topic's importance or seriousness with facts, opinions, statistics, and examples.
- **Satisfaction**—In this step, your job is to satisfy the need you have developed by offering solutions.
- **Visualization**—You need to help your listeners imagine what their lives will be like if they implement the solutions you have offered: how much better their lives might be, or how improved our society might be.
- **Action**—The action step can be part of your conclusion. The point is to encourage your listeners to put your solutions into action.

A brief example will demonstrate how easy it is to frame a speech using these five steps. Briana Christopher brought some of the advertisements campus credit-card hawkers were using to lure students to their credit cards. To call attention to the problem, she used a personal example and cited a statistic that about 80 percent of college students hold at least one credit card.[24]

The need, she said, had to do with the debts students carried. Briana said that on average, each student is likely to carry a credit-card balance of $2,748. Twenty-one percent have piled up credit-card debts of $3,000 to $7,000. From an interview she had with the director of first- and second-year student advising, Briana let her listeners know the range of difficulties students find themselves in, such as severe credit messes, some students using their scholarship and grant money to pay off their debts, and how some students have had to leave school because of credit-card difficulties.

In her satisfaction step, Briana recommended that students have only one credit card, use the card only for emergencies, shop around for a card that has no annual fee and a lower interest rate, pay off the entire balance each month, cap the credit line at $500 to $1,000, and use only a secured credit card in which the credit limit on the card is equal to the money deposited in the bank.

For the visualization step, Briana talked about her own difficulties with her credit card, and she showed her audience members the free and independent feelings they could achieve by following her advice. Having interviewed several other students who were free of credit-card problems, she let her listeners know—from a student's vantage point—what "free of debt" really means.

Briana made her action step specific and direct by, first, repeating her solutions and showing what she, herself, did to take action on each one of them. She took her solutions one step further in her action step by giving her listeners the Bank Rate Monitor's Web site for helping them shop around for the best credit card.

Daquisha Lattrell organizes her speech "Giving Something Back" using the motivated sequence. Hers is the sample speech at the end of this chapter, and she uses her introduction for the attention step and her conclusion for the action step of the sequence. The need, satisfaction, and visualization steps are the three main heads of the body of her speech, and each of the transitions she uses refers to the main heads as her speech progresses.

THE INTERNET AND THE PERSUASIVE SPEECH

The following things persuaders must do to adapt to listeners in the age of the Internet may not be new; they simply require a new emphasis or focus. To be successful, persuaders must:

1. *Create immediate respect and integrity.* Without respect and integrity on the Internet, listeners will mouse click to another source just as easily as they can divert their attention from what is taking place in front of them.

2. *Form an emotional bond with listeners.* With no emotional bond, there is no need for listeners to stay tuned. If you are fired up about what you believe in, your listeners will become fired up as well.

3. *Filter the noise for them by organizing the chaos.* So much information available becomes little more than noise—clutter—to many people.

4. *Put what is most important front and center.* Because it is fast, the Internet has helped nurture short attention spans. When they are drowning in a glut, they need a life preserver in their face.

5. *Offer the necessary facts, figures, and additional information.* Efficiently and effectively offer what they need and want with the necessary support.

6. *Bring in others' ideas and opinions; avoid dominating your speech as the single, sole source of information and opinion.* The Internet offers links; when you link your ideas to those of others, you provide a strong foundation for belief and action. A site with links simply says, "Click here for more information."

7. *Make certain listeners have ways to get further information; give them the citations necessary.* Because they are unlikely to make up their mind on the spot (because they don't have to do so), they need specific instructions on where additional information can be found. The easier it is to get, the more likely it will be sought.

8. *Talk to listeners in a language they can understand.* There can be no ambiguity or misunderstanding, because the connection between persuader and listener is but a mouse-click option. Translate jargon; avoid difficult words; keep it simple.

9. *Help listeners see your solutions or approaches in action—in situations with which they can easily identify.* The Internet is both a verbal and visual medium.

10. *Give listeners freedom.* Avoid high pressure, pushy persuasion. Technology has given customers a greater sense of control. Acknowledge their need to move at their own pace and, thus, release them from their overscheduled, overcommitted, stress-filled lives.

Mooney claims that in today's Internet-dominated world "—what really counts in the long run is the sense of being known as an individual, understood as a unique human being, and treated with the respect that each and everyone of us deserves."[25]

Sample Speech

The following speech was given by Daquisha Lattrell in her summer required speech communication class. Ms. Lattrell is a friend of the authors, and her speech is used here with her permission.

General purpose: To persuade.

Specific purpose: To inspire the class to take an active role in volunteer work.

Central idea: To convince listeners that you can make a difference, that you can begin right here and now, and that you will experience many benefits from your volunteer work.

Giving Something Back

Introduction

I watched my mother prepare, serve meals, and clean up at the local food pantry in the neighborhood where I grew up. These soup kitchens and food pantries feed over 26 million hungry Americans each year.[1] Until I was old enough to help, I would love to sit and chat with the visitors while they ate. One man, I'll call him a V.V., or volunteer veteran, helped with blood donations for the American Red Cross, volunteered as a teacher's aid in the local school, worked as a volunteer shelving books at the local public library, picked up trash for a local parks beautification project, taught basic skills in a nearby prison, and served regularly as part of the "Friends of the Elderly" group visiting seniors who live alone. This was my early introduction to volunteering, and this gentleman was my inspiration. To volunteer, according to the dictionary, is to enter into any service of your own free will, and today I want to encourage you to take an active role in volunteer work.

When I was home for the break, I noticed that my mother had a copy of *Chicken Soup for the Volunteer's Soul,* and in that book I read some of the most inspirational stories about volunteers. It was that book, those stories, and my V.V. (volunteer veteran) that inspired me to choose this topic for this speech. There are more than 200 million volunteers throughout the world,[2] and, according to a report out of UCLA, between 75 and 85 percent of first-year students have performed volunteer work in the past year.[3]

Transition: I want to talk about the need for volunteers, how to become a volunteer, and the benefits you can get from volunteer work.

Body

I. The need for volunteers is great. It makes no difference what your major is, what kind of job you are preparing for, or the nature of your life

---

Daquisha begins her speech with a personal example, but she follows that example immediately with a statistic. What makes this introduction so effective is how she worked different types of volunteering into her experience of talking with V.V. (volunteer veteran).

Notice how quickly Daquisha incorporates a dictionary definition of the word *volunteer* into her opening comments and then states her specific purpose directly.

Daquisha uses statistics, too, as she completes her introduction. Her blend of personal experience and statistics works well to both hold audience attention and call their attention to her topic—volunteerism.

Daquisha uses initial partition to divide her speech into three parts just before beginning the body of her speech.

Sample Speech (continued)

plan; there are volunteer opportunities that are closely related and that need your help.
  A. It could be, for example, civic involvement—the backbone of thriving cities and towns—where you work with the Jaycees, Rotary, Lions, or Kiwanis.
  B. It could be social action where you work as an election volunteer or take part in local party politics. I take great pride, for example, in helping a politician from my district get elected to a state office.
  C. It could be in your neighborhood as my friend the V.V. was fully involved. I have worked in a women's shelter, too. Did you know that more than one million women seek medical assistance for injuries caused by abuse? Another five million will be battered but will not seek treatment.[4]
  D. There are many other areas where your volunteer work will be appreciated—areas such as health, education, arts and sciences (places such as libraries, museums, zoos, botanical gardens, aboretums, and conservatories), the environment, and even global opportunities, too.
  E. In an online article "Colleges Fail to Encourage Volunteerism Among Students," Jack Calareso makes two claims:
    1. "College students seem less and less willing to get involved in serving the common good."[5]
    2. "Volunteering time to engage in community or public service ranks at the bottom of students' priorities."[6]

Transition: There is obviously a great need for volunteers in all segments of our society. But, what can you do about it?

  II. There are many ways you have to get involved in volunteer work. Larson, who is co-chair of the May 4 Task Force and president of the Kent State University chapter of Amnesty International, writes: "I think [students] don't really know how to get involved, and I know our campus does not really encourage involvement."[7] Let me show you how to get involved.
    A. If you are not a volunteer and if you want just a taste of it before committing to any particular group, check out City Cares at **http://www.citycares.org**. It is located in more than 30 major cities, and it is a great way to get involved if you're not sure what you want to

---

During the first four points of her first main head, Daquisha simply discusses various opportunities available for volunteers.

Daquisha found it important not just to outline various opportunities but to more strongly drive her point home with a couple of quotations from Jack Calareso directly related to college students.

Daquisha uses a transition to move her listeners from her "Need" step to the "Satisfaction"—or solutions—step.

Daquisha knows her listeners—and their involvement in the Internet—well. The first four subpoints of her second main head all convey Web sites that Daquisha wrote on a posterboard and placed in the eraser and chalk tray.

       do or if you're just looking for a short-term commitment.[8]
- B. Another Web site that will help you find a short-term commitment is the Points of Light Foundation at **http://www.pointsoflight.org**, which sponsors a variety of annual one-time service opportunities.
- C. To find other opportunities, you can contact your nearest United Way organization or check out the Web site at **http://www.unitedway.org**, or check your local white pages for a listing.
- D. Two of the best Internet resources for finding local volunteer opportunities are **http://www.volunteermatch.org** and **http://www.usafreedomcorps.gov**
- E. Finally, let me remind you that most churches and synagogues will be able to connect you with local volunteer opportunities.

She breaks from her list of Web sites to mention churches and synagogues as places where students might obtain volunteer opportunities.

Transition: All right, you can see what the need is, and all of the Web sites I have listed on this posterboard give you many different ways to get connected. Now, you may wonder why should you get involved?

Daquisha mentions both of her previous main heads, and then forecasts her third one with the question, "Now, you may wonder . . . ?"

III. There are many different benefits you can derive from volunteer work.
- A. Professor Arthur Brooks, a scholar who has studied the link between faith, charity, and politics for many years, writes that "The propensity to give is a 'quality-of-life issue'. . . . Those who give are happier and healthier and their communities are far better places to live."[9]
- B. Dr. Linda Sax, of the Higher Education Research Institute at UCLA, writes that "the effect of performing volunteer work during the college years . . . enhances students' commitment to social activism and involvement in the community after college."[10] What she suggests is that "forming a habit of volunteerism is critical to the long-term development of citizenship."
- C. Hope Egan, author of the book *Volunteering*, lists 14 reasons including meeting new people, making new friends, learning about social issues, developing new skills and talents for your résumé, changing career directions, getting training that will benefit you later, and making a unique contribution, to name a few.
- D. Now, here's a benefit none of you would have guessed. There is a direct inverse

This is Daquisha's visualization step. She lists benefits of volunteering, and the first three (A, B, and C) are all based upon the opinions of experts: Arthur Brooks, Linda Sax, and Hope Egan. This is where she is appealing to the needs of her listeners. Both subpoints A and B appeal to safety needs—security, structure, and order of communities and nation. Her subpoint C appeals, for the most part, to belongingness and love needs. Her subpoint D appeals to the need for self-respect. And her subpoint E rose from self-esteem needs to self-actualization (attitude and enthusiasm for school).

Sample Speech (continued)

relationship between the amount of volunteerism on college campuses and the amount of binge drinking. Based on 17,592 student surveys from 140 colleges, schools with above-average levels of volunteerism were 26 percent less likely to binge drink than students at schools with below-average levels.[11]

E. Just a couple of personal insights here. The heightened self-esteem and satisfaction I derived from volunteering spilled over into my attitude and enthusiasm for school. Also, I developed some business contacts that will open important doors for me in the future.

Transition: Now you see the need, you have several ways to get connected, and you know the benefits; you might wonder what's left.

Conclusion

I know that every day I gain satisfaction from knowing that I'm doing something for someone else. And there is no substitute for that.

Now, let me just talk to the females in my audience for a moment. I don't know how many of you have already discovered your "Mr. Wonderful," but I found mine doing volunteer work. Just his commitment to volunteering alone told me he is generous, giving, and has a tremendous compassion for others. By working with him side-by-side, I got to know his character, his interests, and his little quirks—without having to go through the pressures of blind dates or singles' advertisements.

And, let me end my speech by telling you something else. If it were not for volunteers, and I mean volunteers who really cared, I wouldn't be standing here before you today. I was a homeless orphan who was taken in at a very early age, and later adopted, by a wonderful, caring, generous family. Sure, it's about giving something back, but do you know what: now, more than 20 years later, I still can't explain God's mysterious ways, but I can sure thank my lucky stars for the wonderful generosity of my family of volunteers. If you want to make a difference, volunteer. As the poet Longfellow wrote,

> We can make our lives sublime
> And, departing, leave behind us
> Footprints on the sands of time.

Daquisha has added subpoint D as a bit of fun, and because she knew it would relate directly to her listeners and, thus, hold their attention. Who would think there would be a research connection between volunteerism and binge drinking?

Daquisha wanted to end her main point three with several personal examples. Also, these personal examples led directly into the personal anecdotes she shared in her conclusion.

Notice how, in this transition, Daquisha has tied together the three main heads of the body of her speech, and once again, she stimulates the interest of her listeners with the indirect question, "you might wonder what's left."

She begins her conclusion by expressing her personal feelings about volunteering.

Do you think it's proper for her to talk just to the females in her audience? Do you think the males in her audience would even bother to listen to what she was about to say to the females? In this part of her conclusion, she is appealing specifically to belongingness and love needs.

What do you think of Daquisha sharing her personal experience as a homeless orphan? Was this appropriate? Too personal to share? In the final portion of her conclusion, she appeals to the self-actualization needs of her listeners and the realization of their potential: leaving behind footprints on the sands of time.

Should she have ended the speech with the information about being a homeless orphan? Does the Longfellow quotation add anything to the speech? Does it bring the speech to a final, comfortable, and fitting close?

Speech Reference List

1. Egan, H. (2002). *Volunteering: An easy, smart guide to volunteering.* New York: Silver Lining Books (an imprint of Barnes & Noble), p. 96.

2. Canfield, J., M. V. Hansen, A. M. Oberst, J. T. Boal, T. Lagana, & L. Lagana. (2002). *Chicken soup for the volunteer's soul: Stories to celebrate the spirit of courage, caring and community.* Deerfield Beach, FL: Health Communications, Inc., p. v.

3. Hostetler, M. (2002, April 27). Thirty years of activism at Kent State. *FrictionMagazine.com.* Retrieved March 22, 2005, from **http://www.frictionmagazine.com/politik/activism/kent_state.asp**. Hostetler uses 73 percent. Also see Sax, L. (2005). Citizenship and spirituality among college students: What have we learned and where are we headed? *Journal of College and Character* 2 Higher Education Research Institute, UCLA. Retrieved March 22, 2005, from **http//www.collegevalues.org/articles.cfm?a=1&id=1023**. Sax uses 83 percent.

4. Egan, *Volunteering*, p. 86.

5. Calareso, J. (2004, September 27). Colleges fail to encourage volunteerism among students. *Columbus Dispatch* (editorial). Retrieved March 22, 2005, from **http://www.ohiodominican.edu/president/Volunteerism.shtml**

6. Ibid.

7. Hostetler, Thirty years of activism at Kent State.

8. Egan, *Volunteering*, p. 11.

9. Thomas, J. (2005, February 18). *Data show Americans give to charity, volunteer.* International Information Programs, USInfo.State.gov. Retrieved March 22, 2005, from **http://usinfo.state.gove/xarchives/display.html?p=washfile-english&y=2005&m=February&x=200502181639511CJsamohT5.593508e-02&t=livefeeds/wf-latest.html**

10. Sax, Citizenship and spirituality among college students.

11. Brod, P. (2001, March). It takes a village—alcohol and college students. *Psychology Today* (online article). Retrieved March 22, 2005, from **http://www.findarticles.com/p/articles/mi_m1175/is_2_34/ai_71189895**

Daquisha has used a combination of books and online sources for her topic. Do you think her sources are sufficient—especially when you consider the amount of personal experience she has had with the topic?

Assess Yourself

Are You a Credible Speaker?

For each question circle the numerical score that best rates your performance based on the last or most recent speech you have given: 7 = Outstanding; 6 = Excellent; 5 = Very good; 4 = Average (good); 3 = Fair; 2 = Poor; 1 = Minimal ability; 0 = No ability demonstration.

1. Are you generally perceived to be a person of goodwill?   7 6 5 4 3 2 1 0
   A. Do you treat others courteously?
   B. Do you generally display acceptance, approval, and appreciation?
   C. Do you generally consider yourself equal to others?
2. Did you do things prior to your previous speech to develop your credibility?   7 6 5 4 3 2 1 0
   A. Were you aware of your image in all contacts with your audience members prior to your speech?
   B. Did you make your listeners aware of your qualifications?
   C. Did you set a favorable tone prior to your speech?
3. In your past speech, did you build your credibility through quality communication?   7 6 5 4 3 2 1 0
   A. Did you strive for believability in your message?
   B. Were your feelings, meanings, intentions, and consequences clear?
   C. Did you maintain respect for the thoughts and feelings of your listeners?
4. In your past speech did you intentionally raise your perceived competence by doing the things the listeners perceived as competent?   7 6 5 4 3 2 1 0
   A. Did you quote people who are acknowledged experts on your topic?
   B. Did you list facts and issues pertinent to your topic?
   C. Did you use any of the special vocabulary of the experts?
5. Did you pay special attention to the organization of your speech?   7 6 5 4 3 2 1 0
   A. Did you have—and reveal—one clear, powerful central thesis?
   B. Did you reveal the structure of your speech to your listeners?
   C. Did the pattern of organization you followed remain consistent throughout your speech?
6. Did you mention your personal involvement in, your prior commitment or your active current commitment to the topic of your speech?   7 6 5 4 3 2 1 0
   A. Did you specifically let your listeners know your personal experiences with your topic?
   B. Did you specifically let your listeners know the personal actions you have taken in the past which are clearly compatible with your basic orientation?
   C. Did you tell your audience what you are doing or will do as a consequence of your orientation to your topic?
7. Did you reveal a solid knowledge base on your topic?   7 6 5 4 3 2 1 0
   A. Did you appear qualified, informed, and authoritative?
   B. Did you have fresh, clear, relevant, and specific supporting material?
   C. Did you specifically refer to your research effort during your speech?

8. Did you do things during your speech to build your trustworthiness?　　　7　6　5　4　3　2　1　0
   A. Did you self-disclose—within the limits of interpersonal safety, of course?
   B. Did you compliment your audience?
   C. Did you appear honest, kind, friendly, pleasant, earnest, and sincere?
9. Did you do things deliberately in your speech to appear forceful, bold, and dynamic?　　　7　6　5　4　3　2　1　0
   A. Were you poised, relaxed, and fluent?
   B. Did you reflect a clear emotional commitment to your ideas? Complete ego involvement?
   C. Were your nonverbal cues (face, voice, gestures, and body movement) completely supportive of your ideas?
10. Was the evidence you used in your speech significant, relevant, and interesting to your listeners?　　　7　6　5　4　3　2　1　0
    A. Did you objectively evaluate your evidence in terms of its usefulness?
    B. Did you tell your listeners who the authorities of your evidence were, and why those authorities should be respected?

Go to the *Communicating Effectively* CD-ROM and the Online Learning Center at **www.mhhe.com/hybels8** to see your results and learn how to evaluate your attitudes and feelings.

mhhe.com/hybels8

CHAPTER REVIEW

SUMMARY

Persuasion is the process that occurs when a communicator influences the values, beliefs, attitudes, or behaviors of another person. The focus of persuasion should be on the sender, the receiver, and the message, because all three share in the persuasive process. It is only when all three combine successfully that effective persuasion occurs.

The key to understanding persuasion is influence, the power of a person or thing to affect others—to produce effects without the presence of physical force. Persuasion involves motivation as well. Motivation is the stimulation or inducement that causes a person to act. We are motivated to do what we do in order to reduce tension, meet needs, or achieve goals or because we want personal growth, mastery of the environment, and self-understanding. These are useful motivators for persuaders to keep in mind.

We are more likely to respond to persuasive messages that tap into our values, beliefs, and attitudes. Values are the ideas we have about what is good and what is bad and how things should be. Instrumental values guide people's day-to-day behavior, while terminal values are central to our culture. Beliefs are simple propositions, conscious or unconscious, expressed in what people say or do. People often begin statements of belief with the phrase "I believe that . . . " Attitudes are predispositions to respond favorably or unfavorably toward a person, subject, or situation. Persuaders who are sensitive and responsive to the values, beliefs, and attitudes of listeners are more likely to be successful.

Effective persuasion, even though it happens on a daily basis, is challenging. Speakers who understand why it is difficult to change values, beliefs, and attitudes can put the process into perspective and work to create a receptive mental attitude. Challenges include the sheer amount of persuasion that occurs; how slowly persuasion tends to work; how deeply entrenched values, beliefs, and attitudes may be; laziness; and the desire for freedom of action. These difficulties should increase persuaders' willingness to invest time, effort, and care in their preparation for speeches.

There are specific strategies persuaders can use to be effective. In preparing a speech, you must determine your purpose, analyze your audience, appeal to your audience using logic, appeal to your audience using emotion, use research to prove your points, choose your language carefully, appeal to your audience using your credibility, and structure your material effectively. As in all speaking, you should be ethical by conforming to acceptable and fair standards of conduct.

KEY TERMS AND CONCEPTS

Use the *Communicating Effectively* CD-ROM and the Online Learning Center at www.mhhe.com/hybels8 to further your understanding of the following terms.

Ad hominem 408
Analogy 407
Appeal to authority 408
Appeal to ignorance 408
Attitudes 401
Begging the question 408
Beliefs 400
Bifurcation 408
Causal reasoning 407
Credibility 412
Deductive reasoning 404

Dynamism 413
Emotional appeal 409
Expertise 412
Fallacy 407
False analogy 408
False cause 408
Hasty generalization 408
Hierarchy of needs 409
Inductive reasoning 405
Influence 399
Logical appeal 404

Mob appeal 408
Motivation 399
Naturalistic fallacy 407
Persuasion 398
Premise 407
Question-begging epithets 408
Sweeping generalization 408
Target audience 404
Trustworthiness 413
Values 400

CHAPTER REVIEW

QUESTIONS TO REVIEW

1. Think of a recent persuasive message that you have heard. How did the speaker influence and motivate you?
2. What are the differences among values, beliefs, and attitudes?
3. For you, which values, beliefs, or attitudes are the ones most likely to be stable? Most likely to change?
4. For you, which of the challenges of persuasion listed in the chapter would likely make you most resistant to someone else's persuasion? How might you as a speaker overcome (or approach) this particular challenge?
5. Besides those discussed in this chapter, are there other factors that make persuasion challenging?
6. As a persuader, which strategies do you feel most comfortable using when persuading others?
7. As an audience member, which strategies would work best in speeches trying to persuade you? Or which ones would likely hold your attention better than others?
8. When you compare logic, emotion, and credibility (*logos*, *pathos*, and *ethos*), on which do persuaders most often depend?
9. How do questions of fact, value, and policy differ?
10. If you were speaking on the value of a college education, what techniques for building your credibility would you use if you were talking to a high school audience?
11. Have you ever heard persuaders who were not ethical? What did they do?
12. For you to be ethical in persuasion, what principles should you follow?
13. On a controversial topic, which would work best: a one-sided or a two-sided argument? Why?
14. In what ways has the Internet influenced persuasive communication?
15. Would you likely be persuaded by Daquisha Lattrell's speech? Why or why not?

mhhe.com/hybels8

Go to the self-quizzes on the *Communicating Effectively* CD-ROM and the Online Learning Center at **www.mhhe.com/hybels8** to test your knowledge of the chapter contents.

References

Chapter 1

1. Boyer, P. (2003). *College rankings exposed: The art of getting a quality education in the 21st century.* Lawrenceville, NJ: Thomson/Peterson, p. 119.

2. Boyer, *College rankings exposed*, pp. 100 & 119; Haslam, J. (2003). Learning the lessons—Speaking up for communication as an academic discipline too important to be sidelined. *Journal of Communication Management, 7*(1), 14–20; Tucker, M. L., & A. M. McCarthy, (2003). Presentation self-efficacy: Increasing communication skills through service-learning. *Journal of Managerial Issues, 13*(2), 227–245; Winsor, J. L., D. B. Curtis, & R. D. Stephens. (1997). National preferences in business and communication education. *Journal of the Association of Communication Administration, 3*, 170–179; [No author]. (1992). What work requires of schools: A SCANS report for America. U.S. Department of Labor. *Economic Development Review, 10*, 16–19; Rooff-Steffen, K. (1991). The push is on for people skills. *Journal of Career Planning and Employment, 52*, 61–63; [No author]. (1998, December 29). Report of the national association of colleges and employers. *The Wall Street Journal, Work Week*, p. 1A; Maes, J. D., T. G. Weldy, & M. L. Icenogle. (1997). A managerial perspective: Oral communication competency is most important for business students in the workplace. *Journal of Business Communication, 34*, 67–80; Lankard, B. A. (1960). *Employability—The fifth basic skill.* ERIC Clearinghouse on Adult, Career, and Vocational Education, Columbus, OH (ERIC Document Reproduction Service No. ED 325659).

3. Ford, W. S. Z., & D. Wolvin (1993). The differential impact of a basic communication course on communication competencies in class, work, and social contexts. *Communication Education, 42*, 215–223.

4. Diamond, R. (1997, August 1). Curriculum reform needed if students are to master core skills. *The Chronicle of Higher Education*, p. B7.

5. Combs, P. (2003). *Major in success: Make college easier, fire up your dreams, and get a very cool job.* Berkeley, CA: Ten Speed Press.

6. Berlo, D. K. (1960). *The process of communication: An introduction to theory and practice.* New York: Holt, Rinehart and Winston.

7. Washington, D. (2000). *The language of gifts: The essential guide to meaningful gift giving.* Berkeley, CA: Conari Press.

8. Mehrabian, A. (1981). *Silent messages: Implicit communication of emotions and attitudes* (2nd ed.). Belmont, CA: Wadsworth.

9. Wilder, C. (1979, Winter). The Palo Alto Group: Difficulties and directions of the transactional view for human communication research. *Human Communication Review, 5*, 171–186.

10. Barnes, S. B. (2003). *Computer-mediated communication: Human-to-human communication across the Internet.* Boston: Allyn & Bacon, p. 4.

11. Gilster, P. (1997). *Digital literacy.* New York: John Wiley, p. 15.

12. Nieto, S. (1999, Fall). Affirming diversity: The sociopolitical context of multicultural education. In F. Yeo, The barriers of diversity: Multicultural education & rural schools. *Multicultural education*, 2–7; also in F. Schultz (ed.). (2001). *Multicultural education* (8th ed.), Guilford, CT: McGraw-Hill/Dushkin.

13. Griswold, W. (1994). *Cultures and societies in a changing world.* Thousand Oaks, CA: Pine Forge Press.

14. [No author]. (1999). *Ethical comm: NCA credo for ethical communication.* National Communication Association (NCA). Retrieved November 9, 2004, from **http://www.natcom.org/policies/External/EthicalComm.htm**

15. Ibid.

16. Ibid.

17. Ibid.

Chapter 2

1. Muriel, J., & D. Joneward (1971). *Born to win: Transactional analysis with gestalt experiments.* Reading, MA: Addison-Wesley, pp. 68–100.

2. Keillor, G. (1985). *Lake Wobegon days.* New York: Penguin/Viking Press, pp. 304–305.

3. Boone, M. E. (2001). *Managing inter@ctively: Executing business strategy, improving communication, and creating a knowledge-sharing culture.* New York: McGraw-Hill.

4. Manz, C. C., & H. P. Sims, Jr. (2001). *The new superleadership: Leading others to lead themselves.* San Francisco: Berrett-Koehler, p. 110.

5. Schwalbe, M. L., & C. Staples (1991). Gender difference in self-esteem. *Social Psychology Quarterly, 54*(2), 158–168.

6. Joseph, R. A., H. R. Markus, & R. W. Tafarodi. (1992, September). Gender and self-esteem. *Journal of Personality and Social Psychology, 63*(3), 391–402.

7. Maslow, A. H. (1970). *Motivation and personality* (2nd ed.). New York: Harper & Row.

8. Paul, A. M. (2001, March/April). Self-help: Shattering the myths. *Psychology Today*, 66.

9. Ibid., p. 66.

10. Ibid., p. 66.

11. Johnson, K. (1998, May 5). Self-image is suffering from lack of esteem. *The New York Times*, p. C7.

12. Ratey, J. R. (2001). *A user's guide to the brain: Perception, attention, and the four theaters of the brain.* New York: Pantheon Books, p. 56.

13. Ma, Miranda Lai-yee. (2003). *Unwillingness-to-communicate, perceptions of the Internet and self-disclosure in ICQ.* (A graduation project in partial fulfillment of the requirement for the degree of master of science in New Media, the Chinese University of Hong Kong, Hong Kong.) Retrieved March 20, 2004, from **http://216.239.41.104/search?q=cache:jqalB1tqnocJ:www.com.cuhk.edu.hk/courses/msc/Aca** p. 5 of 37.

14. Tidewell, L. C., & J. B. Walther, (2002). Computer-mediated communication effects on disclosure, impressions, and interpersonal evaluations—Getting to know one another a bit at a time. *Human Communication Research, 28,* 317–348.

15. Ma, Miranda Lai-yee, *Unwillingness-to-communicate,* pp. 20–21.

16. [No author]. (1999, December 28). *External reality and subjective experience.* Western Michigan University. Retrieved November 24, 2004, from **http://spider.hcob.wmich.edu/bis/faculty/bowman/erse.html**

17. Ibid.

18. Yeager, S. (2001, January 1). *Lecture notes: Self-concept.* DeSales University. Retrieved November 24, 2004, from **http://www4.allencol.edu/~sey0/selfla.html**

19. *External reality and subjective experience.*

Chapter 3

1. Morreale, S. (2003, November). Gender and diversity. *Spectra, 39*(11), 5. Morreale cites PEN Weekly NewsBlast, September 19, 2003. Survey by Futrell, Gomez, and Bedden, 2003.

2. Nieto, S. (1999, Fall). Affirming diversity: The sociopolitical context of multicultural education. In F. Yeo, The barriers of diversity: Multicultural education & rural schools. *Multicultural education,* 2–7; also in F. Schultz (ed.). (2001). *Multicultural education* (8th ed.). Guilford, CT: McGraw-Hill/Dushkin.

3. Harris, M. (1983). *Cultural anthropology.* New York: Harper & Row.

4. Gudykunst, W. B., & Y. Y. Kim. (2002). *Communicating with strangers: An approach to intercultural communication* (4th ed.). Boston: McGraw-Hill, p. 122.

5. Carnes, J. (1999). A conversation with Carlos Cortes: Searching for patterns. In Schultz, *Multicultural education,* pp. 50–53. From Cortes, C. (1999, Fall). *Teaching tolerance,* 10–15.

6. Beamer, L., & I. Varney. (2001). *Intercultural communication in the global workplace* (2nd ed). Boston: McGraw-Hill/Irwin, p. 3.

7. Rosaldo, R. (1989). *Culture and truth: The remaking of social analysis.* Boston: Beacon Press.

8. Samovar, L. A., & R. E. Porter. (2001). *Communication between cultures* (4th ed.). Belmont, CA: Wadsworth, pp. 2, 46.

9. Martin, J. N., & T. K. Nakayama. (2001). *Experiencing intercultural communication: An introduction.* Boston: McGraw-Hill.

10. Aseel, M. Q. (2003). *Torn between two cultures: An Afghan-American woman speaks out.* Sterling, VA: Capital Books, p. 67.

11. Schultz, F. (2001). Identity and personal development: A multicultural focus. In Schultz, *Multicultural education.*

12. Martin & Nakayama, *Experiencing intercultural communication,* p. 185.

13. Cruz-Janzen, From our readers; Howard, G. R. (1999). *We can't teach what we don't know: White teachers, multiracial schools.* New York: Teachers College Press.

14. Carnes, A conversation with Carlos Cortes.

15. Schultz, Identity and personal development, p. 113.

16. Martin & Nakayama, *Experiencing intercultural communication,* p. 8.

17. Liu, Jun. (2001). *Asian students' classroom communication patterns in U.S. universities: An emic perspective.* Westport, CT: Ablex. As reviewed by Mary M. Meares, Book Reviews. (2004). *Communication Education, 53*(1), 123.

18. Martin & Nakayama, *Experiencing intercultural communication.*

19. Triandis, H. (1990). Theoretical concepts that are applicable to the analysis of ethnocentrism. In R. Brislin (ed.), *Applied cross-cultural psychology.* Newbury Park, CA: Sage.

20. [No author]. (2001). *Dimensions of culture.* Retrieved December 2, 2004, from **http://cwis.kub.nl/~fsw2iric/vms.htm**

21. Hall, E. T. (1976). *Beyond culture.* New York: Harper & Row, 1983; Hall, E. T. (1994). Context and meaning. In Samovar & Porter (eds.), *Intercultural communication.*

22. Ibid.

23. Chang, I. (2003). *The Chinese in America: A narrative history.* New York: Viking Press, p. xiii.

24. Hofstede, G. (2001). *Culture consequences: International differences in work-related values* (2nd ed.). Beverly Hills, CA: Sage.

25. Hall, *Beyond culture;* Hall, Context and meaning.

26. Martin & Nakayama. (2001). *Experiencing intercultural communication,* p. 44.

27. Ibid.

28. Orbe, M. P. (1998). *Constructing cocultural theory: An explication of culture, power, and communication.* Thousand Oaks, CA: Sage.

29. Adair, N., & C. Adair. (1978). *Word is out.* New York: Dell.

30. Raybon, P. (1996). *My first white friend.* New York: Viking Press.

31. Fadiman, A. (1997). *The spirit catches you and you fall down.* New York: Farrar, Straus & Giroux, p. 182.

32. Raybon, *My first white friend,* pp. 1–2.

33. DuPraw, M. E., & M. Axner. (1997). *Working on common cross-cultural communication challenges: Toward a more perfect union in an age of diversity.* Study Circles Resource Center—AMPU. Retrieved December 2, 2004, from **http://www.wwed.org/action/ampu/crosscult.html**

34. Carnes, A conversation with Carlos Cortes.

35. Pool, K. (2002, February). Valuing diversity. *Personal Excellence,* 13.

36. Cruz-Janzen, From our readers.

37. DuPraw & Axner, *Working on common cross-cultural communication challenges.*

38. Ibid.

39. Gudykunst, W. B., & Y. Y. Kim. (2002). *Communicating with strangers: An approach to intercultural communication* (4th ed.). Boston: McGraw-Hill.

40. Karim, A. U. (2001, April). *Intercultural competence: Moving beyond appreciation and celebration of difference.* Interculturally Speaking, Kansas State University Counseling Services' Human Relations Newsletter, I(1). Retrieved December 2, 2004, from http://www.ksu.edu/counseling/ispeak/people to people.htm

41. Taylor, R. (2001). *Are you culturally competent? (intercultural communication).* Springhouse Corporation. Retrieved December 2, 2004, from http://www.findarticles.com/cf0/m3231/431/74091624/print.jhtml. This World Wide Web article was excerpted and adapted from Taylor, R. (2000). Check your cultural competence. *CriticalCareChoices.* Springhouse, PA: Springhouse Corporation.

42. Maruyama, M. (1970). *Toward a cultural futurology.* Paper presented at the annual meeting of the American Anthropological Association, published by the Training Center for Community Programs, University of Minnesota, Minneapolis, MN. In Martin & Nakayama, *Intercultural communication in context.*

43. Martin & Nakayama, *Experiencing intercultural communication,* p. 320.

44. Hwang, J., L. Chase, & C. Kelly. (1980). An intercultural examination of communication competence. *Communication, 9,* 70–79.

45. Gudykunst & Kim, *Communicating with strangers.*

46. Ibid.

47. [No author]. (2004, February 28). New online friendship community helps like-minded Muslims link up. Associated Press. *The (Toledo) Blade,* p. B5.

Chapter 4

1. Thompson, K., & D. Dathe. (2001). *Moving students toward competent listening: The Thompson-Dathe integrative listening model (ILM).* Convention Paper Resource Center, International Listening Association (ILA). Retrieved December 6, 2004, from http://www.listen.org/pages/cprc_2001.html. The process of remembering has been added to the ILM framework as discussed in this chapter.

2. Friedman, P. G. (1978). *Listening processes: Attention, understanding, evaluation.* Washington, DC: National Education Association, p. 274.

3. Rubin, R. B., & C. V. Roberts. (1987, April). A comparative examination and analysis of three listening tests. *Communication Education, 36,* 142–153.

4. Youaver, J. B. III, & M. D. Kirtley. (1995). Listening styles and empathy. *Southern Communication Journal, 60*(2), 131–140.

5. Kiewitz, C., J. B. Weaver, H. B. Brosius, & G. Weimann. (1997, Autumn). Cultural differences in listening style preferences: A comparison of young adults in Germany, Israel, and the United States. *International Journal of Public Opinion Research, 9*(3), 233–247. Online abstract retrieved December 9, 2004, from http://www3.oup.co.uk/intpor/hdb/Volume_09/Issue_03/090233.sgm.abs.html

6. Ibid.

7. O'Brien, P. (1993, February). Why men don't listen . . . and what it costs women at work. *Working Women, 18*(2), 56–60.

8. Tannen, D. (1999, May 6). Listening to men, then and now. *New York Times Magazine,* 56ff.

9. O'Brien. Why men don't listen, pp. 56–60.

10. Ibid.

11. Golen, S. (1990, Winter). A factor analysis of barriers to effective listening. *The Journal of Business Communication, 27,* 25–36.

12. Burton, J., & L. Burton. (1997). *Interpersonal skills for travel and tourism.* Essex: Addison-Wesley Longman.

13. Purdy, M. (2002). Listen up, move up: The listener wins. Monster Career Center. Retrieved December 9, 2004, from http://content.monster.com/listen/overview/. Copyright 2005—Monster Worldwide, Inc. All Rights Reserved. You may not copy, reproduce or distribute this article without the prior written permission of Monster Worldwide. This article first appeared on Monster, the leading online global network for careers. To see other career-related articles visit http://content.monster.com.

14. Youst, R., & J. C. Pearson. (1994). Antecedent and consequent conditions of student questioning: An analysis of classroom discourse across the university. *Communication Education, 43*(4). CommSearch 95, CD-ROM, National Communication Association, first release (no date).

15. Pryor, B. K., P. Taylor, R. W. Buchanan, & D. U. Strawn. (1980). An affective-cognitive consistency explanation for comprehension of standard jury instructions. *Communication Monographs, 47,* 69

16. Nichols, M. P. (1995). *The lost art of listening.* New York: Guilford Press.

17. Greider, L. (2000, February). Talking back to your doctor works. *AARP Bulletin.*

18. Elias, M. (2003, September 23). The doctor is inattentive: Med students will be tested on empathy, listening skills. *USA Today,* p. 9D.

Chapter 5

1. Ratey, J. J. (2001). *A user's guide to the brain: Perception, attention, and the four theaters of the brain.* New York: Pantheon Books, p. 253.

2. [No author]. (no date). *Let's talk about it: Fostering the development of language skills and emergent literacy.* The Whole Child, For Early Care Providers, (PBS) Public Broadcasting Service. Retrieved December 18, 2004, from http://www.pbs.org/wholechild/providers/talk.html

3. Sapir, E. (1958). The status of linguistics as a science. In E. Sapir, *Culture, language and personality* (ed. D. G. Mandelbaum). Berkeley: University of California Press.

4. Whorf, B. L. (1940). Science and linguistics. *Technology Review, 42*(6), 229–231, 247–248; Whorf, B. L. (1956). *Language, thought and reality* (ed. J. B. Carroll). Cambridge, MA: MIT Press.

5. Paratore, J., & R. McCormack (eds.). (1997). *Peer talk in the classroom: Learning from research.* Newark, DE: International

Reading Association. As reviewed by Hoffman, J. (2004, July). *Communication Education, 53*(3), 297.

6. Hayakawa, S. I. (1991). *Language in thought and action* (5th ed). New York: Harcourt.

7. Cotrell, H. W. (2001). *Spice up that family history.* Retrieved December 2, 2001, from e-mail.

8. Boone, M. E. (2001). *Managing inter@ctively: Executing business strategy, improving communication, and creating a knowledge-sharing culture.* New York: McGraw-Hill, pp. 109–110.

9. [No author]. (2002, April 2). Egg mystery boils down to physics: Mathematicians unravel gyroscope effect. *The* (Toledo) *Blade*, p. 3A.

10. Postman, N. (1992). *Technopoly: The surrender of culture to technology.* New York: Vintage Books.

11. Goffman, E. (1971). *Relations in public.* New York: Basic Books, p. 62.

12. Greif, E. B., & J. B. Gleason. (1980). Hi, thanks, and goodbye: More routine information. *Language in Society, 9,* 159–166.

13. Lutz, W. (1996). *The new doublespeak.* New York: HarperCollins.

14. Bennet, J. (1995, March 29). A charm school for selling cars. *The New York Times,* pp. D1, D8.

15. King, S. (2000). *On writing: A memoir of the craft.* New York: Scribner's, p. 208.

16. Tanno, D. V. (2000). Jewish and/or women: Identity and communicative style. In A. Gonzalez, M. Houston, & V. Chen (eds), *Our voices: Essays in culture, ethnicity, and communication.* Los Angeles: Roxbury., p. 33.

17. Tannen, D. (1990). *You just don't understand.* New York: Morrow, pp. 42–43.

18. Ibid., p. 76.

19. Ibid., pp. 51–52.

20. Mulac, A., J. M. Wiemenn, S. J. Widenmann, & T. W. Gibson. (1988). Male/female language differences and effects in same-sex and mixed-sex dyads: The gender-linked language effect. *Communication Monographs, 55,* 316–332.

21. Tannen, D. (1992, February). How men and women use language differently in their lives and in the classroom. *Education Digest, 57,* 3–6.

22. Turner, L. H. (1992). An analysis of words coined by women and men: Reflections on the muted group theory and Gilligan's model. *Women and Language, 15,* 21–27.

23. Tannen, *You just don't understand,* p. 153.

24. Ibid., p. 245.

25. Ibid., pp. 255–256.

26. Weatherall, A. (1998). Re-visioning gender and language research. *Women and Language, 21*(1), 1.

27. Shaywitz, B. A. (1995, February 16). Sex differences in the functional organization of the brain for language. *Nature, 37*(3), 607–608.

28. Ibid., pp. 89–90.

29. Gurian, M. (2003). *What could he be thinking? How a man's mind really works.* New York: St. Martin's Press.

30. Johnson, C. E. (1987, April). An introduction to powerful talk and powerless talk in the classroom. *Communication Education, 36,* 167–172.

31. Haleta, L. L. (1996, January). Student perceptions of teachers' use of language on impression formation and uncertainty. *Communication Education, 45,* 20–27.

32. Johnson, An introduction to powerful talk, p. 167.

33. O'Connor, S. D. (2003). *The majesty of the law: Reflections of a supreme court justice.* New York: Random House, p. 197.

34. [No author]. (2003, October 9). Foreign languages spoken in U.S. homes on rise. Census Bureau Study. *The* (Toledo) *Blade,* pp. 1, 7.

35. Nelson, M. C. (2004, March 15). On the path: Business's unfinished journey to diversity. *Vital Speeches of the Day, LXX*(11), 337.

36. [No author]. (2004, February 27). English declining as world language. *USA Today,* p. 7A.

37. Ibid.

38. Nelson, *On the path,* p. 339.

39. Hummel, S. (1999, January 25). Do you speak Bostonian? *U.S. News and World Report,* 56–57.

40. Rosen, E. (2000). *The anatomy of buzz: How to create word of mouth marketing.* New York: Doubleday, p. 215.

41. Tannen, *You just don't understand,* p. 62.

42. Penn, C. R. (1990, December 1). A choice of words is a choice of worlds. *Vital Speeches of the Day,* 117.

43. Ibid.

44. Crystal, D. (2000). *The Internet: A linguistic revolution.* Retrived December 18, 2004, from **http://www.crystalreference.com**

45. Crystal, D. (2001). *Language and the Internet.* New York: Cambridge University Press.

46. Crystal, *The Internet: A linguistic revolution.*

47. Essberger, J. (2001). *Speaking versus writing.* For ESL learners. EnglishClub.com. Retrieved December 18, 2004, from **http://learners.englishclub.com/esl-articles/200108.htm**

Chapter 6

1. Mehrabian, A. (1981). *Silent messages: Implicit communication of emotions and attitudes* (2nd ed.). Belmont, CA: Wadsworth.

2. Brody, J. (1992, August 19). Personal health: Helping children overcome rejection. *The New York Times,* p. C12.

3. Flora, C. (2004, May/June). Snap judgments: The once-over. Can you trust first impressions? *Psychology Today,* 60.

4. Boyce, N. (2001, January 15). Truth and consequences: Scientists are scanning the brain for traces of guilty knowledge. *U.S. News & World Report,* 42.

5. Ibid.

6. [No author]. (2004, November 8). They can't tell a lie—some people just know. *The* (Toledo) *Blade,* p. 1D.

7. Ekman, P., & W. V. Friesen. (1969). The repertoire of nonverbal behavior: Categories, origins, usages, and coding. *Semiotica, 1,* 49–98.

8. Goodman, E. (2002, May 1). Some prefer to smile, furrow brows to Botox. *The* (Toledo) *Blade*, p. 11A.

9. Planalp, Communicating emotion in everyday life; Planalp, S., V. L. DeFrancisco, & D. Rutherford. (1996). Varieties of cues to emotion occurring in naturally occurring situations. *Cognition and emotion, 10,* 137–153.

10. Planalp, Communicating emotion in everyday life.

11. Andersen, P. A., & L. K. Guerrero. (1998). The bright side of relational communication: Interpersonal warmth as a social emotion. In Andersen & Guerrero, *Handbook of communication and emotion,* pp. 303–324.

12. Griffin, M. A., D. McGahee, & J. Slate. (1998). *Gender differences in nonverbal communication.* Valdosta State University, Valdosta, Georgia. Retrieved December 28, 2004, from **http://www.bvte.edc.edu/ACBMEC/p1999/Griffin.htm**. Throughout this section, Griffin, McGahee, and Slate site three sources: Burgoon, J. K., D. B. Buller, & W. G. Woodall (1996). *Nonverbal communication: The unspoken dialogue* (2nd ed.). New York: McGraw-Hill; Hanna, M. S., & G. L. Wilson (1998). *Communicating in business and professional settings* (4th ed.). New York: McGraw-Hill; Ivy, D. K., & P. Backlund (1994). *Exploring genderspeak.* New York: McGraw-Hill.

13. Griffin, McGahee, & Slate, *Gender differences in nonverbal communication.*

14. Ibid.

15. Ibid.

16. Hall, E. (1966). *The hidden dimension.* Garden City, NY: Doubleday.

17. Griffin, McGahee, & Slate, *Gender differences in nonverbal communication.*

18. Ibid.

19. Birdwhistell, R. L. (1970). *Kinesics and context.* Philadelphia: University of Pennsylvania Press, p. 117.

20. Addington, D. W. (1968). The relationship of selected vocal characteristics to personality. *Speech Monographs, 35,* 492–505; Pearce, W. B. (1971). The effect of vocal cues on credibility and attitude change. *Western Speech, 35,* 176–184; Zuckerman, M., & R. E. Driver. (1989). What sounds beautiful is good: The vocal attractiveness stereotype. *Journal of Nonverbal Behavior, 13,* 67–82; Zuckerman, M., H. Hodgins, & K. Miyake. (1990). The vocal attractiveness stereotype: Replication and elaboration. *Journal of Nonverbal Behavior, 14,* 97–112.

21. Mehrabian, A. (1968, September). Communication without words. *Psychology Today,* 53; Mehrabian, A. (1981). *Silent messages: Implicit communication of emotions and attitudes* (2nd ed.). Belmont, CA: Wadsworth, pp. 42–47.

22. MacLachlan, J. (1979, November). What people really think of fast talkers. *Psychology Today,* 113–117.

23. Ray, G. B. (1986). Vocally cued personality prototypes: An implicit personality theory approach. *Communication Monographs, 53,* 272; Buller, D. B., & R. K. Aune. (1988). The effects of vocalics and nonverbal sensitivity on compliance: A speech accommodation theory explanation. *Human Communication Research, 14,* 301–332; Street, R. L., & R. M. Brady. (1982). Speech rate acceptance ranges as a function of evaluative domain, listener speech rate and communication context. *Communication Monographs, 49,* 290–308.

24. Burgoon, J. K. (1978). Attributes of a newscaster's voice as predictors of his credibility. *Journalism Quarterly, 55,* 276–281.

25. Street, & Brady, Speech rate acceptance ranges as a function of evaluative domain, pp. 290–308.

26. Buller, & Aune, The effects of vocalics and nonverbal sensitivity on compliance, pp. 301–332.

27. Ray, Vocally cued personality prototypes, p. 273.

28. Berry, D. S. (1992, Spring). Vocal types and stereotypes of vocal attractiveness and vocal maturity on person perception. *Journal of Nonverbal Behavior, 16*(1), 41–54.

29. Burgoon, Buller, & Woodall, *Nonverbal communication,* p. 33.

30. Ekman, P., & W. V. Friesen. (1969). The repertoire of nonverbal behavior: Categories, origins, usages, and coding. *Semiotica, 1,* 49–98.

31. Benton, D. A. (2003). *Executive charisma.* New York: McGraw-Hill, p. 90.

32. Burgoon, Buller, & Woodall, *Nonverbal communication,* p. 42.

33. Ibid.

34. Andersen, P. A. (1999). *Nonverbal communication: Forms and functions.* Mountain View, CA: Mayfield, p. 40.

35. Kendon, A. (1967). Some functions of gaze direction in social interaction. *Acta Psychologica, 26,* 22–63; Exline, R. V., S. L. Ellyson, & B. Long. (1975). Visual behavior as an aspect of power role relationships. In P. Pliner, L. Drames, & T. Alloway (eds.), *Nonverbal communication of aggression.* New York: Plenum, Vol. 2, pp. 21–52; Fehr, B. J., & R. V. Exline. (1987). Social visual interaction: A conceptual and literature review. In A. W. Siegman & S. Feldstein (eds.), *Nonverbal behavior and communication* (2nd ed.). Hillsdale, NJ: Erlbaum, pp. 225–236; Andersen, P. A. (1985). Nonverbal immediacy in interpersonal communication. In A. W. Siegman & S. Feldstein (eds.), *Multichannel integrations of nonverbal behavior.* Hillsdale, NJ: Erlbaum, pp. 1–36; Silver, C. A., & B. H. Spitzberg. (1992, July). *Flirtation as social intercourse: Developing a measure of flirtatious behavior.* Paper presented at the Sixth International Conference on Personal Relationships, Orono, ME.

36. Gudykunst, W. B., & Y. Y. Kim. (1997). *Communicating with strangers: An approach to intercultural communication* (3rd ed.). New York: McGraw-Hill; Jensen, J. V. (1985). Perspective on nonverbal intercultural communication. In L. A. Samovar, & R. E. Porter (eds.), *Intercultural communication: A reader.* Belmont, CA: Wadsworth, pp. 256–272; Samovar, L. A., R. E. Porter, & N. C. Jain. (1981). *Understanding intercultural communication.* Belmont, CA: Wadsworth.

37. Richmond, Y., & P. Gestrin. (1998). *Into Africa: Intercultural insights.* Yarmouth, ME: Intercultural Press, p. 95.

38. Feingold, A. (1990). Gender differences in effects of physical attraction on romantic attraction: A comparison across five research paradigms. *Journal of Personality and Social Psychology, 59,* 981–993.

39. Andersen, *Nonverbal communication*, p. 113.

40. Andersen, P. A. (1998). Researching sex differences within sex similarities: The evolutionary consequences of reproductive differences. In D. J. Canary & K. Dindia (eds.), *Sex differences and similarities in communication*. Mahwah, NJ: Erlbaum, pp. 83–100; Berscheid, E., K. K. Dion, E. H. Walster, & G. W. Walster. (1971). Physical attractiveness and dating choice: Tests of the matching hypothesis. *Journal of Experimental Social Psychology, 7,* 173–189; Berscheid, E., & E. H. Walster (1969, 1978). *Interpersonal attraction* (2nd ed.). Reading, MA: Addison-Wesley; [No author]. (1972, September). Beauty and the best. *Psychology Today, 5,* 42–46, 74; Berscheid, E., & E. H. Walster. (1974). Physical attractiveness. In L. Berkowitz (ed.), *Advances in experimental social psychology*, Vol. 7. New York: Academic Press, pp. 158–215; Brislin, R. W., & S. A. Lewis. (1968). Dating and physical attractiveness: Replication. *Psychological Reports, 22,* 976; Coombs, R. H., & W. F. Kenkel. (1966). Sex differences in dating aspirations and satisfaction with computer-selected partners. *Journal of Marriage and the Family, 28,* 62–66; Walster, E., V. Aronson, D. Abrahams, & L. Rottman. (1966). Importance of physical attractiveness in dating behavior. *Journal of Personality and Social Psychology, 4,* 508–516.

41. Levine, M., & H. E. Marano. (2001, July–August). Why I hate beauty. *Psychology Today,* 41.

42. Dimitrius, J. E., & M. Mazzarella. (1998). *Reading people: How to understand people and predict their behavior—Anytime, anyplace.* New York: Random House, p. 31.

43. [No author]. (2004, January 18). Pay scale follows its natural height. *The* (Toledo) *Blade*, p. 1B.

44. Schwartz, J. (1963). Men's clothing and the Negro. *Phylon, 24,* 224–231.

45. Kelly, J. (1969). *Dress as nonverbal communication.* Paper presented at the Annual Conference of the American Association for Public Opinion Research.

46. Thourlby, W. (1978). *You are what you wear.* New York: New American Library, pp. 143–151.

47. Stolzafus, L. (1998). *Traces of wisdom: Amish women and the pursuit of life's simple pleasures.* New York: Hyperion, pp. 134–135.

48. Joseph, N. (1986). *Uniforms and nonuniforms.* New York: Greenwood Press, pp. 2–3, 15.

49. Ibid., p. 143.

50. Morris, T. L., J. Gorham, S. H. Cohen, & D. Hoffman. (1996, April). Fashion in the classroom: Effects of attire on student perceptions of instructors in college classes. *Communication Education, 45,* 142–148.

51. Joseph, *Uniforms and nonuniforms*, pp. 168–169.

52. Hall, *The hidden dimension*, pp. 116–125.

53. Ratey, J. (2001). *A user's guide to the brain: Perception, attention, and the four theaters of the brain.* New York: Knopf, p. 76.

54. Goleman, D. (1988, February 2). The experience of touch: Research points to a critical role. *The New York Times,* p. C1.

55. Heslin, R. (1974). *Steps toward a taxonomy of touching.* Paper presented at the Western Psychological Association Convention, Chicago, IL, 1974; Winter, R. (1976, March). How people react to your touch. *Science Digest, 84,* 46–56; Thayer, S. (1988). Touch encounters. *Psychology Today, 22,* 31–36.

56. Anastasi, A. (1958). *Differential psychology.* New York: Macmillan; Mehrabian, A. (1970). Some determinants of affiliation and conformity. *Psychological Reports, 27,* 19–29; Mehrabian, A. (1971). *Silent messages: Implicit communication of emotions and attitudes* (2nd ed.). Belmont, CA: Wadsworth.

57. Heslin, *Steps toward a taxonomy of touching;* Winter, R, How people react to your touch.

58. Hickson, & Stacks, *NVC—Nonverbal communication*.

59. Ibid. Many of the facts cited here are quoted directly from the U of C wellness letter.

60. Burgoon, Buller, & Woodall, *Nonverbal communication*, pp. 127–128.

61. Ritts, V., & J. R. Stein. Six ways to improve your nonverbal communications. Faculty Development Committee, Hawaii Community College. Retrieved January 2, 2005, from **http://www.hcc.hawaii.edu/intrnet/committees/FacDevCom/guidebk/teachtip/commun-1.htm**

62. Newberry, B. (2002). *Media richness, social presence and technology supported communication activities in education.* Technology Enriched Learning, University of Kansas. Retrieved January 2, 2005, from **http://learngen.org/resources/module/lgend101_norm1/200/210/211_3.html**

63. Ibid.

64. Ibid.

65. Ibid.

66. Mandel, T., & G. Van der Leun. (1996). *Rules of the net: Online operating instructions for human beings.* New York: Hyperion.

Chapter 7

1. Lindley, C. (1996). *Clyde's corner.* International Personnel Management Association Assessment Council. Retrieved January 5, 2005, from **http://www.ipmaac.org/acn/dec96/clyde.html**

2. Goleman, D. (1995). *Emotional intelligence.* New York: Bantam, p. 179.

3. Ibid., p. 178.

4. Goleman, *Emotional intelligence*.

5. Ibid., pp. 43–44.

6. Ibid., pp. 81–82.

7. Ibid., p. 193.

8. Goleman, D. (1998). *Working with emotional intelligence.* New York: Bantam, pp. 322–223; Covey, S. (1998). *7 habits of highly effective families.* New York: Golden Books, pp. 22–23, 238.

9. Ibid.

10. Ibid., p. 193.

11. Ibid., pp. 86–90.

12. Ibid., pp. 106–110.

13. Ibid., pp. 111–126.

14. Weinberg, G. (2002). *Why men won't commit: Getting what you both want without playing games.* New York: Atria Books, p. 30.

15. Hatfield, E., & R. L. Rapson. (1992). Similarity and attraction in close relationships. *Communication Monographs, 59,* 209–212.

16. Sias, P. M., & D. J. Cahill. (1998). From co-workers to friends: The development of peer friendships in the workplace. *Western Journal of Communication, 62*(3), 173–299.

17. Mantovani, F. (2001). Cyber-attraction: The emergence of computer-mediated communication in the development of interpersonal relationships. In L. Anolli, R. Ciceri, & G. Riva (eds.), *Say not to say: New perspectives on miscommunication*. IOS Press. Retrieved January 2, 2005, from **http://www.vepsy.com/communication/book3/2CHAPT_10.PDF+Revealing+attractiveness+int.CMC&hl=en&start=4**

18. Walther, J. B. (1993). Impression development in computer-mediated interaction. *Western Journal of Communication, 57,* 381–398.

19. Chenault, B. G. (1998). Developing personal and emotional relationships via computer-mediated communication. *CMC Magazine, 5* (online): **http://www.december.com/cmc/mag/1998/may/chenault.html**

20. Baym, N. K. (1995). The performance of humour in computer-mediated communication. *Journal of Computer-Mediated Communication, 1* (online): **http://jcmc.mscc.huji.ac.il/voll/issue2/baym.html**

21. Rubin, R. B., E. M. Perse, & C. A. Barbato. (1998). Conceptualization and measurement of interpersonal communication motives. *Human Communication Research, 14,* 602–628.

22. Goleman, D. (1988, October 7). Feeling of control viewed as central in mental health. *The New York Times,* pp. C1, C11.

23. Ibid.

24. Wolfer, S. (2004, January/February). Save the date: Relationships ward off disease and stress. *Psychology Today, 37*(1), 32.

25. Joinson, A. (2003, November 4). *Intimacy and deception on the Internet: The role of the user, media and context*. Institute of Educational Technology—The Open University (*Instytucie Psychologii Uniwersytetu Gdannskiego*). Retrieved January 3, 2005, from **http://64.233.167.104/search?q=cache:ljEQ9LVhkTUJ:iet.open.ac.uk/pp/a.n.joinson/anima.ppt+motivation+for+using+CMC+for+romance&hl=en&start=9**

26. Marano, H. E. (1997, May 28). Rescuing marriages before they begin. *The New York Times,* p. C8.

27. Ibid.

28. Booher, D. (1996, May). How to master the art of conversation. *Vitality,* 5.

29. Gottman, J. M., & J. DeClaire. (2001). *The relationship cure: A five-step guide for building better connections with family, friends, and lovers*. New York: Crown, p. 4.

30. Ibid., p. 25.

31. Ibid., p. 31.

32. Gordon, T. (1974). *T.E.T.—Teacher effectiveness training*. New York: Wyden.

33. Proctor, R. F. II. (1991). *An exploratory analysis of responses to owned messages in interpersonal communication*. Unpublished doctoral dissertation, Bowling Green State University, Bowling Green, OH, p. 11.

34. Weaver, R. L. II. (1996). *Understanding interpersonal communication* (7th ed.). New York: Harper/Collins, pp. 149–154.

35. Gordon, *T.E.T.,* p. 139.

36. Parks, M. R. (1985). Interpersonal communication and the quest for personal competence. In M. L. Knapp & G. R. Miller (eds.), *Handbook of interpersonal communication*. Thousand Oaks, CA: Sage, pp. 171–201.

37. Littlejohn, S. W. (1992). *Theories of human communication* (4th ed.). Belmont, CA: Wadsworth, p. 274.

38. Miller, G. R., & M. J. Sunnafrank. (1982). All is for one but one is not for all: A conceptual perspective of interpersonal communication. In F. E. X. Dance (ed.), *Human communication theory: Comparative essays*. New York: Harper & Row. All is for one but one is not for all, pp. 222–223.

39. Ibid.

40. Luft, J. (1970). *Group process: An introduction to group dynamics* (2nd ed.). Palo Alto, CA: Science and Behavior Books.

41. Dindia, K., M. A. Fitzpatrick, & D. A. Kenny. (1997, March). Self-disclosure in spouse and stranger interaction: A social relationships analysis. *Human Communication, 23*(3), 388.

42. Barbor, C. (2001, January/February). Finding real love. *Psychology Today,* 42–49.

43. Kimura, D. (1999, Summer). Sex differences in the brain. *Scientific American Presents, 10*(Special Issue, no. 2), 26; Hedges, L. V., & A. Nowell. (1995, July 7). Sex differences in mental test scores, variability, and numbers of high-scoring individuals. *Science, 269,* 41–45; Halpern, D. F. (1992). *Sex differences in cognitive ability* (2nd ed.). Hillsdale, NJ: Erlbaum; Blum, D. (1997). *Sex on the brain: The biological differences between men and women*. New York: Viking Press.

44. Gottman & DeClaire, *The relationship cure,* pp. 65–87.

45. Sommers, C. H. (2000). *The war against boys: How misguided feminism is harming our young men*. New York: Simon & Schuster, p. 87.

46. Goleman, *Emotional intelligence,* p. 131.

47. Wood, J. T. (1997). *But I thought you meant. . . . Misunderstandings in human communication*. Mountain View, CA: Mayfield, p. 69. In D. Vaughan, *Uncoupling: How relationships come apart*. New York: Random House.

48. Sommers, *The war against boys,* p. 151.

49. Levin, J., & A. Arluke. (1985). An exploratory analysis of sex differences in gossip. *Sex Roles, 12,* 281–285.

50. Ibid.

51. McGuinness, D., & J. Symonds. (1977). Sex differences in choice behaviour: The object-person dimension. *Perception, 6*(6), 691–694.

52. Sommers, *The war against boys;* Brody, L. R., & J. A. Hall. (1993). Gender and emotion. In M. Lewis & J. Haviland (eds.), *Handbook of emotions*. New York: Guilford Press, pp. 447–460.

53. Wood, But I thought you meant . . . , p. 69. In Vaughan, *Uncoupling*.

54. Ibid.

55. Ibid.

56. Ibid.

57. Axtell, R. (1997). *Do's and taboos around the world for women in business*. New York: John Wiley, pp. 161–162.

58. Boteach, S. (2000). *Dating secrets of the ten commandments*. New York: Doubleday, p. 165.

59. Fein, E., & S. Schneider. (2001). *The rules for marriage: Time-tested secrets for making your marriage work.* New York: Warner Books, pp. 187–188.

60. Boone, M. E. (2001). *Managing inter@ctively: Executing business strategy, improving communication, and creating a knowledge-sharing culture.* New York: McGraw-Hill, p. 223.

61. Mottet, T. P., & V. P. Richmond. (1998). An inductive analysis of verbal immediacy: Alternative conceptualization of relational verbal approach/avoidance strategies. *Communication Quarterly, 46*(1), 25–40.

62. Burgess, A. (2002, January 26). I vow to thee. *Guardian.* Retrieved March 24, 2003, from **http://www.guardian.co.uk/Archive/Article/0,4273,4342138,00.html**

63. Real, T. (2002). *How can I get through to you? Reconnecting men and women.* New York: Scribner's, p. 198.

64. Ibid., p. 202.

65. Ibid., p. 74.

66. Perrole, J. A. (1991). Conversations and trust in computer interfaces. In C. Dunlop & R. Kling (eds.), *Computerization and controversy.* Boston: Academic Press, pp. 350–363. As cited in Chenault, B. G. (1998, May). Developing personal and emotional relationships via computer-mediated communication. *CMC magazine,* p. 1. Retrieved January 10, 2004, from **http:www.december.com/cmc/mag/1998/chenault.html**

67. [No author]. (2005, January 10), "Numbers," *Time,* 19. From the Stanford Institute for the Quantitative Study of Society.

68. Douglas, J., & S. Singular. (2003). *Anyone you want me to be: A true story of sex and death on the Internet.* New York: Scribner's (a Lisa Drew Book), p. 91.

69. Eitzen, D. Stanley. (2003, December 15). Avoiding trends that deprive us of humanity: The atrophy of social life. *Vital Speeches of the Day, LXX*(5), 144.

70. Greenwald, Rachel. (2003). *Find a husband after 35: Using what I learned at Harvard Business School.* New York: Ballantine Books, pp. 114–135.

Chapter 8

1. Knapp, M., & A. Vangelisti. (1995). *Interpersonal communication and human relationships* (3rd ed.). Boston: Allyn & Bacon.

2. Avtgis, T. A., D. V. West, & R. L. Anderson. (1998, Summer). Relationship stages: An inductive analysis identifying cognitive, affective, and behavioral dimensions of Knapp's relational stages model. *Communication Research Reports, 15*(3), 281.

3. Levine, M., & H. E. Marano. (2001, July–August). Why I hate beauty. *Psychology Today,* 42.

4. Avtgis, West, & Anderson, Relationship stages, pp. 280-287.

5. Ibid., p. 283.

6. Ibid., p. 284.

7. Ibid.

8. Ibid.

9. Ibid.

10. Casto, M. L. (2004). *The 7 stages of a romantic relationship.* The All I Need. Retrieved January 11, 2005, from **http://www.theallineed.com/ad-self-help-2/self-help-010.htm**. This article is adapted from the book: Casto, M. L. (2000). *Get smart! About modern romantic relationships: Your personal guide to finding right and real love.* Cincinnati, OH: Get Smart! Publishing.

11. Avtgis, West, & Anderson, Relationship stages, p. 284.

12. Ibid.

13. Ibid., p. 285.

14. Ibid.

15. Ibid.

16. Ibid.

17. Ibid.

18. Knapp, M. L., R. P. Hart, G. W. Friedrich, & G. M. Shulman. (1973). The rhetoric of goodbye: Verbal and nonverbal correlates of human leave-taking. *Speech Monographs, 40,* 182–198.

19. Banks, S. P., D. M. Altendorf, J. O. Greene, & M. J. Cody. (1987). An examination of relationship disengagement perceptions: Breakout strategies and outcomes. *Western Journal of Speech Communication, 51,* 19–41.

20. Mauchline, P. (2000). *Evaluating whether a potential partner may be the one for you.* The Art of Loving. Retrieved January 8, 2005, from **http://aboutyourbreakup.com/potential.html**. Mauchline lists five questions only. Some of the information here is taken directly from his Web site.

21. Littlejohn, S. W. (1992). *Theories of human communication* (4th ed.). Belmont, CA: Wadsworth, p. 274.

22. Kirshenbaum, M. (1996). *Too good to leave, too bad to stay.* New York: Dutton, p. 94.

23. [No author]. (no date). *Competition and feeling superior to others.* Retrieved January 9, 2005, from **http://mentalhelp.net/psyhelp/chap9/chap9q.htm**. The questions and comments in this section have been taken from this source.

24. Ibid.

25. Lerner, H. (2001). *The dance of connection: How to talk to someone when you're mad, hurt, scared, frustrated, insulted, betrayed, or desperate.* New York: HarperCollins.

26. Infante, D. A. (1995, January). Teaching students to understand and control verbal aggression. *Communication Education, 44*(1), 51.

27. Guerrero, L. K. (1994, Winter). I'm so mad I could scream: The effects of anger expression on relational satisfaction and communication competence. *Southern Communication Journal, 59*(2), 125–141.

28. Kantrowitz, B., & P. Wingert. (1999, April 19). The science of a good marriage. *Newsweek,* 52–57.

29. [No author]. (1993, September–October). The rat in the spat. *Psychology Today,* 12.

30. Tracy, K., D. Van Duesen, & S. Robinson. (1987). "Good" and "bad" criticism: A descriptive analysis. *Journal of Communication, 37,* 46–59.

31. Ibid., p. 48.

32. Alberts, J. K., & G. Driscoll. (1992). Containment versus escalation: The trajectory of couples' conversational complaints. *Western Journal of Speech Communication, 56,* 394–412.

33. Cline, R. J., & B. M. Johnson. (1976). The verbal stare: Focus on attention in conversation. *Communication Monographs, 43,* 1–10.

34. Gibb, J. (1961). Defensive communication. *Journal of Communication, 11,* 141–148.

35. Wieder-Hatfield, D. (1981). A unit in conflict management education skills. *Communication Education, 30,* 265–273.

36. Kantrowitz, & Wingert, The science of a good marriage, 56.

37. Waite, L. J., D. Browning, W. J. Doherty, M. Gallaher, Y. Luo, & S. M. Stanley. (2002, July 11). *Does divorce make people happy? Findings from a study of unhappy marriages.* The Institute for American Values. Retrieved January 11, 2005, from **http://www.americanvalues.org/html/r-unhappyii.html**

Chapter 9

1. [No author]. (2002). *Types of interviews and how to handle them.* CareerJournal.Jobpilot. Retrieved January 17, 2005, from **http://www.jobpilot.co.th/content/channel/journal/typeinterview.html**

2. Morreale, S. (2001, May). Communication important to employers. *Spectra,* 8.

3. Misler, E. G. (1975). Studies in dialogue and discourse: II. Types of discourse initiated by and sustained through questioning. *Journal of Psycholinguistic Research, 4,* 99–121.

4. Campullo, J. L. (no date). *Cultural differences in the workplace: Stereotypes vs. sensitivity.* Fisher & Phillips LLP (Attorneys at Law). Retrieved January 16, 2005, from **http://www.laborlawyers.com/CM/Seminar%20Materials/seminar%20materiala548.asp**, p. 1.

5. [No author]. (2004, March 3). *Workforce diversity issues: The role of cultural differences in workplace investigations.* Cultural Differences in Workplace Investigations. Texas Workforce. Retrieved January 16, 2005, from **http://www.twc.state.tx.us/news/efte/cultural_differences.html**

6. [No author]. (2004, September 1). Studies find women, men motivated on job by differing concerns. *The* (Toledo) *Blade,* p. 8B (originally published in the *Boston Globe*).

7. Tymson, C. (no date). *Business communication: Bridging the gender gap.* Retrieved January 16, 2005, from **http://www.tymson.com.au/pdf/gendergap.pdf**

8. Lifland, S. (2002, February). *Interview with Florence M. Stone.* AMA–American Management Association. Retrieved January 15, 2005, from **http://www.amanet.org/arc_center/archive/experts_feb2002.htm**

9. Wisinski, J. (1993). *Resolving conflicts on the job: A WorkSmart book.* New York: AMACOM, Chap. 1.

10. Dikel, Margaret F. (2003, September). *How to use the Internet in your job search.* The Riley Guide: Execute a Campaign. Retrieved May 7, 2004, from **http://www.rileyguide.com/jobsrch.html**

Chapter 10

1. Sharpe, R. (1999, May 27). *Contributing to online discussions.* University of Plymouth. Retrieved January 20, 2005, from **http://sh.plym.ac.uk/eds/LO/LOnet6.html**

2. Chadwick, T. B. (2001, September 21). *How to conduct research on the Internet.* Infoquest! Information Services. Retrieved January 20, 2005, from **http://www.tbchad.com/resrch.html**

3. Sharpe, *Contributing to online discussions.*

4. [No author]. (2005). *Internet usage statistics: The big picture.* Internet World Stats: Usage and Population Statistics. Retrieved January 20, 2005, from **http://www.internetworldstats.com/stats.htm**

5. [No author]. (2001, January 1). *Help with Internet e-mail and mailing lists.* City of Grand Prarie, Alberta, Canada. Retrieved January 20, 2005, from **http://www.city.grandeprare.ab.ca/h_email.htm#Frinding_And-Subscribing_toMls**

6. Beebe, S. A., & J. T. Masterson. (2002). *Communicating in small groups: Principles and practices* (7th ed.). Boston: Allyn & Bacon.

7. Whetten, D. A., & K. S. Cameron. (1984). *Developing management skills.* Glenview, IL: Scott, Foresman, p. 6.

8. Ibid.

9. Tubbs, S. L. (2003). *A systems approach to small group interaction* (8th ed.). New York: McGraw-Hill.

10. Svinicki, M. (no date). *Using small groups to promote learning: Section 5. Improving specific teaching techniques.* Center for Teaching Effectiveness, the University of Texas at Austin. Retrieved January 19, 2005, from **http://www.utexas.edu/academic/cte/sourcebook/groups.pdf**, p. 1.

11. Wilson, G. L. (2004). *Groups in context: Leadership and participation in small groups* (7th ed.). New York: McGraw-Hill.

12. Beebe & Masterson, *Communicating in small groups.*

13. Ibid.

14. Goleman, D. (1990, December 25). The group and the self: New focus on a cultural rift. *The New York Times,* pp. 37, 41.

15. Ibid.

16. Thelen, H. A. (1997, March). Group dynamics in instruction: Principle of least group size. *School Review, 57,* 142.

17. Lawren, B. (1989, September). Seating for success. *Psychology Today,* 16–20.

18. Beebe & Masterson, *Communicating in small groups,* p. 113.

19. Janis, I. L. (1972). *Victims of groupthink.* Boston: Houghton Mifflin, p. 9.

20. Ibid., p. 3.

21. Greenhalgh, L. (2001). *Managing strategic relationships: The key to business success.* New York: Free Press.

22. Ibid., p. 237.

23. Janis, *Victims of groupthink,* pp. 174–175.

24. Larson, C. E., & F. M. J. LaFasto. (1989). *Teamwork.* Newbury Park, CA: Sage, p. 19.

25. Dyer, W. G. (1985). *Team building: Issues and alternatives* (2nd ed.). Reading, MA: Addison-Wesley, p. 24.

26. [No author]. (no date). *What makes a good team?* Center for Service and Leadership, George Mason University, Fairfax, Virginia. Retrieved January 19, 2005, from **http://www.gmu.edu/student/csl/goodteam.html**

27. Barnett, S. (no date). *Teams in the workplace.* LIS 405. Retrieved January 20, 2005, from **http://lrs.ed.uiuc.edu/students/sbarnett/lis405le/teams.htm**

28. Drucker, P. F. (no date). *There's more than one kind of team.* Retrieved January 20, 2005, from **http://web.cba.neu.edu/~ewertheim/teams/drucker.htm**

29. Hersey, P., & K. H. Blanchard. (1982). *Management of organizational behavior: Utilizing human resources* (4th ed.). Englewood Cliffs, NJ: Prentice Hall.

30. Benne, K. D., & P. Sheats. (1948). Functional roles of group members. *Journal of Social Issues, 4,* 41–49.

31. Ibid.

32. Gahran, Amy (1999, June 20). The content of online discussion groups, Part 1: Introduction. *Contentious.* Retrieved May 11, 2004, from **http://www.contentious.com/articles/V2/2-3/feature2-3a.html**, p. 1.

33. [No author]. (no date). *Types of group communication tools.* University of Illinois. Retrieved March 24, 2003, from **http://illinois.online,uillinois.edu/stovall/GroupTools/GT/index.html**

34. Gahran, The content of online discussion groups.

35. Maeroff, G. I. (2003). *A classroom of one.* New York: Palgrave Macmillan, p. 43.

Chapter 11

1. Arnold, H. J., & D. C. Feldman. (1986). *Organizational behavior.* New York: McGraw-Hill, pp. 120–121.

2. Abrams, R. (1999). *Wear clean underwear: Business wisdom from mom.* New York: Villard Books, p. 36.

3. Cramer, R. J., & T. R. Jantz. (2005). *An examination of personality traits among student leaders and nonleaders.* PSI CHI. The National Honor Society in Psychology, Loyola College. Retrieved January 24, 2005, from **http://www.psichi.org/pubs/articles/article_421.asp**

4. Bennis, W. (1998). *Managing People Is Like Herding Cats.* London: Kogan Page.

5. Burbules, N. C. (1993). *Dialogue in teaching.* New York: Teachers College Press.

6. Doyle, M. E., & M. K. Smith. (2001, September 18). *Shared leadership.* Infed Encyclopedia—The Encyclopedia of Informal Education. Retrieved January 25, 2005, from **http://www.infed.org/leadership/shared_leadership.htm**

7. Zigarmi, P., D. Zigarmi, & K. H. Blanchard. (1985). *Leadership and the one minute manager: Increasing effectiveness through situational leadership.* New York: William Morrow.

8. Hargrove, R. (2001). *E-leader: Reinventing leadership in a connected economy.* Cambridge, MA: Perseus, p. 7.

9. Chang, H. K. (2003, March 14). *Sustainable leadership requires listening skills.* Graduate School of Business, Stanford University. Retrieved January 25, 2005, from **http://www.gsb.stanford.edu/news/headlines/vftt_vanderveer.shtml**

10. Simonton, B. (2003). *Leadership skills—Listening, the most important leadership skill—Don't shoot the messenger.* Retrieved January 25, 2005, from **http://www.bensimonton.com/messenger-leadership-skills.htm**

11. McCutchen, B., & Heller, Ehrman, White, & McAuliffe, LLP. (2003, September). Preserving diversity in higher education. *A Manual on Admissions Policies and Procedures After the University of Michigan Decisions.* Retrieved January 25, 2005, from **lhttp://www.bingham.com/bingham/webadmin/documents/radb5f5a.pdf**.

12. Nelson, C. S. (2004). *What makes a great leader great?* ConcreteNetwork.com. Retrieved January 25, 2005, from **http://www.concretenetwork.com/csn_archive/greatleader.html**

13. Giuliani, R. W. (2002). *Leadership.* New York: Miramax Books, p. 184.

14. Sieler, A. (1999). *Leadership and change.* Observing Differently, Newfield, Australia. Retrieved January 20, 2005, from **http://www.newfieldaus.com.au/Articles/leadership&change.htm**

15. Goleman, D. (1990, December 25). The group and the self: New focus on a cultural rift. *The New York Times,* pp. 37, 41.

16. Deutsch, M. (1973). *The resolution of conflict: Constructive and destructive processes.* New Haven, CT: Yale University Press; Johnson, D. W. (1970). *Social psychology of education.* Edina, MN: Interaction Book Company; Johnson, D. W., & F. Johnson. (1994). *Joining together: Group theory and group skills* (5th ed). Boston, MA: Allyn & Bacon; Johnson, D. W., & R. T. Johnson. (1995). *Teaching students to be peacemakers* (3rd ed.). Edina, MN: Interaction Book Company.

17. Blake, R. R., & J. S. Mouton. (1964). *The managerial grid.* Houston, TX: Gulf Publishing, p. 11; Blake, R. R., & J. S. Mouton. (1978). *The new managerial grid.* Houston, TX: Gulf Publishing.

18. Gahran, A. (1999, June 20). The content of online discussion groups, Part 3: Improving content in the discussion groups you run. *Contentious.* Retrieved May 11, 2004, from **http://www.contentious.com/articles/V2/2-3/feature2-3a.html**

19. Munro, K. (2002, May). Conflict in cyberspace: How to resolve conflict online. *Psychology of Cyberspace.* Rider University. Retrieved May 12, 2004, from **http://www.rider.edu/~suler/psycyber/conflict.html**, p. 1.

Appendix

1. Markoff, J. (2004, December 30). Internet use said to cut into TV viewing and socializing. *The New York Times,* p. C5.

2. Ibid.

3. Chenault, B. G. (1998). Developing personal and emotional relationships via computer-mediated communication. *CMC Magazine.* University of Illinois at Urbana–Champaign. Retrieved November 10, 2004, from **http://www.december.com/cmc/mag/1998/may/chenault.html**

4. [No author]. (1999). *Resource guide: Media literacy.* Ontario, Canada: Ministry of Education; [No author]. (1999, May 30). A

few words about media literacy. Retrieved March 10, 2003, from **http://www.cmpl.ucr.edu'exhibitions/education/vidkids/medialit.html**; Hobbs, R. (1998). Media literacy in Massachusetts. In A. Hart (ed.), *Teaching the media: International perspectives.* Mahwah, NJ: Erlbaum, pp. 127–144.

5. Freed, K. (2002, May 11). Deep literacy: A proposal to produce public understanding of our interactivity. *Media & Education, Media Visions Journal.* Retrieved March 2, 2005, from **http://www.media-visions.com/ed-deeplit.html**

6. Flaherty, L. M., K. J. Pearce, & R. B. Rubin. (1998, Summer). Internet and face-to-face communication. Not functional alternatives. *Communication Quarterly, 46*(3), 250–268.

7. O'Sullivan, P. B. (2000). What you don't know won't hurt me: Impression management functions of communication channels in relationships. *Human Communication Research, 26*(3), 405–406.

8. Barnes, S. B. (2003). *Computer-mediated communication: Human-to-human communication across the Internet.* Boston: Allyn & Bacon, p. 15. Throughout this appendix, I depend heavily on the work of Susan B. Barnes.

9. Mazur, M. A., R. J. Burns, & T. M. Emmers-Sommer. (2000). Perceptions of relational interdependence in online relationships: The effects of communication apprehension and introversion. *Communication Research Reports, 17*(4), 397–406.

10. Barnes, *Computer-mediated communication,* p. 148.

11. Loughlin, T. W. (1993, January). Virtual relationships. The solitary world of cmc. *Interpersonal Computing and Technology: An Electronic Journal for the 21st Century, 1*(1). Retrieved March 20, 2002, from **http://jan.uce.edu/~ipct-j/** (7 pages).

12. Keen, P. G. W. (1988). *Competing in time.* New York: Ballinger.

13. Barnes, *Computer-mediated communication,* p. 116.

14. Ibid., p. 125.

15. Ibid., p. 213.

16. Ibid., p. 230.

17. Rheingold, H. (1993). *The virtual community.* Reading, MA: Addison-Wesley, p. 6.

18. Rheingold, H. (1998). Virtual communities. In F. Hesselbein, M. Goldsmith, R. Beckhard, & R. F. Schubert (eds.). *The community of the future.* San Francisco: Jossey-Bass, p. 116.

19. Barnes, *Computer-mediated communication,* p. 226.

20. Ibid., p. 227.

21. Ibid., p. 227.

22. [No author]. (2004, March 6). You're on. *The (Toledo) Blade,* p. 1D.

23. [No author]. (2004, September 27). Who's blogging now? *Newsweek,* 62.

24. Ibid.

25. Ibid.

26. Mintz, J. (2005, January 21). When bloggers make news: As their clout increases, web diarists are asking: Just what are the rules? (Marketplace) *The Wall Street Journal,* p. 1B.

Chapter 12

1. Tucker-Ladd, C. E. (1996–2000). *Chapter 5: Signs of stress.* Psychological self-help/mental health net. Retrieved February 2, 2005, from **http://www.mhnet.org/psyhelp/chap5/chap5c/htm**

2. Levasseur, D. G., K. W. Dean, & J. Pfaff, (2004, July). Speech pedagogy beyond the basics: A study of instructional methods in the advanced public speaking course. *Communication Education, 53*(3), p. 247.

3. Chadwick, T. B. (2001, September 21). *How to conduct research on the Internet.* Infoquest! Information Services. Retrieved February 2, 2005, from **http://www.tbchad.com/resrch.html**

4. Ormondroyd. J., M. Engle, & T. Cosgrave. (2001, September 18). *How to critically analyze information services.* Olin Kroch, Uris Libraries, Research Services Division, Cornell University Library. Retrieved February 2, 2005, from **http://www.library.cornell.edu/okuref/research/skill26.htm**

5. Cuomo, M. (1998). Graduation speech at Iona College. In A. Albanese & B. Trissler (eds.), *Graduation day: The best of America's commencement speeches.* New York: Morrow, pp. 72–73.

6. Selnow, G. (2000, November 1). The Internet: The soul of democracy. *Vital Speeches of the Day, 67*(2), 59.

7. [No author]. (2004). *Trends Journal.* The Trends Research Institute. Rhinebeck, New York. Retrieved November 3, 2005, from **http://www.trendsresearch.com/**

8. [No author]. (2002). *Trends in college binge drinking during a period of increased prevention efforts: Findings from 4 Harvard School of Public Health College alcohol study surveys: 1993–2001.* School of Public Health, Harvard University. Retrieved March 25, 2003, from **http://www.hsph.harvard.edu/cas/Documents/trends/**

9. Franklin, W. E. (1998, September 15). Careers in international business: Five ideas or principles. *Vital Speeches of the Day,* 64.

10. Ibid., p. 719.

11. Walters, F. M. (2000, December 15). We, the people: Prize and embrace what is America. *Vital Speeches of the Day, 67*(5), 144.

Chapter 13

1. Mann, W., & J. Lash. (2004). *Some facts psychologists know about: Test and performance anxiety.* Psychological Services Center and the Division of Student Affairs and Services, University of Cincinnati. Retrieved November 3, 2005, from **http://www.psc.uc.edu**, p. 3.

2. Probert, B. (2003). *Test anxiety.* University of Florida Counseling Center. Retrieved November 3, 2005, from **http://www.counsel.ufl.edu/selfHelp/testAnxiety.asp**

3. [No author]. (no date). *Health, exercise, diet, rest, self-image, motivation, and attitudes.* Learning Strategies Database, Center for Advancement of Learning, Muskingum College, Muskingum, MI. Retrieved November 3, 2005, from **http://muskingum.edu/~cal/database/Physiopsyc.html**

4. [No author]. (no date). *Dealing with test anxiety.* SUNY Potsdam Counseling Center. Retrieved November 3, 2005, from **www.potsdam.edu/COUN/brochures/test.html**

5. [No author]. (no date). *Study skills for college*. Pennsylvania State University. Retrieved November 3, 2005, from **http://www.bmb.psy.edu/courses/psu16/troyan/studyskills/examprep.htm**

6. *Dealing with test anxiety.*

7. Probert, *Test anxiety.*

8. Mann, & Lash, *Some facts psychologists know about*, p. 3.

9. [No author]. (2002). *Test-taking strategies*. Academic Services, Southwestern University. Retrieved November 3, 2005, from **http://www.southwestern.edu/academic/acser-skills-terstr.html.**

10. Mann & Lash, *Some facts psychologists know*, p. 3.

11. [No author]. (2002, January 17). *Test anxiety*. Counseling Center, University of Illinois at Urbana. Retrieved November 3, 2005, from **http://www.couns.uiuc.edu/brochures/testanx.htm**

12. [No author]. (2001, August 31). *Test anxiety: Overcoming test anxiety*. Counseling Center, University of Florida. Retrieved November 3, 2005, from **http://www.counsel.ufl.edu/selfHelp/testAnxiety.asp**

13. Lamm, R. D. (2003, September 1). Sustainability: The limited use of history in the new world of public policy. *Vital Speeches of the Day, 69*(22), 678.

14. Kreahling, L. (2005, February 1). The perils of needles to the body. (Health & Fitness). *The New York Times*, p. D5.

15. McKerrow, R. E., B. E. Gronbeck, D. Ehninger, & A. H. Monroe. (2003). *Principles and types of speech communication* (15th ed.). Boston: Allyn & Bacon.

16. Gruner, C. B. (1985, April). Advice to the beginning speaker on using humor—What the research tells us. *Communication Education, 34*, 142.

17. Keillor, G. (1998). Commencement address—Gettysburg College. In A. Albanese & B. Triller (eds.), *Graduation day: The best of America's commencement speeches*. New York: Morrow, p. 181.

18. Dilenschneider, R. L. (2001, July 15). Heroes or losers: The choice is yours. *Vital Speeches of the Day, 67*(19), 605.

Chapter 14

1. Knight, B. (2000). *Women who love books too much: Bibliophiles, bluestockings and prolific pens*. Berkeley, CA: Conari Press.

2. Sellnow, D. D., & K. P. Treinen. (2004, July). The role of gender in perceived speaker competence: An analysis of student peer critiques. *Communication Education, 53*(3), 293.

3. Argyle, M. (1991). Intercultural communication. In L. A. Samovar & R. E. Porter (eds.), *Intercultural communication: A reader* (6th ed.). Belmont, CA: Wadsworth, p. 43.

4. Hahner, J. C., M. A. Sokoloff, & S. Salisch. (2001). *Speaking clearly: Improving voice and diction* (6th ed.). New York: McGraw-Hill.

5. [No author]. (2005). *How many online?* ComputerScope, Ltd., Scope Communications Group, Prospect House, 3 Prospect Road, Dublin 9, Ireland. Retrieved February 8, 2005, from **http://www.nua.ie/surveys/how_many_online/**, p. 1.

6. Ibid.

7. Motley, M. T. (no date). *Overcoming your fear of public speaking*. Communication Resource Center for Students, Fundamentals of Communication, Faculty Services Center, Houghton Mifflin Company. Retrieved February 7, 2005, from **http://college.hmco.com/communication/resources/students/fundamentals/fear.html**

8. Ibid.

9. Ibid.

10. Schacter, D. L. (2001). *The seven sins of memory: How the mind forgets and remembers*. Boston: Houghton Mifflin.

11. Manz, C. C., & H. P. Sims, Jr. (2001). *The new superleadership: Leading others to lead themselves*. San Francisco: Berrett-Koehler.

12. Ibid.

Chapter 15

1. Petersen, J. A. (1999, August 12). *Better families*. Quoted on the Christianity New home page, Preaching Resources. Copyright 1996 by *Christianity Today, Inc/LEADERSHIP, 17*(3), 69.

2. Lamm, R. (1998, September 15). Unexamined assumptions: Destiny, political institutions, democracy, and population. *Vital Speeches of the Day, 64*(23), 712.

3. Ehrensberger, R. (1945). An experimental study of the relative effects of certain forms of emphasis in public speaking. *Speech Monographs, 12*, 94–111.

4. [No author]. (2005, February 25). *Visual communication of ideas*. Presentation Helper. Retrieved March 8, 2005, from **http://www.presentationhelper.co.uk/visual_communication.htm**

5. This study was cited in Arredondo, L. (1994). *The McGraw-Hill 36-hour course: Business presentations*. New York: McGraw-Hill, p. 177. Also see Weaver, R. L. II. (2001). *Essentials of public speaking* (2nd ed.). Boston: Allyn & Bacon, p. 186.

6. Knapp, M. L., & A. L. Vangelisti. (1996). *Interpersonal communication and human relationships* (3rd ed.). Boston: Allyn & Bacon.

7. Kluger, J. (2004, December 20). The buzz on caffeine. *Time*, 52.

8. Finerman, E. (1996, March 1). Humor and speeches: A standup history. *Vital Speeches of the Day, 62*(9), 313.

9. Price, Technical presentations, pp. 1–3.

10. Ibid., p. 6.

11. Templeton, M., & S. S. Fitzgerald. (1999). *Schaum's quick guide to great presentations*. New York: McGraw-Hill, pp. 46–48.

12. Ringle, W. J. (1998). *TechEdge: Using computers to present and persuade*. (Essence of Public Speaking Series). Boston: Allyn & Bacon, pp. 120–121.

13. Price, Technical presentations, p. 4.

14. [No author]. (1999, February 4). *Technical presentations*. Toastmasters International. Retrieved March 24, 2003, from **http://www.toastmasters.bc.ca/ed-program/man-technical.html**

15. Tham, M. (1997). *Poster presentation of research work*. Chemical and Process Engineering. University of Newcastle upon Tyne. Retrieved March 24, 2003, from **http://lorien.ncl.ac.uk/ming/dept/tips/present/posters.htm**

16. Birdsell, D. S. (1998). *The McGraw-Hill guide to presentation graphics*. Boston: McGraw-Hill, pp. 8–11.

17. Nordgren, L. (1996, September 23). *Designing presentation visuals*. Media Services. Robert A. L. Mortvedt Library. Pacific Lutheran University. Retrieved March 24, 2003, from **http://www.plu.edu/~libr/media/designing_visuals.html**

18. Dershern, H. L. (1998, June 24). *How to give technical presentations*. Retrieved March 24, 2003, from **http://www.cs.hope.edu/~dershern/reu/howtopresent/**

Chapter 16

1. Rokeach, M. (1968). *Beliefs, attitudes, and values: A theory of organization and change.* San Francisco: Jossey-Bass, p. 124.

2. Bell, P. (2001, July 1). The new entrepreneurship: From exuberance to reality. *Vital Speeches of the Day, 67*(18), 572–575.

3. Haines, M. P. (2001, July 23). Facts change student drinking. *USA Today*, p. 15A.

4. Lane, T. (2001, December 3). Colleges develop better awareness of drinking risks. *The* (Toledo) *Blade*, p. 1A.

5. Ibid., p. 6A.

6. Kluger, J. (2001, June 18). How to manage teen drinking (the smart way). *Time*, 42–44.

7. Lane, Colleges develop better awareness of drinking risks, p. 1A.

8. Waldron, R. (2000, October 30). Students are dying: Colleges can do more. *Newsweek*, 16.

9. Morse, J. (2002, April 1). Women on a binge. *Time*, 56–61.

10. Ibid., p. 56.

11. Haines, M. P. (2001, July 23). Facts change student drinking. *USA Today*, p. 15A.

12. Ibid.

13. Kluger, How to manage teen drinking, p. 43.

14. Haines, Facts change student drinking, p. 15A.

15 Ibid.

16. Lane, Colleges develop better awareness of drinking risks, p. 1A.

17. Haines, Facts change student drinking, p. 15A.

18. Dunn, C. P. (1976). *Logical fallacies in argument*. Department of Management, San Diego State University. Retrieved March 26, 2003, from **http://www.rohan.sdsu.edu/faculty/dunnweb/logicafall.html**. Adapted from Engel, S. M. (1976). *With good reason: An introduction to informal fallacies*. New York: St. Martin's Press, pp. 66–130. These logical fallacies in argument are quoted directly from C. P. Dunn's adaptation.

19. Bauer, J., & M. Levy. (2004). *How to persuade people who don't want to be persuaded*. New York: John Wiley, pp. 17–18. The study cited is Davenport, T., & J. Beck. (2000, September–October). Getting the attention you need. *Harvard Business Review*.

20. Ibid., pp. 17–18.

21. Maslow, A. H. (1970). *Motivation and personality* (2nd ed.). New York: Harper & Row.

22. Tracy, L. (2005, March 1). Taming hostile audiences: Persuading those who would rather jeer than cheer. *Vital Speeches of the Day, 71*(10), 312.

23. Odden, L. R. (1999, March 1). Talk to your children about the tough stuff: We are all in this together. *Vital Speeches of the Day, 65*(10), 301.

24. Thompson, W. N. (1978). *Responsible and effective communication*. Boston: Houghton Mifflin.

25. [No author]. (2004, February). Optimism and longevity: What's the connection? *University of California, Berkeley Wellness Letter, 20*(5), 1.

26. [No author]. (2002, August 28). College education includes lessons in credit cards. *The* (Toledo) *Blade*, p. 7B. *The Blade* cited the *Kansas City Star*.

27. Mooney K. with L. Berghheim. (2002). *The ten demandments: Rules to live by in the age of the demanding customer*. New York: McGraw-Hill, p. 174.

Glossary

A

abstract symbol A symbol that represents an idea. (ch 1) (10)

accent Nonverbal message designed specifically to place stress on the verbal message. (ch 6) (148)

access to roles A characteristic of the Internet that makes it unique from normal face-to-face communication because there are no limitations; whoever has the technical capacity to receive messages with a computer can also send them. (ch 1) (24)

accommodation An approach that works toward getting the dominant group to reinvent, or at least change, the rules so that they incorporate the life experiences of the nondominant group. Something that occurs in groups when people on one side of an issue give in to the other side. (ch 3) (69)

accommodation strategies When people are not part of a dominant culture, those processes people use to get the dominant group to reinvent or change the rules through the use of nonassertive, assertive, or aggressive accommodation. (ch 3) (69-70)

action listening style That kind of listening in which the listener wants precise, error-free presentations and is likely to be impatient with disorganization. (ch 4) (85)

active listening Making a mental outline of important points, thinking up questions or challenges to the points that have been made, and becoming mentally involved with the person talking. (ch 4) (92)

adaptors Nonverbal ways of adjusting to a communication situation. (ch 6) (139)

ad hominem A fallacy that occurs when an argument diverts attention away from the question being argued by focusing instead on those arguing it. (ch 16) (408)

agenda A list of all the items that will be discussed during a meeting. (ch 11) (235)

aggressive talk Talk that attacks a person's self-concept with the intent of inflicting psychological pain. (ch 8) (196)

analogy In reasoning, comparing two similar cases and concluding that if something is true for one, it must also be true for the other. (ch 16) (407)

anecdote A short, interesting story based on an experience. (ch 15) (381-382)

anticipate The first of six steps of the strategic flexibility format in which users think about potential situations and the needs and requirements likely to arise because of them. (ch 1) (6)

anxiety A disturbance that occurs in your mind regarding some uncertain event, misgiving, or worry. (ch 4, 14) (89, 361-363)

appeal to authority A fallacy that occurs whenever an idea is justified by citing some source of expertise as a reason for holding that idea. (ch 16) (408)

appeal to ignorance A fallacy that occurs when an argument is based on an opponent's inability to disprove a conclusion as proof of the conclusion's correctness. (ch 16) (408)

apply The fifth of six steps of the strategic flexibility format in which users, with care, concern, and attention to all the factors that are likely to be affected—including any ethical considerations that may be appropriate—apply the skills and behaviors they have selected. (ch 1) (7)

appraisal interview A type of information interview in which a supervisor makes a valuation by estimating and judging the quality or worth of an employee's performance and then interviews the employee in connection with the appraisal. (ch 9) (212)

articulation The ability to pronounce the letters in a word correctly. (ch 14) (352)

assertiveness Taking the responsibility of expressing needs, thoughts, and feelings in a direct, clear manner. (ch 8) (199)

assess The second of the six steps of the strategic flexibility format in which users take stock of the factors, elements, and conditions of the situations in which you find yourself. (ch 1, 4) (6, 95)

assimilation When nondominants use assimilation, they drop cultural differences and distinctive characteristics that would identify them with the nondominant group. (ch 3) (68)

assimilation strategies When people are not part of a dominant culture, those processes they use to drop cultural differences and distinctive characteristics that would identify them with the nondominant group include the use of nonassertive, assertive, and aggressive assimilation strategies. (ch 3) (68-69)

assumption A taking for granted or supposition that something is a fact. (ch 3) (72)

asynchronous communication Communication in which people are not directly connected with each other at the same time. (ch 1, 10, Appendix A) (23, 251, 277)

attentiveness Focusing on the moment. (ch 14) (346)

attitudes Deeply felt beliefs that govern how one behaves. Also, a group of beliefs that cause us to respond in some way to a particular object or situation. (ch 12, 16) (297, 401)

attractiveness Having the power or quality of drawing, pleasing, or winning. (ch 6) (139-140)

audience analysis Finding out what one's audience members know about a subject, what they might be interested in, and what their attitudes and beliefs are. (ch 12) (295-300)

authoritarian leader One who holds great control over a group. (ch 11) (261-262)

avoidance A refusal to deal with conflict or painful issues. (ch 8) (199)

B

begging the question A fallacy that occurs when an argument, instead of offering proof for its conclusion, simply reasserts the conclusion in another form. (ch 16) (408)

beliefs One's own convictions; what one thinks is right and wrong, true and false. Also, they are classified as statements of knowledge, opinion, and faith. (ch 7, 12, 16) (160, 297, 400-401)

bid A question, gesture, look, touch, or other single expression that says, "I want to feel connected to you." (ch 7) (166)

bifurcation A fallacy that occurs when one presumes that a distinction is exclusive and exhaustive, but other alternatives exist. (ch 16) (408)

blind pane That area in the Johari Window known as an accidental disclosure area. (ch 7) (170)

blog (or Web log) A spontaneous public online journal (or diary) in which Internet users share their lives. (Appendix A) (282-283)

body adornment Any addition to the physical body designed to beautify or decorate. (ch 6) (141-142)

body movement (kinesics) Describes a phenomenon responsible for much of our nonverbal communication. (ch 6) (138)

body (of speech) The main part of the speech. (ch 13) (318)

brainstorming A technique of free association; in groups, when all members spontaneously contribute ideas in a group without judgments being made. The goal of brainstorming is for the group to be as creative as possible. (ch 10) (242)

bulletin boards An online group discussion originally designed for swapping files and posting notices. (ch 10) (251)

C

causal reasoning A logical appeal that pertains to, constitutes, involves, or expresses a cause and therefore uses the word *because*, which is either implicitly or explicitly stated. (ch 16) (407)

cause-and-effect order Organization of a speech around why something is happening (*cause*) and what impact it is having (*effect*). (ch 13) (320)

central idea The essential thought that runs through the speech or communication. (ch 4, 12) (93, 294-295)

channel The route traveled by a message; the means it uses to reach the sender-receivers. (ch 1, Appendix A, ch 12) (10, 277, 300)

chronemics The study of time. (ch 6) (146-147)

clarity That property of style by means of which a thought it so presented that it is immediately understood, depending on the precision and simplicity of the language. (ch 5) (123)

closed-format Interviews that are highly structured. (ch 9) (214)

closed questions Interview questions that are worded in ways that restrict their answers (e.g., questions that can be answered with a yes or a no). (ch 9) (215)

co-culture People who are part of a larger culture but also belong to a smaller group that has some different values, attitudes, or beliefs. (ch 1, 3) (19, 59)

coercive power In an organization, the ability of a leader to punish followers (e.g., by criticizing them, refusing to pay attention to them, using power to demote them, refusing to raise their pay, or firing them). (ch 11) (259)

cognitive development The development of the thinking and organizing systems of your brain that involves language, mental imagery, reasoning, problem solving, and memory development. (ch 5) (108)

cognitive dissonance A psychological theory, applied to communication, that states that people seek information that will support their beliefs and ignore information that does not. (ch 4) (89)

cohesiveness The feeling of attraction that group members have toward one another. It is the group's ability to stick together, to work together as a group, and to help one another as group members. (ch 10) (239)

commitment A strong desire by both parties for the relationship to continue. In groups, it is the willingness of members to work together to complete the group's task. (ch 7, 10) (176, 239)

communication Any process in which people share information, ideas, and feelings. (ch 1) (8)

comparison Supporting material that points out the similarities between two or more things. (ch 12, 15) (304-305, 377)

compatibility Similar attitudes, personality, and a liking for the same activities. (ch 7) (161)

complaint Expression of dissatisfaction with the behavior, attitude, belief, or characteristic of a partner or of someone else. (ch 8) (198-199)

complement Nonverbal cues designed specifically to add to the meaning of a verbal message. (ch 6) (147)

composition The makeup of a thing. (ch 15) (379)

computer (or online) databases A collection of items of information organized for easy access via a computer. (ch 12) (301)

computer-generated graphics Refers to any images created or manipulated via computer—art, drawings, representations of objects, pictures, and the like. (ch 14) (357-359)

computer-mediated communication (CMC) A wide range of technologies that facilitate both human communication and the interactive sharing of information through computer networks, including e-mail, discussion group, newsgroups, chat rooms, instant messages, and Web pages. (ch 1) (18)

conclusion (of speech) In a speech, the closing remarks that tie a speech together and give listeners the feeling that the speech is complete. (ch 13) (327-328)

concrete symbol A symbol that represents an object. (ch 1) (10)

conflict Expressed struggle between at least two individuals who perceive incompatible goals or interference from others in achieving their goals. (ch 11) (269)

conflict resolution Negotiation to find a solution to the conflict. (ch 8) (202-203)

connotative meaning The feelings or associations that each individual has about a particular word. (ch 5) (109)

constructing meaning The complicated and unique process of making sense of the cues, signals, and impulses received. (ch 4) (81-82)

content listening style That kind of listening in which the listener prefers complex and challenging information. (ch 4) (85)

content openness A characteristic of the Internet that makes it unique from normal face-to-face communication because there are no limitations on content. (ch 1) (24)

context High context occurs when most of the meaning of the message is either implied by the physical setting or is presumed to be part of the individual's beliefs, values, and norms. It is considered low context when most of the information is in the code or message. (ch 3) (65)

contrast Supporting material that points out the differences between two or more things. (ch 12, 15) (305, 377)

controlling listeners People who prefer talking to listening and seek to control their listeners by looking for ways to talk about themselves and their experiences. (ch 4) (90)

convergence An aspect of rate (the speed at which one speaks) demonstrated by how one person will accommodate or adapt to another's rate. (ch 6) (137)

conversational quality When speakers talk to audiences in much the same way they talk when they are having a conversation with another person. (ch 14) (345)

costs The problems associated with relationships. (ch 8) (193)

costumes The type of clothing that is a form of highly individualized dress. (ch 6) (141)

creativity The capacity to synthesize vast amounts of information and wrestle with complex problems. (ch 1, 12) (7, 301)

credibility The believability of a speaker based on the speaker's expertise, dynamism, trustworthiness, and ethics. (Appendix A, 16) (281, 415-417)

critical listening Includes all the ingredients for active listening and, in addition, evaluating and challenging what is heard. (ch 4) (92)

critic-analyzers Group members who look at the good and bad points in the information the group has gathered. (ch 10) (245)

criticism A negative evaluation of a person for something he or she has done or the way he or she is. (ch 8) (197-198)

cultural differences Includes not just obvious differences between people from other countries, but also differences based upon income, regional origins, dress code and grooming standards, music preferences, political affiliation, how long an individual has been in this country, skin tone, language ability, religion, etc. (ch 9) (222-223)

cultural identity The degree to which you identify with your culture. (ch 3) (58)

cultural information Information used in making predictions based on a person's most generally shared cultural attributes such as language, shared values, beliefs, and ideologies. (ch 7) (169)

culture The ever-changing values, traditions, social and political relationships, and worldview created and shared by a group of people bound together by a combination of factors (which can include a common history, geographic location, language, social class, and/or religion). (ch 1, 3) (19, 57)

D

deductive reasoning Reasoning from the general to the specific. (ch 16) (404-405)

defensive communication When one partner tries to defend himself or herself against the remarks or behavior of the other. (ch 8) (199-200)

definition Supporting material that is a brief explanation of what a word or phrase means. (ch 12, 15) (305, 376))

delegating That style of situational leadership in which leaders hang back and let members plan and execute the job. (ch 11) (264)

deletions The blotting out, erasing, or canceling of information that makes people's perceptions less than perfect because their physical senses are limited. (ch 2) (46)

democratic leader One who lets all points of view be heard and lets group members participate in the decision-making process. (ch 11) (262)

demographic analysis Reveals data about the characteristics of a group of people, including such things as age, sex, education, occupation, race/nationality/ethnic origin, geographic location, and group affiliation. (ch 12) (297)

demonstration speech A speech that teaches people "how to" perform a process. (ch 15) (375)

denotative meaning The dictionary definition of a particular word. (ch 5) (109)

dialect The habitual language of a community. (ch 5) (120)

digital literacy The ability to understand and use information in multiple formats from a wide range of sources when it is presented via computers. (Appendix A) (277)

directness Being natural and straightforward. (ch 14) (347)

disciplinary interview A type of information interview that concerns a sensitive area, where the employee is notified, and the interview involves hearing the employee's side of the story and, depending on the outcome, instituting disciplinary action. (ch 9) (212)

discrimination The overt actions one takes to exclude, avoid, or distance oneself from other groups. (ch 3) (67)

displays of feelings Face and body movements that show how intensely we are feeling. (ch 6) (138)

distortions The twisting or bending of information out of shape that makes people's perceptions less than perfect because they observe only a small part of their external environment. (ch 2) (46)

dominant culture Includes white people from a European background. (ch 3) (68)

doublespeak A term that refers to euphemisms created by an institution, such as government, to cover up the truth. (ch 5) (114)

dynamism For speakers, a great deal of enthusiasm and energy for their subject. (ch 16) (416-417)

dysfunctional (individual) roles Any role played by a group member that can be characterized as aggressor, blocker, recognition-seeker, self-confessor, playboy or playgirl, dominator, help-seeker, or special-interest pleader. (ch 10) (250-251)

E

elective characteristics The nonverbal, physical characteristics over which you have control such as clothing, makeup, tattoos, and body piercing. (ch 6) (140)

e-mail lists Group discussions that are completely passive; the discussion contributions arrive through e-mail. (ch 10) (251)

emblems Body movements that have a direct translation into words. (ch 6) (138)

emotional appeal A persuasive strategy that focuses on listeners' needs, wants, desires, and wishes. (ch 16) (409)

emotional intelligence The ability to understand and get along with others. (ch 7) (156)

empathic listening Involves trying to understand what others are feeling from their point of view and reflecting those feelings back. (ch 4) (92)

empathy The process of mentally identifying with the character and experiences of another person. (ch 4) (95) The ability to recognize and identify with someone's feelings. (ch 7) (158)

employment interview An interview used by an employer to determine whether someone is suitable for a job. (ch 9) (219-222)

enunciation How one pronounces and articulates words. (ch 14) (352)

ethical communication Communication that is honest, fair, and considerate of others' rights. (ch 1) (20)

ethics Behavior that is in accordance with right principles as defined by a given system of ethics (such as your culture and co-culture), or professional conduct within a specific business environment. (ch 9, 16) (211, 417)

ethnocentrism The belief that one's own cultural group's behaviors, norms, ways of thinking, and ways of being are superior to all other cultural groups. (ch 3) (65)

etymology The study of the origin and development of words. (ch 15) (376-377)

euphemisms Inoffensive words or phrases that are substituted for words that might be perceived as unpleasant. (ch 5) (114)

evaluate The third of the six steps of the strategic flexibility format in which users determine the value and worth of the factors, elements, and conditions to all those involved and how they bear on one's own skills and abilities. (ch 1) (6)

evaluation Determining the value and worth of the factors, elements, and conditions. (ch 4) (82)

evaluative statements Expressions that involve a judgment. (ch 8) (200)

example Supporting material that is a short illustration that clarifies a point. (ch 12) (305)

exit interview A type of information interview that occurs at the termination of an employee's employment, and is designed to resolve any outstanding concerns of employers and employees. (ch 9) (212)

expertise Having the experience or knowledge of an expert. (ch 16) (416)

expert power The influence and power that an expert has because he or she knows more than anyone else. (ch 11) (259)

extemporaneous speaking Speaking from notes. (ch 14) (349)

external noise Interference with the message that comes from the environment and keeps the message from being heard or understood. (ch 1) (11)

extrinsic Means outside the relationship. (ch 8) (193)

extrinsic costs The sacrifices, losses, or suffering as a result of things that occur outside the relationship (could include not having as much time for your friends or sharing your friends with your partner). (ch 8) (193)

extrinsic rewards The gifts, prizes, and recompenses that occur outside a relationship (could include liking the people your partner has introduced you to or the friends he or she hangs out with). (ch 8) (193)

eye messages As an aspect of nonverbal communication, they include all information conveyed by the eyes alone. (ch 6) (139)

F

fable cause A fallacy that occurs when events are causally connected but in fact no such causal connection has been established (ch 16) (408)

fact Something that can be verified in a number of ways. (ch 4) (95)

fallacy An improper conclusion drawn from a premise. (ch 16) (407-409)

false analogy A fallacy that occurs when a comparison between an obscure or difficult set of facts and one that is already known and understood, and to which it bears a significant resemblance, is erroneous and distorts the facts of the case being argued. (ch 16) (408)

feedback The response of the receiver-senders to each other. (ch 1) (11)

femininity versus masculinity That way of contrasting a group of cultures to another group of cultures that involves the division of roles between women and men. (ch 3) (64)

flaming The exchange of rude or hostile messages between online participants. (Appendix A) (282)

flip chart A series of pictures, words, diagrams, and so forth. It is made up of several pages that speakers "flip" through. (ch 14) (354)

follow-up questions Interview questions that are based on the answers given by interviewees and useful when interviewers want interviewees to go into a subject in greater depth. (ch 9) (215)

FOXP2 gene The gene directly linked to developing the fine motor skills needed for the development of language and speech. (ch 5) (107)

framing The way in which messages are divided, arranged, shaped, composed, constructed, and put together as a new whole. (ch 5) (126)

full-sentence outline A complete map of what a speech will look like. (ch 13) (330)

functional leadership When leadership varies with the task of the group and moves from one individual to another as the group finds it suitable. (ch 11) (262)

G

general purpose The intention of the speaker to inform or persuade. (ch 12) (293)

generalizations The process of drawing principles or conclusions from particular evidence or facts that makes people's perceptions less than perfect because once people have observed something a few times, they conclude that what has proven true in the past will prove true in the future as well. (ch 2) (46)

globalization A characteristic of the Internet that makes it unique from normal face-to-face communication because there are no limitations due to borders. (ch 1) (24)

groupthink A group dysfunction in which the preservation of harmony becomes more important than the critical examination of ideas. (ch 10) (239-241)

H

haptics The study of touch. (ch 6) (144)

hasty generalization A fallacy that occurs when an isolated exceptional case is used as the basis for a general conclusion that is unwarranted. (ch 16) (408)

hidden agendas Unannounced goals, subjects, or issues of individual group members or subgroups that differ from the group's public or stated agenda. (ch 11) (267)

hidden pane That area of the Johari Window where self-knowledge is hidden from others—a deliberate non-disclosure area in which there are certain things you know about yourself that you do not want known and deliberately conceal them from others. (ch 7) (170)

hierarchy of needs The relative order of the physical and psychological needs of all human beings. (ch 16) (409-411)

high context versus low context That way of contrasting a group of cultures to another group of cultures that involves the degree to which most of the information is carried in the context (high) or most of the information is in the code or message (low). (ch 3) (65)

hyperpersonal computer-mediated communication (CMC) When the levels of affection and emotion developed through CMC equal or surpass face-to-face communication. (Appendix) (280-281)

hypothetical example An example that is made up to illustrate a point. (ch 12) (305)

I

illustrators Gestures or other nonverbal signals that accent, emphasize, or reinforce words. (ch 6) (138)

immediacy It occurs when the communicator is completely focused on the communication situation. (ch 14) (346-347)

impromptu speaking Speaking on the spur of the moment with little time to prepare. (ch 14) (347)

indirect aggression (also called *passive aggression*) People who use this form of communication often feel powerless and respond by doing something to thwart the person in power. (ch 8) (196)

individualism versus collectivism The way of contrasting a group of cultures to another group of cultures that involves the degree of integration and orientation of individuals within groups. (ch 3) (64)

inductive reasoning Reasoning from the specific to the general. (ch 16) (405-407)

inflection A change in pitch used to emphasize certain words and phrases. (ch 14) (352)

influence The power of a person or things to affect others—to produce effects without the presence of physical force. (ch 16) (399)

information interview An interview in which the goal is to gather facts and opinions from someone with expertise and experience in a specific field. (ch 9) (212)

information-sharing group A type of group that meets to be informed or to inform others, to express themselves and to listen to others, to get or give assistance, to clarify or hear clarification of goals, or to establish or maintain working relationships. (ch 10) (236-237)

informative speech A speech that concentrates on explaining, defining, clarifying, and instructing. (ch 15) (372-373)

initial partition A preview of the main points of a speech at the outset (often, in the introduction of the speech). (ch 13) (323)

instrumental Refers to the basic exchange of goods and services. (ch 8) (193)

instrumental costs The sacrifices, losses, or suffering as a result of exchanging goods and services (could include sharing your belongings). (ch 8) (193)

instrumental rewards The gifts, prizes, and recompenses that occur as a result of the basic exchange of goods and services (could include raising the current level of relational intimacy with one of the rewards being moving in with your partner and sharing in both the rent and the furniture). (ch 8) (193)

Integrative Listening Model (ILM) A framework for assessing listening both systematically and developmentally. (ch 4) (80)

integrity Uprightness of character and honesty. (ch 9) (210)

intercultural communication When a message is created by a member of one culture, and this message needs to be processed by a member of another culture. (ch 1, 3) (19, 60)

internal noise Interference with the message that occurs in the minds of the sender-receivers when their thoughts or feelings are focused on something other than the communication at hand. (ch 1) (11)

interpersonal communication One person interacting with another on a one-to-one basis, often in an informal, unstructured setting. (ch 1, 7) (15, 156)

interview A series of questions and answers, usually exchanged between two people, that has the purpose of getting and understanding information about a particular subject or topic. (ch 9) (211, 220)

intimate distance The distance zone, a range of less than 18 inches apart, that places people in direct contact with each other. (ch 6) (143)

intrapersonal communication Communication that occurs within you; it involves thoughts, feelings, and the way you look at yourself. (ch 1) (15)

intrinsic Means within the relationship. (ch 8) (193)

intrinsic costs The obligation to return the attention, warmth, and affection you receive, and the time you will spend listening, communicating, and self-disclosing. (ch 8) (193)

intrinsic rewards The gifts, prizes, and recompenses that occur within a relationship could include the attention, warmth, and affection you gain from being in a relationship. (ch 8) (193)

introduction (of speech) In a speech, the opening remarks that aim to get attention and build interest in the subject. (ch 13) (323-327)

J

Johari Window A model of the process of disclosure in interpersonal relationships, developed by Joseph Luft and Harry Ingham. (ch 7) (170-171)

K

keyword outline An outline containing only the important words or phrases of a speech that helps remind speakers of the ideas they are presenting. (ch 13) (300)

knowledge class A class of individuals supported solely by its participation in the new information industries with little, if any, reliance upon traditional manufacturing, production, or agriculture. (ch 3) (56)

L

ladder of abstraction A diagram of how we abstract, through language, classifications, types, categories, etc. (ch 5) (109-112)

laissez-faire leader One who does very little actual leading. This leader suggests no direction for and imposes no order on a group. (ch 11) (262)

language environment The environment in which language takes place (e.g., in a classroom). (ch 5) (113)

leader A person who influences the behavior of one or more people. (ch 11) (258)

leadership style The amount of control a leader exerts over a group. (ch 11) (261)

leading questions A question designed to point the interviewee in a particular direction. (ch 9) (215)

learning group The purpose is to increase the knowledge or skill of participants. (ch 10) (237)

legitimate power (also called *organizational power*) Leaders in formal organizations who derive their influence because they are "the boss" or because of the organizational hierarchy and its rules. (ch 11) (259)

leisure clothing The type of clothing that is up to the individual and that is worn when work is over. (ch 6) (141)

listening Includes the processes of listening preparation, receiving, constructing meaning, responding, and remembering. (ch 4) (80)

listening preparation Includes all the physical, mental, and behavioral aspects that create a readiness to listen. (ch 4) (80)

logical appeal An appeal that addresses listeners' reasoning ability. (ch 16) (404-409)

long-term orientation The way of contrasting a group of cultures to another group of cultures that involves the tradeoff between long-term and short-term needs gratification. (ch 3) (65)

M

mailing lists Group discussions that are completely passive; the discussion contributions arrive through e-mail. (ch 10) (251)

main heads or main points The points that reinforce the central idea. All the broad, general ideas and information that support your central idea. (ch 4, 13) (93, 316)

maintenance roles Group members who play these roles focus on the emotional tone of the meeting. (ch 10) (249-250)

manuscript speaking Writing out an entire speech and reading it to the audience from the prepared script. (ch 14) (358)

map versus territory The map is the personal mental approximation and the territory is the actual land or external reality that people experience. Map versus territory simply contrasts the subjective internal experience with the objective external reality. (ch 2) (41-44)

media literacy The ability to access, analyze, evaluate, and communicate information in all its forms—both print and nonprint. (Appendix A) (277)

media richness How much information is carried by a media source. (ch 6) (150)

memory (speaking from) This type of delivery involves writing out the entire speech and then committing it to memory word for word. (ch 14) (348-349)

mental outline A preliminary sketch that shows the principal features of the speech or lecture. (ch 4) (93)

message The ideas and feelings that a sender-receiver wants to share. (ch 1) (9)

metamessage The meaning, apart from the words, in a message. (ch 5) (125)

minor points The specific ideas and information that support the main points. (ch 13) (316)

mixed message A message in which the verbal and nonverbal contradict each other. (ch 6) (135)

mnemonic device A memory trick used to remember factual information. (ch 4) (83-84)

mob appeal A fallacy that occurs when an appeal is made to emotions, particularly to powerful feelings that can sway people in large crowds. (ch 16) (408)

model A replica of an actual object that is used when the object itself is too large to be displayed (e.g., a building), too small to be seen (e.g., a cell), or inaccessible to the eye (e.g., the human heart). (ch 14) (354)

monotone Little variety of pitch in a speech. (ch 14) (352)

motivated sequence Organization of a speech that involves five steps: attention, need, satisfaction, visualization, and action and works because it follows the normal process of human reasoning. (ch 13, 16) (322, 414-415)

motivation The stimulation or inducement that causes people to act. (ch 16) (399)

multimedia Refers to various media (e.g., text, graphics, animation, and audio) used to deliver information. (ch 14) (359)

N

national communities Co-cultural groupings within a country. (ch 3) (62)

natural delivery The collection of speech and actions that best represents your true self—that is, free from artificiality, affectation, and constraint. (ch 15) (386)

naturalistic fallacy A fallacy that occurs when something is identified as being good or desirable because it appears to be a natural characteristic. (ch 16) (407)

netiquette (or net etiquette) It includes the common practices, customs, conventions, and expectations expected of individuals using the Internet. (ch 10) (232)

neutral questions Interview questions that do not show how the interviewer feels about the subject. (ch 9) (215)

neutrality Not taking sides (in a group discussion). (ch 11) (265)

noise Interference that keeps a message from being understood or accurately interpreted. (ch 1) (11)

nondominant culture Includes people of color, women, gays, lesbians, and bisexuals, and those whose socioeconomic background is lower than middle class. (ch 3) (68)

nonelective characteristics The nonverbal physical characteristics over which you have no control and cannot change such as height, body proportion, coloring, bone structure, and physical disabilities. (ch 6) (140)

nonverbal communication Information we communicate without using words. (ch 6) (132)

nonverbal symbol Anything communicated without words (e.g., facial expressions or hand gestures). (ch 1) (10)

norms Expectations that group members have of how other members will behave, think, and participate. (ch 10) (235)

O

objective reality The actual territory or external reality everyone experiences. (ch 2) (48)

objectivity Basing conclusions on facts and evidence rather than on emotion or opinions. (ch 11) (265)

occupational dress The type of clothing that employees are expected to wear, but not as precise as a uniform. (ch 6) (141)

olfactics The study of smell. (ch 6) (145-146)

open-ended questions Interview questions that permit the person being interviewed to expand on his or her answers. (ch 9) (215)

open-format Interviews that are relatively unstructured. (ch 9) (214)

openness The free exchange of ideas within the bounds of reasonable behavior. (ch 9) (211)

open pane The area of the Johari Window that involves information about yourself that you are willing to communicate, as well as information you are unable to hide. (ch 7) (170)

opinion A personal belief. (ch 4) (95)

organizational chart A chart that shows the relationships among the elements of an organization, such as the departments of a company, the branches of federal or state government, or the committees of student government. (ch 14) (354)

outline A way of organizing material so all the parts and how they relate to the whole can be seen. (ch 13) (329-330)

owned message (also known as an I-message) An acknowledgment of subjectivity by a message-sender through the use of first-person singular terms (*I, me, my, mine*). (ch 7) (167-168)

P

pace How quickly or slowly a person speaks. (ch 14) (352)

paralanguage The way we say something. (ch 5, 6) (121, 136-137)

paraphrasing Restating the other person's thoughts or feelings in your own words. (ch 4) (96)

participating That style of situational leadership in which leaders state the problem but immediately consult with group members. (ch 11) (264)

passiveness The suspension of the rational functions and the reduction of any physical functions to their lowest possible degree. (ch 4) (90)

people listening style That kind of listening in which the listener is concerned with the other person's feelings. (ch 4) (85)

perception How people look at themselves and the world around them. (ch 2) (30)

perceptual filters The limitations that result from the narrowed lens through which people view the world. (ch 2) (47)

personal distance The distance zone, a range from 18 inches to 4 feet, that people maintain from others when they are engaged in casual and personal conversations. (ch 6) (143)

personal inventory Appraising your own resources. (ch 12) (291)

persuasion The process of trying to get others to change their attitudes or behavior; also, the process that occurs when a communicator (*sender*) influences the values, beliefs, attitudes, or behaviors of another person (*receiver*). (ch 16) (398)

PETAL In using presentation graphics, (1) develop pertinent materials, (2) choose an engaging format, (3) present your materials in a timely manner, (4) satisfy yourself that they are appropriate to the audience, and (5) ensure that everything is legible. (ch 15) (387)

pitch Highness or lowness of the voice. (ch 6) (137)

place Refers to the physical stage for the speech and the interaction with the audience. (ch 12) (300)

polls Surveys taken of people's attitudes, feelings, or knowledge. (ch 12) (308)

power distance The way of contrasting a group of cultures to another group of cultures that involves social inequality. (ch 3) (63)

powerful talk Talk that comes directly to the point, that does not use hesitation or qualifications. (ch 5) (118)

PowerPoint One of the most widely used software programs designed for use in presentations. (ch 14) (359-360)

prejudice A negative attitude toward a cultural group based on little or no experience. (ch 3) (67)

premise The reasons given in support of a conclusion. (ch 16) (407)

presentation A descriptive or persuasive account that is created to communicate ideas in a compelling and graphic manner (e.g., explain concepts, communicate complex data, make recommendations, or persuade and motivate others). (ch 15) (385-387)

primary questions Interview questions that often come first in the interview or that come first with each new topic the interviewer introduces. (ch 9) (214-215)

problem–solution order Organization of a speech into two sections: one dealing with the problem and the other dealing with the solution. (ch 13) (320-321)

professional communication Communication that is connected with, preparing for, engaged in, appropriate for, or conforming to business professions or occupations. (ch 9) (210)

pronunciation The ability to pronounce a word correctly. (ch 14) (352)

propriety The character or quality of being proper, especially in accordance with recognized usage, custom, or principles. (ch 4) (100)

proxemics The study of how people use space. (ch 6) (142)

psychological information The kind of information that is the most specific and intimate because it allows you to know individual traits, feelings, attitudes, and important personal data. (ch 7) (169)

psychological risk Taking a chance on something new (e.g., on a new person or place). (ch 2) (37)

psychological safety Approval and support obtained from familiar people, ideas, and situations. (ch 2) (37)

psychological sets A type of psychological filter that includes your expectations or predispositions to respond. (ch 2) (45)

public communication The sender-receiver (*speaker*) sends a message (the *speech*) to an audience. (ch 1) (18)

public distance The distance zone, a distance of more than 12 feet, typically used for public speaking. (ch 6) (144)

public-speaking anxiety The disturbance of mind regarding the uncertainty surrounding a forthcoming public-speaking event for which you are the speaker. (ch 14) (361-363)

Q

quality (of voice) Comprised of all voice characteristics: tempo, resonance, rhythm, pitch, and articulation. (ch 6) (137-138)

question-begging epithets A fallacy that occurs when slanted language is used to reaffirm what we wish to prove but have not yet proved. (ch 16) (408)

questions of fact Questions that deal with what is true and what is false. (ch 10, 16) (245, 412)

questions of policy Questions that are about actions that might be taken in the future. (ch 10, 16) (245, 412-413)

questions of value Questions of whether something is good or bad, desirable or undesirable. (ch 10, 16) (245, 413)

R

rapport style A style of communication designed to establish connections and negotiate relationships. (ch 9) (223)

rapport-talk Type of language women use in conversation, designed to lead to intimacy with others, to match experiences, and to establish relationships. (ch 5) (116)

rate (of speech) Speed at which one speaks. (ch 6) (137)

RDAT In using slides in a presentation, read the visual, describe its meaning or significance, amplify it with an explanation or illustration, and, finally, transition to the next slide. (ch 15) (387)

reassess and reevaluate The sixth of six steps of the strategic flexibility format in which users closely examine the results of any steps taken or not taken by them. (ch 1) (7)

receiving The process of taking in, acquiring, or accepting information. (ch 4) (80)

reference list A list of all the material you have used—and only that which you have used—in preparing your speech. (ch 13) (330-331)

referent power When leaders enjoy influence because of their personality. (ch 11) (259)

reflected appraisals Messages we get about ourselves from others. (ch 2) (32)

regrettable talk Saying something embarrassing, hurtful, or private to another person. (ch 8) (197)

regulate Nonverbal cues designed specifically to direct, manage, or control behavior. (ch 6) (147)

regulators (1) Nonverbal signals that control the back-and-forth flow of speaking and listening, such as head nods, hand gestures, and other body movements. (2) Group members who play this role help regulate group discussion by gently reminding members of the agenda or of the point they were discussing when they digressed. (ch 6) (138)

remembering Information that is learned well and stored securely in your memory system. (ch 4) (82)

report style A style of communication designed to preserve independence and negotiate and maintain status. (ch 9) (223)

report-talk Type of language men use in conversation, designed to maintain status, to demonstrate knowledge and skills, and to keep center-stage position. (ch 5) (117)

respect Conveys regard and appreciation of the worth, honor, dignity, and esteem of people. (ch 9) (211)

responding Using spoken and/or nonverbal messages to exchange ideas or convey information. (ch 4) (82)

response to a bid A positive or negative answer to somebody's request for emotional connection. (ch 7) (166)

responsibility Your ability to meet your obligations or to act without superior authority or guidance. (ch 9) (211)

résumé A summary of a person's professional life written for potential employers. (ch 9) (219)

reward power A leader can have an influence if he or she can reward the followers (e.g., through promotions, pay raises, or praise). (ch 11) (259)

rewards The pleasures that come as a result of being in a relationship. (ch 8) (193)

rhetorical question A question that audience members answer mentally rather than aloud. (ch 15) (384)

ritual language Communication that takes place when we are in an environment in which a conventionalized response is expected of us. (ch 5) (113)

roles Parts we play, or ways we behave with others. (ch 1) (14)

rules Formal and structured directions for behavior. (ch 10) (236)

S

Sapir-Whorf hypothesis The language you use to some extent determines—at least influences—the way in which you view and think about the world around you. (ch 5) (108-109)

scripts Lines and directions given to people by parents, teachers, coaches, religious leaders, friends, and the media that tell them what to say, what they expect, how to look, how to behave, and how to say the lines. (ch 2) (32)

select The fourth of six steps of the strategic flexibility format in which users carefully select from their repertoire of available skills and behaviors those likely to have the greatest impact on the current (and future) situations. (ch 1) (7)

selective attention The ability to focus perception. (ch 4) (82)

self-concept How a person thinks about and values himself or herself. (ch 2) (30)

self-disclosure Process by which one person tells another something he or she would not tell just anyone. (ch 7) (168)

self-esteem See *self-concept*.

self-fulfilling prophecies Events or actions that occur because a person and those around her or him expected them. (ch 2) (33)

self-improvement Seeking all means available to improve your professionalism and expertise. (ch 9) (211)

self-perception The way in which one sees oneself. (ch 2) (35)

selling That style of situational leadership in which leaders state the problem and decide what to do, but they sell the other group members on the idea to gain majority support. (ch 11) (264)

semantic noise Interference with the message that is caused by people's emotional reactions to words. (ch 1) (12)

semiopen format Interviews that occur based on a core set of standardized questions that are asked in a standard manner and carefully recorded. (ch 9) (214)

sender-receivers In communication situations, those who simultaneously send and receive messages. (ch 1) (8)

sensory acuity Paying attention to all elements in the communication environment. (ch 1) (11)

separation When nondominants do not want to form a common bond with the dominant culture, they separate into a group that includes only members like themselves. (ch 3) (70)

separation strategies When people are not part of a dominant culture, those processes that people use to get the dominant group to reinvent or change the rules through the use of nonassertive, assertive, or aggressive separation. (ch 3) (70-71)

servant leader Person who works for the well-being and growth of all employees and is committed to creating a sense of community and sharing power in decision making. (ch 11) (259)

setting Where the communication occurs. (ch 1) (12)

shared leadership It occurs when all group or team members assume both decision-making authority and responsibility for the group or team's results. (ch 11) (262)

situational leadership It occurs when leaders adopt different leadership styles depending on the situation. (ch 11) (263)

small-group communication It occurs when a small number of people meet to solve a problem. The group must be small enough so that each member has a chance to interact with all the other members. (ch 1) (17)

small groups Gatherings of 3 to 13 members who meet to do a job, solve a problem, or maintain relationships. (ch 10) (233)

small talk Social conversation about unimportant topics that allows a person to maintain contact with a lot of people without making a deep commitment. (ch 7) (164)

social comparisons When people compare themselves with others to see how they measure up. (ch 2) (33)

social distance The distance zone, a range from 4 to 12 feet, that people are most likely to maintain when they do not know people very well. (ch 6) (143)

social groups Groups designed to serve the social needs of their participants. (ch 10) (236)

social penetration The process of increasing both disclosure and intimacy in a relationship. (ch 7) (168)

social presence The ability of computer-mediated communication users to project themselves socially and affectively (with feeling) into a communication event. (ch 6) (149)

sociological information Information that tells you something about others' social groups and roles. (ch 7) (169)

space and distance Those distances people maintain between themselves and others that convey degrees of intimacy and status. (ch 6) (142-144)

spatial order Organization of a speech by something's location in space (e.g., left to right, top to bottom). (ch 13) (319-320)

specific purpose A statement for a speech that tells precisely what the speaker wants to accomplish. (ch 12) (294)

statistics Facts in numerical form. (ch 12) (306)

stereotypes Oversimplified or distorted views of another race, ethnic group, or culture. (ch 3) (65)

strategic flexibility Expanding your communication repertoire (your collection or stock of communication behaviors that can readily be brought into use) to enable you to use the best skill or behavior available for a particular situation. (ch 1) (6)

stress interview A type of information interview that is sometimes part of the job search and is designed to see how an interviewee acts under pressure. It is designed to give interviewers a realistic sense of their response to difficult situations. (ch 9) (212)

style The result of the way we select and arrange words and sentences. (ch 5) (116)

subjective view The personal, internal, mental map of the actual territory or external reality that people experience. (ch 2) (48)

substantive conflict Conflict that arises when people have different reactions to an idea. Substantive conflict is likely to occur when any important and controversial idea is being discussed. (ch 11) (269-270)

substitute Nonverbal message designed specifically to take the place of a verbal message. (ch 6) (147)

supporting material Information that backs up your main points and provides the main content of the speech. (ch 12) (304-308)

supporting points The material, ideas, and evidence that back up the main heads. (ch 4) (93)

sweeping generalization A fallacy that occurs when a general rule is applied to a specific case to which the rule is not applicable because of specific features of the case. (ch 16) (408)

symbol Something that stands for something else. (ch 1) (9)

supportive behavior A way of avoiding defensive communication by using supportive strategies such as description, problem solving, spontaneity, empathy, equality, or provisionalism. (ch 8) (200-201)

synchronous communication Online group discussion in which group members communicate at the same time. All participants are virtually present at the same time (e.g., in a telephone conversation, a face-to-face encounter, or a real-time, online group format). (ch 1, 10, Appendix A) (23, 251, 277)

T

target audience A subgroup of the whole audience that you must persuade to reach your goal. (ch 2, 16) (296, 404)

task-oriented group A type of group that serves to get something specific accomplished, often problem-solving or decision-making goals. (ch 10) (236)

task roles Roles that help get the job done. Persons who play these roles help groups come up with new ideas, aid in collecting and organizing information, and assist in analyzing the information that exists. (ch 10) (248-249)

team Two or more people with a specific goal to be attained who coordinate their activity among the members to attain their goal. (ch 10) (241)

teamwork The unity of action by a group of workers to further the success of the business or organization. (ch 9) (211)

telling That style of situational leadership in which the leader is focused more on the task and less on the group. (ch 11) (263)

temporality A characteristic of the Internet that makes it unique from normal face-to-face communication because there are no time limitations. (ch 1) (24)

territory Space we consider as belonging to us, either temporarily or permanently. (ch 6) (142)

testimony Another person's statements or actions used to give authority to what the speaker is saying. (ch 12) (307-308)

time The three facets of time that matter in analyzing the speech occasion are: time frame for the speech, time of day, and the length of time of your speech. (ch 12) (300)

time order Organization of a speech by chronology or historical occurrence. (ch 13) (318-319)

time-style listening That kind of listening in which the listener prefers brief and hurried interaction with others and often lets the communicator know how much time he or she has to make the point. (ch 4) (85)

topical order Organization of a speech used when the subject can be grouped logically into subtopics. (ch 13) (322-323)

touch To be in contact or come into contact with another person. (ch 6) (144-145)

transactional communication Communication that involves three principles:(1) people sending messages continuously and simultaneously; (2) communication events that have a past, present, and future; and (3) participants playing certain roles. (ch 1) (13)

transitions Comments that lead from one point to another to tell listeners where speakers have been, where they are now, and where they are going. (ch 13) (328-329)

transpection The process of empathizing across cultures. (ch 3) (73)

trustworthiness In the giving of a speech, the speaker is perceived as reliable and dependable. (ch 16) (417)

U

uncertainty avoidance The way of contrasting a group of cultures to another group of cultures that involves tolerance for the unknown. (ch 3) (65)

uniforms The most specialized form of clothing and that type that identifies wearers with particular organizations. (ch 6) (141)

unknown pane Area of the Johari Window that is known as a nondisclosure area and provides no possibility of disclosure because it is unknown to the self or to others. (ch 7) (171)

Usenet newsgroups Online group discussions that handle individual messages sorted by broad subject areas that can be subscribed to through Internet or corporate network host providers. (ch 10) (251)

V

values A type of belief about how we should behave or about some final goal that may or may not be worth attaining. (ch 16) (400)

verbal symbol A word that stands for a particular thing or idea. (ch 1) (10)

virtual community A group of people who may or may not meet one another face-to-face, and who exchange words and ideas through the mediation of computer bulletin boards and networks. (Appendix A) (282)

vision Foresight, insight, and imagination. (ch 11) (268)

visual support Visual material that helps illustrate key points in a speech or presentation. Visual support includes devices such as charts, graphs, slides, and computer-generated graphics. (ch 14) (353-360)

vividness That property of style by which a thought is so presented that it evokes lifelike imagery or suggestion. (ch 5) (124)

vocal fillers Words we use to fill out our sentences or to cover up when we are searching for words. (ch 6) (138)

volume (of vocal sound) How loudly we speak.(ch 6) (137)

W–Z

Web conferencing or Web forums Online group discussions that use text messages (and sometimes images) stored on a computer as the communication medium. Messages are typed into the computer for others to read. (ch 10) (252)

Web log (or blog) A spontaneous public online journal (or diary) in which Internet users share their lives. (Appendix A) (282-283)

worldview An all-encompassing set of moral, ethical, and philosophical principles and beliefs that governs the way people live their lives and interact with others. (ch 3) (58)

Credits

Photos

Chapter 1
3: John Giustina/Iconica/Getty Images; **10:** Stockbyte/Getty Images; **12** *(left)*: Sven Martson/The Image Works; **12** *(right)*: Rosebud Pictures/Stone/Getty Images; **19:** Digital Vision/Getty Images

Chapter 2
29: Spencer Grant/PhotoEdit Inc.; **34:** David Young-Wolff/PhotoEdit Inc.; **37:** David Young-Wolff/PhotoEdit Inc.; **45:** Ryan McVay/Photodisc Green/Getty Images

Chapter 3
55: Juan Silva/The Image Bank/Getty Images; **58:** Jose Luis Pelaez, Inc./Corbis; **64:** Robert Essel NYC/Corbis

Chapter 4
79: Tom Stewart/Corbis; **93:** Rubberball; **98:** George Shelley/Corbis

Chapter 5
105: Walter Hodges/Stone/Getty Images; **106:** Jim West/The Image Works

Chapter 6
131: Michael Jang/Stone/Getty Images; **140:** Alan Carey/The Image Works; **145** *(left)*: Bob Daemmrich Photography, Inc./The Image Works; **145** *(right)*: Michael S. Yamashita/Corbis

Chapter 7
155: Cassy Cohen/PhotoEdit Inc.; **160:** Steven Rubin/The Image Works; **170:** Rolf Bruderer/Corbis; **174:** Tim Mantoani/Masterfile

Chapter 8
183: Barry Yee/Taxi/Getty Images; **188:** Michael Newman/PhotoEdit Inc.; **198:** David Young-Wolff/PhotoEdit Inc.

Chapter 9
209: Digital Vision/Getty Images; **213:** Karen Preuss/The Image Works; **219:** Michael Newman/PhotoEdit Inc.

Chapter 10
231: Masterfile; **239:** Bob Mahoney/The Image Works; **249:** Loren Santow/Stone/Getty Images

Chapter 11
257: Charles Gupton/Stone/Getty Images; **261:** Michael Goldman/Masterfile; **270:** Mark Richards/PhotoEdit Inc.

Appendix A
280 *(left)*: Comstock/Getty Images; **280** *(right)*: VStock LLC/Index Stock Imagery, Inc.

Chapter 12
289: Pierre Tremblay/Masterfile Corporation; **293:** Ebsin-Anderson/The Image Works; **296** *(left)*: David Butow/Corbis SABA; **296** *(right)*: AP/Wide World Photos; **302:** Jon Riley/Stone/Getty Images; **306:** Jose Luis Pelaez, Inc./Corbis

Chapter 13
313: Michael Newman/PhotoEdit Inc.; **318:** A. Ramey/PhotoEdit Inc.; **324:** Chuck Savage/Corbis

Chapter 14
343: Cleve Bryant/PhotoEdit Inc.; **348:** Barbara Stitzer/PhotoEdit Inc.; **359:** Lon C. Diehl/PhotoEdit Inc.

Chapter 15
371: Michael Newman/PhotoEdit Inc.; **374:** Susan Van Etten/PhotoEdit Inc.; **377:** James Schnepf/Getty Images; **380:** Michael Newman/PhotoEdit Inc.; **385:** Fisher/Thatcher/Stone/Getty Images

Chapter 16
397: Bob Daemmrich/The Image Works; **400:** David Young-Wolff/PhotoEdit Inc.; **401:** A. Ramey/PhotoEdit Inc.; **410:** AP/Wide World Photos; **415** *(left)*: Michael Newman/PhotoEdit Inc.; **415** *(right)*: Bob Daemmrich/The Image Works

Text and Illustrations

Chapter 1
20: "Credo for Communication Ethics" reprinted by permission of National Communication Association, Washington, DC.

Chapter 2
32: Garrison Keillor, "Revival" from *Lake Wobegon Days*. Copyright © 1985 by Garrison Keillor. Used by permission of Viking Penguin, a division of Penguin Group USA Inc. **51:** In *Measures of Personality and Social Psychological Attitudes* by J.P. Robinson, P.R. Shaver, & L.S. Wrightsman, 1991, San Diego: Academic Press (p. 127-31). Adapted from *The Antecedents of Self-Esteem* by S. Coopersmith, 1967, San Francisco: W. H. Freeman and Company. Used by permission of W. H. Freeman.

Chapter 3
75: Adapted from www.literacynet.org/icans. Used by permission of Adult Basic Education Office, Professional Development Services, Washington State ABE Literacy Resource Center, formerly ABLE Network.

Chapter 4
90: Table 4-1 From "A Factor Analysis of Barriers to Effective Listening" by Steven Golen in *Journal of Business Communication*: 27, 25-36 (Winter 1990). Reprinted by permission of the author. **91:** From *Listen Up, Move Up: The Listener Wins* by Michael Purdy. Reprinted by permission of Michael Purdy. **98:** From "Talking Back to Your Doctor Works" by Linda Greider, *AARP Bulletin*: February 2000. Reprinted by permission of Linda Greider. **101:** Adapted from www.literacynet.org/icans. Used by permission of Adult Basic Education Office, Professional Development Services, Washington State ABE Literacy Resource Center, formerly ABLE Network.

Chapter 5
118: From "Sex Differences in the Functional Organization of the Brain for Language" by B.A. Shaywitz, 1995, Nature 37 (3) 89-90. Used by permission of the Nature Publishing Group.

Chapter 7
165: Quotation from Dianna Booher, 1996, *Vitality*, 5. Used by permission of the author. **171:** Table 7-5 Figure from *Group Processes: An Introduction to Group Dynamics* by Joseph Luft, 1984. Mayfield Publishing Company. Reprinted with permission of The McGraw-Hill Companies. **176:** From "An Inductive Analysis of Verbal Immediacy," by T. P. Mottet & V. P. Richmond, *Communication Quarterly*. Copyright 1998 from Communication Quarterly by T. P. Mottet & V. P. Richmond. Reproduced by permission of Taylor & Francis Inc., www.taylorandfrancis.com. **177:** From "Avoiding Trends that Deprive Us of Humanity," by D. Stanley Eitzen, 2003. Reprinted by permission of Vital Speeches of the Day. **179:** Reprinted by permission of Constance Messina.

Chapter 8
192: © 2003 Antoinette Coleman. www.Consum-mate.com, 703-847-1768, Toni@conum-mate.com. All rights reserved. **194:** From *Newsweek*, April 19, 1999. Copyright © 1999 Newsweek Inc. All rights reserved. Reprinted by permission. **205:** The Relational Assessment Questionnaire, adapted from W.E. Snell Jr., 1999. Used by permission of William Snell.

Chapter 9
226: From How to Use the Internet in Your Job Search, by M. F. Dikel, 2003. The Riley Guide: Execute a Campaign. Used by permission of Margaret F. Dikel, author of The Riley Guide (Rileyguide.com).

Chapter 10
243: Table 10-1 From "Brainstorming Guidelines" by J.M. Fritz. Used by permission of Jane Fritz, University of New Brunswick. **253:** Adapted from www.literacynet.org/icans. Used by permission of Adult Basic Education Office, Professional Development Services, Washington State ABE Literacy Resource Center, formerly ABLE Network.

Chapter 11
272: From Conflict in Cyberspace: How to Resolve Conflict Online by Kali Munro, 2002, www.kalimunro.com/article_conflict_online.html. Used by permission of the author. **273:** Adapted from www.literacynet.org/icans. Used by permission of Adult Basic Education Office, Professional Development Services, Washington State ABE Literacy Resource Center, formerly ABLE Network.

Appendix A
279, 282: From *Computer-mediated Communication: Human-to-human Communication Across the Internet* by Susan B. Barnes, 2003. Used by permission of Allyn and Bacon / Pearson Education, Boston, MA. **280:** From "Virtual relationships: The Solitary World of CMC" by T. W. Loughlin, *Interpersonal Computing and Technology: An Electronic Journal for the 21st Century*, 1993. Used by permission of Thomas Loughlin, SUNY Fredonia.

Chapter 12
292: Fig 12-2 From *Analyzing Your Topic*. Research Tutorial for Freshman and Transfer Seminars, Webster University. Used by permission of Webster University, St. Louis. MO. **305:** From "The Internet: The Soul of Democracy," by G. Slenow, 2000. Reprinted by permission of Vital Speeches of the Day. **307:** From "Trends in College Binge Drinking During a Period of Increased Prevention Efforts: Findings from 4 Harvard School of Public Health College Alcohol Study Surveys: 1993-2001." Retrieved 3/25/03 from www.hsph.harvard.edu/cas/Documents/trends/. Journal of American College Health, 2002; 50(5): 203-217. Reprinted by permission of the Helen Dwight Reid Educational Foundation and the author. Published by Heldref Publications, 1319 18th St. NW, Washington, DC 20036. Copyright © 2002. **307:** From William Franklin, President, Franklin International, 2001. Reprinted by permission of Vital Speeches of the Day. **309:** From *Insight vs.*

Desensitization in Psychotherapy by Gordon L. Paul. Copyright © 1966 by The Board of Trustees of the Leland Stanford Jr. University, renewed 1994. All rights reserved. Used with the permission of Stanford University press, www.sup.org.

Chapter 13

317: From "Sustainability," by Richard Lamm, 2003. Reprinted by permission of Vital Speeches of the Day. **319:** From *Public Speaking: Make 'em Wonder*, C. M. McKinney. Advanced Public Speaking Institute. © Tom Antion. Reprinted with permission. **325:** From Commencement address by Robert L. Dilenschneider, 2001. Reprinted by permission of Vital Speeches of the Day. **332:** Fig. 13-2 "Tech Tips for Teachers - Citing Internet Sources" from the Classroom Connect website www.classroom.com/community/connection/howto/citeresources.jhtml, copyright 2004 by Classroom Connect, reprinted by permission of the publishers.

Chapter 14

356: Fig 14-3 From "Snakes Scarier than Public Speaking," USA TODAY. March 26, 2001. Reprinted with permission.

Chapter 15

374: From "Unexamined Assumptions: Destiny, Political Institutions, Democracy, and Population" by Richard Lamm, 1998. Reprinted by permission of Vital Speeches of the Day. **377:** From "The Buzz on Caffeine," © 2002 TIME Inc. Reprinted by permission. **378:** From "Humor and Speeches: A Stand-Up History" by Eugene Finerman, 1996. Reprinted by permission of Vital Speeches of the Day.

Chapter 16

405: From "The New Entrepreneurship" by Peter Bell, 2001. Reprinted by permission of Vital Speeches of the Day. **406:** From "Facts Change Student Drinking," USA TODAY. June 23, 2001. Reprinted with permission. **412:** From "Talk to Your Children About the Tough Stuff: We Are All in This Together" by Lance R. Odden, 1999. Reprinted by permission of Vital Speeches of the Day and the author.

Index

A

Abstract symbols, 10
Accent, 148
Access to roles, 24
Accommodation, 69, 271
Accommodation strategies, 69–70
Action listening style, 85
Active listening, 93–94
Actual object, 353–354
Ad hominem, 408
Adaptation, 176–177
Adaptors, 139
Agenda, 265
Aggressive accommodation, 69–70
Aggressive assimilation, 69
Aggressive separation, 71
Aggressive talk, 196
Aggressor, 250
Analogy, 407
Anatomy of Buzz, The (Rosen), 122
Anecdote, 381
Anticipate, 80
Anxiety, 89, 157, 361–363, 366
Anyone You Want Me to Be (Douglas/Singular), 177
Appeal to authority, 408
Appeal to ignorance, 408
Appearance, 349–350
Applying, 82
Appraisal interview, 212
Appropriate language, 114
Aristotle, 411
Art of Intimacy, The (Coleman), 192
Articulation, 352
Aseel, M. Q., 60, 142
Asher, E., 306
Asian Students' Classroom Communication Patterns in U.S. Universities (Liu), 62–63
Assertive accommodation, 69
Assertive assimilation, 69
Assertive separation, 71
Assertiveness, 199

Assess yourself
  CMC literacy, 284
  confidence as speaker, 309
  cultural awareness, 75
  delivery self-evaluation form, 367
  leadership potential, 273
  listening, 101
  nonverbal communication, 151
  organizing as speech, 339
  professionalism, 227
  public speaking ability, 424–425
  relationship survey, 205
  self-concept, 51
  small-group participation, 253
  speech preparation, 393
  strategic flexibility, 25
  trusting others scale, 179
  verbal communication, 127
Assessment, 80, 95
Assimilation, 68
Assimilation strategies, 68–69
Assumption, 72
Asynchronous communication, 23, 251, 277
Attention-getting devices, 323–326, 381–383. *See also* Speech introduction
Attentiveness, 346
Attitudes, 160, 297, 401
Attraction to others, 159–162
Attractiveness, 139–140
Audience analysis, 295–300
Audience attitudes and beliefs, 297
Audience demographics, 297–299
Authoritarian leader, 261–262
Avoidance, 199, 271
Avoiding stage, 191
"Avoiding Trends That Deprive Us of Humanity" (Eitzen), 177
Axel, R., 145
Axtell, R., 175

B

Baldridge, L., 7
Bar graph, 356

Barbor, C., 173
Barnes, S. B., 281, 282
Barnett, S., 241
Barriers to
  intercultural communication, 66–67
  listening, 89, 90
Bauer, J., 408
Beamer, L., 73
Beck, J., 409
Begging the question, 408
Beginning conversations, 164–165
Beliefs, 160, 297, 400–401
Bell, Peter, 405
Belongingness and love needs, 410
Benne, K., 247
Bennis, W., 260
Benton, D. A., 138
Bethel, Sheila Murray, 402
Bid, 166
Bidding process, 166–167
Bifurcation, 408
Birdwhistell, Ray, 137
Blake, R., 270
Blasphemous words, 114
Blessing for a Long Time: The Sacred Pale of the Omaha Tribe (Ridington/Hastings), 321
Blind pane, 170
Blocker, 250
Blog, 282–283
Body, 318
Body adornment, 141–142
Body language, 350
Body movement, 138–139
Body orientation, 149
Bond, M., 65
Bonding, 188
Booher, D., 164–165
Boone, M., 112, 175
Boteach, S., 175
Bowen, S. P., 116
Brainstorming, 242, 243
Breaking up, 189–191
Bruck, L., 145
Building anticipation, 382
Building suspense, 382

I-1

Buller, D.B., 146
Bulletin boards, 251
Burgess, A., 176
Burgoon, J. K., 146
Burns, R. J., 279
Bush, G. W., 114

C

Cable, D., 140
Cairo, P. C., 266
Cameron, K. S., 233
Care and appreciation, 175
Causal reasoning, 407
Cause-and-effect order, 320, 416
Central idea, 93, 294
Certainty *versus* provisionalism, 201
Chalkboard, 353
Chang, I., 63
Channel, 10, 277, 300
Chart, 354
Chat rooms, 251, 281
Cher, 361
Chinese in America, The (Chang), 63
Choosing a topic, 242–243
Chronemics, 146
Chronological order, 318–319
Churchill, W., 361
Circumscribing stage, 190
Citing sources, 304, 330–333, 338
Clarity, 123–124
Cline, R., 199
Clip art, 358
Closed-format interviews, 214
Closed-questions, 215
Clothing, 140–141
CMC, 18, 161–162, 163
CMC literacy, 277, 284
Co-culture, 19, 59
Coercive power, 259
Cognitive development, 108
Cognitive dissonance, 89
Cohesiveness, 239
Coleman, A., 192
Collaboration, 271, 272
Collectivist society, 235
Colleges, 40, 160
Color, 379
Combs, P., 5
Coming apart, 189–191
Commitment, 176, 203, 239
Communication
   asynchronous, 23, 251
   CMC, 18
   defensive, 199–202
   defined, 8
   effective, 21–23
   elements of, 8–13
   ethical, 20–21
   intercultural, 18–20
   interpersonal, 15–17. *See also* Interpersonal communication
   intrapersonal, 15
   nonverbal. *See* Nonverbal communication
   oral. *See* Public speaking
   professional. *See* Professional communication
   public, 18
   small-group, 17–18. *See also* Small-group participation
   synchronous, 23, 251
   transactional, 13
   verbal. *See* Verbal communication
Communication message, 9–10
Communication orientation, 361
Communication transaction, 13
Community colleges, 160
Comparison, 377
Compatibility, 161
Competition, 271, 272
Complaint, 198–199
Complement, 147
Composition, 379
Compromise, 271, 272
Computer databases, 301
Computer-generated graphics, 357–360
Computer-mediated communication (CMC), 18, 161–162, 163, 277–282. *See also* Internet
Conclusion, 327–328
Concrete symbol, 10
Conditional commitments, 176
Confidence as speaker (quiz), 309
Conflict
   groups, 269–272
   management approaches, 271–272
   online, 272–273
   types, 269–270
   workplace, 224–226
Conflict management, 270–272
Conflict resolution, 202–203
Confucian dynamism, 65
Connotative meaning, 109, 110
Constructing meaning, 81–82
Constructive conflict, 270
Content listening style, 85
Content openness, 24
Context, 60
Contrast, 305, 377
Control, 90, 148, 163, 200
Controlling listeners, 90
Convergence, 137
Conversational encouragement, 175
Conversational focus, 174
Conversational quality, 345
Cortes, C., 61
Costs, 193
Costumes, 141
Creativity, 7, 301

Credibility, 281–282, 412–414
Critic-analyzers, 245, 248–249
Critical listening, 94–95
Criticism, 197–198
Crystal, D., 126
Cultural awareness self-assessment form, 75
Cultural differences, 63–66
Cultural identity, 58–60
Cultural information, 169
Culture, 19, 57. *See also* Intercultural communication
Cyberattraction, 161–162
Cybermotivation, 163

D

Daly, J., 197
Dance of Connection: How to Talk to Someone When You're Mad, Hurt, Scared, Frustrated, Insulted, Betrayed, or Desperate, The (Lerner), 199
Davenport, T., 409
Decision-making groups, 236
Deductive reasoning, 404–405
Defensive communication, 199–202
Defining, 376–378
Definition, 305, 376
Delegating, 264, 269
Deletions, 46
Delivering the speech, 342–369
   anxiety, 361–363, 366
   appearance, 349–350
   body language, 350
   enunciation, 352–353
   eye contact, 350
   facial expression, 350
   gestures, 351
   good delivery, 344–347
   inflection, 352
   Internet resources, 365–366
   microphone, 351
   natural delivery, 386
   pace, 352
   pitch, 352
   posture, 351
   quick guide, 287
   rehearsing the speech, 363–364
   self-assessment (quiz), 367
   types of delivery, 347–349
   visual support, 353–360. *See also* Visual support
   volume, 351
Delivery self-evaluation form, 367
Democratic leader, 262
Demographic analysis, 297–299
Demonstration speech, 375
Denotative meaning, 109, 110
Describing, 378–379

Index   I-3

Destroying relationships, 185
Destructive conflict, 270
Diagram, 354
Dialect, 120, 121
Differentiating stage, 189–190
Digital literacy, 277
Dilenschneider, R. L., 325
Directness, 347
Disciplinary interview, 212
Disclaimers, 119
Discrimination, 67
Displays of feelings, 138–139
Distance zones, 142–144
Distortions, 46
Divorce assumption, 203
Doctor-patient relationship, 99
Dominant- and nondominant-group communication, 68–71
Dominant culture, 68
Dominator, 250
Do's and Taboos Around the World for Women in Business (Axtell), 175
Do's and taboos lists, 73
Dotlich, D. L., 266
Doublespeak, 114
Douglas, J., 177
Dynamism, 413
Dysfunctional roles, 250–251

E

E-Leader (Hargrove), 263
E-mail lists, 251
Eitzen, D. S., 177
Ekman, P., 135, 138
Elective characteristics, 140
Electronic group, 277–282. *See also* Internet
Emblems, 138
Emmers-Somway, T. M., 279
Emotional appeal, 409–411
Emotional disengaging, 224
Emotional expressiveness, 173–174
Emotional intelligence, 156–159
Emotional Intelligence (Goleman), 173
Emotions, 157
Empathic listening, 95–97
Empathy, 95, 158, 200
Employment interview, 219–222
Encouragers, 249
Endurance, 203
Enron, 21
Enunciation, 352–353
Equality, 200–201
Essberger, J., 127
Ethical communication, 20–21
Ethics, 211
  CMC, 283
  persuasion, 414

two-sided speech, 416
verbal communication, 125–126
Ethnic epithets, 114
Ethnocentrism, 66
Etymology, 376–377
Euphemism, 114
Evaluating relationships, 192–195
Evaluation, 82
Evaluative statements, 200
Example, 305, 324–325, 326, 377
Executive Charisma (Benton), 138
Exit interview, 212
Experimenting stage, 186
Expert power, 259
Expertise, 412–413
Explaining, 379–381
Extemporaneous speaking, 349
External noise, 11
Extrinsic costs, 193
Extrinsic rewards, 193
Eye contact, 139, 148, 350
Eye messages, 139

F

Face-to-face communication (FtFC), 276–279
Facial expressions, 148, 350
Fact, 95
Fadiman, A., 71
Fallacy, 407–408
False analogy, 408
False cause, 408
Fast talkers, 137
Feedback, 11
Femininity versus masculinity, 64
Find a Husband After 35 (Greenwald), 178
"Finding Real Love" (Barbor), 173
Finerman, E., 378
Flaherty, L., 278
Flaming, 282
Flip chart, 354
Flora, C., 134
Follow-up questions, 215
Fonda, J., 361
"Forgetting Everything You've Learned" (Muñoz), 389
Four horsemen of the apocalypse, 197
Framing, 126
Franklin, W., 307
Friendship-warmth touch, 145
Friesen, W. V., 138
FtFC, 276–279
Full-sentence outline, 330
Fully led (fully moderated) ODG, 272
Function, 378
Functional leadership, 260, 262
Functional-professional touch, 145

G

Gender
  listening, 87–88
  nonverbal communication, 136
  professional communication, 223
  self-confidence, 36
  verbal communication, 116–119
General purpose, 293
Generalizations, 46
Gestures, 148, 351
Getting attention, 323–326
Getting listeners involved, 383–384
Giuliani, Rudolph, 268
"Giving Something Back" (Lattrell), 419
Globalization, 24
Goleman, D., 156, 158, 173
Golen, S., 89, 90
Gordon, T., 167–168
Gottman, J., 166, 167, 194, 197, 203
Graddol, D., 119
Graham, B., 361
Grammar, 112
Graph, 356–357
Greenhalgh, L., 240
Greenwald, R., 178
Greider, L., 98
Group, 236. *See also* Small-group participation
  electronic, 277–282. *See also* Internet
  small, 233–236. *See also* Small group participation
  types, 236–237
Group conflict, 269–272
Group leadership, 264–270. *See also* Leadership
Group norms, 235
Group roles, 248–251
Group rules, 236
Group size, 237–238
Groupthink, 239–241
Gurian, M., 118
Gutierres, S., 139

H

Hall, E. T., 63, 136, 142
Handouts, 360
Haptics, 144
Hargrove, Robert, 263
Harmonizer-compromisers, 249
Hastings, D., 321
Hasty generalization, 408
Hayakawa, S. I., 109
Hearing, 81
Hedges, 118
Help-seeker, 250
Hesitation forms, 118

Heslin, R., 145
Hidden agendas, 267
Hidden Dimension, The (Hall), 136
Hidden pane, 170
Hierarchy of needs, 409–411
High context *versus* low context, 65
High-feminine cultures, 64
High-masculine cultures, 64
Hofstede, G., 63
Hosted online chats, 251
How to Persuade People Who Don't Want to be Persuaded (Bauer/Levy), 408–409
Humor, 149, 162, 203, 324
Hyperpersonal CMC, 280
Hypothetical examples, 305–306

I

I-message, 167
"I Vow to Thee" (Burgess), 176
Illustrators, 138
Immediacy, 346–347
Impromptu speaking, 347
Improving relationships, 195–202
In the Dressing Room with Brenda (Kinsel), 35
Inappropriate touch, 146
Inclusion, 162
Indirect aggression, 196
Individual roles, 250–251
Individualism versus collectivism, 64
Inductive reasoning, 405–407
Inflection, 352
Influence, 399
Informal groups, 236
Information giver, 248
Information interview, 212–219
    analyzing the interview, 217
    format, 214
    job interview, as precursor to, 217–219
    note-taking, 216
    preparation, 213–216
    questions, 214–215
    tape recorders/video cameras, 216
    types of interviews, 212
Information seeker, 248
Information-sharing group, 236–237
Informative speech, 370–395
    arousing interest, 381–383
    concepts, 376
    defined, 372
    defining, 376–378
    describing, 378–379
    events, 376
    explaining, 379–381
    getting listeners involved, 383–384
    goals, 373–375

Internet, 387–388
    objects, 375
    overarching principles, 376
    processes, 375
    sample speech, 389–392
    topic, 373
Ingham, Harry, 170
Initial partition, 323
Initiating stage, 186
Initiator-expediters, 248
Instrumental costs, 193
Instrumental rewards, 193
Instrumental values, 400
Insulting language, 114
Integrating stage, 187–188
Integrity, 210
Intensifying stage, 187
Interactive writing, 278
Intercultural communication, 18–20, 54–77
    accommodation strategies, 69–70
    assimilation strategies, 68–69
    barriers to, 66–67
    communication model, 62–63
    cultural differences, 63–66
    defined, 60
    effective communication, 56–57
    importance, 60–62
    improving, 72–74
    Internet, 74–75
    listening, 86
    nondominant-/dominant-group communication, 68–71
    nonverbal communication, 134–135
    professional communication, 222–223
    separation strategies, 70–71
    strategic flexibility, 57
    verbal communication, 119–120
Internal noise, 11
Internet. *See also* CMC
    blogs, 282–283
    communication, and, 23–24
    conflict management, 272–273
    credibility, 281–282
    cyberattraction, 161–162
    ESL students, 101
    evaluating information, 302–303
    informative speech, 387–388
    intercultural communication, 74–75
    interpersonal relationships, 177–178, 203–205
    listening, 100–101
    nonverbal communication, 149–150
    ODGs, 251–252, 272
    outline/organization of speech, 331, 333

    persuasive speech, 418
    professional communication, 226
    research, 302
    self-concept, 44–45
    small-group participation, 251–252
    speech delivery, 365–366
    stress management, 366
    verbal communication, 126–127
    virtual communities, 282
"Internet: The Soul of Democracy, The" (Selnow), 305
Internet-based chat tools, 251
Interpersonal communication, 15–17
Interpersonal relationships, 154–207
    adaptation, 176–177
    beginning conversations, 164–165
    bid/bidding process, 166–167
    care and appreciation, 175
    coming apart, 189–191
    commitment, 176
    conflict resolution, 202–203
    conversational encouragement, 175
    conversational focus, 174
    defined, 156
    destroying relationships, 185
    emotional expressiveness, 173–174
    evaluating relationships, 192–195
    improving relationships, 195–202
    Internet, 177–178, 203–205
    Johari Window, 170–173
    know your relationship partner (quiz), 194
    motives for, 163–164
    nonverbal analysis, 175
    owned messages, 167–168
    relationship survey (quiz), 205
    self-disclosure, 168–173
    small-talk, 164–165
    stages of relationships, 185–189
    talking to each other, 164–168
    verbal skills, 173
Interracial marriages, 62
Interview
    appraisal, 212
    defined, 211
    disciplinary, 212
    employment, 219–222
    exit, 212
    format, 214
    information, 212–219. *See also* Information interview
    note taking, 216
    stress, 212–213
    tape recorders/video cameras, 216
    types of questions, 214–215
Interview questions, 214–215
Intimate distance, 143
Intrapersonal communication, 15–17
Intrapersonal evaluation, 202
Intrinsic costs, 193

Index **I-5**

Intrinsic rewards, 193
Ivy League schools, 160

J

James, W., 45
Janis, I., 239
Jargon, 122
Job interview, 219–222
Johari Window, 170–173
Johnson, B., 199
Judge, T., 140
Junior college, 160

K

Keillor, G., 32, 324
Kenrick, D., 139
Keyword outline, 330
Kinesics, 138
King, S., 116
Kinsel, B., 35
Kirshenbaum, M., 193
Knapp, M. L., 185, 197
Korzybski, A., 41

L

"Lacking in Self-Esteem? Good for You!" (Sullivan), 36
Ladder of abstraction, 109, 110
Laissez-faire leader, 262
Lamm, R., 317, 374
Language. *See* Verbal communication
Language and the Internet (Crystal), 126
Language environment, 113
Language in Thought and Action (Hayakawa), 109
Lattrell, D., 419
Leader, 258
Leadership, 256–275
    answers, 268
    approaches to, 261–264
    conflict management, 269–272
    delegating, 269
    diversity, 267
    encouraging social interaction, 269
    establishing procedures, 265
    finding solutions, 265–266
    helping group to progress, 267
    how to become a leader, 259–261
    influence of, 258–259
    listening, 264
    neutrality/objectivity, 265
    personality traits, 260
    questions, 267
    self-assessment (quiz), 273
    styles, 261–264
    vision, 269–270

Leadership (Giuliani), 268
Leadership style, 261–264
Leading questions, 215
Lean media, 150
Learning group, 237
Lecture, 372
Lecture/demonstration, 372
Legitimate power, 259
Legon, Ronald, 252
Leisure clothing, 141
Lerner, H., 199
Leviric, M., 186
Levy, M., 408
Lindley, C., 156
Line graph, 356, 357
Listening, 78–103
    active, 93–94
    barriers to, 89, 90
    critical, 94–95
    culture, 86
    difficulty of, 88–90
    empathic, 95–97
    gender, 87–88
    good/poor listener, 91–92
    hearing, contrasted, 81
    Internet, 100–101
    leadership, 264
    learning to listen, 90–92
    styles, 85
    talking so others will listen, 98–99
Listening preparation, 80
Listening process, 80–82, 83
Listening styles, 85–88
Lists of do's and taboos, 73
Liu, J., 62
Logical appeal, 404–409
Logical fallacies in argument, 407–409
Long-term orientation, 65
Love-intimacy touch, 145
Low-context messages, 66
Low-uncertainty-avoidance cultures, 65
Luft, Joseph, 170
Lying, 135

M

Mailing lists, 251
Main heads, 93
Main points, 316
Maintenance roles, 249–250
Majesty of the Law: Reflections of a Supreme Court Justice, The (O'Connor), 67
Major in Success (Combs), 5, 13
Managing Interactively (Boone), 112
Managing Strategic Relationships (Greenhalgh), 240
Mandel, T., 151

Manz, C., 364
Map is not the territory, 41–44
Marano, H. E., 186
Masculine cultures, 64
Maslow, A., 37, 409
Maslow's hierarchy of needs, 409–411
Mazur, M. A., 279
McKinney, C. M., 319
Meaning, 112–113
Media literacy, 277
Media richness, 150
Mehrabian, Albert, 10, 137
Mental outline, 93
Message, 9–10
Metamessage, 125
Microphone, 351
Miller, G. A., 48, 169
Minor points, 316
Mixed messages, 135
Mnemonic devices, 83
Mob appeal, 408
Model, 354
Moffatt, K., 112
Monotone, 352
Monroe, A. H., 322
Moore, C., 177
Morreale, S., 212
Motivated sequence, 322, 416
Motivating yourself, 157
Motivation, 399
Mouton, J., 270
Multiculturalism, 61, 62. *See also* Intercultural communication
Multmedia, 359
Muñoz, Mauricio Raul, 389
My First White Friend (Raybon), 69

N

Naseeb.com, 75
National communities, 62
National polls, 308
Natural delivery, 386
Naturalistic fallacy, 407
NCA Credo for Ethical Communication, 20–21
Nelson, A., 87, 146
Nelson, M. C., 119
Neutral questions, 215
Neutrality, 200, 265
"New Entrepreneurship, The" (Bell), 405
New Manners for New Times: A Complete Guide to Etiquette (Baldridge), 7
Newberry, Brian, 150
Newsgroups, 251
Nichols, Michael P., 95
Noise, 11–12
Nonassertive accommodation, 69

Nonassertive assimilation, 68–69
Nonassertive separation, 70–71
Nondominant- and dominant-group communication, 68–71
Nondominant culture, 68
Nonelective characteristics, 140
Nonverbal communication, 130–153
    attractiveness, 139–140
    body adornment, 141–142
    body movement, 138–139
    characteristics, 134–136
    clothing, 140–141
    defined, 132
    effective communication, 132–133
    eye messages, 139
    functions, 147–148
    gender, 136
    improving, 148–149
    Internet, 149–150
    paralanguage, 136–138
    smell, 145–146
    space and distance, 142–144
    strategic flexibility, 133–134
    time, 146–147
    touch, 144–145
    verbal communication, contrasted, 134
Nonverbal symbols, 10
Norms, 235
Note-taking skills, 84–85
Numbers, 380

O

Objective reality, 48
Objectivity, 265
O'Brien, P., 88
Obscene words, 114
Observers, 250
Occupational dress, 141
O'Connor, S. D., 67, 88, 119
Odden, L. R., 412
ODGs, 251–252, 272
Olfactics, 145
Omission of sounds, 352
"On the Path" (Nelson), 119
On Writing (King), 116
One-sided vs. two-sided argument, 416
Online attractiveness, 161–162
Online credibility, 281–282
Online databases, 301
Online dating services, 156
Online discussion groups (ODGs), 251–252, 272
Online discussions, 281
Open-ended questions, 215
Open-format interviews, 214
Open pane, 170
Openness, 187, 211

Opinion, 95
Opposite of Fate: A Book of Musings, The (Tan), 122
Oral presentations. *See* Public speaking
Orbe, M. P., 68
Organization, 316–323
Organizational chart, 354, 355
Osmond, D., 361
O'Sullivan, M., 135
Outline, 329–338
Owned messages, 167–168

P

Pace, 352
Paralanguage, 121, 136–138
Paralinguistics, 149
Parallel structure, 317
Paraphrasing, 96
Participating, 264
Passive aggression, 196
Passiveness, 90
Pasteur, L., 6
Patriotism, 66
Patterns of organization, 318–323. *See also* Patterns of organization
    cause-and-effect order, 320
    motivated sequence, 322
    problem-solution order, 320–321
    spatial order, 319–320
    time order, 318–319
    topical order, 322–323
Paul, A., 38
PDA, 134
Pearce, K., 278
Penn, R., 125, 126
People listening style, 85
Perceived gain, 160
Perception, 30, 45–50
Perceptual filters, 47
Perceptual influences, 48–50
Perceptual process, 45–46
Performance orientation, 361
Personal distance, 143
Personal example, 326
Personal happiness, 203
Personal inventory, 291
Persuasion, 398, 399
Persuasive speech, 396–427
    audience analysis, 404
    causal reasoning, 407
    challenges, 401–402
    credibility, 412–414
    deductive reasoning, 404–405
    emotional appeal, 409–411
    ethical principles, 414
    inductive reasoning, 405–407
    Internet, 418

    logical appeal, 404–409
    logical fallacies in argument, 407–409
    one-sided vs. two-sided argument, 416
    order of presentation, 416–417
    purpose, 403–404
    questions of fact, value, policy, 414–415
    reasoning by analogy, 407
    research, 411
    sample speech, 419–423
    strategies of persuasion, 403
PETAL, 387
Physical attraction, 160
Physician-patient relationship, 99
Physiological needs, 409
Pie graph, 357, 358
Pitch, 137, 352
Place, 300
Plagiarism, 21
Playboy, 250
Polls, 308
Positive thinking, 158
Poster, 354
Postman, N., 113
Posture, 138, 149, 351
Power, 259
Power distance, 63
Powerful talk, 118–119
PowerPoint, 359–360
Prejudice, 67
Premise, 407
Presentation, 385–387
Presentations. *See* Public speaking
Primary questions, 214–215
Principles of professional conduct, 210–211
Private schools, 160
Problem analysis, 243–245
Problem identification, 243
Problem-solution order, 320–321, 416
Problem-solving group, 236
Problem-solving outline, 246
Problem-solving process, 241–246
Productive conflict, 270
Professional communication, 208–229
    conflict, 224–226
    cultural differences, 222–223
    defined, 210
    employment interview, 219–222
    gender differences, 223
    information interview, 212–219. *See also* Information interview
    Internet, 226
    principles of conduct, 210–211
    professionalism survey (quiz), 227
    résumé, 219
    what to do, 224
Professional conduct, 210–211

Pronunciation, 352
Propriety, 100
Provisional statements, 201
Proxemics, 142
Proximity, 149, 161
Psychological information, 169
Psychological risk, 37
Psychological safety, 37
Psychological sets, 45
Public communication, 18
Public displays of affection (PDA), 134
Public distance, 144
Public speaking, 286–427
 analyzing the situation, 300
 anxiety, 361–363
 audience analysis, 295–300
 citing sources, 304
 conclusion, 327–328
 confidence as speaker (quiz), 309
 credibility, 412–414
 delivery, 287, 342–369. *See also* Delivering the speech
 getting attention, 323–326
 getting listeners involved, 383–384
 getting started (Internet), 308
 informative speech, 370–395. *See also* Informative speech
 introduction, 323–326. *See also* Speech introduction
 organization, 316–323
 outline, 329–338
 patterns of organization, 318–323. *See also* Patterns of organization
 persuasive speech, 396–427. *See also* Persuasive speech
 preparation, 291–308, 402
 presentation, 385–387
 purpose, 293–295
 quick guide, 286–287
 reference list, 330–331, 332–333, 338
 rehearsing the speech, 363–364
 research, 301–304
 sample speech, 389–392, 419–423
 supporting material, 304–308
 topic, 291–293
 transition, 328–329
Public-speaking anxiety, 361–363
Purdy, M., 91
Purpose, 293–295

Q

Qualifiers, 118
Quality, 137
Question-and-answer session, 384
Question-begging epithet, 408

Question of fact, 245, 414–415
Question of policy, 245, 415
Question of value, 245, 415
Quiz. *See* Assess yourself
Quotation, 326, 327

R

Race and ethnicity. *See* Intercultural communication
Racial epithets, 114
Rahman, M., 75
Rapport style, 223
Rapport-talk, 116–117
Rate, 137
Ratey, J., 45, 106
Raybon, P., 69, 71
RDAT, 387
Reagan, R., 361
Reasoning by analogy, 407
Receiving, 80
Recognition-seeker, 250
Reference list, 330–331, 332–333, 338
Referent power, 259
Reflected appraisals, 32–33
Regrettable talk, 197
Regulate, 147
Regulators, 138, 250
Rehearsing the speech, 363–364
Relationship survey, 205
Relationships. *See* Interpersonal relationships
Remembering, 82
Remembering information, 83–84
Repair attempts, 203
Repeating/reinforcing ideas, 380–381
Report style, 223
Report-talk, 117
Research, 301–304
Respect, 211
Responding, 82
Response to a bid, 166
Responsibility, 211
Responsibility messages, 167
Résumé, 219
Reward power, 259
Rewards, 193
Rheingold, H., 282
Rhetorical questions, 384
Ridington, R., 321
Ritual language, 113–114
Role, 14
"Role of Gender in Perceived Speaker Competence, The" (Sellnow/Treinen), 350
Roosevelt, E., 307
Roosevelt, F. D., 326, 361
Rosen, E., 122
Rubin, R., 278

Rules for Marriage, The (Fein/Schneider), 175
Rules of the Net (Mandel/Van der Leun), 151
Rushdie, S., 122

S

Safety needs, 410
Sample outline, 334–338
Sapir, E., 108
Sapir-Whorf hypothesis, 108
Satanic Verses, The (Rushdie), 122
Schacter, D., 364
Scripts, 32–33
Seating arrangements, 238
Sejinowski, T., 135
Selective attention, 82
Self-actualization needs, 410
Self-assessment. *See* Assess yourself
Self-awareness, 156
Self-concept, 31–41
 assess yourself, 51
 defined, 30
 gender, 36–37
 improving, 38–41
 Internet, 44–45
 psychological risk/safety, 37–38
 reflected appraisals, 32–33
 self-perception, 35–36
 sex, 36–37
 social comparisons, 33–35
Self-confessor, 250
Self-confidence, 36
Self-disclosure, 168–173
Self-esteem needs, 410
Self-fulfilling prophecies, 33
Self-improvement, 211
Self-perception, 35–36
Selling, 264
Sellnow, D. D., 350
Selnow, G., 305
Semantic noise, 12
Semiopen format interviews, 214
Sender-receiver, 8–9
Separation, 70
Separation strategies, 70–71
Servant leaders, 259
Setting, 12–13
Seven Sins of Memory, The (Schacter), 364
Sexual arousal touch, 145
Sexual identity, 36–37
SF, 6–7, 25
Shape, 378
Shared goals, 202
Shared leadership, 262–263
Shaywitz, B., 118
Shaywitz, S., 118
Sheats, P., 247

Shimomura, Y., 112
Sims, H., Jr., 364
Singular, S., 177
Situational leadership, 263–264
6 × 6 rule, 357–358
Size, 378
Slang, 122
Slow talkers, 137
Slurring, 353
Small group, 233–236
Small-group communication, 17–18
Small-group effectiveness, 237–241
Small-group participation, 230–255
    choosing a topic, 242–243
    cohesiveness, 239
    commitment, 239
    dysfunctional roles, 250–251
    effectiveness, 237–241
    finding/evaluating solutions, 245
    group leadership, 264–270
    groupthink, 239–241
    Internet, 251–252, 272
    maintenance roles, 249–250
    meeting place, 238
    problem analysis, 243–245
    problem identification, 243
    reevaluating solutions, 246
    seating arrangements, 238
    size, 237–238
    task roles, 248–249
Small-talk, 164–165
Smell, 145–146
Social comparisons, 33–35
Social distance, 143
Social groups, 236
Social influence, 399
Social penetration, 168
Social-polite touch, 145
Social presence, 149
Sociological information, 169
Sommers, C. H., 118, 173, 174
Sound substitution, 352
Space and distance, 142–144
Spatial order, 319–320
Speaking from a manuscript, 348
Speaking from memory, 348–349
Speaking publicly. *See* Public speaking
Special-interest pleader, 250
Special language, 115–116
Specific purpose, 294
Speech conclusion, 327–328
Speech delivery. *See* Delivering the speech
Speech introduction, 323–326
    example, 324–325, 326
    get attention, 323–326
    humor, 324
    personal example, 326
    quotation, 326
    refer to the occasion, 325
    show importance of subject, 325
    startling information, 325–326
    state purpose, central idea, 323
    tips, 326
Speech outline, 329–338
Speech reference list, 330–333, 338
Speech transitions, 328–329
Spontaneity, 200
Stafford, L., 197
Stage fright, 361–363, 366
Stagnating stage, 190–191
Staring, 139
Startling information, 325–326
Statement of faith, 401
Statement of knowledge, 400
Statement of opinion, 400–401
Statistics, 306–307
Stereotyping, 66
Stevens, L., 177
Stone, D. C., 238
Stone, F. M., 224–225
Strategic flexibility (SF), 6–7, 25
Strategy, 200
Streisand, B., 361
Stress interview, 212–213
Style, 116
Subjective view, 48
Substantive conflict, 269
Substitute, 147
Subtext, 125
Sullivan, A., 36
Superiority *versus* equality, 200–201
Supporting material, 304–308
Supporting points, 93
"Sustainability" (Lamm), 317
Sutherland, D., 361
Swann, W., 38
Sweeping generalization, 408
Symbol, 9–10
Synchronous communication, 23, 251, 277

T

Table, 354–355
Tag questions, 118–119
Taking notes, 84
"Talk to Your Children about the Tough Stuff" (Odden), 412
"Talking Back to Your Doctor Works" (Greider), 98
Talking to each other, 164–168
"Taming Hostile Audiences" (Tracy), 411
Tan, A., 122
Tannen, D., 87, 116–117, 125
Target audience, 296, 404
Task-oriented group, 236
Task roles, 248–249
Team, 241
Team Building (Dyer), 241
"Teams in the Workplace" (Barnett), 241
Teamwork, 211
Teamwork (Larson/LaFasto), 241
Telling, 263–264
Temporality, 24
Terminal values, 400
Terminating stage, 191
Territory, 142
Testimony, 307
Thourlby, W., 141
"Three Out of Four Say Better Communication Equals Greater Employee Retention" (Morreale), 212
Time, 146–147
Time order, 318–319
Time-style listening, 85
Tomlin, L., 361
Topic, 291–293
Topical order, 322–323
Torn Between Two Cultures: An Afghan-American Woman Speaks Out (Aseel), 60, 142
Touch, 144–145
Tracy, L., 411
Traditional leadership styles, 261–262
Transactional communication, 13
Transition, 328–329
Transpection, 73
Treinen, K. P., 350
Trust, 61, 187
Trusting others scale, 179
Trustworthiness, 413
Two-sided speech, 416
Tyco, 21

U

Uncertainty avoidance, 65
Unconditional commitments, 176
Uniform, 141
Universities, 40
Unknown pane, 171
Unled (unmanaged) ODG, 272
Unnatural Leadership: Going against Intuition and Experience to Develop Ten New Leadership Instincts (Dotlich/Cairo), 266
Usenet newsgroups, 251
User's Guide to the Brain, A (Ratey), 106

V

Values, 400
Van der Leun, G., 151
Varner, I., 73

Vaughan, D., 191
Verbal communication, 104–129
  appropriate language, 114
  clarity, 123–124
  culture, 119–120
  effective communication, 107–108
  ethics, 125–126
  gender, 116–119
  how words work, 109–112
  Internet, 126–127
  meaning, 112–113
  metamessage, 125
  nonverbal communication, contrasted, 134
  ritual language, 113–114
  speaking, 120–121
  specialization, 114–115
  strategic flexibility, 108–109
  style, 116
  vividness, 124
  what do you want do say?, 122
  to whom are you talking?, 124–125
  writing, 121–122
Verbal communication self-evaluation form, 127
Verbal symbols, 10
Video, 360
Virtual community, 282
Virtual Community, The (Rheingold), 282
Vision, 269–270
Visual support, 353–360
  actual object, 353–354
  chalkboard, 353
  chart, 354
  computer graphics, 357–359
  diagram, 354
  graph, 356–357
  handouts, 360
  model, 354
  poster, 354
  PowerPoint, 359–360
  presentation, 387
  rules, 360
  table, 354–355
  video, 360
  whiteboard, 353
Visualization, 364
Vividness, 124
Vocal fillers, 138
Voice quality, 137
Volume, 137, 351

W

Walters, F. M., 307
War Against Boys, The (Sommers), 118
War of the Worlds, The, 122
"We, The People: Prize and Embrace What Is America" (Walters), 307
Web conferencing, 252
Web forums, 252
Web log (blog), 282–283
Web rot, 23
Weighing goals against solutions, 202
Weight, 379
Welles, Orson, 122
What Could He Be Thinking? (Gurian), 118
Whetten, D. A., 233
Whiteboard, 353
Whorf, B. L., 108
Who's Who in America, 214
"Why I Hate Beauty" (Leviric/Marano), 186
Wieder-Hatfield, D., 202
Win-win negotiating, 202
Woodall, W. G., 146
Word etymology, 376–377
Work ethic, 203
Workplace communication. *See* Professional communication
WorldCom, 21
Worldview, 58

Y

You are What You Wear (Thourlby), 141
You Don't Say: Navigating Nonverbal Communication Between the Sexes (Nelson), 87, 146
You-message, 167
Young, K. S., 177